A COMPANION *to*

CHAUCER

and his CONTEMPORARIES

A COMPANION *to*
CHAUCER
and his CONTEMPORARIES

TEXTS *&* CONTEXTS

EDITED BY
Laurel Amtower · Jacqueline Vanhoutte

broadview press

Library and Archives Canada Cataloguing in Publication

Amtower, Laurel
        A companion to Chaucer and his contemporaries : texts & contexts / Laurel Amtower and Jacqueline Vanhoutte.

Includes bibliographical references.
ISBN 978-1-55111-796-6

        1. Chaucer, Geoffrey, d. 1400—Criticism and interpretation. 2. English literature—Middle English, 1100–1500. 3. Civilization, Medieval—Sources. 4. Middle Ages—Sources. 5. England—Civilization—1066-1485—Sources. I. Vanhoutte, Jacqueline, 1968– II. Title.
PR1906.5.A48 2009   821'.1   C2009-900150-0

BROADVIEW PRESS is an independent, international publishing house, incorporated in 1985. Broadview believes in shared ownership, both with its employees and with the general public; since the year 2000 Broadview shares have traded publicly on the Toronto Venture Exchange under the symbol BDP.

We welcome comments and suggestions regarding any aspect of our publications—please feel free to contact us at the addresses below or at: broadview@broadviewpress.com / www.broadviewpress.com.

North America
Post Office Box 1243,
Peterborough, Ontario, Canada K9J 7H5

2215 Kenmore Ave.,
Buffalo, New York, USA 14207
tel: (705) 743-8990; fax: (705) 743-8353

customerservice@broadviewpress.com

UK, Ireland and continental Europe
NBN International
Estover Road, Plymouth, UK, PL6 7PY
tel: 44 (0) 1752 202300;
fax: 44 (0) 1752 202330;
enquiries@nbninternational.com

Australia and New Zealand
UNIREPS, University of New South Wales
Sydney, NSW, Australia, 2052
tel: 61 2 9385 0150; fax: 61 2 9385 0155
infopress@unsw.edu.au

Book Design by Black Eye Design.
Printed in Canada

The text is printed on paper containing 100% post-consumer fibre.

10 9 8 7 6 5 4 3 2 1

FSC

Mixed Sources
Product group from well-managed forests, controlled sources and recycled wood or fibre

Cert no. SW-COC-003438
www.fsc.org
© 1996 Forest Stewardship Council

CONTENTS

PREFACE ... 11

CHAPTER 1 ... 13
POLITICS AND IDEOLOGY IN THE FOURTEENTH CENTURY

INTRODUCTION ... 13
    Civil Conflict and the War with France ... 14
    The Plague ... 17
    The Peasant's Revolt ... 22
    The Merciless Parliament and Its Repercussions ... 26
    The Lancasters ... 32
DOCUMENTS ... 36
    Edward III Makes Ready for War (1337) ... 36
    Close Roll (1337) ... 37
    Statutes of the Realm (1340) ... 39
    The Battle of Poitiers. Henry Knighton (1346) ... 39
    The Plague. Henry Knighton (1348-50) ... 40
    The Plague and Its Aftermath. Henry Knighton (1349) ... 41
    Statute of Laborers (1351) ... 42
    Alice Perrers. Thomas Walsingham (late 14THC) ... 45
    The Poll Tax (1380) ... 47
    John Ball. Thomas Walsingham (1381) ... 49
    The Burning of the Savoy. Thomas Walsingham (1381) ... 50
    The King's Dire Straits. Thomas Walsingham (1381) ... 51
    The Death of Wat Tyler. Thomas Walsingham (1381) ... 51
    Richard's Words to the People. Thomas Walsingham (1381) ... 52
    Proclamation for Keeping the Peace within the City (1381) ... 53
    Letter from Richard Revoking Their Liberties. Thomas Walsingham
        (1381) ... 54
    John Ball Letters (1381) ... 54
    A Censure of the Mendicant Friars. Thomas Walsingham
        (late 14THC) ... 56
    The Merciless Parliament (1388) ... 57
    Deposition of Richard II (1399) ... 59
    Henry IV's words to Richard II, upon Richard's Abdication. Froissart
        (1399) ... 62
    Coronation of Bolingbroke (1399) ... 63

Death of Richard II. Froissart (1400) ... 65
St. Joan's Appearance to Deliver France (1429) ... 66

CHAPTER 2 ... 70
"FROM EVERY SHIRES ENDE": THE STRUCTURE OF SOCIETY

INTRODUCTION ... 70
    The Three Estates ... 70
    Social Conflict and Social Change ... 74
    The Situation of Women ... 79
    The Anti-Feminist Tradition ... 85
DOCUMENTS ... 91
    The Treatise on the Laws and Customs of the Realm of England
        Commonly Called Glanville (12THC) ... 91
    The Sumptuary Laws of 1363 and 1463 ... 94
    Apprenticeship Contracts (13THC) ... 98
    The Oath for the Issue of Apprentices (15THC) ... 99
    The Petition of the Tailors against Nicholas Brembre (1386) ... 100
    On Amazons ... 102
    Men, Women, Wives, Husbands, and Servants. Bartholomew Anglicus
        (trans. 1397) ... 105
    The Ballad of the Tyrannical Husband (15THC) ... 110
    Chaucer and the Raptus of Cecily Chaumpaigne (1380) ... 113
    Widows and Clerical Anti-Feminism. Christine de Pizan
        (1405) ... 115
    Fourteenth-Century Court Cases Involving Women ... 121
    First Epistle to the Corinthians (1388) ... 123
    "The Wife Is Subject to the Husband." John Wyclif (c. 1378 and
        1384) ... 124
    The Clerical Tradition on Women ... 125

CHAPTER 3 ... 133
"OF METE AND DRYNK": DAILY LIFE IN MEDIEVAL ENGLAND

INTRODUCTION ... 133
    Medieval London ... 133
    Getting Around ... 139
    The Country ... 141
    Daily Activities ... 149
    Food and Drink ... 153

Medieval Money ... 158
DOCUMENTS ... 161
Coroners' Cases and Court Cases (14ᵀᴴc) ... 161
Of Swine, Bawds, Thieves, and Courtesans (14ᵀᴴc) ... 166
The Goodman's Instructions on Hosting, Cooking, and Serving
(1392–94) ... 168
A Feast Fit for a King (14ᵀᴴc) ... 173
Letters from the Pastons (15ᵀᴴc) ... 174
On Manners (15ᵀᴴc) ... 185

CHAPTER 4 ... 195
"HOOLY THOUGHT AND WERK":
RELIGIOUS LIFE, RITUAL, AND PRAYER

INTRODUCTION ... 195
Popular Religion and Daily Life ... 197
The Clerical Hierarchy ... 203
Anti-Semitism ... 206
Religious Orders and Religious Professionals ... 208
Corruption and Anticlericalism ... 210
DOCUMENTS ... 216
From *On Christian Doctrine*. St. Augustine (*c.* 396–427) ... 216
"Religious Symbolism." William Durandus (1286) ... 218
"The Lives of Spiritual Women." *The Ancrene Wisse* (13ᵀᴴc) ... 219
"Interpretations of Biblical Verse on the Conduct of Women."
The Ancrene Wisse (13ᵀᴴc) ... 221
Alma Redemptoris Mater (11ᵀᴴc) ... 223
A Myrour to Lewde Men and Wymmen (14ᵀᴴc) ... 224
"Against Pilgrimage." Lollardist Treatise (14ᵀᴴc) ... 226
Margery Kempe's Pilgrimage to Rome and Jerusalem. Margery
Kempe (*c.* 1436–38) ... 227
"The Two Powers." Hugh of St. Victor (1134) 229
A Punishment for Lollardy (1389) ... 230
"Epistola 391: On the Jews." Bernard of Clairvaux (early 12ᵀᴴc) ... 232
The Murder of Hugh of Lincoln. Matthew of Paris (1255) ... 232
The Papal Bull Defending the Jews. Gregory X (1272) ... 234
Vox Clamantis. John Gower (*c.* 1380s) ... 236
On the Pope. John Wyclif (1370s) ... 245
Bull of Pope Gregory XI, Against John Wycliffe (1384) ... 246
Twelve Conclusions of the Lollards (1395) ... 247

Against Confession. Lollard Treatise (1394) ... 250
"The Case for Translation." John Wyclif (1370s) ... 250
On Biblical Translation. Lollard Treatise (early 15THC) ... 252
The Constitutions of Archbishop Arundel Against the Lollards
    (1409) ... 253

CHAPTER 5 ... 256
"TROUTHE AND HONOUR, FREEDOM AND CURTEISIE":
WAR, PAGEANTRY, AND THE KNIGHTHOOD

INTRODUCTION ... 256
    The Origins of Chivalry ... 257
    Chivalry and Courtly Love ... 261
    Practicing Knighthood ... 265
    Chivalric Orders ... 267
    Warfare and the Crusades ... 271
    Class Antagonism ... 275
DOCUMENTS ... 277
    The Book of the Order of Chivalry. Ramon Llull (c. 1276, trans.
        1484) ... 277
    The Tree of Battles. Honoré Bonet (1387) ... 279
    Letter of Othea to Hector. Christine de Pizan (1399-1400) ... 280
    The Art of Courtly Love. Andreas Capellanus (1184-86) ... 281
    The Book of Chivalry. Geoffroi de Charny (c. 1350) ... 285
    The Jousts in Smithfield. The Brut, or Chronicles of England
        (1388) ... 286
    Free Companies. Froissart (c. 1356) ... 287
    The Black Prince's Revenge on Limoges. Froissart (1370) ... 288
    Order of the Garter. Froissart (1344) ... 289
    The Condemnation of the Templars (1312) ... 290
    Statute on Livery and Maintenance (1390) ... 291
    The Defender of Peace. Marsilius of Padua (1324) ... 292
    The Conquest of Alexandria. Petrarch (1365) ... 293
    The Capture of Alexandria. Guillaume de Machaut (after 1369) ... 294
    Relations with the Franks. Ousama Ibn Mounkidh (12THC) ... 297
    From Vox Clamantis. John Gower (c. 1380s) ... 298
    The Two Ways. John Clanvowe (late 14THC) ... 299
    Epilogue to the Book of the Order of Chivalry. William Caxton
        (1484) ... 299

CHAPTER 6 ... 303
"GLADLY WOLDE HE LERNE AND GLADLY TECHE":
READING, LITERACY, AND EDUCATION

INTRODUCTION ... 303
 Education ... 306
 The Medieval Commentary Tradition ... 313
 Humanism ... 317
 The Arrival of the Printing Press ... 319
DOCUMENTS ... 323
 The Boke of Curtasye (c. 1460) ... 323
 A Fifteenth Century School Book (late 15TH c) ... 329
 Aristotle's ABC (early 15TH c) ... 331
 Morale Scolarium. John of Garland (13TH c) ... 332
 Rules of the University of Paris (c. 1215) ... 333
 Studies Necessary Before Admission as a Master of Arts, 1431 ... 335
 The Statutes of New College, Oxford (1400) ... 336
 The Study of the French Language and English Law at Oxford
  (1432) ... 337
 The Commons Protest Against the Misbehaviour of the Scholars and
  Clerks of Oxford (1421) ... 338
 Letter to Can Grande. Dante (early 14TH c) ... 338
 The *Philobiblon.* Richard de Bury (14TH c) ... 339
 Genealogy of the Gentile Gods. Giovanni Boccaccio (1360-74) ... 340
 The Prologues and Epilogues. William Caxton (15TH c) ... 343

CHAPTER 7 ... 351
"MAGYK NATUREEL": SCIENCE, MEDICINE,
PSYCHOLOGY, AND ALCHEMY

INTRODUCTION ... 351
 Medieval Science: Theory and Practice ... 352
 The Elements ... 361
 The Humours and Human Temperament ... 364
DOCUMENTS ... 372
 On the Natural Faculties. Galen (170) ... 372
 Of the Four Complexions (14TH c) ... 373
 Of the Science of Physiognomy from the *Secreta Secretorum*
  (1422) ... 374

An Arab Opinion of the Crusaders' Medicine (12THC) ... 379

A Lollard View on Bodily and Spiritual Blindness
(14THC-15THC) ... 381

From *De Coitu* (On Intercourse). Constantinus Africanus
(11THC) ... 382

From *On the Properties of Things*. Bartholomew Anglicus
(13THC) ... 383

Various Remedies. Gilbertus Anglicus (13THC) ... 388

On Lycanthropia (6TH C) ... 390

Two Medical Cases (late 14THC) ... 392

On Natural Magic (16THC) ... 393

On Animals (12THC and 13THC) ... 394

From *The Ordinal of Alchemy*. Thomas Norton (1477) ... 400

"On Dreams." Macrobius (*c.* 395-423) ... 405

CHAPTER 8 ... 413
"To Flaundres wol I go": International
Influences and Exchanges

INTRODUCTION ... 413
Late Medieval Conceptions of the World ... 413
England and the Continent ... 418
The Stranger in Their Midst ... 425
DOCUMENTS ... 431
Information for Pilgrims (*c.* 1500) ... 431
From *Mandeville's Travels* (1356-57?) ... 432
On Various Countries. Bartholomew Anglicus (13THC) ... 440
From *The Libelle of English Policy* (15THC) ... 443
Court Cases (14THC) ... 446
The Murder of Janus Imperial (1379) ... 447
The Rights of Aliens and the Petition of the Hansards (1389) ... 451
The Massacre of the Flemish (1381) ... 453
Mandate of Payment to Geoffrey Chaucer
(11 November 1373) ... 455

BIBLIOGRAPHY ... 458

SOURCES ... 475

PREFACE

*T*his book arose out of our desire to provide an accessible overview of late medieval English culture to students in our literature courses. Like Shakespeare, Chaucer and his contemporaries are of an age as well as for all time; to know about the particulars of a culture is to gain a greater understanding of its "timeless" literature. Over the years, we have come to rely on a few key historical documents that illuminate some of the conflicts and issues of Chaucer's time; documents by contemporary writers on chivalry and knighthood, for example, help clarify the range of complex attitudes Chaucer displays in his own depiction of knights, while theories about physical ailments reveal surprising undertones to such plot devices as January's sudden blindness in the Merchant's Tale.

Our approach to teaching has governed our selection of texts. Throughout this book, we have tried to convey both a broad sense of historical patterns and a sense of the rich variety of interests and details that comprised medieval life. We include passages from medieval "best-sellers" like *Mandeville's Travels* and Anglicus's *Of the Properties of Things*, as well as less familiar selections drawn from a variety of sources, including religious treatises and court records. All of our documents are meant to clarify the subjects addressed in each chapter. Many of our choices will be familiar to scholars of the period, who will approve some selections and mourn the absence of others. Although we have tried to identify and include the passages that would be most helpful, we have, inevitably, been constrained by space and by our own intellectual predilections. Moreover, in a society where the majority was illiterate, and the written record is biased towards a privileged minority, it is nearly impossible to convey common voices. Among the underrepresented are, for example, lower-class medieval women: not only could they not write, but their opinions were for the most part not regarded as important enough to be recorded. In the six hundred years that separate us from Chaucer, all sorts of people—from garbage-collectors to family members to scholarly editors—have made decisions regarding what was and was not worthy of preservation. Their discrimination shapes our understanding of medieval culture as surely as our own.

Despite such limitations, we hope that our samples will offer a supplement to the literature of the period that will both increase enjoyment and enrich understanding. We had to make some difficult decisions not just about which texts to present but also about how to present them. Our decision to translate Middle English works may seem at odds with our desire to preserve what is unfamiliar about medieval English culture.

Several considerations influenced that decision. One of them is that we include selections originally written in other languages, like the Latin or French of the political and clerical elite. Since few scholars and even fewer students are conversant in these languages, we had to use modern translations. But to insist on the Middle English and not the Latin would be to make Macrobius easier to read than Mandeville: Middle English works would seem less accessible, when the contrary was true in medieval English culture. Although some of the documents provided here exist in modern editions, many are not readily accessible, in part because of language issues. By translating these documents and bringing them in conversation with one another, we hope to encourage students of medieval literature to explore further the many primary sources that are now available.

This book would not have been possible without the help of many people. San Diego State University and the University of North Texas have generously provided some of the funding for our research. We are especially grateful to Eric Kuniholm, who graciously translated many Latin sources for us. We would also like to thank our assistants, Karrie Fuller, Kristin Nielsen, Christian Worlow, and Barbara Zimbalist. We owe important debts to the friends, students, and colleagues with whom we discuss medieval literature, including Alexander Pettit, Paul Justice, Nicole Smith, Robert Upchurch, Amy Taylor, Corey Marks, Michael Borgstrom, Lisa Lampert-Weissig, Rich Amtower, Paul Menzer, Jacqueline Vandenberghe, and Paul Vanhoutte. Finally, a special word of thanks to our daughters, Madeleine and Claire, for their patience and forbearance while we were working on this project.

A NOTE ON THE TEXTS

Where a document was translated by us, we indicate this in the headnote prefacing the document in question. The bibliography contains the sources that we consulted for our own translations. Where a document was not translated by us, we include full information on it in the bibliography and also list it in the separate "Permissions and Acknowledgements" section at the end of the book.

All quotations to Chaucer are to *The Riverside Chaucer* (1987), edited by Larry Benson. When the immediate context did not provide clear information regarding the work quoted, we included an abbreviated form of the title in the parenthetical reference, before the line numbers (e.g., WT is "The Wife of Bath's Tale," CYT is "The Canon's Yeoman's Tale," ParsT is "The Parson's Tale," and so on).

CHAPTER I

Politics and Ideology
in the Fourteenth Century

INTRODUCTION

A vital period that produced a self-conscious interest in classicism and the humanities that heralded the Renaissance, the fourteenth and fifteenth centuries also witnessed some of the most provocative crises of Western history. The century was beset by repeated plagues, an extended and economically catastrophic war with France, a religious schism, and social upheavals that climaxed in the Peasant's Revolt. Growing resentment toward the aristocracy challenged long-held notions about the structure of society and the divine role of the king and clergy. Where a fundamental ideology, correlating social and political roles to a Christian sense of rightful place and order, had prevailed for hundreds of years, a new set of possibilities and assertions appeared that tested the traditional feudal framework. Though these changes seemed cataclysmic and possibly even apocalyptic at the time, with many forecasting the dissolution of society and the coming of the Last Judgment, the period nonetheless produced a climate in which dynamic change seemed both possible and even positive. A shortage in labor meant higher wages for those in the lowest tiers of society, which in turn profoundly affected the feudal social structure. Attitudes toward the hierarchy of feudalism, and particularly the expenditures of the aristocracy, became more critical. And a renewed focus on the middle classes and individual potential had a profound and encouraging effect on literature and the arts.

For Chaucer and his contemporaries, the culture of the fourteenth century, with all its attendant uncertainty and possibility, prompted questions about the paradoxes of human life that infused their creative work. Although many late medieval writers, such as the highly moral John Gower, fought to maintain a moralistic ethos that claimed to rise above the calamities of the age, other writers, including Chaucer, the anonymous *Gawain* poet, William Langland, and Thomas Malory, grappled with the issues that these calamities raised. These are the same issues that have come to concern some of the best Western literature ever since: How is it that a single human being can live contentedly with multiple and even contrasting viewpoints—even beliefs—jostling side-by-side in his or her own mind? What causes bitterness? What keeps hope alive for those who suffer loss after loss? Chaucer's Wife of Bath excoriates the traditional misogyny of religious authorities even as she embraces some of the beliefs that lead to antifeminist stereotypes. His Pardoner sees through the hypocrisy of his own profession but becomes enraged when others follow suit. The dreamer of the late medieval poem, *Pearl*, is devastated at the loss of his daughter, but his faith and creative vision provide hope—and even a kind of restoration—in the face of grief. As these examples suggest, the conflict that marked fourteenth-century England also defines its most memorable characters. Although it would be unwise to credit a specific set of events for the unusual condensation of literary genius that we find in England at the end of the fourteenth century, the particular set of political, economic, and religious crises that beset the period helped fuel a prolific and highly creative era.

CIVIL CONFLICT AND THE WAR WITH FRANCE

By the time of Chaucer's birth, around 1345 or so, times seemed fairly auspicious for England. Under the reign of Edward III, England enjoyed military successes against France that led to a sense of prestige felt for many years afterward; prospects had not appeared so good in some time. The 20-year rule of his father, Edward II, had been disastrous on a number of fronts. Edward II had proved himself incapable of managing the unruly Scots, his own subjects, or even, as his ignominious demise suggests, his own wife. Indeed, there had been relatively little opposition when Isabella invaded England with the aid of the Count of Hainault and her lover, Roger Mortimer. Edward II was deposed in 1327 under the charges that he had failed to uphold justice and the common good, and was conveniently murdered shortly thereafter.

Edward III's reign thus began somewhat precariously. Only 14 years old when he attained the throne, Edward's first three years of reign proved little better than his father's. The young king was almost entirely under the control of his avaricious mother and Mortimer, who, like the deposed king they had ousted, hoarded wealth and heaped honorary titles on themselves and their favorites. Indeed, Isabella and Mortimer quickly arranged a betrothal between Edward and Philippa of Hainault—the daughter of the Count who had aided Isabella in her invasion—as a means of further ensuring their influence over the minor regent. The young Edward acted upon his prerogative as king quickly, however. Within three years he threw off the constraints of his mother and her lover: Isabella was honorably confined; Mortimer was executed. Edward immediately turned his attention to restoring social order. He consolidated his bureaucracy and, stressing the interdependency of the monarch and his nobles, gave his lords a voice and opinion in international affairs. This astute blend of statesmanship and diplomacy proved to be Edward's talent and enabled him to reign uncontested for 50 years.

In later years, England would look back upon the reign of Edward III as a golden age of chivalry. It was certainly an era of war. Almost immediately the young king set out to prove English superiority over the Scots, who had, under Robert the Bruce and later his son, David, made serious inroads against the English. Although serious setbacks threatened the war in early years, Edward decisively defeated the Scots at Halidon Hill in 1333, the first victory for England in years.[1] When the Scots later aligned their political forces with the French, Edward declared war against France as well. Ostensibly erupting over the 1337 confiscation of Aquitaine, an English territory, by the French king, Philip VI, the "Hundred Years War," as it has since been dubbed, consisted of an extended series of campaigns that intermittently surged until 1453—roughly 100 years.

The Hundred Years War in many ways defined the sense of national identity that emerges so clearly in the literature. Although France and England were closely aligned in terms of their aristocratic families and heritages (Edward III's mother, Isabella, was, after all, a French princess), the late Middle Ages brought conflicts of interest that sharpened the two nations' linguistic and cultural differences.[2] Since the Norman Conquest of 1066, French had been the official language of English politics and kings. By the fourteenth century, however, the two dynasties had grown irrevocably apart, and no amount of intermarriages, friendly tournaments, or collaborative crusades against common enemies could stem the mutual resentment. The friction that culminated in the Hundred Years War defined differences between the two cultures and separated their languages and traditions, hitherto intertwined, forever after.

During the height of Edward's reign, England enjoyed several important victories over France. The tide initially turned in England's favor at the Battle of Sluys in 1340, when Edward, after successfully convincing the Flemish to join forces against the French, came upon the fleet of the French and their allies, just as they themselves were preparing to invade England. Although hugely outnumbered, Edward's archers were able to decimate the men on the closely packed enemy ships, and the French fleet was virtually destroyed. The victory at Sluys prevented the French from effectively launching an attack on English ground ever after, and it gave England undisputed control over the Channel. Although Edward was unable to follow up on this victory, having run out of funds, later battles solidified his claims against France. The Battle of Crecy (1346) and the Battle of Poitiers (1356), in particular, contributed to a long-lasting sense of national pride. Both confirmed the supremacy of the English longbow and English military tactics over French cavalry. England proved herself the match, and more, of the superior-minded French and, as a result, increased her territories as well as her dominance over the Channel. Even though the Battle of Crecy is often identified as marking the beginning of the end of the chivalric era, it helped establish Edward III as a warrior-king who embodied the knightly ideal. Much of the ideology of chivalry, defined by a sense of honor, loyalty, and truth, was renewed and sustained not only by Edward's successful campaigns but also by the heroic victories of his popular son and heir apparent, Edward the Black Prince.

Indeed, it was the Black Prince—nicknamed, according to legend, for his magnificent black armor—who led an out-numbered English army against superior French forces in the spectacular victory at Poitiers. The king of France was captured during the battle, as were a slew of other French aristocrats, all of whom were later ransomed at a great price. English soldiers were able to carry off vast spoils, which allowed Edward to pay for his war without the need for further taxation. The English victory was conclusive enough that for a time Edward entertained the idea of winning the entire kingdom of France. Instead, however, the two kingdoms eventually drafted the Treaty of Bretigny, which gave Edward sovereignty over large portions of France, including Gascony, Poitou, Limousin, and the Marche—indeed, over the entire southwest quarter of France—as well as several significant counties in the north. In return Edward agreed to give up his claim to the French throne, although, interestingly, he never formally renounced his title.

Although hostilities erupted intermittently between the two countries for years, cultural exchange and mutual admiration, surprisingly, continued—at least on a superficial level. King Jean of France remained a prisoner in England for another four years after his capture—although to call him a hostage overstates the case. While he was in England, the two monarchs met often, dining together, hosting elaborate entertainments, and attracting an enviable entourage of musicians, poets, and other court entertainers to their circle. The influence of French styles upon English literature and art appears in the English poets' imitation of French authors and their genres and rhymes. Even as French culture dazzled the English in their home territory, however, conflict continued in France. Geoffrey Chaucer was captured during an expedition in late 1359 or 1360, apparently while serving under the king's son, Lionel, during his advance through the northwest territories of France. Chaucer remained hostage for weeks at the very least, quite possibly for longer than that. Although he was attached to a prince's retinue, his treatment was undoubtedly less generous than King Jean's was in England. The English were hated by the French, who resented the casualties imposed by English archers and the damage done to their towns and farms. At least one incident is chronicled in which English soldiers were slaughtered by angry French peasants, rather than ransomed as custom dictated.[3] As John M. Bowers suggests, there may be good reason why Chaucer fails to glorify war to the extent of his contemporaries; his own experiences in France and as a hostage may have colored his perception of the martial life.

Nor did later years allay what may have been a covert antagonism Chaucer felt toward the French. The late 1370s, characterized by the aging Edward's sustained withdrawal from public life, witnessed a steady erosion of support for the war. For although the early victories had revived aristocratic ideals and enabled personal heroics, the war was also a costly burden to England. Setbacks and delays offset the much-publicized victories, and the long periods of military mobilization were expensive. More than once Edward's ministers warned him that the people were unable and unwilling to pay the heavy taxes levied to pay for the war effort. But the aristocracy pushed for ongoing campaigns; wars were, after all, full of opportunities for nobles, for whom reputations could be made and fortunes acquired.

The Plague

The corrosive effects of the Hundred Years War on English resources were compounded in 1348, when a "deadly pestilence" struck Europe.

The Black Death, as it since has become known, first appeared in southern Europe and Italy in the spring and summer; by autumn it had spread to England. Introduced by fleas from rats, the plague was transmitted by the various trade ships that navigated the port cities. Three forms of the virus seem to have attacked: bubonic and septicemic forms, spread through direct contact with fleas, and a deadly airborne—or "pneumonic"—form, transmitted by infected people who coughed or otherwise communicated the airborne bacteria through their saliva. The result of this three-pronged attack was a pandemic that spread uncontrollably through the population with fatal consequences in nearly all cases.

According to the chronicler Henry Knighton, the plague entered at Southampton and rapidly swept through England.[4] Nearly the entire town of Bristol was wiped out in a period of only two to three days. Nor was this the only instance of calamity: the plague returned in 1361, 1369, and again in 1375, devastating the local population. Although the privileged died at lesser rates than the poor—they were partially protected by their better living conditions—the plague did not recognize social hierarchies and claimed victims even among the most powerful: John of Gaunt lost Blanche, his beloved Duchess, to the disease around 1368 or 1369. Chaucer's *Book of the Duchess*, probably written to honor Blanche's memory, provides a moving testimony to the grief and despair felt by survivors, and his "Pardoner's Tale" conveys the celerity with which the plague struck. Estimates on the numbers of those killed by the plague are uncertain, but overall the mortality rate seems to have been somewhere between one-third and one-half the existing population. Some towns and communities had much greater losses: Leicester lost 380, Holy Cross 400, and St. Margaret's 700.[5] Moreover, the plague was unusually cruel in its choice of victims. Infants and children were hit especially hard, as were those young adults who lived in close communities such as monasteries or abbeys.[6]

Eyewitness accounts from the period render a harrowing scene. Boccaccio writes that:

> ... its earliest symptom, in men and women alike, was the appearance of certain swellings in the groin or armpit, some of which were egg-shaped whilst others were roughly the size of the common apple. Sometimes the swellings were large, sometimes not so large, and they were referred to by the populace as *gavoccioli*. From the two areas already mentioned, this deadly *gavocciolo* would begin to spread, and within a short time it would appear at random all over the body.

Later on, the symptoms of the disease changed, and many people began to find dark blotches and bruises on their arms, thighs, and other parts of the body, sometimes large and few in number, at other times tiny and closely spaced. These, to anyone unfortunate enough to contract them, were just as infallible a sign that he would die as the *gavocciolo* had been earlier, and as indeed it still was.[7]

As Boccaccio's description shows, symptoms of the illness were unmistakable. Within days of contact with the contagion, buboes—large areas of swelling filled with blood and pus—appeared in the lymph nodes of the body. Victims suffered horribly: they coughed blood; they developed a ghastly smell, like that of decomposing flesh; they acquired the "egg-shaped," tumor-like buboes, for which one strain of the plague is named; and they got purple, bruise-like spots on their necks and backs, "known as 'God's tokens,'" because they signaled a fatal case.[8] High fever, delirium, and vomiting were almost inevitably followed by death. Although estimates of mortality rates have varied, with chances of survival less than 5 per cent for the untreated, victims typically lived no longer than four days; many lived only a few hours. The plague spread, moreover, with alarming speed. Within hours the ill and dying multiplied throughout the cities and villages. Contemporary observers like Boccaccio were struck by the inexplicable randomness of the victims: not only would those who had come in contact with the ill become infected, but so would those who had simply touched the clothing or possessions of the victim. "It was," Knighton wrote, "as if sudden death had marked [people] down beforehand."[9]

Medieval medicine had no explanatory model to account for the indiscriminate virulence of the plague, and, not surprisingly, many people panicked in response to the devastation. Some fled, leaving afflicted members of their families to die alone. Many escaped to the countryside; others tried to isolate themselves from outsiders. Pope Clement VI famously insulated himself within a ring of flames, forbidding any living soul to pass the fiery boundaries. He survived. Bishop Branwardine, newly appointed Archbishop of Canterbury, did not. Within a mere two days of returning to England after his consecration, he succumbed to the disease.

In the absence of any rational explanation, many found scapegoats on which to blame the scourge. In Switzerland, 600 Jews were blamed and burned at the stake. Similar incidents occurred among some 80 other towns across Europe. Having survived the outbreak himself, Pope Clement issued a bull declaring such accusations libelous; the Jews, he pointed out, were suffering as much as the Christians. His efforts did little to appease the need for blame. Not everyone resorted to violence to control their fear; according to Boccaccio, some took a more pious approach, moderating their food and drink, tempering their lifestyles, and remaining indoors. Others, he claims, abandoned themselves to lawless excess, like the three rioters in the Pardoner's pestilence-ridden fictional town. Fearing each day would be their last, these people turned to drinking, gambling, and carousing. Why waste what few days they had left in tending livestock or working in the fields?

The horror of the situation took its toll on what many considered to be basic humanitarian practices and ethics. The sick were left untended as their relatives fled, a signal that familial bonds—the foundation of any social order—had eroded. The traditional respect given to the dead was also lost. Instead of receiving church burials attended by the traditional almsmen, bodies were dumped unceremoniously into nearby gravesites by opportunistic gravediggers, who were the only citizens bold enough to risk contact with the contagion. Reminders of mortality were everywhere, manifesting in a preoccupation with death that created an enormous cultural sense of anxiety and guilt. Representation provided one means of dealing with this. A macabre iconographic tradition developed to help contain and confront the horrific division of the body from the soul. Transi tombs, ornamented with representations of skeletal decay and grinning personifications of Death, replaced the traditional effigial tombs that had commemorated and idealized the body of the living person who had passed on. By 1425, the *Danse Macabre*, in which living humans are depicted dancing with cadavers, became commonplace. Functioning as an allegorical reminder of the fragility of life and the inevitability of death, these images subvert social hierarchies by reminding the viewer that death levels all, regardless of money or status.[10] This role is repeated in the personification of Death in morality plays, such as the late medieval *Everyman*.

The demographic effects of the plague only compounded a sense of the transience and futility of human life. Many cities were left largely depopulated. Chroniclers described deserted villages, buildings left to crumble, livestock wandering aimlessly. Yet this devastating scene, ironically, paved the way for greater social mobility. Many peasants were able to take advantage of the sudden availability of land, either increasing their own holdings by taking over the vacated fields of others or by demanding better terms of their lords for what fields remained. Wages subsequently climbed, because so few remained to produce the essentials required by the survivors. The middle classes acquired some of the goods and luxuries formerly reserved for the aristocracy; some commoners became wealthier even than those with inherited titles. Chaucer's Franklin, whose wealth is such that he can keep his table always at the ready for unexpected callers, is an example of this new kind of status. But the Franklin's concern that gentility is often measured by blood and an inherited title, rather than personal merit, reflects his anxiety over his own ambivalent social stature.

These economic shifts, combined with the general sense of betrayal by the governing orders, fundamentally challenged feudal ideology, as we shall see in the next chapter. The medieval world view was a hierarchical one, depending on the notion that every order and occupation had its place in a triangle of mutual support: the laborers provided the necessary sustenance for the world, the warriors protected and watched over that world, and the preachers provided spiritual counsel and nourishment. This model of society provided a comforting sociological sense that God had a plan that was enacted through mutual service and dedication. The reality too often fell short of this ideal, and the plague brought home the distinction between how things ought to be and how they really were. Although the ruling elite contracted the plague as well, it was the work-ing population, who lacked the resources to leave the close conditions of the cities, that was hit the hardest. Thus, there was a sense of dissatisfaction with the strictly hierarchical sense of world order that had so clearly failed. Many survivors accused the aristocracy and the clergy of not living up to their mandates of guardianship and spiritual counseling. Others blamed the masses for not upholding their proper societal roles or maintaining an appropriate sense of station. Thomas Brinton, bishop of Rochester (1320-89), preached in a sermon on the plague that "the scourges" were the direct result of sin, "since the corruption of lust and the designs of wickedness are greater today than in Noah's time," and since "a thou-sand forms of vice are practiced today which did not exist then."[11] Such moralistic interpretations reveal a widespread conviction that society had become dissolute and that the plague was God's vengeance for a more pervasive lapse in moral behavior. The antidote was moderation and an abstemious lifestyle. John Lydgate, in his *Dietary and a Doctrine for the Pestilence*, advised the avoidance of "incontinence"—by which he meant any overindulgence—either in food or in mirth: "beware of dissipation in your house at night; beware of rare suppers and of great excess."[12] These perspectives might strike us as severe, yet they must have been far prefer-able to the alternative: believing that the suffering inflicted by the plague was meaningless and indiscriminating. In addition, moralistic readings of the plague enabled survivors to channel their anxieties productively into calls for individual or social reformation.

THE PEASANT'S REVOLT

The years following the plague were characterized by a severe shortage in labor. The feudal notion of service depended on the ability of the lords to receive labor and dues from their villeins—the peasantry tied to their estates. Because the plague had decimated the working population, however, those people who had previously lacked power now gained more leverage over their payment and obligations. There was a great demand for skilled labor, but there were too few who could provide it. A succession of statutes aimed at reinstating these services at their pre-plague rates did little to assuage the problem. In 1351, following similar legislation two years earlier, the Statute of Laborers was passed in England, fixing the price laborers could charge for their services and products and blaming them for their "covetise" in exploiting the shortages caused by the plague. However, insofar as some manor houses had lost every one of their laborers, these laws simply could not be implemented. A lord with no villeins was, of course, unable to insist upon his right to revenue.

Among the aristocracy in the latter half of the fourteenth century, then, there was a general sense of anxiety that the peasants should know their place. In addition to those measures that attempted to control wages, additional statutes were passed to legislate what kinds of cloth or clothing the non-aristocracy could wear, signaling a general sense of distress that those of the burgeoning middle class (the merchants, artificers, and citizens of London) were attaining wealth enough to indulge in the same luxury items as the knights and lords (SEE CHAPTER 2). The statute speaks directly against the dress of the non-elite, who were perceived as rebelling against the estate into which they had been born. If everyone were wearing furs and silks, how could the estates be distinguished? How should feudal order be maintained, if the lower orders refused to recognize the prerogative of their "betters"?

At the same time, the peasantry showed an increasing sense of dissatisfaction with a ruling elite that exploited the ideology of the estates system for its own benefit. The glorious years of Edward III's reign were past; by the 1370s, Edward was aging and content to leave more and more of the business of politics to his trusted advisors. Meanwhile, Edward the Black Prince, his eldest son, was suffering from permanent damage to his health from his campaign in Spain (he died in 1376), while his second-eldest,

Lionel of Clarence, had died in 1369. The king surrounded himself with his favorites, who reaped the rewards of privilege for themselves. John of Gaunt, his third-eldest son, took over most of the king's duties, speaking for him in Parliament and exerting a powerful influence in council—roles which earned him increasing suspicion from his peers. The resulting dissatisfaction of the commons was expressed in works such as William Langland's *Piers Plowman*, which came into circulation between 1362 and 1379. A satire of the corruption of both political and religious figures, *Piers Plowman* found its hero in the hard-working figure of the title: Piers, who works to feed both the deserving and the wasteful alike. In particular, *Piers Plowman* parodies the exploits of "Lady Meed" in the royal court. Meed, an allegorical representation of the failures of the "rewards" system of payment, bribes and seduces each of the court figures she encounters while simultaneously protecting the wealthy, who freely rape and plunder the poor. In the allegorical representation of government that preoccupies Passus IV, Meed pays off the poor farmer whose goods have been seized and whose workers have been murdered by predatory aristocrats:

> …Meed, with a self-deprecatory smile, entreated the King's mercy, and offered Peace a present of the finest gold. "Accept this from me, my friend," she said, "a some small amends for all the harm you've suffered. Believe me, I'll guarantee that Wrong will never trouble you in this way again!" (IV.94-97)[13]

Instead of enforcing a system of justice in which criminality is punished regardless of class, the system parodied in *Piers Plowman* allows the aristocracy free rein. Peace, in this sequence, is willing to accept the bribe, because he holds no hope for redress except through compensation. Yet the release of Wrong virtually ensures that such crimes will take place over and over again.

The character of Lady Meed is probably based upon the real-life Alice Perrers, the mistress of the aging Edward III, who was accused in 1376 of misleading the king into expenditures to the degree of financial peril. As in *Piers Plowman*, the king was held blameless, while corruption at court was attributed to the self-serving officials who attended him. Edward managed to avert immediate danger by agreeing to dismiss Perrers and other court advisors in what was later dubbed the "Good Parliament" of 1376.

These reforms were short-lived, however. By that time John of Gaunt effectively held the kingdom and was able to have the acts of the Parliament declared unconstitutional within the year. Edward's death a few months later left the situation at court unresolved. With the Black Prince dead of the disease he had incurred abroad, Richard II, the Black Prince's young son, became king. Only ten years old when he acceded the throne, Richard was too young to rule effectively on his own. The control of the kingdom remained in the hands of magnates—particularly the feared John of Gaunt—who were largely distrusted by the people. Despite Edward's best efforts, dissatisfaction with the excesses of the aristocracy persisted into the reign of his young grandson.

It did not help that England had continued to lose revenue in its war with France. When, beginning in 1379, a series of poll taxes were levied to help offset the debt incurred by the ongoing campaigns, the dissatisfaction of the peasants flared into open anger. The poll tax of 1380, reprinted here, was very regressive: every inhabitant of the realm except for those demonstrated to be beggars had to pay a minimum tax of one groat—the equivalent of one to two days' wages for a skilled laborer (the unskilled made considerably less). This tax was implemented on top of the normal percentage of a rural laborer's work and production already required as part of his seigneurial service. The collection of this tax caused widespread resistance, and when the government attempted to enforce it, violence ensued. On June 10, 1381, an organized band of rebels marched into Canterbury under the leadership of Wat Tyler, imprisoned those they deemed "traitors" to their cause, and beheaded them. Simultaneously rebels attacked in Essex, while poor rioters in London burned the palace of John of Gaunt, the powerful and hated uncle of the young King Richard II. The *Anonimalle Chronicle* claims that an army of 60,000 rebels marched on London on Corpus Christi Day (June 13), razing to the ground the manor houses of hated lords, freeing the prisoners of Fleet Street, and rounding up and killing lawyers and clerks whom they blamed particularly for the government's repressive laws.

The Peasant's Revolt, as these events came to be called, was more than a violent reaction to a harsh tax. It was highly organized and ideologically motivated—held together, indeed, by code words from the popular and inflammatory *Piers Plowman*, which provided the ideological grist to support their anger:

> Where Meed enjoys the favor of the king, heaven help the country! For her favorite is False, and the one who gets injured is Honest Integrity. Jesus, Lord! The whole operation of royal justice is brought to a standstill by her precious stones. She simply tells lies to stop the law taking its course, and Honesty's claims cannot glimpse the light

of day thanks to the rain-cloud of coins she pours upon it. Why, this woman leads the law by the nose! (III.153-62)

In the opinion of the rebels, the country was being mismanaged by the upper classes. They demanded, in addition to restitution for the wrongs of the worst of the criminals, their freedom, an abolition of villeinage, and equality before the law. The rebels held the king himself blameless, however, even as had Langland, targeting instead key advisors from within the court as the real source of corruption. When Richard met with the rebels at Mile End, they declared him their true king and demanded a series of reforms that spoke directly against the prerogatives of the aristocratic class: that they be granted their release from bondage and that the traitors to the realm—including John of Gaunt; Simon Sudbury, the Archbishop of Canterbury; and the man widely held responsible for the poll tax, the king's royal treasurer, Robert Hales—be handed over for punishment.

The king appeared to agree to their requests, promising the rebels their freedom. The rebels then returned to London and, emboldened by the king's promise, burst into the Tower of London and dragged the Archbishop and other councilors to Tower Hill, where they were beheaded. General outlawry took over as the rebels turned against the Flemish and other "aliens" living in London (SEE CHAPTER 8). Hundreds were murdered in the streets and their properties ransacked. The extensive damage put an end to any sympathy that the rebels might have garnered.

According to the records, Chaucer should have been present when the rebels stormed through London, although there is no way of ascertaining whether he was in fact there. In 1381 Chaucer was living in the apartments directly above Aldgate, the entryway the peasants used into the city. He may thus have looked down upon the mob as the insurgents poured through, and he may have witnessed the burning of the Savoy (John of Gaunt's Palace) the opening of the prisons, and the executions of the Archbishop and countless others. He makes no overt reference to that week of terror in his writings, other than to compare the farmhouse ruckus of "The Nun's Priest's Tale" to the killing of the Flemings: "A, benedicitee! –Certes, he Jakke Straw and his meynee / Ne made nevere shoutes half so shrille / Whan they wolden any Flemyng kille, / As thilke day was maad upon the fox."[14] His friend and contemporary, John Gower, was much more strident in his condemnation:

God knows those wild men were deserving of eternal fire and were unreasoning reprobates. O the sorrow in these deeds, O the wicked deeds of sorrow! These foul exploits were more like those of hell than of man. This knavery was not human, for the Devil from the lower worlds was in charge of such rash doings. People were in such a frenzy that the rough mob did not know how to cherish God the Father, for they had lost Christ's love.[15]

The revolt was eventually quelled when the king requested that the leaders of the rebellion meet the king at Smithfield. There Wat Tyler met Richard as if on equal terms, shaking the king's hand and announcing, "Brother, be of good comfort and joyful, for you shall have within the next fortnight 40,000 more of the commons than you have now and we shall be good companions."[16] There was to be no peace, however. A quarrel broke out between Tyler and a yeoman; the mayor of London intervened and killed him (SEE EXCERPT BELOW). Following the loss of its charismatic leader, the rebellion fell apart. Though the violence continued for some days afterward, the aristocracy was able to mobilize and prevent further incidents. Richard revoked what concessions he had made to the rebels with the famous statement, "You have been peasants and peasants you will continue to be; you remain in bondage, not as before, but in comparably worse conditions."[17]

Thus ended what is often considered to be the first popular uprising in England. Although ostensibly few gains were made as a result of the revolt, the consequences were long lasting. Richard never again attempted to institute a poll tax, and the authorities showed considerable awareness about the mood of the general population. This is not to imply that officials were any more liberal than they had ever been—they most certainly were not. Archbishops Courtenay and Arundel, for example, were highly cautious about containing the popular movement of Lollardy, which they suspected could form a huge threat to the accepted hierarchy if left unchecked; eventually Arundel conspired with Henry V to have the movement decisively repressed. Religious and political leaders were simply more wary and a little more careful about maintaining their public images.

THE MERCILESS PARLIAMENT AND ITS REPERCUSSIONS

The Peasant's Revolt marked only the first of a series of crises in Richard's reign. Inheriting the throne at only ten years of age, Richard began his kingship under the stewardship of his uncle, John of Gaunt. Though every effort was made to sustain the pretence that a ten-year-old was capable of ruling efficiently, in reality most matters of governance were carried out by a council nominated from among the upper aristocracy. It was under this arrangement, indeed, that many of the troubles with Richard's nobles were to take shape, as political lines already divided those who were associated with the disliked John of Gaunt from the former supporters of the popular Edward III.

After his triumphant suppression of the Peasant's Revolt, Richard's minority was effectively over, but the realm was still deeply divided. Richard was, by all accounts, an incapable manager of the lords upon whom he depended for support. Possessed of an intrinsic sense of the king's majesty and rights, he insisted on the absolute authority of his office. Brought up in the court of his father, Edward the Black Prince, he had been witness to a style of life in which the prerogative of the royal prince was upheld without question. Edward the Black Prince had been assertive in his insistence on duty and obedience, and his retinue had shown him a deference that seemed to Richard to confirm the notion of a "divine right of kings." The two councilors upon whom Richard most depended for advice and guidance, his old tutor Simon Burley and Michael de la Pole, repeatedly told the commons that the duty of the subject was to obey and that, indeed, there could be no order in the realm without the absolute respect for this rule.[18] This ideological position, ironically, was only reinforced by the events of the Peasant's Revolt. Richard had little tolerance for dissent and compounded his intolerance with near-paranoia over encroachment on what he deemed his prerogative as king. As a result, he alienated some of the most powerful figures of his time, including Thomas Arundel, eventual archbishop of Canterbury, and Thomas Woodstock, the fifth son of the late King Edward.

Richard's intractability toward his barons was especially problematic during his management of the ongoing war with France. His campaigns were noticeably less successful than his grandfather's had been, partly because, after the Peasant's Revolt, there was no money to support troops. Further taxation to raise funds for the war was out of the question. The English thus repeatedly floundered in the 1380s. These disastrous campaigns abroad led to fear of a French invasion at home. In 1385–86, approximately when Chaucer was writing his *Troilus and Criseyde*, England received word that the French king, Charles VI, planned a massive campaign against London. The plan never materialized, but nonetheless 11,000 guards were posted outside London's walls, and the Londoners readied themselves for siege by clearing the immediate perimeter of housing just inside the walls.[19] In the aftermath of these disgraces, Richard attempted to negotiate peace, marrying the six-year-old French princess

Isabella of Valois in 1396 and staging friendly tournaments between the two countries. His efforts earned him the enmity of his lords, however, who were invested in continuing the war. An embarrassing defeat of the combined French and English forces during the crusade at Nicopolis seemed to confirm popular sentiment against Richard's policy abroad.

Matters came to a head in the years leading up to the so-called "Merciless Parliament" of 1388, when the "appellant lords," finding an auspicious period when the powerful John of Gaunt was away at war, accused Richard's closest friends and advisers of exerting treasonable influence over the king. The conciliatory policies of Edward III had ensured a peaceful reign, but at some cost to the purview and authority of the monarch. His grandson, lacking the prestigious military victories that empower a king, paid the price. Emboldened by an increased sense of entitlement, five powerful magnates—Gloucester, Warwick, Arundel, Nottingham, and Henry Bolingbroke (later Henry IV)—united to promote their interests and eliminate Richard's support at court. The enmity aimed at several of the accused seems in some cases deserved: Robert de Vere had been unaccountably favored with honors and estates over more deserving lords; Michael de la Pole, Richard's former chancellor, appears to have conspired repeatedly to have Richard's greatest political enemies put to death; Robert Tresilian, the chief justice of the King's Bench, was accused of corruption and soliciting bribes by numerous parties. The reaction of the Appellants in protecting their interests against such threats is perhaps understandable. Some of the accused, however, such as Nicholas Brembre, the former mayor of London, seem to have been targeted merely because they were close to the king. The object of this reproof was clear: the group of lords who drove the convictions wished to indict Richard's policies and eliminate those whom they felt enjoyed more influence in power than themselves.

At first Richard appeared to assent to the accusations, buying time until the next parliamentary meeting in February. During that time, de la Pole and Neville fled. Robert de Vere, however, decided to take a stand against the Appellants, raising an army in Cheshire and heading south to help support Richard's cause. De Vere was met by the Appellant forces at the historic Battle of Radcot Bridge, where his company was routed by Henry Bolingbroke; de Vere himself fled. The Appellants marched to the Tower of London with 500 armed retainers, accusing Richard of misgovernance and possibly threatening him with deposition. Several chroniclers suggest that Richard was in fact deposed for three days; the only thing that prevented his permanent deposition then and there was the Appellants' quarrel over who should take his place. Divided about the throne as they were, they were united in their desire to have their enemies brought to trial.

All told, eight of Richard's supporters were convicted of treason, including the aging Simon Burley, Richard's boyhood tutor and trusted confidante. As was customary in such situations, their lands were confiscated, and those who hadn't fled were executed. Simon Burley's case was particularly trenchant, given his long-standing loyalty to the king; even the Appellants were divided in their accusations. Events climaxed when Queen Anne herself begged for clemency for the knight, going down on her knees before Parliament. Buttressed by the unhappiness of the commons, however, the chief and highest ranked among the accusers, the Duke of Gloucester, was unmoved, and Burley was sentenced to death. Burley was clearly a victim of his allegiance to the royal family; his condemnation, more than any other during the crisis, gives the Merciless Parliament its name. Richard never forgave the humiliation.

Indeed, the brutal indictments of the Merciless Parliament did little to check royal power. If anything, they only intensified the hostility between Richard and his lords. At first Richard, supported by his uncle John of Gaunt, sought compromise—but not too much. He withdrew from politics for several months, while the Appellants tried, unsuccessfully, to reinvigorate their campaign against France. Emboldened by their purging of the court circle, they sought continental support for an ambitious assault. John of Gaunt, however, remained loyal to the king. Because the most powerful man in England refused to support the wars, other nations hesitated to involve themselves, and the Appellants found themselves increasingly discredited as their promised victories abroad failed to materialize. Meanwhile, emboldened by the lack of public support for the lords, Richard began to look farther afield for his own supporters. Leaving the court of London behind, he turned his attention to normally neglected outer territories such as Cheshire and the northwest midlands, from whom he recruited a private militia that he recognized with his own personal insignia. New magnate families threatened to replace the old in terms of their influence and royal favor.

Tension between Richard and the Appellants thus remained throughout the 1390s. At stake once again was the traditional feudal notion of divine kingship, which clearly troubled even those aristocrats most anxious for a change of leadership. Richard reminded his subjects of the divine ideology underlying his monarchy again and again: through carefully crafted portraiture such as that modeled in the Wilton Diptych, where the Virgin and a host of angels unite to present Richard with the banner of England, and through public acts of piety in which he asserted his devotion to the cults of Mary, John the Baptist, and other popular saints, such as Edmund, widely regarded as the patron saint of England.[20] Richard's beliefs were very likely sincere. There is no reason to attribute his faith to expediency alone. Yet they reinforced an ideological belief that the king's role was approved by God and established a level of harmony that was divinely ordained.

Indeed, whatever problems Richard may have had with his barons, as a patron of the arts he was admirable. The king cultivated a circle of poets to whom he granted appointments and revenues, and who closely followed court politics. The predominant writers of the era seem to have supported him absolutely, with the result that the conflict between the king and his barons reverberated throughout the literary world: Thomas Usk, who claims to have been personally familiar with Chaucer and who writes in praise of him in his *Testament of Love* (1387), was brutally executed in 1388 when he was deemed a traitor for informing on Thomas of Gloucester—he was drawn, hanged, and beheaded with 30 slow strokes of the sword.[21] Other court poets, Chaucer among them, seem to have been able to negotiate through the turbulent times well enough to keep their heads attached. Chaucer benefited from the patronage of Richard and the royal family repeatedly: after first being given considerable responsibilities under Edward III, he was appointed controller of petty customs under Richard in 1382, and he became clerk of the king's works in 1389, overseeing the upkeep and construction of Richard's major castles, manors, and forests. Given the fraught circumstances of the times, it is somewhat surprising that Chaucer weathered the crises so well. He had worked with other victims of the purging, including both Simon Burley and Nicholas Brembre, as part of his various official duties and may even have witnessed their executions. What he thought of these circumstances we cannot know, but certainly his poetry gives some indication. His "Lak of Stedfastnesse," composed in the last decade of the fourteenth century, blames a lack of loyalty for the troubles of the age:

> Somtyme this world was so stedfast and stable
> That mannes word was obligacioun;
> And now it is so fals and deceivable
> That word and deed, as in conclusioun,
> Ben nothing lyk, for turned up-so-doun
> Is al this world for mede and wilfulnesse,
> That al is lost for lak of stedfastnesse. (1–7)

As in many of Chaucer's works, a deliberate lack of specificity makes the target of complaint difficult to ascertain. It seems likely, however, that Chaucer blames Richard's difficulties on the Appellants, whose "lack of steadfastness"—or loyalty—is solely responsible for crisis in the realm. "Lak of Stedfastnesse" clearly establishes Chaucer's presence as a court poet who played a delicate game in trying to retain his position and perhaps his very life in a volatile political environment. The end of the poem addresses Richard directly, urging him to live up to the chivalric ideals of honor and truth threatened by the dominance of meed (rewards). Chaucer suggestively contrasts bribery, conspiracy, and greed to Richard's own characteristics of loyalty, truth, mercy, and compassion, so that by association anyone opposed to Richard's rule—such as the Appellants—is discredited through his or her inability to uphold the chivalric ideal.[22]

In 1396, after Richard had secured his country against the threat of France by marrying Isabella of Valois, he began a counterattack against those who had humiliated him. By most accounts the old diplomacy that had tempered even his worst moments turned now into tyranny. One by one Richard took revenge on his old enemies. Gloucester was murdered in 1397; the Earl of Arundel was executed for treason; Henry Bolingbroke (John of Gaunt's son), Warwick, and Archbishop Arundel, who had pled for the Appellants in 1386, were banished. Richard's behavior was unpredictable and extreme. In 1399, following the death of John of Gaunt, Richard attempted to confiscate Bolingbroke's inheritance and to extend the terms of his banishment from ten years to life. It was this move that undid him. Bolingbroke returned from exile to challenge Richard's claim, and Richard, away in Ireland at the time, found himself surprised as his support disintegrated. Aided by the family of the exiled Arundels, Bolingbroke secretly returned to England with a private army of retainers; making his way north, he secured the help of the most powerful families there. Joined by the forces of the Duke of York, he moved southward and captured Richard's key councilors. Meanwhile, prevented from returning to England by unaccountable delays, Richard lost what support he may have been able to muster as rumors circulated that he had already been killed or captured. Hearing word of Bolingbroke's encroaching army, Richard's nerve broke, and he fled, accompanied, according to the chroniclers, by only a handful of men. He was captured in Conway and deposed, later to die under suspicious circumstances in prison. Bolingbroke was crowned Henry IV in September 1399.

The Lancasters

Henry IV's hold on the English throne was precarious. As noted above, medieval ideology remained firmly committed to the idea of the divine prerogative of kings, even when the immediate desires of those with money and manpower enough provided ample incentive for challenging the monarch. Yet Richard's deposition could be mistaken for little other than an armed takeover. Nor was Henry next in the line of succession. As the son of John of Gaunt, third son of Edward III, Henry's claim to rule fell behind that of Edmund, Earl of March, who was descended from Edward's second son (Lionel). Henry's primary justification for his usurpation thus rested on Richard's unfitness to govern. The imprisoned Richard was forced to voluntarily "resign" the throne and to admit to a host of crimes against the state (SEE EXCERPTS BELOW), including unfair taxation and the abuse of his revenues, unjust sentences against his lords, and general lawlessness and tyranny. Once Richard's resignation was secured, Henry stepped forward to make his own claim, reading from a carefully crafted statement that made clear his legitimacy through Edward III, his grandfather:

> In the name of the Father, of the Son and the Holy Ghost, I,
> Henry of Lancaster, challenge this realm of England ....as that I
> am descended by right line of the blood coming from the good
> lord King Edward III and through the right that God of His grace
> hath sent me with the help of my kin and my friends to recover it,
> the which realm was in point to become undone for the fault of
> governance and the undoing of good laws.[23]

Henry's careful alignment of hereditary bloodline with a righteous moral cause did not go unnoticed by the court poets. Always the reconciler, Chaucer wrote a poem of flattery to the new monarch, acknowledging the strands that both justified and legitimated Henry's position:

> O conquerour of Brutes Albyon,
> Which that by lyne and free eleccion
> Been verray kyng, this song to yow I sende,
> And ye, that mowen alle oure harmes amende,
> Have mynde upon my supplicacion. (22–26)

As an acknowledged Ricardian, Chaucer had to negotiate a difficult set of presumptions. He could not support Henry's claim to lineage, nor denounce Richard for incompetence or wrongdoing, without making his own public support of Richard seem treasonous. His language thus flatters Henry through three separate claims: as warrior and conquerer, as an aristocrat with a kingly lineage, and as a free agent working out his moral goodness on behalf of what he believed to be right. His poem supports and extends Henry's own carefully crafted image by fusing together the paradoxes of the new king's position.[24] Chaucer's success as a negotiator has long been accepted; his survival from Richard's reign into Henry's has been marked as confirmation of his ability to remain impervious to the political threats that ended the lives of so many of his friends and acquaintances. More recently, however, that truism has been contested. After all, Chaucer survived only into the opening months of Henry's reign.[25] He was dead by October 1400, by which time he could not have been much older than 50. Whether he, too, lost his life as a result of the events of that tumultuous year is certainly a possibility.

The truth was that many were uncomfortable with Henry's usurpation. Not only was he not a direct heir to the throne, his right by conquest tacitly made uncertain all the nobles' confidence in the security of their lands and holdings. If a magnate could assume the possession and inheritance of another by force, what insurance did any lord have that something similar would not happen to his own family? Plots to restore Richard's monarchy erupted almost immediately. Within months, several of the lords still loyal to Richard had raised an army in hopes of gaining the deposed king's release. Nor did these end with Richard's mysterious death in prison a year later. Henry's reign was marked by a series of revolts—most notably by Owen Glendower, who styled himself the Prince of Wales and claimed large portions of Wales from England from 1402 to 1406.

Ironically, these internal disputes prevented Henry from renewing the war with France that he and his supporters had believed would restore England and the aristocracy to her chivalric and glorious inheritance. Instead the king maintained an uneasy and not wholly successful truce with France, which meant that he had to give up his dream of asserting himself as a force in Europe. Meanwhile, the French raided the English fleet in the Channel repeatedly and in 1405 threw in their lot with Glendower during his great English campaign. Although Glendower's rebellion was ultimately unsuccessful, Henry's legitimacy as the rightful ruler of England was tenuous, and he spent most of his reign trying to ensure his survival.

His son, Henry V, enjoyed a very different kind of rule. Remarkably, his succession was uncontested. Far from disputing an inheritance that had rested on such insecure grounds, the English now seemed anxious to return to traditional notions of succession and a sense of divine will. Coming to the throne in 1413 at the age of 25, Henry V ruled decisively, recalling a model of kingship that had probably best been exemplified by the old heroes Edward the Black Prince and Edward III. He rapidly put down a serious threat to his authority in the Lollard Uprising of 1415, and, unlike his father, he successfully rekindled the war with France when attempts to reinstate terms approaching the great concessions of the Treaty of Bretigny failed. Using many of the same arguments of his father, Henry V claimed divine right, conquest, and a rightful inheritance as part of his justification for invasion. Raising an army of over 10,000 men, he sailed to France in 1415 and, over the next several months, attained a remarkable series of victories that culminated in the Battle of Agincourt. This battle, commemorated in Shakespeare's *Henry V*, decimated a French force whose eagerness for what many considered a certain glory overpowered the advice of more experienced generals. The great French dukes of Bar, Brabant, and Alençon were killed, while the dukes of Orleans and Bourbon, as well as many other nobles, were taken prisoner.[26] Later victories at Caen and Rouen left England in control of virtually all of Normandy. Henry's negotiation of the Treaty of Troyes, which guaranteed his succession after Charles VI's death as King of France, and his marriage to Katherine, Charles's daughter, marked the zenith of his achievement. Such successes did much to restore the prestige of the monarchy and further legitimized his father's troubling claim to the throne.

Unfortunately, Henry V did not live long enough to enjoy or even solidify his success. Dying in 1422 of dysentery, he left his legacy to his infant son. Within only a few years, the French, led by the spiritual and military force of Joan of Arc, rallied and rebuffed the English campaign. A peasant girl who claimed she heard divine voices directing her private mission to free the French from English oppression, Joan had a volatile effect on the French, uniting dispirited companies and firing them up with her charismatic confidence. After defeating English forces in Orleans, she personally witnessed the crowning of the French dauphin in 1429. This moment has often been mistakenly claimed—by Hollywood and other popularizing sources—as concluding the Hundred Years War and the English claim toward France once and for all; in fact, it was not until 1453 that the war was finally over. Jean herself was captured by the Duke of Burgundy, an ally of the English, and turned over to English forces in 1430. She was tried for heresy by French inquisitors and burned as a witch in 1431; the French aristocracy, many of whom were jealous of her successes, did nothing to save her. Meanwhile, conflict between England and France continued under Henry VI since the English King, perhaps somewhat arrogantly, continued to assert his title as King of France. When Burgundy defected to the French side in 1435, the tide changed irrevocably toward the French. Charles VII of France retook Paris in 1436, and the French regained most of the remainder of their territories over the next decade. The final battle of the Hundred Years War, the Battle of Castillon in 1453, marked not only the end of English aspirations in France, but the beginning of a new age of warfare and weaponry. French cannonry decimated English forces.

The loss of France was nothing short of disastrous for English morale. Having lost territories they had enjoyed for hundreds of years, as well as a hereditary claim to the throne of France on which they had expended a huge amount of money and effort, the English found themselves bereft of European allies, preyed upon in the seas, and facing new enemies at home.[27] The humiliation was virtually complete. Perhaps not surprisingly, a nation already predisposed to violence witnessed fresh internal disputes in the 1450s. Henry VI's loss of his father's legacy had done little to strengthen his position as king. The magnate families quarreled again, and the problematic claim of the Lancasters to rightfully inherit the monarchy was freshly challenged by the Yorkists. The series of wars that resulted from this fresh low point in England's history—dubbed the War of the Roses, alluding to the red and white rose emblems sported by the two warring factions—was fought from 1453 until 1487, when Henry VII, the first Tudor king, defeated Richard III in the famous Battle of Bosworth.

This period has been considered by many to mark the closing of the Middle Ages. A new form of warfare had replaced the old; a dynasty extending back hundreds of years was replaced with the advent of the Tudors. Sir Thomas Malory, who describes himself as a prisoner and who very well may have been a victim of political rivalry during the wars, encapsulates the close of his age with a sense of failure and the loss of an almost divinely appointed sense of legacy:

> Lo ye all Englishmen, see ye not what a mischief was here? For
> he that was the most king and noblest knight of the world, and
> most loved the fellowship of noble knights, and by him they were
> upheld, and might not these Englishmen hold them content with

him ....Alas, this is a great default of us Englishmen, for there may nothing please us no term.[28]

It is perhaps not surprising that William Caxton, England's first printer, chose the *Morte Darthur* for publication in 1485. For him, as for Malory, the glorious feats of chivalry and the great kings of the Middle Ages were irrevocably gone. The old ideologies of loyalty and service, of honor and martial valor, were part of a feudal system of values that had already disintegrated into the past.

DOCUMENTS

EDWARD III MAKES READY FOR WAR (1337)

The Hundred Years War was ignited over a series of tensions regarding England's claims toward France. England itself had strong ties to Normandy and the northern territories of medieval France since the Norman Conquest; many English aristocrats had landholdings in France, which were confiscated first by Philip II and later, in 1337, by Philip VI. Since England had considerable commercial interests in retaining these possessions, hostilities were inevitable.

This document, from *The Brut, or The Chronicles of England*, recounts Edward's attempts to negotiate in Flanders over the French confiscation of Gascony in 1337. These negotiations were largely unsuccessful, and England withdrew its fealty from France. Edward began preparations for war, but his attempt to impose restrictions on French imports and his imposition of new taxes to support the war effort were unpopular moves.

> In the year of our Lord 1337, and of the twelfth year of King Edward, in the month of March, during the parliament at Westminster in Lenten time, King Edward made of the earldom of Cornwall a duchy, the which duchy he gave to Edward his first son with the earldom of Chester. Also King Edward made at that time six other earls, that is for to say, Sir Henry, the Earl of Lancaster's son, Earl of Leichester; William of Bowham, Earl of Northhampton; William of Mountgen, Earl of Salisbury; Hugh of Awdelee, Earl of Glouchester; Robert of Ufforde, Earl of Southfolk; and William of Clyntton, Earl of Huntington. In that same year, it was ordained in that same

parliament, that no man should wear any cloth that was wrought outside of England, such as cloth of gold, of silk, damask, velvet, satin, brocade, nor any such other; not any wilderness in Foreign [lands] beyond the sea, but such as might spend a [a certain portion] of yearly rent: but this ordinance and statute was of little effect, for it was nothing held.

In the thirteenth year of his reign, King Edward went overseas into Brabant, with Queen Philip his wife there bearing child, and at Antwerp; there he dallied more than a year, to treat with the Duke of Brabant and others allied unto him of the charge of the realm of France to King Edward, by right and by heritage, after the death of Carol the great, King of France, brother Germaine of Queen Isabelle, King Edward's mother, the which was held and occupied unrightfully by Phillip of Valois, the Emissary of King Carol: The which duke, and all his, in the foresaid things and in all others thereto longing, with all his men and goods, King Edward found ready unto him, and made and promised him swords, by good faith and trust; and after that, the king hasted him into England again, and left there the queen still behind him in Brabant.

Then in the fourteenth year of his reign, when all the lords of his realm, and others that ought to be at his parliament, were gathered and assembled together in the same parliament, held at London after the feast of Saint Hillary, the King's needs were put forth and promoted as touching the Kingdom of France; for which needs to be sped, the King asked the fifth part of all the movable/portable goods of England, and the wools, and the ninth the sheaf of every corn; and the lords of any town where such things should be taxed and gathered, should answer to the king thereof; and all he had and held at his own lust and will. Wherefore, if I shall acknowledge the very truth, the inner love of the people was turned to hate ...

Close Roll (1337)

The document provided here describes the deterioration of negotiations between England and France and the solidification of Edward's intent to wage war. It makes Edward's position toward France and his grievances therein official: although he recognizes France as a sovereign nation, he seeks to extend English control over the country by marrying his aristocrats into the ruling families of France; he further demands that France return the English possessions seized by Philip and that Philip, in essence, recognize Edward's superior rank.

These are the offers made to the King of France by the King of England, to avoid war.

First, the King of England sent to the King of France various solemn messages, begging him to return to him the lands which he is withholding from him, arbitrarily and against reason, in the Duchy of Guienne; but to these requests the King of France did nothing, until, at last, he promised that, if the King of England would come in his own person, he would do him justice, grace, and favour.

Trusting in this promise, the King of England crossed secretly into France and came to him, humbly requesting the delivery of his lands, offering and doing to the king as much as he ought and more; but the King of France always put him off with words and negotiations, and did nothing for him in fact; and moreover, during the negotiations, wrongfully drew to himself, more and more, the rights of the King of England in the Duchy.

Also, the King of England, seeing the hardness of the King of France, in order to have his goodwill, and that which he wrongfully detains, held out to him the great offers written below, i.e. when one was refused, he put forward another.

First, the marriage of his eldest son, now Duke of Cornwall, with the daughter of the king of France, without taking anything for the marriage.

Item, the marriage of his sister, now Countess of Guelders, with his son, together with a very great sum of money.

Item, the marriage of his brother, the Earl of Cornwall, whom God absolve, with any lady of the blood royal.

Item, to make recompense for the inconvenience, he offered him as much money as he could reasonably demand.

Item, because the King of England was given to understand that the King of France wished to undertake a crusade to the Holy Land, and wished to have the king of England in his company, and therefore he wished to show him grace and favour, the King of England, so that no hindrance of the crusade could be alleged against him, offered to the King of France to go with a large force with him in the crusade; so that, however, before he set off, the French king should make him full restitution of all his lands.

Item, then he offered to go with him on the said crusade, on condition that before he went, the French king should restore half, or a certain part of his lands ....

But the King of France, who was striving by all the means that he could to undo the King of England and his people, so that he could keep what he wrongfully withheld, and conquer more from him, would accept none of these offers; but, seeking his opportunities, busied himself in aid and maintenance of the Scots, the enemies of the King of England, attempting to delay him by the Scottish war, so that he would have no power to pursue his rights elsewhere ....

STATUTES OF THE REALM (1340)

The following document makes Edward's position toward France and his grievances official: France is to recognize itself as a possession of England.

The king to all to whom these letters shall come, greeting. Know that whereas some people do think that by reason that the realm of France has devolved to us as rightful heir of the same, and for as much as we are King of France, our realm of England should be put in subjection to the king and to the realm of France in time to come, we, having regard to the estate of our realm of England and namely that it never was or ought to be in ... the obedience of the kings of France ... will and grant and establish for us and for our heirs and successors, by assent of the prelates, earls, barons, and commons of our realm of England ... that our realm of England and the people of the same, of what estate or condition they be, shall not in any time to come be put in subjection or obedience to us, nor our heirs or successors as kings of France ....

THE BATTLE OF POITIERS. HENRY KNIGHTON (1346)

Before the battle the cardinals went up a nearby hill so that they could see the outcome. At once the first line fell upon the earl of Warwick, but they were quickly struck down by the archers, and the Marshal Clermont was killed, and many others ....The earl of Warwick chased the fugitives, and killed some and took others prisoner. In the mean time the second line of the French came and engaged the prince of Wales, and they fought bitterly under cover of a hedgerow, and the English were exhausted by the intensity of the battle, and their weapons much worn. And so strong and hard was the fight that the archers ran out of arrows, and picked up stones, and fought with swords and lances, and anything that they could find, and they defended themselves with marvelous courage, and at last as God willed it the French took flight.

And then as the English stood wearily refreshing themselves, and hoping to hear that they had overcome all their enemies, there came King Jean of France with a huge force, directing his attack towards the prince, who had a few men with him at that moment, because the rest were pursuing the defeated enemy. But just as the French line bore down, the earl of Warwick returned from the chase with his whole force, and took the French army in the flank, and fought them fiercely. And so by God's grace rather than by human dessert the battle went to the prince, who won a princely victory. And the king was captured, and his younger son, Philippe, and the count of Poitiers, and many great men.

THE PLAGUE. HENRY KNIGHTON (1348-50)

In this year and the next there was a general plague upon mankind throughout the world. It began in India, then spread to Tartary, and then to the Saracens, and finally to the Christians and the Jews, so that in the space of a single year, from one Easter to the next, as the report ran in the papal court, some eight thousand legions of people died suddenly in those distant parts, besides Christians.

The king of Tartary, seeing the sudden and unparalleled slaughter of his subjects, made his way with a great number of nobles towards Avignon, proposing to turn Christian and be baptized by the pope, as he thought that God's judgment had been visited upon his people for their unbelief. Therefore when he had traveled for twenty days and heard that the plague was as fatal to Christians as to other people he shrewdly turned about, abandoned his journey, and hastened to his own country; but the Christians pursued him and slew some two thousand of his people.

There died at Avignon in one day, according to a reckoning made before the pope, 1,312, and on another day four hundred and more.

Of the Dominicans in Provence three of 158 died during Lent, and
of a 140 friars at Montpellier only seven survived. At Magdelaine
only seven friars remained out of eight score (which was enough). At
Marseilles of seven score and ten Minorites, truly, only one remained
to tell the tale (and just as well). Of the Carmelites sixty-six perished
at Avignon before the citizens knew what was happening, for they
were believed to have slain one another. Not one of the Augustinian
friars, nor yet their order, survived in Avignon ...

....Then a lamentable plague traveled by sea to Southampton
and on to Bristol, where almost the whole population of the town
perished, snatched away, as it were, by sudden death, for there were
few who kept their beds for more than two or three days, or even half
a day. And thence cruel death spread everywhere with the passage of
the sun. There died in Leicester, in the little parish of St. Leonard's,
more than nineteen score, 400 in the parish of Holy Cross, and in St.
Margaret's parish 700, and so on in every parish, in great numbers.

THE PLAGUE AND ITS AFTERMATH.
HENRY KNIGHTON (1349)

At that time there was such a shortage of priests everywhere that
many churches were bereft of the divine office: of masses, matins, and
vespers, of sacraments and observances. A man could scarcely retain
a chaplain to serve a church for less than £10, or perhaps 10 marks,
and where one might have had a chaplain for four or five marks, or
two marks and his keep, with such numbers of priests as there were
about before the plague, now in those times there was almost no one
willing to take a vicarage for £20 or perhaps 20 marks. But within
a short time there came into holy orders a great multitude of those
whose wives had died in the plague, many of them illiterate, the
merest laymen, who if they were able to read at all were unable to
understand what they read.

Ox hides fell to a wretched price, namely 12*d*., and yet a pair of
gloves would cost 10*d*., 12*d*., or 14*d*., and a pair of breeches 3*s*. or 4*s*.
In the meantime the king sent word into every shire that mowers
and other workmen should take no more than they had before,
under the penalties laid down in the order, and thereupon made a
statute. Nevertheless the workmen were so puffed up and contrary-
minded that they did not heed the king's decree, and if anyone

wanted to hire them he had to pay what they asked: either his fruit and crops rotted, or he had to give in to the workmen's arrogant and greedy demands.

When it came to the king's notice that they had not obeyed his order, and had given their employees higher wages, he inflicted heavy fines upon abbots and priors, and upon greater and lesser knights, and upon the others, great and small, of the land: from some 100s., from some 20s., and from each according to what he could pay. And he took 20s. from every ploughland in the kingdom, and received not less than a fifteenth would yield.

Then the king caused many labourers to be arrested, and put them in prison. Many ran away, and took to the woods and forests for a time, but those who were caught were grievously fined. And most were sworn that they would not take more than the old established daily rate, and so were freed from prison. And artisans in the boroughs and townships were treated in the same way.

Statute of Laborers (1351)

The Statute of Laborers was the second statute aimed at legislating wages after the Black Death. It proved as unenforceable as its predecessor. Note the tone rebuking the peasantry for laziness and opportunism.

Whereas late against the malice of servants, which were idle, and not willing to serve after the pestilence, without taking excessive wages, it was ordained by our lord the king, and by the assent of the prelates, nobles, and other of his council, that such manner of servants, as well men as women, should be bound to serve, receiving salary and wages, accustomed in places where they ought to serve in the twentieth year of the reign of the king that now is, or five or six years before; and that the same servants refusing to serve in such manner should be punished by imprisonment of their bodies, as in the said statute is more plainly contained: whereupon commissions were made to divers people in every county to inquire and punish all them which offend against the same: and now forasmuch as it is given the king to understand in this present parliament, by the petition of the commonalty, that the said servants having no regard to the said ordinance, but to their ease and singular covetise, do withdraw themselves to serve great men and other, unless they have livery

and wages to the double or treble of that they were wont to take
the said twentieth year, and before, to the great damage of the great
men, and impoverishing of all the said commonalty, whereof the said
commonalty prayeth remedy: wherefore in the said parliament, by
the assent of the said prelates, earls, barons, and other great men, and
of the same commonalty there assembled, to refrain the malice of the
said servants, be ordained and established the things underwritten:

First, that carters, ploughmen, drivers of the plough, shepherds,
swineherds, deies [dairy maids], and all other servants, shall take
liveries and wages, accustomed the said twentieth year, or four years
before; so that in the country where wheat was wont to be given, they
shall take for the bushel ten pence, or wheat at the will of the giver,
till it be otherwise ordained. And that they be allowed to serve by a
whole year, or by other usual terms, and not by the day; and that none
pay in the time of sarcling [hoeing] or hay-making but a penny the
day; and a mower of meadows for the acre five pence, or by the day
five pence; and reapers of corn in the first week of August two pence,
and the second three pence, and so till the end of August, and less in
the country where less was wont to be given, without meat or drink,
or other courtesy to be demanded, given, or taken; and that such
workmen bring openly in their hands to the merchant-towns their
instruments, and there shall be hired in a common place and not privy.

Item, that none take for the threshing of a quarter of wheat or rye
over 2 *d*. ob. [2 1/2 *d*.] and the quarter of barley, beans, pease, and
oats, 1 *d*. ob. if so much were wont to be given; and in the country
where it is used to reap by certain sheaves, and to thresh by certain
bushels, they shall take no more nor in other manner than was
wont the said twentieth year and before; and that the same servants
be sworn two times in the year before lords, stewards, bailiffs, and
constables of every town, to hold and do these ordinances; and that
none of them go out of the town, where he dwelleth in the winter,
to serve the summer, if he may serve in the same town, taking as
before is said. Saving that the people of the counties of Stafford,
Lancaster and Derby, and people of Craven, and of the marches of
Wales and Scotland, and other places, may come in time of August,
and labor in other counties, and safely return, as they were wont to
do before this time: and that those, which refuse to take such oath or
to perform that that they be sworn to, or have taken upon them, shall
be put in the stocks by the said lords, stewards, bailiffs, and constables
of the towns by three days or more, or sent to the next gaol, there to

remain, till they will justify themselves. And that stocks be made in every town for such occasion betwixt this and the feast of Pentecost.

Item, that carpenters, masons, and tilers, and other workmen of houses, shall not take by the day for their work, but in manner as they were wont, that is to say: a master carpenter 3 *d.* and another 2 *d.*; and master free-stone mason 4 *d.* and other masons 3 *d.* and their servants 1 *d.* ob.; tilers 3 *d.* and their knaves 1 *d.* ob.; and other coverers of fern and straw 3 *d.* and their knaves 1 *d.* ob.; plasterers and other workers of mudwalls, and their knaves, by the same manner, without meat or drink, 1 *s.* from Easter to Saint Michael; and from that time less, according to the rate and discretion of the justices, which should be thereto assigned: and that they that make carriage by land or by water, shall take no more for such carriage to be made, than they were wont the said twentieth year, and four years before.

Item, that cordwainers and shoemakers shall not sell boots nor shoes, nor none other thing touching their mystery, in any other manner than they were wont the said twentieth year: *item*, that goldsmiths, saddlers, horsesmiths, spurriers, tanners, curriers, tawers of leather, tailors, and other workmen, artificers, and laborers, and all other servants here not specified, shall be sworn before the justices, to do and use their crafts and offices in the manner they were wont to do the said twentieth year, and in time before, without refusing the same because of this ordinance; and if any of the said servants, laborers, workmen, or artificers, after such oath made, come against this ordinance, he shall be punished by fine and ransom, and imprisonment after the discretion of the justices.

Item, that the said stewards, bailiffs, and constables of the said towns, be sworn before the same justices, to inquire diligently by all the good ways they may, of all them that come against this ordinance, and to certify the same justices of their names at all times, when they shall come into the country to make their sessions; so that the same justices on certificate of the same stewards, bailiffs, and constables, of the names of the rebels, shall do them to be attached by their body, to be before the said justices, to answer of such contempts, so that they make fine and ransom to the king, in case they be attainted; and moreover to be commanded to prison, there to remain till they have found surety, to serve, and take, and do their work, and to sell things vendible in the manner aforesaid; and in case that any of them come against his oath, and be thereof attainted, he shall have imprisonment of forty days; and if he be another time convict, he shall have imprisonment of a quarter of a year, so that at every time that he offendeth and is convict, he shall have double pain: and that the same justices, at every time that they come [into the country], shall inquire of the said stewards, bailiffs, and constables, if they have made a good and lawful certificate, or any conceal for gift, procurement, or affinity, and punish them by fine and ransom, if they be found guilty: and that the same justices have power to inquire and make due punishment of the said ministers, laborers, workmen, and other servants; and also of hostelers, harbergers [those who provide lodging], and of those that sell victual by retail, or other things here not specified, as well at the suit of the party, as by presentment, and to hear and determine, and put the things in execution by the exigend after the first capias,[29] if need be, and to depute other under them, as many and such as they shall see best for the keeping of the same ordinance; and that they which will sue against such servants, workmen, laborers, [and artificers], for excess taken of them and they be thereof attainted at their suit, they shall have again such excess. And in case that none will sue, to have again such excess, then it shall be levied of the said servants, laborers, workmen, and artificers, and delivered to the collectors of the Quintzime [the tax known as the "Fifteenth"], in alleviation of the towns where such excesses were taken.

ALICE PERRERS. THOMAS WALSINGHAM (LATE 14ᵀᴴc)

Although Edward's early reign was unrivaled in its attainment of glory for England, his later years were characterized by a serious decline and a gradual receding from public life. Most notoriously, Edward fell under the influence of Alice Perrers, widely regarded as a corrupt courtier who used her influence for selfish ends. "Lady Meed," in William Langland's *Piers Plowman*, is believed to be based upon her. Our translation is based on Walsingham's *Chronicon Angliae*.

[An account of that shameless, low born harlot, Alice Perrers, her meddling in affairs of state, and how she drained the king of all vigor through *causas venereas*.]

There was at that time in England a certain Alice, an impudent and most shameless harlot, surnamed Perrers. Fortune had elevated her from lowly origins, for she was the daughter of some thatcher or other from the town of Henney. She was neither comely nor beautiful, but knew how to make up for these defects with a flattering tongue. Such is the blindness of fortune, that although she had been the concubine and maidservant of a certain Lombard, for whose household needs she once fetched and bore water on her own back, this woman was promoted to an intimacy with the king that exceeded all expectation, for he loved her more than any other, even while his queen still lived.

After Alice Perrers began her liaison with the king, he became so infatuated that he permitted the most difficult and serious matters of state to be deliberated with her. Once she had begun to entrap the king, and perceived that his mind was at her mercy, she began to intervene unjustly in all his affairs, supporting wrongful suits, and everywhere appropriating others' possessions illegally for her own use. And if anyone seemed ready to confront her, she went straight to the king to effect her purposes lawfully or even unlawfully, abetted by his patronage. Now the people of England had tolerated her these many years, for they heartily loved their king and took care not to offend him; indeed, the English possess a natural affection for their king, more so than any other nation, and once they have admitted a man to royal status, they venerate him always, however grievously he betray them. Therefore, because they knew that the king's preference for this trollop went beyond the bounds of law or honor, they tolerated it until she sullied his reputation among all nations, illegally making herself the most powerful person in England, and polluting almost the whole kingdom with her disgraceful impudence.

Indeed, much does patience and humility abound in the English. This woman's effrontery swelled to such an extent that, without so much as a blush, she took a seat at the courts at Westminster. There she felt no qualms in petitioning the judges, on her own behalf or that of her friends—even on behalf of the king, as if she were some minister charged with his affairs—publicly demanding a favorable outcome for her suits. No surprise then that the judges, motivated by respect for the king or, as is more likely, out of dread of that harlot, rarely dared to render a judgment other than that which she had determined. The English people tolerated these and many other scarcely believable deeds for the longest time. They finally had to decide, although not without scruples of conscience and manifest shame, to give offence to their king rather than to their God. Well they understood how hard it would be for him to accept any accusation or judgment against his Alice! But they strove in the end to act for the good of the king, and not for his damnation.

Therefore, on behalf of the commonwealth, the common knights with Sir Peter de la Mare as their spokesman petitioned John of Gaunt, the Duke of Lancaster, along with his fellow judges to do what was appropriate to remedy her transgressions, and to have Alice Perrers taken away from him, if it could be done within the bounds of propriety and without tarnishing the king's honor any further than it had already been in this and neighboring kingdoms. Not only, they claimed, had she captured and bound the king to her with natural enticements, but also lured him into unnatural lovemaking by means of magical arts, in order that his elderly and depleted body, shriveled of its sexual humors, might be temporarily restored to all its virile force. Thus, she had brought about a double damnation, for she made him an object of contempt for all nations and robbed him almost entirely of his power.

It was revealed moreover, as a result of a diligent investigation by the Commons, that Alice Perrers had been married to Sir William of Windsor, who was then staying in Ireland. The Commons endeavored thence to dispatch her to Ireland, where, with any luck, she might no longer trap the guileless king with her harlot's tricks. First they took care, however, to disclose to the king that his mistress was the wife of another man, and that he had therefore been committing adultery for a long time. When he heard this the king became sore afraid, swearing "by my Holy Lady Mary"—for such was his oath—that he knew not that she was married, and had he known that she had a husband, he would in no way have undertaken his sinful union with her. Nevertheless, he made it known to Parliament that he in no way wanted her put to death for her sins, but that they should rather treat her leniently, out of equal love for the king and for his reputation.

The Poll Tax (1380)

The poll tax of 1380 was the last of a series of regressive tax measures aimed at supporting the unpopular war against France. This tax required even the poorest of the realm to pay a minimum of three groats (the equivalent of three days' labor for a skilled worker), while the wealthy were capped at a maximum tax of 60 groats. This unfair tax measure led to widespread resistance and was directly linked to the outbreak of the Peasant's Revolt.

> The declaration to our lord the king and his council by the commons of England on the matters with which the commons were charged in this present parliament, for various needs which were shown to them as well for the safety of the realm as for the keeping of the sea.
>
> In the first place the lords and commons are agreed that, for the abovesaid needs, contribution should be made by every lay person in the realm, both in franchises and outside, males and females alike, of whatever estate or condition, who has passed the age of fifteen years, of the sum of three groats, except for true beggars, who shall be charged nothing, always providing that the levy shall be made under the regulation and form that each lay person shall be charged equally according to his ability, and in the following manner: that is to say, that for the total sum to be accounted for in each township the well-to-do shall according to their ability help the less; so that the most affluent shall not pay more than the sum of sixty groats for himself and his wife, and no person shall pay less than a groat for himself and his wife; and that no person shall be charged to pay, except in the place where he and his wife and children dwell, or in the place where he remains in service. And that all artificers, labourers, servants, and other lay folk, as well servants dwelling with all prelates and temporal lords whosoever, abbots, priors, clerks of the chancery, common pleas, king's bench, exchequer, receipt and with all other officers, knights, squires, merchants, citizens, burgesses and with all other persons, should, each one of them, be assessed and taxed according to the value of their estate, and in the form aforesaid. And that commission should be given to suitable persons, as well of the shires as of the city and boroughs, to be collectors and controllers of the abovesaid sum, and that they should be sworn to act well and loyal in their offices. And it is not the intention of the said commons to make this present grant except solely for the sustenance of the Earl of Buckingham and the other lords and men in his company in Brittany, and for the defense of the realm, and keeping of the sea. And that this present grant should not be taken or levied in the form or example of any levy of groats before this time, but solely charged on persons who are now alive, so that two thirds shall be paid in

the quinzaine of St. Hilary next coming, and one third at the feat of Whitsuntide next following. And in any event none of the knights, citizens, or burgesses who have come to this present parliament should be made a collector or controller of the aforesaid sums. And that it should please our lord the king and his council to ordain for the said levy that the servants in the king's household as well as those in the households of other lords throughout the realm should be equally charged, according to the intention of this grant.

JOHN BALL. THOMAS WALSINGHAM (1381)

John Ball was one of the charismatic leaders of the Peasant's Revolt. This document describes some of the characteristics of his leadership that led to the events of the uprising.

For twenty years or more, John Ball had always preached in various places the things which he knew would please the common people, disparaging men of the Church as well as secular lords, and so won the good will of the commons rather than approval before God. Indeed, he taught that tithes should not be paid to an incumbent, unless the one who was to give the tithe was richer than the vicar or rector who was to receive it. He also taught that tithes or oblations should be withdrawn from curates if it was an accepted fact that the subject or the parishioner lived a better life than his priest. He further taught that no one was fit for the kingdom of God who had not been born in wedlock. He also preached the perverse doctrines of the perfidious John Wyclif as well as the opinions and false ravings which Wyclif held, and many other things which it would be tedious to relate. Because of these teachings, John Ball had been forbidden by the bishops in whose parishes he had dared to proclaim them, from preaching in their churches in future. So he went into the market-squares and streets, or into the fields, to preach. He did not lack an audience of the common people, for he was ever eager to entice them to listen to what he had to say, by disparaging prelates and by saying things that pleased them.

THE BURNING OF THE SAVOY. THOMAS WALSINGHAM (1381)

The Savoy was John of Gaunt's beautiful palace by the Thames, close to Westminster. The burning of the palace by the mob symbolized the hatred the commoners felt for John of Gaunt; indeed, they blamed him and other corrupt nobles for the deplorable state of England, rather than Richard II himself. This translation is based on Walsingham's *Chronicon Angliae*.

The following day, the day of the feast of Corpus Christi itself, the rebels infiltrated the city of London, and seduced the average simpleton with the lure of freedom and with hatred against so-called enemies of the realm—especially the duke of Lancaster [John of Gaunt], whom they hated most of all. And so they quickly and easily persuaded all the poorer sort to go along with their conspiracy. Then, later that same day, when the hot sun was at the zenith, and the mob had sampled willy-nilly divers wines and rarest liqueurs—for the lords and citizens of London had left all their wine cellars open—becoming as a result not so much drunk as raving, the rebels began to harangue the simpletons at length about these so-called enemies. Following upon this, they massed and rushed for the palace of the duke of Lancaster, the Savoy, not to be compared for its magnificence and nobility with any other dwelling in England, not merely to set it afire and burn it down, but really in order to defy the aforesaid duke, whom they called a public enemy, and to terrorize other so-called enemies.

The common riffraff were so pleased with these exhortations that, considering it particularly shameful were any one else to injure or harm the duke before they did themselves, they rushed to the Savoy like men possessed, cast fire into it from all sides and destroyed it at their leisure. In order to demonstrate to all inhabitants of the realm that they were in no way acting from baser motives, the rebels issued a proclamation that none were to take or hide for their own use anything found there—under penalty of losing their head. They proclaimed instead that the numerous gold and silver vessels to be found at the palace were to be smashed into pieces and thrown into the Thames or the sewers; gold embroidered and silk cloths were to be ripped up and crushed under the heel; rings and other jewelry set with precious stones were to be ground down in mortars, so that they might become of no use henceforth to anyone—and so it was done. They neglected no opportunity to inflict whatever kind of outrage imaginable against the duke: following this, they took one

of his most precious vestments, which we call a "jakke," stuck it on
a lance, and used it as a target for arrows. When, however, they were
scarcely able to damage it with arrowshot, it was taken down and
hewn to pieces with axes and swords.

THE KING'S DIRE STRAITS. THOMAS WALSINGHAM (1381)

Richard's response to the revolt was legendary. Although much of his victory seems somewhat accidental, his words afterward famously reinstated
the feudal estates system and its legitimacy for England. This translation
and the next are based on Walsingham's *Chronicon Angliae*.

> Seeing such crimes being perpetrated, the king and his immediate
> advisors gathered hastily in emergency council. The situation did not
> permit lengthy deliberation, and they were especially confounded
> one and all by the killings of the archbishop of Canterbury and of
> the kingdom's treasurer, who were among the most powerful men
> of the realm; moreover, they feared that if such great men could be
> executed, would even lesser lords be spared by the mob? In order
> to quench the general madness then in full career throughout the
> land, King Richard, following the advice of those nearest to him at
> the time, offered the rebels terms of peace, on condition that they
> desist from burning and tearing down homes, from putting people
> to death, and on condition also that they would return to their own
> homes without more ado, there to be given charters confirming
> the aforementioned peace. The men of Essex accepted these terms
> willingly, for they were already weary of their prolonged labors and
> yearned in part to see their homes, wives, and children once more.
> Nevertheless, while most of them went home, they decided to
> appoint certain of their number to stay behind to receive the king's
> charter. And so it came to pass, even though the Essex contingent
> had left, that the men from Kent remained the whole of the
> following night.

THE DEATH OF WAT TYLER. THOMAS WALSINGHAM (1381)

Although of somewhat tender age, the king was stirred to bold
action, and prompted by the complaints of his knights and esquires,

ordered the mayor of London to arrest Tyler. The mayor, a man of incomparable spirit and audacity, arrested Tyler without hesitation then and there. He struck Tyler a blow on the head that rendered him completely senseless. Tyler was soon surrounded by the others of the king's retinue and pierced through by sword thrusts to several parts of his body. As Tyler fell to the ground from his horse, English knighthood first saw the almost lost hope of resisting the commons restored to them. At once, as the commons contemplated Tyler's ruin, they cried in distress for his death, "Dead is our captain; our leader, treacherously done in. Let us stand together and die with him; to our bows and let us avenge his death like men!" Bows were drawn, and they prepared to shoot. At this the king, with resourcefulness and courage marvelous for so young a man, quickly spurred his horse towards the commons and riding around them said, "What is this, my people? What are you doing? Surely, you do not wish to shoot at your own king? Don't let this move you to rage or sadness—the man that just died was a traitor and nobody. I will be your king, your captain, and your leader. Follow me to that field where you will have whatever it pleases you to seek."

The king acted thus lest the peasants, brought together in their bitterness of spirit, should set fire to the houses at Smithfield where they were when their leader, the aforesaid traitor, was killed. So they followed the king and the knights who were with him to an open field, not yet fully decided or certain whether they should have killed the king, or instead assent to everything and return home with a royal charter.

RICHARD'S WORDS TO THE PEOPLE.
THOMAS WALSINGHAM (1381)

Men were therefore sent to the king, who was then staying at Waltham, to ask him if he was intending to allow them to enjoy that liberty; and further to request that their liberty should be equal to that of the lords, and that they should not be forced to attend courts except only the view of frankpledge twice a year. The king and the council, which was then with him, were absolutely amazed at such temerity, and hesitated for some time as to what reply to give, until the king himself made the following reply. "What wretches you are, hateful on land and sea, and not worthy to live, who demand to be made equal to your lords. You would certainly have been punished with a most ignominious death, if we had not determined to observe the rights of envoys. As you have come here as envoys, you will not die at this present time, but will go on enjoying life, so that you may give a true report of our reply to your fellows. Give this message then to your compatriots on behalf of the king. You have been peasants and peasants you will continue to be; you remain in bondage, not as before, but in comparably worse conditions. As long as we live to be able to ensure this, and while by God's grace we rule over this kingdom, we shall strive with our mind, our strength, and our resources to keep you in subjection ... "

Proclamation for Keeping the Peace within the City (1381)

Although the Revolt was put down relatively quickly, it was months before peace was restored throughout the realm. The following provides some indication of the measures Richard felt compelled to take to ensure peace in city limits.

Richard II, A.D. 1381.

Be it proclaimed on behalf of our Lord the King, for the safekeeping of the peace, that no one repairing unto the City, after he shall have taken up his lodging there, shall go armed, or shall carry upon him, or have carried after him, a sword, unless he be a knight. And that no one shall go with armor for the body, save only the peers of the realm, and a knight or esquire of the household and retinue of our Lord the King; on pain of forfeiture of such armor, and of imprisonment. And that no foreigner shall be found wandering in the City by night after 6 of the clock; or shall go out of his hostel before 6 of the clock in the morning, on the same pain. And that each hosteller shall warn his guests of this Ordinance, and shall harbor no one for whom he will not answer, on the pain thereon ordained.

Injunctions Issued by the Mayor, For Keeping the Peace Within the City; And for Keeping Watch and Ward at the City Gates

....We do direct and command you, on your oath, and on pain of forfeiting as much as unto our Lord the King and to the City you

may forfeit, that, all excuses set aside, you do cause the Gate of
Aldgate this Saturday next to be guarded throughout the day, and
the night following, by four men sufficiently well armed, and four
archers, of the people of your Ward; that so, no stranger enter there
through the same, with any armor, unless he be a gentlemen, or else
an archer, who will say upon his faith that he has now come unto
our said Lord the King, to go forth with him against his rebels. And
that the said four men-at-arms and four archers of Tower Ward are
to come and take the same guard of the gate, in manner aforesaid.
And any person of your Ward whom you shall find rebellious or
disobedient in keeping guard in manner aforesaid, you are to have
forthwith arrested and taken to prison, as being a rebel, and disloyal
to our said Lord the King, and to the City aforesaid. And this you are
in no manner to omit, on the peril which awaits the same.

LETTER FROM RICHARD REVOKING THEIR LIBERTIES. THOMAS WALSINGHAM (1381)

Although Richard promised the remission of bondage to the commoners,
he revoked his promise as soon as the leaders of the Peasant's Revolt were
imprisoned and/or executed. His famous words, below, chillingly promise
enduring servitude to the poorest of England's people.

> We further forbid them from refusing, as they did extraordinarily
> during the times of the troubles, to carry out their aforesaid tasks,
> customs, and services, or from delaying on any pretext carrying
> them out for us or their aforesaid lords. They are not to demand,
> appropriate or lay claim to anything, whether liberties or privileges,
> other than they reasonably had before the aforesaid troubles. Those
> who have in their possession in safe keeping the aforesaid letters of
> our granting freedom and pardon are immediately to return them
> and restore them to our possession and that of our council, for them
> to be cancelled...

JOHN BALL LETTERS (1381)

The John Ball letters, circulated in the months preceding the Peasant's
Revolt, are especially interesting for their invocation of terms from the

popular literary text, *Piers Plowman*. The first selection blames government ills on "Hob the Robber"—a figure who closely echoes "Rob the
Robber" from *Piers Plowman*. Hob is thought to refer to Robert Hales,
the treasurer of the kingdom under Richard II and the force behind the
hated poll tax. Among the advisors who fled with Richard to the Tower
when the rebels surged through the streets of London, Hales was summar-
ily executed, along with the Archbishop of Canterbury, Simon Sudbury.

> John the Shepherd, some time Saint Marie's priest of York, and now
> of Colchester, greets well John Nameless, and John the Miller, and
> John Carter, and bids them that they beware of guile in the borough,
> and stand together in God's name, and bid Piers Plowman go to his
> work, and chastise well Hob the Robber, and take with you John
> Trewman and all his fellows, and no more, and look sharp to one
> head (leader), and no more.

> When Adam delved and Eve spun,
> Who then was a gentleman?

> Man beware and be no fool:
> Think upon the ax, and of the stool.
> The stool was hard, the ax was sharp,
> The fourth year of King Richard.

> Johan the Miller hath ground small, small, small;
> The King's Son of heaven shall pay for all.
> Be wary before ye be of woe;
> Know your friend from your foe.
> Have enough, and say "Ho!"
> And do well and better, and flee sin,
> And seek peace, and hold you therein.

> Now reigns pride in price,
> Covetousness is held wise,
> Lechery without shame,
> Gluttony without blame:
> Envy reigns with treason,
> And sloth is taken in great season;
> God bring relief, for now is time.
> Amen.

Jack Carter prays you all that you make a good end of what you have begun, and do well and always better and better, for at the evening men hurry the day. For if the end be well, then all is well. Let Piers the plowman my brother dwell at home and bid us come, and I will go with you and help that I may fetch your meat and your drink, that none of you will fail. Look that Hob the Robber be well chastised for losing your grace; for you have a great need to take God with you in all your deeds. For now is the time to beware.

John Ball greets you all well and would you understand, he has rung your bell.
Now right and might,
Will and skill
God speed everyone.
Now is time, Lady, to help Jesus your son, and your son to his Father, to make a good end, in the name of the Trinity that is begun, Amen, Amen, per charity, Amen.

A Censure of the Mendicant Friars. Thomas Walsingham (late 14ᵀᴴc)

Several chroniclers conjectured as to why the events of 1381 and other calamities occurred, blaming events on a general dissolution of society or on the more specific failures of the clergy.

To me, moreover, it seems that the causes are not simply such as listed above. More generally, one should attribute these troubled times to the sins of all the land's inhabitants, and include the Mendicant Orders in particular as aggravating causes of the unrest. These had forgotten what they originally professed, or even to what purpose Orders such as theirs had been instituted: to be poor—because their founders, those most holy men, had so wished it—and to be entirely divested of all worldly possessions so that (to speak candidly) they might have nothing they might be loath to lose. But now, jealous of possessions, they countenance the mighty for their crimes, foment error in the common crowd, and glorify both for their sins. And so that they might acquire and amass riches, they—who have renounced possessions and sworn to persevere in poverty—affirm instead that what is good is evil; assert that if evil, it is good. Thus, they seduce the nobility with praise, the people with lies, and drag both into perdition with themselves. Although they make a profession of truth, the Mendicant Orders are so defiled by their perverse lifestyle that nowadays there is a common saying that plays on the logic of sound argument: "He is a friar, therefore a liar"—both formally valid and true to fact, just as it was once customary to adduce, "He is a man, therefore mortal." Lest we appear, however, to have written these things out of spite, let us confess ourselves all to be at fault, and make amends for those sins which we have knowingly committed. And let us beseech God most fervently for peace and charity, so that he may bring about peace and truth in our time.

The Merciless Parliament (1388)

The following account, from the continuation of Ranulf Higden's *Polychronicon*, describes the crisis of 1388 that led to the execution of Richard II's favorites at court. As the selection below shows, Richard's nobles were threatened by his exclusion of their council for his political decisions; they wanted to limit the extent of his power outside their direct control. The Appellants were careful to direct their complaints not against the king, however, whose prerogative as ruler of England was established by the divine right of kings. Instead they directed their wrath at his personal friends, including Simon Burley, who had been the king's tutor in his youth.

> When the lords heard how the king had uttered threats against them, they proposed to depose him, both because he had not kept the agreement made with them, and also because it appeared that he preferred to govern through false traitors rather than through his most faithful friends the lords and nobles of the realm. They were resisted by the Earl of Warwick, who opposed this view in the following speech. "Far be it from me," he said, "that I should see such a glorious prince born from such a noble stock, and sprung from such a noble stem, to whom I and the other lords of the realm did homage and swore fealty at the coronation, now deposed and cast down ... Indeed such an act would be a disgrace to us and an eternal

reproach to our posterity. Therefore withdraw your minds from this intention and give them to the virtuous work of resisting the Duke of Ireland, that perfidious traitor, who with a strong and powerful band coming from Cheshire through the middle of England is striving to reach the king, and may be bringing to us danger and ruin ...." This advice pleased all the lords and they all agreed to do this, the contrary motions being entirely annulled ....

After some period of time, however, the nobles recanted and resolved to approach the king again.

On the morrow the lords sent to the king asking him to give up those persons accused of treason or to give security to them with a warrant for charging such persons wherever they might be found in England. To this he replied that he did not know of such persons, nor was he willing to grant a warrant for them to be charged, for greater and many things had been done to them without a warrant. But the lords were not content with such replies, and said indeed that they wished to have a speedier conclusion on these matters. The more famous bishops of all England, the Duke of York, the Earl of Northumberland and the rest of the temporal lords were arbitrators and pacifiers between the king and the aforesaid lords, and morning and evening every day negotiated earnestly between them for peace and concord. At last they induced them to come to the king to speak with him. Therefore the lords came on the sixth day after Christmas to the Guildhall of London where in the presence of the mayor and community of the city they declared how and under what form and wherefore they were doing these things and they rode there with a great multitude. When they had done this they came to the Tower of London with 500 men well armed, and seeing the king seated in the room next to the chapel on his throne under a canopy they made due obeisance, that is with a three-fold prostration to the ground. Then the king nodded to them and they modestly arose and started to converse with him. But the tumult of the people outside disturbed them and so with the king's consent they went into the chapel, where they spoke strongly to the king about his conduct towards them; first, in contravening his own oath, not keeping those things which he had promised; secondly, plotting death at once against his nobility; thirdly, in defending false traitors to the destruction of himself and the subjugation of the whole kingdom. They said many more things there which have not been repeated in public. But finally they asserted that it was necessary for him to correct these errors and to submit himself to the rule of the lords. But if he refused to do this, he must know that his heir was undoubtedly of full age, and wished freely for the good of the realm and its salvation to obey them and to be governed under their rule.

The king was stupefied and said that he wished to submit himself to them as was fitting in lawful things and to be governed by their wise counsel, saving his crown and royal dignity, and he affirmed this on his own oath. When this had been done, the lords said that he must not deceive them in any way in these promises nor henceforth change his will by force or guile in these matters, if he wished to enjoy his regality and crown in the future....

...They deprived Sir Simon Burley of the custody of Dover Castle and Sir John Beauchamp, then steward of the household of the king, they removed from his office. And on the first of January they held a council at Westminster and caused many to be arrested, that is, Sir Thomas Tryvet, Sir Simon Burley, Sir John Beauchamp, Sir Nicholas Daggeworthe, Sir William Elkham, Sir James Berners, Sir John Salisbury and Sir Nicholas Brembre. Also Dom Richard Medford, Dom Richard Clifford, and Dom John Lincoln, clerks, who were all sent for safe custody to various fortresses by the aforesaid lords until the next parliament.

DEPOSITION OF RICHARD II (1399)

The events of the Merciless Parliament were only the beginning of many years of tension between Richard and the Appellants. Richard's capture at Conway led rapidly to Henry's claim to the throne of England. Tantamount to Henry's claim were the accusations of treason and unjust rule.

> ...And he [Richard] absolved his lieges and made renunciation and cession, and swore this... and he signed it with his own hand, as is more fully contained in the schedule, of which the tenor follows in these words...
>
> And immediately he added to the aforesaid renunciation and cession, in his own words, that if it were in his power the Duke of Lancaster should succeed him in the realm....
>
> 1. In the first place the king is indicted on account of his evil rule, that is, he has given the goods and possessions which belong to the crown to unworthy persons and otherwise dissipated them

indiscreetly, and therefore has imposed collections and other grave and insupportable burdens on his people without cause. And he has perpetrated innumerable other evils. By his assent and command certain prelates and other lords temporal were chosen and assigned by the whole parliament to govern the realm; and they faithfully labored with their whole strength for the just government of the realm. Nevertheless the king made a conventicle with his accomplices and proposed to accuse of high treason the lords spiritual and temporal who were occupied for the good of the realm; and in order to strengthen his evil design he violently forced the justices of the realm by fear of death and torture of body to destroy the said lords.

2. Also the king caused the greater part of his justices to come before him and his adherents secretly at Shrewsbury, and he induced, made and compelled them to reply singly to certain questions put to them on behalf of the king, touching the laws of the realm. This was contrary to their wishes, and other than what they would have replied if they had been free and not under compulsion. By color of these replies the king proposed to proceed later to the destruction of the Duke of Gloucester, the Earls of Arundel and Warwick and other lords, against whom the king was extremely indignant because they wished the king to be under good rule but with divine help and the resistance and power of the said lords opposing him, the king could not bring his scheme into effect.

4. [Although the king in full parliament and with its assent pardoned the Duke of Gloucester and the Earls of Arundel and Warwick, and for years acted in a friendly way towards them, nevertheless he carried venom in his heart, and when the opportunity came he had the Duke of Gloucester murdered, the Earl of Arundel beheaded and the Earl of Warwick and Lord Cobham sentenced to perpetual imprisonment.]

5. [At the time when Gloucester, Arundel and Warwick were condemned, the king, in order to fulfill his harmful designs on others, caused a great multitude of malefactors to be raised in the county of Chester. These ruffians caused many injuries to the king's subjects, as murders, beatings, woundings, robberies, rapes and other excesses, for none of which would the king give justice to plaintiffs.]

7. Also, after many of these people had made fines and redemptions, they sought from the king letters patent of general pardon, concerning the above; but they could secure no advantage from these letters of pardon until they had paid new fines and redemptions to save their

lives; by this they were much impoverished. On account of this the royal name and estate were brought into great disrepute.

8. By color of this concession the persons thus deputed proceeded with other matters touching generally that parliament—and this at the will of the king, in derogation of the estate of parliament, and a great damage to the whole realm, and a pernicious example. And in order that those persons might seem to have a certain color and authority for such deeds, the king caused the rolls of parliament to be deleted and changed to suit his purposes, against the intention of the commission.

9. [Contrary to his coronation oath he had denied justice to Henry duke of Lancaster.]

10. Also, although the crown of England and the rights of the crown, and the same realm, have been so free for all time past that neither the lord high pontiff nor anyone else outside the kingdom ought to intermeddle with the same, yet the king, in order to strengthen his erroneous statutes, begged the lord pope to confirm the statutes ordained in the last parliament. On which the king sought for apostolic letters, in which grave censures were threatened against all who presumed to contravene the statutes in any way ...

16. Also, the king refused to keep and defend the just laws and customs of the realm, but according to the whim of his desire he wanted to do whatever appealed to his wishes. Sometimes—and often when the laws of the realm had been declared and expressed to him by the justices and others of his council and he should have done justice to those who sought it according to those laws—he said expressly, with harsh and determined looks, that the laws were in his own mouth, sometimes he said that they were in his breast, and that he alone could change or establish the laws of his realm. And deceived by this idea, he would not allow justice to be done to many of his lieges, but compelled very many persons to desist from suing for common justice by threats and fear.

It seemed to all the estates who were interrogated thereupon, singly and in common, that those accusations of crime and defaults were sufficient and notorious enough for the deposition of the king; and they also considered his confession of inadequacy and other matters contained in the renunciation and cession, publicly announced: whereupon all the estates unanimously agreed that there was abundant reason for proceeding to deposition, for the greater security and tranquility of the realm and the good of the kingdom ....

And at once, it being manifest from the foregoing transactions and by reason of them that the realm of England with its appurtenances was vacant, Henry Duke of Lancaster, rising in his place, and standing erect so that he might be seen by the people, and humbly making the sign of the cross on his forehead and his breast, and invoking the name of Christ, claimed the realm of England, vacant as aforesaid, along with the crown and all its members and appurtenances, in his mother tongue....

HENRY IV's WORDS TO RICHARD II, UPON RICHARD's ABDICATION. FROISSART (1399)

By this act, you will do much to appease the hatred which many of the English feel for you. It was to end the disorders which had arisen in the country through the breakdown of the judicial system that I was sent for from beyond the sea, and for that reason that the people wish to make me king. Strong rumors are going about the country that I have always had a better claim to the crown than you. When our grandfather, King Edward of happy memory, raised you to the throne, this was pointed out to him, but he always had such affection for his son the Prince of Wales that no one could dissuade him from his purpose of making you king. If you had then followed the example of the Prince and had heeded good advice, as a true son should endeavor to do to the best of his ability, you would still be king and in possession of all your powers. But you have always done the opposite, and now the rumor is, throughout England and beyond, that you are not the son of the Prince of Wales, but of some clerk or canon. I have heard from certain knights who were in the household of my uncle the Prince that when the Prince felt that his marriage was a failure because your mother was a first cousin of King Edward and he was beginning to conceive a great dislike for her because she bore him no children... she, who had won him in marriage by guile and cunning, was afraid that my uncle the Prince would find some pretext for divorcing her. So she arranged to become pregnant and gave birth to you, and to another before you. The first died too young for any opinion to be formed of him, but about you, whose habits and character are so different from the warlike nature of the Prince, it is said in this country and elsewhere that your father was a clerk or canon. At the time when you were conceived and born at Bordeaux on the Gironde there were many young and handsome ones in the Prince's household. That is what people are saying in this country, and you certainly seem to prove it, having always tended to favor the French and to desire peace with them to the prejudice and dishonor of England. Because my uncle of Gloucester and the Earl of Arundel wisely and loyally remonstrated with you and tried to preserve the honor and achievements of their fathers, you treacherously had them killed. For my part, I have taken you under my protection and I will defend you and prolong your life, through human pity, as far as I can. I will plead your cause before the Londoners and the heirs of those whom you unjustly put to death.

CORONATION OF BOLINGBROKE (1399)

Henry's claim to the throne of England was based on three carefully constructed claims: his rightful heritage, his conquest of England as a knight and warrior, and Richard's free acknowledgement of his fit rule. These claims were no doubt coerced from Richard and remain an excellent example of Henry's anxiety regarding his claim.

In the year of Our Lord 1399, on the last day of September, a Tuesday, Henry, Duke of Lancaster, held a parliament in the Palace of Westminster outside London. In this parliament were assembled the prelates and clergy of most of England, the dukes, earls, and nobles of the realm, and also the commons of each town, in numbers proportionate to the size of the towns. Before that assembly Duke Henry made his claim to the throne of England, putting forward three titles to the office of king: first, by right of conquest; secondly, because he said he was the rightful heir; thirdly, because King Richard of Bordeaux had resigned the crown to him of his entire free will in the presence of prelates, dukes and earls in the hall of the Great Tower of London.

Having put forward these three titles to the crown, Henry Duke of Lancaster asked the people of England there assembled to say what their will was. They answered with one voice that their will was that he should be their king and that they would have none other....

....After dinner that Sunday the Duke left the Tower again for Westminster, riding bare-headed and wearing the King of France's emblem round his neck. With him were his son the prince, six dukes,

six earls, eighteen barons and a total of eight to nine hundred knights.
The King had put on a short doublet of cloth-of-gold in the German
style. He was mounted on a white charger and wore the blue garter
on his left leg. He rode right through the city of London and was
escorted to Westminster by a great number of nobles with their
men wearing their various liveries and badges, and all the burgesses,
Lombards and merchants of London, and all the grand masters of
the guilds, each guild decked out with its particular emblems. Six
thousand horses were in the procession. The streets through which
the Duke passed were covered and decorated with various kinds of
hangings and on that day and the next white and red wine flowed
from nine fountains in Cheapside, each with several jets.

....All the way from the Palace to the Abbey a canopy of indigo-
colored silk supported on four silver rods and with four jingling
golden bells was carried over the Duke's head by four citizens of
Dover, as was their right. On one side of him was borne the Sword
of the Church and on the other the Sword of Justice. The first was
carried by his eldest son the Prince of Wales and the second by
Henry Percy, Earl of Northumberland and Constable of England ....
At about nine o'clock the whole procession entered the Abbey,
in the middle of which was a throne upholstered in cloth-of-gold
standing on a high platform covered with crimson cloth. On this the
Duke mounted and took his seat. He was now in royal state, except
that he was wearing neither the cap nor the crown. The Archbishop
of Canterbury then mounted the platform and at each of the four
corners of it in turn explained to the people how God had sent them
a man to be their lord and king ....

When this had been done, the Duke came down from the throne
and went to the altar to be consecrated. Two archbishops and ten
bishops were there to perform the ceremony. Before the altar his
royal robes were taken off, leaving him naked to the waist, and he
was anointed in six places, on his head, his chest, on both shoulders,
on his back between the shoulders, and on his hands. Then a cap was
put on his head and meanwhile the clergy chanted the litany and
the office which is used for consecrating a font. The King was then
dressed in ecclesiastical robes like a deacon; crimson velvet shoes like
those of a prelate were put on his feet and then spurs with points and
no rowels. The Sword of Justice was drawn from its sheath, blessed
and handed to the King, who re-sheathed it. It was then girded on
him by the Archbishop of Canterbury. Next the crown of St. Edward,

which has three arches, was brought and blessed and placed on the King's head by the Archbishop. After the mass had been sung, the King left the Abbey in this regalia and found outside the Constable of England with his lieutenant and the Marshal of England, who together cleared the way for the return to the Palace.

In the center of the Palace was a fountain from which white and red wine flowed through numerous jets. The King went through the hall to his private room, then came back to the hall for the dinner .... Halfway through the dinner there came in a knight of the name of Dymoke, in full armor and riding a horse, with both of them, horse and rider, covered in mail with crimson trappings. The knight was ready to take up a challenge and another knight went before him carrying his lance. He wore a naked sword at one side and a dagger at the other, and he handed the King a parchment saying that if any knight, squire or gentleman cared to say or maintain that King Henry was not the rightful king, he was ready to fight him there and then in the King's presence, or whenever it pleased the King to appoint a day. The King had this challenge cried by a herald-at-arms at six different places in the hall, but no one came forward.

DEATH OF RICHARD II. FROISSART (1400)

Richard's death in prison remains a mystery. It was suggested that he starved himself to death while imprisoned, but historians are largely convinced that he was murdered to ensure Henry's claim.

> It was said to the King: "Sire, as long as Richard of Bordeaux is alive, neither you nor the country will be secure."
>
> The King replied: "I think you are right. But for my part I will never put him to death, since I took him under my protection. I will keep my promise to him until it becomes apparent that he is behaving treasonably."
>
> The King's knights said: "It would be better for you if he were dead rather than alive. As long as the French know that he is there they will want to make war on you. They will hope to restore him to the throne, because he is married to the King of France's daughter."
>
> To this the King of England made no reply, but went out of the room and left them talking together. He went to see his falconers and, placing a falcon on his wrist, became absorbed in feeding it.

Not many days afterward a true report ran through London that Richard of Bordeaux was dead. From what cause and how it happened I did not know at the time when I wrote these chronicles. His body was placed on a hearse with a black canopy over it. Four black horses were harnessed to it, led by two grooms in black, and four black-clad knights followed behind. So he left the Tower of London where he had died and was taken right through London at a walking-pace until they reached Cheapside, the main street of the city.... Some were moved to pity to see him in that state, but others not. These said that for a long time past he had well deserved to die.

....I and everyone else saw Richard of Bordeaux on the throne of England for twenty-two years and, while he was still alive, the crown passing back to the House of Lancaster, when King Henry, in the circumstances I have related, became King of England. He had never thought of the crown nor would have done if Richard had behaved in a kinder and more friendly way towards him; and then it was the Londoners who made him King, to repair the great wrongs done to him and his children, which had aroused their sympathy.

When the hearse, with Richard of Bordeaux on it, had been in Cheapside a full two hours, it moved on. The drivers drove it forward and the four knights walked behind. When they were outside London their servants met them with their horses. They mounted and rode on more rapidly, until they reached a village called Langley thirty miles from London, where there is a manor belonging to the King and Queen. There King Richard of Bordeaux lies buried. May God have mercy on his soul.

St. Joan's Appearance to Deliver France (1429)

The story of Joan of Arc, her humble background and immense faith, is well known. The following document, from the French chronicler Waurin, describes Joan's appearance before the king and her perseverance despite his and his nobles' doubts.

In that year, which was then reckoned one thousand four hundred and twenty eight, while Orleans was besieged, there came to King Charles of France, at Chinon where he was then staying, a young girl who described herself as a maid of twenty years of age or thereabout named Joan, who was clothed and habited in guise of a man, born

in the parts between Burgundy and Lorraine at a town named
Domremy very near Vaucoulleurs. This Joan had remained a long
time at an inn and she was very bold in riding horses and leading
them to drink and also in performing other feats and exercises which
young girls are not accustomed to do; and she was sent to the king
of France by a knight named Sir Robert de Baudricourt, captain
of the place of Vaucoulleurs appointed on behalf of King Charles.
This Sir Robert gave her horse and five or six companions, and
likewise instructed her, and taught her what she ought to say and do,
and the way in which she could conduct herself, since she asserted
that she was a maid inspired by divine providence, and sent to King
Charles to restore him and bring him back into the possession of all
his kingdom generally, from which he was, and she said, wrongfully
driven away and put out. And the maid was, at her coming, in very
poor estate; and she was about two months in the house of the king,
whom she many times admonished by her speeches, as she had
been instructed, to give her troops and aid, and she would repel and
drive away his enemies, and exalt his name, enlarging his lordships,
certifying that she had had a sufficient revelation concerning this;
but whatever she could say at this beginning neither the king nor
those of his council put much faith in her words or admonitions.
And she was then considered at court only as one deranged and
deluded, because she boasted herself as able to achieve so great an
enterprise, which seemed to the great princes a thing impossible,
considering that all they together could not effect it; and so her
words were turned into folly and derision, for it seemed indeed to
the princes that it was a perilous thing to believe on account of
the blasphemy which might follow upon it from the speeches or
scoffs of the people, as it is a great reproach to a wise man to fall
into deception through believing too readily, especially in perilous
matters. Nevertheless, after the maid had remained a good space at
the king's court in the state that I have mentioned, she was brought
forward and aided, and she raised a standard whereon she had painted
the figure and representation of Our Lord Jesus Christ; indeed, all
her words were full of the name of God, wherefore a great part of
those who saw her and heard her speak, like fools, had great belief
that she was inspired by God as she said, or hesitated about it; and
she was many times examined by famous clerks and men of great
authority in order to inquire and know more fully her intention, but
she always held to her purpose, saying that if the king would believe

her she would restore him to his dominion. Maintaining this purpose she accomplished some operations successfully, whereby she acquired great renown, fame, and exaltation....

NOTES

1   Scott L. Waugh, *England in the Reign of Edward III* (Cambridge: Cambridge UP, 1991) 14.

2   Earl Jeffrey Richards, "The Uncertainty in Defining France as a Nation," in *Inscribing the Hundred Years' War in French and English Cultures*, ed. Denise N. Baker (Albany, NY: State U of New York P, 2000) 127-57.

3   John M. Bowers, "Chaucer After Retters: The Wartime Origins of English Literature," in *Inscribing the Hundred Years' War*, ed. Denise N. Baker (Albany, NY: State U of New York P, 2000) 94-95.

4   Colin Platt, *King Death: The Black Death and Its Aftermath in Late-Medieval England* (Toronto: U of Toronto P, 1996) 5.

5   Henry Knighton, *Knighton's Chronicle 1337-1396*, trans. G.H. Martin (Oxford: Clarendon P, 1995) 99.

6   Platt 17.

7   Giovanni Boccaccio, *The Decameron*, trans. G.H. McWilliam (1972; New York: Penguin Books, 1995) 5.

8   John Kelly, *The Great Mortality: An Intimate History of the Black Death, the Most Devastating Plague of All Time* (New York: HarperCollins, 2005) 20-23.

9   Kelly 192.

10   Paul Binski, *Medieval Death: Ritual and Representation* (Ithaca, NY: Cornell UP, 1996) 157.

11   Cited in John B. Friedman, "Henryson's *Testament of Cresseid* and the *Judicio Solis*," *Modern Philology* 83.1 (1985): 12-21.

12   John Lydgate, *The Minor Poems of John Lydgate*, ed. Henry Noble MacCracken, EETS o.s. 192 (London: Oxford UP, 1934): 702, 706.

13   William Langland, *Piers Plowman: A New Translation of the B-Text*, ed. A.V.C. Schmidt (Oxford and New York: Oxford UP, 1992), 38.

14   Geoffrey Chaucer, *The Riverside Chaucer*. Ed. Larry Dean Benson. 3rd ed. (Boston, MA: Houghton Mifflin, 1987), ll. 3393-97.

15   John Gower, *Vox Clamantis*, in *The Major Latin Works of John Gower*, trans. Eric W. Stockton (Seattle, WA: U of Washington, 1962) 72.

16   A.R. Myers and David C. Douglas, eds., *English Historical Documents* 1326-1485 (New York: Routledge, 1969) 136.

17   Thomas Walsingham, *The St. Albans Chronicle: The* Chronica Maiora *of Thomas Walsingham*, Vol. I: 1376-1394, ed. and trans. John Taylor, Wendy R. Childs, and Leslie Watkiss (Oxford: Clarendon P, 2003) 515.

18   Nigel Saul, *Richard II* (New Haven, CT: Yale UP, 1997) 119.

19 Bowers 107.

20 Saul 310.

21 Thomas Usk, *The Testament of Love*, ed. R. Allen Shoaf (Kalamazoo, MI: Medieval Institute Publications, 1998) 7.

22 See Paul Strohm, *Hochon's Arrow: The Social Imagination of Fourteenth-Century Texts* (Princeton, NJ: Princeton UP, 1992) 72.

23 Stowe MS 66, quoted in Strohm, *Hochon's Arrow* 83.

24 Strohm, *Hochon's Arrow* 88–89.

25 Terry Jones argues that Archbishop Arundel negotiated Chaucer's early death in *Who Murdered Chaucer* (New York: St. Martin's P, 2003).

26 Maurice H, Keen, *English Society in the Later Middle Ages,* 1348-1500 (London and New York: Penguin Books, 1990) 359.

27 Keen, *English Society in the Later Middle Ages* 407.

28 Sir Thomas Malory, *Le Morte Darthur*, ed. Helen Cooper (Oxford: Oxford UP, 1998) 507.

29 A "capias" is a writ commanding certain kinds of legal action.

CHAPTER II

"From Every Shires Ende"

The Structure of Society

INTRODUCTION

THE THREE ESTATES

*T*he English poet John Dryden famously praised Chaucer for the generosity of his vision in *The Canterbury Tales*: "here," he said, "is God's plenty."[1] Indeed, Chaucer's pilgrims represent many of the categories that, according to contemporary orthodoxies, composed medieval society. The most influential model for society in the late Middle Ages divided all human beings into three estates: the priestly or clerical order, the knightly order, and the peasantry—or, to use a common restatement, men who pray, men who fight, and men who labor. Chaucer's Parson, his Knight, and his Ploughman are, arguably, idealized representations of each estate. According to the ideal, each estate was responsible for the performance of certain duties. Those who belonged to the clerical class were charged with maintaining the society's spiritual welfare; those who belonged to the military class were charged with defending and policing that society; and those who belonged to the laboring classes were charged with its material upkeep. Members of different estates were ideally bound to one another by mutual obligation; a "bond of trust," for example, should exist between lord and tenant (SEE *The Treatise on the Laws and Customs of England*, BELOW). Although to moderns the idea of trust and the notion of mutual obligation might sound egalitarian, the three-estate model of society was profoundly hierarchical. The first estate, the clergy, had a monopoly on spiritual authority (for more on this, SEE CHAPTER 4) and the second estate, the "warriors"—who were often elided with the nobility—on political authority. Given that these groups comprised only about 5 or 6 per cent of the actual population, the vast majority of English people owed, according to this idea of society, obedience and deference to their superiors.

The role of the common people was to work hard to keep their masters in the style to which they were accustomed. The three-estate model defined the well-ordered and cohesive society as one in which individuals performed their duties according to their station. During the fourteenth century, England was still feudal in the sense that a large portion of its laboring class owed services and dues, rather than money rents, to their lords. The three-estate model's understanding of the relationship between commoner and lord was a reflection of this traditional manorial system in which lords owned the land that the peasants cultivated. By the end of the Middle Ages, the manorial system had dwindled into insignificance, and money rents became the economic norm. The ideals associated with the earlier manorial culture nevertheless retained their ideological appeal throughout this period. One fourteenth-century homilist preached that:

> He that is not labouring in this world on studying, on prayers, on preaching for help of the people—as it falleth to priests; nor in ruling the people, maintaining them and defending them from enemies, as it falleth to knights; nor labouring on earth in divers crafts, as it falleth to labourers: when the day of reckoning cometh, right as he lived here without labour, so shall there lack the reward of the "penny," that is, the endless joy of heaven.[2]

Here as in other medieval sources, the social order is seen as an emanation of the divine order, and a lack of obedience to your lord is repaid by the Lord. This notion of social order puts a heavy stigma on the disobedient and the rebellious: those who fail to remain in their assigned place are rebels not just against society but against nature and against God. The most frequently cited passage on this issue was from 1 *Corinthians*, where Paul urges the virtue of abiding in the place to which you have been called: "Each man, in what calling he is called, in that dwell he" (SEE BELOW).

The three-estate model served the upper echelons of medieval society well. It protected their privileges by placing a high value on obedience and stability, and it designated the forces that challenged the status quo—change, innovation, and social mobility, among others—as evils. As we saw in the previous chapter, late medieval society was marked by numerous crises, like the plague, that caused radical changes. Not surprisingly, aristocrats took measures to defend what they saw as their prerogatives. Both the Royal Ordinance of Labourers of 1349 and the Statute of Labourers of 1351 attempted to arrest social mobility by fixing salaries: citing the "the malice of servants ... not willing to serve after the pestilence," these laws ordered "men as women" who were "bound to serve" to serve and to receive only the wages that obtained before the plague took its toll on the English population. The language of the Statute of Labourers clearly invokes the three-estate model of society and just as clearly brands departures from it as malevolent. Those who refused "to do and use their crafts and offices in the manner they were wont to" were to be "punished by fine and ransom, and imprisonment after the discretion of the justices." In the years that followed, the government repeatedly passed legislation that imposed versions of the three-estate model. The Statute of Additions of 1413, for example, stipulated that people be identified by their estate in legal cases. The sumptuary laws (SEE BELOW), meanwhile, dictated who could wear what according to social status. Addressing what it characterized as "the outrageous and excessive apparel of diverse people, against their estate and degree, to the great destruction and impoverishment of all the land," the 1363 law spelled out what kind of clothing was appropriate for each estate. Yeomen, for example, were restricted to cloth worth 40 shillings or less and were expressly forbidden to wear ornamentation, like jewelry or embroidered material. In 1463, the government passed more sumptuary laws, which stipulated, among other things, that only members of the royal family could wear purple silk, while knights and those below them should wear jackets "of such length that the same may cover [their] privy members and Buttocks."

The characters of late medieval literature are often judged by the standards invoked in legislation like the Statute of Labourers. In the morality play *Mankind* (c. 1465–70), for example, the central character's frustration with the farming life leads him to seek the company of the vices New Guise and Nowadays, who flout social as well as clerical authority. They convince Mankind to abandon his sensible farmer's weeds for the fashionable wear of a man-about-town. The change in costume symbolizes a complex change in social and spiritual condition: as Mankind dons his shortened jacket, he tries to leave behind his place as farmer, and his desire for social mobility in turn results in his spiritual fall. Mankind's short coat is not just symbolic of his desire to quit the farming life—according to the 1463 law, it infringes on a privilege reserved for peers. Mercy, the play's priest-like virtue, clarifies what is at stake: the vices "know full little what is their ordinance [place]" and that makes them "worse than beasts," who at least follow their "natural institution" (164–66). Mercy further reminds the audience that "this condition of leaving" your ordained place is tantamount to "felony or treason" and warns of the judgment awaiting those who disobey in the afterlife.[3]

Even as they attempt to bring matters into conformity with the idea of the three estates, late medieval laws remind us that minutely observed gradations existed within medieval society: the aristocracy included, for example, esquires, knights, barons, earls, and dukes. Although a mere esquire like Chaucer enjoyed gentle status like John of Gaunt (Chaucer's brother-in-law and, arguably, his patron), the powerful Duke of Lancaster was in many ways in a class of his own (England at the time had only one other duke). Huge differences also obtained between the experiences of poor parsons and rich prelates and between villeins (or serfs) and franklins or urban craftsmen. Villeins—also referred to sometimes as bondmen and naïfs—lived on the properties of the lords and were tied to the land. They did not even own themselves. But the commoners also included wealthier farmers and franklins, who had substantial landholdings; men, like Chaucer's Reeve, whose skills had earned them an office or a privileged place in the lord's retinue; and urban craftsmen and traders, whose standard of living reflected the profitability of their business rather than their status as commoners. In other words, the non-aristocratic classes showed a wide variation in terms of wealth, status, and standards of living.

As the legislation of the late fourteenth century makes clear, rich merchants and landholders were putting the three-estate model under increasing strain. Although the idea of manual work was always linked to membership in the third estate, the more affluent commoners were not always easily discernible from the lowliest members of the gentle classes, who were defined by their right to bear arms, and who therefore considered themselves members of the second estate. Esquires, for example, were only granted gentility in the late fourteenth century. Their claim to a shared status with knights and barons was based in part on income. Some esquires, like Chaucer, earned their newly elevated position through meritorious service—work, in other words. As Paul Strohm notes, "the increasingly complicated category of esquire suggests the unusual flux within the middle strata during the second half of the fourteenth century."[4] Chaucer's family history exemplifies this new phenomenon: his father was a wine merchant; he became an esquire; and his son, Thomas, was knighted.

What made an arms-bearing esquire different from a successful merchant was not always clear—a fact that the legislation acknowledged by allowing wealthy commoners privileges comparable to those of gentle status. Note, however, that in order to wear the garb of an esquire, a merchant had to be worth a considerable £500 to the esquire's £100. Gentility still had its privileges. As our excerpts from the sumptuary laws show, all aspects of clothing were imbued with social and symbolic significance—one reason that medieval writers like Chaucer and the Gawain poet share so many details about their characters' apparel and that playwrights like the author of *Mankind* feature so many costume changes. Much could be conveyed about characters by the simple means of clothing them.

SOCIAL CONFLICT AND SOCIAL CHANGE

Although the three-estate model of society retained its ideological strength and imaginative appeal in late medieval society, it failed to provide a reliable description of social realities (if indeed it ever had). The *Canterbury Tales* registers the tensions that resulted from this disjunction. At the beginning, the narrator promises to let us know what the "condicioun" of each pilgrim *seems* to be. He then defines "condicioun" in terms of "what degree" the pilgrims are and what "array" they wear (GP 38-40). These lines invoke the three-estate model and recall the sumptuary laws' linkage of apparel and class status. However, by stressing interpretative ambiguity—"condicion" as a matter of seeming rather than being—Chaucer also allows that social status, far from being a divinely ordained given, may be achieved through the manipulation of "array." The pilgrims, too, provide ample commentary on designations of status, and common voices often criticize aristocratic ideals or lay claim to aristocratic privileges. The Miller's refusal to observe degree when it comes to the order of story telling is only the most egregious example of this phenomenon. How Chaucer views these upstarts can be hard to ascertain; for every critic, like D.W. Robertson, who argues that Chaucer is conservative, another critic, like David Aers, sees him as potentially subversive.[5] Chaucer's sociopolitical ambiguity may result from an aesthetic preference for presenting multiple viewpoints, or from a tendency towards political cautiousness, or from shifting empathies generated by his ambiguous position as an esquire. Whatever the cause, England's most talented poet clearly understood that his country was undergoing a massive social transformation and that social mobility was one of the major factors of that transformation.

Polemicists, preachers, and parliamentarians tried very hard to bring social realities back into conformity with traditional understandings of society. However, late medieval English authorities could not legislate social change away, since it sprang from sources beyond governmental control. Foremost among these was the plague which, as we saw in the last chapter, decimated the English population in the fourteenth century. The plague's most lasting influences were social and economic. William Langland saw the devastation as an expression of God's wrath against sinful humanity: in *Piers Plowman*, "pestilence" serves as a specific punishment for human pride.[6] But the plague also made new kinds of pride—as expressed in the acquisition of luxury goods, for example—possible. Both Langland and Gower lament the newfound appetite of peasants and laborers for white bread and meat, foods previously reserved for the wealthier members of society. In our documents, Anglicus warns that servants who get used to such dainty foods are likely to refuse to remain in their place. The English peasants and laborers who did not succumb to the plague did indeed go on to enjoy a much higher standard of living than their ancestors. The dwindling population enabled wage earners to command ever higher wages. After crop prices started falling in 1375, and the higher wages led to real purchasing power, the commoners began reaping even greater socio-economic benefits from the plague. The poor were better able to feed, clothe, and house themselves; some were even able to afford nonessential goods and services that they had never enjoyed before.[7]

By encouraging new patterns of consumption, the higher wages that peasants and laborers earned contributed to the urbanization of England. To be sure, other forces were a factor, such as the rapid growth of the textile industry during the second half of the fourteenth century. Despite the fact that towns and cities suffered higher death rates from the plague because of unsanitary conditions, commoners were drawn to the urban centers, where they learned and practiced the trades and crafts made ever more profitable by the burgeoning economy. Some became merchants whose wealth rivaled that of the aristocrats and whose status, as we saw earlier, called into question the viability of the three-estate model. These merchants often commanded considerable power at the level of city government, where they served as jurors, aldermen, and mayors. Affluent towns and cities could become incorporated by royal charter; in these cases, the towns became self-governing, and officials had the right to represent the town legally and to purchase and sell property in its name. The governments of medieval towns were oligarchic, drawing their officials from among the most powerful townsmen. Wealth was almost always a criterion for political office. In London, that meant officials were often members of the most affluent companies, like the grocers or drapers. Significantly, the Mayor of London—the premier political office open to a member of the third estate—was charged the same amount as an earl, £4, in the poll tax of 1379.[8]

That the Mayor could command such a sum is one sign of his status; that he would be compared to an earl is another. The essential distinction between gentleman and commoner did not disappear; nevertheless, the equivalences that laws like the poll tax drew between the various estates eroded the differences between them. The wealthiest merchants often married their daughters to the lower gentry, a practice that further confounded class distinctions. Successful urbanites also bought up land, thereby converting their capital into the source of revenue traditionally associated with the gentry.[9] Some of the most powerful of the London merchants even got knighted, thereby officially laying claim to gentle status. Nicholas Brembre, for example, was a wealthy grocer who bought up several estates in the country and who served two terms as Mayor of London (Brembre was also Chaucer's superior at Customs). An avid partisan of Richard II, Brembre was knighted by the king for services rendered during the Peasant's Rebellion of 1381. He thus achieved what must have been the dream of many medieval merchants: he became a gentleman.

To paraphrase the Wife of Bath, in the towns and cities of late medieval England, those with an eye for "profit" could clearly raise their status and guarantee their own "ese." It is surely no accident that the ambitious and profit-minded Wife is herself an adept cloth-maker, whose work rivals that of "Ypres and Gaunt" (WP 447-48), the Flemish towns that had traditionally produced the best textiles. The economically minded urban population is the one most fully represented in *The Canterbury Tales*, and not without reason. Chaucer's choice offers another index of the heightened visibility of this group in late medieval England. The "middle strata" arrived at their new-found power in part by privileging peer relations over hierarchical ones. Medieval merchants and craftsmen organized themselves into groups, referred to variously as "crafts," "fraternities," "mysteries," "companies," or "fellowships." The guilds were self-governing bodies that protected the interests of their members: they charged dues, fixed wages and prices, instituted regulations, set and enforced standards, obtained privileges like monopolies, and controlled competition from nonmembers. Some companies even issued liveries—like the liveries that aristocrats gave to their retainers—to their members.[10] All these factors contributed to the development of a corporate sense of identity, based on shared economic success and social ambition.

Although these companies included stratification—between masters and apprentices, between younger and older members, and between more and less successful members—they also promoted the development of a shared professional identity. Each group took its name from a common service performed (like the painters) or from a common commodity sold (like the grocers or the fishmongers). As the name "mystery" suggests, trade secrets were jealously guarded, which helped those in the know feel a sense of connection to one another. Apprentices were expected to swear oaths of secrecy before gaining access to their profession's "mysteries." When they had done so, they became for all intents and purposes part of their master's family, sometimes literally so, when they married the master's daughter. Contemporary wills, in which masters left significant bequests to former apprentices, suggest that the relationship between master and apprentice was often marked by affection. Apprentices normally served seven- to ten-year contracts with their masters; during that time, they often received no other payment than room and board. Their education and the promise of membership in the guild, with all the advantages it brought, was reward enough for the successful apprentice.

The literature of the period calls attention to the new modes of identification and allegiance associated with the flowering of the urban guilds. Chaucer's Haberdasher, his Carpenter, his Weaver, his Dyer, and his Tapester, for example, all signal their membership in "a solempne and greet fraternitee" (GP 365) by wearing livery. The narrator clarifies that these guildsmen are politically and socially ambitious—they want to be aldermen, and their wives want to be called "madame." The "greet fraternitee" that bound English townsmen to one another is also evident in the production of the Corpus Christi cycles, which recount sacred history, from the creation of the world to the Last Judgment, in a series of pageants. Performed in English towns from the fourteenth century well into the sixteenth century, these costly productions were made possible by the new-found prosperity of medieval guilds. In towns like York, Coventry, and Chester, each "mystery" took responsibility for a pageant: the guild covered the costs of the production, and its members performed in the plays (which are sometimes referred to as "mystery plays," although the term is probably a reference to their performance of spiritual mysteries). When the York pinners and painters put on "the Crucifixion," they demonstrated their ability to function as a fraternity; given the subject of their pageant, they also advertised more technical abilities. The sometimes queasy correspondence between pageant and mystery—for example, the butchers of York put on Christ's death and burial, the bakers of Chester the Last Supper, and the shearmen of Coventry the shepherds' play— offered opportunities for social and economic advancement, as well as for spiritual reflection. The Chester bakers may have distributed loaves to the audience during the performance of their pageant, a medieval ana- logue for the "free samples" offered by today's supermarkets. The fact that the cycles involved the participation of the entire town made them, as Mervyn James argues, ritualized assertions of local coherence. These plays "incorporate[d]" individual members and guilds into "the wholeness of the social body" while ensuring "subordination to its head":

> In towns like York and Chester, characterized by numerous crafts and
> guild organizations ... the play cycles provided a mechanism ... by
> which the tensions implicit in the diachronic rise and fall of
> occupational communities could be confronted and worked out.
> In addition, they made available a means by which visual and
> public recognition could be given to changes in the relationships
> of superiority, dependence, or cooperation which existed between
> occupations.[11]

The towns' apparent reluctance to give these plays up after the Protestant Reformation (the last performance of the Chester Cycle was in 1575) is one sign of their effectiveness as vehicles for the expression of an emergent sense of civic and professional identity.

Although only one in seven commoners lived in urban areas, the urbanites came, over the course of the fourteenth century, to command substantial economic and political clout. Their increased social visibility resulted from a variety of factors. The high customs levied on foreign cloth to pay for the Hundred Years War, for example, helped make the native English cloth industry the economic powerhouse it became in the four- teenth century. The plague was probably the most significant influence in creating new social and economic opportunities. The various epidemics made the accumulation of property easier, not just by causing an increase in individual incomes, but also by narrowing the pool of potential heirs and rivals. According to many scholars, the fourteenth century was a "golden age" for laborers. This assessment needs to be balanced by the rec- ognition that the improved economic circumstances resulted from severely adverse conditions, including, most obviously, the high mortality rate. The commoners' new economic power came, ironically enough, at the price of their loved ones' deaths.

The Situation of Women

And what about women? Did they, too, benefit from the upheavals of the fourteenth century? The answers to those questions are hard to obtain, because of the legal doctrine of coverture. This doctrine enshrined the view that the wife was an extension of her husband. Just as the Church considered a married woman to be "one flesh" with her husband, the Common Law considered a married woman or *femme covert* ("covered woman") to be the same person as her husband. For all intents and purposes, the husband owned his wife and her property. Note, for example, that in one of the court cases we reproduce below, Joan is considered her husband's property, along with "the woolen and linen cloths, silver plate, dishes, pewter saltcellars and iron and brass pots and pans" that Thomas Norwich allegedly pilfered. As objects owned by their husbands, married women had no legal agency—and therefore few legal recourses—of their own. They could not own property or sign contracts; even small purchases technically required the permission of their husbands. According to the *Treatise on the Laws and Customs of England*, under English law the husband enjoyed near total control: "legally a woman is completely in the power of her husband ... [and even] her dower and all other property are clearly deemed to be at his disposal" (SEE BELOW).

Because of the labor shortage, some women did secure employment in male fields in the aftermath of the plague. The powerful merchants of the Staple, for example, included two women in the fifteenth century.[12] And in post-plague Leicestershire, women mowed, ploughed, and fixed roads.[13] But these were exceptions, and most women who worked outside the home still had traditionally female occupations, like spinning, brewing, and retail (the Chester Cycle offers a memorable representation of a late medieval alewife, sent to hell for her dubious trade practices). The differing tools associated with male and female labor, the plough or sword and the distaff, were used as stable signifiers of sexual difference throughout this period. The Chester Cycle's "Slaughter of the Innocents," for example, turns this biblical episode into a battle of the sexes by pitting the soldiers' swords against the mothers' distaffs. A few professions were traditionally open to women only, with midwifery and the silk trade on one end of the spectrum and prostitution on the other. But even when a profession was exclusive to women workers, these often failed to organize into guilds and to develop the sort of professional identity that helped their male counterparts thrive. Women were admitted to the male-dominated guilds only if they inherited membership from their husbands or fathers. The guilds made concerted efforts to exclude single women (or *femme sole*, the legal status attaching to a woman who was not under the authority or "cover" of a husband), which might account for the dwindling participation of women in the trades after 1480. Still, in the towns and cities of medieval England, enterprising women "appear to have enjoyed more freedom and respect in practice than they were ascribed in theory or in law." [14] Matters stood differently in the country. The majority of peasant women were unpaid domestic workers. As the "Ballad of the Tyrannical Husband" illustrates, this work was often undervalued and extensive. It included not only tasks we normally consider part of housewifery, like cooking and child rearing, but also entailed other forms of labor, nowadays performed by professionals, like making butter, making clothes, and brewing ale. Clearly, medieval housewives had no time to be desperate (for more about their daily life, SEE CHAPTER 3).

As guild practices regarding female membership suggest, late medieval women's status depended on that of their husbands or fathers. The sumptuary statutes also exemplify the tendency to see women in terms of their male relations; the 1363 statute, for example, repeats the refrain "that their wives, daughters, and children, be of the same condition in their vesture and apparel." Should a daughter marry down, she would presumably be legally obligated to have her wardrobe follow suit (whether this happened in practice is an entirely different matter). The literature of the period tends to reinforce the idea that women are extensions of their male relatives. It identifies men by social rank or professional occupation but women according to their marital status only. Many works do not even give female characters names, other than their husband's (e.g., Noah's wife in the Cycle plays or Bercilak's lady in *Sir Gawain and the Green Knight*). The division of women into "maiden, wife, or widow"—by far the most common way of categorizing women in the Middle Ages—provides further evidence of the primacy of marital status in determining medieval women's identities. The "Ballad of the Tyrannical Husband," for example, takes the position that "all women that to this town belong" are either "maidens, widows, [or] wives." Although the narrator is sympathetic to the plight of women, whom he claims are often undeservedly blamed, he uses a system of categorization that does for gender relations what the three-estate model did for class relations. It expresses a conservative ideal, against which the actions of actual women might be measured. As the tripartite division of womankind suggests, medieval women ideally passed from the control of fathers to the control of husbands, enacting the "normal steps in an unfolding life pattern" that would take them from daughter to wife to widow.[15] All women fit the category of "maiden" at one stage of life, but this category was transitional, covering the years between sexual maturation and sanctioned sexual consummation. While premarital sex seems to have been widely tolerated among the peasants, marriage was nevertheless the social destiny for young women in the Middle Ages.

Even the Wife of Bath, who apparently has some skill in textile manufacturing, is identified primarily in terms of her relationship to men. Alison's eagerness to acquire a new husband may well have to do with retaining her social status; certainly, she seems alert to the connection between social and marital status. As Christine de Pizan points out to her fellow widows in the excerpt below, "those who honored you during the lifetime of your husbands, who may well have been officials or men of importance, now will pay little attention to you and barely even bother to be friendly." Widowhood could entail a radical drop in social status, although it also involved some advantages. Legally speaking, widows had far more rights than married women. They could inherit and trade property, for example, as well as sign contracts, which is one reason that, as Christine suggests, they needed to be prepared for legal entanglements. Widows also exerted more control over their children's marriages as well as over any remarriage of their own. Because men's occupations tended to put them in the way of danger and early death, there were far more widows than widowers in medieval England. Unlike Chaucer's Alison, many of them chose to remain unmarried, no doubt because the status of widow gave them a degree of control over their life that they had never before experienced.[16] Wealthy widows were probably the women with the most access to freedom in medieval societies.

Ironically, according to many Christian authorities, marriage was not an ideal state at all: God preferred virgins. He had created marriage as a sanctioned alternative to unlicensed fornication; as Paul put it succinctly, "better to be wedded than to be burnt" (SEE OUR EXCERPT FROM *Corinthians* 1:7). Admittance into a convent or an abbey was one of the few ways in which women might achieve status or find a meaningful form of work outside marriage. Many nuns chose the religious life for spiritual reasons. Jerome (SEE THE EXCERPT BELOW) depicted virginal perfection as the surest avenue to heavenly reward for women: "Christ," he writes, "loves virgins more than others." But elsewhere he also emphasized the difficulties facing women who chose this route: "if you walk laden with gold, you must beware of a robber. This mortal life is a race. Here we struggle, that elsewhere we may be crowned. No one walks without anxiety amid serpents and scorpions." While the cloistered life offered some protection against sexual assault, it also offered women avenues not elsewhere available to them, like the pursuit of knowledge and the assumption of responsibility. A handful of religious women, like the anchoress and mystic Julian of Norwich (1342-c.1416), even achieved a measure of personal fame. While many medieval nuns hoped to attain spiritual heights like Julian, some no doubt had more pragmatic purposes in mind, like escaping unwanted marriages. Joining the convent was in fact "one of the most common and practical strategies of avoiding forced marriage" throughout the Middle Ages.[17]

As the fine manners and worldly pretensions of Chaucer's Prioress suggest, the option of the convent was primarily limited to women from the upper echelons of society. Novices who wished to join a convent had to provide a dowry, a practice which in effect ruled out the participation of lower class women. Unlike aristocratic women, who lived a life of comparative leisure, lower class women were also expected to work, and they were crucial to the functioning of the farm as an economic unit. Most rural women married since the position of servant—the main alternative form of employment—was usually a temporary one, restricted to the teenage years. Those women who were unable to secure a husband were left with few attractive options; they relied on the mercy of male relatives, they became servants at the manor, they found employment in town, or they turned to prostitution. Estimates of how many women remained unmarried in the late Middle Ages tend to be low; Barbara Hanawalt, for example, cites a figure of less than 7 per cent.[18] There are few mentions of celibate women in official records, and few female literary characters fit the description of "permanently celibate" (again, the exceptions are mainly of the religious variety—saints whose commitment to celibacy makes them spiritual rather than social ideals). The common law had little to say about single women and covered mainly the rights of wives and widows. By obtaining the legal designation of *femme sole*, women could trade and make contracts like men. Many of the women designated in this way, however, were widows or wives whose husbands had agreed to this legal status for business reasons. As the near invisibility of single women in medieval culture suggests, a failure to negotiate the transition from maid to wife in early English society could lead to harsh social repercussions. Those few female characters in medieval literature who seem to be neither maiden, wife, nor widow include the witch in *Gawain* and the prostitute in *Piers Plowman*. Adult women who remained unmarried were considered an anomaly, and anomalies do not generally garner much approval in conservative societies.

The institution of marriage, which defined most women's experiences, enforced contemporary orthodoxies regarding male dominance. Documents of the period situate authority in the husband: his role is to rule and the wife's role is to obey. A favorite metaphor, derived from Paul's fifth letter to the Ephesians, expresses the power relationship between husband and wife in terms of the human anatomy. As Anglicus puts it "For in might and strength a man surpasses a woman, and a man is the head of a woman, as the apostle says. Therefore a man is held to rule his wife, as the head has the cure and rule of all the body" (SEE BELOW). Few quarreled with this view. John Wyclif, for example, was entirely orthodox in his opinions regarding marriage: "See now how the wife owes to be subject to the husband, and he owes to rule his wife, and how they both owe to rule their children in God's law. First Saint Peter bids that wives be subject to their husbands" (SEE BELOW). The subjection of women was even likened by some writers to that of domestic animals. So an affluent Parisian bourgeois, in instructing his wife how to behave, finds no better model for her to emulate than that of a dog: "even if his master whip him and throw stones at him, the dog followeth, wagging his tail and lying down before his master to appease him, and through rivers, through woods, through thieves and through battles followeth him."[19] Wives were expected to obey their husbands unquestioningly, even if these husbands issued orders that were irrational or unjust. The author also clarifies by analogy that the beating of a disobedient wife was an acceptable practice; Jankyn, who beats the Wife of Bath so badly that she loses her hearing in one ear, would not be perceived as an ogre by Chaucer's original audience. It was a husband's right to correct a disobedient wife. His status as her master was legally established: a wife who killed her husband was not guilty just of homicide but of petty treason, for killing her lord and master. In marriage, the husband exercised an authority over his wife comparable to that of the king over his subjects.[20]

To be sure, not all medieval marriages adhered to the hierarchical model set forth in authoritative texts. Many peasant marriages, for example, functioned much more like partnerships, as spouses worked together in their different domains to maintain the family's precarious economic position. To some extent, the dominant discourse on marriage did also emphasize mutuality when it came to sexual obligation; in these matters, as St. Paul asserted, the "husband [should] yield debt to the wife, and also the wife to the husband. The woman has not power of her body, but the husband. And the husband has not power of his body, but the woman." The sexual obligation that came with marriage is often referred to in medieval texts; it is, for example, a primary concern for Marjorie Kempe, whose desire for celibacy conflicted with her duty to her husband. Husband and wife were also enjoined by various authorities to love one another—but medieval definitions of marital love were shot through by power structures. The husband manifested his love by taking care of his wife and restraining from abusing her, while the wife manifested her love by her meekness and complete obedience. As this formulation suggests, the ideal servant and the ideal wife had many points in common, including the total subjection to their lord's authority. Despite the emphasis on some mutual obligations, the modern ideal of marriage as a partnership between equals who choose one another because of personal attraction finds little counterpart in medieval culture.

If people married to avoid a worse hell, they also married to have children and to secure their financial or political situation. Male farmers needed wives to tend to housework when they were in the fields, and they needed children to help them with fieldwork. After enumerating her many responsibilities, Gill, in "The Second Shepherd's Play," notes that "Full wofull is the householde / That wantys a woman" (420-421). Although male aristocrats did not need to marry to secure domestic help, they used marriage to consolidate their wealth or power and to ensure the continuance of their dynasty. The opinion of privileged women regarding their potential partners was often not consulted in matters of marriage; marriage for love was, insofar as it occurred at all, associated with the non-propertied class. Although by law aristocratic girls could not be married until they had reached puberty, set at 12 years of age, they could be betrothed as early as seven years old.[21] Sometimes, of course, the needs of the families coincided with the tastes of the couple: arranged marriages did not preclude affectionate bonding.

An aristocratic bride's obedience and chastity were prized, since land could not be willed but passed according to the system of primogeniture, from father to first-born son. When no son survived to inherit, the property passed to the daughters, and the crown as well as the aristocracy took a keen interest in such heiresses.[22] John of Gaunt's first marriage to Blanche of Lancaster, in 1359, was by all accounts a happy one; it also secured him a vast fortune and the Dukedom of Lancaster. His second marriage, to Constance, the heiress apparent of the deposed King of

Leon and Castile (1372), furthered his political aspirations (he wanted to become a king). When in 1396 Gaunt chose as his third wife Catherine de Roet Swynford, a member of the minor gentry who had been his mistress for many years, everyone was probably shocked. This marriage to a known adulteress brought Gaunt no advantages, so that it must have been made out of personal considerations. Gaunt even legitimized the bastard children that had been born from his illicit union with Catherine (this act—entered into without political motivations—secured the crown for Gaunt's descendants, the Tudors). If Gaunt's first two marriages followed the pattern for aristocrats, his final marriage offers an apt reminder that there are always exceptions to generalizations, especially when it comes to affairs of the heart.

The Anti-Feminist Tradition

Medieval literature reflects contemporary attitudes towards marriage in a number of ways. Most medieval characters marry for reasons other than love—for procreation and sexual pleasure (January in "The Merchant's Tale") or for money (the Wife of Bath), for example. Aristocratic female characters often marry under the direct orders of male relatives, as do Emily in "The Knight's Tale" and Custance in "The Man of Law's Tale." Their lower-class counterparts in the Cycle Plays, meanwhile, have marital relationships strained by economic hardship. Mak in "The Second Shepherd's Play" complains about how much his wife eats, while Gill reflects on his ingratitude for the many tasks she performs. Neither mentions love as a significant component of their marriage. The genres that consistently celebrate romantic love, like the romance, tend to emphasize the incompatibility of marriage—which makes husbands lords over their wife—with love. "The Franklin's Tale" is the exception that confirms this rule. Dorigen and Arveragus recognize that "Love wil nat been constreyned by maistrye" (FT 764) and is therefore unlikely to survive the constraints of marriage. When they decide to marry anyhow, they make a complex agreement designed to protect their love from the power structures that normally inhered in medieval marriage.

Although he can be as ambiguous about gender as he is about class, Chaucer has a particular interest in the power differentials between men and women. Perhaps this interest stemmed from his own biography: he was, in 1380, accused by one Cecily Chaumpaigne of *raptus*. Medieval scholars have long dealt with this troubling historical datum by insisting that *raptus* could mean either rape or abduction; however, a document recently brought to light suggests that it was indeed about what we would call rape. The case was settled out of court. Cecily Chaumpaigne released Chaucer from the accusation, and the incident remains cloaked in mystery.[23] As works like *Troilus and Criseyde*, "The Wife of Bath's Tale," and "The Franklin's Tale" suggest, Chaucer was fascinated throughout his career with the closely related issues of female consent and female agency. At times, his works betray a generous sympathy for women, who "are born to thralldom and penance / And to been under mannes governance" (MLT 285-86). January's fantasies about the total subjugation of his future wife, for example, are so ridiculous (MerT 1341-51) that they legitimate May's trespasses against him before she even commits them. But Chaucer also endorses the idea that the wife should be subject to the husband. The Parson, for example, explains

> how that a womman sholde be subget to hire housbonde, that telleth Seint Peter. First, in obedience. And eek, as seith the decree, a womman that is wyf, as longe as she is a wyf, she hath noon auctoritee to swere ne to bere witnesse withoute leve of his housbonde, that is hire lord; algate, he sholde be so by resoun. She sholde eek serven hym in alle honestee, and been attempree of hire array. I woot wel that they sholde setten hir entente to plesen hir housbandes, but nat by hire quentnise of array ... (ParsT 929-31)

A good wife was sober, quiet, chaste, obedient, homebound, and modest. The Parson voices no original sentiment here, as the agreement among the authors excerpted in this chapter shows. In keeping with these widely shared values, Griselda in "The Clerk's Tale" insists that she is her husband's "owene thing," to do with as he lists (652). One reason for the popularity of this tale in the Middle Ages—the author of *Le Ménagier de Paris* tells it, as do Boccaccio and Petrarch—is that Griselda, in her unquestioning subjection to her tyrannical and capricious husband, embodied a shared cultural ideal of womanly excellence. Those who diverged from this ideal made themselves vulnerable to a series of degrading accusations, including that of being shrewd and lewd, scolds and whores.

The topic of feminine divergence from the norm brings up the Wife of Bath. Alison's passionate advocacy for female sovereignty has struck some modern readers as proto-feminist (e.g., Carolyn Dinshaw).[24] And, indeed, the Wife appears to be a perceptive critic of her culture's habitual misogyny. Her insistence that her own experience, for example, is a match for clerical authority recalls Christine de Pizan's description of her struggle to reconcile her first-hand knowledge of women with the clerics' misogynistic assertions about them (SEE OUR EXCERPT). But, for all her proto-feminist credentials, Alison is also constituted of those very misogynistic stereotypes that she criticizes: she is wanton, ignorant, talkative, and spectacularly unchaste. Note, for example, the extensive correspondence between the gossipy and verbally aggressive Alison and the bad wife described by Anglicus:

> No man has more wealth than he that has a good woman to wife.
> Nor no man is more wretched neither, has woe and sore, than
> he that has an evil wife, crying, jangling, chiding and scolding;
> drunken and unsteadfast and contrary to him; costly, stout and gay;
> envious, annoying, and leaping over lands and countreys; and sneaky,
> suspicious, and wrathful (SEE BELOW).

Far from questioning stereotypes, Chaucer's Wife may well confirm them.

The legal and social subordination of women to men in medieval culture reflect what Chaucer's contemporaries held as truth: women were inherently inferior to men. They were, as Custance puts it, "born" to this condition of inferiority. Medieval subjects believed feminine inferiority to be a fact of nature. As Anglicus explains it,

> The male surpasses the female in perfect complexion (and in
> working [acting], in wit and discretion, in might and in lordship ...)
> for in comparison to the female the male is hot and dry, and
> the female the reverse. In the male, there are virtues formal and
> of shaping and working [or action]; and in the female, material,
> suffering, and passive.

Women were by nature in need of direction. The opposition of passive and active permeates medieval thinking on the subject of gender differences and sexuality. When Anglicus says, for example, that the man has the virtue of "shaping" whereas the woman is "material," he makes reference, among other things, to the contributions of each to procreation. The woman provided the "matter" for the child but the father shaped or formed it. Sexuality was generally conceived of in terms of male activity and female receptivity. Even the apparently aggressive Wife of Bath imagines herself as suffering her old husband to "do hys nycetee" (WP 412). With Jankyn, she experiences more pleasure but still relies on a fundamentally passive conception of herself as the text that he "glose[s]."

Women's inferior status in medieval society was justified not just by reference to their inherent passivity but also by clerical models of women's sinfulness. In the history of women's oppression in Western culture, interpretations of Genesis have consistently played a significant role. Because Eve was created after Adam, she was held to be less like God. Most authorities also assigned more blame to Eve for the Fall, since she instigated it. Since all women derived from Eve, the argument went, they perforce shared in her inferiority and her corruptibility. In the authoritative texts of medieval culture—produced by male clerics—women could be good, like Mary, or bad, like Eve. Both positive and negative role models attempted to circumscribe feminine behavior and to enforce a rigid understanding of female virtue. Some Church Fathers, like the influential and deeply misogynistic Jerome, excelled at illustrating the virgin/whore dichotomy by examples of good (silent, chaste, and obedient) and bad women (all the others). No doubt this rhetorical habit contributed to the development of a formal debate in the later Middle Ages on the nature and status of women. Often referred to as the *Querelle des Femmes*, or the quarrel about women, this debate provided writers with an impressive series of colorful *exempla*, drawn from biblical and classical traditions. These include the chaste martyrs that Dorigen cites as "ensamples" (1419) in "The Franklin's Tale," the wise women that January describes when contemplating marriage, and the wicked wives that Jankyn likes to read about in the "The Wife of Bath's Prologue." Entire works were dedicated to the elaboration of these *exempla*, including, most famously Boccacio's *De Claris Mulieribus* (1361-62), Chaucer's *The Legend of Good Women* (1380-87), and Christine de Pizan's *The Book of the City of Ladies* (1405).

It could be argued that, in the cult of the Virgin Mary and the female saints, the Church challenged the poor opinion that medieval thinkers held of women. The medieval cycle plays, for example, devote a great deal of attention to the tribulations of the Virgin, who acts as heroine to Christ's hero. But female worthies were often worshiped precisely for their embodiment of fundamentally female qualities, like their chastity and their ability passively to endure suffering. Many virtuous female characters in medieval literature—Mary in the cycle plays, the women in *The Legend of Good Women*, and Griselda and Custance in *The Canterbury Tales*—also fit this paradigm. The appreciation for such women in medieval culture may have given actual women a mode of affirming their own value; certainly, images of the Virgin did much to glorify motherhood. But these representations tended to enforce rather than challenge fundamental gender roles: women were praised for emulating these role models and thus for adhering to narrow notions of female virtue.

The clerical authorities justified the subjugation of women not just through the deployment of positive and negative models but also through direct teaching. The biblical passages that the Wife refers to in her prologue all featured prominently in the Church's discourses on female inferiority. So did the pronouncements of Church Fathers like Jerome and Augustine. Anglicus provides an example of how these various authorities could be woven together to form the case against women:

> Therefore a man surpasses a woman in reason, in sharpness of wit, and understanding. So says Augustine. And by the authority of the apostle he sets a man before a woman in dignity and worthiness of the image and likeness of God. In this dignity a man surpasses a woman in authority and might of sovereignty. Authority of teaching and of sovereignty is granted to man, and denied and prohibited to woman as for custom and usage. As in *Corinthians* 1:6, the apostle says: I suffer not a woman teach in church, for it is written: under man's power thou shalt be, and he shall be thy lord. (*Genesis* 3)

Paul, whom Anglicus here cites, was the go-to man on female subjection. The comment about prohibiting women from teaching in church, for example, was interpreted to be a prohibition against public speech and public office more generally. Even the dissident English preacher Wyclif fully approved the Church's more misogynistic teachings. We have reproduced some of his writings on marriage, as well as his translation of the first letter to the Corinthians, with its implication that for a man even to touch a woman was defiling.

The unanimous condemnation of women by Church authorities must have been an additional burden on actual women. Unfortunately, the prohibition against public speech ensured that, a very few exceptions aside, women did not write, so that we do not have a record of their opinion on the matter. No doubt Chaucer's Wife is right to suggest that "if wommen hadde written stories, / As clerkes han withinne hire oratories, / They wolde han written of men moore wikkednesse / that al the mark of Adam may redresse" (WP 693-96). Certainly Christine de Pizan, one of the few exceptional women, thought long and hard about this issue. She wondered "how it happened that so many different men—and learned men among them—have been and are so inclined to express both in speaking and in their treatises and writings so many wicked insults about women and their behavior....They all concur in one conclusion: that the behavior of women is inclined to and full of every vice." Doubtless there would have been no debate if some had not rushed to the defense of women (including Christine herself). But those who pleaded the case of women, as Chaucer does in *The Legend of Good Women*, rarely challenged received notions of feminine virtue and feminine vice. They just claimed that many women were virtuous by these widely accepted standards. Chaucer praises the Egyptian queen Cleopatra—a favorite *exemplum* on both sides of the argument—not for her political acumen but for her total subjection to Antonius. Cleopatra wishes to show herself "unreprovable" in her "wyfhod" (691), and so "naked, with ful good herte, / Among the serpents in the pit she sterte" (696-97). This cheerfully compliant suicide, buried in the serpentine symbols of phallic power, is a long ways away from the historical queen or from Shakespeare's later representation of this queen as a masterful political artist.

What the effect of all the negative writing about women and sexuality had on the lives of actual women is hard to say. The written record was produced by a tiny, almost entirely male, and almost entirely celibate fraction of the population. Even though clerics unanimously recoiled at the idea of fornication, the majority of the population obviously engaged in it. Medieval secular literature provides many euphemisms and metaphors for sexual congress that suggest a far more positive valuation of the experience (in "The Miller's Tale," for example, Nicholas and Alison "maken melodye") than found in clerical discourse. The assumption that women were inferior may have been shared by all; however, it's unlikely that everyone took this assumption to the extremes espoused by the likes of St. Jerome and Jacques de Vitry. Educated women like Christine, who were the most likely to be exposed to clerkly diatribes about women, and who felt most keenly the intellectual restrictions imposed on them, suffered directly from clerical misogyny. But Christine concludes that the misogynistic writings contained "absurdities" that had little to do with the majority of women's daily experiences. Although most written sources from the period are heavily influenced by clerical misogyny, lower-class wills also tell a different story. They suggest that most men trusted their wives enough, for example, to make them the executors of their wills. Many men sought to ensure that their widows would be well rewarded for their contributions to married life.[25] Probably the qualities by which a woman was judged in the lower classes were different as well. The documentary evidence suggests that many peasant marriages were marked by shared goals and responsibilities, as well as by a sense of trust and mutual respect. From these lower-class marriages, our own ideal of the companionate marriage eventually emerged. → THE LOWER CLASS MARRIAGES SHARED MORE EQUALITY / TRUST / LOVE.

Documents

The Treatise on the Laws and Customs of the Realm of England Commonly Called Glanville (12ᵗʰc)

This treatise, often attributed to one of Henry II's legal advisors and experts, Ranulf de Glanville (d. 1190) is the first systematic attempt to record and describe English common law. Our excerpts describe the status of villeins in medieval England, the bond that obtains between a lord and his tenant, and the rights of the wife regarding her dower.

The Ways in which a Person Can Be Made Free

A person of villein status can be made free in several ways. For example, his lord, wishing him to achieve freedom from the villeinage by which he is subject to him, may quit-claim him from himself and his heirs; or he may give or sell him to another with intent to free him. It should be noted, however, that no person of villein status can seek his freedom with his own money, for in such a case he could, according to the law and custom of the realm, be recalled to villeinage by his lord, because all the chattels of a villein are deemed to such an extent the property of his lord that he cannot redeem himself from villeinage with his own money as against his lord. If, however, a third party provides the money and buys the villein in order to free him, then he can maintain himself for ever in a state of freedom as against his lord who sold him.

When anyone quit-claims his villein from himself and his heirs, or sells him to a third party, he who has achieved freedom in this way can maintain it for ever against his lord and any of his lord's heirs, provided that he proves it in court by a charter or other lawful means; the proceedings may even result in battle if anyone denies that he has been freed from villeinage, provided that a suitable witness who saw and heard him freed is willing to prove his freedom in court. It should, however, be noted that anyone may make his villein free as against himself or his heirs, but not as against others.

For if anyone formerly a villein, who has been freed in this way, is produced in court to make proof as a champion or to wage law, he can lawfully be excluded if his villein status is raised as an objection and proved, even if he has been made a knight since he was freed.

If any villein stays peaceably for a year and a day in a privileged town and is admitted as a citizen into their commune, that is to say, their guild, he is thereby freed from villeinage.

THE WAYS IN WHICH PEOPLE BECOME VILLEINS

Some persons are villeins from the moment of birth, for example a person born of a villein father and a villein mother, or one born of a free father and a villein mother; even to one born of a free mother and a villein father the same conclusion about civil condition applies. Therefore, if a free man marries a villein and lives on a villein tenement, so long as he is bound in this way by the villein tenure he loses, as a villein, all legal rights. If children are born of the villein of one lord and the villein woman of another they will be equally divided between the two lords.

PLEAS OF DOWER

The word "dos" has two meanings. In common English law usage it means that which a free man gives to his wife at the church door at the time of his marriage. For every man is bound both by ecclesiastical and by secular law to endow his wife at the time of his marriage. When a man endows his wife either he nominates certain property as dower, or he does not. If he does not nominate dower, then one-third of the whole of his free tenement is deemed to be her dower, and the reasonable dower of any woman is one-third of the whole of the free tenement of which her husband was seised in demesne at the time of the marriage. If, however, the husband nominates dower and it amounts to more than one-third, it cannot stand at such a level, but will be measured up to one-third; for a man can give less but not more than one-third of his tenement in dower.

INCREASE IN DOWER AS A RESULT OF LATER ACQUISITIONS

It sometimes happens that a husband who has a little land can increase the dower by adding one-third or less of his later acquisitions. However, if nothing was said about acquisitions when the dower was originally assigned, then, even if the husband had little land at the time of the marriage and afterwards acquired much land, no more can be claimed in dower than one-third of the land which he had at the time of the marriage. I state the same rule when a man who has no land endows his wife with money or other chattels and afterwards acquires many lands and tenements, for nothing can in future lawfully be claimed as dower from these acquisitions. For it is a general rule that however much dower and of whatever kind is assigned to a woman, if she consents to this arrangement of dower at the church door she cannot in future lawfully claim any more as dower.

It should be known that a woman cannot alienate any of her dower during the life of her husband. For since legally a woman is completely in the power of her husband, it is not surprising that her dower and all her other property are clearly deemed to be at his disposal. Therefore any married man may give or sell or alienate in whatever way he pleases his wife's dower during her life, and his wife is bound to consent to this as to all other acts of his which do not offend against God. Indeed, to such an extent is a woman bound to obey her husband that if he wishes to sell her dower and she opposes him, and afterwards the dower is in fact sold and purchased, she cannot when her husband is dead claim the dower from the purchaser if she confesses, or it is proved against her, in court that it was sold by her husband against her will.

The Bond of Trust Arising from Lordship and Homage Should Be Mutual

The bond of trust arising from lordship and homage should be mutual, so that the lord owes as much to the man on account of lordship as the man owes to the lord on account of homage, save only reverence. Therefore if anyone gives to another a tenement in return for service and homage, and a third party afterwards proves his right to it against the tenant, the lord will be bound to warrant him that tenement or give him equivalent lands in exchange. But the rule is different in the case of a person who holds his fee as his inheritance from another to whom he has done homage for it, for even if he loses the land the lord will not be bound to give him equivalent lands in exchange.

The Sumptuary Laws of 1363 and 1463

Sumptuary laws are laws designed to curb excessive expenditure. Although they have become mainly associated with clothing, they can also address matters like food consumption, as the first few lines that we reproduce from the 1363 laws show. The sumptuary laws of late medieval England are instructive in a number of ways. Most obviously they tell us something about the fashions of the time, like the one for long-toed, phallic-shaped shoes, with which the 1463 law takes issue. Because clothing was closely linked to status, these laws also reveal the complex system of gradation that determined the structure of English society. The fact that the government felt the need to regulate what people wore suggests that this system of gradation was under some pressure by upstarts. By setting up equivalencies between wealthy citizens and those of gentle status, the sumptuary laws also acknowledge and try to control one source of this social change: the increasingly powerful middle class. The laws are reproduced in their entirety in the second volume of *Statutes of the Realm* (1810).

Excerpts from the Laws Passed under Edward III (1363)

Item, For the outrageous and excessive apparel of diverse people, against their estate and degree, to the great destruction and impoverishment of all the land, it is ordained that grooms, as well as servants of lords, as they of mysteries, and artificers, shall be served [to eat] and drink once a day of flesh or of fish, and the remnant [of] other victuals, as of milk, butter, and cheese, and other such victuals, according to their estate. And that they have clothes for their vesture, or hosing, whereof the whole cloth shall not exceed two marks, and that they wear no cloth of higher price, of their buying, nor otherwise, nor nothing of gold nor of silver embroidered, enameled, nor of silk, nor nothing pertaining to the said things; and their wives, daughters, and children of the same condition in their clothing and apparel, and they shall wear no veils passing 12 *d.* a veil.

    Item, That people of handicraft, and yeomen, shall take nor wear cloth of an higher price for their vesture or hosing, than within forty shillings the whole cloth, by way of buying, nor otherwise; nor stone, nor cloth of silk nor of silver, nor girdle, [knife, button,] ring, garter, nor brooch, ribbon, chains, nor no such other things of gold nor of silver, nor no manner of apparel embroidered, enameled, nor of silk by no way; and that their wives, daughters, and children, be of the same condition in their vesture and apparel; and that they wear no veil of silk, but only of yarn made within the realm, nor no manner of fur, nor of budge [a type of fur, usually made from sheepskin, used as trimming on gowns], but only lamb, rabbit, cat, and fox.

Item, That esquires and all manner of gentlemen, under the estate of a knight, which have no land nor rent to the value of an hundred pounds by year, shall not take nor wear cloth for their clothing or hosing of a higher price, than within the price of four marks and a half the whole cloth, by way of buying nor otherwise; and that they wear no cloth of gold, nor silk, nor silver, nor no manner of clothing embroidered, ring, [buttons,] nor brooch of gold, ribbon, girdle, nor none other apparel, nor harness, of gold nor of silver, nor nothing of stone, nor no manner of fur; and that their wives, daughters, and children be of the same condition, as to their vesture and apparel, without any turning up or trimming or border; and that they wear no manner of apparel of gold, or silver, nor of stone. But that esquires, which have land or rent to the value of 200 marks by year and above, may take and wear cloths of the price of 5 marks, the whole cloth, and cloth of silk and of silver, ribbon, girdle, and other apparel reasonably garnished of silver; and that their wives, daughters, and children may wear fur turned up of miniver [a white fur with black spots], without ermine or letuse [white or light grey fur trims], or any manner of stone, but for their heads.

Item, That merchants, citizens and burgesses, artificers, people of handicraft, as well within the city of London, as elsewhere, which have clearly goods and chattels, to the value of £500, and their wives and children, may take and wear in the manner as the esquires and gentlemen which have land to rent to the value of £100 by year; and that the same merchants, citizens, and burgesses, which have clearly goods and chattels, to the value of £1000 and their wives and children may take and wear in the manner as esquires and gentlemen, which have land and rent to the value of £200 by year. And no groom, yeoman, or servant of merchant, artificer or people of handicraft shall wear otherwise in apparel than is above ordained of yeomen of lords.

Item, That knights, which have land or rent within the value of £200 shall take and wear cloth of 6 marks the whole cloth, for their vesture, and of none higher price. And that they wear not cloth of gold, nor cloths mantle, nor gown furred with miniver nor of ermines, nor no apparel embroidered of stone, nor otherwise; and that their wives, daughters, and children be of the same condition; and that they wear no turning up of ermines, nor of letuses, nor no manner of apparel of stone, but only for their heads. But that all knights and ladies, which have land or rent over the value of 400 mark by year, to the sum of £1000 shall wear at their pleasure, except ermines and letuses, and apparel of pearls and stone, but only for their heads.

Item, That clerks, which have degree in any church, cathedral, collegial, or schools, or clerk of the King, that have such estate that requires fur, shall do and use according to the constitution of the same; and all other clerks, which have 200 marks of land by year, shall wear and do as knights of the same rent; and other clerks within the same rent, shall wear as the esquires of £100 of rent: and that all those, as well knights as clerks, which by this ordinance may wear fur in the winter, in the same manner shall wear linen clothing in the summer.

Item, That carters, ploughmen, drivers of the plough, oxherds, cowherds, shepherds, and all other keepers of beasts, threshers of corn, and all manner of people of the estate of a groom, attending to husbandry, and all other people, that have not forty shillings of goods, nor of chattels, shall not take nor wear no manner of cloth, but blanket, and russet wool of twelve-pence; and shall wear the girdles of linen according to their estate; and that they come to eat and drink in the manner as pertains to them, and not excessively. And it is ordained, that if any wear or do contrary to any of the points aforesaid, then he shall forfeit against the King all the apparel that he hath so worn against the form of this ordinance.

Excerpts from the Laws Passed under Edward IV (1463)

Item, Pray the Commons in the said Parliament assembled, to our said Sovereign Lord the King, to reduce to his gracious remembrance, that in the times of his noble progenitors divers ordinances and statutes were made in this realm of England for the apparel and array of the commons of the same realm, as well of men as of women, so that none of them ought to use nor wear any inordinate and excessive apparel, but only according to their degrees; which statutes and ordinances notwithstanding, for default of punishment and putting them in due execution, the Commons of the said realm, as well men as woman, have worn and daily do wear excessive and inordinate array and apparel, to the great displeasure of God, and impoverishing of this realm of England and to the enriching of other strange realms and countries, to the final destruction of the husbandry of this said realm. Our said Sovereign Lord the King, by the advice and assent of the said Lords, and at the special request of the said Commons assembled in the said Parliament, and by authority of the same, hath ordained and established, that no knight under the estate of a lord, other than lords' children, nor no wife of such knight, from the Feast of the Purification of our Lady, which shall be in the year of our Lord God one thousand four hundred sixty-five, shall wear any manner cloth of gold, or any corsets wrought with gold, or any fur of sable; and if any such knight do the contrary, or suffer his wife or child, the same child being under his rule or governance, to do the contrary, that then he shall forfeit for every such default £20 to the King. And also that no bachelor knight, nor his wife, from the said feast, shall wear any cloth of velvet upon velvet, but such knights which be of the Order of the Garter, and their wives, upon pain to forfeit to the King's use every such default twenty marks. And also that no person under the state of a Lord, from the said feast, wear any manner cloth of silk, being of the color of purple; upon pain to forfeit to the King for every default £10. And also that no esquire or gentleman, nor none other under the degree of a knight, nor none of their wives, except the sons of lords and their wives, and the daughters of lords, esquires for the King's body, and their wives, shall wear from the said feast any velvet, satin branched, nor any counterfeit cloth of silk resembling to the same, or any corsets wrought like to velvet or to satin branched, or any fur of ermine; upon pain to forfeit for every default ten marks to the King's use.

And also he hath ordained and established, that no yeoman, nor none other person under the same degree, from the said Feast of Saint Peter called *ad vincula*, which shall be in the year of our Lord 1465, shall use nor wear in array for his body, any bolsters nor stuffing of wool, cotton, nor cadas [material made out of silk and cotton for stuffing doublets], nor any stuffing in his doublet, but only lining according to the same; upon pain to forfeit to the King's use for every such default six shillings and eight-pence. Also our said Sovereign Lord the King, by the advice and assent aforesaid, hath ordained and established, that no knight under the estate of a lord, esquire, gentleman, nor none other person, shall use or wear from the Feast of All Saints, which shall be in the Year of our Lord 1465 any gown, jacket, or coat, unless it be of such length that the same may cover his privy members and buttocks; upon pain to forfeit to the king for every default twenty shillings. Also by the assent aforesaid, it is ordained, that no taylor after the said Feast, shall make to any person, any gown, jacket, or coat of less length, or doublet stuffed, contrary to the premises, upon the same pain for every default. And also hath ordained and established, in the said present Parliament, that no knight under the estate of a lord, esquire, gentleman, nor other person, shall use nor wear, after the said Feast of Saint Peter, any shoes or boots having peaks passing the length of two inches; upon pain to forfeit to the King for every default three shillings and four-pence. And if any shoemaker make any peaks of shoes or boots after the said Feast of Saint Peter, to any of the said persons, contrary to this Ordinance, he shall likewise forfeit to the King for every default four shillings four-pence.

APPRENTICESHIP CONTRACTS (13THC)

Those eager to learn a trade or craft in the Middle Ages served as apprentices to a master. Most apprentices were in their early teens when they started. Their contract, for seven to ten years, took them to adulthood. Normally, apprentices lived with their masters; as might be expected, close bonds often developed between apprentices and the families hosting them. An apprenticeship was an education in the "mysteries" of a particular trade—it was not a form of wage-labor, although some masters no doubt abused the situation and had their apprentices perform menial work. Those sponsoring apprentices had, as the following documents show, to provide surety in case the apprentice should fail to fulfill the terms of his or her contract. Both contracts, one from Arras and one from Marseilles, show normal agreements reached between a master weaver and the sponsors of apprentices. In one case, the master promises to house the apprentice; in the second, the master provides room, board, and clothing.

> Be it known to present and future aldermen that Ouede Ferconne apprentices Michael, her son, to Matthew Haimart on security of her house, her person, and her chattels, and the share that Michael ought to have in them, so that Matthew Haimart will teach him to weave in four years, and that he (Michael) will have shelter, and learn his trade there without board. And if there should be reason within two years for Michael to default she will return him, and Ouede Ferconne, his mother, guarantees this on the security of her

person and goods. And if she should wish to purchase his freedom for the last two years she may do so for thirty-three solidi, and will pledge for that all that has been stated. And if he should not free himself of the last two years let him return, and Ouede Ferconne, his mother, pledges this with her person and her goods. And the said Ouede pledges that if Matthew Haimart suffers either loss or damage through Michael, her son, she will restore the loss and damage on the security of herself and all her goods, should Michael do wrong.

April the ninth. I, Peter Borre, in good faith and without guile, place with you, Peter Feissac, weaver, my son Stephen, for the purpose of learning the trade or craft of weaving, to live at your house, and to do work for you from the feast of Easter next for four continuous years, promising you by this agreement to take care that my son does the said work, and that he will be faithful and trustworthy in all that he does, and that he will neither steal nor take anything away from you, nor flee nor depart from you for any reason, until he has completed his apprenticeship. And I promise you by this agreement that I will reimburse you for all damages or losses that you incur or sustain on my behalf, pledging all my goods, etc.; renouncing the benefit of all laws, etc. And I, the said Peter Feissac, promise you, Peter Borre, that I will teach your son faithfully and will provide food and clothing for him.

The Oath for the Issue of Apprentices (15ᵗʰ c)

The following, from *The Life and Typography of William Caxton* (1861), is an example of the oaths required of apprentices prior to entering into service. Note the emphasis on keeping the "mysteries" of the trade a secret and on obeying the various rules and regulations. The mercers were a powerful company of cloth merchants, who exported domestic wool and imported luxury fabrics from abroad. Those initiated into their trade stood to do well indeed.

You shall swear that you shall be true unto our liege lord the king, and to his heirs, the kings. You shall also be obedient and ready to come at all lawful summons & warning of the Wardens of the Mercery when and as often as you be duly admonished & warned by them, or by any of them, by their beadle, or by any other in their name, lawful excuse always excepted. All ordinances & rules by the fellowship of the mercers, ordained, made and established and here after for the well worship & profit of the said fellowship to be made, you shall hold & keep. All... necessary ordinances and councils for the welfare of the said fellowship and the secrets thereof to you showed, you shall keep secret & hold for counsel, and nor them nor any of them to discover or show by any means or color unto any person or persons of any other fellowship. You shall also be contributory to all charges to you put by the wardens & fellowship & to bear & pay your part of charge set for your degree like as other of the same fellowship shall do for their degree. Moreover you shall not depart out of the said fellowship for to serve nor you shall not accompany you with any person or persons of any other fellowship where through prejudice & hurt may in any wise grow unto the said fellowship of the mercery. And on this you shall swear that during the time of your service you shall neither buy nor sell for your own self nor for any other person nor that you shall receive any goods or merchandise by any color belonging unto any other person than only to your master which that you now serve or shall serve within the fellowship of your mercery except by his special license & will. And also that you shall not take any shop house, chamber seller, nor warehouse, by any color for to occupy, buying and selling until such time as that you have been with the wardens of the mercery for the time being and by one of them for shop-holder admitted, sworn and entered. Nor that you shall take nor have any apprentice, or any servant, for to occupy until he by you be unto one of the said Wardens for apprentice first presented & by the said Warden so admitted. All which points & any of them to your power well & truly you shall hold & keep so help you God etc.

THE PETITION OF THE TAILORS AGAINST NICHOLAS BREMBRE (1386)

Sir Nicholas Brembre was a wealthy grocer, whose influence in his own guild procured him the position of Mayor of London in 1377. The grocers were among the most powerful companies in medieval London; throughout his career, Brembre worked to secure their interests and those of the larger companies like the fishmongers. He also served as collector of customs, a position that made him for several years Geoffrey Chaucer's direct superior. An avid partisan of Richard II, Brembre was knighted by the king for services rendered during the Peasant's Rebellion of 1381. In what his opponents argued was a rigged election, he was named Mayor again in 1383. Ten companies belonging to a rival faction filed petitions with Parliament accusing Brembre of tyrannical abuse of office in 1386; the petition here reproduced is from the tailors, who charged him with stealing their charter and violating the rights—like the rights to choose their masters and to regulate their trade—first granted to them by the king in 1327 and confirmed by Edward III in 1341. Brembre was accused of treason by the Merciless Parliament in 1387. Although he tried to claim the privileges of gentle status at his trial, including that of trial by combat, he was drawn and hung in 1388, a fate reserved for commoners.

> Also the said suppliants complain against Nicholas Brembre that with the others his accomplices he took upon himself royal authority in that whereas a charter was granted by the progenitor of our lord the king to the mystery of the Taylors of London as by the copy of the same the charter fully makes mention, the which copy follows: "Edward by the grace of God king of England and France and lord of Ireland to all to whom the present letters shall come, Greeting. We have inspected the letters patent which we lately under the seal then used by us in England caused to be made in these words: 'Edward by the grace of God king of England, lord of Ireland, and duke of Aquitaine to all to whom the present letters shall come, Greeting. We have been supplicated by the Taylors and Linen Armourers of our city of London through a petition exhibited before us and our council in our present parliament that whereas they and their predecessors belonging to the same mysteries in the City aforesaid have always hitherto since time immemorial been accustomed once in the year to have and to hold their guild within the same City, and in the same guild to make rules for their mysteries and to order the condition of their servants belonging to the same mysteries, and to correct and amend the shortcomings of the same for the common weal, as well of the men of the same City as of those resorting together to the same. And now, during some time, all those, both strangers and others, who have claimed to belong to those mysteries have at their will taken shops in the City aforesaid and have practiced those mysteries by the hands of such unruled strangers and uncorrected from their defaults very many losses have often times resulted to many of the City as to others, to the scandal of the honest men of the same mysteries.

Our will is to approve the guild aforesaid and to confirm it to the men of the mysteries aforesaid abiding in the said City to be held to themselves and their successors in perpetuity, we assenting to their supplication in this behalf do by tenor of these presents receive and approve the aforesaid guild. Willing and granting for us and our heirs that the men belonging to the mysteries aforesaid in the City aforesaid and their successors may be able to have and hold their guild once in the year, as hath of old been accustomed to be done; and in it, to order and make rules for their mysteries and to correct and amend the defaults of their servants aforesaid by the view of the Mayor of the City aforesaid for the time being, or of any whom he shall have deputed in his place, and by the more worthy and sufficient men belonging to those mysteries according as they may see should be done to the greater weal of the commonality of our people, and that none hold a counter or shop touching those mysteries within the liberty of the City aforesaid unless he be free of that City, and that no one be admitted to that freedom on behalf of those mysteries unless he be testified to by worthy and loyal men of the same mysteries as being good, faithful and fit for the same. In witness thereof we have caused these our letters patent to be made. Witness ourself at Westminster on the tenth day of March in the first year of our reign. Now we have thought fit that the tenor of our letters aforesaid should be exemplified under the seal now used by us in England. In testimony thereof we have caused these our letters of patent to be made. Witness ourself at Langley on the sixth day of February in the fifteenth year of our reign over England but the second of our reign over France." The which charter the said Sir Nicholas Brembre took out of the possession of the said mystery against the crown of our lord the king and yet detains the said charter. Wherefore may it please our very excellent and very dread lord the king and the very noble lords of this present parliament to make due remedy for this horrible trespass done against the crown of our lord the king and the law of the land as a work of charity.

ON AMAZONS

The first appearance of Amazons—a mythic tribe of women warriors—in Western literature coincides with its inception, at the end of the eighth century or the beginning of the seventh century BC, in the great Homeric epic, *The Iliad.* They have been popular figures in the Western imagination ever since. No doubt our fascination with the Amazons, whose nation is usually situated in the East, in modern-day Turkey, has to do with their inversion of the "normal" gender structures that obtain in Western societies. References to the Amazons abound in medieval literature, including, for example, in Chaucer's "Knight's Tale," where Theseus's marriage to Hippolyta symbolizes his conquest of "al the regne of Femenye" (866). Below, we include two important medieval sources of Amazon lore. The first is *The Voyage and Travel of Sir John Mandeville* (1356-57?), purportedly written by a knight from St. Albans, England. Our second excerpt is from Christine de Pizan's equally influential *The Book of the City of Ladies* (c. 1405).

From The Travels of
Sir John Mandeville (1356-57)

Next to Chaldea is the land of Amazon, which we call the Maiden Land or the Land of Women; no man lives there, only women. This is not because, as some say, no man can live there, but because the women will not allow men to rule the kingdom. There was once a king in that land called Colopheus, and there was once men living there as they do elsewhere. It so happened that this king went to war with the King of Scythia, and was slain with all his great men in battle with his enemy. And when the Queen and the other ladies of that land heard the news that the King and the lords were slain, they marshaled themselves with one accord and armed themselves well. They took a great army of women and slaughtered all the men left among them. And since that time they will never let a man live with them more than seven days, nor will they allow a boy child to be brought up among them. But when they want to have the company of man, they go to that side of their country where their lovers live, stay with them eight or nine days and then go home again. If any of them bears a child and it is a son, they keep it until it can speak and walk and eat by itself and then they send it to the father—or they kill it. If they have a girl child, they cut off one of her breasts and cauterize it; in the case of a woman of great estate, the left one, so that she can carry her shield better, and, in one of low degree, they cut off the right, so that it will not hinder them shooting—for they know very well the skill of archery. There is always a queen to rule that land, and they all obey her. This queen is always chosen by election, for they choose the woman who is the best fighter. These women are

noble and wise warriors; and therefore kings of neighboring realms
hire them to help them in their wars. This land of the Amazons is an
island, surrounded by water, except at two points where there are two
ways in. Beyond the water live their lovers to whom they go when it
pleases them to have bodily pleasures with them.

FROM THE BOOK OF THE CITY OF LADIES. CHRISTINE DE PIZAN (1405)

When the women of the place saw that they had all lost their
husbands and brothers and male relatives, and only old men and
children were left them, they courageously assembled and took
counsel among themselves and decided finally that thenceforth they
would maintain their dominion by themselves without being subject
to men, and they promulgated an edict whereby no man was allowed
to enter into their jurisdiction. In order to maintain a succession,
they would go into neighboring lands during certain times of the
year and then return; if they then gave birth to males, they would
send them to their fathers, but if their offspring were females, they
would raise them. To carry out this ordinance, they selected two of
the most noble ladies from among them and crowned them queens,
the first of whom was named Lampheto and the second Marpasia.
Once this was accomplished, they banished all the remaining males
from their land, and afterward they armed themselves and in large
battalions constituted solely of ladies and maidens, they advanced on
their enemies and laid waste to their lands with fire and the sword,
and no one could resist them. In short, they exacted a most fine
revenge for their husbands' deaths. And in this way the women of
Scythia began to carry arms and were then called Amazons, which
actually means the "breastless ones," because they had a custom
whereby the nobles among them, when they were little girls, burned
off their left breast through some technique so that it would not
hinder them from carrying a shield, and they removed the right
breast of commoners to make it easier for them to shoot a bow. They
so delighted in the vocation of arms that through force they greatly
increased their country and their dominion, and their high fame
spread everywhere....

The news of their power reached the land of Greece, which was
quite distant, as well as the report of how these ladies never stopped
invading and conquering but went everywhere, laying waste to
lands and countries if they did not immediately surrender, and of

how there was no force which could resist them. The Greeks were frightened by this news, fearing that the power of these women might at the same time extend even to their own land.…

Hercules said that it would not be wise to wait until the Amazons came to them, and that therefore it was by far the best thing to invade them first. In order to accomplish this, he had a fleet armed and he assembled a large mass of noble youths to go there in great strength. When the valiant and brave Theseus, who was king of Athens, learned this news, he said that Hercules would never go without him and so assembled his army with that of Hercules, and thus they put to sea in large numbers, heading for the land of Amazonia. When, after a short while, they had approached Amazonia, Hercules, notwithstanding his fabulous strength and boldness and his large army of such valiant soldiers, did not dare to come into port nor to land during the day, so much did he fear the great power and daring of these women. This would be fantastic to repeat and hard to believe if so many historical writings did not attest to it, that a man who could not be conquered by the power of any creature feared the strength of women. So Hercules, as well as his army, waited until dark night had come, and then, at the hour when all mortal creatures should rest and sleep, these men streamed out of the ships and entered the country and began to put different cities to the torch and to slay all those women who were caught off-guard, unarmed.… [Afterward Theseus and Hercules capture the two great maidens, Hippolyta and Menalippe. The queen of the Amazons petitions for their return and is constrained to make peace on their behalf, but finally allows Theseus to marry Hippolyta and take her into his own country.]

Men, Women, Wives, Husbands, and Servants. Bartholomew Anglicus (trans. 1397)

The Franciscan Bartholomew Anglicus's *On the Properties of Things* was among the most widely read books of the late Middle Ages. Anglicus was a highly respected scholar, teaching at the University of Paris, one of the foremost medieval centers of learning. He describes the city as a medieval counterpart to classical Athens, a "mother of wisdom." As this comparison suggests, the friar based his understanding of the world on classical as well as Christian authorities. His encyclopedia collects learning on a range of subjects, from manners to metals. The sixth book concerns the "state of men, general and specific." In it, Anglicus provides definitions and descriptions of gender distinctions as well as of social roles and occupations. Although the original work dates to the mid-thirteenth century, one of Richard II's courtiers, Thomas, Lord Berkeley commissioned a vernacular translation from his chaplain, John Trevisa, in 1397. Our translated excerpts are based on Trevisa's translation.

OF MALES

A male is called *masculus*, and *masculus* is the diminutive of *mas, maris*, and in all kind of beasts the male has the principal, touching the worthiness of *sexus*, that is distinction of male and female. So says Isidore. The male surpasses the female in perfect complexion (and in working, in wit and discretion, in might and in lordship—in perfect complexion) for in comparison to the female the male is hot and dry, and the female the reverse. In the male, there are virtues formal and of shaping and working and in the female, material, suffering, and passive. Therefore ... Aristotle says that a man is, as it were, form and shape; and a woman, as it were, patient and suffering. Also the male surpasses in terms of a natural disposition towards actions, for generally the disposition towards action is stronger in the male than in the female, for in him is more virtue and strength. And therefore a man is called *vir* in Latin, and has the name of surpassing strength. So says Isidore. For the sinews and brawn of men are grounded in great strength and are able to perform strong works and deeds. The bones of males are strong, great, and firm in the joints; and therefore they are naturally strong to all manner strong works and deeds. Also Constantine says that in males the hearts be large and great. Therefore they are able to take on much plenty of spirit and of blood; and so for great abundance of blood a man is more bold and hardy than a woman, for in her the cause is contrary. And because of the strength of his heat and the virtue of his dry complexion, no man has the passion menstrual, as women have. All the superfluousness that is bred in men's bodies turns into hairs or is voided by the business of work or is wasted by strength and might of heat.

Also the conditions of man and woman are diverse in terms of discretion of wit. For in all kind of beasts the male is more crafty and alert than the female to avoid and to escape treachery, griefs, and perils. So says Aristotle ... Therefore a man surpasses a woman in reason, in sharpness of wit, and understanding. So says Augustine.

And by the authority of the apostle he sets a man before a woman in dignity and worthiness of the image and likeness of God. In this dignity a man surpasses a woman in authority and might of sovereignty. Authority of teaching and of sovereignty is granted to man, and denied and prohibited to woman as for custom and usage. As in *Corinthians* 1:6, the apostle says: I suffer not a woman teach in church, for it is written: under man's power thou shalt be, and he shall be thy lord (*Genesis* 3).

Of Men

A man is called *vir* in Latin, and has that name of might and virtue and strength. So says Isidore. For in might and strength a man surpasses a woman, and a man is the head of a woman, as the apostle says. Therefore a man is held to rule his wife, as the head has the cure and rule of all the body. And a man is called *maritus*, as it were warding and defending the mother, for he takes so the charge, the ward, and the keeping of his wife that is mother of children, and is called *sponsus* also, and has that name of *spondere*, for he pledges and obligates himself. For in the contract of wedding he pledges his truth; and obliges himself to lead his life with his wife without departing; and to pay debts to her and to keep to her faith and company; and that he shall leave her for none other. A man has so great love to his wife that because of her he adventures himself to all perils, and sets her love before his mother love, and for to dwell with his wife he forsakes his father and mother and his country, as our lord says: Herefore a man shall forsake father and mother and abide with his wife.

Before the wedding the spouse tries to win the love of his spouse that he woos with gifts, and certifies of his will with letters and messengers and ... gives many gifts and much good and cattle, and pledges even more. And to please her, he puts himself to various plays and games among gatherings of people; and uses often deeds of might and of mastery; and makes himself gay and seemly in diverse clothing and array. And all that he is prayed to give or to do for her love, he gives and does anon with all his might; and grants no boon but that is prayed in her name and for her love. He speaks to her pleasingly; and beholds her in the face with pleasing and glad cheer and with a sharp eye; and assents to her at the last; and tells openly his will and his assent in presence of her friends; and espouses her with a ring and takes her to wife, and gives her great gifts in token of

the contract of wedding; and makes to her charter and deeds of grant
and of gifts; and makes revels and feasts of spousals, and gives many
good gifts to friends and guests, and comforts and gladdens his guests
with songs and pipes and with instruments of music. And hereafter
he brings his spouse into the privity of his chamber, and takes her as
fellow and makes her fellow in bed and at board. And then he makes
her lady of his money and of his men. Then he has her cause as much
to heart as his own, and takes the charge and keeping of her. And for
special love he corrects her if she does amiss, and takes heed of her
bearing and going, of speaking and looking, and of her passing and
coming again and entering.

No man has more wealth than he that has a good woman to
wife. Nor no man is more wretched neither, has woe and sore,
than he that has an evil wife, crying, jangling, chiding and scolding;
drunken and unsteadfast and contrary to him; costly, stout and gay;
envious, annoying, and leaping over lands and countries; and sneaky,
suspicious, and wrathful.... In a good spouse and wife needs these
conditions: that she be busy and devout in God's service; meek and
serviceable to her husband, and fair speaking and goodly to her men;
merciful and good to wretches that are needy; easy and peaceable to
her neighbors; ready, aware, and wise in things that shall be avoided;
rightful and patient in suffering, busy and diligent in her doings and
deeds, mannerly in address, sober in moving, wary in speaking, chaste
in looking, honest in bearing, sober in going, shamefast among the
people, merry and glad with her husband, and chaste in private. Such
a wife is worthy to be praised, that tries more to please her husband
with being meekly covered than with being gaily pleated, and
wrapped more with virtues than with fair and gay clothing. She uses
the goodness of matrimony more because of children than of fleshly
liking ... a good wife be this enough at this time.

OF THE PROPERTIES OF BAD SERVANTS

Hereto shall be put the conditions of an evil servant for he is noxious
to other men in many things. For he is often a drunkard and then he
neglects and forseeks his lords' goods and cattle or takes it thievishly
and spends it. *Proverbs* 30: A drunken workman shall not be rich.
Also he is slow and idle, and then he loses in idleness the time that
is granted to work in, as the husband said to servants: Why stand ye
here all day idle? And *Ecclesiastes* 32: Set you thy servant to work
that he be not idle, so it is seemly for him. Also he is a great spender

of his lord's good and cattle, and spends and wastes all; *Matthew* 18: the rent gatherer was defamed to his lord that he had wasted his good and cattle. Also he [the bad servant] is slow, sleepy, and listless, and neglects all his lords needs and leaves them undone....

They [bad servants] are hard of heart and malicious, yet they covet and desire to have grace (and though he get grace he doth no grace) from other men. *Matthew* 20: Wicked servant, I forgave thee all the debt for which thou prayest me. [The bad servant is] also unaware and unadvised, forgetful and ignorant, he has no mind that he shall give to his lord accounts of his outrage ... an evil speaker and tall teller of all things and namely he speaks evil of his lord.... *Ecclesiastes* 7: Hire not a servant that speaks [evil] to thee. Also, if he is delicately treated, he mistreats and withstands his lord. *Proverbs* 29: Who that nourishes his servant delicately he shall find him rebel. And it behooves not a servant to have liking of dainty things.

OF THE GOOD SERVANT

The condition of a good servant stands in diverse doings, for a good servant will be teachable and is quick to understand.... It is seemly that a servant be merry and glad of cheer in his service, for all the service displeases if the servant have not glad cheer; *Genesis* 45: And we shall be glad and serve the king.... Also he is good and gracious to speak with, and servants are well loved if they are goodly and good to speak with. Therefore it is said of David that served Saul, *Kings* 1:1, David was loved of all the people, and most of the king's servants. And there it is said: Lo, thou pleases the king and all his servants love thee. Also he is manly, bold, and hardy, and puts himself against the enemies of his lord.... And he is trusty and true in a thing that is entrusted to him, and busy to pursue his lord's needs ... [And he] is meek and crafty to procure the profit of his lord, and he takes more heed to multiply ... his lord's good and cattle than his own, for in multiplying of his lord's cattle he procures his own profit....

Also a good servant is wise and wary and curious to give accounts and reckoning of what he has taken and delivered of his lord's good and cattle. For he hopes certainly to have mead and reward for good accounts.... A true servant that dreads his lord and knows his coming does not dispose himself to bed nor to sleep before the coming of his lord; *Luke* 12: Well is the servant that his lord finds waking when he cometh. Also a busy servant [and loving] wakes when other men sleep, to keep the coming of his lord.... Also a good servant ceases

never to work. He is never idle but always busy about the profit of
his lord, for whether he eats or fasts, sleeps or wakes, his wit and
thought is always to ordain and to do the profit of his lord....Also
a good servant is never costly to his lord in meat and drink, nor in
clothing, but sometime he holds himself paid with an old cloth of his
lord's all the year long. He knows that he shall have more of his lord
when his service comes out, for in the law it is commanded that a
lord shall not let his servant go from him in the seventh year without
[meat] and drink and clothing over his chief covenant, *Exodus* 21
and *Deuteronomus* 25.

A servant that is virtuous and well taught in manner and thoughts
is often gracious and well-loved of lords. Therefore a wise servant
does his business to serve his lord courteously and curiously for
sometimes a lord loves cleanness more than service, *Psalms*: He that
proceeds in the clean way served me; *Ecclesiastes* 7: if you have a wise
servant, be he to thee as thine own soul, *et cetera*. Also a good servant
begrudges nothing nor complains against his lord when he [that is,
the lord] blames him and tells him his faults. For he knows well that a
good lord would not blame his servant wrongfully and such blaming
turns to his profit....

THE BALLAD OF THE TYRANNICAL HUSBAND (15THC)

This Middle English lyric depicts with sympathy the difficult life of many
peasant women, whose work was never done, even though their husbands
might accuse them of being lazy. Women were responsible for tending to
children and for what might be loosely described as "housework." As this
poem makes clear, the latter category included everything from making
dinner to brewing ale to spinning cloth. Our translated excerpt is based on
Thomas Wright and James Halliwell's transcription from a late fifteenth-
century manuscript.

Jesus that art gentle, for joy of thy dame,
As thou wrought this wide world, in heaven is thy home,
Save all this company and shield them from shame,
That will listen to me and tend to this game.

God keep all women that to this town belong,
Maidens, widows, and wives among;

For much they are blamed and sometimes with wrong,
I take witness of all folk that hear this song.

Listen, good sirs, both young and old,
By a good husband this tale shall be told;
He wedded a woman that was fair and bold,
And had good enough to go as they would.

She was a good housewife, courteous and clever,
And he was an angry man, and soon would be set on fire,
Chiding and brawling, and behaved like a fiend,
As they that often will be wroth with their best friend,

Till it befell upon a day, short tale to make,
The goodman would to the plow, his horse he goes to take;
He called forth his oxen, the white and the black,
And he said, "dame, make our dinner in time, for God's sake."

The goodman and his lad to the plow be gone,
The goodwife had much to do, and servant had she none,
Many small children to keep besides herself alone,
She did more then she might within her own home.

Home come the goodman early on in the day,
To look that all things were according to his say,
"Dame," he said, "is our dinner made?" "Sir," she said, "nay;
How would you have me do more then I can?"

Than he began to chide and said, "Evil must thee be!
I would thou should all day go to plow with me,
To walk in clothes that be wet and muddy,
Than should thou know what it were a plowman to be."

Than swear the goodwife, and thus began she to say,
"I have more to do then I do may;
And you should follow me fully one day,
You would be weary of your part, my head dare I lay."

"Weary! In the devil's name!" said the goodman,
"What hast thou to do, but sit here at home?

Thou goest to thy neighbors' house, one by one,
And sits there jangling with Jack and with John."

Then said the goodwife, "you must miss everything!
I have more to do, who so knows all;
When I lie in my bed, my sleep is but small,
Yet early in the morning you will me up call.

"When I lie all night waking with our child,
I rise up at morning and find our house wild;
Then I milk our cattle and bring them to the field,
While you sleep full still, also Christ me shield!

"Then make I butter further on the day;
After make I cheese,—these hold you a play;
Then will our children weep and up must they,
Yet while you blame me for our good, and any be away.

"Whan I have so done, yet there comes more even,
I give our chickens meat, or else they will be lean:
Our hens, our capons, and our ducks by the teen,
Yet tend I to our goslings that goeth on the green.

"I bake, I brew, it will not else be well;
I beat and I beat flax, as ever have I health:
I comb the fibers, I separate and I clean,
I tease the yarn and arrange it and spin it on the wheel."

"Dame," said the goodman, "the devil have thy bones!
Thou needs not bake nor brew in a fortnight past once;
I say no good that thou dost within this wide home,
But ever thou excuseth thee with grunt and groan."

"Give a piece of linen and will I make once a year,
For to clothe our selves and our children in all;
Else we should go to the market, and by it full dear,
I am as busy as I may in every year.

"When I have so done, I look on the sun,
I prepare meat for our beasts against that you come home,

And meat for our selves lest there be none,
Yet I have not a fair word when I have done.

"So I look to our good without and within,
That there be none away neither more nor less,
Glad to please you to pay, lest any battle begin,
And for to chide thus with me, in faith you be in sin."

Then said the goodman in a grieved tone,
"All this would a good housewife do long before it were prime;
And since the good that we have is half deal thine,
Thou shalt labor for thy part as I do for mine."

"Therefore, dame, make thee ready, I warn thee, anon,
Tomorrow with my lad to the plow thou shalt gone;
And I will be housewife and keep our house at home,
And take mine ease as thou hast done, by God and Saint John!"

"I grant," said the goodwife, "as I understand,
Tomorrow in the morning I will be walking:
Yet will I rise while you be sleeping,
And see that all things be ready laid to your hand."

Chaucer and the Raptus of Cecily Chaumpaigne (1380)

On 1 May 1380, a document was enrolled in the court of Chancery in which a Cecily Chaumpaigne released Geoffrey Chaucer from all legal actions concerning her rape, or, as the document puts it, "*raptus meo.*" We reproduce it here in our own translation (for the original Latin document, see *Chaucer Life Records*). The release was witnessed at court by several of Chaucer's known associates, all men of some power and status. That Cecily acted as her own agent in the matter suggests she had no male guardian or husband; according to Derek Pearsall, this would make her at least twenty-one years of age.[26] Because the Latin word "raptus" can mean abduction or rape, some scholars argue that Chaucer was released from charges of abduction rather than rape. However, documents in the case suggest that the matter was settled out of court and that Cecily Chaumpaigne was paid through intermediary the substantial sum of £10. The documentary record leaves all possibilities open: Chaucer may have raped Cecily, he may have committed some other offense against her, or he may have been the innocent victim of a blackmailing scheme. According to Christopher Cannon, someone went out of their way to cover up the nature of the original accusation: the phrase "de raptus meo" in the original document was "so bold that three days later, whether by coercion, persuasion, or some more complicated manipulation in the court of the king, this strong word—this mention of rape—had to be quietly, emphatically, retracted."[27] Our second excerpt reprints his translation of the "cleaned up" version of the Chaumpaigne release.

> Let it be known altogether by me, Cecily Chaumpaigne, daughter
> of the late William Chaumpaigne and Agnes his wife, that I have
> remitted, released, and quitclaimed in perpetuity for myself and
> my heirs to Geoffrey Chaucer, armsbearer, all manner of action
> concerning my rape, or any other matter with whatever conditions
> there were, which I have had, do have, or shall have been able to have
> from the beginning of the world to the making of these presents.
> With these witnesses: William Beauchamp, then chamberlain of the
> lord King, Sir John Clanvowe, Sir William Neville, knights John
> Philipott and Ricardo Morel. Given at London, the first day of
> May in the third year of the reign of Richard the second after the
> conquest.

> Be it remembered that Cecily Chaumpaigne, daughter of the late
> William Chaumpaigne and Agnes his wife, on the Monday next
> before the feast of Pentecost in this same term comes before the
> lord king in her own person and proffers here in court a certain
> writing which she acknowledges to be her own deed, and asks that
> it be enrolled, and it is enrolled in these words: Let all men know
> by (these) presents that I Cecily Chaumpaigne, daughter of the late
> William Chaumpaigne and Agnes his wife, have remitted, released,
> and quitclaimed in perpetuity entirely for myself and my heirs to
> Geoffrey Chaucer, esquire, all manner of actions both concerning
> felonies, trespasses, accounts, debts and any other actions whatsoever
> that I ever have had, do have, or shall have been able to have against
> the said Geoffrey from the beginning of the world until the day
> of the making of (these) presents. In testimony of which I have
> placed my seal on (these) presents. With these witnesses: Sir William
> Beauchamp, then chamberlain of the lord king, Sir John Clanvowe,

Sir William Neville, knights, and others. Given at London, the first day of May in the third year of the reign of Richard the second after the Conquest.

Widows and Clerical Anti-Feminism. Christine de Pizan (1405)

Christine de Pizan (1365–*c.*1430) was a member of the French intelligen-tsia. Her father, a scholar and astrologer who worked for the French court, gave his daughter a thorough education of the sort not usually reserved for women. Christine married Étienne de Castel, another courtier, when she was 15 years old. The marriage was both happy and short-lived. Widowed at 25, Christine turned to writing to support herself and her children. She is regarded as the first European woman to earn her living by writing; not surprisingly, many of her works focus on issues of significance to women. *The Treasury of the City of Ladies* (*c.* 1405) provides a detailed categoriza-tion of the roles that women performed in medieval society. Christine draws on her own bitter experience as a widow in our first excerpt. Our second excerpt, from *The Book of the City of Ladies* (1405), responds to Boccacio's *On Famous Women* specifically and to clerical anti-feminism more generally by celebrating women's contributions to society.

Advice to Widows
Dear friends, we pity each one of you in the state of widowhood because death has deprived you of your husbands, whoever they may have been. Moreover, much anguish and many trying problems afflict you, affecting the rich in one manner and those not rich in another. The rich are troubled because unscrupulous people commonly try to despoil them of their inheritance. The poor, or at least, those not at all rich, are distressed because they find no pity from anyone for their problems. Along with the grief of having lost your mate, which is quite enough, you also must suffer three trials in particular, which assault you whether you are rich or poor.

First is that, undoubtedly, you will find harshness and lack of consideration or sympathy everywhere. Those who honored you during the lifetime of your husbands, who may well have been officials or men of importance, now will pay little attention to you and barely even bother to be friendly. The second distress facing you is the variety of lawsuits and demands of certain people regarding debts, claims on your property, and income. Third is the evil talk of people who are all too willing to attack you, so that you hardly know what you can do that will not be criticized. In order to arm you with the sensible advice to protect yourself against these, as well as other overpowering plagues, we wish to suggest some things you may find useful....

Against the coldness you undoubtedly will find in everyone—the first of the three tribulations of widowhood—there are three possible remedies. Turn toward God, who was willing to suffer so much for human creatures. Reflecting on this will teach you patience, a quality you will need greatly. It will bring you to the point where you will place little value on the rewards and honors of this world. First of all, you will learn how undependable all earthly things are.

The second remedy is to turn your heart to gentleness and kindliness in word and courtesy to everyone. You will overcome the hard-hearted and bend them to your will by gentle prayers and humble requests.

Third, in spite of what we just said about quiet humility in words, apparel, and countenance, nevertheless you must learn the judgment and behavior necessary to protect yourself against those only too willing to get the better of you. You must avoid their company, having nothing to do with them if you can help it. Rather, stay quietly in your own house, not involving yourself in an argument with a neighbor, not even with a servingman or maid. By always speaking quietly while protecting your own interests, as well as by mingling little with miscellaneous people if you don't need to, you will avoid anyone taking advantage of you or ruining you.

Concerning the lawsuits which may stalk you, learn well how to avoid all sorts. They damage a widow in many ways. First of all, if she is not informed, but on the contrary is ignorant in legal affairs, then it will be necessary for her to place herself in the power of someone else to solicit on behalf of her needs. Those others generally lack diligence in the affairs of women, willingly deceiving them and charging them eight crowns for six. Another problem is that women cannot always come and go at all hours, as a man would do, and therefore, if it is not too damaging for her, it may be better to let go some part of what is her due rather than involve herself in contention. She should consider circumspectly any reasonable demands made against her; or if she finds herself obliged to be the plaintiff, she should pursue her rights courteously and should attempt alternatives for achieving her ends. If assailed by debts, she must inform herself of what rights her creditors have and make an appropriate plan of action....

....If, in spite of all this, she is obliged to go to court, she should understand three things necessary for all who take action. One is to act on the advice of wise specialists in customary law and clerks who are well versed in legal sciences and in the law. Next is to prepare the case for trial with great care and diligence. Third is to have enough money to afford all this. Certainly if one of these things is lacking, no matter how worthy the cause, there is every danger the case will be lost....

If it is necessary for her to do these things, and if she wishes to avoid further trouble and bring her case to a successful conclusion, she must take on the heart of a man. She must be constant, strong, and wise in judging and pursuing her advantage, not crouching in tears, defenseless, like some simple woman or like a poor dog who retreats into a corner while all the other dogs jump on him. If you do that, dear woman, you will find most people so lacking in pity that they would take the bread from your hand because they consider you either ignorant or simpleminded, nor would you find additional pity elsewhere because they took it. So do not work on your own or depend on your own judgment, but hire always the best advice, particularly on important matters you do not understand.

....Because widowhood truly provides so many hardships for women, some people might think it best for all widows to remarry. This argument can be answered by saying that if it were true that the married state consisted entirely of peace and repose, this indeed would be so. That one almost always sees the contrary in marriages should be a warning to all widows. However, it might be necessary or desirable for the young ones to remarry. But for all those who have passed their youth and who are sufficiently comfortable financially so that poverty does not oblige them, remarriage is complete folly. Though some who want to remarry say there is nothing in life for a woman alone, they have so little confidence in their own good sense that they will claim that they don't know how to manage their own lives. But the height of folly and the greatest of all absurdities is the old woman who takes a young husband: There a joyful song rarely is heard for long. Although many pay dearly for their foolishness, nobody will sympathize with them—for good reason.

On the Anti-Feminists

One day as I was sitting alone in my study surrounded by books on all kinds of subjects, devoting myself to literary studies, my usual habit, my mind dwelt at length on the weighty opinions of various authors whom I had studied for a long time. I looked up from my book, having decided to leave such subtle questions in peace and to relax by reading some light poetry. By chance a strange volume came into my hands, not one of my own, but one which had been given to me along with some others. When I held it open and saw from its title page that it was by Matheolus, I smiled, for though I had never seen it before, I had often heard that like other books it discussed respect for women. I thought I would browse through it to amuse myself. I had not been reading for very long when my good mother called me to refresh myself with some supper, for it was evening. Intending to look at it the next day, I put it down. The next morning, again seated in my study as was my habit, I remembered wanting to examine this book by Matheolus. I started to read it and went on for a little while. Because the subject seemed to me not very pleasant for people who do not enjoy lies, and of no use in developing virtue or manners, given its lack of integrity in diction and theme, and after browsing here and there and reading the end, I put it down in order to turn my attention to more elevated and useful study. But just the sight of this book, even though it was of no authority, made me wonder how it happened that so many different men—and learned men among them—have been and are so inclined to express both in speaking and in their treatises and writings so many wicked insults about women and their behavior. Not only one or two and not even just this Matheolus (for this book had a bad name anyway and was intended as a satire) but, more generally, judging from the treatises of all philosophers and poets and from all the orators—it would take too long to mention their names—it seems that they all speak from one and the same mouth. They all concur in one conclusion: that the behavior of women is inclined to and full of every vice. Thinking deeply about these matters, I began to examine my character and conduct as a natural woman and, similarly, I considered other women whose company I frequently kept, princesses, great ladies, women of the middle and lower classes, who had graciously told me of their most private and intimate thoughts, hoping that I could judge impartially and in good conscience whether the testimony of so many notable men could be true. To the best of my knowledge, no

matter how long I confronted or dissected the problem, I could
not see or realize how their claims could be true when compared
to the natural behavior and character of women. Yet I still argued
vehemently against women, saying that it would be impossible that
so many famous men—such solemn scholars, possessed of such deep
and great understanding, so clear-sighted in all things, as it seemed—
could have spoken falsely on so many occasions that I could hardly
find a book on morals where, even before I had read it in its entirety,
I did not find several chapters or certain sections attacking women,
no matter who the author was. This reason alone, in short, made me
conclude that, although my intellect did not perceive my own great
faults and, likewise, those of other women because of its simpleness
and ignorance, it was however truly fitting that such was the case.
And so I relied more on the judgment of others than on what I
myself felt and knew. I was so transfixed in this line of thinking
for such a long time that it seemed as if I were in a stupor. Like a
gushing fountain, a series of authorities, whom I recalled one after
another, came to mind, along with their opinions on this topic. And
I finally decided that God formed a vile creature when He made
woman, and I wondered how such a worthy artisan could have
deigned to make such an abominable work which, from what they
say, is the vessel as well as the refuge and abode of every evil and vice.
As I was thinking this, a great unhappiness and sadness welled up in
my heart, for I detested myself and the entire feminine sex, as though
we were monstrosities in nature....

So occupied with these painful thoughts, my head bowed in
shame, my eyes filled with tears, leaning on the pommel of my chair's
armrest, I suddenly saw a ray of light fall on my lap, as though it were
the sun. I shuddered then, as if wakened from sleep, for I was sitting
in a shadow where the sun could not have shone at that hour. And
as I lifted my head to see where this light was coming from, I saw
three crowned ladies standing before me, and the splendor of their
bright faces shone on me and throughout the entire room. Now no
one would ask whether I was surprised, for my doors were shut and
they had still entered. Fearing that some phantom had come to tempt
me and filled with great fright, I made the Sign of the Cross on my
forehead.

Then she who was the first of the three smiled and began to
speak, "Dear daughter, do not be afraid, for we have not come here
to harm or trouble you but to console you, for we have taken pity on

your distress, and we have come to bring you out of the ignorance
which so blinds your own intellect that you shun what you know for
a certainty and believe what you do not know or see or recognize
except by virtue of many strange opinions. You resemble the fool
in the prank who was dressed in women's clothes while he slept;
because those who were making fun of him repeatedly told him he
was a woman, he believed their false testimony more readily than the
certainty of his own identity. Fair daughter, have you lost all sense?
Have you forgotten that when fine gold is tested in the furnace, it
does not change or vary in strength but becomes purer the more
it is hammered and handled in different ways? Do you know now
that the best things are the most debated and the most discussed?
If you wish to consider the question of the highest form of reality,
which consists in ideas or celestial substances, consider whether the
greatest philosophers who have lived and whom you support against
your own sex have ever resolved whether ideas are false and contrary
to the truth. Notice how these same philosophers contradict and
criticize one another, just as you have seen in the Metaphysics where
Aristotle takes their opinions to task and speaks similarly of Plato and
other philosophers. And note, moreover, how even Saint Augustine
and the Doctors of the Church have criticized Aristotle in certain
passages, although he is known as the prince of philosophers in
whom both natural and moral philosophy attained their highest level.
It also seems that you think that all the words of the philosophers are
articles of faith, that they could never be wrong. As far as the poets of
whom you speak are concerned, do you not know that they spoke
on many subjects in a fictional way and that often they mean the
contrary of what their words openly say? One can interpret them
according to the grammatical figure of antiphrasis, which means,
as you know, that if you call something bad, in fact, it is good, and
also vice versa. Thus I advise you to profit from their works and to
interpret them in the manner in which they are intended in those
passages where they attack women. Perhaps this man, who called
himself Matheolus in his own book, intended it in such a way, for
there are many things which, if taken literally, would be pure heresy.
As for the attack against the estate of marriage—which is a holy
estate, worthy and ordained by God—made not only by Matheolus
but also by others and even by the Romance of the Rose where
greater credibility is averred because of the authority of its author,
it is evident and proven by experience that the contrary of the evil

which they posit and claim to be found in this estate through the obligation and fault of women is true. For where has the husband ever been found who would allow his wife to have authority to abuse and insult him as a matter of course, as these authorities maintain? I believe that, regardless of what you might have read, you will never see such a husband with your own eyes, so badly colored are these lies. Thus, in conclusion, I tell you, dear friend, that simplemindedness has prompted you to hold such an opinion. Come back to yourself, recover your senses, and do not trouble yourself any more over such absurdities. For you know that any evil spoken of women so generally only hurts those who say it, not women themselves."

Fourteenth-Century Court Cases Involving Women

The following sampling of court cases illustrate the position of women in regards to the English law during the late Middle Ages. In all but one case, the woman is treated as an extension of her husband. The one exception is that of Joan Gade, an unmarried woman who accuses her lover of having killed their son. In the 14 September 1365 case, Joan Lord was the victim of an attack, but her husband brought the bill of complaint against the assailant. The two last examples treat women as one of several objects purloined from male victims. Note that in the last case, in which the wife is taken away by force, the abduction (and possible rape) is nonetheless considered a crime against the husband, not the wife.

2 April 1365

Joan Gade came into court and charged William Beneyt, fuller, with having killed their son, and with using threats to her, though he had previously promised to marry her. The said William, being summoned, produced the boy alive in court. The woman then asked that the man should find sureties for keeping the peace, which he did forthwith, *viz.* Nicholas Potyn and Walter Parker. The man made a similar demand as regards the woman, and as she was unable to find mainpernors [persons who take on the legal obligation to ensure that a prisoner will appear in court on the day mandated] she was committed to prison, where she remained till 30 April, when Thomas de Claveryng, saddler, and John Tiryngton, mason, mainprised [the act of being a mainpernor] her.

14 SEPTEMBER 1365

Edmund Lord of Candlewickstreet Ward brought a bill of complaint against John Fraunceys, cordwainer, of Clement's Lane, whom he charged with having drawn a knife called a "*broche*" against the plaintiff's wife, Joan, and with having beaten her so as to cause a miscarriage, the cause of the quarrel being that Joan had demanded payment of 18½d. from Emma, the defendant's wife, who also had attempted to assault her, and had used villainous language to her.

The defendant appeared by attachment and admitted the assault and drawing the knife (for which he paid a fine of half-a-mark to the Chamber) but denied having caused the miscarriage, and on this charge put himself on the country; and the plaintiff did likewise. The jury found him guilty of the matters which he had confessed, but not guilty of causing the miscarriage, so far as they could ascertain among themselves. He was accordingly set free.

18 DECEMBER 1374

John Loryng, William Neweman, Richard Bereford, William Stratford, and Robert Buckston were indicted with others, not taken, for having been present with arms to give assistance to a certain John Spencer and others, who had gone with swords and bucklers and cuirasses, called "*jakkes*," under their outer garments to the inn of John Godard, hosteler, in the parish of St Peter's Cornhill, where they broke into a chamber occupied by Katherine de Brewes and carried her out, dragging her along the floor by her arms and clothes, naked upwards to the waist and with her hair hanging over her bosom, until the neighbors, aroused by the cries of her servants and herself, came and rescued her.

The accused denied the charge and put themselves on the country. They were found not guilty and acquitted.

9 JULY 1382

Thomas Norwich, chaplain, was attached to answer Henry de Wilton in a plea of trespass, wherein the latter complained that the defendant on divers occasions between 1 Aug. 1381 and 8 July 1382 by force and arms against the peace had eloigned [removed] and carried away the plaintiff's wife Joan, woolen and linen cloths, silver plate, dishes, pewter saltcellars and iron and brass pots and pans.

A jury brought in a verdict that as regards the wife, she was nothing but a common strumpet, and so there was no eloigning, but the defendant was in possession of certain goods belonging to the plaintiff of the value of 60s., some of which Joan had brought to him and the rest he had himself taken. It was considered that the defendant pay 60s. damages and restore the goods, in default of which he was committed to prison.

8 August 1382

John Hankyn, fishmonger, was attached to answer Richard Elme, baker, in a plea of trespass, wherein the latter complained that on 30 Sept. 1381 the defendant by force and arms, to wit swords, had taken, abducted and carried away the plaintiff's wife Alice, together with 6 woollen cloths of blanket worth £40, 4 mazers with silver bands worth 12 marks, 2 pieces of silver worth 30s. and 8 gold rings worth 10 marks.

The defendant pleaded not guilty and put himself on the country. On 8 Aug. a jury of St Botolph's Bishopsgate found that as regards the mazers, silver pieces, and rings he was not guilty, but guilty of eloigning the wife and carrying away the woollen cloths, to the plaintiff's damage 200 marks. Accordingly it was considered that the plaintiff recover the damages taxed by the jury, but that he be in mercy for his false claim concerning the mazers *etc.*

First Epistle to the Corinthians (1388)

The misogynistic attitudes that led medieval clerics to vilify women and condemn marriage had their roots in the Bible, especially in the writings of St. Paul. One of the most frequently referenced passages in medieval culture was from *Ephesians* 5:23: "For the husband is the head of the wife, even as Christ is the head of the church: and he is the saviour of the body." Another is the passage from *Corinthians* 1:7, on conjugal obligations and on the desirability of marriage more generally speaking. These verses also include the famous reference to servants favored of conservative commentators in the Middle Ages. We reproduce a version based on the first English Bible, known as the Wyclif Bible for its associations with the dissident preacher John Wyclif, and his followers, the Lollards.

But of the ilk things that ye have written to me, it is good to a man to touch not a woman. But for fornication, each man has his own wife, and each woman has her own husband. The husband yield debt to the wife, and also the wife to the husband. The woman has not power of her body, but the husband. And the husband has not power of his body, but the woman.

Do not ye defraud each to other, but peradventure of consent to a time that ye give attention to prayer. And once more turn ye again to the same thing, lest Satan tempt you for your incontinence. But I say this thing as giving leave, not by commandment. For I will that all men be as myself. But each man has his proper gift of God, one thus and another thus. But I say to them that are not wedded and to widows, it is good to them if they dwell so as I. That if they contain not themselves, be they wedded, for it is better to be wedded than to be burnt.

Each man, in what calling he is called, in that dwell he. Thou, servant, art called, be it no charge to thee. But if thou may be free, then rather use thou. He that is a servant, and is called in the Lord, is a freeman of the Lord. Also, he that is a freeman and is called, is the servant of Christ. With price ye are bought. Do not ye be made servants of men. Therefore, each man, in what thing he is called a brother, dwell he therein with God. But of virgins, I have no commandment of God, but I give counsel as he that has mercy of the Lord, that I be true.

"THE WIFE IS SUBJECT TO THE HUSBAND." JOHN WYCLIF (*c.* 1378 AND 1384)

The dissident preacher John Wyclif (1330–84) was an Oxford-educated cleric, who is best known for his proto-Protestant positions on matters like the relationship between church and state, the relative importance of the Word, and the significance of the Eucharist (Wyclif denied the doctrine of transubstantiation), as well as for his association with the first vernacular English Bible. However radical Wyclif's views on doctrinal matters were, he was a conservative when it came to gender, as this excerpt from a treatise entitled "Of Wedded Men and Wives and of their Children Also" shows. Our translation is based on the edition of this late fourteenth-century treatise by Herbert E. Winn.

See now how the wife owes to be subject to the husband, and he owes to rule his wife, and how they both owe to rule their children in God's law. First, Saint Peter bids that wives be subject to their husbands, in so much that if any believe not by word of preaching, that they be won without word of preaching to the holy living of women, when men urge the chaste living of women. And these women should not have ... adornment of hair, nor garlands of gold, nor over precious or curious clothing, but they should have a clean soul, peaceable and meek and obedient, which is rich in the sight of God. And sometime holy women, hoping in God, honored him in this manner, and were subject to their own husbands as Sara, Abraham's wife, obeyed to Abraham, calling him lord; and women doing well are ghostly spiritual daughters of Sara. All this says Saint Peter.

Also Saint Peter speaks thus of husbands and wives: I will that men pray in each place, lifting up clean hands, that is, clean works, without wrath and strife. Also I will that women are in decent clothing, with shame-fastness and soberness adorning them or making them fair, not in braided hair, nor in gold, nor in precious stones, or pearls, nor in precious cloth, but that which becomes women, promising pity, through good works. A woman owes it to learn in silence, with all obedience and subjection. But Paul says: I suffer not a woman to teach, that is, openly in church, as Paul says in an epistle to Corinthians; and I suffer not a woman to have lordship in her husband, but to be in silence or stillness.

The Clerical Tradition on Women

The excerpts below, taken from various Church authorities, illustrate the anti-feminist tendencies of clerical writing on women. Although Jerome eventually regretted writing his *Against Jovinian*, it was one of many authorities included in books like the one that Chaucer's Jankyn likes to read to the unruly Wife of Bath. We also provide an excerpt from *The Lamentations of Matheolus*, the book that Christine de Pizan discusses in the excerpt above.

From "Against Jovinian." *Jerome* (*c.* 393)

Let us turn back to the chief point of the evidence: "It is good," he [St Paul] says, "for a man not to touch a woman." If it is good not to touch a woman, it is bad to touch one: for there is no opposite to goodness but badness. If it be bad and the evil is pardoned, the reason for the concession is to prevent a worse evil. But surely, a thing which is only allowed because there may be something worse has only a slight degree of goodness. He would never have added "let each man have his own wife," unless he had previously used the words "but, because of fornications." Do away with fornication, and he will not say "let each man have his own wife." Just as though one were to lay it down: "It is good to feed on wheaten bread, and to eat the finest wheat flour" and yet, to prevent a person pressed by hunger from devouring cow-dung, I may allow him to eat barley. Does it follow that the wheat will not have its peculiar purity, because such a one prefers barley to excrement? That is naturally good which does not admit of comparison with what is bad, and is not eclipsed because something else is preferred.

At the same time, we must take note of the Apostle's prudence. He did not say, "it is good not to have a wife," but, "it is good not to touch a woman": as though there were danger even in the touch; as though he who touched her would not escape from her who "hunts for the precious life," who causes the young man's understanding to fly away. "Can a man take fire in his bosom, and his clothes be not burnt? Or can one walk upon burning coals and his feet not be scorched?" As then he who touches fire is instantly burned, so by the mere touch the peculiar nature of man and woman is perceived, and the difference of sex is understood....

"Defraud ye not one the other [of marital obligations] except it be by consent for a season, that ye may give yourselves unto prayer." What, I pray you, is the quality of that good thing which hinders prayer? Which does not allow the body of Christ to be received? So long as I do the husband's part, I fail in continency. The same Apostle in another place commands us to pray always. If we are to pray always, it follows that we must never be in the bondage of wedlock, for as often as I render my wife her due, I cannot pray....

Then come the words, "But I say to the unmarried and to widows, it is good for them if they abide even as I. But if they have not continency, let them marry: for it is better to marry than to burn." Having conceded to married persons the enjoyment of wedlock and pointed out his own wishes, he passes on to the unmarried and to widows, sets before them his own practice for imitation, and calls them happy if they so abide. "But if they have not continency, let them marry," just as he said before, "[to avoid] fornication," and "Lest Satan tempt you, because of your incontinency." And he gives a reason for saying "If they have not continency, let them marry," namely, "It is better to marry than to burn." The reason why it is better to marry is that it is worse to burn. Let burning lust be absent, and he will not say it is better to marry. The word *better* always implies a comparison with something worse, not a thing absolutely good and incapable of comparison. It is as though he said, "it is better to have one eye than neither, it is better to stand on one foot and to support the rest of the body with a stick, than to crawl with broken legs"....

Christ loves virgins more than others, because they willingly give what was not commanded them. And it indicates greater grace to offer what you are not bound to give, than to render what is exacted of you. The Apostles, contemplating the burden of a wife, exclaimed, "If the case of a man is so with his wife, it is not advantageous to marry." Our Lord thought well of their view. "You rightly think," said He, "that it is not expedient for a man who is hastening to the kingdom of heaven to take a wife: but it is a hard matter, and all men do not receive the saying, but only they to whom it has been given. Some are eunuchs by nature, others by the violence of men. Those eunuchs please me who are such not of necessity, but of free choice. Willingly do I take them into my bosom who have made themselves eunuchs for the kingdom of heaven's sake, and in order to worship me have renounced the condition of their birth."

FROM "SERMON 66." *Jacques de Vitry* (EARLY 13ᵀᴴ C)

It is clear that however much a married couple is equal as regards the carnal debt, in other things the husband is his wife's head, to rule her, correct her (if she strays), and restrain her (so she does not fall headlong). For hers is a slippery and weak sex, not to be trusted too easily. Wanton woman is slippery like a snake and as mobile as an eel; so she can hardly be guarded or kept within bounds. Some things are so bare that there is nothing by which to get hold of them. Just as whoever tries to grasp a sunbeam opens his hand to find it holds nothing, and just as a round glass container lacking handles to hold is not easily grasped by the hand and quickly slips away, so it is with woman: roving and lecherous once she has been stirred by the devil's hoe. Put a frog on a silk cloth and it'll never rest until it jumps back into the mud; it cannot stay in a clean place.

She will bring tears to your eyes—but *their* eyes are schooled in weeping. Do not believe her, because "the iniquity of a man is better than a well-meaning woman." When the time comes she will spread her wings, since if an opportunity discloses itself she'll fly off and quit. In this respect woman can be called a virtuoso artist, as they say; because she has one skill—that is, one way of deceiving—more than the devil.

THE LAMENTATIONS OF MATHEOLUS.
Jehan le Fèvre (c. 1371-72)

ON WIDOWS As soon as her husband is in his coffin, a wife's only thought day and night is to catch another husband. She observes convention by weeping, but after three days can't wait to be remarried. If her children wish to claim their share of the goods and money they have inherited from their father, there's not one of them who doesn't pay dearly for it. She disagrees with everything they say, argues, and is good at reproaching them, saying "I would already be married if it were not for your objections, for this has already happened to me three or four times. Now I'm having to dispute with you; what wretched progeny I have borne." Then she curses the fruits of her womb and tells them that, despite their objections, without delay or further procrastination, she will marry one of her suitors, who will protect her rights for her. And she is so eager to marry that she takes a husband who brings about her ruin: who spends and squanders her money, an unbridled spendthrift, who will not be restrained as long as she still has something in the loft. He leaves her with neither a penny nor halfpenny, neither land, vineyard, nor house which he hasn't sold; everything has been spent. Then, when she sees how she has been used, she complains to her children and weeps for her first husband. Such tears, may God help me, with which women reproach their most recent husbands, are an indictment against the heat of their loins. Their frivolity does not excuse them.

I don't think there is a more foolish woman than a widow all dolled up; she doesn't think of herself as past it, she often transforms and changes her appearance, adopting different hairstyles. She paints her face, rearranges her hair, wears make-up, adorns herself. One moment she is willing, the next she isn't; now she's friendly, now hostile; first she quarrels with one person then with another, praising one to the skies and piling scorn on another. And if ever out of habit many men waste their time with her, she is still too dissolute, abandoning the flower for the flames. In this way she proves to be naïve and foolish, resembling the dung-beetle, which leaves the perfume of the flowers to follow in the wake of carts, wallowing in horse shit. And just like the she-wolf on heat, that always takes the worst male as her mate, so the widow always chooses badly.

Alas, things used to be different. A wife used to lament her husband's death and remain in mourning for a full year. Now she waits no more than three days; you'd be hard pressed to find anyone waiting longer! For as soon as her first husband slips into everlasting sleep and has been disposed of in the ground, his wife begins to wage war, refusing to give up until she has found another man to stuff her tights again, for she is incapable of remaining alone. And I don't believe for a moment that she will wear black clothes to encourage mourning. Instead she will don a silk dress to indicate her joy. This is no more nor less than a disgrace. There is no bridle nor halter that could ever restrain her. She is forever coming and going; no man would ever be able to confine her to her room or to her house. She wants to be seen everywhere, so driven is she by her ardour. The burning lust of widows is an affront to decency; they creep and climb on to rooftops just like the frogs of Egypt; they are not interested in beds or couches unless there is a man with them. Who would have thought they would be like this? Saint Acaire preferred to be the protector of madmen and the insane rather than to be responsible for widows. Anyone who looks into the matter knows that he was right. For these women are mad and know no bounds and so he didn't wish to be their patron. Widows are a base and immoral lot, while a madman in chains can do no harm.

ON WOMEN AND LECHERY People say that women are lecherous. On the surface, these words sound insulting. However, with due respect to all ladies, it is necessary to speak as one finds, and so that you don't think that I have made this up, I shall provide you with an example. Queen Semiramis introduced a general law that every woman should take as her husband whomsoever she liked and that they would be allowed to do this without any regard to consanguinity. This precaution was to her own advantage for, as we learn from history, she married her own son. Heavens, this law was very shameful indeed, dirty, vile, and incestuous. And Pasiphaë, another queen, lay down under a bull disguised in a hollowed out wooden cow. This was barefaced lechery. Just like a brutish animal, Pasiphaë placed her crotch where there was a crack in the artificial cow to receive the bull's prick. It is quite right that she has the reputation of a whore. Scylla committed an outrageous act for which she deserved to be hated and disgraced throughout the world. She burned with passion for Minos; her ardor was so insane and ill-fated that she cut off her own father's head. Her lust burned hotter than stubble. Minos won Scylla and the whole kingdom. Because Scylla was cruel, outrageous, and lecherous and had a reputation for treachery, she shares her name with one of the perils of the sea.

No fever has a hotter flame than that of a woman on heat. Their ardor is more bitter and violent than toothache or other affliction. Myrrha was not afraid of what people might say. She slept with her father and accepted intercourse with him, which so dishonored him. The daughters of Lot sinned too, for they slept with their father. If Myrrha lay with her father, Biblis did so with her brother. It would be almost impossible for me to remain silent on this subject; Canace lay with Macareus, receiving her brother carnally in debauchery, which was her downfall. Phaedra, the daughter of the king of Crete, was not very discreet in love. She loved with an illicit passion, besotted by Hippolytus, the son of her husband Theseus. When she had had the last remnants of that old pot she turned to her stepson for some banging. Venus turned her into a crazed stepmother. Phyllis committed a horribly devilish act. You would never find another woman so insane, so wretched, so mad, so out of control because of her passion. She abandoned herself to shameful dishonor when she hanged herself because of Demophöon. I don't know what made her hang herself; all I know is that she couldn't wait because she was overcome with despair and her beloved did not seem to be coming. Nine times she went to the seashore, then she hanged herself with her girdle. Dido, the queen of Carthage, also went too far because of Aeneas, her guest, who had dipped into her bread-basket. There's much to criticize in Dido's actions. When she saw Aeneas out at sea on his way to Lombardy, she did a terrible and reckless thing. Aware that she was heavy with child, weeping, lamenting, and insane with love, she took destiny into her own hands by killing herself, using Aeneas' sword. Ill-fated was the hour when she was born. I could list many more examples, but I shan't do so for brevity's sake.

If there is anyone who says that women with their tits and boobs are colder than the male, let him lose his purse and its contents. If anyone has come to this conclusion, he hasn't looked at the evidence carefully enough. For, by Saint Acaire of Haspre, their lust is much stronger than ours and turns into greater ardor. A woman underneath a man gets very excited. But let's say no more about it at present. The great authorities on the subject put forward many reasons for this and say that women burn more passionately, and more frequently spill their own blood than men, and are quicker to desire union with the male. Uguccione himself claims that she is more eager to consummate the relationship; for the word "woman" (*femme*) comes from the Greek "fire" (*fos*), because she burns more than a man, or from "thigh" (*femur*) via "breeches" (*femourailles*). Women have heat in their loins and adore the "thigh" game. Even supposing that you could find some who are frigid, cold humours are difficult to digest and such matter needs to be purged through bonking—for desperation gets even an old woman going, whose desire is that much keener since it stems from frigidity. They are by nature very weak and frail and more fragile than glass. Ovid says that woman is only chaste when no man courts or chases her. Given their lust, the pope has granted them permission to marry without delay in order to pay the tribute their flesh demands. For otherwise they would hardly manage to wait and would offer or sell themselves to all comers.

Notes

1   John Dryden, "The Preface to Fables Ancient and Modern," in *John Dryden* (New York: Oxford U, 1987) 563.

2   Quoted in Keen, *English Society in the Later Middle Ages* 2.

3   Paul Strohm, *Social Chaucer* (Cambridge, MA: Harvard UP, 1989) 9.

4   Paul Strohm, *Social Chaucer* (Cambridge, MA: Harvard UP, 1989) 9.

5   D.W. Robertson, *A Preface to Chaucer: Studies in Medieval Perspectives* (Princeton, NJ: Princeton UP, 1962); David Aers, *Chaucer* (Brighton: Harvester, 1986).

6   Bryon Lee Grigsby, *Pestilence in Medieval and Early Modern English Literature* (New York: Routledge, 2004) 103-06.

7   Barbara Hanawalt, *The Ties that Bound: Peasant Families in Medieval England* (New York: Oxford UP, 1986).

8   Keen, *English Society in the Later Middle Ages* 9.

9   Christopher Dyer, *Standards of Living in the Later Middle Ages: Social Change in England, C. 1200-1500*, Cambridge Medieval Textbooks (Cambridge and New York: Cambridge UP, 1989) 22-24.

10 Sylvia Thrupp, *The Merchant Class of Medieval London* (Chicago, IL: U of Chicago P, 1948) 3, 12-13.

11 Mervyn James, "Ritual, Drama, and Social Body in the Late Medieval English Town," *Past and Present* 98 (1983): 8, 15.

12 Kay E. Lacey, "Women and Work in Fourteenth and Fifteenth Century London," in *Women and Work in Pre-Industrial England*, ed. Lindsey Charles and Lorna Duffin (London: Croom Helm, 1985) 24–83.

13 Mavis E. Mate, "Work and Leisure," in *A Social History of England 1200-1500*, ed. Rosemary Horrox and W. Mark Ormrod (Cambridge: Cambridge UP, 2006) 282.

14 Lacey 25, 57.

15 Olwen Hufton, *The Prospect Before Her: A History of Women in Western Europe* (New York: Alfred Knopf, 1996) 255.

16 Hanawalt, *The Ties That Bound* 220.

17 Jane Tibbets Schulenburg, "The Heroics of Virginity: Brides of Christ and Sacrificial Mutilation," in *Women in the Middle Ages and the Renaissance*, ed. Mary Beth Rose (Syracuse, NY: Syracuse UP, 1986) 54.

18 Hanawalt, *The Ties That Bound* 142.

19 *The Goodman of Paris: A Treatise on Moral and Domestic Economy by a Citizen of Paris*, trans. Eileen Power (New York: Harcourt Brace, 1928) 108.

20 Peter Coss, "An Age of Deference," in *A Social History of England 1200-1500*, ed. Rosemary Horrox and W. Mark Ormrod (Cambridge: Cambridge UP, 2006) 49–50.

21 Peter Coss, *The Lady in Medieval England* 1000-1500 (Mechanicsburg, PA: Stackpole Books, 1998) 87.

22 Bruce Campbell, "The Land," in *A Social History of England, 1200-1500*, ed. Rosemary Horrox and W. Mark Ormrod (Cambridge: Cambridge UP, 2006) 198.

23 Christopher Cannon, "*Raptus* in the Chaumpaigne Release and a Newly Discovered Document concerning the Life of Geoffrey Chaucer," *Speculum* 68 (1993): 74–94; and Christopher Cannon, "Chaucer and Rape: Uncertainty's Certainties," *Studies in the Age of Chaucer* 22 (2000): 67–92.

24 See Carolyn Dinshaw, *Chaucer's Sexual Poetics* (Madison, WI: U of Wisconsin P, 1989).

25 Hanawalt, *The Ties That Bound* 153.

26 Derek Albert Pearsall, *The Life of Geoffrey Chaucer: A Critical Biography,* Vol. 1: (Oxford and Cambridge, MA: Blackwell, 1992) 136.

27 Cannon 94.

CHAPTER III

"Of Mete and Drynk"
Daily Life in Medieval England

INTRODUCTION

MEDIEVAL LONDON

*L*ocated at the geographical and cultural center of England, late medieval London was a fortified town of about 50,000 inhabitants. Although to us moderns, used to our vast metropolises, this number seems small, London had almost five times the population of York and Norwich, the next largest towns in England. Some 70 or 80 church steeples made up the medieval equivalent of the London skyline. These parish churches tended to the spiritual welfare of all citizens, obviously, but they also helped ensure the physical welfare of the city's many poor and indigent, who congregated near places of worship to receive alms from church-goers. Londoners clearly had an attachment to their own neighborhoods—they preferred to attend services near home.

The city was divided into 24 such neighborhoods or wards (25 after 1394). Each ward had its own alderman, or head, as well as its own watch, which patrolled the streets and enforced the laws, like the one setting a curfew at night. The mayor of London was "elected" from among the aldermen every year. Although this practice sounds democratic, city government was in fact in the hands of a small oligarchy. For one thing, only about one in four adult men were full citizens (a status denied to women, children, servants, apprentices, clergymen, and aliens). Only citizens were allowed to vote in city elections and to trade freely. The business restrictions on aliens (anyone who was not a citizen of London) were so severe that most adult males who were not freemen were forced to work for freemen. One of the surest paths to freedom and citizenship was through membership in the guilds, and the more powerful guilds—like the Mercers (traders in luxury fabrics) and the Grocers—accordingly exerted undue influence over the election and appointment of officials. Becoming the alderman of a ward was a crucial step to political power in medieval London, which is why Chaucer's five guildsmen aspire to the position. The wardmoot, presided over by the alderman, was the city's basic unit of administration and enforcement: it appointed ward officials, ensured that businesses followed city regulations, and arbitrated disputes among the locals.

Every London ward developed a distinct cultural atmosphere, reflecting its particular preponderance of businesses. Birds of a feather tended to flock together in medieval towns—Londoners involved in the book trade, for example, gathered around St. Paul's, while the mercers, the goldsmiths, and other traders in luxury goods were to be found on West Cheap. The congregation of like businesses in one area of town helps explain how guilds could take control of city government. As might be expected, some neighborhoods, like those of the merchants, were also more pleasant than others, like those of the butchers. The butchers near Newgate apparently made a practice of washing the entrails of the beasts they slaughtered on a city quay—judging by the complaints, this must not have been a pretty sight.[1] Place names frequently gave an indication of the business transacted there. Londoners who wished to buy fish would head to Fish Market, for example, where the fishmongers and their wives plied their trade. The Vintry, the ward where Chaucer was born and bred, was associated with the wine trade (John Chaucer, Chaucer's father, was a vintner or wine merchant). Its location near the quays was a preferred one for all merchants, who wanted access to the boats that transported their goods. By medieval standards, the Vintry was cosmopolitan, since it was home to many of the city's foreign immigrants, including Italian wine merchants. Growing up there must have helped equip Chaucer for his travels abroad and for his enduring love of Italian literature.

First-time visitors to medieval London would have been awed by its various sights. On the west side of town, the house of the Black Friars and the Cathedral of Saint Paul testified to the power of God and His ministers; on the east side, the royal palace of the Tower testified to that of the monarch and his minions. In between were a variety of dwellings, from the rough shacks of the very poor, to the three-storey houses of the middling sort, to the court-yarded palaces of the very rich. The storeyed houses in which most people lived were spaced closely together and leaned over the narrow streets. Each of these houses provided living quarters for families, as well as rooms for servants, apprentices, renters, and lodgers. Many had shops or taverns on the first floor, and signs advertising wares and services or naming the establishment stuck out from the buildings into the streets. Taverns would often announce their presence by an "alestake," a pole hung with leaves. Repeated ordinances trying to regulate the length of "alestakes" suggest that they were a nuisance to riders and other people attempting to use the streets.[2]

Living conditions were very congested. The majority of Londoners lived within one square mile or so—the space enclosed on one side by the Thames and on the other sides by the city walls. Given those circumstances, only the prosperous could afford dwellings large enough to allow for something like privacy. A successful vintner like John Chaucer, for example, might have a reception hall in his house where he received customers, a cellar that contained his collection of wines, some living and dining rooms where the women and children spent their days, as well as a kitchen and a number of bedrooms. Most families, however, had to make do with just one or two rooms and a kitchen; sometimes, family members even shared a bed. Because they were expensive, beds were among the most cherished possessions of medieval families. Other furnishings were basic, including some chests, tables, and chairs. Those wishing to display their success also invested in luxury items like decorated salt cellars or Flemish tapestries.

The congested living conditions generated a number of problems for the city. Sewage and garbage were inevitable points of contention. The inhabitants of any given house used a communal privy, often located in the yard or in the basement floor. Although some of the better houses had privies that emptied out over streams, most had to be drained by "gong farmers" at the cost of two shillings per ton. Many conflicts—like the one involving John Stockyngbury's "large dung heap" (SEE BELOW)—concerned the disposal of garbage and sewage. Those with no immediate access to privies used the street, as did London's substantial animal population. One of the major differences between modern cities and their medieval counterparts is the presence in the latter of what we would consider farm animals. Besides the various beasts of burden, pigs also roamed the streets, making the most of the garbage available everywhere. In 1332, one such pig wandered into an unattended shop and bit a newborn in the face. The baby died later that night.[3] In addition to inflicting harm on the city's inhabitants, the animals left their own distinct droppings and odors. Despite the city's best efforts—it passed ordinances, outlawed pigs, punished wrongdoers, built public privies, and employed rakers (who raked or scraped refuse off the streets)—nasty smells pervaded medieval London.

From a modern perspective, it might be hard to understand why so many people moved from the country into the city. London's streets were crammed with refuse and its buildings with rodents, which meant that the city was particularly hard-hit by the plague. During epidemics, the overabundance of dead bodies added the stench of decay and decomposition to the city's usual smells. In addition to its unsanitary conditions, the city was beset by urban conflicts. The various city factions and guilds were regularly at odds with one another; class tensions ran high, especially during the troubled political times of the 1380s; and crime was a recurrent problem. Fraud was rampant: butchers sold rotten meat, bakers cheated on the size of their breads, and tavern owners sold adulterated ale or used thick-bottomed measuring cups to fool their customers.[4] Unscrupulous merchants engaged in price gouging, a practice that got Nicholas Sardouche into repeated trouble with the law during the late 1360s. Although he was able to procure a legal pardon, Sardouche was subsequently murdered under suspicious circumstances during a street brawl. Then as now, urban conditions encouraged high levels of violent crime. Tempers flared often and easily, abetted by the large amounts of ale that the London population consumed daily. The court records include many cases in which disputes over trivial matters—a small sum of money, a perceived insult—boiled over into physical violence.

But London had many redeeming aspects as well. Whereas modern citizens tolerate a high level of noise pollution, the loudest noises in medieval London came from the church bells. Although they were resented by some, the city's immigrants brought with them a diversity of tastes, ideas, and cultures, which helped make the city the most stimulating place in England. London was also a consumer's paradise. The city's taverns and ale-houses tended to the thirsty with wine and ale, while its street vendors plied the hungry with fresh fruit, hot pies, and roasted eel. London's shopkeepers offered a fabulous array of luxurious goods for purchase: lace from the Low Countries, wine from France, oranges and lemons from Spain, spices and peppers from the Orient. Many of these goods were not obtainable elsewhere in England; even when a particular product was available in the country, it was of lower quality. Margaret Paston claimed that she could get "neither good cloth nor good frieze" in her own town. Her letters to her husband John, an esquire and lawyer with frequent business in London, routinely include requests for clothes or specialty foods. During one of her pregnancies, Margaret begged John to "send me dates and cinnamon as hastily as you may," signing herself "your groaning wife."[5] London had goods enough to satisfy the most capricious appetites.

For those with no money to spend, London street life presented plenty by way of diversion. Although some aristocrats had access to coaches, these could only travel along big thoroughfares. Traffic on other streets consisted mainly of pedestrians and people on horseback. On long summer nights, Londoners lived in these streets: children played there, their parents gossiped, young men gambled, prostitutes solicited business, and thieves stole from them all. The legal records contain vivid glimpses of this aspect of urban life; for example, John Cheddele was accused by neighbors of being a "common player of dice by night and a constant nightwalker." According to the jury's findings in the case, "John used to stand in the street at night and accost the daughters, wives and serving-maids of citizens, against the latter's will, and take them off to lie with him" (SEE Court Cases and Coroners' Cases BELOW). The streets seem to have brought pleasure and danger in equal measures. There was always something worth observing. The castigation of a common criminal—a routine event—was one occasion for spectacle, since public ridicule was a component of many punishments. A pillory at Cornhill was reserved for those who violated city ordinances, including the ones against indecency and against selling rotten meat. One law stipulated, for example, that

> any woman [who] shall be found to be a common courtesan, and if the same shall be attainted, let her be taken from the prison unto Aldgate, with a hood of ray [darnel straw?], and a white wand in her hand; and from thence, with minstrels, unto the thew,[6] and there let the cause be proclaimed…. (SEE BELOW)

The gallows at Tyburn offered up gorier sights to those so inclined: traitors were hung, disemboweled, and quartered, and heretics were burned, all before appreciative crowds. Frequently, minstrels accompanied criminals to the site of their shame in order to draw onlookers.

Not all forms of official urban entertainment involved cruelty. On feast days, Londoners donned their best clothes and gathered in the happening parts of town—around St. Paul's, Cheapside, or the Guildhall—for mummings, parades, pageants, and processions. The revelry might include the election of a boy bishop on St. Nicholas Day (6 December); a parade led by the giants Gog and Magog on Midsummer's Night's Eve; or a procession by the Skinners, who marched bearing torches and accompanied by chanting priests on Corpus Christi Day. Elaborate tableaux and pageants welcomed a new king into the city. On some festive occasions, like the entry of Edward I's second queen in 1299, the fountains and conduit which normally made drinking water available to the populace ran with wine, and everyone, rich or poor, had a chance to get drunk.[7] When London found itself in trouble with Richard II in 1392, it put on a splendid show for him: the conduit ran again with red and white wine; the streets were decorated with precious fabrics; and a child disguised as an angel offered the king and queen golden crowns, as well as various other gifts. The king forgave his theatrically gifted subjects and restored the city's liberties. Medieval Londoners shared such a "passion for pageantry" and processions that the city kept at its disposal a whole range of theatrical properties, which were put to use at the merest hint of a festive event.[8] On occasions like Midsummer and St. Peter's Day, people also decorated their houses with flowers and boughs, hung lanterns from the roofs, and lit bonfires in the streets. The rich provided food for the poor, so that no one was left out of the festivities.[9] Along with economic opportunities, London offered many pleasures—no wonder country people kept coming to the city to replenish its population, even during the worst of the plague years.

Most people entered London through one of its seven gates, which were closed at night in observance of the curfew. These gates were big enough to provide comfortable housing to some Londoners, like Chaucer, who lived over Aldgate from 1374-86. Newgate contained lodgings of a different sort—the prison where Sir Thomas Malory (d. 1471?) probably composed his *Morte Darthur* (1469-70?). Aside from the gates, the only other access to the city was by boat or by ferry across the Thames. Only one bridge—the famous London Bridge—allowed pedestrian traffic across the Thames. London Bridge was a destination in itself for medieval pleasure-seekers: it contained over 100 shops where customers could buy a variety of merchandise. People could also gaze on the heads of traitors, displayed as a warning on the bridge. Those wanting more thrills still went on from London Bridge to Southwark, a suburb on the other side of the Thames, which was known for prostitution and bear-baiting, activities that had been outlawed in London proper. The inn where Chaucer's pilgrims first meet, the Tabard, is located in this outlying area. Not surprisingly, some aristocrats preferred playing grounds of their own, near the city but far enough away to avoid the filth, the hubbub, and the plague. Many great lords—secular and religious—built palaces along the river, on the Strand (or "beach") near Westminster, the seat of royal government. The Savoy, the fabulous residence of John of Gaunt, which was destroyed during the Peasant's Rebellion of 1381, was one of these palaces. London's lawyers also valued proximity to royal power: the Inns of Court, where Chaucer's Manciple works, were also near Westminster. The east and the north of the city offered a sharp contrast to the prestige and power of the west. There, in the medieval equivalent of the ghettos, the disenfranchised residents of this urban world—the permanently poor, the low-level criminals, the recent transplants—had their homes.

GETTING AROUND

Chaucer's Host urges the pilgrims to join forces in their journey from London because traveling together would result in the "myrthe" and "confort" of all (GP 773). He might also have urged their safety. The roads that connected London to the rest of the country presented travelers with multiple hazards. The roads themselves were primitive by our standards, and, according to court records, often in a state of disrepair. Some had potholes big enough that they caused carts to overturn.[10] People sometimes drowned in these large pits or in the ditches that drained water from roads.[11] No reliable maps existed to lead travelers safely to their destination, and only an occasional signpost helped guide the lost. Travelers often had to rely on guides and locals to help them identify the correct route, as Margery Kempe did when she hired a Dover man to take her to Canterbury.[12] The most ominous dangers of the road were the highwaymen, who lurked among the bushes, surprising travelers along their routes. Highwaymen were less likely to attack large groups than single persons; by traveling together, Chaucer's pilgrims lessen their chances of an unwanted encounter with outlaws. Chaucer was himself a victim of highwaymen: in 1390, he was robbed of his horse, his goods, and over £20—a huge sum—near Hatcham in the county of Surrey.[13] Medieval literature often invokes the dangers of the roads. In "The Wife of Bath's Tale," a knight sees "a mayde walkynge hym beforn, / Of which mayde anon, maugree hir heed, / By verray force, he rafte her maydenhed" (885–87). These lines present rape as a banal crime of opportunity—just as richly dressed merchants invited theft, women traveling alone invited rape.

The wide appeal of the legendary Robin Hood suggests that there was some sympathy in medieval culture for those driven to commit felonies on the king's highways. The stories about Robin Hood, who lives with his "merry men" in the king's woods, where he dines on the king's poached deer, imagine a utopian alternative to the rigid hierarchies of medieval society. The first dated reference we have to the outlaw hero, who steals from the rich and gives to the poor, is in *Piers Plowman* (1377). Many late medieval ballads, verse narratives, and plays, like *Robin Hood and the Sheriff of Nottingam* (1475), celebrated his adventures. By the end of the fifteenth century, he had also become closely associated with popular festivities on May Day.[14] Larceny appears to have been a common way of supplementing family income in rural England, and the folklore about Robin Hood turns the act of theft into a practical response to medieval society's inequities.

Apparently the dangers of travel were offset by its benefits, since late medieval English roads were well-traveled. Even the lowliest peasants had occasion to go to the nearest market town in order to sell any surplus and to purchase the few necessary items that they could not manufacture themselves, like tools. Coaches were rare—most people traveled by foot or on horseback. A healthy pedestrian could cover 15 to 20 miles a day. Where modern tourists can get from London to Canterbury in an hour, pilgrims in Chaucer's time would thus have taken two or three days. Those on horseback might cover an additional 10 miles a day but unless they had the means of changing horses along the way, they would have to feed, water, and rest their animal. A number of options were open to medieval travelers whose trips required an overnight stay. Monasteries were tasked with hospitality, among other duties, and travelers traditionally found a safe haven there (today, European monasteries on some pilgrimage roads, like the one to Santiago de la Compostela, continue to harbor pilgrims). Some locals took in guests, but it might not always have been easy to tell whether these hosts acted out of charitable or mercenary motives. Many stories, like "The Reeve's Tale" and *Sir Gawain and the Green Knight*, focus on the ambiguities of this situation: they concern guests cheated by hosts, hosts cheated by guests, or both. Those able to afford private lodgings in a well-known inn probably chose to pay for this comfort whenever possible. Others opted for shared rooms or even shared beds in inns or taverns.

People transporting goods overland did so themselves, by means of baskets, or they relied on a cart or pack animals. By far the fastest and most economical way of transporting goods, however, was by water. Some people, known as carriers, made the transportation of goods and objects a profession.[15] Others had different professional reasons for traveling, like the friars, the pardoners, and the king's messengers. Ambitious employees of both Church and State had to accept a certain amount of mobility; you could not become a cardinal if you stayed in your home town. Chaucer traveled on state business in England and abroad throughout his life. There were nonprofessional reasons for traveling as well: people traveled to see relatives or friends; healthy pilgrims traveled in hope of contact with the sacred; and sick pilgrims traveled in hope of a cure. The relics belonging to St. Thomas à Beckett housed in the Cathedral at Canterbury, to cite a relevant example, drew those afflicted by epilepsy, leprosy, and blindness. As Chaucer repeatedly suggests, "wandrynge by the weye" (GP 467) was also an end in itself. Then as now, people liked the opportunities for new encounters and new experiences that journeys afforded.

THE COUNTRY

Despite the sophistication of its court and its larger towns, late medieval England was an agricultural country at heart. A large majority of its inhabitants—about six out of seven—lived in the country, and those who made it big in town almost invariably converted their capital back into land, since ownership of land was the premier method of achieving prestige in late medieval society. Any division between town and country in the Middle Ages is thus to some extent artificial. A constant exchange of goods—produce and meat from the country, manufactured goods from the towns—ensured a network of roads and connections between any given medieval town and its surrounding countryside. People from the country came to town regularly for markets, feasts, and fairs. Seasonal holidays, like May Day, a celebration of fertility associated with the Virgin Mary, or Michaelmas (29 September), a celebration of harvest associated with the archangel Michael, were observed all over England. Indeed, medieval towns moved to the rhythms of the agricultural year just as surely as the country did: early summer brought scarcity while, in good years, harvest-time brought plenty for all. The produce available in town markets was the one currently being harvested in the surrounding countryside, and a bad harvest claimed victims in town as well as in the country. The importance of the country is evident even in the courtliest of the medieval literary genres, the romance. In *Sir Gawain and the Green Knight*, the green knight is associated with seasonal fertility and rebirth. Bercilak is a country lord, whose robust strength compares favorably to the effete courtliness of Arthur's knights.

Like the characters in *Mankind* and *Piers Plowman*, virtually all commoners living in the country subsisted by working the land. England included a variety of landscapes, both hospitable and inhospitable to cultivation: fields and pastures, but also marshes, moors, heaths, forests, and cliffs. Some areas, like the midlands and the southern counties, were more arable and fertile than others, like the wild coastlines of Cornwall and the moors of the northern counties. Usable land was divided in roughly three categories: arable land for cultivation of crops, grazing land for pasturing animals, and wooded land for timber and fuel. The ratios between these three types shifted throughout the late medieval period in response to changes in the populations of human beings and, as the wool trade flourished, of sheep. In the mid- to late fourteenth century, for example, the plague caused the human population to dwindle to about 2.2 million from about 4 million. As some villages disappeared altogether and their arable lands returned to pasture, the ratio of arable to pastured land went from 1:1 to 1:2. Herding sheep requires much less in way of human labor than growing crops. In response to the surplus of land and the shortage of labor, landlords began to enclose grazing land that had previously been in common use, because sheep in enclosures required even less human supervision. The population of sheep went up accordingly; one estimate places its peak between 8 and 10 million.[16] There were far more sheep in late medieval England than people. It wouldn't have been difficult for those putting on the Wakefield cycle's comic masterpiece, "The Second Shepherd's Play," to secure a live sheep for its performance. Although enclosures did not cause huge problems while labor supply was low, the practice became increasingly controversial as the human population rebounded from the plague in the fifteenth and sixteenth centuries. The Wakefield cycle was performed throughout the fifteenth century; in its pageant on the killing of Abel, the rivalry between Cain, a ploughman bitterly angry at his Lord, and Abel, a shepherd in favor with the same Lord, might well reflect some incipient tensions regarding the use of land.

Most people working the land were at the mercy of two powerful forces—the weather and the lord of the manor. The latter often seemed as implacable as the former. Manors varied greatly in kind, in size, and in customs. A manor was a section of land, technically granted by the crown to a landlord, in return for his services—of a military variety in the case of secular lords and of a religious variety in the case of ecclesiastical lords. Landlords could have only one manor and be resident on it, or they could hold several manors at once, in which case they might appoint reeves or family members to supervise in their absence. Just as the ward was the basic administrative unit in London, the manor was the basic administrative unit in the country. Manors had their own courts, where the lord presided and dispensed justice. Depending on the manor's size, the lord might have officers, called bailiffs, to assist him in his business, which included punishing violations of manorial law, settling local disputes, and raising public taxes. Peasants who wished to make a complaint in manorial court had to pay a fee to do so; this was a way of limiting tendentious cases, while increasing the lord's revenue. Whipping was a common punishment in England's manorial courts, as were fines, which further augmented the lord's revenues. Petty crime could be a lucrative business for manorial lords: in 1301-02, for example, the powerful Bishop of Winchester made £550 from fines levied against his tenants, an enormous sum which nevertheless constituted only 10 per cent of his gross income.

The bulk of most manors' revenue was from the cultivation of the land. Normally the lord reserved part of the land for his own use—the *desmene*—and the rest was used by his tenants, who owed him dues in the form of goods, labor services, and/or rent in return. At the opening of the "Second Shepherd's Play," a shepherd's complaints about the cold weather shade almost imperceptibly into a criticism of feudal relations:

> Lord, what these weders are cold! And I am ill happyd.
> I am nerehande dold, so long have I nappyd.
> My legys thay fold, my fingers ar chappyd.
> It is not as I wold, for I am al lappyd
> In sorrow.
> In stormes and in tempest,
> Now in the eest, now in the west,
> Wo is him has never rest
> Midday nor morrow!
>
> Bot we sely husbandys that walkys on the moore,
> In faith, we are nerehandys outt of the doore.
> No wonder, as it standys, if we be poore,
> For the tilthe of oure landys lyis fallow as the floore,
> As ye ken.
> We are so hamyd,
> Fortaxed and ramyd,
> We are amide handtamyd
> With thise gentlery-men.[17]

The shepherd goes on to object specifically to maintenance, the system by which a manorial lord extended his protection and gave fees and liveries (distinctive uniforms, sometimes decorated with his insignia or coat of arms) to retainers or servants, in return for their loyalty and services.

In the late Middle Ages, the authority of manorial lords declined as a result of their own decreased control over their tenants and the simultaneous increase of royal control and authority. Maintenance, which is often referred to as a form of "bastard feudalism," helped lords resist this process by expanding their retinue and affinity—and thus their power base. In the fifteenth century, the powerful Earl of Warwick brought some 600 liveried servants with him to Parliament.[18] He had, in other words, the equivalent of a small, personal army. As the Wakefield shepherd points out, the lord's protection was sometimes used as a cover for dubious activities, like the illegal collection of goods or services. The government was cognizant of the problem. As early as 1390, it passed an ordinance trying to regulate the practice and curb the worst abuses of those "encouraged and emboldened in their aforesaid maintenance and wrongdoing because they are in the retinues of lords and others."[19]

In addition to the rents and revenues they earned from the cultivation of the land, landlords charged for a variety of services, like the pasturing of animals on meadows, the gathering of wood from their woodland, or the obligatory use of their mills. Depending on the type of manor, some lords benefited from *droits de Seigneurs* over their tenants, that is, customary dues, fees, and taxes. The description of Chaucer's Reeve gives some idea of what was entailed in the management of a manor:

> Wel koude he kepe a garner and a bynne;
> There was noon auditour koude on I wynne.
> Wel wiste he by the droghte and by the reyn
> The yeldynge of his seed and of his greyn.
> His lordes sheep, his neet, his dayerye,
> His swyn, his hors, his stoor, and his pultrye
> Was holy in this Reves governynge. (GP 5593-99)

If those managing manors worried about the weather, like the peasants did, the managers also worried about the honesty of the tenants. One of the Reeve's talents as a supervisor is his ability to make underlings "adrad of hym as of the deeth" (605). Absentee landlords were more vulnerable to being cheated, a privilege Chaucer's "ful riche" Reeve has apparently reserved for himself (GP 609).

As we saw in Chapter 2, tenants could be unfree—villeins or bondsmen—or they could be free. In the former case, they were unable to move, sell their holdings, or marry without the lord's permission. Where free tenants could rely on the royal courts for justice, villeins were entirely subject to their landlords (the end of villeinage also spelled the end of the manorial court system). Landlords received special dues from villeins, like *merchet* (the fine owed on the marriage of a bondswoman) and *heriot* (a death duty, in which the lord took the best beast of the deceased). If tenants had a range of duties and obligations, so did landlords. Landlords exercised judicial control, provided military protection, managed resources, and took care of the infrastructure (like the roads and bridges).[20] A medieval lord was a patriarch, in the sense that he served as a father to his subordinates whether they were family members, tenants, or, in the case of magnates, vassals.[21] The common analogy between father and lord reveals that relations between father and child were marked by power hierarchies in the late Middle Ages; the younger John Paston, for example, routinely addressed his father as "right reverend and worshipful father," beseeching him "lowly of his blessing."[22] The fact that metaphors of feudal lordship were applied to God suggests that love, ideally, informed the bonds between master and servant. In contemporary letters, the formulaic modes of address emphasized love and obedience in equal measure. When requesting a favor from John Paston, for example, the higher ranked Earl of Oxford mentions his affection for his "well-beloved" correspondent, even while stressing that he has always found Paston "right trusty."[23] Paston occasionally practiced good lordship himself. On being informed that one of his manors was under threat of attack, he instructed his wife "nevertheless ye be a gentlewoman, and it is worship for you to comfort your tenants; wherefore I would ye might ride to Hellesdon and Drayton and Sparham, and tarry at Drayton and speak with them, and bid them hold with their old master till I come."[24] Ideally, being of the gentle class entailed an obligation to protect and care for those who served you.

In reality not all lords cared about the comfort and safety of their tenants, of course. The manorial system lent itself readily to abuses, one reason for the explosive violence of the Peasant Rebellion in 1381 and of Cade's Rebellion in 1450. What was so shocking about these rebellions is that they happened at all. The price for rebellion was very high—petty traitors and traitors alike were put to death in medieval England—and there was far less violent resistance to the system than we might expect. Those who did protest did not usually object to the system itself but to abuses of it. There are some cases of tenants murdering their lord: Sir Thomas Murdak of Edgecote, for example, was brutally murdered by 15 people associated with his household, including his wife Juliana, on 11 April 1316. He cannot, given the level of complicity, have been a popular man with his servants.[25] Most dissatisfied underlings, however, relied on nonviolent means of addressing their situation: they refused to work unless the lord compensated them properly, or they ran away without paying *chevage*, the fee that villeins owed to the lord for leaving the manor. Free men could also rely on the royal court system for redress.

Although the manorial system seems arbitrary and degrading, it did provide tenants with a measure of protection, even against their own landlords. Custom was king in the manorial courts, and prudent landlords were careful not to violate it. If unfree tenants observed manorial law and custom, they could not easily be evicted, nor could the fees the landlord assessed be easily increased.[26] Money rents for villeins were accordingly low, at least before the plague made land so abundant that landlords were forced to drop the rents of their free tenants. Labor services, meanwhile, were often commuted. When a lord did insist on them, he might be expected to provide services in return, most commonly in the form of bread and ale. At harvest time, when peasants were most likely to be asked to do "boon" work for the lord, food rewards could be very generous; one lord, for example, promised a dinner of soup, bread, beef, and cheese, with all the ale the tenants could drink.[27] A lord needed his tenants to cultivate his land, and it was in his best interest to treat them relatively well. Although the land ultimately belonged to the lord, tenants could tradi-tionally pass their right to cultivate the land on to their children and heirs, as long as appropriate death duties were paid. It was therefore possible for a person or a family to accumulate substantial landholdings and become comparatively wealthy from its cultivation. After the plague, this indeed became a common phenomenon and a contributing factor in the gradual demise of the manorial system over the course of the fifteenth century.

A lord's household comprised his wife, his and other noble chil-dren, extended family members, servants, and tenants, all of whom were considered subject to his authority. The size of a household depended on the rank and wealth of its lord: a mere knight might have 12 to 15 people, where a duke or earl might command over 100. The king's household in the fourteenth century included about 400 people.[28] Unlike most aris-tocrats, who were surrounded by extended kin and tended by servants, and who often sent their own children to be educated by other nobles, peasants lived in single-family dwellings. All but the youngest members of the family contributed something to the household economy. Children might be asked to watch the geese or gather the eggs, while their fathers worked the field and their mothers brewed ale. Tasks were apportioned not just according to age but also according to gender: men worked out of the house, women took care of domestic matters. Male and female forms of labor were essential to the economic survival of the household as a whole. When Mak, in "The Second Shepherd's Play," complains that his wife does nothing but play, she pointedly asks: "Why, who wanders? Who wakys? Who commys? Who gose? / Who brewys? Who bakys?" (415). Peasant women were medieval society's factotums: they prepared meals, tended to the house, raised the children, spun yarn for making clothes, washed the clothes, watched the poultry, made butter and cheese, worked the vegetable garden, gathered nuts and berries, and so on and so forth. At harvest time women might also have to join their husbands in the field. The bulk of England's food was produced by these husbands, the plough-men idealized by Chaucer and Langland. They performed the heavy work of plowing, sowing, and harvesting. Aside from field work, male peasants contributed to the household in many other ways, doing basic repairs, for example, or slaughtering animals.

Most of the peasant dwellings were gathered together in villages, each with its own church, which was the center of social and spiritual life. Along with the manor house, the church was the only structure in the vil-lage built to last. The tenant farmers' houses were impermanent buildings, good for one generation or so. Each was situated on a plot of land, which might contain a garden for growing vegetables and some outbuildings, like a barn. Fruits and vegetables—mostly apples and pears, beans, peas, cabbages, and onions—were grown for the family's own consumption, although any excesses might be sold at market. The poorest peasants had the smallest homestead; their cottages were huts, really, with one or two rooms and a small garden. Cottagers had only a few acres to their names, not nearly enough for subsistence (a family needed at least five and up to 15 acres). Peasant houses were made out of widely available materials, including timber, local stone, and wattle and daub. Most of them had clay floors, laid with straw, which meticulous housewives swept out and replaced when it became dirty from mud and animal droppings. Furniture was sparse and functional, with some peasants sleeping on straw pallets rather than beds. At the center of each house was a hearth, where peas-ants built the fires used for light, heat, and cooking. The fires also posed a hazard, given that floors and roofs were frequently covered in straw.

Peasants usually supplemented their income by hiring them-selves out as day laborers or by practicing a craft. Mak, in "The Second Shepherd's Play," relies on another popular means of making ends meet in medieval cottages—theft. As the Wakefield pageant leads us to expect, the most commonly stolen items were livestock—horses, oxen, pigs and sheep. Beasts were peasants' most valuable asset: they were used for work (oxen and horses), for meat (all farm animals), for cheese and milk (cows and sheep), and for leather and wool (sheep).[29] Although the Wakefield Cain complains bitterly about his poverty, he is identified by his servant as a yeoman, or substantial landholder, and he comes on stage driving his plough-team of horses. Many peasants could not have afforded such a luxury.

Like cottagers, tenants with more acreage sought to supplement their income by earning wages or by engaging in various so-called "cottage industries," like making linen thread.[30] Men might round meals off with fishing or a bit of poaching from the lord's hunting chases. Although peasants were legally forbidden to hunt animals like deer and boar, they were allowed to supplement their diet with small animals. John Wheeler, who died catching pigeons in the bell tower, was probably trying to provide protein for his family's supper (SEE Court Cases and Coroners' Cases BELOW). The better-off peasants had bigger houses than the cottagers, although they often shared the extra space with the pigs and chickens that roamed in and out of the living spaces.

Peasant houses in the Middle Ages were not necessarily pleasant places to be, and villagers spent a great deal of time outside. When they were at leisure, people congregated near the church, in the streets, or, where these existed, in taverns, ale houses, and village greens. Like their urban counterparts, peasants seem to have enjoyed gossiping, carousing, and playing together. Although villagers competed with each other for scarce resources, they also had to share many of them, like the grazing pastures and the meadows, which were held in common. Inevitably peasants had to rely on one another's help—at harvest time, when some women worked in the fields, teenage girls might watch their neighbor's smaller children, for example, in exchange for borrowing his beasts of burden. The ability to collaborate was necessary to survival, and the conditions of life in medieval villages therefore must have encouraged a sense of community and neighborliness. Certainly these are the values celebrated in Langland's Piers, Chaucer's Ploughman, and the Wakefield cycle's Abel. Although it renders the frustrations of the farming life in sympathetic detail, the Wakefield pageant suggests that Cain's hostility to any form of community—he greets his brother by inviting him to "com kis mine ars" (59)—contributes to his poor harvests.

Daily Activities

One of Chaucer's most charming lines concerns a character's morning routine: "Up roos the sonne, and up roos Emelye" (KT 2273). Like the radiant Emily, the majority of late medieval people rose at or before dawn, when the village church bells would ring matins. The first task was preparing the house for the day, which entailed getting water for daily ablutions, lighting the fire, and making breakfast. Sometimes animals had to be tended to as well. According to "the Ballad of the Tyrannical Husband" (SEE CHAPTER 2), the early riser in peasant households was the wife:

> Whan I lie all night waking with our child,
> I rise up at morning and find our house wild;
> Then I milk our cattle and bring them to the field,
> While you sleep full still, also Christ me shield!

A teenage child or, in wealthier households, a servant might also be assigned these tasks.

The choice beverage, at breakfast and throughout the day, was ale (tea and coffee were not introduced to England until the mid-seventeenth century), or, for those who could afford it, wine. The medieval diet relied heavily on grains, eaten in the form of rye or wheat bread and cereals or porridge. The kind of bread people ate for breakfast depended on their income—the most expensive breads were made out of whole-meal flour, from which the bran had been removed; the least expensive ones from dark rye.[31] The "wastel" or white bread that Chaucer's Prioress feeds to her dogs (GP 147) was a luxury that many humans could not afford in medieval England. Although traditionally the peasants ate the darker breads, after the plague brought them greater affluence, some ate the more luxurious wheaten breads of their betters, or so claimed conservative critics like John Gower and William Langland. At breakfast, that bread might be accompanied with some cheese, for those who had livestock, or fruit, for those who had gardens.

What medieval people put on when they got dressed in the morning depended not just on gender (as it still does in our society) but also on station. Aristocrats displayed their coat of arms on their clothing or shields. Members of the clergy announced their vocation by their hair tonsures. Nuns, monks, and friars also donned colored habits—long tunics and cowls, with wimples, veils, and linen bands for the nuns—associated with their particular order. The so-called Black Friars were Dominicans, for example, while the White Friars were Carmelites. The liturgical vestments that priests wore to say mass were so richly embellished as to rival those of kings; however, when they went about their business outside of church, priests wore more sober street clothes. The exceptions were cardinals, the princes of the Church, who signaled their status by wearing red fur-lined cloaks and broad red hats.[32] The association of cardinals to the color red proved enduring; the dapper American songbird named after the high-ranking clergymen owes his name to his crimson colors.

Peasants also revealed their status by the colors they most often wore—white or grey garments, left undyed, or blue, produced by dyeing clothes in woad, the cheapest dye used in the Middle Ages. Poor people wore simple, functional garments, without ornamentation: men wore breeches, loose tunics or shifts, covered by a tunic-length jacket, and hats or hoods; women wore long, loose, A-shaped gowns, linen kerchiefs or woolen hoods, and sleeveless jackets or cloaks. To protect their gowns, women wore aprons almost all the time. Men occasionally donned these as well, as when slaughtering animals or working a craft like blacksmithing. Peasant clothing for winter was made of rough wool; in summer, it was likely made out of hemp, which was cheaper than linen. Both men and women wore stockings or hose and leather or wooden shoes. Peasant budgets did not allow for many changes in clothing, and people wore individual pieces until they became frayed, faded, and torn. Being poor meant looking drab in the Middle Ages.

Fashion got progressively more complicated, more colorful, and more decorative as people's means increased. Brightly colored cloths and ornaments were traditionally associated with the privileged classes; some colors—like purple—were even restricted to the royal family. Technically only free men who were not members of the clergy were allowed to bear arms, and swords were reserved for knights. Note that Chaucer's Yeoman violates several of these precepts: he wears bright green, he has a silver ornament, and he carries a sword. Then as now, people did not necessarily conform to rules, which was one reason for the anxiety of the authorities on the matter of dress. The male clerics cited in Chapter 2, for example, worried about women's dress; John Wyclif articulates the common view that "women should not have ... adornment of hair, nor garlands of gold, nor over precious or curious clothing." He would not have approved of the Wife of Bath, who sets out for Canterbury all decked out in new shoes, a broad hat, and closely tied scarlet hose. Because of the stress on women's modesty, the length of their garments emphasized coverage. Variations were a factor of the tightness of the bodice, the cut of the neckline, the length of the sleeves, and the extent of the embellishments. Headgear was one way a woman could show an extravagant sense of fashion—as the Wife, with her broad hat and her body-length "coverchiefs" (GP 453), does. The fashion for strange headdresses reached its apogee in the fifteenth century, when some women wore a "horned headdress," sometimes topped with a veil and a coronet.[33] The scarlet fabric that the Wife favors for her hose also constitutes a flamboyant choice, since it makes use of the most expensive dye available.[34] By advertising her financial status through her clothes, the Wife hopes to lure a new husband.

Although the *types* of garment worn by the more privileged members of society were similar to those of the peasants, their *appearance* was another matter altogether. The late medieval period is associated with the beginning of fashion, in that the cut on male garments began to change regularly, and it became a sign of privilege in itself to own a trendily cut garment. In the late fourteenth century, fashion emphasized a short cut and a tight fit for the jerkin or doublet (Chaucer's Squire wears such a fashionable jacket). This garment might also be padded or slashed, depending on the current fashions. A real vogue existed as well for parti-colored or motley fabrics, which were expensive because they were made of different fabrics sewn together laboriously by hand. Chaucer's Merchant, with his forked beard, his motley coat, and his Flemish beaver hat makes quite a fashion statement. Observing the latest trends enabled the privileged to distinguish themselves from poor relations and to favor certain retainers or servants, who often were gifted old clothes. Other sartorial signs of status included embellishments such as brooches and jewels, decorated buttons, embroidery, silk ribbons, girdles or belts, and lace or fur trims. Belts developed a special significance as aristocratic symbols of protection and virtue—one reason that Gawain so readily accepts the girdle "Of a gay green silk, with gold overwrought, / And the borders all bound with embroidery fine" offered by Bercilak's lady.[35] Material, too, mattered. Clothing of any sort was expensive in the Middle Ages, but fashionable clothing was prohibitively expensive. Silk, cloth of silver, cloth of gold, and furs like ermine and miniver (the hide of a small grey and white squirrel) were reserved for the most privileged members of society, as the sumptuary laws, discussed in Chapter 2, suggest. That the authorities attempted to regulate the wearing of such fabulous materials by commoners is a measure of their increasingly destabilizing affluence. Chaucer's Parson shares this anxiety; in his tale, he inveighs passionately against what he considers wasteful spending on contemporary fashions.

Once he had his breakfast and had dressed—soberly if he was a peasant, richly if he was a merchant, and sumptuously if he was a courtier—the medieval man would head out for the day's business. Especially in the country, daily schedules revolved around the rising and setting of the sun, even after mechanical clocks became more common in the fourteenth and fifteenth centuries. Not all days were working days, however; on Sundays and feast days, commoners were able to enjoy more pleasurable activities like games (dice, cards, blind man's buff, "tables" or backgammon), sports (ball games, swimming, wrestling, archery), and dances. Then as now, people also celebrated days off by eating and drinking together. Those who had access to towns caught performances by jugglers, minstrels, and traveling entertainers on fair and market days. More brutal pastimes available in urban centers included bear-baiting, cock-fighting, and dog-fighting. The former consisted of watching a bear tied at a stake being attacked by dogs. Since bears were not native to England, they had to be imported, at some expense, specifically for the purpose of being put to such torture. In addition to these various pastimes, certain feast days were associated with particular activities, like the fertility dances around the Maypole and the election of a queen on May Day or the processions and plays on Corpus Christi Day. One scholar estimates that the "no-work" days (Saturdays, Sundays, and feast days) could add up to 115 a year for some.[36] Most peasants would, of course, have to do a bare minimum of work, like feeding the animals, even on those days.

Only those who did not work—those of gentle status—were able to engage in purely pleasurable activities on a daily basis. Some of their pastimes, like hunting, horse-back riding, and jousting, served a function in that they prepared England's warrior class for meeting its duties. Many aristocrats kept hawks, hounds, and horses—and the requisite servants to tend to them—precisely for this purpose. These three types of animals came, therefore, to be closely associated with the aristocracy; the peregrine falcon, in "The Squire's Tale," for example, is clearly of noble provenance. Given the need for specialized caretakers (greyhounds were handled by servants known as fewterers, while the berners managed the running hounds), hunting was not cheap.[37] In 1345-46, Thomas de Berkeley spent a total of £174, or 13 per cent of his substantial income of £1308, on his horses and falcons. The expense was presumably worth it, since hunting—the sport of kings—was also a confirmation of masculine status in medieval society. The king reserved large sections of land, called royal forests, as game preserves, and his magnates had to obtain his permission to maintain hunting grounds of their own. Medieval romances, like Chaucer's

The Book of the Duchess and *Sir Gawain and the Green Knight*, reflect the importance of the hunt to aristocratic values. *Gawain* presents Bercilak as a masculine ideal in part because of his skills in the sport. Aristocratic boys were trained to hunt at an early age, as this activity was thought to develop the courage, strength, and individual prowess of the ideal warrior. Chess, a war game that hones strategic skills while providing an orthodox image of the social order, also featured prominently in the education of noble children and in the entertainments of their parents.[38] It is no accident that Chaucer's Black Knight, a figure for the aristocratic and warlike Gaunt, thinks of his lady's death in terms of a game of chess with "fals Fortune" (*The Book of the Duchess* 618), who steals his "fers" or queen (*The Book of the Duchess* 654). Not all aristocratic pastimes were warlike in nature, of course. Noble men and women also sought to entertain themselves by employing artists, writers, musicians, acrobats, and jesters. They played instruments and read books; they kept pet dogs and birds; they indulged in tennis and dancing; and, like their lower-class counterparts, they ate and drank.

FOOD AND DRINK

Food was of paramount importance in medieval society. Whether the day was for work or for sporting, it was punctuated by two more meals after breakfast—dinner (anywhere from 9 or 11 a.m.) and supper (as early as 3 p.m. in winter), with dinner usually being the more substantial of the two.[39] Although eating was necessary for survival, it was also, for all classes, a social occasion. In the Chester Cycle's "Shepherd's Play," three shepherds congregate to share their supper, which one of them describes as a source of "solace"(101), that is, of pleasure and comfort. His friend agrees, noting that "in good meat there is much glee" (112). Although the occasion is festive (the audience may indeed have shared in the feast), what the shepherds eat gives an indication of the ingredients that made up the peasant diet: "bread this day was baken, / onions, garlick, and leeks"; butter; green cheese (a fresh cheese); ale; a pudding; an oat-cake; a "sheep's head soused in ale"; a pig's snout; milk curds; a pig's foot; some pig tripe, liver, and entrails; bacon, ham, and a tongue (113-45). Most everyday meals were heavier on complex carbohydrates and included less meat. Peasants who had no livestock would eat meat very rarely. Pigs were the most popular form of meat for the lower classes because they were almost completely comestible, a fact attested to in the number of pig organs and parts devoured by the Chester shepherds. Many peasants also kept poultry, so that eggs were an additional source of protein, as were fish, shellfish, and various cheeses. In addition to the onion family, common vegetables included parsley, peas, beans, carrots, radishes, and cabbages (no potatoes, tomatoes, or corn which are New World foods). Soup, broths, and stews were a favored way of preparing and preserving food in peasant kitchens. When the harvests were good, the peasant diet was thus more whole-some and nutritious by modern standards than the meat-heavy diet of the wealthier members of society.

One's status in medieval society could be measured by the quantity of meat one ate; indeed, the sumptuary laws of 1363 even attempted to make this measure official by restricting the lower classes' consumption of meat and fish to once daily. Existing accounts of gentle households include references to a wide variety of meats and hardly any vegetables. In 1512, for example, the household of the Earl of Northumberland intended to eat 49 deer, "123 cows, 667 sheep, 25 pigs, 28 veal calves, 60 lambs," as well as rabbits and various kinds of fowl.[40] Many types of birds were consumed, including the pigeons and pheasants consumed by today's gourmets but also the much stronger flavored herons and peacocks. A favorite mode of presentation for banquets found the cooked bird reconstituted to look like the live one, feathers and all. People did not shirk, as we do, from the recognition that meat came from animals, and most animals were served intact and carved at the table, often by the lord himself. Whereas nowadays some wealthy people distance themselves altogether from the preparation of food, medieval aristocrats also participated in the production of food for their tables by their hunting activities. Among their favorite prey were hares and deer, as well as wild boar. One of the major differences between commoner and aristocratic diets is that aristocrats ate game regularly. A statute passed by Richard II's government in 1390 made it illegal for most Englishmen to hunt rabbits, hares, or deer.[41] When in late medieval plays and ballads Robin Hood and his friends dine on venison, they are thus not "roughing" it in our sense at all—they are eating food reserved by law for their betters. No doubt the element of transgression made deer taste even better to those commoners who poached it.

Besides status, two other factors allowed medieval gourmets greater access to gustatory variety—money and location. Most people in the country rarely paid for food; instead, they grew it, caught it, raised it, and exchanged it. In the towns, as might be expected, food was more often purchased (although even there most people grew some herbs and veg-etables in their gardens). Fishmongers offered many different kinds of fish for sale, much of it preserved through drying or brining processes, but some of it fresh. Oysters, considered an expensive treat nowadays, were comparatively cheap at 4*d.* a bushel. The demand for fish was always high, because religious regulations required people to eat fish rather than meat during Lent, as well as on the eve of major holidays and every Wednesday, Friday, and Saturday. Understandably enough, on other days, people preferred to eat meat. Many ready-made foods—handy for those with no kitchens or unexpected guests—were available in town, like pies and roast meats.[42] Towns also had a far greater range of available foods, including spices and delicacies like strawberries and exported oranges. The lucky few in the country with the means of obtaining these wares were eager to do so. As we saw earlier, Margaret Paston often requested that her husband send her food from London, including some of the basic ingredients for making medieval desserts: cinnamon, sugar, and almonds. The latter, combined, make marchpane (marzipan or almond paste), a favorite sweet of the time, which was sometimes sculpted into elaborate table decorations. The practice survives in modern Europe; on 6 December, for example, Belgian bakeries sell marzipan figurines of St. Nicholas, complete with his bishop's miter.

Medieval culinary traditions have enjoyed a long afterlife in Europe, especially in the northern countries like England, Belgium, Germany, and the Netherlands. English puddings and Belgian beef stews rely on the dried fruit—prunes, dates, figs, and raisins—featured in many medieval dishes, both sweet and savory. The basic spices favored in northern European cuisines were also the ones in most common use in the English Middle Ages: black pepper, cinnamon, nutmeg, mace, ginger, cloves, and saffron (then as now, the most expensive spice for purchase). Hippocras, a sweetened, spiced wine often served with dessert, might contain a variety of these spices, including pepper, cinnamon, ginger, cloves, nutmeg, and cardamom. Meats were either roasted or cooked in sauces made of wine, ale, or blood. Pies and tarts were also popular, as were custards and jellies. Many dishes combined sweet and savory flavors, like "frumenty," a desert mentioned in the *Menagier de Paris*, which was made of almonds, wheat, milk, eggs—and venison. There was clearly nothing bland about the way medieval food tasted.

In most houses meals were fairly simple occasions. People would eat out of wooden trenchers they had made themselves, with knives and spoons (made out of wood, horn, or, in rare cases, silver). In upper-class households, however, festive meals were complicated, ritualized occasions that nourished more than stomachs and showcased more than just the cook's skills. Careful attention was paid to the aesthetics of eating. The lord's wealth and status might be evidenced in the elaborateness of the meal, the expensive platters and drinking cups, or the decorated salt cellar placed near him on the table. Those who could afford it took a special pleasure in elaborate-looking food—it was wrapped in decorated pastries, dyed in vivid colors, shaped into sculptures, strewed with flowers, or theatrically reconstituted to look alive. Unlike in humbler homes, tables were laid with tablecloths and napkins, as well as cups, spoons, and trenchers. The latter were usually made out of bread, with the "upper crust" reserved for the lord or highest ranking table guest.[43] The order of seating followed social hierarchy: one's place at the table reflected one's place in the household. Food was also served, as the *Gawain* poet puts it, "to each man ... in order of rank" (*Gawain* 1006). Highly ranked guests and the host might get platters to themselves, but most people would share common platters and even drinking cups. The meals thus encouraged the development of intimacy and community, even as they reinforced social hierarchies.

Courtesy manuals, like the ones excerpted at the end of this chapter, helped youngsters learn the rules that governed proper behavior in aristocratic households. Dinner guests always waited for the lord to sit and for the lord to begin eating before doing so themselves. Given that relations of service marked every level of society, the only Englishman who never had to wait for anyone was the king. In Richard II's presence, even a powerful magnate like his uncle John of Gaunt would have to wait. By waiting, guests confirmed their host's status and bore vivid witness to his or her power. At meals, as under all circumstances in the Middle Ages, deference to rank was fundamental to courteous behavior. People were expected to behave in a subdued and appropriate fashion, talking neither too loudly nor too softly. Before eating, people washed their hands in a ceremonial fashion at the table, using water brought by servants. While rank was observed in the order of hand-washing, these ablutions also had practical applications. Forks were rare in the Middle Ages, and even at the best tables, eating was mainly done with one's fingers. What further rules existed would be considered rudimentary by today's Miss Manners. For example, guests who had to blow their noses and didn't have handkerchiefs were expected to use their fingers and wipe these off on their own clothes, not on the napkin or the tablecloth.[44] According to late medieval etiquette, guests should also keep their hands clean, out of common dishes or plates, and out of their noses; and they should not blow on their food, lest their bad breath ruin the appetites of their neighbors.[45] Chaucer's Prioress is obviously familiar with many of these rules:

At mete wel ytaught was she with alle;
She leet no morsel from her lippes falle,
Ne wette her fyngres in hir sauce depe;
Wel koude she carie a morsel and wel kepe
That no drope ne fille upon hire brest
In curtesie was set ful muchel hir lest.
Hir over-lippe wiped she so clene
That in hir coppe ther was no ferthyng seen
Of Grece, when she drunken had her draughte. (GP 127-34)

Whether a nun should pay quite so much attention to courtesy is of course a good question.

After grace was said, the meats were carved according to elaborate protocols, with the best piece reserved for the person of highest rank. The host usually carved himself, although on occasion an honored guest might perform this duty; carving was considered a privilege, which every aristocratic man should be able to handle.[46] Most courses were meat or fish-based; servants replaced trenchers and filled cups with wine and ale as needed. On grand occasions, like marriages, there might be more than 20 courses served. The first few days that Gawain spends at Bercilak's castle are filled with such feasting, "with soups of all sorts, seasoned with skill, / Double-sized servings, and sundry fish, / Some baked, some breaded, some broiled on coals, / Some simmered, some in stews, steaming with spice, / And with sauces to sup that suited his taste" (*Gawain* 889-93). Meals like the ones enjoyed by Gawain usually finished with cheese and fruit, served with hippocras [spice-flavored wine]; another ritualized hand-washing ceremony concluded the event. The entertainment between courses formed part of the feast; Gawain mentions the "many fair sports; / Amid the meal and after, melody sweet, / Carol dances and Christmas songs" (*Gawain* 1654-1655). These "fair sports" were frequently not just musical but also theatrical in nature; an early word for plays, "interludes," may refer to their performances between courses at banquets.[47] Pageants, which featured elaborate sets rolled in on wagon-type structures, were also popular. At the court of Henry VIII, for example, one entertainment featured a "riche Mount ... set full of riche flowers of silk," from which dancers, including the king himself, emerged.[48]

Although the descriptions of food and feasting in *Gawain* might at first strike us as trivial, hospitality was taken seriously in the Middle Ages. Keeping a good table was a sign of gentility and magnanimity. By feeding people, a lord showed his ability to care for and protect them—to function, that is, as a viable patriarch. He also demonstrated the vastness of his network of relations, while putting individual guests under further obligation to him. Once he has eaten, Gawain recognizes that he is now "bound and beholden" (*Gawain* 1040) to Bercilak, that "master of men" (*Gawain* 849). Hosting was both means and proof of power. A great deal of capital and labor went into the production of ceremonial meals; the greater the household, and the richer the lord, the more splendid and fabulous the meal could be. As Christopher Dyer shows, the "largest single item in aristocratic budgets was food."[49] Even if the bulk of the food was raised or grown on the lord's estates, many specialty items—spices and wine, for example—were purchased. The preparation and serving of the food also required the lord to keep multiple servants for these purposes: cooks, obviously, but also bakers, butlers, kitchen maids, table servants, and laundresses. The thirteenth-century Countess of Pembroke, Joan de Valence, kept a household staff of 85, 28 of whom were charged with preparing and serving food.[50] Each of these had to be trained to perform their function adequately. And entire rooms in the house had to be devoted to making meals: butteries and pantries and kitchens and wine cellars. For those aspiring to be a great host, like Chaucer's Franklin, keeping a house where it snows meat and drink was an expensive proposition (GP 345).

MEDIEVAL MONEY

Because it can be hard for modern students to discern the value of money in Chaucer's England, we list some wages, incomes, and prices below. There were 20 shillings (designated as *s*.), or 240 pence (designated as *d*.), to a pound (designated as £) in medieval England. Each shilling was therefore worth 12 pence. The mark was valued at two-thirds of a pound. The amount that Chaucer lost to highwaymen, £20, was the equivalent of one year's income for someone of his rank or ten years' income for a laborer. Note that daily wages often included non-monetary compensation, like food and drink. After the plague, employers routinely were forced to pay more than the wages fixed by law.[51]

Estimated daily wages for fourteenth-century craftsmen (e.g., masons)	5d.–6d.
Estimated daily wages for fourteenth-century farm laborers	3d.–4d.
Estimated income required to support a gentleman	£10
Estimated income required to support an esquire	£20
Lowest landed income set by law for knights, after 1292	£40
Estimated average landed income of barons, circa 1300	£200–£500
Landed income of the Duke of Lancaster, in 1361	£8,380
Landed income of the English crown, circa 1300	£30,000
Income of the Bishopric of Ely, 1454	£2,224
Maintenance fees paid to retainers, circa 1461	£2–£10
Room and board for one lady for one year, circa 1311	50s.
Food expenses in an esquire's house, with a total income of £50	£24
Food expenses in Thomas de Berkeley's household, 1345-6	£742

Loaf of bread	½d.
Butter, 1 pint	1½d.
Loin of beef	5d.
Ham	1s.
10 eggs	1d.
6–10 herring	1d.
Bushel of mussels or oysters	4d.
Gallon of wine	3d.–10d.
Cinnamon, 1 pound	1s.
Saffron, 1 pound	12s.–15s.
1 pound candles	2d.
1 ax	5d.
Cheap cloth, per yard	2½d.
Fine linen, per yard	1s.
Fine woolens, per yard	3s.–5s.
Silk, per yard	10s.–12s.
Fur trimming for one garment	£2–£3
Shoes	4d.–5d.
Tunic	1s. 4d.

DOCUMENTS

CORONERS' CASES AND COURT CASES (14TH C)

Few of the documents that have come down to us offer reliable evidence
regarding material conditions of life in the Middle Ages; court records
offer one notable exception (the others being letters, SEE BELOW, and wills).
The following cases offer tantalizing glimpses into the daily life of English
citizens. The first three are from the coroners' rolls and concern suspicious
deaths in the country. The other cases are all from London. Given that
these ended in court, the conflicts described in these records illustrate the
sort of disagreement that often led to violence in medieval England. In
addition to documenting the activities of an energetic criminal element,
these cases also give us information about a whole range of things, from the
preferred pastimes of young men, to the dangers of being a housewife, to
the wholesale price of woad (the dye most frequently used in cheap cloth).

THE DEATH OF ISABEL SHERMAN

Inquest was taken at Burford on Friday next after the feast of St.
Bartholomew the Apostle in the second year of King Richard
the Second before John Hardy, the king's coroner in Oxfordshire,
concerning the death of Isabel, John Sherman's wife, on view of
her body, by the oath of [12 men]. They say on their oath that it
happened at Burford at the hour of prime on Thursday next after
the said feast that Isabel, while engaged in brewing, took a ladder
and mounted it in order to procure wood in an upper room above a
boiler full of hot water. And her feet slipped from the ladder, and she
fell into the boiler, and her whole body was scalded. In this condition
she lingered until the hour of vespers of the said day, and then she
died, but she received the rites of the church. The furnace was worth
six shillings and eight pence. And the four wardmen of the said town
with their wards, having been similarly charged, examined, and sworn
for this purpose, agree expressly with the said inquest.

THE DEATH OF JOHN WHEELER

Inquest was taken at Ensham on Wednesday next after Easter in the
twelfth year of King Richard the Second before John Carswell, the
king's coroner in Oxfordshire, concerning the death of John Wheeler,
whose body was viewed on the said day, by the oath of [12 men]
together with four townships, to wit, Stanton Harcourt, Cassington,

Church Handborough, Yarnton, and Ensham. They say on their oath
that on Tuesday next after Easter John Wheeler went into the gallery
of a bell-tower to catch pigeons, and by mischance he fell into the
choir of the church soon after the hour of noon. His whole body
was crushed, and so he died; no one was guilty of his death. At length
John Crips came and found the said John Wheeler thus lying dead;
he raised the hue forthwith, and the hue was pursued in due form;
and he found pledges to come at any time and place to do all things
required by law, namely John Spearman and Henry Porter. And the
four townships agree with this verdict in all things.

The Death of John Swale

Inquest was taken at Marston on Tuesday next after the Holy Trinity
in the twentieth year of King Richard the Second before Robert of
Lockwood, one of the king's coroners in Staffordshire, on view of the
body of John Swale, by the oath of [12] jurors of four neighboring
townships. They say on their oaths that on Monday next after the
said feast in the said year and place Nicholas of Cheddleton was
going along the king's highway with linen and woollen cloths and
other goods, when he was met by certain thieves who tried to kill
and rob him. And the said Nicholas in self-defense struck one of the
robbers, named John Swale, right over the head with a staff worth a
penny, of which blow he died forthwith, but he had the rites of the
church and was buried. And immediately after the said felony the
said Nicholas fled with all his goods and chattels, etc.

Adam Ryebred, London, 22 November 1381

Adam Ryebred of Spalding was brought before the Mayor and
Aldermen on a charge of wandering through the city begging and
pretending that he was unfit for work, whereas, upon examination of
his body, it was manifest that he was strong and lusty, capable of labor
and able to earn his food and clothing and a reasonable wage in any
part of the kingdom, and thus he was defrauding genuine beggars and
poor people, and deceiving the public. The said Adam did not deny
it. Accordingly he was sworn not to beg within the liberty of the city
henceforth, under penalty of the pillory if he were convicted thereof.

John Stockynbury, London, 13 May 1382

John Stockyngbury was brought before the Mayor and Aldermen
for having a large dung heap on the banks of the Thames next to

his house at Billingsgate, to the detriment of the Thames water, the
damage of the commonalty, and the disgrace of the city. He prayed for
a reasonable amount of time to remove it and cleanse the place, and
agreed of his own free will to pay the chamberlain, Richard Odyham,
the sum of £10, if this were not done before the Feast of the Nativity
of St. John the Baptist [24 June]. He undertook further to construct a
wharf on the site before Michaelmas under penalty of £20.

Robert atte Wode, London, 8 August 1382

An inquest was taken before the Mayor and Aldermen to discover
what evildoers and disturbers of the peace had molested foreigners
bringing fish to the city for the use of the king, his magnates, and
commonalty, or what other persons had been molested on account
of these foreigners, contrary to the ordinance made and proclaimed
by the Mayor, Aldermen, and Common Council. The jury said on
oath that a certain Robert atte Wode, fishmonger, on Wednesday last
struck a certain Alice Yonge on Cornhill, because she was talking
there with a foreigner belonging to her own district, who had
brought fish for sale, and because she had brought water for him to
wash his hands and had invited him to come and have a drink with
her. They said further that John Ditton, fishmonger, aided and abetted
the said Robert.

John de Lubek, London, 20 November 1364

Baldewyn de Freville, knight, complained to the Mayor and
Aldermen that when he was passing through Cheap on business of
the Prince of Wales, he was rudely stopped by John de Lubek, saddler,
and charged with owing the said John, as executor of the will of John
de Blythe, a sum of money, which he was told he would have to pay
whether he wanted to or not. To this he had answered that to his
knowledge he owed nothing to any citizen of London, but if money
had been borrowed for his use by servant Gilbert, he was quite
willing to answer before the Mayor and Aldermen, whose duty it was
to administer the laws of the City.

The said John Lubek, on being summoned to court, denied
the charge of insulting behavior and put himself on the country. A
jury was summoned from Cheap, and he was committed to prison
meanwhile for lack of mainprise. When questioned about the debt,
he produced the will of the above-mentioned John de Blythe, saying
at the same time that it had been enrolled in the Husting on Monday

the eve of St Margaret [20 July]....The will was examined by the Court, when it was found that the surname of "Lubek" and also the endorsement relating to the date of enrolment had been erased, and when search was made on the Roll, no enrolment could be found on the date alleged. Under these suspicious circumstances, the will was retained by the Mayor and Aldermen for further examination....

John de Pikenham, London, 19 March 1366

Godescalcus Sadeler, merchant of Almaine [Germany], brought a bill of complaint to the effect that he had bought 13 barrels of woad from John de Pikenham, which woad lay in the cellars of Geoffrey de Ditton. As soon as the bargain was made and Geoffrey had handed over the keys, the plaintiff had put his mark on the woad. But afterwards, when he went to see his woad, he found that the lock had been forced and that two of the barrels had been removed by the said Geoffrey, to his damage £100....

The defendant Geoffrey, who appeared on summons next day, pleaded that long before the alleged sale the vendor John owed him and another person the sum of £71 and had deposited the woad in his premises as security for the debt, and that the plaintiff had acquired the key by showing a false token to his servant. As the plaintiff refused to return the key, he had broken open the door, taken out two casks and placed them in premises nearby as security for the debt. He demanded judgment whether any action lay against him personally.

The plaintiff protested that he did not admit that the casks of woad had been deposited as security or that there was any debt as alleged. The defendant, he asserted, had let the premises to John de Pikenham, who had informed him of the sale and asked that the key should be handed over to the plaintiff, and the key had been duly handed over by the defendant's servant in the Ropery. He prayed that the matter might be inquired into by the country, and the defendant did the same. Thereupon the plaintiff claimed that as he was a foreigner, a moiety of the jury should consist of merchants of Almaine. Accordingly a jury drawn from the Ropery and foreign merchants was empanelled as follows: Richard Cras, William Aumesbury, John Bradle, William Chaundeler, Andrew Yerdele, Hugh Skynnere, Henry Brok, Godescalcus Cameshed, Aluin Wynter, John Benynghof, Gurrod Myneshaghen, and John Pette. Their verdict was in accordance with the plaintiff's pleadings, and they valued the two casks at £28. Judgment was given that the plaintiff recovers the two casks or their value and damages taxed at 6s. 8d. and that the defendant be in mercy. The plaintiff remitted the damages in court.

Nicholas Sardouche, London, 29 November 1368

On Wednesday after the Feast of St Katherine [25 November] came certain women called "Silkwomen" and delivered to the Mayor and Aldermen a bill complaining that whereas within the last fifteen days the pound of raw silk was worth 14s., Nicholas Sardouche, Lombard, by his crafty and evil design, embraced all the silk which he could find for sale in London and refused to sell it for less than 18s., and further that he daily spied out all aliens bringing such merchandise to London and either embraced it or caused them to sell it at a higher price than they would otherwise have done, to the great damage of the said women and the whole realm, wherefore the complainants prayed for a remedy, that they might not have cause to complain elsewhere.

Nicholas Sardouche, London, 1 December 1368

By virtue of this bill precept was issued to summon the said Nicholas for Friday after the Feast of St Andrew the Apostle [2 December]. He made default and order was given to distrain him by his chattels for the Saturday. On that day he appeared and, on being questioned, declared that his master and his partners in foreign parts had warned him by letter that divers bales of silk and other merchandise had been lost and stolen on their way to Bruges, on account of which they thought the price of silk ought to be much dearer in the future and that he ought to buy as much silk as he could. Accordingly he had bought all the silk he could find in the hands of strangers, both to sell it in the City at a profit and to export it abroad for resale. He was not aware that he had committed any trespass in doing so, and he was willing to sell that silk to anyone at 16s. the lb. Being further asked by the Court what quantity of silk he had bought, and from whom, and where it was weighed, he said he had bought 59 lbs of raw silk from Paul Penyk, Lombard, and 80 lbs of colored silk from Dyne Sanoche, Lombard, and that the whole of this silk was weighed in his house by his own balance and not by the common balance of the City ordained for weighing silk.

Inasmuch as, among other ancient ordinances made for the benefit of the King and his people in the City, it was ordained that all silk and merchandise of the same character exposed for sale in the City ought to be weighed at the common balance of the City established for that purpose under penalty of forfeiture of such merchandise weighed otherwise, and since the said Nicholas had confessed that he had bought the aforesaid silk from Paul and Dyne, alien merchants, for further sale or transference for sale to foreign parts, and had weighed it with his own balance against the aforesaid ordinance, and because the Mayor and Aldermen wished for further information as regards giving judgment in the matter, a day was given to the said Nicholas to hear judgment on Monday after the Feast of St Andrew the Apostle [4 December].

John Cheddele, London, 21 December 1371

John Cheddele was indicted in Billingsgate Ward in the Wardmoot of John Wroth, Alderman, held on Sunday the Feast of St Thomas the Apostle ... by oath of twelve men, as being a common player of dice by night and a constant nightwalker to the nuisance of the neighbors, and also for having entered the house of James Skynnere, in John Wroth's Rents, against the will of the same John and James, and for having there eloigned and hidden both the goods and the wife of the said James.

The accused denied the charges and put himself on the country. He was mainprised by William Swayn, tailor, and William Toukesbury, and a jury was summoned. The jurors brought in a verdict that the said John used to stand in the street at night and accost the daughters, wives, and serving-maids of citizens, against the latter's will, and take them off to lie with him; further that he entered the house of James Skynnere by night and there lay with James' wife Mary, but he was not guilty of taking away any of his goods. As regards dicing by night, he did not play more than was seemly, but his general behavior against the peace was a nuisance to the neighbors and he was not fit to reside in the Ward. The Court acquitted him as regards the dice and the goods, and committed him to prison on the other matters of which he was convicted.

Of Swine, Bawds, Thieves, and Courtesans (14th c)

The following laws, registered in the famous *Liber Albus* or the *White Book* of the City of London, show how the authorities tried to control the sometimes chaotic conditions of life in England's largest city and illustrate the types of punishment meted out to those who violated the city's ordinances.

Of Swine (Edward I)

And that no swine shall be found about the streets or about the lanes in the City, or in the suburbs, or in the fosses of the said city, from this time forward. And if swine shall be found in the places aforesaid, they may be killed by those by whom they shall be so found; and those who kill them, shall have them freely and clearly without any challenge thereof; or else the swine shall be bought back by him who owns it at the price of four pence. And he who shall wish to feed a pig, must feed it in his house.

Of Thieves and Courtesans (Edward I)

And whereas thieves and other persons of light and bad repute are often, and more commonly, received and harbored in the houses of women of evil life within the City than elsewhere, through whom evil deeds and murders, by reason of such harboring, do often happen, and great evils and scandals to the people of the City—the King doth will and command, that from henceforth no common woman shall dwell within the walls of the City. And if any such shall hereafter be found within the City residing and dwelling, she shall be imprisoned forty days. And let the Warden cause search to be made throughout the City in the best manner that he shall see fit, where such women are received, and who they are; and then, when they shall be found, let their limits be assigned unto them. And let no [such person] from henceforth wear miniver [a kind of fur] or cendal [silk] on her dress or on her hood; and if any one shall do so, let her lose the miniver and the cendal. And as to such miniver and cendal, let the same be forfeited unto the sergeant who shall have found such woman and have taken her in such guise.

Of a man who is ... a Whoremonger or Bawd, and of his Punishment (Richard II)

In the first place, if any man shall be found to be a common whoremonger or bawd, and shall of the same be attainted, first, let all his head and beard be shaved, except a fringe on the head, two inches in breadth; and let him be taken unto pillory, with minstrels, and set thereon for a certain time, at the discretion of the Mayor and Aldermen.

If any woman shall be found to be a common courtesan, and if the same shall be attainted, let her be taken from the prison unto Algate, with a hood of ray, and a white wand in her hand; and from thence, with minstrels, unto the thew, and there let the cause be proclaimed; and from thence, through Cheap and Newgate to Cokkeslane, there to take up her abode.

The Goodman's Instructions on Hosting, Cooking, and Serving (1392-94)

Le Ménagier de Paris was written by an affluent and highly educated Parisian husband for the edification of his much younger wife (she was probably around 15 at the time of composition, whereas he was probably about 60). According to his prologue, he wrote the treatise at his wife's request, so that she should know how to please him. The author is aware that his young wife is likely to marry again after his death; and, indeed, he cites among his motivations for composition his need to insure that her second husband will think well of the training she received at his hand. The following excerpts, based on Eileen Power's translation of *The Goodman of Paris*, provide advice specifically on how to run the kitchen and the dining room of a well-to-do household.

How to Order Dinners and Suppers

After these things it behooves to tell and speak of certain general terms that be used in the feat of cookery, and afterwards to show how you may know and choose the viands [products] wherewith the cook works, as follows:

Primo, in all sausages and thick pottages, wherein spices and bread be brayed, you should first bray [crush] the spices and take them out of the mortar, because the bread which you bray afterwards requires that which remains from the spices; thus naught is lost that would be lost if it were done otherwise.

Item, spices and bindings put into pottages ought not to be strained; nonetheless do so for sauces, that the sauces may be clearer and likewise the more pleasant.

Item, know you well that pea or bean pottages or others burn easily, if the burning brands touch the bottom of the pot when it is on the fire.

Item, before your pottage burns and in order that it burn not, stir it often in the bottom of the pot, and turn your spoon in the bottom so that the pottage may not take hold there. And *note* as soon as you shall perceive that your pottage burns, move it not, but straightaway take it off the fire and put it in another pot.

Item, note that commonly all pottages that be on the fire boil over, and fall onto the said fire, until salt and grease be put into the pot, and afterwards they do not so.

Item, note that the best caudle [a warm drink, sometimes thickened with gruel, intended for the sick or the pregnant] there is, is beef's cheek washed twice in water, then boiled and well skimmed.

Item, one may know whether a coney [rabbit] be fatted, by feeling his sinew or neck betwixt the two shoulders for there you may tell if there be much fat by the big sinew; and you can tell if he be tender by breaking one of his back legs.

Item, note that there is a difference among cooks between "sticking" and "larding," for sticking is done with cloves and larding with bacon-lard.

Item, in pike the soft-roed are better than the hard, save when you would make rissoles [minced pie] thereof.... Of pike one speak of a hurling pike, a pickerel, a pike, a luce.

Item, fresh shad comes into season in March.

Item, carp should be very well cooked, or otherwise it is dangerous to eat it.

Item, plaice be soft to the touch and dab the contrary.

Item, at Paris the cooks of roast meat fatten their geese with flour, neither the fine flour nor the bran, but that which is between the two which is called the pollen; and as much of this pollen as they take, they mix an equal amount of oatmeal therewith, and mix with a little water, and it remains of the thickness of paste, and they put this food in a dish on four feet, and water beside and fresh litter everyday, and in fifteen days the geese be fatted. And *note* that their litter make them to keep their feathers clean.

Item, to give the flavor of game to capons and hens, it behooves to bleed them by cutting their throats and straightaway put them and cause them to die in a bucket of very cold water, and they will be as high on the same day as though two days killed.

Item, you may tell young mallards from old ones, when they be the same size, from the quills of the feathers, which be tenderer in the young birds than in the old. *Item,* you may tell the river mallard, because they have sharp black nails and they have also red feet and the farmyard ducks have them yellow. *Item,* they have the crest or upper part of the beak green all along, and sometimes the males have a white mark across the nape of the neck, and they have the crest feathers very wavy.

Item, Ring doves be good in winter and you may tell the old ones for that the mid-feathers of their wings be all of a black hue, and the young ones of a year old have the mid-feathers ash colored and the rest black.

Item, you may know the age of a hare from the number of holes that be beneath the tail, for so many holes, so many years.

Item, the partridges whose feathers are close set and well joined to the flesh, and be orderly and well joined, as are the feathers of a hawk, these be fresh killed; and those whose feathers be ruffled the wrong way and come easily out of the flesh and be out of place and ruffled disorderly this way and that, they be long killed. *Item,* you may feel it by pulling the feathers of the belly.

Item, the carp which hath white scales and neither yellow nor reddish, is from good water. That which hath big eyes standing forth from the head and palate and tongue is joined, is fat. And *note* if you would carry a carp alive the whole day, wrap it up in damp hay and carry it belly upmost, and carry it without giving it air, in a cask or bag.

The season for trout begins in [*blank*] and lasts until September. The white trout be good in winter, and the red [salmon-]trout in summer. The best part of the trout is the tail and of the carp it is the head.

Item, the eel which hath a small head, loose mouth, shining skin, undulating and glistening, small eyes, big body and white belly, is fresh. The other has a big head, yellow belly and thick brown skin.

Hereafter follow diverse dinners and suppers of great lords and others and notes, whereupon you may choose, collect, and learn whatsoever dishes it shall please you, according to the seasons and to the meats which are native to the place where you may be, when you have to give a dinner or a supper.

Sample Dinner for a Meat Day served in Thirty-one Dishes and Six Courses

First course. Grenache wine and roasts, veal pasties, pimpernel pasties, black-puddings and sausages.

Second course. Hares in civet and cutlets, pea soup, salt meat and great joints, eels and other fish.

Third course. Roast: coneys [rabbits], partridges, capons etc., luce, bar, carp and a quartered pottage.

Fourth course. River fish à la dodine [in a sauce made of almonds, garlic, and eggs], savory rice, a bourrey [a dish of cut and boiled meat] with hot sauce and eels reversed.

Fifth course. Lark pasties, rissoles, larded milk, sugared flans.

Sixth course. Pears and comfits [a sweetmeat usually made out of fruit and sugar], medlars and peeled nuts. Hippocras and wafers.

Sample Fish Dinner for Lent

First course and service. Cooked apples, large Provençal figs roast, with bay leaves thereon, watercress and sorrel with vinegar, pea soup, salted eels, white herring, gravy on fried salt and freshwater fish.

Second course. Carp, luce, soles, roach, salmon, eels.

A Wedding Feast for 40 Guests

Service: Butter, none, because it is a feast day. *Item,* cherries, none, because none were to be had; and for this course not.

Pottages: Capons with blancmange [a dish composed of minced meat (usually fowl), cream, eggs, almonds, and sugar], pomegranates, and red comfits thereon.

Roast: On each dish a quarter of a kid; a quarter of kid is better than lamb; a duckling, two spring chickens and sauce thereto; oranges, cameline [an Italianate sauce], verjuice [the acidic juice of green fruits like crab apples, used as a condiment], and fresh towels and napkins therewith.

Entremets: crayfish jelly, loach [a kind of fish], young rabbits and pigs. Dessert: furment [a dish made out of wheat, milk, and sweet ingredients] and venison. Issue: Hippocras and wafers. Sally-Forth: wine and spices.

Service Required for a Wedding Feast

First, there is needed a clerk or varlet to purchase greenery, violets, chaplets, milk, cheese, eggs, logs, coal, salt, vats, and washing tubs both for the dining hall and for the butteries, verjuice, vinegar, sorrel, sage, parsley, fresh garlic, two brooms, a shovel, and other small things.

Item, a cook and his varlets, who will cost two francs in wages without other perquisites, but the cook will pay varlets and porters, and there is a saying "the more covers, the more wages."

Item, two knife-bearers, whereof one is to cut up bread and make trenchers and saltcellars of bread and they shall carry the salt and the bread and the trenchers to the tables and shall make for the hall two or three receptacles, wherein to throw the large scraps, such as sops, cut or broken bread, trenchers, pieces of meat and other things; and two buckets for casting away and receiving broth, sauce, and liquid things.

Item, one or two water-carriers be needed. *Item,* a big and strong sergeant to guard the portals.

Item, two esquires of the kitchen and two helpers for the service of the kitchen, one of whom shall go bargain for the kitchen things, pastry and linen for six tables; for the which there be needed two large copper pots for twenty covers, two boilers, four strainers, a mortar and pestle, six large cloths for the kitchen, three large earthenware pots for wine, a large earthenware pot for pottage, four wooden basins and spoons, an iron pan, four large pails with handles, two trivets, and an iron spoon. And he shall likewise purvey the pewter vessels; to wit ten dozen bowls, six dozen small dishes, two dozen and a half large dishes, eight quart [pots], two dozen pint [pots], two alms-dishes.

Item, concerning the house; wherein be it known that the hôtel de Beauvais cost Jehan du Chesne four francs; tables, trestles, and such five francs; and the chaplets cost him fifteen francs.

And the other esquire of the kitchen or his helper shall go with the cook to the butcher, the poulterer, the spicer, etc., to purvey and choose the things, have them borne home and pay for the carriage thereof; and they shall have a hutch shutting with a key, wherein they shall keep the spices etc., and they shall distribute all things according to reason and measure. And afterwards they or their helpers shall gather up that which remains and put it away safely in baskets in a closed hutch, to prevent waste and excess.

Two other esquires be needed for the service of the dining hall, and they shall give out spoons and collect them again, give out goblets, pour out whichsoever wine be asked for by the guests at table and collect the vessels again.

Two other esquires be needed for the wine cellar, who shall give out wine to be carried to the dresser, the tables, and elsewhere, and they shall have a varlet to draw the wine.

Two of the most honest and skilled esquires shall accompany the bridegroom and shall go with him before the dishes.

Two stewards to seat the guests and make them rise, and a sewer and two servants for each table, who shall serve and take away, throw the remnants into the baskets and the sauces and broths into the buckets and pails and receive and bring the dessert dishes to the esquires of the kitchen or others that be ordained to keep them and they shall carry nought elsewhere.

The office of steward is to purvey saltcellars for the high table; goblets, four dozen; covered gilt goblets, four; ewers, six; silver spoons, four dozen; silver quart [pots], four; alms dishes, two; comfit dishes, two.

A Feast Fit for a King (14ᵀᴴc)

The following is a description of a feast for a king from a fourteenth-century manuscript on English cookery. The "subtleties" are presumably clever and spectacular foods of some sort.

This is the purveyance for the feast for the king at home for his own table:

Venison with furmenty in pottage, boar's heads, great flesh, swan roasted, capons roasted in hot grease, pesson [fish], pike, and 2 subtleties.

Pottage called blundsorre, pottage called jelly, pigs roasted, cranes roasted, pheasants roasted, herons roasted, peacocks roasted, bream, broken brawn, rabbit roasted, & 1 subtlety.

Pottage called bruet of Almayne, new lombard, venison roasted, egret roasted, peacocks roasted, partridges roasted, pigeons roasted, rabbits roasted, quails roasted, larks roasted, a meat called pain puff, perches ... and 2 subtleties.

LETTERS FROM THE PASTONS (15THC)

The Pastons belonged to the lower gentry. Their letters provide a trove of information about the habits, concerns, and anxieties of affluent families in the late Middle Ages. John Paston was a lawyer, who spent much of his time in London on business, leaving his wife in charge in the country. Margaret Paston wrote to her husband about problems with tenants, recently purchased horses, and local and national politics. The civil wars of the fifteenth century leave their mark in Margaret's purposefully oblique references to the "desire" of the Duke of York and to the loyalties of the various people around her. These letters also show the structures of obedience and affiliation that marked social and familial relationships in medieval England. For the ideal conjunction of love and obedience, see the Duke of Suffolk's letter of advice to his son, which was copied into the Paston papers. Of course ideal and reality often failed to meet, as is evidenced by the Pastons' difficult relationship with their eldest son. John Paston's letter begging his father for money should still strike a chord with many children; Margaret's desperate attempts to mediate between father and son should strike a chord with modern mothers; and John Paston's anger at his son, who seems to want to "dwell again in your house and mine, and there eat and drink and sleep," should strike a chord with many fathers.

FROM AGNES PASTON TO WILLIAM PASTON, ON THE FIRST MEETING BETWEEN JOHN PASTON AND HIS FUTURE BRIDE, MARGARET, SOMETIME BEFORE 1440

Dear husband, I recommend me to you, etc. Blessed be God, I send you good tidings of the coming and the bringing home of the gentlewoman that you know of from Reedham this same night, according to appointment that ye made there for yourself.

And as for the first acquaintance between John Paston and the said gentlewoman, she made him gentle cheer in gentle wise, and said he was verily your son; and so I hope there shall need no great treaty betwixt them.

The parson of Stockton told me, if ye would buy her a gown, her mother would give thereto a goodly fur. The gown needs for to be had; and of color it would be a goodly blue, or else a bright sanguine [red].

I pray you do buy for me two pipes of gold. Your stews do well. The Holy Trinity have you in governance. Written at Paston, in haste.... etc. Yours, Agn. Paston.

FROM MARGARET PASTON TO JOHN PASTON, 28 SEPTEMBER 1343

Right worshipful husband, I recommend me to you, desiring heartily to hear of your welfare, thanking God of your amending of the great disease that ye have had. And I thank you for the letter that ye sent me, for by my troth my mother and I were not in heart's ease from the time that we knew of your sickness, till we knew verily of your amending.

My mother behested another image of wax of the weight of you, to our Lady of Walsingham, and she sent four nobles to the four orders of friars at Norwich to pray for you, and I have behested to go on pilgrimage to Walsingham and to St Leonard's for you. By my troth, I had never so heavy a season as I had from the time that I knew of your sickness till I knew of your amending; and yet my heart is in no great ease, nor not shall be till I know that ye be very hale. Your father and mine was this day seven-night [a week ago] at Beccles, for a matter of the Prior of Bromholm, and he lay at Gelderstone that night, and was there till it was nine of the clock and the other day. And I sent thither for a gown, and my mother said that I should have then, till I had been there anon, and so they could none get.

My father Garneys sent me word that he should be here the next week ... and they should have me home with them; and so God help me, I shall excuse me of my going thither if I may, for I suppose that I shall readilier [more readily] have tidings from you here than I should have there. I shall send my mother a token that she took me, for I suppose that the time is come that I should send it her, if I keep the behest that I have made; I suppose I have told you what it was. I pray you heartily that ye will vouchsafe to send me a letter as hastily as ye may, if writing be none disease to you, and that ye will vouchsafe to send me word how your sore doth. If I might have had my will, I should have seen you ere this time; I would ye were at home (if it were your ease, and your sore might be as well looked to here as it is there ye be now) lever than a gown, though it were of scarlet. I pray you, if your sore be whole and so that ye may endure to ride when my father come to London, that ye will ask leave and come home when the horse should be sent home again; for I hope ye shall be kept as tenderly here as ye be at London. I may none leisure have to do write half a quarter so much as I should say to you if I might speak with you. I shall send you another letter as hastily as

I may. I thank you that ye would vouchsafe to remember my girdle, and that ye would write to me at the time, for I suppose that writing was none ease to you. Almighty God have you in His keeping, and send you health. Written at Oxnead, in right great haste, on St Michael's even. Yours, M. Paston.

MARGARET PASTON TO JOHN PASTON, SOMETIME IN 1449

Right worshipful husband, I recommend me to you, and pray you to get some crossbows and windas [a tool for bending crossbows] to bind them with, and quarrels; for your houses here be so low that there may none man shoot out with no long bow, though we had never so much need.

I suppose ye should have such things of Sir John Fastolf ye would send to him; and also I would ye should get two or three short pole-axes to keep with doors, and as many jacks, and ye may....

Purry fell in fellowship with William Hasard at Quarles's, and told him that he would come and drink with Partrich and with him, and he said he should be welcome. And after noon he went thither for to espy what they did, and what fellowship they had with them; and when he came thither the doors were fast closed, and there were none folks with them but Mariot, and Capron and his wife, and Quarles's wife, and another man in a black hood somewhat halting; I suppose by his words that it was Norfolk of Gimmingham. And the said Purry espied all these foresaid things.

And Mariot and his fellowship had much great language that shall be told you when ye come home.

I pray you that ye will vouchsafe to do buy for me one lb. almonds and one lb. of sugar, and that ye will do buy some frieze to make of your children's gowns, ye shall have best cheap and best choice of Hays's wife as it is told me. And that ye will buy a yard of broad cloth of black for a hood for me of 44*d.* or four shillings a yard, for there is neither good cloth nor good frieze in this town....

The Trinity have you in His keeping, and send you good speed in all your matters.

THE COPY OF A NOTABLE LETTER, WRITTEN BY THE DUKE OF SUFFOLK TO HIS SON, GIVING HIM THEREIN VERY GOOD COUNSEL, 30 APRIL 1450

My dear and only well-beloved son, I beseech Our Lord in heaven, the maker of all the world, to bless you, and to send you ever grace to love Him and to dread Him; to the which, as far as a father may charge his child, I both charge you, and pray you to set all your spirits and wits to do, and to know His holy laws and commandments, by the which ye shall, with His great mercy, pass all the great tempests and troubles of this wretched world.

And that also, wittingly, ye do nothing for love nor dread of any earthly creature that should displease Him. And there as any frailty makes you to fall, beseech His mercy soon to call you to Him again with repentance, satisfaction, and contrition of your heart, never more in will to offend Him.

Secondly, next Him above all earthly things, to be true liegeman in heart, in will, in thought, in deed, unto the King our uttermost high and dread sovereign lord, to whom both ye and I be so much bound to; charging you, as father can and may, rather to die than to be the contrary, or to know anything that were against the welfare or prosperity of his most royal person, but that as far as your body and life may stretch ye live and die to defend it, and to let his Highness have knowledge thereof in all the haste ye can.

Thirdly, in the same wise, I charge you, my dear son, always, as ye be bounden by the commandment of God to do, to love, to worship, your lady and mother; and also that ye obey always her commandments, and to believe her counsels and advices in all your works, the which dread not but shall be best and truest to you. And if any other body would steer you to the contrary, to flee the counsel in any wise, for ye shall find it naught and evil.

Furthermore, as far as father may and can, I charge you in any wise to flee the company and counsel of proud men, of covetous men, and of flattering men, the more especially and mightily to withstand them, and not to draw nor to meddle with them, with all your might and power. And to draw to you and to your company good and virtuous men, and such as be of good conversation, and of truth, and by them shall ye never be deceived nor repent you of.

Moreover, never follow your own wit in no wise, but in all your works, of such folks as I write of above, ask your advice and counsel; and doing thus, with the mercy of God, ye shall do right well, and live in right much worship, and great heart's rest and ease.

And I will be to you as good lord and father as my heart can think.

And last of all, as heartily and as lovingly as ever father blessed his child in earth, I give you the blessing of Our Lord and of me, which of His infinite mercy increase you in all virtue and good living. And that your blood may by His grace from kindred to kindred multiply in this earth to His service, in such wise as after the departing from this wretched world here, ye and they may glorify Him eternally amongst His angels in heaven. Written of mine hand, the day of my departing from this land, Your true and loving father, Suffolk.

MARGARET PASTON TO JOHN PASTON, 21 OCTOBER 1460
Right worshipful husband, I recommend me to you. Please it you to know that I received your letter that ye sent me by Nicholas Colman on Sunday last past. And as for the matter that ye desired me to break of to my cousin Rookwood, it fortuned so that he came to me on Sunday to dinner soon, after that I had your letter; and when we had dined, I moved to him thereof in covert terms, as Playter shall inform you hereafter. And as I thought by him, and so did Playter also by the language that he had to us, that he would be as faithful as he could or might be to that good lord that ye wrote of, and to you also, in anything that he could or might do in case were that he were set in office, so that he might aught do; and thereto he said he would be bound in £1,000, if he was so much worth.

As for the other that ye desired I should move to of the same matter, meseemeth he is too young to take any such things upon him; and also I know verily that he shall never love faithfully the other man that ye desired that he should do, for when he remembers the time that is past, and therefore I spake not to him thereof.

This day was held a great day at Acle before the under-sheriff and the under-escheator for the matter of Sir John Fastolf's lands; and there was my cousin Rookwood and my cousin John Berney of Reedham, and divers other gentlemen and thrifty men of the country; and the matter is well sped after your intent, blessed be God! As ye shall have knowledge of in haste.

I suppose Playter shall be with you on Sunday or on Monday next coming if he may. Ye have many good prayers of the poor people that God should speed you at this Parliament; for they live in hope that ye should help to set a way that they might live in better peace in this country than they have done before, and that wools should be purveyed for, that they should not go out of this land, as it hath been suffered to do before, and then shall the poor people more live better than they have done by their occupation therein. Thomas Bone hath sold all your wool here for 20d. a stone, and good surety found to you therefore, to be paid at Michaelmas next coming; and it is sold right well, after that the wool was for the most part right feeble.

Item, there be bought for you three horses at St Faith's fair, and all be trotters, right fair horses, God save them, and they be well kept.

Item, your mills at Hellesdon be let for twelve marks, and the miller to find the reparation. And Richard Calle hath let all your lands at Caister; but as for Mauteby lands, they be not let yet. William White hath paid me again this day his £10, and I have made him an acquittance thereof, because I had not his obligation.

There is great talking in this country of the desire of my Lord of York. The people report full worshipfully of my Lord of Warwick. They have no fear here but that he and other should show too great favor to them that have been rulers of this country before time.

I have done all your errands to Sir Thomas Howes that ye wrote to me for. I am right glad that ye have sped well in your matters betwixt Sir Philip Wentworth and you, and so I pray God ye may do in all other matters to His pleasance.

As for the writings that ye desired that Playter should send you, Richard Calle told me that they were at Harry Barber's, at the Temple Gate.

The mayor and the mayoress sent hither their dinners this day, and John Damme came with them, and they dined here. I am beholden to them, for they have sent to me divers times since ye went hence. The mayor said that there is no gentleman in Norfolk that he would do more for than he would for you, if it lay in his power to do for you.

J. Perse is still in prison, but he will not confess more than he did when ye were at home. Edmund Brome was with me, and told me that Perse sent for him for to come speak with him; and he told me that he was with him and examined him, but he would not be aknow to him that he had no knowledge where no goods was of his master's more than he had knowledged to you. He told me that he sent for him to desire him to labor to you and to me for him if ye had been at home; and he told me that he said to him again that he would never labor for him, but he might know that he were true to his master, though it lay in his power to do right much for him. I suppose it should do none harm though the said Perse were removed further. I pray to God give grace that the truth may be known, and that the dead may have part of his own goods. And the blessed Trinity have you in His keeping. Written in haste, at Hellesdon, the Tuesday next after St Luke. By yours, M.P.

JOHN PASTON TO HIS FATHER,
JOHN PASTON, 23 AUGUST 1461

Most reverend and worshipful father, I recommend me heartily, and
submit me lowlily to your good fatherhood, beseeching you for
charity of your daily blessing. I beseech you to hold me excused that
I sent to you none erst no writing, for I could not speed to mine
intent the matters that ye sent to me for. I have labored daily my
Lord of Essex, Treasurer of England, to have moved the King both
of the manor of Dedham and of the bill copy of the court roll every
morning afore he went to the King, and often times inquired of
him and he had moved the King in these matters. He answered me
nay, saying it was no time, and said he would it were as fain sped as
I myself, of times delaying me, that in truth I thought to have sent
you word that I felt by him that he was not willing to move the
King therein. Nevertheless, I labored to him continually, and prayed
Berners, his man, to remember him of it. I told often times to my
said Lord that I had a man tarrying in town that I should have sent
to you for other sundry matters, and he tarried for nothing but that
I might send you by him an answer of the said matters; other times
beseeching him to speed me in these matters for this cause, that ye
should think no default in me for remembering in, the said matters.

And now of late, I remembering him of the same matter, inquired
if he had moved the King's Highness therein; and he answered me
that he had felt and moved the King therein, rehearsing the King's
answer therein; how that when he had moved the King in the said
manor of Dedham, beseeching him to be your good lord therein,
considering the service and true part that ye have done and owe to
him, and in especial the right that ye have thereto, he said he would
be your good lord therein, as he would be to the poorest man in
England. He would hold with you in your right; and as for favor, he
will not be understood that he shall show favor more to one man
than to another, not to one in England.

And as for the bill copied of the court roll, when he moved to
him of it, he smiled and said that such a bill there was, saying that
ye would have oppressed sundry of your countrymen of worshipful
men, and therefore he kept it still. Nevertheless, he said he should
look it up in haste, and ye should have it.

Berners undertook to me twice or thrice that he should so have
remembered his lord and master that I should have had it within two
or three days. He is often times absent, and therefore I have it not

yet; when I can get it, I shall send it you, and of the King's mouth, his name that take it him.

I send you home Peacock again. He is not for me. God send grace that he may do you good service; that, by estimation, is not likely. Ye shall have knowledge afterward how he hath demeaned him here with me. I would, saving your displeasure, that ye were delivered of him, for he shall never do you profit nor worship.

I suppose ye understand that the money that I had of you at London may not endure with me till that the King go into Wales and come again, for I understand it shall be long ere he come again. Wherefore I have sent to London to mine uncle Clement to get an hundred shillings of Christopher Hansson your servant, and send it me by my said servant, and mine harness with it, which I left at London to make clean.

I beseech you not to be displeased with it, for I could make no other remedy but I should have borrowed it of a strange man, some of my fellows, which I suppose should not like you an ye heard of it another time. I am in surety where as I shall have another man in the stead of Peacock.

My Lord of Essex says he will do as much for you as for any esquire in England, and Berners his man telleth me, saying, "Your father is much beholden to my Lord, for he loveth him well." Berners moved me once, and said that ye must needs do somewhat for my lord and his, and I said I knew well that ye would do for him that lay in your power. And he said that there was a little money betwixt you and a gentleman of Essex called Dyrward, saying that there is as much between my said Lord and the said gentleman, of the which money he desires your part.

It is talked here how that ye and Howard should have striven together on the Shire day, and one of Howard's men should have stricken you twice with a dagger, and so ye should have been hurt but for a good doublet that ye had on at that time. Blessed be God that ye had it on! No more I write to your good fatherhood at this time, but Almighty God have you in His keeping, and send you victory of your enemies, and worship increasing to your life's ending. Written at Lewes, on St Bartholomew's eve, By your servant and elder son, John Paston.

MARGARET PASTON TO JOHN PASTON (HER SON), 15 NOVEMBER 1463

I greet you well, and send you God's blessing and mine, letting you know that I have received a letter from you, the which ye delivered to Master Roger at Lynn, whereby I conceive that ye think ye did not well that ye departed hence without my knowledge. Wherefore I let you know I was right evil paid with you. Your father thought, and thinks yet, that I was assented to your departing, and that hath caused me to have great heaviness. I hope he will be your good father hereafter, if ye demean you well and do as ye ought to do to him; and I charge you upon my blessing that in anything touching your father that should be his worship, profit, or avail, that ye do your devoir and diligent labor to the furtherance therein, as ye will have my good will, and that shall cause your father to be better father to you.

It was told me ye sent him a letter to London. What the intent thereof was I know not, but though he take it but lightly, I would ye should not spare to write to him again as lowly as ye can beseeching him to be your good father; and send him such tidings as be in the country there ye be in, and that ye ware of your expense better and ye have been before this time, and be your own purse-bearer. I trust ye shall find it most profitable to you.

I would ye should send me word how ye do, and how ye have shifted for yourself since ye departed hence, by some trusty man, and that your father have no knowledge thereof. I durst not let him know of the last letter that ye wrote to me, because he was so sore displeased with me at that time.

Item, I would ye should speak with Wykes, and know his disposition to Jane Walsham. She hath said since he departed hence, but she might have him she would never be married; her heart is sore set on him. She told me that he said to her that there was no woman in the world he loved so well. I would not he should jape her, for she means good faith; and if he will not have her, let me know in haste, for I shall purvey for her in other wise.

As for your harness and gear that ye left here, it is in Dawbeney's keeping; it was never removed since your departing, because that he had not the keys. I trust it shall appear but-if [only if] it be taken heed at betimes. Your father knows not where it is.

I sent your grey horse to Ruston to the farrier, and he says he shall never be naught to ride, neither right good to plough nor to cart; he says he was splayed, and his shoulder rent from the body. I know not what to do with him.

Your grandam would fain hear some tidings from you. It were well done that ye sent a letter to her how ye do as hastily as ye may. And God have you in His keeping, and make you a good man, and give you grace to do well as I would ye should do. Written at Caister, the Tuesday next before Saint Edmund the King. Your mother, M. Paston.

John Paston to His Father, John Paston, 1464

Right reverend and worshipful father, I recommend me unto you, beseeching you lowly of your blessing, desiring to hear of your welfare and prosperity, the which I pray God preserve unto His pleasance, and to your heart's desire; beseeching you to have me excused that ye had no writing from me since that I departed from you. For so God me help, I sent you a letter to London anon after Candlemas, by a man of my Lord's; and he forgot to deliver it to you, and so he brought to me the letter again, and since that time I could get no messenger till now.

As for tidings, such as we have here I send you.

My Lord and my Lady are in good health, blessed be God, and my Lord hath great labor and cost here in Wales for to take divers gentlemen here which were consenting and helping unto the Duke of Somerset's going; and they were appealed of other certain points of treason, and this matter. And because the King sent my Lord word to keep this country, is cause that my Lord tarry here thus long. And now the King hath given my Lord power whether he will do execution upon these gentlemen or pardon them, whether that him list; and as far forth as I can understand yet, they shall have grace. And as soon as these men be come in, my Lord is purposed to come to London, which I suppose shall be within this fortnight. The men's names that be impeached are these: John Hanmer and William his son, Roger Puleston, and Edward of Madoc; these be men of worship that shall come in.

The commons in Lancashire and Cheshire were up to the number of 10,000 or more, but now they be down again; and one or two of them was headed [beheaded] in Chester as on Saturday last past....

And other tidings have we none here, but that I suppose ye have heard before. I suppose verily that it shall be so nigh Easter ere ever my Lord come to London, that I shall not mowe [no more] come home to you before Easter; wherefore I beseech you that ye will vouchsafe that one of your men may send a bill to mine uncle Clement, or to some other man, who that ye will, in your name, that they may deliver me the money that I am behind of this quarter since Christmas, and for the next quarter, in part of that sum that it pleased you to grant me by the year. For by my troth, the fellowship have not so much money as we weened to have had by right much; for my Lord hath had great costs since he came hither.

Wherefore I beseech you that I may have this money at Easter, for I have borrowed money that I must pay again after Easter. And I pray to Almighty God have you in keeping. Written in the castle of the Holt, in Wales, the first day of March. Your son and lowly servant, John Paston, the Youngest.

JOHN PASTON TO MARGARET PASTON AND OTHERS, 27 JUNE 1465

... *Item*, as for your son, I let you know I would he did well; but I understand in him no disposition of policy, nor of governance as man of the world ought to do, but only lives and ever hath as man dissolute without any provision, nor that he busies himself nothing to understand such matters as a man of livelihood must needs understand; nor I understand nothing of what disposition he purposes to be, but only I can think he would dwell again in your house and mine, and there eat and drink and sleep. Therefore I let you know, I would know him ere he know mine intent, and how well he has occupied his time now he hath had leisure. Every poor man that has brought up his children to the age of twelve year waits then to be helped and profited by his children, and every gentleman that hath discretion waits that his kin and servants that lives by him and at his cost should help him foreward. As for your son, ye know well he never stood you nor me in profit, ease, or help to the value of one groat, saving at Calcote Hall when he and his brother kept it one day against Debenham; and yet was it at three times the cost that ever Debenham's sons put him to. For by their policy they keep Cotton at my cost and with the profits of the same. Wherefore give him no favor till ye feel what he is and will be....

Item, Calle sends me word that Master Philip has entered in Drayton in my Lord Suffolk's name, and hath other purpose to enter in Hellesdon, and he [Calle] asks my advice; which is that ye comfort my tenants and help them till I come home, and let them know I shall not lose it, and that the Duke of Suffolk that last died would have bought it of Fastolf, and, for he might not have it so, he claimed the manor, saying it was one Pole's, and, for his name was Pole, he claimed to be heir. He was answered that he came nothing of that stock, and whomsoever were kin to the Poles that owned it it hurt not, for it was lawfully bought and sold, and he never claimed it after. *Item*, I am in purpose to take assize against him at this time, and else I would have sent thither straight by a letter of attorney to enter in my name. Nevertheless ye be a gentlewoman, and it is worship for you to comfort your tenants; wherefore I would ye might ride to Hellesdon and Drayton and Sparham, and tarry at Drayton and speak with them, and bid them hold with their old master till I come, and that ye have sent me word but late, wherefore ye may have none answer yet. And inform them as I have written to ye within; and say openly it is a shame that any man should set any lord on so untrue a matter, and special a priest; and let them know as soon as I am come home I shall see them.... God keep you. Writ the Thursday before St Peter's day. John Paston.

On Manners (15ᵗʰ c)

The first excerpt, from a poem entitled *The Babees Book: Or a "Lytyl Reporte" of How Young People Should Behave*, is from 1475; the second, from a poem by Richard West entitled *The Booke of Demeanor and the Allowance and Disallowance of Certaine Misdemeanors in Company* [1619] dates from the Renaissance. Both manuals convey through rhyme basic rules about comportment for children. *The Babees Book* includes marginal comments that clarify the main moral for each stanza; we have tried to reproduce this format in our translations, based on Frederick Furnivall's edition of both poems.

FROM *The Babees Book*

....

At every time obey unto your lord | Bow to your lord
when you answer.

When ye answer, else stand ye still as stone

But if he speak; look with one accord

That if ye see come in any person | If any one better than
yourself comes in,

Better than ye, that ye go back at once | retire and give place
to him.

And give him place;
your back eek in no way

Turn on no wight, as far forth as ye may. | Turn your back on
no man.

....

Give that your lord also ye see drinking, | Be silent while your
lord drinks, not

Look that ye be in right stable silence | laughing, whispering,
or joking.

Without loud laughter or jangling,

Roving, japing, or other insolence.

If he command also in his presence | If he tells you to sit
down, do so at once.

You for to sit, fulfill his will by life,

And for your seat look not
with others [to] strive....

....

If that your lord his own cup wants to command

If your lord offers you his cup,

To you to drink, rise up when ye it take,

rise up, take it with both hands,

And receive it goodly with both your hands;

Of it also to no one other proffer ye make,

offer it to no one else, but give it back to

But unto him that brought it ye it take....

him that brought it.

Before him stand until he command you sit,

Stand by your lord till he tells you to sit,

With clean hands, ay, ready him to serve;

When ye be seated, *your* knife with all your wit,

then keep your knife clean and sharp

Unto your self both clean and sharp conserve,

That honestly you may your own meat carve.

to cut your food.

Let courtesy and silence with you dwell,

Be silent, and tell no nasty stories.

And foul tales look no one to other tell.

Cut with your knife your bread, and break it not;

Cut your bread, don't break it.

A clean Trencher before you eek you lay,

And when your potage to you shall be brought,

Lay a clean trencher before you, and eat your broth with a spoon,

Take you spoons, and sup by no way,

don't sup it up.

And in your dish lay not your spoon, I pray,

Don't leave your spoon in your dish.

Nor on the board leaning be ye not seen,

But from en-browning the cloth ye keep clean.

Don't lean on the table, or dirty the cloth.

Out over your dish your head ye not hang,

And with full mouth drink in no wise;

Your nose, your teeth, your nails, from picking,

Don't hang your head over your dish, or eat with a full mouth, or pick your nose, teeth, and nails,

Keep, at your mete, for so teach the wise.

Eek ere ye take in your mouth, you advise,

So much meat but that ye right well may

or stuff your mouth so that you can't speak.

Answer, and speak, when men speak to you.

When ye shall drink, your mouth cleanse
with a cloth;

Your hands eke that they in no manner

En-brown the cup, for then should no one
be loath

With you to drink that be with you in fere.

The salt also touch not in his salter

With no kinds of meat, but lay it honestly

On your Trencher, for that is courtesy....

Wipe your mouth
when you drink,

and don't dirty the
cup with your hands.

Don't dip your meat
in the salt-cellar,

And, sweet children, for whose love now I
write,

I you beseech with very loving heart,

To know this book that ye set your delight;

And mightyful god, that suffered pains
smart,

In courtesy he make you so expert,

That through your nurture and your
governance

In lasting bliss ye may your self advance!

Sweet children,

I beseech you

know this book, and
may God make you
so expert therein

that you may attain
endless bliss.

FROM THE *Booke of Demeanor*

Stand straight upright, and both thy feet
    together closely standing,
Be sure on it, ever let thine eye
    be still at thy commanding.

Observe that nothing wanting be
    which should be on the board.
Unless a question moved be,
    be careful: not a word....

Let not thy brows be backward drawn,
    it is a sign of pride,
Exalt them not, it shows a heart
    most arrogant beside.

Nor let thine eyes be gloating down,
    cast with a hanging look:
For that to dreamers doth belong,
    that goodness cannot brook.

Let forehead joyful be and full,
    it shows a merry part,
And cheerfulness in countenance,
    and pleasantness of heart.

Nor wrinkled let thy countenance be,
    still going to and fro:
For that belongs to hedge-hogs right,
    they wallow even so.

Nor imitate with Socrates,
    to wipe thy snivelly nose
Upon thy cap, as he would doe,
    nor yet upon thy clothes.

But keep it clean with handkerchief,
    provided for the same,
Not with thy fingers or thy sleeve,
    therein thou art too blame....

If thou of force do chance to sneeze,
    then backwards turn away
From presence of the company,
    wherein thou art to stay....

Keep close thy mouth, for why, thy breath
    may hap to give offence,
And other worse may be repaid
    for further recompense....

To laugh at all things thou shalt hear,
    is neither good nor fit,
It shows the property and form
    of one with little wit....

If spitting chance to move thee so
    thou canst it not forbear,
Remember do it modestly,
    consider who is there.

If filthiness, or ordure thou
    upon the floor doe cast,
Tread out, and cleanse it with thy foot,
    let that be done with haste....

To belch or bulch like *Clitipho*,
    whom *Terence* has set forth,
Commends manners to be base,
    most foul and nothing worth.

If thou to vomit be constrained,
    avoid from company:
So shall it better be excused,
    if not through gluttony....

Let not thy privy members be
    laid open to be viewed,
It is most shameful and abhorred,
    detestable and rude.

Retain not urine nor the wind,
    which doth thy body vex,
So it be done with secrecy,
    let that not thee perplex.

NOTES

1   Peter Hammond, *Food and Feast in Medieval England* (1993; Stroud, Gloucestershire: Sutton Publishing, 2005) 44. Our description of medieval London reflect facts and information made available in Derek Pearsall, *The Life of Geoffrey Chaucer: A Critical Biography*, Blackwell Critical Biographies (Oxford and Cambridge, MA: Blackwell, 1992), as well as in the range of the sources cited below.

2   Hammond 50.

3   Charles Pendrill, *London Life in the 14th Century* (New York; Adelphi, 1925) 11.

4   Pendrill 194.

5   *The Paston Letters,* ed. John Warrington, rev. ed. (London: J.M. Dent and Sons, 1956) Vol. 1: 24, #24 (1449); Vol 1: 20, #20 (31 January [?] 1449).

6   A punitive device for female offenders consisting of a raised platform with an attached post to which the transgressor would be tied.

7   Pendrill 40.

8   Pendrill 54-57.

9   Barbara Hanawalt, *Growing Up in Medieval London: The Experience of Childhood in History* (New York: Oxford UP, 1993) 38; Mate 276-92, 280.

10   Hanawalt, *Growing Up in Medieval London* 26.

11   H.S. Bennett, *The Pastons and Their England: Studies in an Age of Transition,* 2nd ed. (Cambridge: Cambridge UP, 1951) 134.

12   Wendy R. Childs, "Moving Around," in *A Social History of England, 1200-1500,* ed. Rosemary Horrox and W.M. Ormrod (Cambridge and New York: Cambridge UP, 2006) 260-75.

13   Martin M. Crowe and Clair C. Olson, eds., *Chaucer Life Records* (Oxford: Clarendon P, 1966) 477.

14   *Robin Hood and the Friar, PLS Performance Text #3,* ed. Mary Blackstone (Toronto: Poculi Ludique Societas, 1981).

15   Bennett 160-62.

16   Campbell 187-88.

17 "The Second Shepherd's Play," in *Medieval Drama*, ed. David Bevington (Boston, MA: Houghton Mifflin, 1987) 1-18. References to this work are from this edition.

18 Frances Elizabeth Baldwin, *Sumptuary Legislation and Personal Regulation in England* (Baltimore, MD: Johns Hopkins P, 1926) 73.

19 *Statutes of the Realm*, 12 vols. (London: Record Commission, 1810-28) 2: 74.

20 Campbell 200.

21 Peter Coss, "An Age of Deference," *A Social History of England, 1200-1500*, ed. Rosemary Horrox and W.M. Ormrod (Cambridge: Cambridge UP, 2006) 46.

22 John Paston to John Paston, 1 March 1464, in *The Paston Letters* 1: 238, #231.

23 The Earl of Oxford to John Paston (1449-51?), in *The Paston Letters* 1: 43, #39.

24 *The Paston Letters* 2: 16, #247.

25 Peter Coss, *The Lady in Medieval England* (Mechanicsburg, PA: Stackpole Books, 1998) 131-36.

26 Campbell 210.

27 Hammond 33.

28 Christopher Dyer, *Standards of Living in the Later Middle Ages: Social Change in England c. 1200-1500* (New York: Cambridge UP, 1989) 50.

29 Hanawalt, *Growing Up in Medieval London* 117.

30 Hanawalt, *Growing Up in Medieval London* 115-16.

31 Hammond 45-46.

32 Françoise Pipponier and Perrine Mane, *Dress in the Middle Ages*, trans. Caroline Beamish (New Haven, CT: Yale UP, 1997) 115, 120.

33 Baldwin 91.

34 Pipponier and Mane 74-81, 16.

35 Pipponier and Mane 61; *Sir Gawain and the Green Knight*, trans. Marie Boroff (New York: Norton, 1967) 1832-33. All references to *Gawain* are to this edition.

36 Mavis E. Mate, "Work and Leisure," in *A Social History of England*, ed. Rosemary Horrox and W. Mark Ormrod (Cambridge: Cambridge University Press, 2006) 281.

37 Albert Compton Reeves, *Pleasures and Pastime in Medieval England* (Stroud, Gloucestershire: Alan Sutton, 1995) 103, 107.

38 Compton Reeves 106, 77.

39 Hammond 104.

40 Hammond 71.

41 Compton Reeves 200.

42 Hammond 49.

43 Hammond 107.

44 Norbert Elias, *et al.*, *The Civilizing Process: Sociogenetic and Psychogenetic Investigations*, rev. ed. (Oxford and Malden, MD: Blackwell, 2000) 56.

45 Hammond 117.

46 Elias 101.

47 Glynne Wickham, "Introduction," *English Moral Interludes* (London: J.M. Dent and Sons, 1976) vii.

48 Edward Hall, *Hall's Chronicle; Containing the History of England, During the Reign of Henry the Fourth, and the Succeeding Monarchs, to the End of the Reign of Henry the Eighth, in Which Are Particularly Described the Manners and Customs of Those Periods.* (1809; New York: AMS Press, 1965) 535.

49 Dyer, *Standards of Living* 55.

50 Hammond 150.

51 Figures are based on Pendrill 170–85; and Dyer, *Standards of Living* 27-48, 61–62, 79.

CHAPTER IV

Hooly Thought and Werk

Religious Life, Ritual, and Prayer

INTRODUCTION

Despite their materialistic interests, the pilgrims of the *Canterbury Tales* move through a profoundly spiritual world, engaging constantly with religious figures and preoccupations. Several pilgrims themselves belong to ecclesiastical orders, but even for those who don't, the presence of religion is tangible. Most of the tales are casually sprinkled with reference to churchly issues, events, and people. John, of "The Miller's Tale," boards a student who reads theology and predicts a second flood, while a monk in "The Shipman's Tale" dupes a friend and his wife. A cleric in "The Franklin's Tale" practices the art of illusion, while another cleric marries the Wife of Bath. The stories of the religious professionals are, of course, saturated with the spiritual issues that most concern them: the nature of chastity, the attaining of absolution, the testing of faith. The pilgrims tell saints' lives and miracle stories, exempla and allegories. No matter how corrupt the teller, thoughts of the eternal are never far away.

Reminders of the spiritual realm were everywhere in the medieval world, from the village bells that rang on the hour to signal the recitation of daily prayers, to the friars who regularly visited to take confession and give blessing. Biblical *exempla* and maxims punctuated the patterns of thought and the structure of ordinary events; even everyday activities were fixed within the context of the sacred. This was an environment populated by spiritual figures with highly specialized occupations and functions— friars, pardoners, parsons, and summoners, among others—who moved ponderously through the lives of the more secular. Religious symbolism and biblical echoes permeate the literary landscape, and stories resonate with a theological significance beyond what their plots might at first suggest. Seemingly innocuous decorations such as flowers, headpieces, and jewelry often carried spiritual significance; lilies and daisies were associated with the Virgin Mary, for example, as were pearls. Even head coverings or haircuts could contain a spiritual reference: the docked style worn by the Reeve of the *Canterbury Tales* suggests his identification with the friars. These spiritual allusions reflect the culture and sensibility of the Middle Ages, echoing the miscellany of modes of religious practices that marked the age.

Western Europe was dominated by the rule of the Western Catholic Church, whose center in Rome influenced both political and individual life, and whose ideology and world-view were diffused through religious imagery. Although spiritual life in England was mediated largely through the local parishes, the general structure that regulated and informed local practice had been in place for hundreds of years. Contemporary issues and thinkers sometimes altered the surface, but years of tradition and administration gave the medieval church and its flock a sense of permanence and comfort. Public displays of devotion were common, but piety was found in the home, too, in the form of daily prayers and even, for those able to afford them, books of hours, filled with the Hours of the Virgin and other saints, special prayers and hymns, a calendar of special saint's days, scriptural meditations, and whatever other personal forms of devotion a reader might wish to use for private devotion. A variety of didactic means, ranging from sermons to the yearly cycle of miracle plays, supplied lessons in the symbolic artifacts that suggested the invisible presence of the sacred world beyond. Worship provided a source of solace and comfort in the medieval world, as well as an ideal of inner perfection to which many aspired. The institutions that supported the church—the clerical hierarchy itself, but also the guilds and the economic and political dynasties—held a virtual monopoly over educational practice, manuscript production, and the circulation of books and knowledge until the fifteenth century, forming a dominant religious sensibility that functioned almost as a screen through which even the most radical voices were filtered.

Thus, as D. W. Robertson has argued, we can read almost every literary event in the Middle Ages through a sacred veil.[1] Chaucer's Miller isn't just a drunken peasant who stirs up the storytelling contest by interrupting his better, the Monk; he also embodies what would be instantly recognizable to a medieval audience as the deadly sins of Gluttony, Pride, and, arguably, Avarice. The Man in Black in Chaucer's *Book of the Duchess* surely represents the political figure of John of Gaunt, but his heavily stylized description and surroundings also suggest a retreat into the sin of Despair. Chanticleer, the vainglorious rooster of "The Nun's Priest's Tale," can be seen as a kind of Adam in that he, too, falls prey to the bad advice of his wife, while the gardens in which the lovers meet in both "The Franklin's Tale" and "The Merchant's Tale" remind readers of the Garden of Eden and mankind's subsequent fall from grace. Even romantic love allegorically illustrates the Christian ideal of charity, and almost every poem, no matter how witty or how removed from religious concerns, can be read in terms of an overarching Christian lesson that reconstitutes what might seem a purely secular interest.

Popular Religion and Daily Life

Despite the religious controversies of the age, the daily life of the medieval layman remained governed by religious rhythms, ranging from such mundane reminders as the temporal division of the days and weeks, to the religious feasts and holidays and the prayers that punctuated and informed the "thoroughfare" of life. The local parish church that could be found in every medieval village comprised, to a great extent, the center of the social community. Not only did the unlettered laity learn its scriptural lessons in the form of sermons and other readings from the parish priests and itinerant clergymen, whose duty it was to provide spiritual knowledge and solace to their flock, but the church also provided the most available space for neighborly interaction and commerce. Even the most ribald and secular of the medieval tales, like the fabliaux told by Chaucer's Miller and the Reeve, are littered with reminders of the religious world that structured medieval inner life. In "The Reeve's Tale," the miller Simkin's wife is a parson's daughter, raised in a nunnery; when she and her husband wish to flaunt their wealth to their fellow townsmen, they do it on holy days, which provide the opportunity to dress in scarlet petticoats. In "The Miller's Tale," Absolon uses his clerkly position to waft his incense toward the pretty ladies of the parish. John the Carpenter mentions seeing a body being borne to the church, then worries that another Noah's flood will carry off his young wife. Absolon's shoes are carved like the windows of St. Paul's, and all the characters swear by theological names, invoking by turns their favorite saints (St. Thomas!, St. Frideswide!), or God, Christ, or the devil.

The central experience of the medieval churchgoer involved attending mass at the local church. Every village had its own church, and cities
had many—one for every neighborhood. By the late Middle Ages, the
Sunday mass was a majestic and ritualized event. The service was initiated
by a processional around the church, during which the laity were sprinkled with holy water. A series of scriptural readings came next, followed by
prayers for both the living and the dead. On major feast days a creed (or
statement of faith) would be read, followed by the sharing of Communion.
The central feature of the mass was the Eucharist: the taking of the wafer,
or "body of Christ," during Communion. Orthodox belief decreed that
the consecrated wine and bread—or "host"—were transformed into the
real and actual blood and body of Christ during this ritual. Although
most medieval laymen did not participate themselves in the taking of the
Eucharist, they witnessed it during the mass and identified it as the central
miracle of Christianity: that is, the moment in which the sacred and the
temporal converged most fully to demonstrate the power of belief in the
salvation of the soul. Indeed, everything about the service, including not
only the rituals but also the iconography of the church, the craftsmanship
and beauty of the vestments and the rich sacred vessels, attested to the
honor due to God and inspired awe among the congregation. The wealthy
had their own chapels in which they could take their devotions; indeed,
the pious elite could partake in as many as five masses a day, customized for
their particular needs.[2] Special masses were also said for sacred occasions,
including matrimony, baptism, confirmation, and funerals.

The primary concern of the medieval church was for preparing the
soul for the transition to the next world. This concern manifested itself
in a number of beliefs, practices, and sacraments, including the sacred
rituals of baptism, confirmation, Eucharist, penance, the Anointing of the
Sick, marriage, and the Holy Orders, believed to have been recognized by
Christ. Although early reformist movements—including, much later, the
Protestant Reformation—challenged many of these beliefs, these rituals
and core celebrations comprised the most elemental feature of the religiosity that characterized medieval life. Confession, for example, had been
institutionalized since the early thirteenth century. Not only were medieval citizens expected to attend mass, but they also had to make a thorough
reckoning of their sins to the local parish priest, who was entrusted with
instructing them on how to overcome temptations and compensate for
transgressions. Monetary offerings ensured that priests and friars would say
prayers after a parishioner's death to shorten the length of time inevitably
spent in purgatory—that realm between heaven and hell that provided for

the purification of any unrepented sins. Numerous manuals on confession and penitence survive, providing detailed explanations of the forms of contrition and their genuineness. Confessors expressed an interest not in the types of sins committed but rather in the deeper psychological impulses that caused the misdeed in the first place. The Seven Deadly Sins—Gluttony, Lust, Sloth, Avarice, Wrath, Envy, and Pride—represented the kinds of feelings that led to acts that could threaten eternal salvation. Penance manuals frequently point to the sins as a way of organizing the various venial acts that can be committed in the course of an ordinary life. Chaucer's "Parson's Tale," a long treatise on penance and contrition, is organized in large part according to the Seven Deadly Sins and their remedies; *Piers Plowman* features the Seven Deadly Sins as part of an allegory of the failure of society and government; and Gower's *Confessio Amantis* organizes its collection of tales as examples of each of the sins.

The infusion of the religious into daily life also occurred in other prominent ways. One of the conspicuous differences that distinguishes modern from medieval life, for example, is our concept of time. The modern world divides the year into fixed categories, months, and numbers; we think of these dates as absolute, and we organize our lives in accordance with them. For the medieval world, however, these divisions were much more fluid and reflected a living mirror of sacred time. Much of the emphasis on the living and mobile liturgical year that characterized time for the medievals is foreign to us. The only major religious holidays still recognized by the modern Western age are Christmas and Easter, the latter of which is a moveable religious holiday determined by the lunar calendar. When we think of those feast days, we imagine concrete dates: Christmas always occurs on the December 25, while Easter occurs in March or April. In the Middle Ages, however, religious feast days marked the passing of the seasons and the years. Many of these days were moveable and dictated by seasonal and lunar events. Medieval time was imagined as part of a natural and changing cycle. The religious calendar year was organized in large conceptual terms around the events that chronologically represented the life of Christ:

Advent, or the events leading to Christ's coming
Christ's nativity and birth
The circumcision
Epiphany, or the baptism of Christ and the adoration of the Magi
Lent, or the 40-day fast of Christ

Palm Sunday, during which Jesus re-entered Jerusalem after his
period in the desert
The Last Supper
The betrayal and crucifixion
The resurrection
The ascent into heaven
Pentecost (Whitsunday), the day on which the Holy Ghost
descended upon the Apostles

Large or significant events in the Middle Ages are frequently remembered
as occurring "on Whitsunday," "after Pentecost," and the like. These major
holidays were often the occasion for civic celebrations; the Chester Cycle,
for example, was produced initially on the feast of Corpus Christi and later
on Whitsunday. The daily calendar was also largely conceptualized in terms
of lesser feast days; in the Paston Letters, for example, a legal document
refers to a payment coming due on All Saint's Day, while the chancery
documents denote official dates as occurring "On St. Michael's Day," "St.
Luke's Day," and so on. Frustratingly for modern readers, these feast days
are not absolute. Calendars were idiosyncratic and varied from region to
region and year to year. Although the feast days of saints fill every day of
the year, which saints and feasts had primacy over others depended on
the locale and its specific traditions. A feast day for a certain saint might
be recognized on a different day in Rome than in York.

A similar concept informs the passing of the hours during the day.
Most people did not have access to a clock, so they measured time instead
by the tolling of the local church bells or by reference to the sun, which
itself routinely invoked a theological context. Church bells rang throughout the day, signaling the passing of important hours of mass. The church
divided the day into canonical hours, each corresponding both to an event
in the life of Christ and to a corresponding prayer that should be uttered
at that moment:

Matins, or the hour just after midnight
Lauds, daybreak
Prime, around 6 a.m.
Terce, midmorning
Sext, the noon hour
None, midafternoon;
Vespers, early evening
Compline, the hour just before bedtime.

The practice of dividing the day into canonical hours had originally begun in the monasteries as a means of regulating private devotion, but it soon became a standardized means of referring to the passing of time. At least some of the mass hours translated into common instruments of measure in everyday speech. Thus, we see Chaucer's Chaunticleer "feathering" his wife 20 times "before pryme" (or before 6 a.m.) and Alisoun and Nicholas frolicking until "the belle of laudes." The numerous references to events occurring after "none" also reveal a more relative perception of the passing of time, as well as the theological framework in which it unfolds. Ideally, the tolling of church bells reminded the devout layman to pause to recite a brief prayer throughout the day. Although it is unlikely that many were able to adhere to such a strict religious regimen, that spiritual reminder was always there. And when we see references in the literature to the specific hours of "Vespers" and "Matins," the religious context of prayer is nearly always present; unlike the other canonical hours, which became commonplace markers of time, these terms tend to be invoked in literature only when prayer is specifically involved.

The annual journey of life was also punctuated by the coming of familiar and pleasurable spiritual events. The religious pilgrimage that frames the *Canterbury Tales* is an example of both a common practice and the conflicting motivations that accompanied it. By the late Middle Ages, the practice of pilgrimage had become a controversial topic. Ostensibly a journey of penance or devotion to pay homage to a revered saint, pilgrimage was excoriated by the reformers, who saw in these annual treks to churches and shrines an opportunity for exploitation, drunkenness, and corruption. The aim of a pilgrimage might be the shrine of St. Thomas at Canterbury, as in Chaucer, or it might entail the long and expensive journey to Rome or Jerusalem, as undertaken by Margery Kempe. Certainly a thriving industry had arisen to support the annual throngs of pilgrims who passed through well-rehearsed routes. Hostels and inns housed and fed the travelers; trinkets and other souvenirs were manufactured to sell to pilgrims once they reached their destinations; even churches and cathedrals came to rely on the donations and monies that flooded into their treasuries from the pilgrims who freely spent once they arrived at their designated shrines. The Veronica and the pilgrim's badges worn by the corrupt Pardoner point clearly to the mercantile side of pilgrimage; the collection of badges for their own sake signaled bragging rights for all the trips undertaken and as such seem suspiciously unspiritual. Yet as an allegory for the journey that is human life, as people traveled from birth to death seeking salvation, and as an opportunity to travel and to experience new places, tastes, and people, pilgrimage married the best of both worlds. It brought together the quest for the spiritual and the pleasure of the material, providing solace both of a spiritual and physical sort. Pilgrimage enabled religious withdrawal and contemplation, but it also lent comfort and conviviality to the very human group of travelers that united for the trip.

Inextricably tied to the notion of pilgrimage was the cult of saints, whose shrines and relics made a site worthy of a pilgrimage. In addition to the canonical saints, such as Catherine, Jerome, and Francis, medieval England (and, indeed, medieval Europe) had a wealth of its own local saints, many of whom had lived in or near the parish area and whose miracles had become widely associated with that particular locale. St. Frideswide, a Mercian princess from the early eighth century, was associated with the Oxford area. St. Brigid, who died in 525, had been an abbess in Kildare; sites associated with her, including a healing well, were popular with pilgrims. The cult of St. Dunstan, who had been Archbishop of Canterbury in the tenth century, sprang up almost immediately after his death, making Canterbury (and Glastonbury, which also claimed to have his body) a popular pilgrimage site. Dunstan's popularity was eclipsed by Thomas Becket, whose martyrdom under Henry II made him an instant national hero. The Pilgrims' Way—the pilgrimage route from London to Canterbury to visit the shrine of Becket—was one of the most important in medieval Europe.

Although the journey might well be diverting, most medieval pilgrims traveled out of an authentic desire to venerate the saints. The remains of saints, however fragmentary they might be, provided a symbolic connection to the otherworld, acting as a portal from which to pass from the known to the unknown. To touch the relic was to come in physical, tangible contact with utter sanctity; according to contemporary beliefs, each relic directly conferred the spiritual and intellectual essence of the living person from which it had come. Upon visiting important pilgrimage sites, and encountering in person the presence of the saint or martyr, some pilgrims experienced ecstasies or visions. Margery Kempe, for example, describes falling into hysterical fits of weeping before the tomb of Jesus, during which she claimed to see and feel the crucifixion of Christ:

> Then they went to the church of the Holy Sepulchre in Jerusalem.... And this creature wept and sobbed as plenteously as though she had seen our Lord with her bodily eyes suffering his Passion at that time.

Before her in her soul she saw him in truth by contemplation, and
that caused her to have compassion. And when they came up on to
the Mount of Calvary, she fell down because she could not stand or
kneel, but writhed and wrestled with her body, spreading her arms
out wide, and cried with a loud voice as though her heart would
have burst apart, for in the city of her soul she saw truly and freshly
how our Lord was crucified.[3]

Although Margery's dramatic affective response to sacred sights is
extreme even for the Middle Ages, the metaphoric sensation of presence
that pilgrimage sites, shrines, and relics conveyed was a real phenomenon.
Moreover, these also functioned as *memento mori*, reminders of the ongoing
cycle of life and death, which provided perspective and inspired gratitude
for the gifts of health or fortune. To some extent the veneration of relics
crossed the line into superstition. Relics were invariably associated with
miracles and healing powers, and carrying a fragment of the true cross or
a sliver of the bone of a patron saint guaranteed the safety and health of
the wearer. The Pardoner of the *Canterbury Tales* freely intermingles folk
superstition with religious belief; his false relics, he claims, function like
charms, healing the diseases of cattle and curing jealousy. The Pardoner's
shenanigans fool no one on the pilgrimage; the medieval world was well
aware of the potential for fraud. The presence of charlatans did not dilute
the faith in real relics, however, which possessed a charged spirituality that
can hardly be overstated.

The Clerical Hierarchy

The medieval world was also reminded of its spiritual mission by a broad
administrative infrastructure. Theoretically, the church in England was a
separate body from the political one. Medieval laymen were, in essence,
governed by two distinct bodies—one political, deriving from the monarch and his aristocrats, and one religious or "clerical," derived from the
pope and mediated through a bureaucratic hierarchy over which the pope
at least nominally retained authority. Historically these two authoritative
bodies were in a constant state of tension as monarchs struggled to retain
the balance of power and authority over church decisions.

 The highest ranking members of the church were deeply entrenched
in their own politics, and despite the separation of the ruling hierarchies,
the intervention of the church in the state could be seen at almost every
level. The Archbishop of Canterbury—Courtenay from 1381 to 96 and the

formidable Thomas Arundel from 1397 to 1414—was arguably the most influential man in the state after the king. In theory, at least, the arch-bishop—who was elected by the monks at Canterbury—had a power that lay completely outside royal influence and prerogative. However, the two strongholds frequently found mutual interests. The highest levels of the clergy drew mainly from noble families, and these clergymen retained familial interests even in their religious environments. The clergy, more-over, participated in Parliament. The bishops and higher ecclesiasts took their place in the House of Lords, while the lower clergy had representa-tion in the House of Commons. There the clergy could maintain their influence over politics, pressuring the crown for legislation that would benefit the church and expressing their views on various political issues. Representation in the House of Commons decreased through the four-teenth century as "Convocations" (the equivalent of a clerical parliament, where similar debate over political matters and taxation occurred) took over as a venue for expressing the church's views.

In his adulthood, Chaucer witnessed the comings and goings of four different archbishops, whose approaches and attitudes toward the way in which the people practiced their daily worship varied widely. Under the reign of Edward III, the scholarly Simon Langham, appointed archbishop in 1366, was a vigilant custodian of religious practice in England, denounc-ing anti-papal criticism and suppressing the early radical movements that were eventually to lead to the Peasant's Revolt. Langham earned the disapproval of Edward, however, when he accepted the dignity of car-dinal without consulting with the king first. Edward III proclaimed that Langham had forfeited his see upon acceptance of his new title and took the opportunity to seize the revenues of Canterbury—always a tempting source of monies to bolster the royal coffers.

From that period on the archbishops were expected to function as pawns for the monarchy. Langham was succeeded by William Whittlesea, then by Simon Sudbury in 1375, whom the king (now Richard II) appointed Chancellor of England only five years later. People perceived the church in England—the spiritual shepherd to the people—as having sold itself for personal gain. *Piers Plowman*'s lengthy tirades against the clergy and its indebtedness to Lady Meed reflect the common disgust toward these events. It did not help that Sudbury was responsible for levy-ing the king's unpopular poll tax. When the Peasant's Revolt erupted in 1381, Sudbury was among the most prominent to be executed. England's population wanted its clergy to take its spiritual responsibilities seriously: politics and religion were expected to be exclusive domains. Later archbishops—William Courtenay and Thomas Arundel—were somewhat more careful about privileging the interests of their governed body over personal gain. Insofar as both men were rigid in their defense of orthodoxy and quick to punish perceived offenders, this change of attitude may or may not have resulted in a change for the better.

Corresponding to the double-rule of the church and state was a two-part judicial system, in which the secular courts oversaw one kind of law, the religious courts another. Whereas the secular courts enforced what we would today call "criminal" law—crimes against property, persons, and the government—church courts had jurisdiction over a wide swath of "moral" issues, such as marital complaints, wills and testaments, tithing obligations, and, to some extent, even matters of debt. Decisions in the church courts were binding, and so, as might be imagined, their presence ensured the authority of the officials who empowered them.

Such facts explain the deep fear and resentment that would have been experienced in the fourteenth century upon the appearance of the local summoner, who "summoned" the laity to the church courts for moral crimes. Chaucer's tales reflect some of these concerns. In "The Friar's Tale," a corrupt summoner can trump up all sorts of false charges against which there are very few means of defense; when he accuses a chaste widow of adultery, for example, there is little the blameless widow can do to prove her chastity other than to assert repeatedly that she is innocent. Various punishments awaited the hapless few who committed moral crimes. In 1388, Archbishop Courtenay compelled William Smyth and Roger Dexter, along with Dexter's wife, to parade through the streets "in their undershirts and drawers" for practicing Lollardy.[4] This sentence was arguably rather light, however, considering that practitioners of Lollardy could be—and later were, in great numbers—put to death. The archbishop could also mete out punishments for lesser crimes than heresy; in one instance he excommunicated three squires who forced one of his messengers to eat the wax that sealed the parchment.[5] One could also be summoned to answer to the archbishop for abandoning a marriage, for refusing to pay adequate tithes, for doing physical or property damage to any member of the clergy, or even for encroaching in any way on the authority given to any of the clergy's officers in upholding clerical law.

ANTI-SEMITISM

For the most part, religious difference was not tolerated in the Middle Ages. A case in point is the extreme intolerance, demonstrated over and over again in secular writing as well as religious texts, shown toward the Jews. Chaucer's Prioress tells a disturbingly anti-Semitic tale, in which the Jews of a near-Eastern city murder a young boy for singing the "Alma Redemptoris" in their earshot. The tale is a reminder, she says at her conclusion, of the murder of Hugh of Lincoln, "slain also by the accursed Jews" (PT 684-85). Much has been written on how to interpret Chaucer's attitude toward these lines, for the intolerance displayed in them seems at odds with the generosity toward other perspectives shown in his other writings. Critics have been reluctant to attribute such an intolerant and harsh point of view to an author who seems so tolerant in most other areas. Yet anti-Semitism was an acceptable stance in medieval England, supported by official Christian exegesis and a tradition of political intolerance. Indeed, the Jews had been banished from England for nearly 100 years by the time of the tale's writing, after one of the most notorious miscarriages of justice witnessed during the late Middle Ages.

The incident, mentioned by the Prioress at the end of her tale, occurred when the body of young Hugh of Lincoln was found in the well of a Jewish citizen, Jopin (or "Copin"). Under torture, Jopin was induced into claiming that the Jews had crucified the boy during a bizarre ritual and that, moreover, such practices were not uncommon. Not surprisingly, widespread horror resulted, which only exacerbated a religious intolerance that was already well-established. Despite being promised his life, Jopin was dragged behind a horse through the town and then subsequently hanged, and the Jews of Lincoln—many of whom were not residents, but visitors—were collectively apprehended and taken to London. Eighteen of them were executed for refusing to admit to the crime. The others were eventually pardoned and released, probably because the king, Henry III, whose brother was in possession of the Jewry at the time, relied on the Jews as a source of income. The incident was not forgotten, however, and the king did little to dispel increasing hostility. In 1290 the Jews were officially expelled from England; increased repression and expulsions in other major European cities followed throughout the fourteenth century.

The Prioress's careless attitude toward the Jews reflects what was probably a widespread sentiment among the English during Chaucer's time. Did Chaucer himself share her views? As Lee Patterson has pointed

out, acts against the Jews were promoted by monarchs as a means of align-
ing themselves with Christian values; Richard II, for example, liked to
array himself in portraiture as a crusading knight, because "banishing the
infidel" promoted his interests in styling himself as a Christian king. [6] An
anti-Semitic position was certainly considered unproblematic in England
during the time of Chaucer's productive years. Yet Chaucer's travels in
Europe throughout the 1380s and 1390s would have exposed him to some
extraordinarily unjust situations, including the massacre of the Jews in
Spain in 1391 and the abrupt expulsion of the Jews from France in 1394.
He likely interacted personally with Jews, especially while he worked
in Navarre in the 1360s. In Navarre, Jews and Muslims were integrated
and practiced a wide variety of occupations—Navarre had Jewish scribes,
Jewish courtiers, and Jewish actors. Chaucer would also have been witness to the highly politicized attacks that the Spanish king, Henry "The
Bastard," who usurped the throne from England's ally, Pedro of Castile,
made upon Jewish communities as a specific response to the fact that
Pedro had a Jewish mother. [7] Nor, according to the Jewish chroniclers,
were the English entirely innocent; they, too, participated in attacks and
forced conversions. The hypocrisy of the English position would not have
gone unnoticed, especially given that the official ecclesiastical position
preached tolerance to the Jews. Gregory X had even issued bulls denounc-
ing anti-Semitic acts as being contrary to Christianity, and questions about
faith, tolerance, and peace appear elsewhere in the theological debates.

The literature of the age, too, shows a wider variety of attitudes
toward the Jews than England's official position might suggest. The writings of Boccaccio give some indication of the range of stereotypes, as well
as the hypocrisy involved in stereotyping. In *Decameron* 1.2, Abraham,
an upright citizen and a Jew, is appalled by the corruption he sees in
Rome, although the ability of his Christian friend to retain his belief
in the face of such wrongdoing is, ironically, enough to convert him. In
Decameron 1.3 the stereotype of the miserly Jew is superficially retained:
Melchizedek is characterized as "such a miserly fellow that he would
never hand (money) over of his own free will." [8] Yet those Christians who
surround him are greedier and more willing to manipulate their victims.
Melchizedek is wise enough that he sees through the ruses of the great
Saladin. When Saladin tries to trap him into arguing over the logic of
ancient religious law, Melchizedek responds with a complicated metaphor that both acknowledges different approaches to faith and advocates
tolerance. Beginning with a parable of three rings, each of great value and
yet each indistinguishable from the others, Melchizedek concludes:

> And I say to you, my lord, that the same applies to the three laws
> which God the Father granted to His three peoples, and which
> formed the subject of your inquiry. Each of them considers itself the
> legitimate heir to His estate, each believes it possesses His one true
> law and observes His commandments. But as with the rings, the
> question as to which of them is right remains in abeyance.[9]

Tolerance and coexistence are not only possible but necessary, Melchizedek
points out, because neither the Jews, the Christians, nor the Saracens possess proof of superiority. His remarkable response is both generous and
thought-provoking enough that the wise Saladin immediately admits his
own ulterior motive in asserting the stereotype in the first place, and the
two become fast friends. Boccaccio's tale testifies to the ambivalence present in the Middle Ages about Judaism. The message, it would seem, is that
openness and understanding bridge gaps across widely different practices
and peoples. In Boccaccio's world it takes two outsiders—Saladin is, in
the eyes of the medieval world, a Saracen—to realize that communication
can create such fast bonds.

Medieval literature was thus not afraid to explore compassion toward
the Jews nor, for that matter, to the Saracens. Whether Chaucer shared his
Prioress's anti-Semitism, or whether his own reading and extensive experience abroad would have provided him the same ironic perspective in this
story that he shows in his other tales, then, remains an open question. What
we do know is that even the most orthodox of writers found the debate
complicated enough to defy simple responses or attitudes.

RELIGIOUS ORDERS AND RELIGIOUS PROFESSIONALS

There were a great many religious officials in the Middle Ages, each of
whom had their own jurisdiction over highly specialized areas of spiritual
governance. One of the most visible characteristics of the motley group
of pilgrims who accompany the narrator to Canterbury is the variety of
religious professions on parade there: the aforementioned Summoner, but
also the Monk, the Friar, the Pardoner, the Parson, the Prioress, the nuns,
and the Nun's Priest. Each of these professions represents a tightly defined
sphere of influence and authority. The clerical bureaucracy was made up of
a complex administrative body responsible for overseeing large areas and
populations. Its largest unit was the diocese, which in England was (and
still is) overseen by the heads of the two largest geographical provinces of
Canterbury and York. The archbishops of these two regions had seniority

over all other English clerics and were responsible for the various "sees" that fell within their geographical domain. Where Canterbury had 18 sees, York had three. A bishop—essentially the next in command—presided over each diocese, which contained further subdivisions; the diocese was made up of archdeaconries, supervised by a bishop-appointed archdeacon, and the archdeaconry was made up of deaneries, supervised by a dean. At the smallest level of organization was the parish, which was headed by a parish priest or parson, the loweliest clergyman in the clerical chain. The parish was directly responsible for religious management of the people and the general care of souls. Over 8,800 parishes flourished in England by the end of the fourteenth century.

Complicating this basic administrative structure were the religious houses, whose clerical authority lay somewhat alongside and independent of the ecclesiastical hierarchy. Among these higher regular orders, vows of celibacy and mindful poverty were required. As their model for this kind of obedience, monks and nuns chose the enclosed life of the monastery and cloister, a lifestyle intended to echo Jesus' period in the desert. The idea was that they would live in isolation, following vows of poverty through self-subsistence and spending their days in prayer and spiritual work. The friars, on the other hand, modeled their path after the wanderings of the apostles, traveling among the people to preach and take confession, living off the charity of others. Both monks and friars belonged to an "order," that is, a religious community under a specific ascetic rule that provided a structure and way of spiritual living. When Chaucer says of the Friar that "of the orders foure" was there no "that kan so muchel of daliaunce and fair langage," he refers to the four mendicant orders to which a friar in the Middle Ages in England might belong—the Augustinians, the Carmelites, the Franciscans, or the Dominicans—and whose expansion into England took hold in the late thirteenth century, so that by the writing of the *Canterbury Tales* they were so numerous that they could be found, as the Wife of Bath complains, "in every bussh or under every tree" (WT 879).

Some of these religious orders were subject to the administrative control of the episcopate as described above (the archbishop, for example, had the authority to visit and critique the religious houses). In other cases, however, it was the other way around: the religious house—that is, the abbey or cathedral—had control over the parish and collected monies from it. The intricate bureaucracy of the church and its various institutions made the chain of command somewhat elastic, opening its members to the various concerns of worldly competition for control and the monies that went with it (although the clergy made up less than 5 per cent of the overall population, they held over 25 per cent of the nation's wealth).[10]

These various religious occupations provided career opportunities for those who otherwise might have few options for advancement. Men, in particular, could pursue clerical training and from there proceed either into the priesthood or into a nonreligious administrative position in government or an aristocratic household. With an education from one of the universities, a bright or well-connected young man could seek out a position in which he might be able to help manage the affairs of either a nobleman or even a higher ranking religious official. Such positions invariably required patronage; very little in the Middle Ages was gained through hard work alone. But talent and diligence might win the admiration of someone who could help out a career, and from there one might eventually even be able to procure a benefice.

Those without a university education or aristocratic background were less able to rise up the ecclesiastical ladder. However, the lower echelons of the clergy, including the parsons, parish priests, and chaplains, allowed those of modest origins to make a small stipend caring for the spiritual welfare of everyday people. They took confession, said the mass, and offered spiritual guidance, both in the local noble households and in the parish villages. Some education was required; at each level members of the minor clergy took an examination that ensured at least some literacy and training (although complaints about the woeful Latin and training of the clergy after the Black Plague were numerous). There are complaints in the late fourteenth century about those who were concerned more for their wages than for the salvation of souls, but serious and well-meaning spiritual providers could nevertheless be found among the minor orders. Such a one presumably inspired Chaucer's Parson, who seeks no benefice or career advancement and who models, as best he can, the life he preaches.

CORRUPTION AND ANTICLERICALISM

Of course, as is clear from the discussion above, the reality was that not every religious figure adhered to the ideal. Complaints about the corruption of the clergy are numerous in the late fourteenth century, many of these appearing in a standard format and structure that has come commonly to be known as "estates satire." William Langland's *Piers Plowman* and John Gower's *Vox Clamantis* (excerpted below) are famous examples of this genre, which analyzes society in terms of the various "estates" of warrior, preacher, and laborer and the degrees to which the individualized professions fall from those ideals. Both Langland and Gower complain of clergymen who know little Latin and who are generally inept at their spiritual duties. In this passage from *Piers Plowman A*, the noble king rejects wrongdoing, especially those who would use "meed" or compensation to buy out wrong's crimes. Reason supports him in this act:

> "Counsel me not," said Reason, "to have compassion at all
> Until lords and ladies all love the truth....
> Till clerks and knights speak with more courtesy,
> And repent of their ribaldry and repeat it no longer;
> Till priests ponder their preaching and apply it to themselves,
> And by their example inspire us to good ... " (IV.100–108)

Incompetence and what seemed to be a lackadaisical attitude toward clerical duty were widespread problems after the Plague. The shortage of educated clergy resulted in the rise of those whom many considered detrimental to the spiritual care of their flock. As *Piers Plowman* suggests, however, the more troubling problem was the glaring corruption of the late fourteenth century: the clergy no longer followed "truth," but answered the call of "meed." Estates satire abounds in similar examples.

Several factors contributed to this growing sense of disenchantment with the organized church, including the Great Schism of 1378, when the papacy became divided between Avignon and Rome; the practice of selling papal indulgences to help pay for church improvements; and the flagrant selling of church benefices (or "simony"). Dante includes a special place deep in Hell for the simonists, whom he plants head downward into deep holes in the earth, while their feet, flailing wildly above, are continually burnt with fire. Dante classifies simony as a sin of fraud resulting from extreme cupidity; the simonists debase both the church they are chosen to represent and the people they are supposed to heal.

Even more problematic were the selling of pardons, or "indulgences." An indulgence was the equivalent of penance; the indulgence would relieve the sinner of years spent in Purgatory. Commercialized mid-fourteenth century by Pope Clement VI, the sale of indulgences arose out of the church's need for funds. Although special indulgences had been granted for centuries to reward Christians for services like participating in the Crusades, in the late Middle Ages these rewards began to be granted for special "almsgiving"—monetary acts of charity that benefited the church. In other words, a certain sum of money "charitably" contributed to the church could result in years off from Purgatory. Of course, outrage quickly rose at the idea that heavenly grace might be sold. But many, anxious for their eternal souls, readily embraced the practice, as the Pardoner of Chaucer's *Canterbury Tales* attests.

The Great Schism crystallized the ongoing problems with papal authority. Although the official dates of the schism span from 1378 to 1417, when first two and then three rivals claimed the title of pope, the tensions and the vying for power that led to the schism reflected the political aspirations of the European nations and went far back in time. The papacy had been moved from Rome to Avignon in 1309 under Pope Clement V, and the French monarch had enjoyed a long-standing influence over papal decisions because of it. Gregory XI moved the papacy back to Rome in 1377, but when he died only a year later, the French were still anxious to reassert their prerogative. The College of Cardinals elected an Italian pope in 1378 but invalidated their own election only a short while later. Thus Europe became split between two living popes, each of whom claimed legitimate election. England, the Holy Roman Empire, and almost all of Italy supported Urban VI in Rome, while France, Scotland, Naples, Sicily, and Spain sided with Clement VII in Avignon. The problem was not resolved until the Council of Constance (1414-17), which finally deposed all the claimants and elected a new pope, Martin V, instead.

The troubles of the papacy reverberated throughout the medieval world in almost irreparable ways. For one thing, it became abundantly clear that the highest levels of the church had become unacceptably politicized. How could the pope, the highest level of authority sanctioned to ensure the safety of the world's souls, claim to be the elected official of God when it was not entirely clear who had been elected? Given the crises and corruption that percolated throughout the authorized church, it is perhaps not surprising that spirituality in the late Middle Ages increasingly focused on individual and private forms of devotion.

In some cases, these new forms of devotion led to the outright rejection of the institutions and hierarchies of the Catholic Church. Among the most prominent dissenters was John Wyclif, an Oxford theologian who had been passed by on numerous occasions for religious offices. Recognized even during his own lifetime for his brilliance in theology and scholastic learning, Wyclif achieved political influence quickly under Edward III, who appointed him as his representative for important papal negotiations in 1374. Wyclif criticized the rampant corruption among the clergy, despising the opulent lifestyles that many church officials had adopted in blatant contrast to their vows of poverty and abstinence. The crisis in

Avignon seemed a bitter confirmation of what was already patently clear: the medieval church had forgotten its mission and had instead turned toward serving its own corrupt officials. Wyclif's criticism went much farther than merely targeting individuals, however. He advocated a return to the simple and direct form of religion that he saw encouraged in scripture. He wrote unflinchingly that the church had no need for a pope at all, nor indeed for that administrative hierarchy of friars, monks, priests, and other officials who "mediated" between scripture and the people. He believed that laymen should have direct access to scripture and should be able to read it for themselves in their own language. Perhaps most controversially, Wyclif wrote against the doctrine of transubstantiation, arguing that the entire elaborate belief system premised on the Eucharist was based on a misreading of the Last Supper. Wyclif also had a direct role in the first translation of the Bible into English; a translation of the four Gospels and possibly some of the later books of the New Testament was completed under his initiative by 1388. As the documents below show, Wyclif's beliefs were forceful and uncompromising. Many of the elaborate practices of late medieval religiosity, he attested, had become cumbersome, and he showed no hesitation in letting his opinions be known.

Not surprisingly, the established church did not take this criticism lightly. Wyclif's career stalled as he incurred the wrath of officials whose positions were threatened by the appeal his arguments had among both the nobles and the common people. Although he enjoyed the patronage and support of John of Gaunt, who encouraged his outspokenness against the church for his own political and financial reasons, Wyclif was summoned before William Courtenay—at that point the bishop of London—in 1377 on the charge of heresy. He escaped serious consequence on this occasion, largely because of the patronage of the powerful Gaunt. In the aftermath of the Peasant's Revolt, however, with Courtenay now elected archbishop, Wyclif was not so lucky. His fundamental propositions—particularly those dealing with the transformation of the Eucharist and his views on the administration of the church—were condemned in 1382 as erroneous and heretical.

The influence of Wyclif and his followers upon contemporary anticlerical literature has been much debated. While it cannot be denied that anticlerical attitudes are omnipresent in the second half of the fourteenth century, as we have noted already in the examples of *Piers Plowman*, the *Vox Clamantis*, and the *Canterbury Tales*, whether that sentiment was directly due to the influence of Wyclif or the pervasive dissatisfaction of the period is difficult to determine. John Ball confessed to being a follower of Wyclif during his imprisonment, and it seems probable that Ball gained at least some encouragement and justification for his political and religious opinions from Wyclif's London sermons. Yet scholars have generally assumed that economic and social factors were more responsible for the revolt than these sermons. However the case may be, the attitudes expressed in all of these texts are a product of the social conditions of the times, and their mutual influence fueled an increasing sense of the need for reform.

Certainly the condemnation of 1382 did little to quell the momentum that arose from Wyclif's teachings. The religious movement of Lollardy disseminated his opinions among laymen and appealed to pious members among both the gentry and the literate middle class, who circulated scriptural readings translated into English and formed local groups to read and discuss them. Indeed, the Lollards went to a great deal of effort to produce copies of translations for popular consumption, and they were no less outspoken than Wyclif in condemning some of the more flagrant abuses of the authorized church and of the people who practiced according to its teachings. In addition to their more orthodox reformist assertions, the Lollards also believed that anyone should have the right to preach, including women, and that the church should not have the reserved right of appointing the shepherds to take care of the spiritual flock. Divine inspiration, they asserted, was a better source of truth than the ecclesiastical hierarchy.

It is not clear how pervasive the Lollard movement was, nor how many practitioners there were. In actuality it was probably quite limited. Conformity to the dominant religious practice was expected among the laity, and difference was, for the most part, not tolerated; under Archbishop Arundel, especially, open adherence to the movement became increasingly dangerous. The mystic Margery Kempe describes having been accused on more than one occasion of Lollardy, sometimes to such an extent that she feared for her very life. Her autobiography, dictated to a priest many years after the events she recounts, maintains her adherence to accepted doctrine, despite her insistence on her obligation to speak of her visionary experiences.

As the accusations against Margery illustrate, the Lollard movement became an increasingly disturbing entity to the established church, which was threatened by the notion that an uninformed laity might take doctrine into its own hands. Religious officials were right to be alarmed, for the Lollards were outspoken in their insistence that the Church's authoritarian hold on knowledge and access to religious literature amounted to little more than a will to power over others. Among the Twelve Conclusions of the Lollards (SEE BELOW) is a paragraph condemning the practice of confession. Mandating confession, the Lollards held, concentrated too much power into the hands of a religious official who may or may not have had the education and the best interests of the parishioner at heart:

> That auricular confession which is said to be so necessary to the salvation of a man, with its pretended power of absolution, exalts the arrogance of priests and gives them opportunity of other secret colloquies which we will not speak of; for both lords and ladies attest that, for fear of their confessors, they dare not speak the truth.[11]

The document goes on to imply that corrupt confessors take advantage of the secrets revealed by their flock to extort bribes or even sexual favors. The church's interest in insinuating itself into the private minds of individuals, the Lollards averred, manifested more often as manipulation and abuse than as an interest in the ultimate salvation of the soul.

Indeed, much of the Lollard's criticism was directed toward the accumulation of power and money by the established church. Particularly offensive to the church was the Lollards' assertion—following Wyclif—that the clergy should not own property and that established endowments by the aristocrats and gentry should be abolished. In 1409, as a means of controlling the movement, Archbishop Arundel passed legislation banning the possession or reading of any scripture translated into English. This move was supported by Henry IV, who shared the ecclesiastical fear that Lollardy constituted a threat to the entire notion of class and property. Insofar as the Lollards seem to have been instructed to recant or flee rather than to martyr themselves, the ownership of suspect books seemed the readiest means by which to identify potential heretics. The burning of books following a conviction of heresy was normal. When, in 1414, the Lollard knight Sir John Oldcastle attempted a coup against Henry, these fears seemed more than justified. The movement was put down, Oldcastle was executed, and Lollardy was thenceforth rigorously suppressed. Another small rebellion ensued in 1431, but for the most part the movement was forced underground.

Why didn't Lollardy succeed? A variety of factors probably contributed to the movement's demise, including an overall inability to disseminate information widely. The Reformation inspired by Martin Luther in 1517 had the advantage of the printing press; printing came too late to benefit Lollardy in the aftermath of Arundel's barriers against unmediated scripture. Also important to the later movement were the increased numbers of those who were able to read, which resulted in the growing independence of education from the church. As Anne Hudson remarks in *The Premature Reformation*, "As long as the church retained almost complete dominance in schooling, any reform movement that brushed with heresy could gain no direct advantage from wider educational opportunities; even elementary instruction could become a vehicle for reinforcement of orthodoxy and of the ecclesiastical status quo."[12]

Had Wyclif and his followers been able to implement a coherent program of reform during the late Middle Ages, the changes to the practice of religion would likely have been profound and probably much more so than the reformist changes that came about under Thomas Cromwell and Henry VIII in the 1530s. The Eucharist would have been established primarily as a memorial and figurative event; predestination, with its implication of a priesthood of the elect, would have diminished the power of all sacraments and physical manifestations of the temporal church. Scripture, placed at the center of worship and made available to all, would have displaced the recitation of the offices, and Puritan-style preaching, readings, and discussion would have dominated the mode of spiritual education. Some Lollard proposals, including the disendowment of the regular clergy and the payment of mass priests, were implemented under Henry VIII's reforms, but the idea of a complete separation between church and state, and the confinement of the clergy to spiritual matters, was not fully implemented until the Commonwealth. The Lollard rejection of images, pilgrimages, and church ornamentation found only partial implementation in the sixteenth-century reforms; only the more extreme Puritan groups were ever to fully support these ideas in force.

❧

DOCUMENTS

FROM *On Christian Doctrine*. ST. AUGUSTINE (*c.* 396-427)

Although it is a very early work, *On Christian Doctrine* may be the single most influential text on interpretation for medieval writers. St. Augustine posited two important claims: first, that sacred truths are to be understood on a figurative rather than a literal level and that those who fail to understand language on this level condemn their very souls; and, second, that the works of the pagan authors could legitimately be reinterpreted according to a Christian and theological set of precepts in order to glean their moral value. This conviction encouraged scholastic thinkers to write extensive commentaries on classic works, relocating them in a Christian context (SEE CHAPTER 6).

II.X

There are two reasons why things written are not understood: they are obscured either by unknown or by ambiguous signs. For signs are either literal or figurative. They are called literal when they are used to designate those things on account of which they were instituted; thus we say *bos* [ox] when we mean an animal of a herd because all men using the Latin language call it by that name just as we do. Figurative signs occur when that thing which we designate by a literal sign is used to signify something else; thus we say "ox" and by that syllable understand the animal which is ordinarily designated by that word, but again by that animal we understand an evangelist, as is signified in the Scripture, according to the interpretation of the Apostle, when it says, "Thou shalt not muzzle the ox that treadeth out the corn."

II.XL

If those who are called philosophers, especially the Platonists, have said things which are indeed true and are well accommodated to our faith, they should not be feared; rather, what they have said should be taken from them as from unjust possessors and converted to our use. Just as the Egyptians had not only idols and grave burdens which the people of Israel detested and avoided, so also they had vases and ornaments of gold and silver and clothing which the Israelites took with them secretly when they fled, as if to put them to a better use. They did not do this on their own authority but at God's commandment, while the Egyptians unwittingly supplied them with things which they themselves did not use well. In the same way all the teachings of the pagans contain not only simulated and superstitious imaginings and grave burdens of unnecessary labor, which each one of us leaving the society of pagans under the leadership of Christ ought to abominate and avoid, but also liberal disciplines more suited to the uses of truth, and some most useful precepts concerning morals....

III. V

For at the outset you must be very careful lest you take figurative
expressions literally. What the Apostle says pertains to this problem:
"For the letter killeth, but the spirit quickeneth." That is, when
that which is said figuratively is taken as though it were literal, it is
understood carnally. Nor can anything more appropriately be called
the death of the soul than that condition in which the thing which
distinguishes us from beasts, which is the understanding, is subjected
to the flesh in the pursuit of the letter....There is a miserable
servitude of the spirit in this habit of taking signs for things, so that
one is not able to raise the eye of the mind above things that are
corporal and created to drink in eternal light.

"RELIGIOUS SYMBOLISM." WILLIAM DURANDUS (1286)

William Durandus wrote his *Rationale Divinorum Officiorum* ("The
Symbolism of Churches and Church Ornaments") in the late thirteenth
century. It provides a sense of the rich overlay of meaning that religious
symbols carried for the medieval mind.

Sometimes also representation is made of the four living creatures
spoken of in the visions of Ezekiel and the aforesaid John: the face
of a man and the face of a lion on the right, the face of an ox on
the left, and the face of an eagle above the four. These be the Four
Evangelists. Whence they be painted with books by their feet,
because by their words and writings they have instructed the minds
of the faithful, and accomplished their own works. Matthew hath the
figure of a man, Mark of a lion. These be painted on the right hand:
because the nativity and the resurrection of Christ were the general
joy of all: whence in the Psalms: "And gladness at the morning." But
Luke is the ox: because he beginneth from Zachary the priest, and
treateth more specially of the Passion and Sacrifice of Christ: now
the ox is an animal fitted for sacrifice. He is also compared to the ox,
because of the two horns, as containing the two testaments; and the
four hoofs, as having the sentences of the four Evangelists. By this
also Christ is figured, who was the sacrifice for us: and therefore the
ox is painted on the left side, because the death of Christ was the
trouble of the apostles. Concerning this, and how blessed Mark is
depicted, in the seventh part. But John hath the figure of the eagle:

because, soaring to the utmost height, he saith, "In the beginning was the word." This also representeth Christ, "Whose youth is renewed like the eagle's": because, rising from the dead, He ascendeth into heaven. Here, however, it is not portrayed as by the side, but as above, since it denoteth the ascension, and the word pronounced of God. But how, since each of the living creatures hath four faces and four wings, they can be depicted, shall be said hereafter....

And note that the patriarchs and prophets are painted with wheels in their hands. Some of the apostles with books and some with wheels: namely, because before the advent of Christ the faith was set forth under figures, and many things were not yet made clear; to represent this, the patriarchs and prophets are painted with wheels, to signify that imperfect knowledge. But because the apostles were perfectly taught of Christ, therefore the books, which are the emblems of this perfect knowledge, are open. But because some of them reduced their knowledge in writing, to the instruction of others, therefore fittingly they are represented with books in their hands like doctors. So Paul, and the Evangelists, Peter, James, and Jude. But others, who wrote nothing which has lasted, or been received into the canon by the Church, are not portrayed with books, but with wheels, as a type of their preaching. Whence the Apostle to the Ephesians, "And he gave some apostles, and some prophets, and some evangelists, and some pastors and teachers for the work of the ministry."

But the Divine Majesty is also portrayed with a closed book in the hands: "which no man was found worthy to open but the Lion of the tribe of Juda." And sometimes with an open book: that in it every one may read that "He is the Light of the world": "and the Way, the Truth, and the Life": and the Book of life [is also portrayed]. But why Paul is represented at the right, and Peter at the left of the Saviour, we shall show hereafter.

"The Lives of Spiritual Women." *The Ancrene Wisse* (13TH C)

Despite our modern tendency to focus on the abuses of the medieval church, religious sensibility was a strong component of premodern identity. The following extract, from the mid-thirteenth century *Ancrene Wisse*, illustrates a spiritual approach for women who devote themselves to the anchoritic life. Written for three women of some education and social expectation, who have chosen to "enclose" themselves from the living and dedicate themselves to a religious and chaste existence, the text provides a warm understanding of human life and what it means to give up participation in the world. Based loosely on the "rules" guiding solitary life for recluses, the *Ancrene Wisse* is less a rule than a guidebook, offering advice, solace, and moral edification for those who dedicate themselves to a spiritual existence. As such its piety and the forms of devotion it advocates are fairly representative of lay devotional practices in the late Middle Ages.

> *Omnia custodia serva cor tuum quia ex ipso vita procedit* (*Proverbs* 4:23). "Protect your heart well with every kind of defense, daughter," says Solomon, "for if she is well locked away, the soul's life is in her." The heart's guardians are the five senses, sight and hearing, tasting and smelling, and the feeling in every part. And we must speak of all of them, for whoever protects these well does as Solomon commands: protects well their heart and their soul's health. The heart is a most wild beast and makes many a light leap out. As St. Gregory says, *Nichil corde fugiatus,* "nothing flies out of a person sooner than their own heart." David, God's prophet, at one time mourned that she had escaped him: *Cor meum dereliquit me* (*Psalm* 39:13), that is, "My heart has fled from me." And another time he rejoices and says that she has come home: *Invenit servu tuus cor suum* (2 *Samuel* 7:27)—"Lord," he says, "my heart has come back again; I have found her." When so holy a man and so wise and so wary lets her escape, anyone else may anxiously dread her flight. And where did she break out of David, the holy king, God's prophet? Where? God knows, at the window of his eye, because of one sight that he saw while looking out just once, as you will hear after.
>
> Therefore my dear sisters, love your windows as little as you possibly can. Let them all be little, the parlor's smallest and narrowest. Let the cloth in them be of two kinds: the cloth black, the cross white, both inside and outside. The black cloth symbolizes to the world outside that you are black and unworthy, and that the true sun has burned you outwardly, and so made you as outwardly unlovely as you are, with the gleams of his grace (*Canticles* 1:5). The white cross is proper to you. For there are three crosses, red and black and white. The red is proper to those who are ruddied and reddened as the martyrs were through the shedding of their blood for God's love. The black cross is proper to those who are doing their penance in the world for terrible sins. The white cross is rightly proper to

white maidenhood and to purity, which it is very hard to keep well. By a cross, hardship is always to be understood—so the white cross symbolizes the defense of white chastity, which it is very hard to protect well. The black cloth, apart from its symbolism, does less harm to the eyes and is thicker against the wind and harder to see through, and keeps its color better against the wind and other things. Look that your parlor cloth is fastened on every side and well-attached, and guard your eyes there in case your heart flies out and goes away as it did from David, and your soul sickens as soon as she is gone.

"Interpretations of Biblical Verse on the Conduct of Women." *The Ancrene Wisse* (13ᵗʰc)

Also of interest in the *Ancrene Wisse* are the commonplace interpretations of biblical verse which lay the fault for sexual temptation on women. It does not matter how the woman feels or thinks, the anonymous author says explicitly, but rather what desire her body elicits in others. Thus, it is the woman's prerogative to control the sight of men who might desire her by concealing her body, which is a trap or "pit" into which all fall and metaphorically experience the correlating pit of hell. In this understanding, Eve's taking of the apple is to be understood as a kind of giving in to sexual temptation: her eyes lead her to desire the apple, and the apple corresponds to lust or physical desire. Similarly, Bathsheba is to blame for David's lust: he sees her naked body bathing, and her body tempts him to sin. In *Sir Gawain and the Green Knight*, Gawain blames all women for men's sexual transgressions, pardoning both Adam and David for succumbing to physical desire because of the "wiles" of women.

> Of Eve our first mother it is written that sin found its very first entry into her through her sight … that is, "Eve looked on the forbidden apple and saw it was fair; and she began to delight in looking at it, and set her desire on it, and took and ate of it, and gave it to her husband." See how Holy Writ speaks and how profoundly it tells the way sin began, thus: sight went before and made a way for harmful desire—and the act that all humanity feels came after it.
>
> This apple, dear sister, symbolizes all the things that desire and the delight of sin turn to. When you look at a man, you are in Eve's situation: you look at the apple. If someone had said to Eve when

she first cast her eye on it, "Ah, Eve, go away, you are looking at your death," what would she have answered? "My dear sir, you are wrong, why are you challenging me? The apple that I look on is forbidden me to eat, not to look at!" Thus would Eve readily enough have answered. O my dear sisters, Eve has many daughters who follow their mother, who answer in this way: "But do you think," someone says, "that I will leap on him just because I look at him?" God knows, dear sister, stranger things have happened. Eve your mother leapt after her eyes, from the eye to the apple, from the apple in paradise down to the earth, from the earth to hell, where she lay in prison four thousand years and more, she and her husband both, and condemned all her offspring to leap after her to death without end. The beginning and the root of all this sorrow was one light look; just so, as it is often said, much comes from little. So let every weak woman fear greatly—seeing that she who had just then been wrought by the hands of God was betrayed through a single look, and brought into deep sin which spread over all the world.

.... "A maiden, Jacob's daughter, called Dinah," as it tells in Genesis, "went out to look at strange women"—yet it does not say that she looked at men. And what do you think came of that looking? She lost her maidenhood and was made a whore. Therefore, because of that same act, the pledges of high patriarchs were broken and a great city was burned, and the king, his son, and the citizens were slain, the women led away. Her father and her brothers were made outlaws, noble princes though they were. This is what came of her looking. The Holy Spirit caused all such things to be written in the book to warn women of their foolish eyes. And take note of this; that this evil caused by Dinah did not come from the fact that she saw Hamor's son, whom she sinned with, but came from her letting him lay eyes on her—for what he did to her was very much against her will at first.

In the same way Bathsheba, by uncovering herself in David's sight, caused him to sin with her, a holy king though he was, and God's prophet. Now, here comes a weak man—though he holds himself estimable if he has a wide hood and a closed cloak—and he wants to see some young anchoresses. And he just has to see whether her looks please him, she whose face has not been burnt by the sun—as if he was a stone! And he says she may confidently look upon holy men—yes, someone like him, with his wide sleeves. But, arrogant sir, have you not heard about David, God's own darling? –Of whom God himself said *inveni virum secundum cor meum* (*Acts* 13.22): I have found," he said, "a man after my own heart." This man, whom God himself in this precious saying declared a king and a prophet chosen above all, this man, because of one look cast on a woman as she washed herself, let out his heart and forgot himself, so that he did three immeasurably serious and mortal sins: with Bathsheba, the lady he looked at, adultery; on his faithful knight, Uriah her lord, treachery and murder (2 *Samuel* 11). And you, a sinful man, are so brazen as to cast foolish eyes upon a young woman! Yes, my dear sisters, if anyone is eager to see you, never believe good of it, but trust him the less. I would not have it that anyone see you unless he has special leave from your director. For all the three sins I have just spoken about, and all the evil caused by Dinah that I spoke about before, all came about not because the women looked foolishly on men, but because they uncovered themselves in the sight of men, and did things through which they had to fall into sin.

For this reason it was commanded in God's law that a pit should always be covered, and if anyone uncovered a pit and a beast fell in, the one who had uncovered the pit had to pay for it (*Exodus* 21:33-34). This is a most fearsome saying for a woman who shows herself to the eyes of men. She is symbolized by the one who uncovers the pit; the pit is her fair face and her white neck and light eyes, and her hand, if she holds it out in his sight. And also her words are a pit, unless they are well-chosen. Everything to do with her, whatever it may be, which might readily awaken sinful love, our Lord calls all of it a pit. This pit he commanded to be covered, lest any beast fall in, and drown in sin.

Alma Redemptoris Mater (11ᵗʰc)

The "Alma Redemptoris Mater," chanted in Chaucer's "Prioress's Tale" by the young Christian boy, was a popular medieval antiphon praising the Virgin Mary. Traditionally sung at Compline, the song is attributed to Hermannus Contractus, who based the words upon the writings of some of the early church fathers.

> As I lay upon a night,
> My thought was on a maiden so bright,
> That men call Mary, full of might,
> Redemptoris Mater.

To her came Gabriel with light
And said: Hail be thou, blissful wight!
To be called now art thou named
Redemptoris Mater.

At that word that lady bright
Anon conceived God full of might;
Then men know well that she is called
Redemptoris Mater.

When Jesu on the rood was fastened,
Mary was doleful of that sight
Till she saw Him rise upright,
Redemptoris Mater.

Jesu, that sittest in heaven light,
Grant us to come before Thy sight
With that maiden that is so bright,
Redemptoris Mater.

A Myrour to Lewde Men and Wymmen (14TH c)

This extract, from an anonymous late fourteenth-century treatise on devotion, provides the official and doctrinal stance toward pilgrimage as a spiritual journey that symbolically embodies the long passage of life as a quest for God.

> For it is so that all mankind in this world is not but in exile and wilderness out of his natural country, or as is a pilgrim or a wayfaring man in a strange land where he may in no manner abide, but of necessity every day, every hour and every time is passing on his way, as Holy Writ witnesses and says thus: *Non habemus hic manentem civitatem, sed futuram inquirimus,* "We have here no city or place of dwelling or abiding," that is to understand no place that we may, "but we seek another that is going to come." And that is but one of two cities, of the which that one city may be called the city of Jerusalem, that is to say the city of peace, and that other the city of Babylon, that is to say confusion. And by this city of Jerusalem, that

city of peace, may be understood the endless bliss of heaven, where
there is endless peace, joy, and rest without hindrance. And this city of
Babylon, that is confusion, it may be understood the endless pain of
hell, where all manner of confusion, shame and disgrace, sorrow and
woe, shall be without end.

And since then all of a man's living in this world is not but a
going or a moving either way to one of these two cities, that is to say
to endless bliss or to endless pain, the holy doctor Saint Augustine in
his meditations teaches us and says thus: with vigilance, taking busy
mind, sovereign effort, and continual busyness, it behooves us to learn
and inquire by what manner and by what way we may shun the pain
of hell and purchase the bliss of heaven; for that pain, he says, may
not be shunned nor that joy purchased except by the way we know.
And as we may see these two cities are contraries in their conditions
each to the other, so be the roads that lead to them each contrary
to the other; which roads be not else except that one that leads to
endless bliss is virtues and virtuous living, and that other that leads to
endless pain is sin and sinful living.

And because a man may not know in which of these two ways he
goes in, nor hitherward he is but he knows what virtue is and what
sin is, therefore this writing is made for lewd and meanly lettered
men and women in such tongue as they can best understand, and
may be called a mirror to lewd men and women in which they may
see God through steadfast belief and himself through meekness, and
what is virtue and what is sin. And for this or no other good deed
may be done without the help and grace of almighty God that of his
endless goodness will send to a man plenteously through holy desire
and devout prayer—as our Lord Jesus Christ promises us in many
places of the gospel, and to that end he taught his holy apostles and
by them us all, how we should pray and what—therefore this writing
shall begin with that holy prayer that Christ himself made and taught,
that is the Pater Noster, as the gospel bears witness. And first in this
writing shall be showed the profit and fruit and the dignity of the
holy prayer the Pater Noster; afterward the seven askings that are in
the Pater Noster; and the seven gifts of the Holy Ghost that we ask
thereby; and the seven head sins that the seven gifts put away; and the
seven virtues that the seven gifts set in the place of the seven sins; and
the seven joys of heaven that the seven virtues bring to us; and also
the seven rewards that bring to thee the seven joys of heaven.

"AGAINST PILGRIMAGE." LOLLARDIST TREATISE (14THC)

This contrasting document, from a fourteenth-century Lollard text, shows the other side of pilgrimage. Pointing to the decadent inns, restaurants, and jollities that might accompany a group of pilgrims along their route, the text is a nice illustration of the realities of medieval life on the road. Our translation is based on Anne Hudson's edition of Wycliffite texts.

These pilgrimages and offerings seem brought up of caution of the fiend and his covetous and worldly clerks, for commonly such pilgrimages be in the maintaining of lechery, of gluttony, of drunkenness, of extortions, of wrongs, and worldly vanities. For men that may not hunt their lechery at home as they would, for fear of lords, or magistrates, and for clamor of neighbors, they cast many days before and gather what they may, sore pining themselves to spare it, to go out of the country in pilgrimages for fair images, and lie in the going in lechery, in gluttony, in drunkenness, and maintain falseness of hostelers, of cooks, of taverners, and vainly spend their good and leave the true labor that they should do at home in help of themselves and their neighbors, boasting of their gluttony when they come home, that they never drank but wine in all the journey, by which misspending great parties of the people fare war in their household the half year after, and in hap become in debt that they never quit. But men that do extortions and falsely get cattle be lightly assailed hereof, and charged in confession to do such pilgrimages and offerings. And some men do it of their own great will rather to see fairer countries than for any sweet devotion in their souls to God or to the saints that they seek. And thus is true satisfaction lost, and foul wrongs and extortions maintained, and the poor people wickedly piled; and these high synagogues have been repositories of thefts and nourishing of sins by privileges and subtle hypocrisy. And hereby these churches that should be houses of devout prayer and holiness, they have been made dens of thieves and synagogues of Satan's; and this is commonly the fruit of these pilgrimages and offerings.

Margery Kempe's Pilgrimage to Rome and Jerusalem. Margery Kempe (*c.* 1436-38)

Margery Kempe was a mystic and a reformer, who claimed during her latter life to have vivid visions of Christ. She was an outspoken critic of the hypocrisy and abuse of her times, as well as an enthusiastic pilgrim, undertaking long and hazardous pilgrimages to famous sites in the Holy Land. The following is a description of her reaction to the sight and presence of holy relics and places during her trips to the Church of the Holy Sepulchre and the Mount of Calvary.

> When this creature with her fellowship came to the grave where our Lord was buried, anon, as she entered that holy place, she fell down with her candle in her hand and she should have died for sorrow. And after she rose up again with great weeping and sobbing as though she had seen our Lord buried even before her. Then she thought she saw Our Lady in her soul, how she mourned and how she wept over her son's death, and then was our lady's sorrow her own sorrow. And so over all wherever the friars led them in that holy place she always wept and sobbed wonderfully, and especially when she came where our Lord was nailed on the cross. There she cried and wept without measure so that she might not restrain herself. Also they came to a stone of marble that our Lord was laid on when he was taken down off the cross, and there she wept with great compassion, having mind of our Lord's Passion. Afterwards she was given communion on the Mount of Calvary, and then she wept, she sobbed, she cried so loud that it was a wonder to hear it. She was so full of holy thoughts and meditations and holy contemplations in the Passion of our Lord Jesus Christ and holy dalliance that our Lord Jesus Christ relayed to her soul that she could never express them after, so high and so holy they were. Great was the grace that our Lord showed to this creature while she was in Jerusalem three weeks. Another day early in the morning they went again to the great hills. And her guides told where our Lord bore the cross on his back, and where His Mother met with Him, and how she swooned, and how she fell down also. And so they went forth all the morning until they came to Mount Syon. And ever the creature wept abundantly all the way that she went for compassion of our Lord's Passion. In the Mount Syon is a place where our Lord washed his disciples' feet, and a little from there he made his Last Supper with his disciples. And

therefore this creature had great desire to be given communion in that holy place where our merciful Lord Christ Jesus first consecrated his precious body in the form of bread and gave it to his disciples. And so she was with great devotion, with plenteous tears, and with noisy sobbing, for in this place is plenary remission. And so is in other four places in the temple. One is in the Mount of Calvary; and another at the grave where our Lord was buried; the third is at the marble stone that his precious body was laid on when it was taken off the cross; the fourth is where the holy cross was buried, and in many other places of Jerusalem. And, when this creature came into the place where the apostles received the Holy Ghost, our Lord gave her great devotion. Afterward she went to the place where our Lady was buried, and as she kneeled on her knees the time of hearing two masses, our Lord Jesus Christ said unto her, "Thou comst not hither, daughter, for any need but for merit and for reward, for thy sins were forgiven thee ere thou came here, and therefore thou comst hither for increasing of thy reward and of thy merit. And I am well pleased with thee, daughter, for thou standest under obedience of Holy Church and that thou will obey thy confessor and follow his council, which through authority of Holy Church has pardoned thee of thy sins and dispensed with thee that thou should not go to Rome nor to Saint James unless thou wish to thyself. Not withstanding all this, I command thee in the name of Jesus, daughter, that thou go visit these holy places and do as I bid thee, for I am above all Holy Church and I shall go with thee and keep thee right well." Then our Lady spoke to her soul in this manner, saying, "Daughter, well art thou blessed, for my son Jesus shall flow so much grace into thee that all the world shall wonder of thee. Be not ashamed, my beloved daughter, to receive the gifts which my son shall give thee, for I tell thee in truth they shall be great gifts that he shall give thee. And therefore, my beloved daughter, be not ashamed of him that is thy God, thy Lord, and thy love, no more than I was when I saw him hanging on the cross, my sweet son, Jesus, for to cry and to weep for the pain of my sweet son, Jesus Christ; Mary Magdalene was not ashamed to cry and weep for my son's love. And therefore, daughter, if thou will be able to partake in our joy, thou must be able to partake in our sorrow." This sweet speech and dalliance had this creature at our Lady's grave, and much more then she could ever rehearse. Afterward she rode on an ass to Bethlehem and when she came to the temple and the crib where our Lord was born, she had great devotion, much speech, and dalliance in her soul, and high ghostly comfort with much weeping and sobbing so that her fellows would not let her eat in their company. And therefore she ate her meals alone. And then the Grey Friars who had led her from place to place received her into them and set her with them at the meals that she should not eat alone. And one of the friars asked one of her fellowship if that was the woman of England the which they had heard speak with God. And, when this came to her knowledge, she knew well that it was truth that our Lord said to her ere she went out of England, "Daughter, I shall make all the world to wonder of thee, and many men and many women shall speak of me for love of thee and worshipping me in thee."

"The Two Powers." Hugh of St. Victor (1134)

This is a fairly early text for our period of inquiry, but it illustrates the distinction between the two kinds of law and adjudication recognized in the Middle Ages. Hugh of St. Victor's *On the Sacraments of the Christian Faith*, from which this excerpt is taken, was well-known in the Middle Ages, and his work is regarded as having been highly influential on the thought and writings of Chaucer.

> For there are two lives, the one earthly, the other heavenly; the one corporeal, the other spiritual; one by which the body lives from the soul, the other by which the soul lives from God. Both have their own good by which they are invigorated and nourished, so that they can subsist. The earthly life is nourished by earthly goods; the spiritual life is nurtured by spiritual goods. To the earthly life pertain all things that are earthly, to the spiritual life all goods that are spiritual. Now, that in both lives justice may be preserved and utility flourish, at first those have been distributed on each side who would acquire the goods of each according to necessity or reason by zeal and labor.
>
> Then there are others who by the power of the office committed to them dispense according to equity, that no one may step over his brother in business but justice may be preserved inviolate. On this account powers were established in both peoples distributed according to both lives. Indeed, among the laics [laypersons], to whose zeal and providence those things which are necessary for the earthly life belong, is earthly power. But among the clerics to whose

office look those things which are the goods of the spiritual life, is
divine power. Thus the one power is said to be secular; the other
is called spiritual. In both powers are diverse grades and orders of
powers; yet in both they are distributed under one head and, as it
were, deduced from one beginning and referred to one. The earthly
power has as its head the king. The spiritual power has the highest
pontifex. To the powers of the king pertain all things that are earthly
and made for the earthly life. To the power of the highest pontifex
pertain all things that are spiritual and attributed to the spiritual life.
Now the more worthy the spiritual life is than the earthly and the
spirit than the body, so much does the spiritual power precede the
earthly or the secular in honor and in dignity.

For spiritual power has also to establish earthly power in order to
exist, and it has to judge it, if it has not been good. Indeed, it itself
was established first by God and when it goes astray it can be judged
by God alone, just as it is written: "The spiritual man judgeth all
things, and he himself is judged by no man." Now, it is manifestly
declared among that ancient people of the Old Testament where the
priesthood was first established by God that spiritual power, in so
far as it looks to divine institution, is both prior in time and greater
in dignity; afterwards indeed royal power was arranged through
the priesthood at God's order. Wherefore, in the Church sacerdotal
dignity still consecrates regal power, but sanctifying it through
benediction and forming it through institution. If then, as the Apostle
says, "He who blesses is greater, and he who is blessed less," it is
established without any doubt that earthly power which receives
benediction from the spiritual is thought inferior by law.

A PUNISHMENT FOR LOLLARDY (1389)

The ecclesiastical authorities were granted enormous power to enforce
their laws and public belief. In "The Register of William Courtenay,"
excerpted below, William Smyth, Roger Dexter, and Alice Dexter are
excommunicated and publicly humiliated for practicing Lollardy. As the
final paragraph shows, the three were also put at considerable physical risk,
since they were required to parade nearly naked through the town in the
wintry month of November.

On the Sunday following their return to their homes, each of them shall walk in front of the procession in the collegiate church of St. Mary's in Newark, William and Roger in their undershirts and drawers, Alice in her shift, with feet and heads bare; said William with an image of St. Catherine, Roger and Alice with crucifixes in their right hands, and each of them carrying in their left hands candles of one-half pound weight. They will genuflect and devoutly kiss those images three times, once at the beginning of the procession, again when it is half completed, and again at the end, in reverence to the crucifix, in memory of His passion, and in honor of the Virgin. They will enter said church with the procession and will stand before the image of the crucifix while high mass is being sung, with their images and candles in their hands as indicated. At the conclusion of the mass of the day, said William, Roger, and Alice will offer these [candles] to the celebrant of the mass.

Then on the Saturday following, in the open public square or marketplace of said village of Leicester, the same William, Roger, and Alice, wearing as before nothing beyond their underwear, and with said images in their right hands, will kiss these three times while genuflecting, once at one end of the marketplace, again at the middle, and finally at the farther end. William, because he has had some education, will recite with devotion an antiphon and the collect of the feast of St. Catherine, said Roger and Alice, being illiterate, will recite the Lord's prayer and Ave Maria. On the Sunday immediately following they will stand in the parish church of said village and do in all respects as they did the preceding Sunday in the collegiate church. The candles they will be carrying, they will humbly and devoutly offer to the vicar or chaplain who celebrated the mass.

Because the said penitents may suffer bodily injury from standing so long uncovered during the present cold weather, we are willing to so moderate the severity of this penance, that after they have entered said churches, while they are hearing mass, they may put on what additional clothes they may need, providing, however, that their feet and heads remain uncovered.

"EPISTOLA 391: ON THE JEWS."
BERNARD OF CLAIRVAUX (EARLY 12THC)

This early letter, written by the Cistercian monk Bernard of Clairvaux in the early twelfth century, justifies anti-Semitism even while promoting tolerance; that is, acts of violence against the Jews are not condoned, despite the difference in belief.

> The Jews are for us the living words of Scripture. They are dispersed all over the world so that by expiating their crime they may be everywhere the living witnesses of our redemption….It is an act of Christian piety both to "vanquish the proud" and also "to spare the subjected," especially those from whom we have a law and a promise, and whose flesh was shared by Christ Whose name be forever blessed.

THE MURDER OF HUGH OF LINCOLN.
MATTHEW OF PARIS (1255)

The following account of the tragic murder of Hugh of Lincoln and its aftermath is recorded by Matthew of Paris in his Chronicles. The account is fairly uncritical and supports the official anti-Semitic stance of the time. However, a close reading reveals inconsistencies hidden between the lines that might indicate ulterior motives for the scapegoating that ensued.

> When Lent drew near, the king with great urgency demanded from the oft-impoverished Jews the immediate payment to him of eight thousand marks, on pain of being hung in case of nonpayment. Seeing that nothing but ruin and destruction were impending, the Jews unanimously replied to this demand in the following terms: "Your Majesty, we see that you spare neither Christians nor Jews, but make it your business on divers pretexts to impoverish all: no hope remains to us of breathing freely; the pope's usurers have supplanted us; therefore permit us to depart from your kingdom under safe conduct, and we will seek another abode of some kind or other." When the king was told of this speech, he exclaimed in a querulous tone, "It is no wonder that I covet money…." Becoming, then, a second Titus or Vespasian, he (the king) sold the Jews for some years to his brother Earl Richard, that the earl might disembowel those whom the king had skinned. However, the earl spared them

out of consideration for the diminution of their power and their ignominious poverty.

At this time, the king used all the means in his power to delay and impede the election of an archbishop of York, in order that he might the longer, and with greater freedom, pillage the possessions of that archbishopric . . . . This attempt fails and Master Sewal is nominated to the office.

In this same year, about the time of the festival of the apostles Peter and Paul, the Jews of Lincoln stole a boy of eight years of age, whose name was Hugh; and, having shut him up in a room quite out of the way, where they fed him on milk and other childish nourishment, they sent to almost all the cities of England where the Jews lived, and summoned some of their sect from each city to be present at a sacrifice to take place at Lincoln; for they had, as they stated, a boy hidden for the purpose of being crucified . . . .

The boy's mother had been for some days diligently seeking after her absent son, and having been told by the neighbours that they had last seen him playing with some Jewish boys of his own age, and entering the house of one of that sect, she suddenly made her way into that house, and saw the body of the child in a well, into which it had been thrown . . . . [She summons the citizens of the city.] There was present at this scene one John of Lexington, a man of learning, prudent and discreet, and he thus addressed the people: "We have already learned," said he, "that the Jews have not hesitated to attempt such proceedings as a reproach and taunt to our Lord Jesus Christ, who was crucified"; then addressing a Jew who had been seized upon, and the one whose house the boy had gone into whilst at play, and who was therefore an object of greater suspicion than the others, he said to him: "Wretched man, do you not know what a speedy death awaits you? Not all the gold of England will avail to ransom you, and save you from your fate. However, I will tell you, undeserving as you are, how you may preserve your life and prevent your limbs from being mutilated. Both of these I will guarantee to you, if you will without fear or hesitation disclose to me, without any falsehood, all that has happened on this occasion." The Jew, whose name was Copin, thinking he had found a means of escape, then said, "My lord John, if by your deeds you will repay me for my statements, I will reveal wonderful things to you." Then, being urged on and encouraged by the eloquence of John to do so, he continued: "What the Christians say is true . . . ." [Copin now tells an amazing story of how the boy was crucified by the Jews, but how the earth kept miraculously "vomiting forth" his body so that it could not be hidden.] "...Almost all the Jews of England agreed to the murder of this boy, of which they are accused; and from almost every city of England in which Jews dwell...." After he had given utterance to these words and to other ravings, he was tied to a horse's tail and dragged to the gallows, where he was delivered over body and soul to the evil spirits of the air. The rest of the Jews who had participated in this crime, to the number of 91, were carried to London in carts, and consigned to close imprisonment; and if they were perchance pitied by any Christians, they did not excite any tears of compassion among the Caursins, their rivals....

Afterwards, on an inquisition made [by] the king's justiciaries, it was discovered and decided that the Jews of England had by common consent crucified and put to death an innocent boy....On St. Clement's day, eighteen of the richer and higher order of Jews of the city of Lincoln were dragged to new gibbets, erected especially for the purpose, and were hung up, an offering to the winds. More than eighty others also were kept in close confinement in the Tower of London, awaiting a similar fate.

The Papal Bull Defending the Jews. Gregory X (1272)

In response to vicious attacks upon Jewish communities in the late thirteenth century, Gregory X issued a papal bull prohibiting attacks against Jews and protecting the Jews from false testimony. Notice that Gregory specifically forbids Christians from making accusations against Jews; testimony is valid only if a Jew himself testifies.

Gregory, bishop, servant of the servants of God, extends greetings and the apostolic benediction to the beloved sons in Christ, the faithful Christians, to those here now and to those in the future.... Although [the Jews] prefer to persist in their stubbornness rather than to recognize the words of their prophets and the mysteries of the Scriptures, and thus to arrive at a knowledge of Christian faith and salvation; nevertheless, inasmuch as they have made an appeal for our protection and help, we therefore admit their petition and offer them the shield of our protection through the clemency of Christian piety.

In so doing we follow in the footsteps of our predecessors of blessed
memory, the popes of Rome—Calixtus, Eugene, Alexander, Clement,
Celestine, Innocent, and Honorius.

We decree moreover that no Christian shall compel them or any
one of their group to come to baptism unwillingly. But if any one of
them shall take refuge of his own accord with Christians, because of
conviction, then, after his intention will have been manifest, he shall
be made a Christian without any intrigue. For, indeed, that person
who is known to have come to Christian baptism not freely, but
unwillingly, is not believed to possess the Christian faith.

Moreover no Christian shall presume to seize, imprison, wound,
torture, mutilate, kill, or inflict violence on them; furthermore no
one shall presume, except by judicial action of the authorities of the
country, to change the good customs in the land where they live
for the purpose of taking their money or goods from them or from
others.

In addition, no one shall disturb them in any way during the
celebration of their festivals, whether by day or by night, with clubs
or stones or anything else. And no one shall exact any compulsory
service of them unless it be that which they have been accustomed
to render in previous times. Inasmuch as the Jews are not able to
bear witness against the Christians, we decree furthermore that the
testimony of Christians against Jews shall not be valid unless there
is among these Christians some Jew who is there for the purpose of
offering testimony.

Since it happens occasionally that some Christians lose their
Christian children, the Jews are accused by their enemies of secretly
carrying off and killing these same Christian children and of making
sacrifices of the heart and blood of these very children. It happens,
too, that the parents of these children or some other Christian
enemies of these Jews, secretly hide these very children in order that
they may be able to injure these Jews, and in order that they may be
able to extort from them a certain amount of money by redeeming
them from their straits.

And most falsely do these Christians claim that the Jews have
secretly and furtively carried away these children and killed them,
and that the Jews offer sacrifices from the heart and the blood of
these children, since their law in this matter precisely and expressly
forbids Jews to sacrifice, eat, or drink the blood, or to eat the flesh

of animals having claws. This has been demonstrated many times at our court by Jews converted to the Christian faith; nevertheless very many Jews are often seized and detained unjustly because of this.

We decree, therefore, that Christians need not be obeyed against Jews in a case or situation of this type, and we order that Jews seized under such a silly pretext be freed from imprisonment, and that they shall not be arrested henceforth on such a miserable pretext, unless— which we do not believe—they be caught in the commission of the crime. We decree that no Christian shall stir up anything new against them, but that they should be maintained in that status and position in which they were in the time of our predecessors, from antiquity till now.

We decree in order to stop the wickedness and avarice of bad men, that no one shall dare to devastate or to destroy a cemetery of the Jews or to dig up human bodies for the sake of getting money. Moreover, if any one, after having known the content of this decree, should—which we hope will not happen—attempt audaciously to act contrary to it, then let him suffer punishment in his rank and position, or let him be punished by the penalty of excommunication, unless he makes amends for his boldness by proper recompense. Moreover, we wish that only those Jews who have not attempted to contrive anything toward the destruction of the Christian faith be fortified by the support of such protection....

Vox Clamantis. JOHN GOWER (*c.* 1380s)

The following excerpts, from John Gower's *Vox Clamantis*, were written shortly after the Peasant's Revolt of 1381. The work begins with a description of the revolt, then blames events on a falling off from the appropriate professions that he believed to be divinely prescribed. Although the *Vox Clamantis* critiques each of the estates in turn, these excerpts focus on the abuses of the clerical estate. Chaucer's portraits of the Monk and the Friar in *The Canterbury Tales* are particularly indebted to Gower's descriptions; some, such as Chaucer's comparing of the monk out of his cloister to a fish out of the sea, are close paraphrases of Gower.

AGAINST THE PRIESTS
BOOK III, CHAPTER 27. Here he speaks of the spiritual worthiness of priests, and of how they accomplish more than others, if they

perform their duties well. Otherwise, they furnish more opportunity for transgression through their own bad examples.

A priest's honor is great, and his power is even greater, if he remains pious and good, and far removed from vices. With their hands they perform the rites of the highest sacrament, through which the flesh is made one with God by a word. And they can take away the sin for which our first parent fell by the sacred purification of baptism. They also celebrate our marriages according to the new law, and if they seek after righteousness, they will not engage in anything idle. They also offer pardon to those confessing they have fallen, and they provide an erring man a return to God. They also give us to partake of the heavenly host, and afterwards on our deathbed their unction awaits us. They also must assist the dead and buried, and offer up pious prayers in their masses.

They are the salt of the earth, by which we on earth are seasoned; without their savor man could scarcely be seasoned. Elisha healed the waters with the salt he cast into them, and no bitter taste remained in them. The salt signifies the knowing discretion of the just man, whereby the man of discretion may season his people. They are the light of the world. For this reason, if they are in darkness, we in the world stand blind and uncertain. As God has declared, he shall be cursed who puts any stumbling block before a blind man that is hurt by it. He who has placed obstacles before a blind man shall, by his cursed deeds, show the pathway to sin.

They are Jacob's ladder with its many steps, reaching to the heights of heaven; by them the pathway will lie revealed. They are a holy mountain; through them every man of faith must mount the peak of virtues. They are our counsel, the right way to on high, the teachers of the law, and our new way of salvation. These good men close heaven and open it wide to people, and they can subject everything to themselves. It was said unto them, "Multiply, and yield much fruit." These words have reference to good morals. It was said unto them, "Replenish the earth." Note what is said unto you: be full of good fruits in the Church.

No worthless person should come before God, for no one lacking in virtue should be near God. So the priest should reconcile both the righteous and the sinful to God and pour forth the frankincense of prayers to heaven. Let him pray lest the just man fall away from justice, and let him pray that the dissolute man may rise up and weep over his extreme wickedness. O what a shameful thing it is when a priest is like an ass, unversed in morals and lawlessly wild! Priests are like the stars of the sky in number, but scarcely two out of a thousand shine with light. They neither read the Scripture nor understand them. Nevertheless, being tonsured, these men are apart from the common herd, and they think this is enough. There are some like this; and there are others whom an ardent virtue distinguishes in the Church, and who do many good works. Noah sent forth a raven and it did not return. He sent forth a dove and it did return. Similarly, in the church there are ravens and doves. The good ones are without gall, while the bad ones are full of gall. "Tomorrow at prime," they sing, since they are slow to reform themselves; but the day of judgment often does away with such people. Such are the black ones whom the bonds of this world shackle, and who are unwilling to thirst after the promised kingdom of God. [As for] the priest who upholds the laws of his order and who imparts holy teachings by both action and example, no esteem is too high for him, even when he is not held in honor by his order. Praise from the people is not enough for him, but God's praise is. I maintain that among the clergy, for those whom an ardent virtue shows to be good and true, their thanks shall be larger than they deserve.

AGAINST THE MONKS

BOOK IV, CHAPTER I. Since he has discussed the waywardness of the clergy, to whom he looks especially for guidance for our souls, he now intends to discuss the waywardness of men in monastic orders. And he will speak first of monks and others who get possession of temporal goods. While commending, to be sure, the sanctity of their order, he rebukes in particular those whose actions are just the contrary.

There are also cloistered men of diverse kind, concerning whom I wish to write the little I know. As their actions show, some of them are noted for property and some of poverty, but the poverty is feigned to too great an extent. A monastic order is good in itself, but we say that those who betray it are evil. I believe that those who live faithfully in their cloister and who cannot be held guilty of worldly love are blessed. A religious order will recognize as holy men those who put their hand to the plow without looking back. God is present among the monks who are willing to enter monasteries apart from mankind, and the fellowship of heaven is theirs. When a man undertakes to love two opposing things equally, the one love will detract from the effectiveness of the other. I accordingly direct my words to those who presume to mask their faces under the shadow of a religious order, yet inwardly commit worldly sins. And no one else is going to be hurt by what I have written; instead, every man shall bear his own burden. Nothing that I write is my own opinion; rather, I shall speak what the voice of the people has reported to me.

There are certainly monks whom ownership of property has made a claim on, men whom no religious order can hold in check through moral precepts. For some men of property seek the leisure of an order so that they cannot suffer any hardships. They avoid being hungry, and slake their thirst with wine. They get rid of all cold with their warm furred cloaks. Faintness of the belly does not come upon them in the hours of the night, and their raucous voice does not sing the heights of heaven in chorus with a drinking cup. A man of this kind will devour no less than several courses at table, and empties a good many beakers in his drinking. Then he believes he has grown sick and demands to be made well again; and in such fashion does he devote himself to his sports. Indeed, it is only with difficulty that this man of professed vows is to be worn out from drinking; thus, master monk is willing to appear before God while in his cups. And while you are bringing him wine, he allures women to himself; wanton monasteries now furnish these two things together. If he can get to heaven after being inflamed with passion even while in his vestment; and if his gluttony can gain a place among those above, then I think that the monk distinguished on these two counts will stand as Peter's fellow-citizen in the vault of the skies.

AGAINST THE WEALTH OF THE MONKS

BOOK IV, CHAPTER 2. Here he speaks of the monks who, contrary to the decrees of their order, are the first to abandon the virtue of self-restraint and partake again and again of the delights of the flesh.

Things which are dead by no means belong with the living; and no one who renounces the world does not return to worldly behavior. No matter how much he seems to be a sheep, neither tonsure nor the humblest garb is any help at all to him, if he is a wolf. For men can be deceived, but no one can deceive Christ, Who deceived no man. Indeed, He condemns the pretense of feigned religion and reckons its work as nothing. Nevertheless, a monk withdraws from the world nowadays only in respect to his dress, and thinks that a religious order is sufficient for him in outer appearance alone. The vestments will be the monk himself, and his thoughts will wander about in the world, heeding nothing beyond the material wealth of his order. Since he knows that bodies seldom thrive properly on slender rations for the belly, such a monk demands plentiful sustenance for his gullet. And the more food he eats the more he craves, so that his belly may enjoy its pleasures, with the help of his gullet. Unmindful of his father, who used to bear burdens on his shoulders, the monk lugs the finest wines about in his belly. Such a man pours the fruit of the vine into his stomach as if it were a flagon, and he is not one to allow any place in his swelling paunch to be empty.

A monk ought to shun wine for many reasons, one of them being lest his flesh yearn for debauchery. A man should not spoil the good works of his brothers in religion, or sit around in a drunken state or have a fever from it. Nevertheless, the monk cares about nothing except stuffing his worthless body, yet his soul goes hungry every day. In these times snow-white bread, delicate wine, and meats provide monks with daily feasts. Just see how the cook bakes and roasts, freezes and melts, grinds and presses, strains and tests his performances. If a gluttonous monk can fatten his paunch, he thinks there is nothing in Holy Writ to the effect that one should work. Scorning manna, this kind of people demands that its cooking pots be black [with constant use], and prefers its vices to virtues. Lest hunger might weaken these fat fellows, their belly's harlot gluttony crams their faint stomachs full. A monk does not know what ought to be honored, but what ought to be esteemed for the belly. This, he says, is the way, the life, the salvation. When the bell rings for the dinner pot, he runs at a fast clip, and not one crumb from the table escapes him. But when the sluggard gets up at night and comes to prayers at a slow pace, he tries to be last.

When their order began, monks' homes were caves; now a grand marble palace sets them off. They used to have no steaming kitchen, and no cook served them delicacies roasted or baked by the fire. In former times no boiled food or dishes loaded with meat made monks fat. Bodily gluttony did not affect their souls, nor were they inflamed by lust of the flesh to seek out debauchery on the sly. They who used to cover their bare bodies with the skins of animals now cover them more comfortably with wool. Herbs used to furnish their food, a spring their drink, and a base hair shirt their clothing, yet there was no grumbling in those days. There was no envy or splendor

in a monastery then; he who was the greater served as did the lesser.
There was no great quantity of silver or chain of gold that could
corrupt their holy state then. Money did not touch their pockets,
nor wine their palates, and no carnal flame burned in their loins.
They had a holy spirit which served their resolution well, and which
persevered successfully in the work it undertook.

They were righteous men who shunned the world and who
were burdened with no love of sins. The world did not draw them
away from the right path, and the flesh did not beckon them toward
heinous evils. They put aside all the vanities which the world affords,
and yearned only for the God of heaven. It was no disgrace then to
take one's rest upon straw or to put hay under one's head. The forest
was their home, herbs were their food, and leafy boughs were their
bedding, which the earth furnished without their even asking. The
hazel then flourished among them in high esteem, and the sturdy
oak yielded splendid treasures. They gathered the fruits of the arbutus
and mountain, which were seasoned neither with salt nor with spices.
And although they partook of acorns from Jove's spreading tree, they
grew strong from these foods. Contented with the modest things
produced by Nature of her own accord, they sent forth their humble
prayers to God on high. Admirable sowers of the seeds of justice
then, now they reap their fruits eternally a hundred-fold. But that
ancient salvation of souls, which religious orders once possessed, has
perished, undermined by the weakness of the flesh.

Against the Monks Who Wander Outside the Monastery

Book IV, Chapter 5. Here he speaks of how monks ought not to
wander around outside the monastery.

The sea is the proper habitat of a live fish, and the monastery is
the right home for a monk. Just as the sea will not keep dead fish, so
the monastery casts out evildoing monks. A fish ought not to be out
of the water, nor ought a monk to be away from his cloisters, unless
you return to them, O monk in holy orders. If there were a fish that
forsook the waters of the sea to seek its food on land, it would be
highly inappropriate to give it the name of a fish; I should rather
give it the name of a monster. Such shall I call the monk who yearns
for worldly delights and deserts his cloister for them. He should not
rightly be called a monk but a renegade, or what God's wrath brands
as a monster of the Church. As for those who still remain within the

monastery, yet with wandering minds look back on the world with new love in their hearts, their transgression disgraces such men in the eyes of God. Because of this they lose their cloister's rightful rewards. It is not a wise man who amasses goods for himself of several years and dissipates them in only one day. The monk who makes the rounds of town and country quite frequently commits a fault for which he perishes as a sinner. In spite of this, there are only a few at present who do not give over their errant hearts to sensual pleasures. Solomon said that a man's foolish attire, which is outwardly visible, tells what is within. But although a monk should array himself with humble garb, nevertheless you now see many sumptuous things on his back.

AGAINST THE FRIARS

BOOK IV, CHAPTER 16. I grant that the functions of the original order were holy, and that in the beginning its founders were pious. A friar remains blessed who follows after them, who in renouncing the world seeks to reach God, who adopts monastic poverty for himself and bears it voluntarily, and who patiently undertakes the work of his order. Such a man is indeed to be praised for his high merits, for the earth is restored through his prayers. But he who disguises his outer appearance in the order and lacks its true essence, he who preaches outwardly yet inwardly yearns for riches—to such men of the present this book offers its message, since the voice of the people furnished the things for it to say.

The throng of friars overflows the mendicant order; the original rule is dead, inundated by them. These men, who used to bear hardships pleasing to God in accordance with the vow of their order, are becoming soft. For the first time they are giving themselves a name which must be described as "headless"; those upon whom everyone confers opulence call themselves "inopulent." The friars maintain that they are disciples of Christ and that they are pursuing all their duties after His example. Their false faith claims this, but this is sufficient unto them, as those who know the Scriptures say. They are now acting like people who have no property, yet under a pauper's guise they grab everything. I do not know whether it is a sign of favor or doom for these friars, but all the world abounds with them. They hold the Pope in their hands; he mitigates the hardships of their order and decrees that more and more things are now permissible. And if the papal authority rejects their suits, their perverse order will secretly make them lawful. There is no king nor prince nor great man in the world who should not confess his secrets to them.

And so the mendicants are mightier than lords, and from the world they secretly usurp what their order plainly forbids. I would say that these men are not disciples but rather gods: both life and death bring money to them. For a friar demands that he himself bury the dead bodies of those to whom he attached himself as a confessor, if they were dignitaries. But if it should be a poor [man's] body, he makes no claim at all, since his piety takes no cognizance of anything unless there is money in it. They refuse to baptize mere faith, since a matter of business with no money in it will not be esteemed or performed at their hands. Just as a merchant buys every kind of goods in order that he can make a great deal for himself out of a great many people, so the greedy friar embraces every worldly cause in order that he may enjoy his various gains. They are men whom the grasping world has not frightened away; on the contrary, it shows a high regard for them, and has surrendered up its affairs to them. It is obvious that these converted men are subverted, so they should derive their true reputations from their deeds. Thus the pharisaical branch has cut itself off from its source of life, and its fruit is pungently bitter to the taste.

Against Hypocritical Friars

Book IV, Chapter 17. Here he speaks of the friars who hypocritically rebuke the people's sins when preaching in public, but nevertheless promote them zealously in private with blandishments and satisfaction.

A friar's assiduous hypocrisy sows his words in order that his harvest of profit in the world may thrive through them. He thunders out fearful sermons as he publicly damns the practice of sin, like a very servant of God. But like a servant of Satan, he furnishes glosses for them when it comes to sit down for a while in private chambers. His gentle blandishment is soothing to the ear [of] those whom his deep, resounding voice has goaded before. And thus does this sinner cater to sins for others, for by encouraging vice he gets a profit from it. A friar knows well that when sin dies, then his revenue dies for all time. Tell me where a friar will come three times, unless he may take away money. He does not return by the road where his lot is unprofitable. If you took away crime from the friar's foundations, their house which was lofty for so long would fall without struggle.

O how the words of the prophet Hosea are verified! Thus did he speak the truth: "A certain tribe will arise on earth which will eat up the sin of my people and know much evil." We perceive that this prophecy has come about in our day, and we give credit for this to the friars. No matter what is necessary for their sustenance, fate provides everything for them through sins. There are no such sensuous pleasures as sometimes fail to yield a crumb to friars, if they are confessors. Notice that doves come to spotless quarters, and that an unclean tower does not harbor such birds. Similarly, no house except those of tycoons provides friars of today with guest accommodations where they wish to stay on. Ants never make their course toward empty granaries, and a wandering friar will not come near when one's wealth is lost. With no thought of the blooms which it bore before, they disdain the thorn when the roses have fallen off. In this way do the friars scorn the favors of friendship from a man formerly rich, when he can give no more.

Many are friars in name but few by rights. As some say, Falseness is their prophet. Their cloak's appearance is poor, but their money box is rich. They hide their shameful deeds under sanctimonious words. Poor without poverty and holy without Christ, thus does a man who is lacking in goodness stand out as eminently good. They call upon God with their lips, yet they venerate gold in their hearts, and on every side they seek to learn the way to it. The Devil has placed everything under their foot, but their pretended sanctity does not teach them how to hold on to anything. Thus does one who "scorns" the world grasp in turn at the things of the world, while his sheep's clothing conceals a hostile wolf. And thus the people, deluded by pretenses, will think of men whom deceitfulness inwardly rules as outwardly holy. There is scarcely a one who reproaches the falseness of another; rather, each contributes to the trickery so that they may be the more deceiving. Driven by the same vice, they are thus tainted the more, and they taint all the earth with their dishonesties. In any event, may the Lord repress those whom He knows to be sinning at this time against the age-old faith. I do not ask that they be destroyed, but that the weak be strengthened, and that they submit to the original way of life which their order imposed.

ON THE POPE. JOHN WYCLIF (1370s)

The Great Schism inspired a number of anti-papal statements. The following is John Wyclif's rejection of a clerical hierarchy—particularly one headed by the pope—that separates people from their religion. Our translation is based on Winn's edition.

Some think it great evidence, that if the Pope canonized this man (Peter), then he must needs be a saint in Heaven. But let these men believe what they will. Well I know that these popes may err and sin as Peter did, and yet Peter dreamed not thus, to show that men become saints in Heaven. But it may happen that many men who are canonized by these popes are damned in hell, for they deceive and are deceived. We affirm it not as belief, that if a man is chosen Pope, then he is chosen to bliss, even as here he is called "Most Blessed Father." And many believe because of their works that they are the deepest damned in hell. For they charge themselves as hypocrites, both in office and in name, and so they sit in the first place here, and at the last day of doom they shall be in the last place, that is, the deepest place of hell. We hold ourselves in bonds of belief that stand in general words and in conditional words, and we judge not their folly. But we may say by supposing, that we guess that this is so, and whoever has more evidence, his part should sooner be supposed.

But here there are three great heresies that deceive many men. First, men suppose that each pope is the "Most Blessed Father," but this speech lasts but a while, so that the pope may advance men. But here we say truly, that these men that call themselves blessed, deceive themselves and flatter themselves, for they hope to have the profit of them. For whither is this Pope most blessed in this life or after this life? He is not blessed in this life, for bliss falls to the other life, and this life is full of sorrow and sin, so that bliss suffers not with it. And if men speak largely, many men are here more blessed than the Pope, for highness of estate makes not a man blessed by himself, for otherwise each pope would be blessed, even if he were falsely chosen by fiends, and Judas Escariot should be blessed, for he was chosen by Christ Himself....

Bull of Pope Gregory XI, Against John Wycliffe (1384)

Wyclif was compelled to answer to charges in 1384. The following document makes clear which of the reformations Wyclif called for were unacceptable to the church. Under the threat of excommunication and the charge of heresy, Wyclif recanted on all accounts.

We are compelled to wonder and grieve that you, who, in consideration of the favors and privileges conceded to your University of Oxford by the apostolic see, and on account of your familiarity with the Scriptures, in whose sea you navigate, by the gift of God, with auspicious oar, you, who ought to be, as it were, warriors and champions of the orthodox faith, without which there is no salvation of souls—that you through a certain sloth and neglect allow tares to spring up amidst the pure wheat in the fields of your glorious University aforesaid; and what is still more pernicious, even continue to grow to maturity. And you are quite careless, as has been lately reported to us, as to the extirpation of these tares; with no little clouding of a bright name, danger to your souls, contempt of the Roman Church, and injury to the faith above mentioned. And what pains us the more, is that this increase of the tares aforesaid is known in Rome before the remedy of extirpation has been applied in England where they sprang up. By the insinuation of many, if they are indeed worthy of belief, deploring it deeply, it has come to our ears that John de Wyclif, rector of the church of Lutterworth, in the diocese of Lincoln, Professor of the Sacred Scriptures (would that he were not also Master of Errors), has fallen into such a detestable madness that he does not hesitate to dogmatize and publicly preach, or rather vomit forth from the recesses of his breast, certain propositions and conclusions which are erroneous and false. He has cast himself also into the depravity of preaching heretical dogmas which strive to subvert and weaken the state of the whole church and even secular polity, some of which doctrines, in changed terms, it is true, seem to express the perverse opinions and unlearned learning of Marsilio of Padua of cursed memory, and of John of Jandun, whose book is extant, rejected, and cursed by our predecessor, Pope John XXII, of happy memory. This he has done in the kingdom of England, lately glorious in its power and in the abundance of its resources, but more glorious still in the glistening piety of its faith, and in the distinction of its sacred learning; producing also many men illustrious for their exact knowledge of the Holy Scriptures, mature in the gravity of their character, conspicuous in devotion, defenders of the Catholic Church. He has polluted certain of the faithful of Christ by sprinkling them with these doctrines, and led them away from the right paths of the aforesaid faith to the brink of perdition.

Wherefore, since we are not willing, nay, indeed, ought not to be willing, that so deadly a pestilence should continue to exist with our connivance, a pestilence which, if it is not opposed in its beginnings, and torn out by the roots in its entirety, will be reached too late by medicines when it has infected very many with its contagion; we command your University with strict admonition, by the apostolic authority, in virtue of your sacred obedience, and under penalty of the deprivation of all the favors, indulgences, and privileges granted to you and your University by the said see, for the future not to permit to be asserted or proposed to any extent whatever, the opinions, conclusions, and propositions which are in variance with good morals and faith, even when those proposing strive to defend them under a certain fanciful wresting of words or of terms. Moreover, you are on our authority to arrest the said John, or cause him to be arrested and to send him under a trustworthy guard to our venerable brother, the Archbishop of Canterbury, and the Bishop of London, or to one of them.

Besides, if there should be, which God forbid, in your University, subject to your jurisdiction, opponents stained with these errors, and if they should obstinately persist in them, proceed vigorously and earnestly to a similar arrest and removal of them, and otherwise as shall seem good to you. Be vigilant to repair your negligence which you have hitherto shown in the premises, and so obtain our gratitude and favor, and that of the said see, besides the honor and reward of the divine recompense.

Twelve Conclusions of the Lollards (1395)

Not unlike the 95 Theses, which would later be famously nailed on the church door in Wittenburg by Martin Luther, the Twelve Conclusions of the Lollards were affixed to the doors of St. Paul's Cathedral and Westminster Abbey, the foremost churches of London, in 1395 as an assertion of the abuses of the religious and secular clergy. The document is

addressed to Parliament, and King Richard II found it alarming enough
that he demanded abjurations from the leaders of the sect upon his return
from Ireland later that year. This translation is based on Anne Hudson's
edition.

> We poor men, treasurers of Christ and his apostles, denounce to the
> lords and the commons of the Parliament certain conclusions and
> truths for the reformation of the holy church of England, the which
> has been blind and leprous many years through the maintenance of
> the proud prelate, borne up with the flattering of private religion,
> the which is multiplied to a great charge and onerous to her people
> in England.
>
> When the church of England began to dote in temporality after
> her stepmother, the great church of Rome, and churches were slain
> by appropriation to diverse places, faith, hope, and charity began to
> fly out from our church, for pride with his sorry genealogy of deadly
> sins challenges the title of heritage. This conclusion is general and
> proved through experience, custom, and manner...
>
> The second conclusion is this. Our usual priesthood, which
> began in Rome, feigned from a power higher than angels, is not the
> priesthood which Christ ordained to his apostles...
>
> The third conclusion, sorrowful to hear, is that the law of
> continence annexed to the priesthood, that in prejudice of women
> was first ordained, induces sodomy throughout Holy Church....
>
> The fourth conclusion that harms the innocent people is this: that
> the feigned miracle of the sacrament of bread induces all men but
> a few to idolatry, for they believe that God's body, that never shall
> be out of heaven, by virtue of the priest's words should be enclosed
> essentially in a little bread that they show to the people....
>
> The fifth conclusion is this: that exorcisms and hallowing made in
> the church with wine, bread and wax, water, salt and oil and incense,
> the stone of the altar, on the vestments, miter, cross, and pilgrim's
> staves, be the very practice of necromancy rather than of holy
> theology....
>
> The sixth conclusion that maintains much pride is that a king and
> a bishop all in one person, a prelate and a justice in temporal cause, a
> curate and an officer in worldly service, make every realm according
> to God's realm....The corollary is that we, procurators of God in his
> cause, pursue to this Parliament that all manner of curates both high

and low should be fully excused from temporal offices, and occupy themselves with their curacy and nothing else.

The seventh conclusion that we mightily affirm is that special prayers for dead men's souls made in our church, preferring one name more than another, is the false grounding of deeds of alms, on which alms houses in England are wickedly based....

The eighth conclusion necessary to tell the beguiled people is that the pilgrimage, prayers, and offerings made to blind roods and to deaf images of tree and stone, are nearer in kin to idolatry and far from the deeds of alms....

The ninth conclusion that holds the people low is that the articles of confession that are said to be necessary to the salvation of man, with a feigned power of absolution, enhances priests' pride, and gives them opportunities for private callings other than what we well now say....

The tenth conclusion is that manslaughter by battle of pretense of law of righteousness for temporal causes or spiritual, without special revelation, is expressly contrary to the New Testament, which is a law of grace and full of mercy. This conclusion is openly proved through the example of Christ's preaching here on earth, who most taught to love and have mercy on his enemies, and not to slay them....The corollary is: it is a holy robbing of the poor people when lords purchase indulgences *a pena et a culpa* [without punishment or blame] to those who help the host [of armies], and gather to slay the Christian men in far lands for God's temporality, as we have seen. And knights that run to heathendom to get themselves a name through slaying men get much in spite of the King of Peace, for through meekness and suffering our belief was multiplied, and fighters and manslayers Jesus Christ hates and menaces. *Qui gladio percutit, gladio peribit* [he who smites with his sword shall be slain].

The eleventh conclusion is shameful to speak of, that a vow of continence made in our church of women, who are fickle and imperfect in nature, is the cause of bringing about a most horrible sin possible to mankind. For the slaying of children before they have been christened, abortion and destroying of kindred through medicine is full sinful...

The twelfth conclusion is that the multitude of craftwork is not needed that is commonly used in our churches, nourishing much sin in waste, curiosity and disguise...

AGAINST CONFESSION. LOLLARD TREATISE (1394)

Yearly confession had been mandatory in England since the Fourth
Lateran Council of 1215. This paragraph comprises one part of the Lollard
Conclusions of 1394. What is interesting is the author's condemnation
of confession as something that actually promotes licentiousness and, it
implies, sexual harassment of the laity by the priests. Priests who know
others' secrets have too much power over them; too frequently, the secret
hideaways of the confessional thus become spaces for eliciting more liai-
sons from parishioners who are afraid that their secrets might be made
public. The document thus points both to the corruption of the clerics and
the failure of the institution for promoting spiritual well-being.

> That auricular confession which is said to be so necessary to the
> salvation of a man, with its pretended power of absolution, exalts
> the arrogance of priests and gives them opportunity of other secret
> colloquies which we will not speak of; for both lords and ladies attest
> that, for fear of their confessors, they dare not speak the truth. And
> at the time of confession there is a ready occasion for assignation
> that is for "wooing," and other secret understandings leading to
> mortal sins. They themselves say that they are God's representatives
> to judge of every sin, to pardon and cleanse whomsoever they please.
> They say that they have the keys of heaven and of hell, and can
> excommunicate and bless, bind, and loose, at their will, so much so
> that for a drink, or 12 pence, they will sell the blessing of heaven
> with charter and close warrant sealed with the common seal. This
> conclusion is so notorious that it needs not any proof.

"THE CASE FOR TRANSLATION." JOHN WYCLIF (1370s)

Wyclif is perhaps best known for his call for an English translation of the
Bible. In the first document below, Wyclif defends the case for translation
and draws attention to the claim that the suppression of the knowledge of
the Gospel abetted the abuses of the friars, whose authority could remain
unchallenged as long as people failed to understand the lack of biblical
basis for their order. The second document, an anonymous treatise written
for the Lollards, makes translated texts a central tenet of the movement:
ordinary people, the Lollards believed, had the right to have direct access
to the Bible. This translation is based on Anne Hudson's edition.

And hear the friars with their followers, saying that it is heresy
to write God's law in English, and to make it known to ignorant
men....

It seems first that the knowledge of God's law should be taught in
that tongue by which it is more known, for this knowledge is God's
word. When Christ says in the Gospel that both heaven and earth
shall pass, but His words shall not pass, he understands by His words
His knowledge. And thus God's knowledge is Holy Writ, that may in
no way be false. Also the Holy Ghost gave to the apostles knowledge
on Whit Sunday for to know all manners of language, to teach the
people God's law thereby, and so God wished that the people be
taught God's law in diverse tongues. What man, on God's behalf,
should reverse God's ordinance and His will?

And for this reason Saint Jerome traveled and translated the Bible
from diverse tongues into Latin, that it might be afterwards translated
into other languages. And thus Christ and his apostles taught the
people in that language that was most known to the people. Why
should men not do so now?

And hereto the authors of the new law, that were apostles of Jesus
Christ, write their Gospels in diverse tongues that were more known
to the people.

Also the worthy realm of France, notwithstanding all prevention,
hath translated the Bible and the Gospels, with other true sentences
of the doctors, out of Latin into French. Why should Englishmen
not do so? As lords of England have the Bible in French, so it is
not against reason that they have the same sentences in English; for
God's law would be better known, and more believed, for oneness of
knowledge, and more accord would be between the realms....

Some men say that the friars and their followers travel, in
this case, for three reasons, that I will not affirm, but God knows
whether they are true. First they wished to be seen as so necessary
to the Englishmen of our realm that singularly in their wit lies the
knowledge of God's law, to tell the people God's law in whatever
manner they should wish. And the second reason hereof is...friars
wish to lead the people in teaching them God's law, and thus they
will teach some things, hide others, and shorten some. For then the
faults in their own lives should be less known to the people, and
God's law should be untruly known both by the clerks and by the
commons. The third reason that men may see stands in this way, so
they say: all these new orders (of friars) fear that their sins should

be known, and how they are not grounded (authorized) by God to come into the church; and thus they desire out of fear that God's law not be known in English; thus they might put heresies in men if English told other than what they were saying.

ON BIBLICAL TRANSLATION. LOLLARD TREATISE (EARLY 15THC)

This treatise, the original of which has been reproduced in Anne Hudson's edition of Wycliffite texts, proves that each nation may lawfully have holy writ in their mother tongue.

> Since that the truth of God stands not in one language more than another, but whoso lives best and teaches best pleaseth most God, of what language that ever it be, therefore the law of God written and taught in English may edify the common people, as it doeth clerks in Latin, since it is the sustenance to souls that should be saved. And Christ commanded the gospel to be preached, for the people should learn it, know it, and worship thereafter. Why may we not then write in English the gospel and all holy scripture to edification of Christian souls, as the preacher showeth it truly to the people? For, if it should not be written, it should not be preached. This heresy and blasphemy should Christian men put from their hearts, for it springs from the fiend, father of losses (John in the eighth chapter) ....
>
> Oh! Since a craft of great subtlety is much praised by worldly men, much more should the glorious law of God be loved and praised of Christ's children, for all things that men needeth, both bodily and ghostly [spiritually] is contained in this blessed law, and especially in the gospel. And therefore Christ in the hour of his ascension commanded to his disciples to preach it to all people – but, we be sure, not only in French nor in Latin, but in that language that the people use to speak, for thus he taught himself. And here is a rule to Christian folk of what language so ever they be: it is a high sacrifice to God to know holy writ and to do thereafter, where it be taught or written to them in Latin or in English, in French or in Dutch, or in any other language after the people hath understanding. And thus clerks should be glad that the people know God's law, and they themselves busily by all the good means that they might, should occupy them to make the people know the truth of God's law. For this was the cause that Jesus became man and suffered and died on

the tree, so that by keeping of his lore the people might rise from ghostly dead and come to the bliss that never shall have end. And give any clerk opposed this and so concluded, who shall be damned but such a quick fiend? And therefore said Christ to the father of such clerks, "Not only in bodily bread liveth man but in each word that cometh out of God's mouth," the which word is the sustenance of Christian men's souls. For right as bread strengthens man's body to travail, so the word of God maketh said man's soul in the Holy Ghost, and strong to work thereafter. And this bread is more needful than is the first bread, as the soul of man is worthier than his body. For when the body shall lie stinking in the grave, then the soul that loved this bread and lived thereafter shall be in endless bliss with Jesus their spouse. And thus if, through negligence of our bishops and prelates and other false teachers that are in the church, the truth of God's word be not shown to the people, pray we Jesus Christ bishop of our souls that he ordain preachers to warn us to leave our sins by preaching of his law, and that, as he inspired the prophets with wisdom and knowledge and taught the apostles the way of all truth, so lighten he our hearts with understanding of his love and grant us grace to live thereafter both in word and work. For those that contradict the gospel and the epistle and do not want to let it to be preached and pursued ... love not Christ; wherefore, if they would but amend themselves while they have time, they shall die in their sins ....

THE CONSTITUTIONS OF ARCHBISHOP ARUNDEL AGAINST THE LOLLARDS (1409)

The following excerpt, taken from Arundel's register, identifies Lollardy as a heresy. This treatise seeks to stamp out the heresy by abolishing various Lollard practices, including the transmission of spiritual documents written in English, preaching on the part of the laity without authorization of the church, meeting secretly to discuss theology, or even knowing about or hiding information about those meetings or practitioners.

> 1. ... No one should preach without licence, except a person privileged in law.
> 2. If anyone should preach in any church, graveyard, or other place in the province of Canterbury without licence, that church, graveyard, or other place should *ipso facto* lie under an interdict ....

4. No preacher ... is to teach or preach ... concerning the sacrament of the altar, matrimony, or any other sacrament of the church anything other than what has been resolved by Holy Mother Church.
5. ... Masters teaching in arts or grammar, or instructing any others whatsoever in elementary knowledge, shall not meddle at all with matters of the Catholic faith, the sacrament of the altar, or other sacraments of the Church, or any theological matter, contrary to the determination of the Church; nor shall they expound holy scriptures, except the meaning of the text, as was accustomed to be done of old.
6. ... No book or tract composed by John Wyclif or anyone else in his time or since then ... shall henceforth be read in schools, halls, hostels, or other places whatsoever in our province, nor shall anything be taught according to them, unless it has first been examined by the university of Oxford or Cambridge, or at least twelve persons from them whom we ... shall cause to be elected ...
7. ... No one henceforth shall translate any text of Holy Scripture into the English language on his own authority, by way of book, booklet, or tract ... under pain of the greater excommunication ....
8. No one ... of whatever grade, estate, or condition he may be ... shall assert or propose any conclusions or propositions sounding contrary to the Catholic faith or good rules, beyond the necessary teaching of his faculty, in schools or outside, in disputing or communicating, and whether a disclaimer is made or not ...
9. No one shall presume to dispute publicly or secretly about articles determined by the Church, as in decrees, decretals, and our provincial constitutions ... except to have a true understanding of them and this expressly ....

NOTES

1   D.W. Robertson, *A Preface to Chaucer: Studies in Medieval Perspectives* (Princeton, NJ: Princeton UP, 1962).

2   Henrietta Leyser, "Piety, Religion, and the Church," in *The Oxford Illustrated History of Medieval England*, ed. Nigel Saul (Oxford: Oxford UP, 1997) 204.

3   *The Book of Margery Kempe*, trans. B.A. Windeatt (London: Penguin, 1985) 104.

4   "The Register of William Courtenay," in Joseph Dahmus, *William Courtenay: Archbishop of Canterbury 1381-1396* (University Park, PA: The Pennsylvania State UP, 1966) 145-46.

5   "The Register of William Courtenay" 121.

6   Lee Patterson, "The Living Witnesses of Our Redemption: Martyrdom and Imitation in Chaucer's Prioress's Tale," *Journal of Medieval and Early Modern Studies* 31.3 (2001): 538.

7   Patterson, "The Living Witnesses" 537.

8   Boccaccio 42.

9   Boccaccio 44.

10 A.J. Pollard, *Late Medieval England 1399-1509* (New York: Longman, 2000) 204.

11 Henry Gee and William John Hardy, *Documents Illustrative of English Church History* (New York: Macmillan, 1896) 130.

12 Anne Hudson, *The Premature Reformation: Wycliffite Texts and Lollard History* (New York: Oxford UP, 1988) 512.

CHAPTER V

"Trouthe and Honour, Freedom and Curteisie"
War, Pageantry, and the Knighthood

Introduction

C haucer's Knight has long been considered the epitome of gracious and humble chivalry. He upholds the values of loyalty, generosity, honor, and courtesy; instead of comporting himself arrogantly or ostentatiously, like other aristocrats, he shows humbleness and devotion. The knight Arveragus, in Chaucer's "Franklin's Tale," holds similar values, upholding the integrity of an implied promise even when he is threatened with infidelity. His comportment is so very astonishing that eventually everyone in the tale strives to be counted as "free"—and presumably as chivalric—as he.

It would be difficult to overstate the importance that chivalry played in shaping the late medieval imagination. As a code of conduct that modeled courteous behavior both on the battlefield and in human relationships, chivalry defined the estate and social identity of the aristocratic knight. At its best, chivalry provided a model that encouraged warrior-knights to inhibit selfish desires and rise above petty human interaction. Not every example of knighthood in *The Canterbury Tales* is positive, however; Chaucer explores the chivalric code not only through characters who embody its ideals but also through those who merely pretend to them. If Arveragus and the Knight arguably model the chivalric ideal at its very best, the knight in "The Wife of Bath's Tale" is a rapist, who has to learn to listen to "what women want" in order to save his life. And although the Knight of the General Prologue himself seems to exemplify

the ideal, his chivalric tale introduces two charac⌐
parameters of chivalric behavior only imperfe⌐
define themselves by a rigidly codified standard
ing, and dying for a courteous lady whom they
distance and who does not even know they e⌐
the chivalric ideal demonstrates the limits of a masculine ⌐⌐⌐
that, in Lee Patterson's words, "foreclose(s) self-reflection and critical distance."[1] Such contradictory literary examples show how difficult it is to
characterize medieval chivalry: even those who aspired to the ideal had a
mixed understanding of it.

The Origins of Chivalry

The prestige that accompanied the station of the aristocratic knight was a
long time in the making. Most scholars agree that there is some corollary
between the rise of courtly vernacular literature and the development
of the ideals and behaviors that came to be associated with aristocratic
knights. They disagree, however, as to whether the courtly literature preceded the social behavior or whether it merely mirrored it. Certainly we
do know that the rise of the knights as a landed upper class—the class later
to be established as the "nobility," who lived off the labor of others and
who expected to participate to some extent in government—occurred
gradually in the centuries after Charlemagne. By amassing titles and property, the rewards for war pillage and service, a class initially constituted of
the rough warrior/servants surrounding the king gradually turned into a
landed, wealthy elite. As the territories and power of the early medieval
kings increased, this class of warriors became the administrative retinue
upon which the king depended to protect and control his lands. In the
eleventh century the introduction of stirrups led to a mounted cavalry
who could use lances, and thus our idea of the medieval knight was born:

> Imagine a military force of the period. It presents a dual aspect.
> On the one hand there is a body of infantry as ill-equipped for
> attack as for defense, slow in advancing to the assault and slow in
> flight, and quickly exhausted by long marches on wretched tracks
> or across-country. On the other hand, looking down from their
> chargers on the poor wretches who, "shamefully" as one court
> romance puts it, drag their feet in the dust and mire, are stalwart
> soldiers, proud of being able to fight and maneuver swiftly, skillfully,
> effectively—the only force, indeed...which it is worth the trouble

of counting when assessing the numerical strength of an army. In a civilization where war was an everyday matter, there was no more vital contrast than this.[2]

By the eleventh century this class of warriors had not only begun to take on the status of nobility, but had also undertaken legal steps to protect its social privilege. Although the process of separation from the lower orders of society was not uniform across Europe, we can roughly trace the jagged process of gentrification. The concern for ensuring that knighthood be conferred not solely on the basis of valor alone increased in the twelfth century, when several prominent groups of "villeins," or unfree men who were bound to vassalage under the feudal system, claimed the status of knight.[3] As knighthood shaded into nobility, the title of "knight" became a hereditary right, and pedigrees were established to guarantee an elite ancestry.[4] In 1186 Frederick Barbarossa, king of Germany and Roman emperor, decreed that the oath of knighthood could only be taken by sons of knights. Other monarchs followed suit, so that by the end of the twelfth century, the knighthood had become the domain exclusively of the aristocracy. Anyone could fight in the wars, in other words, but bondsmen were prohibited from rising up the ranks or from ever taking the oath of knighthood. A distinction arose between knights and members of the lower classes, who provided the bulk of the militia. Knights were "free," property-owning cavalrymen, whose relative wealth allowed them to purchase the equipment necessary to the station—the helmet and mail, the horse and its equipage, and the arms. Bondsmen could take up arms, but after the twelfth century, they could not rise to the higher ranks.

Ideological markers of status and distinction accompanied the historical transformation of this class of warriors into an aristocracy. The first dubbing ceremony publicly conferring knighthood as a signal rank was recorded in 1128 in Rouen (in modern-day France). The ceremony was secular but nonetheless imbued with Christian symbolism, which underscored the blessed condition of the knight. The initiate took a ritual bath, symbolizing baptism, dressed in the finest clothes, and appeared before the king, who personally girded him with a special sword. Feasts and tournaments followed.[5] Later ceremonies included a blessing of the sword and oaths of loyalty to king and to God. Although such ceremonies were not regulated by the church, they demonstrated the nobility's interest in legitimating itself as a special class, protected and even ordained by God. An abundance of writing sustained this claim. Bernard of Clairvaux, writing in the early twelfth century on the newly formed Knights Templar, declared that the Christian knight had God on his side, and that in fighting Christian battles he "ceaselessly wages a twofold war both against flesh and blood and against a spiritual army of evil in the heavens."[6] John of Salisbury, writing a few years later, took Bernard's claims even further, declaring without irony (or any reference to history) that the origin of the Christian knight coincided with the coming of Christianity itself. The military oath, he claimed, extended back to the first Christian emperors. Because the knight was a protector of both secular and eternal law, he should receive the same devotion as any steward of God.[7] Within a century, the drive to establish a mythic origin for knights had reached almost ludicrous dimensions. Ramon Llull, a Spanish knight writing in 1276, imagined knighthood as a special corps of quasi-divine men, willed by God to conquer injustice and falseness: "And therefore the people were divided into groups of one thousand. And from each thousand was chosen one man who more than all the others was most loyal, most noble in courage, best instructed, and best mannered."[8] By the late thirteenth and early fourteenth centuries, knights had achieved a near-heroic status.

What drove this idealization of the warrior was, in part, the vernacular romance. Appearing as a relatively new genre in the twelfth century, the vernacular romance concerned the acts and ideals of knights, modeling a form of ideal chivalric behavior that rapidly became adopted as a social reality. Authors such as Chrétien de Troyes and Marie de France focused on knights who tempered their military prowess with courtesy and deference toward women, both of which implied empathy and an attention to the needs of others. The knight Erec, in Chrétien de Troyes' twelfth-century romance, for example, speaks politely, serves his queen and wife well, defends their honor on multiple occasions, gives generously of his own wealth, and rights social wrongs. He is not perfect in the beginning of the tale: he loves his wife to such an extent that he risks losing his own honor before his men. But he listens to criticism and corrects his own flaws, so that by the end of the romance, his kingly robes, embroidered with a cosmic depiction of the seven liberal arts, reflect the knightly perfection that he has acquired. Guigemar and Lanval, knights in the romances of the roughly contemporary author Marie de France, exhibit similar qualities. Their social demeanor and humility are emphasized over their martial capability. Indeed, the knight who has right on his side need never fear defeat, for God is always on the side of the righteous. Thus, the romances imply, attention to that inner sense of conviction and selflessness eventually guarantees martial success. The outer perfection reflects the inner virtue.

To a large extent, the ritualized code of conduct associated with the knighthood had to do with mitigating the propensity to violence and aggression that in actuality made the knight good at what he did. This attention to the manners and demeanor appropriate to a knight in service of a king demonstrates a marked shift in emphasis on the part of vernacular writers. A gentle bearing and noble aspect were products of a refined set of manners associated with court. It has been speculated that these clerkly writers were consciously dedicated to educating and socializing the rough breed of warriors who made up the king's retinue. Social harmony depended on the cultivation of manners and respect among a group more used to violence and conflict than to conversation.[9] Because of the fraught power relationship between the king and his nobles, the courtier's success hinged on his ability to negotiate conversational and behavioral nuances. Any perceived infraction against loyalty could result in a death sentence, so that those eager to survive learned how to moderate their tempers and choose their words carefully. The romances provided a hero worthy of emulation in the Christian knight who defends justice, receives the respect of his peers and superiors, and earns the love of the most beautiful lady in court. The romances also modeled a kind of behavior that differentiated this new class of knights from the rough laborers; in these works, knights are *noble*, not only in blood, but in action. For a relatively new social class aspiring to legitimate its claims both by blood and by merit, the romances provided a powerful and persuasive model.

This legitimating impulse can be found in the popular romance motif of the "fair unknown," in which a young man enters the court, refuses to divulge his identity, and sets about proving his knightly valor through his own deeds. After proving his physical worth, the young man modestly admits his noble blood. Probably the most famous example is the "Tale of Gareth" in Malory's *Morte Darthur*. Gareth is the nephew of King Arthur, but is unknown when he first appears at court. Because he has such a handsome and aristocratic bearing, all the knights agree that he must be noble, but Gareth refuses to confirm his heredity, instead taking on the job of the kitchen boy until a young woman arrives at court seeking a knight to free her imprisoned sister. Gareth volunteers, proves his merit in many fights against knights, and returns triumphantly on the arm of the beautiful Lyonesse at the end of the tale. He thus fulfills the fantasy of all knights: that the knightly merits discernible to all are not only based on personal worth but are also a product of his noble bloodline. Variants of the "fair unknown" motif appear in the Tristan romances; the story of Galahad; the Perceval legends; and even, with a slight twist, in Chaucer's

"Knight's Tale," when Arcite, having fled prison, returns to Theseus's court to be near Emily, and rises up through the ranks despite his alleged lack of relations simply because of his innately noble bearing.

CHIVALRY AND COURTLY LOVE

The combination of noble blood and noble bearing is captured in the Middle English word "gentilesse," a richly associative word, from which the modern "gentleman" descends, that signifies not just gentility, but gentle behavior. Chaucer's Knight is "a verray, parfit gentil knight" (GP 72); he is a "true" knight, meaning that his nobility is signaled not only by his station but by his identity and comportment. In *Sir Gawain and the Green Knight*, Gawain's shield is blazoned with a pentangle signifying the five knightly virtues—loyalty, generosity, courtesy, "clanes" (cleanness), and "pité" (compassion). Notably absent are attributes that we nowadays identify with knights, such as personal honor, courage, or strength. Instead, the poem emphasizes virtues that bespeak the need for understanding and protecting the interests of others over the interests of the self. Compassion requires that one look outward, beyond the immediate rewards that come the way of the wealthy, and instead think of the social good.

Upholding such high-mindedness is easier said than done, of course; even Gawain finds himself falling short of the ideal despite his determination to enact it. In its disenchantment, *Sir Gawain and the Green Knight* reflects late fourteenth-century complaints about a militia that failed to uphold the ideal virtues described and celebrated in courtly literature. Some of the best romances address the difficulty of making reality conform to the ideal. In "The Wife of Bath's Tale," for example, a very imperfect knight—convicted of rape and ungrateful to his benefactress—is reminded of what it is he is supposed to value, namely, gentle manners and humility. In this and other tales Chaucer unpacks the word "gentilesse" in all its permutations, making it clear that the birthright of gentility should be used with godly grace:

> ... Gentillesse nys but renomee
> Of thyne auncestres, for hire heigh bountee,
> Which is a strange thing to thy persone.
> Thy gentillesse cometh fro God allone.
> Thanne comth our verray gentillesse of grace;
> It was no thyng biquethe us with oure place. (WT 1159-1164).

Ancestral gentility and behavioral gentility, as the loathly lady points out, are two very different things, and having one does not guarantee the other. Nor does a legacy endow one with the right to boorishness. Chaucer's comments on chivalry and its practitioners appear relatively late in the Middle Ages, when the prerogative of the nobility was so firmly established that the disparity between literary heroes and actual knights was blatant. Yet the chivalric ideal retained its imaginative power, despite the failure of individuals to conform to it. The Canterbury pilgrims and their tales thus display a range of possible relations between fantasy and reality: if the Knight exemplifies the ideal, for instance, his son, the Squire, seems more intrigued with the trappings of knighthood than with its lofty aspirations. Yet even this difference between father and son might be due to the relatively peaceful nature of the times rather than to a wholesale rejection of chivalric ideals. The Squire, unlike his crusading father, has had the opportunity to practice his craft only in tournaments and lesser venues. In the same way, circumstances might mitigate our assessment of the Knight. His lack of knowledge about women is not particular to him; obviously, it is a widespread phenomenon. And the Knight, at least, is able to recognize a truth when he hears it. The story ends with the optimistic promise that he has learned something about the world and will redeem his past errors.

A prominent feature of the ideal knight is his ability to love. The term "courtly love" refers to the ritualized form of service and devotion that a knight owes to his lady. This form of love derived almost entirely from the literature of the troubadours and the vernacular romances, which stylized love as a form of obedience modeled after the obedience that vassals owed to a lord.[10] The term given to this stylized form of behavior is no mere abstraction, however. In the twelfth century courtly love was specifically named and theorized as an ennobling force:

> Oh what a wonderful thing is love, which makes a man shine with
> so many virtues and teaches everyone, no matter who he is, so many
> good traits of character! There is another thing about love that we
> should not praise in few words: it adorns a man, so to speak, with the
> virtue of chastity, because he who shines with the light of one love
> can hardly think of embracing another woman, even a beautiful one.[11]

Andreas Capellanus's *Art of Courtly Love*, from which the above passage is taken, is an odd and contradictory work; many, in fact, have wondered if the treatise was intended to be ironic. Whatever its intentions, it clearly addresses matters of interest among twelfth-century court patrons, who desired stories and treatises about actions that glorified the courtier-knight in general. A key feature of Capellanus's courtly love is that it belongs in the domain of the aristocratic and the mannered. Knights are capable of heightened feelings because they are noble people; only superior beings are capable of such fine feelings.[12] Despite its pretension to private passion, courtly love is relentlessly public: that he pines for love demonstrates the knight's innate nobility.

Love itself is expressed as a form of abjection. The lover grows pale, loses sleep, and even comes close to dying because of his suffering. All see, and admire, his pain. The knight in love is capable of enduring years of service for his lady, no matter how unresponsive she is. In ideal situations, this service has positive and productive social effects, but in some cases, as in the cruel Guinevere's love for Lancelot, the lady may abuse her powers and demand extreme forms of humiliation and subjection as proof of her lover's devotion. Again and again in the *Morte Darthur* Guinevere whimsically signals her lover that he should deliberately lose tournaments and suffer public defeat. By enacting these public gestures, the knight affirms his innate gentility. Because it is readily apparent that he loves, his refined sensibility is on display as a public marker of his noble character and status.

As the example of Lancelot and Guinevere suggests, courtly love is typically also adulterous. It is thus secretive and characterized by long periods of separation, which extend the protagonist's suffering and provide additional opportunities for knightly service. The knight who cannot be with his lady channels his energies into helping others instead—typically other ladies in distress, but also other nobles and even common citizens subject to injustice or threat. The vernacular romances frequently correlate these acts of service with the passions of the knight. It is not unusual for the fictionalized knight to require that his defeated opponent return to his lady to recount the story of his defeat publicly before her. This ensures that the lady recognizes that the knight's positive social service has in effect been done for her alone, but insofar as the deed is recounted publicly, it also validates the knight's honor and reputation at the court.

The thin line that separates courtly devotion from self-glorification in twelfth- and thirteenth-century works did not go unnoticed by later writers. Christine de Pizan's *Book of the Duke of True Lovers* portrays courtly love as an exclusively male prerogative, which glorifies the suitor at the expense of the beloved. In a telling passage, the young Duke, who has become enamored with a lady, describes his personal transformation to idealized perfection through love:

> I did not yet feel the fierce assault of burning desire, which assails
> lovers, making them tremble and burn, grow pale, thirst, and become
> agitated. That had not yet come to pass. For at that time I thought
> only of how I would be elegant and dashing, how I would have a
> beautiful mount and expensive clothing, and how, avoiding stinginess,
> I would share my wealth generously...In order to acquire the ways
> of love I took pains to learn how to sing and dance, and to take up
> arms. I thought that by pursuing love, arms, and valor, honor would
> surely come, and so it truly does.[13]

We learn a lot about the Duke and his desires in this passage, and very little about the lady he claims to love. This lady, as it turns out, is not at all pleased at the attention from her suitor. She reminds him of the potential consequences that his attention will bring her as a married woman, and begs him repeatedly to pursue unmarried women instead. Although she eventually succumbs to his feelings, her honor requires that the affair remain unconsummated. Even then, the mutually honorable affection they eventually accept as a compromise brings nothing but pain, because their feelings can never be consummated. Christine thus reveals the unromantic flipside of the courtly love fantasy: lovers can choose adultery, or they can choose chaste resistance and the ensuing stagnation. Neither option is very satisfying.

Indeed, marriage is only occasionally an option for lovers in the romances. As Capellanus writes in *The Art of Courtly Love*, "When made public love rarely endures"; marriage, in other words, is too public a venue for such fine feelings as love.[14] Whether Capellanus was serious or not when he wrote these words, the vernacular romances certainly insist that love—and the chivalric feats it inspires—belongs to those unshackled by wedlock. In the *Morte Darthur*, marriage effectively exempts a knight from participating in court tournaments and other functions; Sir Gareth, once he weds his beloved damsel, must content himself with merely watching the feats of the other knights.[15] Unmarried women, however, are necessary commodities: they witness and verify the acts of the knights they accompany, and, in several cases, Malory's knights are loath to proceed before they have first procured a lady to accompany them on their travels.

The lady, then, might be seen as the logical extension of the knight's courtliness embodied in the opposite sex—in Chrétien de Troye's twelfth-century romance *Erec*, the beautiful Enide is even described as Erec's mirror. The more beautiful the lady is, the more worthy, by association, the knight. This equation reaches its more extreme form in Chaucer's

"Knight's Tale," where the two imprisoned knights, Palamon and Arcite, become sworn enemies when both fall in love with the noble Emily. Undaunted by the fact that they have never met the damsel at stake and indeed have only seen her from across a great distance, the rivals embark upon a campaign that lasts over seven years and only ends when one of them dies. Courtly love and service are components of the chivalric identity. "A man moot nedes love, maugree his heed," as Arcite himself warns (KT 1169).

Practicing Knighthood

Chaucer's interest in the various ways in which the aristocracy performed its chivalric function is reflected in the social reality of the late fourteenth century. Edward the Black Prince, the eldest son of Edward III, was regarded by his contemporaries as the embodiment of the noble warrior. The chronicler Froissart referred to him as "the flower of chivalry"; Thomas Walsingham called him "a second Hector."[16] Establishing his reputation as a valiant leader and warrior at the Battle of Crecy when he was only 16, Edward continued on to impressive victories at Poitiers—during which he captured King John of France—and in Spain. The Black Prince was in every way the model knight: he loved lavish display and took part often in tournaments and jousts. Yet he was also apparently very pious and bore himself with a humility that was remarked on by his contemporaries. His devotion to the cult of the Trinity was well-known. He held feasts every year in honor of Trinity Sunday, and his portraits—found in pilgrim's badges or in his biography by Sir John Chandos, who accompanied him on several of his campaigns—shows him kneeling before the Trinity.[17] The Black Prince also made large bequests to the order at Ashridge and was an avid and reverent defender of the abbot of St. Albans. In all, his reputation echoed the ideal of valor tempered with extreme piety and humility espoused by Chaucer in his portrait of the Knight.

So venerated was the Black Prince that when he died after a protracted illness, his passing was recorded as nothing short of calamity, or so the St. Alban's Chronicle suggests:

> On his death the hopes of the English utterly perished; for while he was alive they feared no enemy invasion, while he was with them they feared no hostile encounter. Never, while he was with them, did they suffer the disgrace of a campaign that had been unsuccessful or abandoned .... Despite his serious illness because of which he could

hardly stay on his horse for an hour, he was such an inspiration to his men that they considered that it was impossible for any city to withstand their force.[18]

As our chapters on politics and religion indicate, modern historians are more skeptical about the prince's campaigns than Edward's contemporaries. His intervention in the Spanish campaigns was brutal, and his victorious sieges in France employed the standard burn-and-pillage policy. Yet except for a few complainers, the people of the fourteenth century cared little about such casualties of war. Edward was a national hero, whose personal conduct brought honor to the entire nation.

Both the Black Prince and Edward III, his father, used the chivalric ideal as a form of propaganda, staging tournaments reminiscent of the romances and making use of elaborate symbolism and literary conventions. The tournament had its practical justification: knights needed opportunities to train. Jousting allowed knights to practice the mounted charge and use of the lance, while hand-to-hand combat tested swordsmanship and other necessary battle skills. All-out melees might also be staged, in which groups of knights practiced "jousts of war," much like the staged battle between the forces of Palamon and Arcite before the court of Theseus in "The Knight's Tale." These tournaments were not at all safe. Numerous young men met their ends participating in staged tournaments, which caused the censure of some contemporaries. Yet these unfortunate deaths did not temper the predominant public enthusiasm for such lavish spectacles at all. These staged events had important aesthetic and ideological components, so that no expense was spared. Knights dressed in their best finery, which incorporated symbolism that reinforced their loyalties and aristocratic associations. Sometimes knights donned costumes or participated incognito; jousts during Edward III's tenure included elaborate masquerades that reflected contemporary religious and foreign policy, such as the tournament at Smithfield in 1343, in which a body of knights posed as the pope and all his cardinals.[19]

Tournaments encouraged knights to show the courtesy modeled in the romances. Strict rules of conduct regulated the treatment of a fallen opponent, and the values of loyalty and valor could be demonstrated in the knight's deference to his colleagues and superiors. Knights also paid ritual obeisance to the ladies who sat in observance in the lists. In return, the ladies and the higher nobility were expected to show their generosity toward their servants and retainers in the form of lavish gifts and praise. The Windsor tournament, held in 1344, was even more ideologically inspired than its Smithfield predecessor: knights were staged into a "round table" suggesting King Arthur's fellowship, took mass in the chapel, and made oaths echoing that of Arthur's knights before undertaking the quest for the Holy Grail.[20]

CHIVALRIC ORDERS

Edward's Order of the Garter, founded in 1348, institutionalized his claims to a chivalric identity. The order is associated with a story—almost certainly apocryphal—that confirms Edward's courtly pretensions: while dancing before the court, a lady lost her garter, much to the amusement of lookers-on. Edward, however, gallantly retrieved the garter and returned it with the words, "*Honi soit qui mal y pense*"—evil to him who thinks evil of it. These words became the motto of the Order of the Garter, which itself continued the chivalric themes of Arthurian romance. The original members of the order were drawn from the participants in the recent victories at Crecy and Calais. Those associated specifically with the division of the Black Prince were honored with stalls in the Black Prince's side of the Chapel of St. George.[21]

The imagery and ideal of chivalry associated with the Order of the Garter provided a fertile source of symbolism and allusion for imaginative literature. *Sir Gawain and the Green Knight*, for example, concludes with Arthur and his entire court donning the green girdle that signifies Gawain's humility, an act many have taken to signify as homage to the very similar garter that functions as the central symbol of Edward's humility. The motto of the Order of the Garter is inscribed beneath the last line of the poem in the manuscript, making the connection more explicit. The poem *Winner and Waster* makes an even more direct connection, invoking the blue and gold colors of the order, as well as its famous motto, in its description of the noble king's environment and retinue:

> At the crest of a cliff a cabana was raised,
> All adorned with red was the roof and the sides,
> With English coins full bright, beaten of gold,
> And each one gaily surrounded with garters of India blue,
> And each with a garter of gold adorned full rich.
> Then were there words in the web woven up high,
> Painted of blue, with points between,
> That were formed full fair upon French letters,

And it was all one saying in the English tongue:
"Shame has the knight that any harm thinks."[22]

By endowing the just king with the symbolism and ideals of the Order of
the Garter, the anonymous author validates his fictional character as having
the chivalric sense of justice appropriate to a judgment on the virtues of
expenditure and moderation.

Although the Order of the Garter was the most prestigious of the
orders founded in fourteenth-century England, it was only one of many.
Knightly orders and confraternities proliferated in the latter Middle Ages.
The Order of the Band was founded in Castile in 1330. France had the
Company of the Star, Naples the Order of the Knot.[23] In addition to these
secular orders, important crusading orders existed, such as the Knights of
the Temple and the Knights of the Hospital, both founded in the early
twelfth century. The latter orders were committed to the conquest of
Jerusalem and the Holy Land. More so than the secular orders, the members of the religious confraternities committed themselves—at least in the
early years of their inceptions—to living the role of the Christian knight.
The orders were conceptualized along the principles of a monastic community, so that the knights took vows of chastity and poverty in addition
to swearing their fealty to Christendom.

Such ideals might inspire the founding of an order, but often the
years dimmed the original vision. During the 200-year period in which
they flourished, the Templars, in particular, amassed great wealth, largely
from their unscrupulous sacking of Mediterranean cities. The rise of religious and secular chivalric orders was thus accompanied by a fair amount
of criticism from skeptics who pointed toward the wealth and prestige
of the orders and the sense that these institutions promoted the self-
entitlement of an already arrogant class. The Templars and the Hospitallers
were targeted in part because of the wealth they acquired through their
crusading campaigns in the Middle East and their powerful position as the
"bankers" of the kings of continental Europe. The Templars were abolished as an order in 1312 by Pope Clement V, following a trial during
which many of their leaders confessed, under torture, to heretical practices, including idol-worship, desecrating the cross, and homosexuality.
Historians have argued that Philip IV of France, who initiated the accusations against the Templars, had much to gain by dismantling the order
and confiscating its wealth. However, the attitudes that contributed to
the persecution of the Templars were complicated and far-reaching; the

conviction that the crusading orders were in need of serious reform had much to do with the distrust that contributed to their suppression.

The dramatic downfall of the Templars did not signal the end of chivalric orders in general, however. If anything, the creation of martial organizations increased in the following years. As the number of chivalric orders proliferated, so too did the granting of liveries, which mimicked them in form if not in ideology. Whereas membership in an order involved the taking of oaths and cleaving to a particular ideal of chivalric identity and behavior, assuming a livery or a badge signaled merely the association with a particular lord and membership in his own private militia. The distribution of badges as a means of establishing ties of loyalty and public markers of belonging was extremely popular in the late Middle Ages as a means of quickly forming temporary bands of retainers to enforce dominion throughout a lord's territories. John of Gaunt bestowed collars to his retinue; the minor aristocracy indulged in the practice as well.

The bestowing of liveries met with considerable protest on the part of the Commons (SEE ALSO CHAPTER 2). Formal petitions were introduced in Parliament during the reigns of Edward III, Richard II, and Henry IV. The Commons objected that the practice appropriated the emblems of chivalry to enforce a purely martial order over territories. Maintenance, the Commons charged, had little to do with the chivalric code and everything to do with exerting power over the weak.[24] It was not unusual for petty lords to form their own militias to enforce private laws on their own lands. The enlisted men that constituted these militias, emboldened by their badges, used their affiliation with the local magnate to exploit the weak; the emblem of military identity enabled a form of brute rule.

One of the more controversial uses of livery occurred when Richard II began designating his own private militia with White Hart badges in the last years of his reign. After the Merciless Parliament cost him his London supporters, Richard turned to other resources and began recruiting his retinue from the northwest, which had historically been removed from the culture and politics of London. His presence in the North may explain a small surge of literary efforts in the area, especially in the genre of romance. Most of these works are of interest only to specialists, but several—notably *Sir Gawain and the Green Knight* and *Pearl*—are among the best works of the age. Richard developed relationships with many of the wealthy families in the area, including the family of Sir John Stanley, Knight of the Garter and controller of the wardrobe, and Lawrence Booth, later to become chancellor of England.[25] Along with John de Macclesfield, another native of the northwest, Stanley was instrumental in seeking out hundreds of Cheshire archers and retainers for Richard's bodyguard under his personal insignia of the white hart.[26]

The lengthy contact with Richard's court retinue left a mark on northwest England. It is tempting to conclude that the detailed knowledge the *Gawain*-Poet displays about courtly protocol derives from direct contact with Richard's retinue in the northwest. The poem's date of composition, with *terminus ad quem* of 1400, potentially coincides with the period in which Richard actively attempted to shape the perception of his kingship through dramatic displays of courtly power and to recruit broadly from magnates in Cheshire and its environs, the area in which the *Gawain*-Poet flourished. Richard's founding of the Order of the White Hart, in particular, perpetuated the careful mythos of the monarch and marked the king's new favorites for recognition. Established in 1390, even while the House of Commons was expressing its concern over the use of badges and livery, the Order of the White Hart threatened to replace the highly venerated Order of the Garter with this new group of men specially selected for their loyalty to Richard and their opposition to the nobles of London. Not surprisingly, the magnates back in London were offended. Could the reference to the Order of the Garter at the end of *Sir Gawain and the Green Knight* refer more broadly to the new elite King's Order of the White Hart and to elite aristocratic orders in general? Richard's new favorites incurred the resentment of his peers, as discussed in Chapter 1; according to local accounts, they were "beast-like" in manner yet haughty in disposition, considering themselves "the equals and companions of lords."[27] The shift in royal focus led to concern among the traditional nobility because it instilled an artificially inflated sense of worth or personal value based on membership within a select group—concerns directly engaged in *Sir Gawain and the Green Knight*.

Richard was specifically named in Parliament's complaint about liveries in 1389. Eager to show a willingness to cooperate, the king agreed to give up the badges to set an example for others.[28] This move was overtly political, intended more to force his recalcitrant lords to give up their own military retinues than to initiate peace, and the appellant lords were, as he anticipated, reluctant to agree. Parliament accepted his efforts, however, and all members of the lower estates and all warriors who contracted for less than a lifetime's service were forbidden to wear livery badges.

As the conflict about liveries and the ambivalent portrayals in literature suggest, then, medieval citizens themselves recognized that a martial identity—especially one legitimated through special emblems or orders—often produced a sense of entitlement that was at odds with the noble aspirations of the chivalric ideal. Yet, despite individual corruptions, the idea of knighthood continued to resonate in late medieval literature. Even as knightly practices attracted critics, the culture continued to strive for an ideal that had not yet lost its force.

Warfare and the Crusades

Despite the emphasis on love in courtly literature, the true calling of the knight, of course, was warfare. The latter half of the fourteenth century offered many opportunities for defending the king's land and extending Christian aspirations in the Mediterranean. The ongoing series of battles most frequently associated with the medieval knight are undoubtedly the Crusades, initiated in the late eleventh century under Pope Urban II. A product of the growing militarization of medieval society and the need to occupy a restless militia during times of relative peace, the First Crusade gave the growing European warrior class an arena in which to prove their nobility and a unifying sense of mission.

The First Crusade corresponded with the period in which knights were achieving social dominance. During this time the term *miles*, or "knight," was beginning to circulate in reference to that new warrior class.[29] Conventional scholarly opinion holds that the call to crusade galvanized a class and a society already used to violent means for upholding justice; trial by combat or ordeal, for example, was a common means of resolving dispute. The underlying belief was that God ensured the victory of the righteous. If righteousness was proved by strength, then that was part of natural law. Supporting this inherent doctrine was Urban II's analogy of the crusade to the pilgrimage. According to this logic, knights who undertook the journey to Jerusalem followed a traditional pilgrimage route; thus, their military agenda only furthered their spiritual journey to salvation. Those who undertook the crusade were promised the equivalent of a bulk forgiveness for all sins previously committed and confessed, because, Urban suggested, the undertaking was so difficult and came at such personal sacrifice that it amounted to a form of extended penance.[30]

The justification for the crusade did much to promote the idealization of the Christian knight who defended both God and king. Knights were not alone in undertaking the crusade; members of all walks of society participated, albeit at lower martial levels, but the crusades were the domain and privilege of the knightly class. The First Crusade proved to be only a beginning; throughout the next several hundred years, Christian warriors laid siege to the Holy Land, sometimes to the great shame of Christendom. After the Third Crusade failed to recapture the Holy Land, for example, Pope Innocent III rekindled the mission in the early thirteenth century. Things went awry when the crusaders were diverted by Prince Alexius Angelus of Byzantium, who had been forced to flee from the city because of what he characterized as his uncle's unlawful usurpation. Promising the crusaders ample payment and additional soldiers for the mission to Jerusalem, Alexius convinced the crusaders to spend a winter in Constantinople, so that he could raise the necessary monies. When he refused to compensate his defenders, hostilities broke out between the Western Catholic crusaders and the Eastern Orthodox Byzantines. The crusaders turned on Alexius, pillaging the land in what Robert of Clari rationalized as just payment for services rendered.[31]

The sack of Constantinople that followed has been almost uniformly regarded as a low point in the crusades. Constantinople was the wealthiest and most sophisticated city of the Middle Ages, and it was destroyed by Christians turning on Christians. The motive was purely mercenary, as the wealth of the city was freely looted and its beautiful buildings burned. Much of the great art of the ancient world was destroyed or melted for gold. The ideological argument that had protected the Christian knight and glorified his motives was thus exposed as a cover for mercantilism, and relations between the East and the West deteriorated, exacerbating tensions that are still with us today.

Despite the criticism that the sack of Constantinople caused, the crusades continued into the fourteenth century, although the later expeditions were less clear in their mission than their predecessors. For one thing, the target was no longer Jerusalem, since the Holy Land had been lost. Instead, the targets became the pockets of infidels in outlying countries of central Europe. Additionally, these later crusades failed to achieve the massive momentum that united knights from across different nations; instead, they were largely organized by local rulers who lacked international backing.[32] Because the ideological sensibility that drove the knight to prove his worth in crusade remained, however, the knights of the wealthiest and most established families typically continued to undertake a crusade as a matter of course. The two powerful sons of King Edward III, Edward the Black Prince and Thomas of Woodstock, went on crusade, as did the Lancasters, the Beauchamps, the Bohuns, the Percies, and the Despensers. Henry Bolingbroke, later Henry IV, went on crusade in Prussia in the early 1390s. Chaucer declares his Knight to have participated in a number of well-known battles, including crusades in Alexandria, Prussia, and Spain. These historical events were not well chronicled in Chaucer's time, nor did they receive much fanfare back home. Still, insofar as the crusades defined the identity of the European knight, the Knight's participation in these campaigns signals his commitment to public duty and to the cross. His immediate undertaking of a pilgrimage further serves as a reminder of the noble and spiritual calling of the knighted aristocracy.

Scholars have nonetheless found some ambiguities in Chaucer's portrayal of the Knight. The campaigns that he has supposedly undertaken are problematic, like all the later crusades, insofar as their ideological motivations and bloody consequences did not always cohere with a spiritual agenda. Accordingly, Chaucer's references to these expeditions have incited a great deal of scholarly debate about his own attitudes toward knights and their crusades. The campaigns in Prussia, for example, seem to have been packaged as something of a vacation; instead of large-scale battles, visiting knights were treated to feasts, hunts, and contests with the possibility of awards and accolades designed for the purpose. After a few weeks the "crusaders" were able to return home with all the glory of their earlier crusading ancestors.[33] The Battle of Algeciras in 1343—in which Chaucer's Knight participates—was less a crusade than a diplomatic mission during which England negotiated with Alfonso XI of Castile for a valuable military alliance. The crusading mission seems to have been almost entirely absent on that occasion, although chroniclers from Castile acknowledge that the English knights saw themselves as fighting the enemies of God.

Two of the Knight's crusades have been particularly marked for criticism. Peter of Cyprus's campaigns in Satalia and Alexandria, in 1361 and 1365 respectively, did little toward the cause of recapturing Jerusalem but jeopardized important trade relations between the Europeans and the Mediterranean peoples for years to come. The crusade originated as a preemptive attack against the Mamluks, who had plans to conquer Cyprus, a central commercial port between the Middle East and Europe. Peter, thinking strategically, planned a frontal attack, characterizing his own campaign to the European nations as a crusade against the "Saracens," as Muslims were called. Originally both Italy and France seized upon Peter's cause as a way to get rid of the marauding Free Companies—bands of mercenary knights who organized themselves after hostilities during the Hundred Years War had temporarily ceased. These unemployed knights freely raided their own home countries and as such posed a serious domestic threat. England, however, proved considerably more cynical than France and Italy, and Edward III refused to participate, despite Peter's urging.

Edward allowed English crusaders to join Peter if they wished, but he provided no revenues in support of the campaign. Edward's known ambivalence toward the crusade must complicate our view of Chaucer's motives for listing it as one of his Knight's campaigns. If the crusade was not explicitly endorsed by England, then why was the Knight present? Did he sell himself as a mercenary to Peter of Cyprus? This question cannot be answered satisfactorily, since even at the time no one's agenda was entirely clear. There is also some indication that Pope Urban himself was deceived as to Peter's ultimate plans; the senate in Italy claimed five years later that Peter had explicitly promised not to enter Alexandria until after October 1365, a promise which, if made, he certainly broke.[34] Nonetheless, Urban promised full indulgences to all the mercenaries, probably as an incentive for Free Companies in Italy to take part as well.

When the crusaders eventually broke through the walls of the beautiful city of Alexandria, they destroyed everything in their path, executing Muslims without pity, including those who sought sanctuary in the mosques, and destroying what they could not take for themselves. Contemporary Arab accounts describe the crusaders as merciless, a claim that even the French poet Machaut, despite his nationalistic defense of the crusade, does not deny (SEE BELOW). The reckless destruction worked against the invaders, who, in burning the city gates, left themselves open for counterattack. Within days of the city's capture, the Alexandrians began returning, and the looters, having gotten what they had come for, saw no reason to stay. Peter of Cyprus had hoped to use Alexandria as the base camp for further expeditions into Egypt and eventually the Holy Land; within a week, however, his knights returned home with their booty—led, according to the eyewitness Philip de Mézières, by the English—and he went with them.

The fact that Chaucer claims the siege of Alexandria as one of his Knight's campaigns is certainly troubling, given the week-long rampage in which many of the knights indulged. Although *The Canterbury Tales* describes its Knight as a perfect embodiment of chivalry, he does keep company with those who flouted its ideals and used them for mercantile purposes or for vainglory. Still, despite the apparently mercenary nature of these campaigns and the problematic issue of a crusade against Christians, chivalric ideology seems to have remained an important part of the drive to participate. The campaign was given a propagandistic spin by such writers as Machaut and Philip de Mézières, who unquestioningly praised Peter of Cyprus. The victory in Alexandria was seen as a victory against the Infidel, and many found as much satisfaction in this achievement as in the taking of Jerusalem during the First Crusade. Peter himself—despite a tyrannical domestic side that led to his assassination a few years later—was celebrated as the model Christian knight. Chaucer circulated among knights who had fought in the siege and were proud of their part in the taking of Alexandria, and Thomas Walsingham cites the siege with admiration in his chronicle of the times.

Class Antagonism

The disparity between the actual practices of real knights and the ideals espoused by the heroes of the vernacular romances was patently obvious to late fourteenth-century authors. Increasingly the writing of the period explored both the ideology of the knighthood and the mechanisms by which that ideology was instituted. Chaucer's depiction of the contest between Palamon and Arcite shows, for example, an astute awareness of the private drives that are only superficially concealed by the respectable veneer of courtly love. The temples of Venus and Mars, where the knights pray, are littered with destructive examples of narcissism, lust, and conquest. At the end of the tale, when Theseus proclaims that it is always best to make a virtue of necessity, Arcite's less-than-glorious death is transformed into an epic passing. The spectators pour wine, milk, and honey into the burning pyre and tear pieces of their own clothing for the fuel. The scene becomes an enactment of myth in the making, as Arcite is transformed from a hapless man who falls off his horse into a heroic lover and conqueror. This is the work of fiction, which exalts the craft of violence and in so doing legitimates the aristocratic hierarchy. The knight John Clanvowe—a personal acquaintance of Chaucer—avers as much in his work, *The Two Ways*:

> And the world also greatly honors those who would be avenged proudly and spitefully upon every wrong that has been said or done of them. And of such people men write books and songs and read and sing about them so as to remember their deeds that much the longer on earth, for that is what worldly men desire greatly: that their name might last long after them upon earth.[35]

Clanvowe's suspicions were not far off the mark: the libraries of some of the most prominent of the crusaders contained copies of romances, and their houses were adorned with tapestries commemorating the crusades.[36] Nor was Clanvowe alone in his suspicion of the ideological machine. John

Wyclif, the Oxford theologian and reformer, was equally disdainful in his condemnation of knights:

> Lord! What honor is it to a knight that he kills many men? Well I
> know that the hangman kills many more, and with more justice,
> and therefore more right, and so they should be praised more than
> such knights. And the butcher of beasts does his office many times
> with right and charity, and therefore does it well; but there is not as
> much evidence that the butcher of his brother slays men in charity,
> and therefore not so justly. Why should not this butcher, since he
> does better, be praised more than this knight that the world glorifies?
> Since the more virtuous deed is the more to be praised. And
> therefore it were better to be a butcher of beasts than to be a butcher
> of one's brother, for the latter is more unnatural. The suffering of
> Christ is much to be praised, but the slaying of his tormentors is
> odious to God.[37]

Clearly, as Wyclif and his contemporaries pointed out, there was a need for self-reflection. Social and economic changes in the fourteenth century encouraged widespread questioning of aristocratic privileges. The legal records are rife with complaints from commoners who suffered theft, rape, and other abuses at the hands of marauding knights. No wonder, then, that so many of Chaucer's tales should concern themselves with the definition of the word "gentilesse." The very notion of inherited gentility, as the Peasant's Revolt showed, was at stake. A number of social factors contributed to this sense of dissatisfaction; foremost among them was the Hundred Years War which, by Chaucer's time, was not going well.

Even as skepticism developed regarding the behavior of aristocrats, the idea of chivalry continued to play an important role in the imagination of fourteenth-century authors. The chivalric ideal represented masculine aristocratic perfection, and even the most skeptical writers seemed anxious to maintain their faith in the capacity for human goodness. That ideal continued to resonate despite the social realities of the times. Clanvowe himself was living proof that the ideal vision of service might co-exist with a critical assessment of aristocratic behavior. A pious Lollard, Clanvowe adhered to the conviction that a knight served God by serving his king and country. He very likely viewed his own participation in the crusades in this light; the crusade, in addition to continuing what the late Middle Ages still saw as the just war against the infidel, also afforded a journey of penance and devotion that was a reminder of the life to come.

Such inconsistencies perhaps point to the paradox at the heart of the medieval attitude toward the knighthood. While mercenaries were deplored, a "gentil knyght" such as Chaucer's still inspired awe and admiration. Though knights were as susceptible to variation in temperament and behavior as other human beings, their noble calling and the sacrifice inevitably required of them compelled the respect and fired the imagination of their contemporaries.

Documents

The Book of the Order of Chivalry.
Ramon Llull (*c.* 1276, trans. 1484)

The extraordinary Ramon Llull (1232-1315) was a gifted philosopher, troubadour, and knight. Born in the Balearic Islands, Llull wrote in the Catalan language, although he was fluent in Arabic and Latin as well. He was a tutor for James II of Majorca and traveled extensively on various diplomatic missions throughout his life. His elaborate justification for the privileges of knighthood verges on the mythical.

> When charity, loyalty, truth, justice, and verity failed in the world, then began cruelty, injury, disloyalty, and falseness. And therefore was error and trouble in the world in which God hath created man with the intention that by the man He be known, loved, feared, served, and honored. In the beginning, when wrongfulness had come to the world, justice returned, by order, as the honor toward which it was accustomed. And therefore all the people were divided by thousands. And from each thousand was chosen a man most loyal, most strong and of the greatest courage, and better instructed and mannered than all the others.
>
> Afterward was inquired and reckoned which beast was most fitting, most fair, most courageous, and strongest to withstand travail, and most able to serve the man. And then it was found that the horse was the most noble and most fitting to serve man. And because men chose the horse among all the beasts and gave him to this same man chosen among a thousand, that man was named "chevalier" (which is a knight in English), after the horse, which is called "cheval" in French. Thus was that most noble man given the most noble beast.

It behooved after this that there should be chosen all the armor such as is most noble and most fitting for battle, that defends the man from death. And these arms were given to and appropriated by the knight.

Thence whoever would enter into the order of chivalry must think upon the noble origin of chivalry. For if it were not so, he should be contrary to his order and to his beginnings. And therefore it is not a fitting thing that the order of chivalry receive his enemies in honor, nor those who are contrary to its beginnings, with love and fear beginning against haste and misprision. And therefore it behooves that the knight who is noble in courage and custom and bounty, and honor so great and so high, be made by election, and by his horse and by his arms be loved and feared by the people. Through love he restores charity and instruction, and through fear he should restore verity and justice. And in as much as a man has more wit and understanding and has a stronger nature than a woman, he is that much better than a woman. For if he were not more puissant and different as to be better than a woman, it would follow that bounty and strength of nature were not contrary to bounty of courage and to good works. Thus a man by his nature is appareled so as to have a noble heart and to be better than the woman. In like wise he has more inclination for vice than a woman. For if it were not thus, he should not be worthy of his greater merit to be good—more than the woman.

....So high and noble is the order of chivalry that it is not sufficient that there be knights as the most noble persons, nor that there be given to them the most noble beast, and the best and most noble arms. But it behooves also that he be made lord of many men. For in seigniory is as much noblesse as in servitude there is subjection. So if you take the order of knighthood, and are a vile and wicked man, you do great injury to all your subjects and to your fellows who are good. For according to the vileness which you have, and your wickedness, you should be put under a serf or bondman. And because of the nobility of knights who are good, it is not fitting nor worthy that you be called a knight. Election, horse, and arms suffice not for the high honor which belongs to a knight, but it behooves that there be given to him a squire and a servant who can take care of his horse. And it behooves also that the common people work the land to bring forth fruits and goods whereby the knight and his beasts have their living, and that the knight rest himself and sojourn according to his noblesse, and that he comport himself upon his horse either by hunting or in other ways that please him, and that he ease himself and delight in things for which his men have labored and pained.

Clerks study doctrine and science how they may know God and love Him, to the end that they may give doctrine to the lay and bestial people and by good examples [show them] to know, love, serve, and honor God, our glorious Lord. And so that they may do these things ordinately, they attend the schools. Then just as clerks, by their honest life, good example, and learning have their orders and office to incline the people toward devotion and a good life, in like manner the knights, through their nobility in courage and by force of arms maintain the order of chivalry and hold this same order so that they may incline the small people, by fear that makes them dread doing wrong to each other.

....So high and so honored is the order of chivalry that for a squire it suffices not that he care for horses, learn to serve a knight, and go with him to tourneys and battles, but it is necessary that there be held for him a school of the order of knighthood, and that the science be written in books, and that the art be demonstrated and read in the way other sciences are read. The sons of knights should learn first the science that pertains to the order of chivalry, and after they become squires they should ride through divers countries with the knights.

The Tree of Battles. HONORÉ BONET (1387)

Honoré Bonet was a French cleric, known for his writings on international law. *The Tree of Battles*, from which the following excerpts are taken, offers a practical guide to the social and professional obligations of knights, free of metaphysical pretense.

Now we must see what are the qualities of all good knights, and what their duties are.

And I tell you that the first and principal thing is that they should keep the oath which they have made to their lord to whom they belong, and to whom they have sworn and promised to do all that he shall command for the defense of his land, according to what is laid down by the laws. He is no true knight who, for fear of death, or of what might befall, fails to defend the land of his lord, but in truth he is a traitor and forsworn. A knight must be obedient to him who is acting in place of his lord as governor of the host, and if he is not obedient to him he is no good knight but is overbearing and insolent. And knights, especially those who are in the king's service, or in a lord's, should in thought and deed be occupied only with the practice of arms, and with campaigning for the honour of their lord, and for his peace, as says the law. They must always carry out the orders of him who takes the place and guards the interests of their lord, and if a knight acts contrary to such command he must lose his head.

Further, the laws say that a knight must not till the soil, or tend vines, or keep beasts, that is to say, be a shepherd, or be a matchmaker, or lawyer; otherwise he must lose knighthood and the privileges of a knight. And he should never, if he is a paid soldier, buy land or vineyards while he is in service, and what he does buy must belong to his lord. If you wish to know why this was so ordained, I tell you that it was that knights should have no cause to leave arms for desire of acquiring worldly riches.

....War is not an evil thing, but is good and virtuous; for war, by its very nature, seeks nothing other than to set wrong right, and to turn dissension to peace, in accordance with Scripture. And if in war many evil things are done, they never come from the nature of war, but from false usage ....Thus we must understand that war comes from God, and not merely that He permits war, but that He has ordained it; for God commanded a man called Joshua that he should do battle against his enemies, and advised him how he should set an ambush for the discomfiture of his enemies. Further, we say that our Lord God Himself is lord and governor of battles. And for this reason we must accept and grant that war comes from divine law, that is, the law of God: for the aim of war is to wrest peace, tranquility, and reasonableness, from him who refuses to acknowledge his wrongdoing.

Letter of Othea to Hector. CHRISTINE DE PIZAN (1399-1400)

Christine de Pizan (1364-1430) was one of the few women writers of the Middle Ages to achieve the recognition of her contemporaries. First circulated in the French court, her works were widely translated. *The Letter of Othea to Hector*, from which this extract is taken, combined allegories and stories of the Greek and Roman gods with moral interpretations. It was one of her most popular works, surviving in 43 manuscripts.

> As by the great knowledge and high power of God all things are created, rationally so must all things lead at the end to him, and because our spirit, which God created in his image, is of the things created the most noble after the angels, an appropriate thing it is and necessary that it be adorned with virtues by means of which it may be guided to the end for which it was fashioned. And in that it [the spirit] may be hindered by the ambushes and assaults of the enemy from hell, who is its mortal adversary and often turns it away from the attainment of its beatitude, we may call human life virtuous chivalry, as the Scripture says in several places. And as all terrestrial things are fallible, we must have in continual memory the future time which is without end. And in that it is the great and perfect chivalry, and all else is of no comparison, and for which the victorious will be crowned in glory, we will take the manner of speaking of the chivalrous spirit; and this be done for the praise of God principally and for the profit of those who will read this present treatise.

The Art of Courtly Love. ANDREAS CAPELLANUS (1184-86)

Little is known of Andreas Capellanus, other than that he flourished in the late twelfth century in Champagne, France. *The Art of Courtly Love* was probably written under the direction of the Countess Marie of Troyes (sister to Eleanor of Aquitaine), who encouraged courtly vernacular writers in her court. Although some scholars speculate that much of Andreas's work is intended to be satiric, *The Art of Courtly Love* functioned for later generations as a sort of textbook on love.

CHAPTER I.I

Love is a certain inborn suffering derived from the sight of and excessive meditation upon the beauty of the opposite sex, which causes each one to wish above all things the embraces of the other and by common desire to carry out all of love's precepts in the other's embrace.

That love is suffering is easy to see, for before the love becomes equally balanced on both sides there is no torment greater, since the lover is always in fear that his love may not gain its desire and that he is wasting his efforts. He fears, too, that rumors of it may get abroad, and he fears everything that might harm it in any way, for before things are perfected a slight disturbance often spoils them....

CHAPTER I.IV

Now it is the effect of love that a true lover cannot be degraded with any avarice. Love causes a rough and uncouth man to be distinguished for his handsomeness; it can endow a man even of the humblest birth with nobility of character; it blesses the proud with humility; and the man in love becomes accustomed to performing many services gracefully for everyone. O what a wonderful thing is love, which makes a man shine with so many virtues and teaches everyone, no matter who he is, so many good traits of character! There is another thing about love that we should not praise in few words: it adorns a man, so to speak, with the virtue of chastity, because he who shines with the light of one love can hardly think of embracing another woman, even a beautiful one. For when he thinks deeply of his beloved the sight of any other woman seems to his mind rough and rude....

CHAPTER I.VI

It remains next to be seen in what ways love may be acquired. The teaching of some people is said to be that there are five means by which it may be acquired: a beautiful figure, excellence of character, extreme readiness of speech, great wealth, and the readiness with which one grants that which is sought. But we hold that love may be acquired only by the first three, and we think that the last two ought to be banished completely from Love's court....

CHAPTER II.I

Now since we have already said enough about acquiring love, it is not unfitting that we should next see and describe how this love may be retained after it has once been acquired. The man who wants to keep his love affair for a long time untroubled should above all things be careful not to let it be known to any outsider, but should keep it hidden from everybody; because when a number of people begin to get wind of such an affair, it ceases to develop naturally and even loses what progress it has already made. Furthermore a lover ought to appear to his beloved wise in every respect and restrained in his conduct, and he should do nothing disagreeable that might annoy her. Moreover every man is bound, in time of need, to come to the aid of his beloved, both by sympathizing with her in all her troubles and by acceding to all her reasonable desires. Even if he knows sometimes that what she wants is not so reasonable, he should be prepared to agree to it after he has asked her to reconsider. And if inadvertently he should do something improper that offends her, let him straightway confess with downcast face that he has done wrong, and let him give the excuse that he has lost his temper or make some other suitable explanation that will fit the case. And every man ought to be sparing of praise of his beloved when he is among other men; he should not talk about her often or at great length, and he should not spend a great deal of time in places where she is. When he is with other men, if he meets her in a group of women, he should not try to communicate with her by signs, but should treat her almost like a stranger, lest some person spying on their love might have opportunity to spread malicious gossip. Lovers should not even nod to each other unless they are sure that nobody is watching them. Every man should also wear things that his beloved likes and pay a reasonable amount of attention to his appearance—not too much, because excessive care for one's looks is distasteful to everybody and leads people to despise the good looks that one has. If the lover is lavish in giving, that helps him retain a love that he has acquired, for all lovers ought to despise all worldly riches and should give alms to those who have need of them. Nothing is considered more praiseworthy in a lover than to be known to be generous, and no matter how worthy a man may be otherwise, avarice degrades him, while many faults are excused if one has the virtue of liberality. Also, if the lover is one who is fitted to be a warrior, he should see to it that his courage is apparent to everybody, for it detracts very much from the good character of a man if he is timid in a fight. A lover should always offer his services and obedience freely to every lady, and he ought to root out all his pride and be very humble. He ought to give a good deal of attention to acting toward all in such a fashion that no one may be sorry to call to his mind his good deeds or have reason to censure anything he has done....

CHAPTER II.VIII: THE RULES OF LOVE

    I. Marriage is no real excuse for not loving.

    II. He who is not jealous cannot love.

    III. No one can be bound by a double love.

    IV. It is well known that love is always increasing or decreasing.

    V. That which a lover takes against the will of his beloved has no relish.

    VI. Boys do not love until they arrive at the age of maturity.

    VII. When one lover dies, a widowhood of two years is required of the survivor.

    VIII. No one should be deprived of love without the very best of reasons.

    IX. No one can love unless he is impelled by the persuasion of love.

    X. Love is always a stranger in the home of avarice.

    XI. It is not proper to love any woman whom one would be ashamed to seek to marry.

    XII. A true lover does not desire to embrace in love anyone except his beloved.

    XIII. When made public, love rarely endures.

    XIV. The easy attainment of love makes it of little value; difficulty of attainment makes it prized.

    XV. Every lover regularly turns pale in the presence of his beloved.

    XVI. When a lover suddenly catches sight of his beloved, his heart palpitates.

    XVII. A new love puts to flight an old one.

    XVIII. Good character alone makes any man worthy of love.

    XIX. If love diminishes, it quickly fails and rarely revives.

    XX. A man in love is always apprehensive.

    XXI. Real jealousy always increases the feeling of love.

    XXII. Jealousy, and therefore love, are increased when one suspects his beloved.

    XXIII. He whom the thought of love vexes eats and sleeps very little.

    XXIV. Every act of a lover ends in the thought of his beloved.

    XXV. A true lover considers nothing good except what he thinks will please his beloved.

    XXVI. Love can deny nothing to love.

    XXVII. A lover can never have enough of the solaces of his beloved.

    XXVIII. A slight presumption causes a lover to suspect his beloved.

xxix. A man who is vexed by too much passion usually does not
love.
xxx. A true lover is constantly and without intermission possessed
by the thought of his beloved.
xxxi. Nothing forbids one woman being loved by two men or one
man by two women.

The Book of Chivalry. Geoffroi de Charny (*c.* 1350)

Geoffroi de Charny (d. 1356) was one of the most celebrated knights of
his time; he was twice named the keeper of the *oriflamme,* the banner of
the king of France, and he died at his king's side in the historic battle of
Poitiers. His treatise on the practice and highest ideals of chivalry was
written for France's Company of the Star.

Deeds of Arms at Tournaments

We should then talk of another pursuit at which many men-at-arms
aim to make their reputation: that is at deeds of arms at tournaments.
And indeed, they earn men praise and esteem for they require a
great deal of wealth, equipment, and expenditure, physical hardship,
crushing and wounding, and sometimes danger of death. For this
kind of practice of arms, there are some whose physical strength, skill,
and agility enable them to perform so well that they achieve in this
activity such great renown for their fine exploits; and because they
often engage in it, their renown and their fame increases in their own
territory and that of their neighbors; thus they want to continue this
kind of pursuit of arms because of the success God has granted them
in it. They content themselves with this particular practice of arms
because of the acclaim they have already won and still expect to win
from it. Indeed they are worthy of praise; nevertheless he who does
more is of greater worth.

Men-at-Arms Who Undertake Distant Journeys and Pilgrimages

We shall first consider those who aim to make their reputation by
a great enterprise, undertaking distant journeys and pilgrimages in
several faraway and foreign countries; they may thereby see many
strange and unusual things at which other men who have not
traveled abroad would wonder because of the strange marvels and

extraordinary things described by those men who have seen them; and those who listen can scarcely believe what they hear, and some say mockingly that it is all lies. And it should seem to all men of worth that those who have seen such things can and should give a better and truer account of them than those who will not or dare not go there, that such people lie. We should therefore be glad to listen to, behold, and honor those who have been on distant journeys to foreign parts, for indeed no one can travel so far without being many times in physical danger. We should for this reason honor such men-at-arms who at great expense, hardship, and grave peril undertake to travel to and see distant countries and strange things, although, to tell the truth, among all those who are intent on distant journeys, there are some who make a habit of it and who always want to go and see new and strange things and do not stay anywhere long and cannot find and take part in armed exploits as often as others who do not seek out such very distant journeys and who stay longer in one place and wait for the opportunity to perform great deeds of arms in war. It may well happen that in making these distant journeys they may from time to time encounter some fine adventure, but not very often, for when, in the midst of a time of peace, it is possible to go where one would not dare to go equipped for war nor as a man-at-arms, but only as a pilgrim or a merchant. It seems therefore to some that one does not come across opportunities to practice the military art so often in this way of life as might be encountered in another way of life. Nevertheless one should honor and respect such men who subject themselves in this way to physical danger and hardship in order to see these strange things and make distant journeys. And they find satisfaction in doing this because of the wondrously strange things which they have seen and still want to see. And indeed it is a fine thing, but nevertheless I say: he who does more is of greater worth.

The Jousts in Smithfield.
The Brut, or Chronicles of England (1388)

The following extract describes the attention given to the symbolic design and pageantry of the medieval jousts.

In this aforesaid parliament, and in the twelfth year of King Richard's reign, he let cry and ordain general justice, that is called a tournament, of lords, knights, and squires. And these jousts and tournaments were held at London in Smithfield, of all matter of strangers, of what land and country they were, and thither they were right welcome; and to them and to all others was held open household and great feasts; and also great gifts were given to all manner of strangers. And they of the king's side were all of one suit: their coats, their armor, shields, and their horse and trappings, all was white harts, with crowns about their necks, and chains of gold hanging there upon, and the crown hanging low before the hart's body: the which hart was the king's livery that he gave to lords and ladies, knights and squires, for to know his household from other people.

And at this first coming to their jousts, twenty-four ladies led these twenty-four lords of the Garter with chains of gold, and all in the same suit of harts as it is aforesaid, from the Tower on horseback through the city of London into Smithfield, there the jousts should be done. And these feasts and jousts were held generally, and to all those that would come, of what land or nation that ever they were; and this was held during twenty-four days, of the king's own cost; and these twenty-four lords to answer to all manner of people that would come thither. And thither came the Earl of St. Poule of France, and many other worthy knights with him of divers parties, full well arrayed. And when these feasts and jousts were done and ended, the King thanked these strangers and gave them many great gifts; and then they took their leave of the King and of other lords and ladies, and went home again unto their own country, with great love and much thanks.

Free Companies. Froissart (*c.* 1356)

The Free Companies were bands of mercenary knights who pillaged the European countryside when they were not able to find gainful employment through warfare. As such they exemplify knighthood at its worst.

At that time also there arose another company of men-at-arms and irregulars from various countries, who subdued and plundered the whole region between the Seine and the Loire. As a result, no one dared to travel between Paris and Vendome, or Paris and Orleans, or Paris and Montargis, and no one dared to remain there. All the inhabitants of the country districts fled to Paris or Orleans. This company had a Welsh captain called Ruffin, who had himself made a knight and became so powerful and rich that his wealth was uncountable. These companions often carried their raids almost to Paris, or at other times towards Orleans or Chartres. No place was safe from being attacked and pillaged unless it was very strongly defended....They ranged the country in troops of twenty, thirty or forty and they met no one capable of putting up a resistance to them. Elsewhere, along the coast of Normandy, there was a larger company of English and Navarrese pillagers and marauders commanded by Sir Robert Knollys, who conquered towns and castles in the same way and also found no one to oppose them. This Sir Robert Knollys had been following this practice for a long time and had acquired at least a hundred thousand crowns. He had a large number of mercenaries at his command and paid them so well that they followed him eagerly.

These activities of what were known as the Free Companies, who attacked all travelers carrying valuables, began under the administration of the Three Estates.

THE BLACK PRINCE'S REVENGE ON LIMOGES. FROISSART (1370)

Edward the Black Prince was an English hero, but his actions were not always above censure. The following account depicts one of his merciless rages.

> You would have then seen pillagers, active to do mischief, running through the town, slaying men, women, and children, according to their orders. It was a most melancholy business; for all ranks, ages, and sexes cast themselves on their knees before the prince, begging for mercy; but he was so inflamed with passion and revenge that he listened to none, but all were put to the sword, wherever they could be found, even those who were not guilty; for I know not why the poor were not spared, who could not have had any part in this treason; but they suffered for it .... Upwards of three thousand men, women and children were put to death that day.

ORDER OF THE GARTER. FROISSART (1344)

The following account by Froissart describes the institution and symbolism of Edward III's Order of the Garter.

At that time King Edward of England conceived the idea of altering and rebuilding the great castle of Windsor, originally built by King Arthur, and where had been first established the noble Round Table, from which so many fine men and brave knights had gone forth and performed great deeds throughout the world. King Edward's intention was to found an order of knights, made up of himself and his sons and the bravest and noblest in England and other countries too. There would be forty of them in all and they would be called the Knights of the Blue Garter and their feast was to be held every year at Windsor on St. George's Day. To institute the feast, the King called together the earls, barons, and knights of the whole country and told them of his intentions and of his great desire to see them carried out. They agreed with him wholeheartedly, because they thought it an honorable undertaking and one which would strengthen the bonds of friendship among them.

Forty knights were then chosen from among the most gallant of them all and these swore a solemn oath to the King always to observe the feast and the statutes, as these were agreed and drawn up. In the castle of Windsor, the King founded and had built the Chapel of St. George and established canons to serve God in it, giving them a generous endowment. In order to make the feast known in all countries, the King sent his heralds to announce it in France, Scotland, Burgundy, Hainault, Flanders, and Brabant, and also in the German Empire. All knights and squires who wished to come were given safe-conducts for fifteen days after the feast for their return home. There were to be jousts against forty home knights, challenging all comers, and forty esquires as well. The feast was to be held on the following St. George's Day in the year 1344, at Windsor Castle. The Queen of England was to be there accompanied by three hundred ladies and young girls, all of noble or gentle birth, and all similarly dressed.

THE CONDEMNATION OF THE TEMPLARS (1312)

The following excerpt is taken from Pope Clement V's bull suppressing the Order of the Templars.

....Indeed a little while ago, about the time of our election as supreme pontiff... we received secret intimations against the master preceptors, and other brothers of the order of Knights Templar of Jerusalem and also against the order itself. The men had been posted in lands overseas for the defense of the patrimony of our lord Jesus Christ, and as special warriors of the Catholic faith and outstanding defenders of the Holy Land seemed to carry the chief burden of the said Holy Land.... For all these reasons we were unwilling to lend our ears to insinuation and accusation against the Templars; we had been taught by our Lord's example and the words of canonical scripture.

Then came the intervention of our dear son in Christ, Philip [IV], the illustrious king of France. The same crimes had been reported to him. He was not moved by greed. He had no intention of claiming or appropriating for himself anything from the Templars' property; rather, in his own kingdom he abandoned such claim and thereafter released entirely his hold on their goods. He was on fire with zeal for the orthodox faith, following in the well-marked footsteps of his ancestors. He obtained as much information as he lawfully could, then, in order to give us greater light on the subject, he sent us much valuable information through his envoys and letters. The scandal against the Templars themselves and their order in reference to the crimes already mentioned increased. There was even one of the knights, a man of noble blood and of no small reputation to the order, who testified secretly under oath in our presence, that at his reception the knight who received him suggested that he deny Christ, which he did, in the presence of certain other knights of the Temple; he furthermore spat on the cross held out to him by this knight who received him. He also said that he had seen the grand master, who is still alive, receive a certain knight in a chapter of the order held overseas. The reception took place in the same way, namely with the denial of Christ and the spitting on the cross, with quite two hundred brothers of the order being present. The witness also affirmed that he had heard it said that this was the customary manner of receiving new members: at the suggestion of the person receiving the profession or his delegate, the person making profession

denied Jesus Christ, and in abuse of Christ crucified spat upon the
cross held out to him, and the two committed other unlawful acts
contrary to Christian morality, as the witness himself then confessed
in our presence.

We were duty-bound by our office to pay heed to the din of such
grave and repeated accusations....

Statute on Livery and Maintenance (1390)

The following document is excerpted from Parliament's censure of the
distribution of badges and liveries for the creation of private militia.

Whereas ... in many of our parliaments previously held ... grievous
complaint and great clamour has been made to us by the lords
spiritual and temporal, as well as by the commons of our realm, of
the great and outrageous oppressions and maintenance done in injury
to us and to our people in various parts of the same realm, by various
maintainers ... procurers and embracers of quarrels and inquests
in the countryside, of whom many are the more emboldened and
encouraged in their maintenance and evil deeds because they are
of the retinue of lords and others of our said realm with fees, robes,
and other liveries called liveries of company. [Therefore] we have
ordained and strictly enjoined, by the advice of our Great Council,
that no prelate or any other man of Holy Church, or any bachelor, or
esquire, or any other of less estate, shall give any kind of such livery
called livery of company; and that no duke, earl, baron, or banneret
shall give such livery of company unless he is retained with him for
the term of his life in peace and war by indenture, without fraud or
malice, or unless he is a servant and family retainer dwelling in his
household; and no such noble shall give such a livery to any "valet"
called a yeoman archer nor to any other person of lower estate than
esquire unless he is a family servant living in the household. And that
all lords spiritual and temporal and all others of whatever condition
they may be shall eject completely all such maintainers ... of
quarrels ... from their fees, robes, and all manner of liveries, and from
their service, company, and retinue, without receiving any such into
their retinue in any way whatsoever in the future .... And that if
any lord should eject any such maintainer ... from his company for
this cause, that then no other lord shall retain or receive him in his

retinue or company in any way; and that none of our lieges ... shall
undertake any quarrel but his own, nor maintain it by himself or by
another, neither in private nor openly; and that all those who use and
carry such livery called livery of company contrary to this ordinance
shall give them up entirely within ten days of the proclamation of
this ordinance, on pain of imprisonment, fine, and ransom, or of
being punished in any other manner according to what may be
recommended to us and to our council.

Given under our great seal at Westminster, May 12, 1390

The Defender of Peace. MARSILIUS OF PADUA (1324)

Marsilius of Padua (1275-1343) was an Italian philosopher who was outspoken in his criticism both of the Pope and of the crusades in general.

But now we come to what is the most vicious and most gravely
harmful of all the acts of this present Roman bishop: an iniquitous
practice which we have briefly mentioned above, and which no one
who desires to cling to the law of love can pass over in silence. I refer
to those acts of his whereby he brings about the eternal confusion
and destruction of "all Christ's sheep," who he says were entrusted
to him that he might feed them with salutary doctrine. For again
putting "good for evil and light for darkness," he has issued oral and
written pronouncements "absolving from all guilt and punishment"
every soldier, in cavalry or in infantry, that has waged war at a certain
time against those Christian believers who maintain steadfast and
resolute subjection and obedience to the Roman ruler; and by
himself or through others this Roman bishop has issued oral and
written proclamations making it lawful to attack in any way, to rob,
and even to kill these faithful subjects, as being "heretics" and "rebels"
against the cross of Christ. And, what is horrible to hear, this bishop
declares that such action is just as pleasing in God's sight as is fighting
the heathen overseas, and he has this declaration published far and
wide by false pseudo-brethren who thirst for ecclesiastic office. To
those whom physical disability prevents from participating in such
criminal action, he grants a similar fallacious pardon if they have up
to the same time gotten others to perpetrate these outrages in their
place or if they have paid to his vicious collectors a sufficient sum for

this purpose. But no one should doubt that, according to the Catholic religion, this empty and ridiculous pardon is utterly worthless, nay, harmful, to men who fight in such a cause. Nevertheless, by vocally granting something that is not in his power, the bishop dupes simple men into carrying out his impious desires, or rather he seduces and misleads them to the eternal perdition of their souls. For when men, unjustly invading and attacking a foreign land, disturb the peace and quiet of innocent believers, and, even though they well know that their victims are true Catholics, nevertheless rob and kill them because they are defenders of their own country and loyal to their true and legitimate ruler, then such aggressors are fighters not for Christ but for the devil. For they commit rapine, arson, theft, homicide, fornication, adultery, and practically every other kind of crime. And hence it is indubitably certain that the proper desert of such men is not pardon but rather prosecution and punishment by eternal damnation. And yet they are misled into perpetrating these crimes by the words and writings of the very man who calls himself (although he is not) Christ's vicar on earth.

The Conquest of Alexandria. Petrarch (1365)

The conquest of Alexandria, listed by Chaucer as one of his Knight's expeditions, is described by the poet Petrarch in a letter to his friend and fellow author, Boccaccio. Petrarch defends the holy mission of the crusade, but blames the knights who accompanied Peter for their lack of valor and duty.

> The conquest of Alexandria by Peter I, king of Cyprus, was a great and memorable achievement, which would have created a powerful basis for the spread of our religion if only the valor demonstrated in its capture had been matched in its holding. Peter himself, it is said, was not found lacking, but his army, drawn together largely from northern peoples, who begin undertakings well but cannot sustain them, was to blame.
>
> These northerners followed the pious king not from piety but from avarice. They deserted him at his moment of success, departing with their booty and frustrating his pious vow while satisfying their own greed.

The Capture of Alexandria.
Guillaume de Machaut. (after 1369)

Guillaume de Machaut (d. 1377) was one of the most celebrated poets in France. His lyric poetry and dream-visions greatly influenced Chaucer's early work. This long narrative poem recounts the crusade in Alexandria, pouring praise upon Peter of Cyprus. It also graphically depicts some of the horrors of the campaign.

6. The Attack on Tripoli and Ayas (1367)

The hunt
Took a long time. So very many men
Did Peter and his forces slash and gut,
They covered all that space with Saracens,
Bloody and dead. No one could ever know
How many bodies lay there, mouths agape,
Scattered between the galleys and the town.

The king stood outside Tripoli.
Inside some twenty thousand strove to keep him out.
With all their might. But they may show their teeth –
In came the king and in came all his men.
So many did he slaughter at the gate
That even the bravest of the Saracens
Would have been glad to be in India.
All day he killed and killed, and all his men
Laid waste and sacked the town. When that was done,
The whole place sacked and ravaged and destroyed,
The king set it alight. As he could see,
They'd never hold it, and the night was near.
He had the trumpet blown to sound Recall
And bring his scattered men in from the town;
All over it, they were. So they came in
Each burdened with rich plunder; every lad
And page was hugely wealthy. Now the king,
Noble, brave-hearted, joyful, found he'd lost
Only one knight, also some nine or ten
Men who'd gone rushing in like fools among
Buildings and streets they didn't know. The king
Was never able to find out from those

Present that day, what happened to these men,
Whether they died or were held prisoner.
So Tripoli was taken and destroyed,
Laid waste, then set alight and burned.

Two
And now
I want to tell you what this town is like,
And where it's placed. It lies in a wide plain
Close to the sea, easily visible,
And rising in the centre are two round hills,
Quite small and pretty, round, not very high;
On one side there stands a castle, not at all
Ill-placed or ugly. All around both hills
Houses are built. The town's circumference
Measures three leagues or more; remarkably
Densely inhabited, it's not at all enclosed.
Sweet-smelling gardens ring it round about;
So delicate and fragrant is the air
You think yourself in some spice-merchant's shop,
Just from the scent of all the fruits and plants
Set by the hands of the Saracens. You'll find
In plenty every fruit tree, every graft,
Each stock, each plant, each herb and root from which
Medicines can be obtained. All flourish there,
Planted and tended by the Saracens.
Among them fountains flow, sparkling and clean,
Sugar grows there and cinnamon and more
Spices besides, all good and fair, and yet
They have no river there, no, not at all.

Three
But the king,
Noble and lion-hearted, being there
Beyond the sea among the Saracens,
Hopes he can bring support. So he sets out
From Tripoli and goes, joyful yet sad
(he's often sad), to hurt his enemies
and help the Armenian king. But none the less
he's very pleased that he took Tripoli.

Along the coast he rides in war. No house,
Stone, clay or wood, is spared; he burns them all.
Often his sword is bloody; everyone
Whom he can find, he kills. He fights his way
On towards Ayas, killing Saracens
And setting fires ablaze—what more's to say?
Three good towns the valiant king destroyed:
Tortosa, Baniyas, Latakia,
And many other places, large and small.
No one need peel a clove of garlic there,
Everyone's dead, cinders, nobody spared,
No prisoners taken. Then as night drew on,
The king retreated to the boats and made
His men do so as well. But every day
They ranged the land, destroying the Saracens.

FOUR
Now can you find a king who could do this,
To whom God gave such grace that he could fight
One to a hundred and still always win?
His enemies, I mean, were never less
In number than a hundred to each one
Of his. Let's think what Alexander did,
And Hector too, never less great than he,
And those fine men of long ago, whose names
I gave above. (But Hector was supreme—
No battle honour ever ranks with his.)
If our king had his rights, he would be named
Tenth worthy, with those nine. And when this book
Is finished, I shall add his name to theirs,
Because he's valiant, staunch, a cheerful friend,
Generous and loyal, truthful, just and wise,
Intelligent – examine him, you'll see
That he has every trait nature can use
To make a perfect man. I could go on,
But never could sufficiently describe
The virtue, honour, sense and worth which form
His goodness.

Relations with the Franks.
Ousama Ibn Mounkidh (12ᵗʰ c)

Viewpoints on the crusades exist on the other side, too, written by Arab chroniclers and eyewitnesses to the events. The following early document, written by a Syrian prince and diplomat, illustrates the intolerance and inhospitality shown by the Christian occupiers to the indigenous Muslims.

It is always those who have recently come to live in Frankish territory who show themselves more inhuman than their predecessors who have been established amongst us and become familiarized with the [Muslims].

A proof of the harshness of the Franks ... is to be seen in what happened to me when I visited Jerusalem. I went into the mosque al-Aqsa. By the side of this was a little mosque which the Franks had converted into a church. When I went into the mosque al-Aqsa, which was occupied by the Templars, who were my friends, they assigned me this little mosque in which to say my prayers. One day I went into it and glorified Allah. I was engrossed in my praying when one of the Franks rushed at me, seized me, and turned my face to the east, saying, "That is how to pray!" A party of Templars made for him, seized his person, and ejected him. I returned to my prayers. The same man, escaping attention, made for me again and turned my face round to the east, repeating, "That is how to pray!" The Templars again made for him and ejected him; then they apologized to me and said to me, "He is a stranger who has only recently arrived from Frankish lands. He has never seen anyone praying without turning to the east." I answered, "I have prayed sufficiently for today." I went out and was astonished to see how put out this demon was, how he trembled and how deeply he had been affected by seeing anyone pray in the direction of the *Kiblah*.

The Franks understand neither the feeling of honor nor the nature of jealousy. If one of them is walking with his wife and he meets another man, the latter takes the woman's hand and goes and talks to her while the husband stands aside waiting for the end of the interview. If the woman prolongs it unreasonably, the husband leaves her along with her companion and goes back ....

FROM *Vox Clamantis*. JOHN GOWER (*c.* 1380s)

John Gower's *Vox Clamantis*, in addition to satirizing the clergy, also attacks the warrior estate. The list of knightly abuses is long; here, Gower specifically targets the quest for fame and love.

CHAPTER 5.5

Here he speaks of those knights of whom one will engage in feats of arms for the sake of a woman's love and another for the sake of worldly fame. In the end, however, both things pass away in vain, without the reward of divine commendation.

One part of the knightly estate seeks after woman's love, and another, what the world's lofty praise may extol to it. Everywhere the knight aspires to and tries for new favor so that he may have fame. But God knows by what right he desires honor, if the world or woman's love will bestow it. If he wishes worldly praise, then he pours out the wealth of Croesus in order that his lofty praises may be sounded, because of his gifts. Then he sows gold, clothes, gems, and horses like grain, in order that a crop of praises may grow in his ear.

But if a knight chooses a woman's love for himself, then he will pay for it more dearly than with his wealth. He will give up so many good things for it – his body, his soul, his property, everything that Nature or God has imparted to him. Nevertheless, when he shall have done with his troublesome doings, yet at the same time every fickle compliment deceives him; and when neither the prattling talk of the world reaches his ears nor virtuous love bestows its treasures upon him, then the dupe will say, "Alas, how wicked Fortune is! For all my labor turns out fruitless after such a long time." The man who laments for himself in this foolish way is too late, for he himself is the cause of his suffering, and not another.

The world brings heavy burdens, but woman brings heavier ones. It moves along, while she rushes; it buffets, while she kills. When a knight thinks he has vanquished a woman's power, and with tender affection she grants everything he has asked, then he himself is thoroughly defeated, just when he thinks he is thoroughly victorious, and the conquered woman reconquers him. And even if the knight chooses worldly fame, surely it passes away vainly in a short time.

O why does a knight whose worldly honor remains without God's esteem seek such honors for himself? Why does he believe that the words of the prattling mob are an honor, and wish to possess them at the price of death? Then, too, he fears nothing when he is overcome by a woman, whereby he, guilty before God, loses a wealth of honor. So why does a knight's undaunted courage wish in vain for things which are senseless? His praises are sung in vain, unless God is the author of them. And that honor which is noised about apart from God is a disgrace. A knight is eager for any kind of praise or honor, when God knows he is unworthy of it.

The Two Ways. JOHN CLANVOWE (LATE 14ᵀᴴC)

John Clanvowe (1341-91) was a knight-courtier who seems to have epitomized the ideal of chivalry. A Knight of the Chamber under Richard II, Clanvowe served during the Hundred Years War and went on several crusades. He composed two substantial works, *The Book of Cupid*, a long narrative poem, and *The Two Ways*, a religious piece in which he refers sympathetically to the Lollards. Our translation is based on the edition by V.J. Scattergood.

> The world considers to be honorable those who are great warriors and fighters and who destroy and take over many lands, and who waste and give away many of the profits to those who have enough already, which are squandered outrageously in food, drink, clothing, building, luxurious living, sloth, and many other sins. And the world also greatly honors those who would be avenged proudly and spitefully upon every wrong that has been said or done of them. And of such people men write books and songs and read and sing about them so as to remember their deeds that much the longer on earth, for that is what worldly men desire greatly: that their name might last long after them upon earth. But howsoever the world judges these aforesaid people, we learn well that God is the sovereign truth and a true judge who considers them very shameful ...

EPILOGUE TO THE *Book of the Order of Chivalry*. WILLIAM CAXTON (1484)

Our final document appears at the end of an age. Here Caxton laments the passing of a chivalric ideal that he believed held great force for many people. This excerpt concludes his edition of Ramon Llull's *Book of the Order of Chivalry*.

Here ends the *Book of the Order of Chivalry* ... which book is not requisite to every common man to have, but to noble gentlemen that by their virtue intend to come and enter into the noble order of chivalry, the which in these late days has been used according to this book heretofore written, but forgotten, and the exercise of chivalry not used, honored, nor exercised as it has been in ancient times, at which time the noble acts of the knights of England that used chivalry were renowned through the universal world.

... O ye knights of England, where is the custom and usage of noble chivalry that was used in the days; what do ye now but go to the baynes [baths] and play at dice. And some, not well advised, use not honest and good rule against the order of knighthood. Leave this; leave it and read the noble volumes of the Sangreal of Lancelot, of Galahad, of Tristram, of Per se Forest; of Perceval; of Gawain, and many more. There shall ye see manhood, courtesy and gentleness. And look in the latter days of the noble acts since the conquest, as in King Richard Coeur de Lyon's days, Edward I and III and his noble sons, Sir Robert Knolles, Sir John Hawkwood, Sir John Chaundos, and Sir Gaultier Manuy. Read Froissart and also behold that victorious and noble King Harry V and the captains under him, his noble brethren the Earl of Salisbury, Montague and many others, whose names shine gloriously by their virtuous noblesse and acts that they did in honor of the order of chivalry.

Alas, what do ye but sleep and take ease, and are disordered from chivalry? I would demand a question, if I should not displease, how many knights there are now in England that have the use and exercise of a knight, that is, to know that he knows his horse and his horse him, that is to say he being ready at a point to have all things that belong to a knight, a horse that is broken in according to his hand, his armor and harness fitting and sitting, so forth, etc. I suppose that a due search should be made. There should be many found that lack. The more pity. I would it pleased our sovereign lord that twice or thrice in a year, or at least once, he would do cry to the Justice of the Peace to the end that every knight should have horse and harness, and also the use and craft of a knight, and also to tourney one against another, or two against two, and the best to have a prize, a diamond or jewel such as should please the prince. This should cause gentlemen to resort to the ancient custom of chivalry to great fame and renown, and also to be always ready to serve their prince when he shall call them or have need. Then lately every man that is come of noble blood and intends to come to the noble order of chivalry, read this little book and do thereafter in keeping the lord and commandments therein comprised. And then I doubt not he shall attain to the order of chivalry, et cetera.

Notes

1   Lee Patterson, *Chaucer and the Subject of History* (Madison, WI: U of Wisconsin P, 1991) 168.

2   Marc Bloch, *Feudal Society*, Vol. 2, trans. L.A. Manyon (Chicago, IL: U of Chicago P, 1961) 291.

3   Richard Barber, *The Knight and Chivalry* (New York: Charles Scribner's Sons, 1970) 11.

4   Bloch 283-89.

5   Maurice Keen, *Chivalry* (New Haven: Yale UP, 1984) 64-65.

6   Bernard of Clairvaux, "In Praise of the New Knighthood," in *The Works of Bernard of Clairvaux*, vol. 7, trans. Conrad Greenia (Kalamazoo, MI: Cistercian Publications, 1977) 134.

7   John of Salisbury, *The Policraticus*, trans. Cary J. Nederman (Cambridge: Cambridge UP, 1990) 115.

8   Ramon Llull, from *The Book of the Order of Chivalry*, in *Chaucer: Sources and Backgrounds*, ed. Robert P. Miller (New York: Oxford UP, 1977) 181.

9   This is the thesis of C. Stephen Jaeger's book, *The Origins of Courtliness: Civilizing Trends and the Formation of Courtly Ideals 939-1210* (Philadelphia, PA: U of Pennsylvania P, 1985).

10 C.S. Lewis, *The Allegory of Love* (Oxford: Oxford UP, 1936) 2.

11 Andreas Capellanus, *The Art of Courtly Love*, trans. John Jay Parry (New York: Columbia UP, 1990) 31-32.

12 C. Stephen Jaeger, *Ennobling Love: In Search of a Lost Sensibility* (Philadelphia, PA: U of Pennsylvania P, 1999).

13 Christine de Pizan, *The Book of the Duke of True Lovers*, trans. Thelma S. Fenster (New York: Persea, 1991) 57.

14 Capellanus 185.

15 Dorsey Armstrong, "Gender, Marriage, and Knighthood: Single Ladies in Malory," in *The Single Woman in Medieval and Early Modern England: Her Life and Representation*, eds. Laurel Amtower and Dorothea Kehler (Tempe, AZ: MRTS, 2003) 41-61.

16 Thomas Walsingham, *The Chronica Maiora of Thomas Walsingham*, trans. David Preest (Woodbridge: The Boydell P, 2005) 27.

17 Richard Barber, *Edward, Prince of Wales and Acquitaine* (New York: Charles Scribner's Sons, 1978) 241.

18 Thomas Walsingham, *The St. Albans Chronicle: The Chronica Maiora of Thomas Walsingham*, ed. and trans. John Taylor, Wendy R. Childs, and Leslie Watkiss (Oxford: Clarendon P, 2003) 37.

19 Juliet Vale and Malcolm Vale, "Knightly Codes and Piety," in *The Age of Chivalry: Art and Society in Late Medieval England*, ed. Nigel Saul (Leicester: Brockhampton P, 1995) 30.

20 Vale and Vale 32.

21 Keen, *English Society in the Later Middle Ages* 142.

22 Warren Ginsburg, ed., *Wynnere and Wastoure and The Parlement of the Three Ages*. TEAMS Middle English Texts (Kalamazoo, MI: Medieval Institute Publications, 1992) ll. 59-68.

23 Keen, *Chivalry* 179.

24 Strohm, *Hochon's Arrow* 59.

25 Michael J. Bennett, "*Sir Gawain and the Green Knight* and the Literary Achievement of the North-West Midlands: The Historical Background," *Journal of Medieval History* 5 (1979): 76.

26 T.F. Tout, *Chapters in the Administrative History of Medieval England: The Wardrobe, the Chamber and the Small Seals*, Vol. 4 (New York: Manchester UP, 1967) 199.

27 Thomas Walsingham, quoted in Bennett, "*Sir Gawain*," 79-80.

28 Saul 201.

29 Marcus Bull, "Origins," in *The Oxford Illustrated History of the Crusades*, ed. Jonathan Riley-Smith (Oxford: Oxford UP, 1995) 20.

30 Bull 31.

31 Robert of Clari, *The Conquest of Constantinople*, trans. Edgar Holmes McNeal (1936; New York: Columbia UP, 2005) 85.

32 Christopher Tyerman, *England and the Crusades 1095-1588* (Chicago, IL: U of Chicago P, 1988) 265.

33 Tyerman 267.

34 Kenneth M. Setton, *The Papacy and the Levant, 1204-1571*, Vol. 1 (Philadelphia, PA: The American Philosophical Society, 1976) 262.

35 John Clanvowe, *The Works of Sir John Clanvowe*, ed. V.J. Scattergood (Cambridge: D. S. Brewer, 1975); our translation.

36 Tyerman 261.

37 John Wyclif, *Wyclif: Select English Writings*, ed. Herbert E. Winn (London: Oxford UP, 1929); our translation.

CHAPTER VI

"Gladly Wolde He Lerne and Gladly Teche"

Reading, Literacy, and Education

INTRODUCTION

*C*haucer's Clerk is described as a bookish man, who would rather have "twenty books, clad in black or red" at his bedside table than fancy clothes or instruments. Although he possesses learning enough to earn himself a decent living,

> ...Yet hadde he but litel gold in cofre;
> But al that he myghte of his freendes hente,
> On bookes and on lernynge he it spente. (CT 298–300)

Scholars have pointed toward the clerk as an example of one of the "idealized" portraits in *The Canterbury Tales*. The clerk does not fall into an easy social category: he isn't a preacher, a warrior, or a laborer. He is instead a learner or a "philosopher," and as such he represents a relatively new medieval focus on books and intellectual training as a measure of status and honor.

Chaucer may have identified with this particular character on many levels. He himself was something of a "clerk," occupying a middle space in the late medieval social spectrum. He was not an aristocrat, but he worked for the aristocracy and traveled in aristocratic circles; he spoke the language of the aristocracy and he understood them, but he would never be one of them. Although Chaucer apparently did not attend university, unlike his clerk, he was obviously trained enough in legal and financial matters to be sent overseas on diplomatic missions of some urgency, as well as to assume the title "Clerk of the King's Works" from 1389 to 1391. His reading, like his clerk's, was wide-ranging and encompassed several languages. *The Book of the Duchess* and *House of Fame* describe his narrator-persona's bedroom as containing stacks of books, and in *The Book of the Duchess* Geffrey calls for a servant to bring him more reading material to help him sleep. Chaucer knew Latin and French well enough to produce sophisticated translations of works from both languages, and he seems to have had a fairly good reading knowledge of Italian as well.

How pervasive was this level of education? What kinds of gentle-men acquired it? By the late Middle Ages, the English and Europeans were becoming increasingly bookish, and education was beginning to acquire a status of its own. Although education was much less systematized in the late Middle Ages than it is now, and was by no means mandatory nor even available to all, there was considerable interest in making sure that those classes with leisure and money enough acquired the learning necessary to further their family interests. The degree of literacy in medieval England is difficult to estimate; numbers have ranged from approximately 50 per cent of the male population to considerably lower.[1] The difficulty of coming up with a concrete number reflects a number of factors. For one thing, medieval England had its own standard of evaluating whether a person was literate or not: the term *literati* referred explicitly to a person who could read Latin, and *illiterati* to someone who could not, although the latter may very well have been able to read and write English. In addition is the question of what precisely we mean by literacy: many people could sign their name to a business document, but that was the extent of their writing skills. Thus, the vast numbers of signatures we find surviving on manuscripts do not necessarily correspond to a population of competent readers. What we might label as "reading competency" belonged to a much smaller proportion of the population, people who had the luxury of reading for entertainment and whose demand for books created a market for such poets as Chaucer and John Gower. Most of these readers probably had some formal education, which very likely would have included some instruction in language. A more sophisticated level of competency still was expected for the educated professionals, such as clerks or lawyers who depended on written language to transact business. These highly literate professionals were fluent in Latin and French—the official languages of religion and politics—and their professional services were very much in demand, so much, in fact, that if a charged criminal could plead "benefit of clergy"—that is, if he could read Latin—he was *ipso facto* released and held innocent of the accusation.[2]

By the fourteenth century a degree of literacy was necessary for the basic operation of society, and special persons dedicated to the reading, writing, and analysis of texts, whether for religious or secular purposes, were in great demand. Many guilds demanded basic literacy as a requirement for apprenticeship, and anyone with ambition needed literacy in the English language at a minimum, preferably with a little Latin and some accounting as well. At the most elementary level of household management, reading and writing had a practical purpose: signing documents and agreements, ordering merchandise, and keeping accounts of household and farmyard goods. Such simple documents were, for the most part, written in English. At more sophisticated levels, however, such as the ones obtaining in juridical or ecclesiastical institutions, documents might be in Anglo-French, in English, or in Latin. An ability to decode and interpret complicated texts on a very close level was essential to the smooth running of most major medieval institutions, whether they were secular or spiritual.

That the late Middle Ages was characterized by its awareness of its own textual dependence can be illustrated by the increasing role that the law played in medieval culture. M.T. Clanchy has shown how medieval England increasingly relied on documentation as a means of understanding and legitimating interrelationships between individuals and their community's interests. The difficulty of texts, and their vulnerability to misreading, misappropriation, and disputation, frequently generated the need for a professional trained in the art of textual analysis. As medieval society developed increasingly complex structures, more and more texts were generated. Trade agreements needed to be drawn up; taxation and imports needed to be documented. Lawyers became involved in diplomatic roles, in negotiating terms of peace, and in drawing up contracts between nations and magnate families. All of this activity indicates an increasingly literate response to a very textual society—a society concerned with staking out the minute differences of ambivalent statements and in clarifying each of the discrepancies that might arise between two parties in highly specific and technical language. In such an environment, private agendas provided more and more motivation for interpreting the law in idiosyncratic and often self-promoting ways.

EDUCATION

The increasing demands of administration and commerce meant that the need for literacy was recognized fairly early in the Middle Ages. Although probably a great deal more education occurred in the medieval home than in modern ones, public schools did become available gradually as towns amassed the resources to provide them. By the fourteenth century, public schools catered even to the lower strata of society. Most of these charged a fee, but by the end of the century, some were free. These schools, managed normally by secular priests or clerks but sometimes by a layman, were accessible to all the young boys who could afford them, regardless of class. Wills of the fourteenth century show a marked interest on the part of parents in the advancement of their children through education or apprenticeships. Agreements for apprenticeships often included stipulations that ensured that the child would be taught as he learned his given trade. The lowest level of public schools, the grammar schools, taught reading and some Latin; children attended these schools probably from the ages of seven to ten. In the absence of standardized textbooks, children—like Chaucer's "little clergeon" from "The Prioress's Tale"—were taught the alphabet, simple prayers and songs, and eventually church precepts. A few students continued to secondary schools, which taught Latin and literature. Some subcategories of grammar schools focused on teaching the specialized language necessary for business administration. Particularly in demand were people who understood law, which required both a mastery of Latin, usually achieved only at the university level, and a period of apprenticeship at court.

For a boy like Geoffrey Chaucer, growing up in the 1350s after the first epidemic of the plague, education probably began at a grammar school associated with a local church. St. Paul's Cathedral, only minutes away from Chaucer's childhood home on Thames Street, had a grammar school that was intended to prepare students for the cathedral school. Because it had a large library consisting of encyclopedias, standard classic authors like Ovid and Virgil, and "florilegia" (extracts from the great works), many scholars think that St. Paul's was most likely where Chaucer received his early schooling. There he would have been exposed to many of the works that influenced his later writings. Since all of the cathedrals and many of the churches in London had similar schools attached to them, this conjecture cannot be proved. Chaucer would have learned his "Alma Mater," the Paternoster, and the Creed at St. Paul's or another such school, in Latin and by memory, as a way of learning the basics of Latin itself. Rote learning was, indeed, the mainstay of grammar-school education. Like the little clergeon in "The Prioress's Tale," medieval schoolboys probably had little real understanding of the texts they were supposed to memorize. They were expected to recite and to respect the written word, not to think.

Upper-class girls may have had some form of education, too, but for the majority education would have been limited in comparison to what boys received. Many pictures from the period show the popular image of St. Anne teaching the Virgin to read, indicating that mothers may have had the major responsibility for instructing their daughters, at least in the basic skills of literacy. However, the payment records for grammar schools suggest that at least some girls attended these schools alongside the boys for the first four or five years, where they would have picked up some Latin, French, and perhaps some practical math. In addition, we have evidence for the existence of one medieval schoolmistress in England, which leaves open the possibility that girls may have had their own institutions for education.[3]

Many educational manuals and primers survive from the period, indicating a popular interest in the upbringing and training of upwardly mobile youths. Some of these are directed specifically at parents for the proper training of their children, such as the courtesy books that instruct the proper forms of virtue and etiquette expected of a child in society, as discussed in Chapter 3. Proper reverence for authority is an ongoing theme: *The Book of Courtesy*, cited below, advises children "Thy father and mother, with mild speech, / In worship and serve with all thy might / That thou dwell the longer in earthly light."[4] *The Babees Book* aims itself at children who might find a position in a noble household, reminding them to "take no seat, but be ready to stand until you are bidden to sit down. Keep your hands and feet at rest; do not claw your flesh or lean against a post, in the presence of your lord, or handle anything belonging to the house."[5] Chaucer's sententious Physician puts the responsibility for teaching these niceties squarely onto the parents:

> Ye fadres and ye moodres eek also,
> Though ye han children, be it oon or mo,
> Youre is the charge of al hir surveiaunce,
> Whil that they been under youre governaunce.
> Beth war, if by ensample of youre lyvynge,
> Or by youre necligence in chastisynge,
> That they ne perisse. (PhT 93–9)

The Physician's advice echoes that offered in the moral treatise "Sans Puer ad Mensam": "A rod reformeth all their negligence. / In their courage no rancour doth abide. / Who spareth the rod all virtues sets aside."[6] Sober dignity was the proper end of education, where the child learned to put away childish things, to accept the burdens of adulthood, and to revere the authority of medieval teachings.

Educational manuals from the period also include medieval horn-books, upon which the alphabet was inscribed above a Latin Paternoster. Children would memorize the alphabet by associating each letter with an appropriate word from the Paternoster, pronouncing each letter and its phonetic sound equivalent in turn. A sixteenth-century comedy illustrates the process by which students linked letters first to syllables and then to words through a spelling of the word "pater":

Lo, he hath forgotten, you may see,
The first word of his abc.
Hark, fool, hark! I will teach thee:
P, a, pa; t, e, r, ter.[7]

A child might also learn to read from a primer, from which he or she memorized basic church songs and prayers. Children were thus expected to learn to read by what we might call a "whole language" approach: entire words were learned through memorization and context rather than through phonics. These primers remind us that the primary purpose for reading was to enable the medieval layman to read prayers and to read them in Latin, the language of the Church.

Learning to read was made particularly difficult insofar as it required spelling things out in a language other than English. Latin was familiar to medieval children; even the illiterate were accustomed to making at least the basic formal prayers in Latin rather than in English. But most laymen were not fluent in Latin, and learning their letters in the Latin language probably did little to advance their skill. Those who had professional aspirations needed more formal study than the basic primers afforded. Schoolmasters were not unsympathetic to the problems of learning to read in a foreign language. Texts were developed that helped students overcome some of the difficulties. One type of manual, the *vulgaria*, consisted of various phrases and paragraphs intended to help children learn Latin through colloquial translation exercises that represented familiar situations. These were written by schoolmasters, sympathetic to the difficulties of learning the language, specifically for their own students. Some of the paragraphs for translation in the *vulgaria* are clearly moral and didactic, such as this one from the fifteenth-century schoolmaster cited in our documents section:

> I have this thought: that there is nothing better nor more profitable in bringing a man to knowledge than to mark such things as are left by the good authors, and I mean not all, but the best, and though to follow as closely as a man's mind will allow him. And he that does this, and besides which gives himself to exercise, cannot but become wise.[8]

Others are much more colloquial, even risqué. Some of the entries of a later *vulgaria,* written in the sixteenth century, include such ribaldries as "you stink" and "you are a false knave."[9] The books also make frequent reference to the fact that discipline took the form of beatings:

> I played my master a merry prank yesterday, and therefore he hath taught me to sing a new song today. He hath made me to run a race that my buttocks doth sweat a bloody sweat. The more instantly that I prayed him to pardon me, the faster he laid upon. He hath taught me a lesson that I shall remember whiles I live.[10]

In other instances, *vulgaria* comment on the sights of London (Whittinton remarks on the grisly number of heads mounted over London Bridge), on how students' days began, on how correspondence with parents and requests for more funds might unfold, and the like. The miscellanies are interesting because they show that the teachers of the Middle Ages had a sincere interest not only in educating but in keeping up the interest of their students. The books reveal something of the process that took place within the classroom, and they acknowledge the relationship between the schoolmaster and the boys under his care. Moreover, the *vulgaria* show something of the variegated concerns of aspiring medieval youth. They remind us that students' ambitions were broad and included secular interests in addition to the religious sentiments that dominate the official curriculum and perhaps provide a misguided assumption about medieval concerns.[11]

Chaucer's own literacy in Latin was competent but possibly not comfortable, which confirms the theory that his education was directed at secular rather than religious interests. As Derek Pearsall points out, Chaucer uses French translations of Latin sources whenever he can, preferring, for example, the French *Ovide Moralise* to the original Latin of Ovid.[12] This would indicate that his education was practical and oriented toward a career as a civil servant rather than as a churchman and that, as a corollary, his advanced education was less likely to have occurred in the universities than in the households of the aristocratic patrons with whom we know he was associated during his adolescence. Some scholars have speculated that Chaucer attended the Inns of Court, the institution that provided a professional education for those inclined toward law or other non-ecclesiastical clerical functions. However, that theory has been difficult to prove, insofar as the Inns of Court only appear as a regulating body in the mid-fourteenth century, and no records exist affirming any formalized level of training until after 1400. More likely Chaucer picked up his skills from practice and his erudition from private study.

The university was reserved for the higher forms of learning—that is, the study of theology, canon and civil law, and the rhetorical and dialectical arts—and by the late Middle Ages, a university education had largely become a prerequisite for entry into the king's service or the church. Those who could attend university had a very different experience from what we associate with higher learning today. Certainly the modern university system shares many features with its medieval counterpart; the liberal arts curriculum, the lecture system, and the division between undergraduate and graduate studies all have their origins in the Middle Ages. Yet much of what we associate with the university—the uniquely designated space for the buildings, the elaborate administrative structure—were absent in medieval times. For the most part the curriculum focused on the seven liberal arts, consisting of the *trivium* (grammar, rhetoric, and dialectic), and the *quadrivium* (geometry, music, arithmetic, and astronomy). At the more advanced levels, theology, natural and moral philosophy, law, and medicine were added. The method of education for the student combined attendance at a faculty member's lectures, either in rented halls or in one of the few buildings actually owned by the university, with participation in an active form of staged, scholarly debate, in which scholars demonstrated their mastery of the books by engaging and attacking their opponents through lively argument and logic. Students had to participate for at least one year in public debates in order to qualify for the undergraduate degree.[13] By Chaucer's time, a rigorous final examination was also required to ensure that the material had been mastered before graduation.

A university education was designed to take approximately nine years to complete if a scholar continued all the way through to his graduate studies, longer if the student wished to continue on to the doctorate in theology.[14] By the thirteenth century, all grammar school teachers were expected to have a master of arts that qualified them to teach. After the plague, however, a shortage in educated clergy necessitated the formation of shorter courses of study. The bachelor of arts was established as one of these, granting the degree to those who had completed four years of study; the master of grammar (or "MGramm") involved an even shorter period of university work.

These curricular developments evolved slowly over a 100-year period. In their early years of existence, the universities were organized almost entirely around the charismatic energy of a famous teacher, who would teach out of a cathedral, an available hall, or even his own living quarters to whatever students sought him out. The University of Paris, the first university and the oldest in existence, had its origins in the early twelfth century, when learning—that is, Roman law, medicine, and classical philosophy—flooded Western Europe in the form of manuscripts translated into Latin by the Arab scholars of Spain and the Mediterranean. Aristotle, Ptolemy, Euclid, Galen, and Hippocrates became available to the West for the first time. Students wanted access not only to the material but also to scholars who could provide commentary that would help clarify these difficult works. The brilliant Peter Abelard was the intellectual force that drew legions of students to Paris in the early twelfth century; in Bologna, the famous scholar of law, Irnerius, established the reputation of the university there.

In its earliest years, then, the medieval university bore little similarity to the bureaucratic institution with which we are now familiar. Instead, individual scholars relied on talent and training to attract paying students, who eventually formed classes that in turn became standardized into a curriculum. Standardization of the curriculum and process occurred only gradually. At the University of Bologna, famous for the study of law, student guilds, similar to labor unions, formed for the protection of student rights, setting regulations for their professors that would guarantee a certain amount of work for the fees they were paid and negotiating lodging and the price of books with the local townsmen. In response, the professors formed their own guild, which measured student competency (via an examination before students were allowed to attend lectures), decided upon a curriculum, and licensed professors to teach. Although Bologna established a model which guided many other universities in their curricular and administrative decisions, the institutional procedure in Paris and Oxford was set by the masters themselves, who appointed officers—such as the dean, the rector, and the provost—with different degrees of responsibility and oversight to administer the programs. Within 100 years this administrative unit had developed into a system of "colleges" (such as Merton and Balliol at Oxford) that organized and housed the students who gathered to learn there.

Organization into different colleges caused its own set of problems, encouraging students to form rivalries amongst each other and with the townspeople with whom they lodged and dealt. Jacques de Vitry, in his account of students at the University of Paris, writes that the college system at Paris—which was divided into "nations" such as the "English," the "Normans," and the "Romans"—incited a life devoted less to learning than to competitive pursuits:

> Almost all the students at Paris, foreigners and natives, did absolutely nothing except learn or hear something new. Some studied merely to acquire knowledge, which is curiosity; others to acquire fame, which is vanity; others still for the sake of gain, which is cupidity and the vice of simony. Very few studied for their own edification, or that of others. They wrangled and disputed not merely about the various sects or about some discussions; but the differences between the countries also caused dissensions, hatreds, and virulent animosities among them and they impudently uttered all kinds of affronts and insults against one another.
>
> They affirmed that the English were drunkards and had tails; the sons of France proud, effeminate and carefully adorned like women. They said that the Germans were furious and obscene at their feasts; the Normans, vain and boastful; the Poitevins, traitors and always adventurers. The Burgundians they considered vulgar and stupid. The Bretons were reputed to be fickle and changeable, and were often reproached for the death of Arthur. The Lombards were called avaricious, vicious, and cowardly; the Romans, seditious, turbulent, and slanderous; the Sicilians, tyrannical and cruel; the inhabitants of Brabant, men of blood, incendiaries, brigands, and ravishers; the Flemish, fickle, prodigal, gluttonous, yielding as butter, and slothful. After such insults from words they often came to blows.[15]

The assumption that students were rowdy, drunk, and pugnacious was borne out by numerous incidents, documented in the rolls and records, of brawling and various other petty crimes. As a student, the French poet François Villon was forced to flee Paris after killing a priest during a brawl. Several students died during the repeated student riots in Oxford, and students were known to attack each other with weapons or pelt their lecturers with stones when provoked.[16] Chaucer's students in "The Reeve's Tale," with their determination to demonstrate their cleverness against the cheating Symkin, exemplify the stereotypes of behavior even in the Middle Ages: "Testif they were, and lusty for to pleye," full of "myrthe and revelrye" (RT 4004-4005). They certainly knew how to brawl: after first taking advantage of the miller's daughter as revenge for their host's treatment of them, the students end up in a fisticuff free-for-all in which everyone gets hurt. As is often the case in town and gown conflicts, the citizens are as guilty as the students. Symkin takes pride in routinely cheating the college and its students of their fair share of grain, re-enacting a frequent complaint on the part of real students that the townspeople who hosted them took advantage of their visitors' more marginal position and connections.

The Medieval Commentary Tradition

Of course, the records document only those students who transgressed norms, while ignoring the vast majority of "povre scolars" who were serious about their vocation and who obeyed the law. The serious student had much to occupy his time, for the examination process was rigorous, and, if a scholar expected to achieve any serious reputation in his field, he had to produce a serious body of writing, normally on questions of logic. Traditionally scholarly writing and analysis took the form of extensive commentaries, through which the academic expounded upon the major points of a great theological, philosophical, or classical work. The most famous of all the commentaries was the *Glossa Ordinaria*, an enormous compendium of writings on the vulgate Bible, based on the interpretive strategies of patristic fathers such as Jerome and Ambrose. By the fourteenth century, lengthy commentaries were also being written on pagan works by authors such as Ovid and Aesop. Ostensibly the purpose of writing the commentary was to "universalize" the text—to take a particular piece of classical or theological writing and to apply standardized techniques and formulaic interpretations upon it that distilled what we might today consider a vast range of meanings down to a doctrinal message or import. In other words, the particular was de-emphasized in favor of the universal; individual experience was less valued than authority. Ironically, of course, what was more at stake in the commentaries was establishing the authority of the scholar, whose reputation might be staked upon the production of this scholastic work. These commentators are the very scholars referred to by the Wife of Bath, when she remarks that "Men may devyne and glosen up and doun" and yet still never interpret the Bible correctly. To "gloss" meant to interpret or comment upon a text; the commentators, in providing their scriptural glosses, essentially fixed the range of meaning that an ambiguous biblical event or parable might carry.

The purpose of the commentary was to analyze the style or didactic mode by which the material was treated. By meticulously dividing and subdividing the text's form and organizational structures, the commentator would whittle away the excess so as to reveal the hidden theological or moral meaning inside. Thus the acts of *dispositio, divisio,* and *distinctio*— "arrangement," "division," and "discrimination"—were the key tools of exegesis, exegesis itself being a form of interpretation almost exclusively aimed at deriving a figurative or theological secondary meaning.

The theological agenda was primary to the act of interpretation. Commentaries usually began with a prologue that applied an Aristotelian schema of categorization by "cause" to a weighty work in order to reveal its purpose and utility. The "efficient cause" referred to the intention of the author, who provided the authority by which the commentator himself could speak; the "material cause" assessed the materials with which that author worked; the "formal cause," the lengthiest portion of the commentary, analyzed the literary structure and arrangement of the contents; and the "final cause" summed up the ethical and moral usefulness of the work overall. By elaborating on the four causes that determined the production and meaning of a work of literature or philosophy, scholars would schematically analyze both a text's affective impact on public morals and ethics, and the role it played in terms of the larger field of knowledge in which it participated. Discussions of genre, allegory, ethics, and morality would be worked into this larger philosophical sense of how all things in the universe were supposed to be explained.

The scholastic approach seems incredibly dry to modern readers. Yet it constitutes a sophisticated approach to literary analysis that exposes a great deal about medieval attitudes toward aesthetics and literature. For medieval scholars, classification and subclassification were ways of defining the world and making it understandable. By breaking things into smaller and smaller parts, one could begin to understand, theoretically, the operation of the whole. More importantly, by taking texts apart and breaking them down, then reconstructing them into a shape that fit a theologically predefined position, scholars also appropriated them for their own contexts and uses. The role of the exegete—that is, the scholar who performed exegesis—was not to restore the cultural differences to the text in order to understand the past and its lessons. Rather, his purpose was to erase any cultural or religious beliefs that might conflict with the doctrinally approved Christian position. Thus, even the most provocative and potentially seditious authors, such as the naughty Ovid, whose works influenced Chaucer possibly more than any other classical author, could be reclaimed for theology by an efficacious exegete.

The purpose of medieval commentary was less to understand the text as it was originally written than to reframe it for another agenda. The fourteenth-century commentator and mythographer Pierre Bersuire remarked outright that "falseness can be constrained to serve truth," especially when explicating those "poems, enigmas, and fables" that otherwise threaten to seduce the imagination.[17] Even the explication itself might be subjected to further explication, as new generations of scholars came forward to revise the needs of both texts and glosses for their own needs. Scholasticism later became associated with some of the worst of the errors of medieval philosophy; it was almost unanimously repudiated by the early modern humanists who succeeded the scholastics.

How much influence did the scholastic ventures of the universities have on secular authors and poets such as Chaucer? For the most part, contemporaries ridiculed university scholars for promoting an impossibly illogical form of language and belief. Yet one university movement, nominalism, deserves some mention. Nominalism was a philosophic movement that gained fresh currency in the fourteenth century under such philosophers as William Ockham and, later, Ralph Strode. A subcategory of the study of logic, nominalism focused on the way knowledge is ordered and presented. Asserting that universal concepts about God, existence, and divine being were represented merely by words that had no real independent existence, nominalism was opposed to the more prevailing theological position of "realism," which held that God's son was the Logos and that God's Word was reality incarnated. The nominalist position held that the study of logic, which dealt with categorizing reality according to concepts of likeness and difference, dealt purely within the system of signs, not with reality. In a radical departure from orthodoxy, nominalists believed that common concepts such as "greenness" or "unity" were word categories that signified relations between things and that did not necessarily correspond to real existing categories or forms. Things exist outside the words we give them, certainly. Facts are not at issue; the way we interpret and analyze them is. For the nominalists, ideas and concepts are products of our interior mental landscape and its signifying systems, rather than of any intrinsic characteristics of the things in themselves.

The nominalist position challenged the orthodoxy in many important ways, because it dangerously separated human ways of conceptualizing things from divine will. It was one thing to discuss the inaccessibility of divine knowledge, but it was altogether another to insist that all human concepts and laws are based in a very human language, distinct from God's planned reality. If all discussion of the divine Logos and God's will turned out to be based on corrupt human interpretations, then what was the real truth? How could the ideological belief in the divine right of kings be upheld? Was the pope divinely appointed, or was he, as William of Ockham himself proclaimed, a heretic who failed to learn from his own errors? Not surprisingly, William got into trouble for his views. He was compelled to respond to questioning in Avignon (though his views were never officially condemned); when he later fled, fearing for his life, he was excommunicated. His ideas influenced many later thinkers, however, including John Wyclif, Robert Holcot, and Ralph Strode, the friend to whom Chaucer dedicates *Troilus and Criseyde*.

As a writer profoundly interested in language and its relation to truth, Chaucer may have found much to intrigue him in nominalism. He frequently draws attention to the images and phantasms of dreams in order to provide a wholly secular and humanistic material for his fictions. His characters repeatedly question the authority of scholastic philosophy, separating God's original Word and will from the centuries of commentary that followed. The Wife of Bath's well-known mantra— "experience, though noon auctoritee were in this world, is right ynogh for me" (WP 1-2)—neatly bisects assertions about truth from the real thing. Other characters, too—like the narrators of the dream poems, Melibee, or Chanticleer—gloss texts according to personal interpretation to inform their experiences instead.[18] No text deflates the truth content of words more than the *House of Fame*, which posits that words are no more than "broken air" and as such should carry little authority:

> Soun ys noght but eyr ybroken;
> and every speche that ys spoken
> Lowd or pryvee, foul or fair,
> In his substaunce ys but air. (765-768)

Indeed, the *House of Fame* shares much of its skepticism about language and the force of tradition with some of the nominalist thinkers of

Chaucer's age. In a world in which lies and self-interest are preserved and glorified as readily as facts and moral action, how can any belief in the ontology of language be sustained?

HUMANISM

The scholastic method of glossing texts had profound implications for philosophy and considerable influence on professional interpretation. By the early fourteenth century authors in the secular languages, who read for personal rather than professional reasons, also began to write about books and the art of interpretation, adding a different perspective that was to eventually overtake scholasticism, especially in the arts. We might say that the most profound difference between the reading strategies of the humanists and that of the scholars was that the humanists were more interested in the role of the individual reader—the individual who *reads*—than in the recognition of *auctoritas*, or traditional authority, in measuring a book's effect on human action. In other words, the humanists saw personal benefits in reading that were actuated in the living world. Reading was, for them, a pleasurable and personally enriching experience. This belief was counter to the more orthodox opinion that any reading should be undertaken exclusively with an eye toward eternal salvation and God's will.

One of the most influential of the new humanists was the great Italian poet Dante Alighieri, who introduced a highly personalized interest in his identity as an author and in how his works might be viewed by others. The *Vita Nuova*, an account of his early years as a poet and of his love for Beatrice Portinari, combines a series of sonnets for interpretation with the personal context from which they emerged. After circulating his first sonnet—inspired by a dream he had had about his beloved Beatrice— the poet describes its reception and interpretation by others:

> This sonnet was answered by many possessing a variety of opinions, among whom was the one I call my first friend, who composed a sonnet which begins: "I think that you beheld all worth." My sending the sonnet to him resulted in the forming of our friendship. The true interpretation of the dream I described was not perceived by anyone then, but now it is very clear to even the least sophisticated.[19]

In this passage the poet observes that both the meaning of the sonnet and even the position of the speaker are misunderstood when a poem is circulated in isolation. The *Vita Nuova* provides the personal context normally separate from isolated stanzas of poetry. The addition of personal information enriches Dante's seemingly conventional poems and extends their potential meaning beyond the structural and stylistic analyses he also provides in his work. In other words, the personal meaning that the poem carries for both author and audience matters. The *Vita Nuova* functions in many respects as a kind of training in interpretation, where the poet calls for his audience to submit to the poetry and to read his sonnet sequence not in isolation but as part of an unfolding drama in which the poet describes his own transformation, a transformation that may resonate with others.

This kind of reading represents a very different trend from that followed by professional glossators. Dante views reading and writing as highly personal and transformative experiences that have value in the human world. The sacred remains of primary concern, but the human world is richly fulfilling, as well. Dante's human ethos is echoed in the works of later Italian writers. Petrarch, considered one of the first of the Italian Humanists, makes an even more explicit claim for poetry's power:

> In truth, poetry is not in the least contrary to theology. Does this astonish you? I might almost say that theology is the poetry of God. What else is it if not poetry when Christ is called a lion or a lamb or a worm? In Sacred Scripture you will find thousands of such examples too numerous to pursue here. Indeed, what else do the parables of the Savior in the Gospels echo if not discourse different from ordinary meaning or, to express it briefly, figurative speech, which we call allegory in ordinary language? Yet poetry is woven from this kind of discourse, but with another subject. Who denies it?[20]

Petrarch staked an ideological claim for poetry that was nothing short of revolutionary. He was not just advocating for his own poems; although we remember him for his sonnets, he was known primarily to his contemporaries as a classical scholar and translator. As such, he sought to renew interest in the great literary works of Roman antiquity. Authors had certainly made tentative claims for the value of these secular works in the past, but never had they encroached on the territory of theology. Augustine, in his *Confessions*, had rejected the classical authors as reading that distracted him from the contemplation of God; for nearly 1,000 years no thinker challenged his view on the matter. Petrarch's celebration of literary values was catching, however, and by the mid-fourteenth century, humanist ideas had achieved some cultural cachet. The great humanist, scholar, and churchman Richard de Bury declares that

> ... in books I find the dead as if they were alive; in books I foresee things to come; in books warlike affairs are set forth; from books come forth the laws of peace. All things are corrupted and decay in time; Saturn ceases not to devour the children that he generates; all the glory of the world would be buried in oblivion, unless God had provided mortals with the remedy of books.[21]

De Bury's *Philobiblon* grants reading for personal pleasure enormous ethical value. For him reading fires the imagination and connects cultures and peoples thousands of worlds apart. It is perhaps not surprising that a man like Richard should share such a reading philosophy with his contemporaries. Like both Dante and Petrarch, he had a long international career that encompassed various political situations in several countries; he was well-traveled, well-connected, and well-read. Bishop of Durham and tutor to Prince Edward of Windsor (later Edward III), he was also a trusted public official who traveled widely on diplomatic missions, including several missions to Rome during which he acted as ambassador to Pope John XXII. These journeys both exposed him to the humanistic movement emerging in Italy—indeed, his meeting with Petrarch is recounted in Petrarch's own letters—and served as a metaphor for the act of reading itself. Reading, for him, was like travel in that it broadened the mind, spanned countries and oceans, and brought together intellects separated by hundreds of miles of distance. The *Philobiblon* was directed toward other readers who might find, as he himself did, a kind of intellectual transcendence that occurred only through reading for purely personal and aesthetic reasons.

The Arrival of the Printing Press

Throughout the fourteenth and fifteenth centuries books were increasingly perceived as markers of status. The educated were either already part of an aristocratic ruling class or had access to aristocratic circles; owning books, whether or not one was literate enough to read them independently, was itself a symbol of the prestige that ordinarily only belonged to those elite circles. Manuscript books enjoyed a tangible rise in retail during this period as well. Book artisans proliferated: in 1373 the scriveners established their own professional guild outside the cathedrals and universities, and in 1403 the illuminators and Writers of Text-Letters formed their own guilds. A guild of "book artisans," which combined the separate professional functions, was established in 1403.[22] The rise in professionals dedicated to the production of more and more books attests to the demand for books in private circles.

A vibrant urban trade was a necessary precondition for the invention and spread of the printing press. This trade was driven by enthusiastic readers such as Richard de Bury, who made an urgent argument for the production of new works. *The Philobiblon* pointed to the importance not just of reading books but of making books in order to keep tradition and history alive:

> Of making many books there is no end. For as the bodies of books, seeing that they are formed of a combination of contrary elements, undergo a continual dissolution of their structure, so by the forethought of the clergy a remedy should be found, by means of which the sacred book paying the debt of nature may obtain a natural heir and may raise up like seed to its dead brother, and thus may be verified that saying of Ecclesiasticus: His father is dead, and he is as if he were not dead; for he hath left one behind him that is like himself. And thus the transcription of ancient books is as it were the begetting of fresh sons, on whom the office of the father may devolve, lest it suffer detriment.[23]

Just as the human body dies and lives again in the next generation, so too does the physical structure of books decay over time and become renewed through continual transcription. Thought evolves as books are not only recopied but reformulated for succeeding generations. According to Richard de Bury, the evolution of books is like the evolution of fathers and sons "on whom the office of the father may devolve": each new version of the tradition is not just an identical replication of its predecessor, but a transformation of it, kept alive by the production of new books.

Given his views on the matter, Richard must have approved the fact that the *Philobiblon* was itself reprinted multiple times over the next several hundred years in countries as far apart as England, Cologne, Spires, and Paris. Certainly his praise for the art of the book and his interest in the value of reading embodied and encouraged a growing interest in owning books. The personal encounter with the text that de Bury validates is echoed not only by later authors but especially by printers, who of course were invested in establishing a sense of reading's relevance to supply book-buying consumers.

The invention of the printing press is attributed to Johannes Gutenberg in the 1440s; his first book, the Gutenberg Bible, was printed in 200 copies on borrowed funds during the 1450s. The press, which introduced the innovation of moveable metal type that could be set into templates and arranged in an infinite variety of words and pages, enabled multiple copies to be printed from a single block of text. Given that a monk or professional copyist might take several years to produce a single copy of a text, which then would cost the equivalent of a modern-day automobile, printing revolutionized literary culture in an almost unfathomable way. A single block of print could produce thousands of copies in a single day. Thus, not only were people suddenly able to afford books that had previously been the exclusive right of the privileged, but books that hitherto had existed only in a few scattered copies were now readily printed and made available for popular scrutiny.

Following Gutenberg's venture in Mainz, printers spread outward to set up presses in Cologne, Strasbourg, Rome, and finally France and Flanders. London was introduced to the printing press by William Caxton, who learned the trade in 1473 while living in Bruges as a foreign merchant and an active member of the Merchant Adventurers, a trade association that controlled trade regulations and agreements between England and Scotland and their European trading partners. Caxton most likely learned the trade from the Bruges printer Colard Mansion, who provided him with the materials he needed to establish a print in England, and who cast the types according to his own models.[24] Mansion worked with Caxton in the production of his first printed work, *The Recuyell of the Historyes of Troyes*, which he not only printed, but also translated and edited. Caxton brought the press to England around 1476, setting up shop in Westminster. He was a savvy businessman, and his business concentrated on producing books that were not available through the already-existing tradesmen. Thus, he specialized in a new market—books written in English. Caxton produced all of the major English works of his time, including Chaucer's *Canterbury Tales*, the *House of Fame*, and his translation of the *Consolation of Philosophy*.[25]

Richard de Bury's influence can be recognized in the long, highly personalized prologues Caxton wrote for many of his editions. These prologues justify his choice of materials and explain his process of translation and editing. Like de Bury, Caxton was interested in providing a personal framework for his printed editions that helped readers to understand his own interest in the works and perhaps even feel some of that interest themselves. Although his prologues often gesture toward the universal moral appeal that literature holds, the emphasis is more on the personal and the colloquial than on the logical and analytical. An example is his prologue to the *Aenead*, a work he painstakingly translated from the French in order to introduce the English to something of both European and French values.

> ... I had great pleasure, because of the fair and honest terms and words in French, which I never saw to-fore like, nor none so pleasant nor so well ordered, which book as me seemed should be much requisite to noble men to see as well for the eloquence as the histories.[26]

Caxton's personal pleasure in coming across a new text to share with the English public is very different from the scholastic approach of dividing and analyzing. Yet Caxton, too, saw important universal lessons in literature—he simply localized these large-scale interests in terms of nation and culture. As Governor of the English Nation at Bruges and diplomat for trade relations regarding a commercial treaty between England and Burgundy, Caxton recognized that England needed to wake up to the possibilities of international communication and innovation. In his prologue to his edition of the *Aenead*, he pointed to French books as being particularly worthy of emulation. If France surpassed England in its cultural awareness, it was, Caxton believed, because the French read more often and more carefully, and valued reading more than his own native countrymen. In addition, Caxton's works often comment on the theme of alienation and fragmentation in English politics. He thought that this factionalization resulted from the many dialects of the language, which isolated rather than united the English people. A common national vision and culture would provide the uniting glue that would draw different interests and locales together. Voicing an opinion similar to that in a passage from Malory's *Morte Darthur*, which also laments the lack of steadfastness among Englishmen, Caxton blamed this disharmony on the lack of English participation in international culture and international history:

> For we Englishmen be born under the domination of the moon, which is never steadfast, but ever wavering, waxing one season and waneth and decreaseth another season, and that common English that is spoken in one shire varyeth in another.[27]

By printing books in English, Caxton addresses this problem and helped establish a common culture and a common set of cultural goals for England. He dedicates his edition of the *Aenead* to Henry VII's son Arthur, heir to the throne of England, as a means of insisting on impressing on his readers the similarity between their reading tastes and those of the aristocracy. By calling on their desire to emulate the gentry, Caxton invites his readers to read the *Aenead* with some attention and care. Reading connotes not just political expediency, not just participation in a communal European history, but also the achievement of social status. Those who read—and who are, moreover, educated readers, who have bothered to go over their "Virgil, or the Epistles of Ovid"—are informed and can inform others. Only through the establishment of a community of like-minded readers, Caxton implies, might England as a nation step up to the international plate and participate on an equal footing with Italy and France.

Caxton's writings point toward a new international concern that takes hold beginning in the early fourteenth century for elaborating a culture of reading on an international and intercontextual level. The Caxtons, de Burys, and Chaucers of the Middle Ages were naturally conversant in multiple languages and traditions; when they transposed and translated other works, they did so with great attention to their various purposes and associations. The very difference that they found in the European milieu intrigued these later writers, sometimes more than the familiar classical traditions. Certainly, Caxton, Chaucer, and company participated in Latin clerical culture, and probably they even believed in the transcendence of the divine over the humanistic. Yet the great variety of human achievement, as it was recorded in the works of contemporary European authors, breathed life into their works and lent an urgency to their pleas to read books.

Documents

The Boke of Curtasye (*c*. 1460)

This extract is from an anonymous narrative poem providing advice on living in a wealthy household. The first book instructs household officers and servants on appropriate manners and comportment, while the second book offers advice about schooling, church behavior, and the like. Our translation is based on Frederick Furnivall's edition of the book.

THE SECOND BOOK
(WHAT YOU LEARN IN GRAMMAR SCHOOL)
If you are a young infant,
And think about being in school,
These lessons shall thy master advance thee towards,
The cross of Christ assist thee in all thy work;
Since thy *Pater Noster* he will teach thee,
As Christ's own apostles do to preach;
After thy *Ave Maria* and thy *Creed*,
That shall save thee at the judgment of dread;
Then after to bless thee with the trinity,
In *nomine patris* he will teach thee;
Then with Mark, Matthew, Luke, and John,
With *per crucis* and the high name;
To shrive thee in general thou shall learn
Thy general Confession and absolution in fear.
To seek the kingdom of God, my child,
I thereto advise you not to be unrestrained.
Therefore worship God, both old and young,
To be strong in body and soul alike.
When thou come through the church door,
Take the holy water standing on the floor;
Read or sing or say prayers
To Christ, for all thy Christian companions;
Be courteous to God, and kneel down
On both knees with great devotion.
To man thou shall kneel upon one,
The other thou shall hold to thyself alone.
When your ministers are at the high altar,
With both hands serve thou your priest in fear,
The one to make steadfast the other
Lest thou fail, my dear brother.
Another courtesy I will teach thee,
Thy father and mother, with mild speech,
In worship and serve with all thy might,
That thou dwell the longer in earthly light.
To another man do no more amiss
Then thou wish be done by others;
So Christ thou please, and get the love
Of men and God that sits above.

Be not too meek, but in moderation hold thee,
For else a fool you will be called.
He that will incline to righteousness,
As holy writ says is good and fine,
His seed shall never go seek for roasted meat,
Nor suffer moaning for any shameful deeds.
To forgive thou shall haste thee;
To look to vengeance thou come on last;
Draw thee to peace with all thy strength;
From strife and discord draw thee on length.
If a request is asked of thee for God's sake,
And the desired thing whereof to take,
Give him good words of fair manner,
With glad semblance and pure good cheer.
Also of service thou shall be free
To every man in his degree.
Thou shall never lose for being kind;
That which one forgets, another has in mind.
If any man has parted with thee in gifts,
With him thou make an even share;
Let it not hang in hand for deceit,
Thou art uncourteous if thou do it.
To saints if thou thy journey have promised,
Thou shall fulfill it with all thy might,
Lest God strike thee with great vengeance,
And thrust thee into sore penance.
Believe not all men that speak fair,
Whether it be commons, burgesses, or mayor;
In sweet words the serpent was closest,
Ever deceitful and blamed;
Therefore thou art of Adam's blood,
With words be wary, unless thou be angry:
A short word is commonly true
That first slides from man's tooth.
Look that thou never become a liar,
Keep thy word for all and some.
Laugh not too often for any solace,
For no kind of mirth that any man confuses;
Whose laws all that men may see,
A shrew or a fool he seems to be.

Three enemies in this world there are
That desire to mislead all men,—
The devil, the flesh, the world also,
That make very great woe for mankind:
If thou may destroy these three enemies,
Thou may be secure of heaven's bliss.
Also, my child, against thy lord
Look thou strive with no type of words,
Nor lay thou any wager with him,
Nor at the dice play with him.
He that thou know of greater state,
Be not his fellow in rest or dissension.
If thou are stationed in a strange country,
Make sure no fire then falls to thee,
Nor take anymore tasks in hand
Then thou may have honor of all in land.
If thou see any man fall by the street,
Laugh not thereat in dry or wet,
But help him up with all thy might;
As Saint Ambrose teaches thee is right;
Thou that stands so sure in his seat,
Be ware lest thy head fall to thy feet.
My child, if thou stand at the mass,
At understanding both more and less,
If the priest advises not at thy liking,
Reprove him not, but hold thee still.
To any creature if you show thy council,
Be ware that he be not a shrew,
Lest he slander thee with tongue
Among all men, both old and young.
Beckoning, pointing with a finger, use thou not,
And secret whisperings look thou refuse.
If you meet knight, man, or knave,
Hail him anon, "sir, God save you."
If he speaks first upon the meeting,
Answer him gladly without more.
Go not forth as a dumb man,
Since God has left the tongue to speak;
Lest men say to a relation or friend,
"Yond is a man without mouth."

Speak never dishonestly of womankind,
Nor let it ever run in thy mind;
The book calls him a churl in cheer,
That speaks villainy about women individually:
For we are all born of women,
And our fathers before us;
Therefore it is a dishonest thing
To speak of them with any contempt.
Also a wife is, as right befalls
To worship her husband both day and night,
To his bidding be obedient,
And to serve him without offence.
If two brothers are at debate,
Look thou further neither in their hate,
But help to staunch them in their malice;
Then thou art friend to both indeed.
If thou go with another at the gate,
And ye are both of one estate,
Be courteous and let him have the way,
That is no villainy, and men say to me;
And he who comes of great lineage,
Go not before thou are bidden;
And if he is thy master,
Go not before, for courtesy,
Neither in field, wood, or land,
Nor go even with him, unless he commands.
If thou shall go on pilgrimage,
Be not the third fellow for health or woe;
Three oxen in plough may never draw well,
Neither craft, right, or law.
If thou are offered to drink of cup,
Drink not all of it, nor in any way sip;
Drink politely and give it again,
That is a courtesy, to speak plainly.
In bed if it befalls thou to be in lodgings,
With fellow, master, or kin,
Thou shall inquire to be courteous
In what part of the bed he will lie;
Be honest and lay thyself far from him,
Thou art not wise unless thou do so.

With any men, both far and nigh,
The journey to go, look thou be wise
To ask his name, and who he is,
Whither he goes: keep well these three.
With friars on pilgrimage if thou go,
What they wish to do, thou will also;
Also in night thy rest,
And await the day as a true man's deed.
In no sort of house where there is a red man,
Nor woman of the same color indeed,
Take never thy lodging despite any kind of need,
For those are folk that are to be dreaded.
If any through sternness opposes thee,
Answer him meekly and make him an explanation:
But explanatory words that are false,
Forsake, and all that is amiss.
Also if thou have a lord,
And stand before him at the table,
While thou speak, keep well thy hands,
Thy feet also let stand in peace,
His need for courtesy he might break,—
Stirring fingers, toes when he shall speak.
Be stable of cheer and somewhat light,
Nor over all wander thou thy sight;
Stare not on walls with thine eye;
Far or nigh, low or high;
Let not the post become thy staff,
Lest thou be called a silly fool;
Nor pick thou ever thy nostril
With thumb or finger, as a young child;
Clothe not thy arm or claw it,
Bow not down thy head too low;
While any man speaks with great attention,
Hearken his words without distress.
By street or way if thou shall go,
From these two things keep thee from,
Neither to harm child nor beast,
With casting, turning west or east;
Change thou not in face color,
For lightness of word in hall or bower;

If thy visage changes for naught,
Men say "the trespass thou has wrought."
Before thy lord, make not faces
If you wish to take courtesy with thee.
With hands unwashed take never thy meal;
From all these vices look thou keep thyself.
Look thou sit—and make no strife—
Where the host commands, or else the wife.
Eschew the highest place with pleasure,
Unless thou be bidden to therein.
Of courtesy here ends this second part,
The heavenly Christ might our souls fly!

A Fifteenth Century School Book (late 15ᵗʰc)

The extracts that follow were composed as exercises by the schoolmaster of a grammar school in Oxford for the use of his students in learning Latin. Each extract provided a realistic and everyday scenario that the schoolboy would translate into Latin. Although these extracts are not, strictly speaking, nonfiction, they are intended to be practical and realistic, and many of them may even be drawn from real-life models. As such they provide a rare sense of what it was like for the schoolboy inside the classroom. The examples selected below provide some sense of the value grammar had to the curriculum overall and how it was perceived to be the structural basis of the liberal arts. They also offer some descriptive sense of the schoolboy's environment and his tools for learning: he had a pen and a pen case; a Latin book; a set of exercises he was expected to have completed; and, possibly, a nearby library from which other books could be borrowed for classroom use. He was also surrounded by temptations like the taverns and the fairs that threatened to interrupt his course of study.

75. It is a heavy situation that children, in their best and most fit age to learn grammar, are taken from it and set to sophistry, where for the lack of the one they shall be deceived in both.

79. It is no little thing what authors a child is accustomed to in youth, for then the mind of a young man is as wax, apt to accept all things. Whatsoever is printed in him, he receives it, and that which is first received is hard to forget. Wherefore if a man or a child learns

good authors while he is young, he will not stray lightly from them, and if he learns evil and barbarities, he will stick more by them.

80. Would to God that I had spent the years in good learning that I have lost ignorantly in evil grammar!

81. I have ever had this in mind, that there is nothing better nor more profitable to bring a man to wisdom than to mark such things as are left of the good authors, and I mean not all, but the best, and those to follow as closely as a man's mind will allow him. And he who besides gives himself to exercise, he cannot choose but be most wise.

91. Methinks you lack many things that are needed by a good scholar: first, a pen case and an inkhorn, and then books, and yet furthermore, the which is first and chief and surpassing all the precepts of the masters and other doctrines, exercise and diligence in the Latin language.

137. The rules that I must say to my master are scarcely half written, wherefore I am worthy to be beaten.

147. If scholars that have good wits would give themselves to their books, they could not choose but be wise. And so we see it daily proved in those that so doth, for there are many that have noble wits and trust their wit too much and put no diligence to it in the world, and therefore they are deceived often in the end, and those who are dull exceed them.

187. My master sent me to inquire of a certain man of whom I should ask the keys of the library to be brought to him, and I could not find him anywhere. I came again to my master and then I missed my Latin book, but I cannot tell whether I lost it running or left it in the Tavern.

231. Many scholars of this university would spend wastefully all their father's goods in jokes and trifles at the fair if they had the liberty to do so. For these Londoners are so crafty and so wily in dressing their gear up so gloriously that they deceive us scholars easily.

272. It is no marvel that the old authors, such as Virgil and Tully and many others of the Romans, were more eloquent than authors are nowadays, for they set in their minds so greatly toward knowledge that no desire for goods, nor fleshly voluptuousness, nor greed for honor, nor vainglory in battle, nor any worldly labor could trouble their minds, but gave themselves utterly to virtue, putting away all manner of things which might draw them from study.

Aristotle's ABC (early 15ᵗʰc)

An original version of this work can also be found in Furnivall's edition.

> Whoever wishes to be wise, and desires worship,
> Learn he one letter, and look on another
> Of the a.b.c. of Aristotle: argue not against that:
> It is council for right many clerks and knights a thousand,
> And also it might amend a man full often
> For to learn lore of one letter, and save his life;
> For too much of anything was never wholesome.
> Read often on this scroll, and rule thou thereafter;
> Whoever is grieved in his soul, govern him better;
> Blame he not the man that this a.b.c. made,
> But know his wicked will and his work after;
> It shall never grieve a good man though the guilty be mended.
> Now hearken and hear how I begin.

> A   too amorous, too adventurous, nor argue too much.
> B   too bold, nor too busy, nor blabber too much.
> C   too courteous, too cruel, nor care too sorely.
> D   too dull, nor too dreadful, nor drink too often.
> E   too elenge [wretched], too excellent, not too earnest either.
> F   too fierce, too familiar, but friendly of cheer.
> G   too glad, nor too glorious, and hate thou jealousy.
> H   too hasty, nor too hardy, nor too heavy in thine heart.
> I   too jetting [capering], too jangling [chatty], nor jape [deceive] too often.
> K   too kind, nor too keeping [restrained], and be ware of knave habits.

L   too loath for to lend, nor too liberal of goods.

M   too meddlesome, nor too merry, but as measure will allow.

N   too noisy, too nice, nor use any new customs.

O   too orped [bold], nor too overthwart [angry], hate thou oaths.

P   too pressing, not too privy with princes or with dukes;

Q   too quaint, nor too quarrelsome, but queeme [satisfy] well your
    sovereigns.

R   too riotous, too reveling, nor rage not too rudely.

S   too strange, nor too stirring, nor stare too strangely.

T   too contentious, nor too talkative, for temperance is best.

V   too venomous, nor too vengeful, and avoid all villainy.

W   too wild, nor too wrathful, neither waste, nor wade too deep,
    For a measurable mean is ever the best of all.

Morale Scolarium. JOHN OF GARLAND (13ᵀᴴC)

John of Garland (1190-1270) was a prolific philologist whose works on
grammar and poetics were widely followed in the late Middle Ages. This
work is like many similar texts on proper comportment, both in school
and out of it.

> Regard as models of deportment the graven images of the churches,
> which you should carry in your mind as living and indelible pictures.
> Cherish again the violets of civility without blemish so that, when
> your blindness has vanished, the eyes of your soul may have no
> wasting disease. Be not a fornicator, O student, a robber, a deceitful
> merchant, a champion at dice. In the choir stalls a cleric should
> chant without noise and commotion. I advocate that the ordinary
> layman, who does not sing, be kept out of the choir. A student, who
> is a churchman, is expected to follow good custom, to be willing
> to serve, to fee the notary who has drawn up a charter for him, to
> gladden the giver. Do not constantly urge your horse on with the
> spur, which should be used only on rare occasions. Give your horse
> the reins when he mounts an incline; fearing a serious accident,
> avoid crossing swollen rivers, or the Rhine. If a bridge is not safe,
> you should dismount and let the horse pick his way over the smooth
> parts. Mount gently on the left stirrup. Select beautiful equestrian
> trappings suitable to your clerical station. Ride erect unless you are
> bent by age. If you are of the elect you should have a rich saddle

cloth. The cross should be exalted, the voice be raised in prayer, Christ should be worshipped, the foot should be taken out of the stirrup. The horseman will descend from his horse and say his prayers; no matter how far he then will travel, he will ride in safety. He who wishes to serve should be quick, not go to sleep, and not give way to anger against his lord. Avoid drunkards, those who indulge in secret sin, those who like to beat and strike, those who love lewdness, evil games, and quarrels. Passing a cemetery, if you are well-bred, and if you hope for salvation, you pause to pray that the dead may rest in peace. Have nothing to do with the prostitute, but love your wife; all wives should be honored but especially those who are distinguished by virtue. A person who is well should not recline at table in the fashion of the ancients. When you walk after dinner keep on frequented streets, avoid insincere speeches. Unless you wish to be considered a fool learn to keep your mouth shut in season. Stand and sit upright, do not scratch yourself.

Rules of the University of Paris (*c.* 1215)

Robert, servant of the cross of Christ by divine pity, cardinal priest of the title, St. Stephen in Mons Caelius, legate of the apostolic see, to all the masters and scholars of Paris, eternal greeting in the Lord. Let all know that, since we have had a special mandate from the pope to take effective measures to reform the state of the Parisian scholars for the better, wishing with the counsel of good men to provide for the tranquility of the scholars in the future, we have decreed and ordained in this wise:

No one shall lecture in the arts at Paris before he is twenty-one years of age, and he shall have heard lectures for at least six years before he begins to lecture, and he shall promise to lecture at least two years, unless a reasonable cause prevents, which he ought to prove publicly before examiners. He shall not be stained by any infamy, and when he is ready to lecture, he shall be examined according to the form which is contained in the writing of the lord bishop of Paris....And they shall lecture on the books of Aristotle on dialectic old and new in the schools ordinarily and not ad cursum. They shall also lecture on both Priscians ordinarily, or at least on one. They shall not lecture on feast days except on philosophers and rhetoric and the quadrivium and Barbarismus, and ethics, if it please

them, and the fourth book of the Topics. They shall not lecture on
the books of Aristotle on metaphysics and natural philosophy or on
summaries of them or concerning the doctrine of Master David of
Dinant or the heretic Amaury or Mauritius of Spain.

In the *principia* and meetings of the masters and in the
responsions or oppositions of the boys and youths there shall be no
drinking. They may summon some friends or associates, but only a
few. Donations of clothing or other things, as has been customary, or
more, we urge should be made, especially to the poor. None of the
masters lecturing in arts shall have a cope [mantle] except one round,
black, and reaching to the ankles, at least while it is new. Use of the
pallium is permitted. No one shall wear with the round cope shoes
that are ornamented or with elongated pointed toes. If any scholar
in arts or theology dies, half of the masters of arts shall attend the
funeral at one time, the other half the next time, and no one shall
leave until the sepulture is finished, unless he has reasonable cause....

Each master shall have jurisdiction over his scholar. No one shall
occupy a classroom or house without asking the consent of the
tenant, provided one has a chance to ask it. No one shall receive
the licentiate from the chancellor or another for money given or
promise made or other condition agreed upon. Also, the masters and
scholars can make both between themselves and with other persons
obligations and constitutions supported by faith or penalty or oath in
these cases: namely, the murder or mutilation of a scholar or atrocious
injury done a scholar, if justice should not be forthcoming, arranging
the prices of lodgings, costume, burial, lectures and disputations, so,
however, that the university be not thereby dissolved or destroyed.

As to the status of the theologians, we decree that no one shall
lecture at Paris before his thirty-fifth year and unless he has studied
for eight years at least, and has heard the books faithfully and in
classrooms, and has attended lectures in theology for five years before
he gives lectures himself publicly. And none of these shall lecture
before the third hour on days when masters lecture. No one shall be
admitted at Paris to formal lectures or to preachings unless he shall
be of approved life and science. No one shall be a scholar at Paris
who has no definite master.

Moreover, that these decrees may be observed inviolate, we
by virtue of our legatine authority have bound by the knot of
excommunication all who shall contumaciously presume to go
against these our statutes, unless within fifteen days after the offence

they have taken care to emend their presumption before the university of masters and scholars or other persons constituted by the university. Done in the year of Grace 1215, the month of August.

STUDIES NECESSARY BEFORE ADMISSION AS A MASTER OF ARTS (1431)

Since no one is thought worthy to receive the honour of master in any faculty or science unless he has been a studious and diligent disciple for a sufficient length of time in the same, then because the professor of the liberal arts is recognized to adorn in honourable mastership seven of the arts and three of the philosophies jointly and separately, the price of that work is that each person who wishes to climb to the honour of the master's chair shall before his admission to this pass through the public and teaching schools of philosophy for a suitable length of time, learning effectively the seven liberal arts and the three philosophies. Therefore we decree that those who are presented for inception in arts and philosophy shall have completed the form laid down for determining bachelors in the hearing of books, and in the schools of arts they shall have heard ordinarily and attentively the seven liberal arts and the three philosophies for the terms of eight years, each term containing at least thirty reading days according to the form, ascending by degrees; Grammar, for one year, that is Priscian, in greater or lesser form; Rhetoric for three terms, that is, the Rhetoric of Aristotle, the fourth part of the Topics of Boethius, or the Nova Rhetorica of Cicero, or the Metamorphoses of Ovid, or the poetry of Virgil; Logic for three terms, for example, the books De Interpretatione or three first books of the Topics of Boethius, or the books of the Priora or Topica of Aristotle; Arithmetic for one year, that is Boethius; Music for one year, that is Boethius; Geometry for two terms, that is the books of geometry of Euclid or the Perspective of Vitellio; Astronomy for two terms, that is "The Theory of Planets" or Ptolemy in "Almagesta"; Natural Philosophy for three terms, that is the books of Physics, or "Of heaven and earth" or "Of the properties of elements" or "Of the properties of meteors" or "Of vegetables and plants" or "Of the soul" or "of animals" or some of the small books, from the text of Aristotle; Moral Philosophy for three terms, that is the Ethics of the Politics of Aristotle; Metaphysical Philosophy for three terms, that is the book, the Metaphysics of Aristotle; but if he has first determined, he shall be compelled to hear the Metaphysics for only two terms, so that if any of the liberal arts are not ordinarily read in schools appointed for this purpose then it shall be heard by a bachelor extraordinary reading for the above time prescribed for the same art, when a suitable time for them shall have been freed for this purpose.

The Statutes of New College, Oxford (1400)

In the first place then … we decree and also ordain that our college at Oxford shall consist in and of the number of one warden and seventy poor needy scholars clerks to study in these sciences and faculties, and as the college itself will consist of divers persons whom it will collect into one, so in the same college there shall, by God's grace, flourish different sciences and faculties, namely, of philosophy, civil and canon law, and above all … of holy theology …

We have therefore decreed that of the scholars clerks aforesaid it shall be the duty of ten, and they shall be bound, to attend lectures on civil law, and another ten on canon law and to study effectively in the law faculty, separately unless this is impracticable for the reasons stated below.

The rest of the number, namely fifty, shall diligently attend lectures in and learn arts, or philosophy and theology. We allow, however, that two of them may employ themselves and attend to the science of medicine, as long as they shall be actual regent doctors in that faculty, and two others only may employ themselves in the science of astronomy.

We do not wish however that anyone should turn to the faculty of medicine without the will and consent of the warden and the dean of the faculty of theology and that only if he has first really incepted in the faculty or science of arts, and completed the course prescribed in the University of Oxford. And we wish that these students in the faculty of medicine, unless actually regent doctors in the same faculty, shall pass to the study of theology and become proficient in the same.

Decreeing and also ordaining that above and beyond the number of one warden and seventy scholars aforesaid there shall be always and continuously ten priests and three clerks, paid servants of the chapel, daily serving in the same, of sufficient learning and

good standing and upright life, having good voice and sufficiently
instructed in reading and singing; also sixteen boys sufficiently taught
to read and sing....

The Study of the French Language
and English Law at Oxford (1432)

Also since it is consonant with reason, and found in the more ancient
statutes, that any scholar learning any art for which no ordinary
lecture exists ought to attend the ordinary lecture of that faculty or
subject which is nearest to the art which he is learning; so because
the art of writing and reciting and speaking the French language, in
which there are no ordinary lectures, is nearer to the arts of grammar
and rhetoric than to other subjects and faculties, therefore the
university ordains and decrees that every scholar learning to write or
recite or speak French or to compose charters and other writings of
this kind, or the mode of pleading English law, provided that they are
competently instructed in grammar, shall attend the ordinary lectures
of the artists reading grammar or rhetoric, paying fees to them as
to their own masters; so that no one teaching any of these arts shall
instruct anyone in any way for any of these subjects during the
ordinary hours of the Faculty of Arts in full term, and let those who
teach such subjects be admitted to the teaching of such arts by the
chancellor, in the presence of proctors, and let them swear to observe
the statutes, privileges, customs, liberties, and other rules of the
university; with the grammarians they shall be under the supervision
and rule of the supervisory grammar masters; and let them pay 13s 4d
annually to the masters in arts, in recompense for the damage done
by them to the teaching of the masters; to the payment of this sum
all such teachers shall contribute in proportion to the number of
their scholars, and if there is only one such teacher, he shall pay the
whole sum himself, as is accustomed for the highest payment by the
grammarians to the masters in arts; provided always that the whole
sum collected from all the scholars of the faculty for their masters
shall be equally divided amongst all the regent masters of arts giving
ordinary lectures in the same and giving ordinary lectures in the
philosophies for the form of inceptors, since God, nature, and the law
obviously persuade us to distribute emoluments equally among men
of equal honour and equal status.

THE COMMONS PROTEST AGAINST THE MISBEHAVIOUR OF THE SCHOLARS AND CLERKS OF OXFORD (1421)

In "The Reeve's Tale," two students butt heads with an arrogant miller, who resents their scholastic pretensions. Conflicts between town and gown were not uncommon in the Middle Ages, as the document below shows.

> May it please the very wise commons of this present Parliament to consider how a great number of scholars and clerks of the University of Oxford, who are unknown, and armed and arrayed in manner of war, have often dispossessed and ousted several men of the shires of Oxford, Berkshire, and Buckinghamshire of their lands and tenements and have made to the dispossessed persons ... great threats to beat and kill them ... and also chase with dogs and greyhounds in various warrens, parks, and forests in the shires aforesaid, and take, as well by day as by night, does, hares, and rabbits, and menace the keepers foresters, and parkers their servants and deputies, to beat and kill them, and also by force have taken clerks who have been convicted of felony out of the custody of the ordinary, and have brought the said prisoners with them and let them go free ....

Letter to Can Grande. DANTE (EARLY 14ᵗʰC)

Whether or not Dante actually wrote the *Letter to Can Grande* or whether the letter was written by a contemporary is a matter of dispute. Regardless, the letter delineates the various allegorical levels that underlie the *Divine Comedy*.

> 7. For the clarification of what I am going to say, then, it should be understood that there is not just a single sense in this work: it might rather be called *polysemous*, that is, having several senses. For the first sense is that which is contained in the letter, while there is another which is contained in what is signified by the letter. The first is called literal, while the second is called allegorical, or moral, or anagogical. And in order to make this manner of treatment clear, it can be applied to the following verses: "When Israel went out of Egypt, the house of Jacob from a barbarous people, Judea was made his sanctuary, Israel his dominion." Now if we look at the letter alone, what is signified to us is the departure of the sons of Israel from

Egypt during the time of Moses; if at the allegory, what is signified
to us is our redemption through Christ; if at the moral sense, what
is signified to us is the conversion of the soul from the sorrow
and misery of sin to the state of grace; if at the anagogical, what is
signified to us is the departure of the sanctified soul from bondage to
the corruption of this world into the freedom of eternal glory. And
although these mystical senses are called by various names, they may
all be called allegorical, since they are all different from the literal or
historical. For allegory is derived from the Greek *alleon*, which means
in Latin *alienus* ("belonging to another") or *diversus* ("different").

8. This being established, it is clear that the subject about which these
two senses play must also be twofold. And thus it should first be
noted what the subject of the work is when taken according to the
letter, and then what its subject is when understood allegorically. The
subject of the whole work, then, taken literally, is the state of souls
after death, understood in a simple sense; for the movement of the
whole work turns upon this and about this. If on the other hand the
work is taken allegorically, the subject is man, in the exercise of his
free will, earning or becoming liable to the rewards or punishments
of justice.

The Philobiblon. Richard de Bury (14thc)

What Love is Reasonably Due to Books

Again, no one doubts that happiness is better than riches. But
happiness consisteth in the operation of that noblest and diviner
power that we have, when the mind is wholly free for contemplating
the truth of wisdom, which is the most delectable of all operations
next to virtue, as the chief of philosophers determines in the tenth
book of his *Ethics*. On this account philosophy, as he conformably
writes, appears to possess marvelous pleasures from its purity and
certainty. Now the contemplation of truth is never more perfect
than through books, for the act of imagination while continued by
a book does not allow the action of the mind upon truths it beholds
to be interrupted. Wherefore books appear to be the most immediate
instruments of speculative pleasure. Hence Aristotle, the sun of
philosophic truth, after defining the principles of choice, teaches
that in itself it is more desirable to be a philosopher than to be rich,

although on occasion, according to circumstances, as in the case of one in need of the necessities of life, it may be more desirable to be rich than to be a philosopher (the third of the Topics).

Still again, since books are our most agreeable teachers, as the preceding chapter assumes, it is right to pay to them both the love and the honor due a master. Finally, as all men by nature desire knowledge, and as by books we can obtain the knowledge of the ancients, which is to be chosen above riches, what man that liveth true to nature would not have a hungering for books? And though we know that swine despise pearls, the judgment of a wise man is in no way altered by this, that he should not gather the pearls that lie before him. More precious then than all wealth are the libraries of wisdom, and all the things thou canst desire are not to be compared unto her (the third chapter of Proverbs). Whosoever, then, confesseth himself zealous for truth, for happiness, for wisdom, or for knowledge, or even for the faith, must needs make himself a lover of books.

Genealogy of the Gentile Gods. GIOVANNI BOCCACCIO (1360-74)

Giovanni Boccaccio (1313-75) is best known as the author of the *Decameron*, a collection of tales framed by a narrative in which ten storytellers escape from plague-ridden Florence. He was also the author of a wide variety of other works, including the *Genealogy of the Gentile Gods*, a compendium of Greek and Roman mythology. Here he expounds on a justification for reading secular literature that presages the humanist impulses of the Renaissance.

CH. IV.VII: THE DEFINITION OF POETRY, ITS ORIGIN, AND FUNCTION

This poetry, which ignorant triflers cast aside, is a sort of fervid and exquisite invention, with fervid expression, in speech or writing, of that which the mind has invented. It proceeds from the bosom of God, and few, I find, are the souls in whom this gift is born; indeed so wonderful a gift it is that true poets have always been the rarest of men. This fervor of poesy is sublime in its effects: it impels the soul to a longing for utterance; it brings forth strange and unheard-of creations of the mind; it arranges these meditations in a fixed order, adorns the whole composition with unusual interweaving of words and thoughts; and thus it veils truth in a fair and fitting garment of fiction. Further, if in any case the invention so requires, it can arm kings, marshal them for war, launch whole fleets from their docks, even counterfeit sky, land, and sea, adorn young women with flowery garlands, portray human character in its various phases, awake the idle, stimulate the dull, restrain the rash, subdue the criminal, and distinguish excellent men with their proper share of praise: these, and many other such, are the effects of poetry. Yet if any man who has received the gift of poetic fervor shall imperfectly fulfill its function here described, he is not, in my opinion, a praiseworthy poet. For, however deeply the poetic impulse stirs the mind to which it is granted, it very rarely accomplishes anything commendable if the instruments by which its concepts are to be given shape are deficient. I mean, for example, the precepts of grammar and rhetoric, an abundant knowledge of which is required. I grant that many a man already writes his mother tongue admirably, and indeed has performed each of the various duties of poetry as such; yet over and above this, it is necessary to know at least the principles of the other liberal arts, both moral and natural, to possess a strong and abundant vocabulary, to be familiar with the monuments and relics of ancient civilizations, to have in one's memory the histories of the nations, and to be familiar with the geography of various lands, of seas, rivers, and mountains.

Ch. IX: It is Rather useful Than Damnable to Compose Stories

Of fiction I distinguish four kinds: The first superficially lacks all appearance of truth; for example, when brutes or inanimate things converse. Aesop, an ancient Greek, grave and venerable, was past master in this form; and though it is a common and popular form both in city and country, yet Aristotle, chief of the Peripatetics, and a man of divine intellect, did not scorn to use it in his books.

The second kind at times superficially mingles fiction with truth, as when we tell of the daughters of Minyas at their spinning, who, when they spurned the orgies of Bacchus, were turned to bats; or the mates of the sailor Acestes, who for contriving the rape of the boy Bacchus, were turned to fish. This form has been employed from the beginning by the most ancient poets, whose object it has been to clothe in fiction divine and human matters alike; they who have followed the sublimer inventions of the poets have improved upon them; while some of the comic writers have perverted them, caring more for the approval of a licentious public than for honesty.

The third kind is more like history than fiction, and famous poets have employed it in a variety of ways. For however much the heroic poets seem to be writing history—as Vergil in his description of Aeneas tossed by the storm, or Homer in his account of Ulysses bound to the mast to escape the lure of the Sirens' song—yet their hidden meaning is far other than appears on the surface. The better of the comic poets, Terence and Plautus, for example, have also employed this form, but they intend naught other than the literal meaning of their lines. Yet by their art they portray varieties of human nature and conversation, incidentally teaching the reader and putting him on his guard. If the events they describe have not actually taken place, yet since they are common, they could have occurred, or might at some time. My opponents need not be so squeamish—Christ, who is God, used this sort of fiction again and again in his parables!

The fourth kind contains no truth at all, either superficial or hidden, since it consists only of old wives' tales.

Ch. XII: The Obscurity of Poetry is Not Just Cause for Condemning It

If by chance in condemning the difficulty of the text, they really mean its figures of diction and oratorical colors and the beauty which they fail to recognize in alien words, if on this account they pronounce poetry obscure—my only advice is for them to go back to the grammar schools, bow to the ferule, study, and learn what license ancient authority granted the poets in such matters, and give particular attention to such alien terms as are permissible beyond common and homely use. But why dwell so long upon the subject? I could have urged them in a sentence to put off the old mind, and put on the new and noble; then will that which now seems to them obscure look familiar and open. Let them not trust to concealing their gross confusion of mind in the precepts of the old orators; for I am sure the poets were ever mindful of such. But let them observe that oratory is quite different, in arrangement of words, from fiction, and that fiction has been consigned to the discretion of the inventor as being the legitimate work of another art than oratory. "In poetic narrative above all, the poets maintain majesty of style and corresponding dignity." As saith Francis Petrarch in the Third

Book of his *Invectives*, contrary to my opponents' supposition. "Such majesty and dignity are not intended to hinder those who wish to understand, but rather propose a delightful task, and are designed to enhance the readers pleasure and support his memory. What we acquire with difficulty and keep with care is always the dearer to us," so continues Petrarch. In fine, if their minds are dull, let them not blame the poets but their own sloth. Let them not keep up a silly howl against those whose lives and actions contrast most favorably with their own. Nay, at the very outset they have taken fright at mere appearances, and bid fair to spend themselves for nothing. Then let them retire in good time, sooner than exhaust their torpid minds with the onset and suffer a violent repulse.

But I repeat my advice to those who would appreciate poetry, and unwind its difficult involutions. You must read, you must persevere, you must sit up nights, you must inquire, and exert the utmost power of your mind. If one way does not lead to the desired meaning, take another; if obstacles arise, then still another; until, if your strength holds out you will find that clear which at first looked dark. For we are forbidden by divine command to give that which is holy to dogs, or to cast pearls before swine.

The Prologues and Epilogues. William Caxton (15ᵗʰc)

The following extracts are taken from the prologues and epilogues William Caxton wrote for his various editions. Each provides a justification for the text, as well as a sense of the work's importance for late medieval culture.

Prologue to *Reynard the Fox* (1481)

In this history are written the parables, good learning, and diverse points to be marked, by which points men may learn to come to the subtle knowledge of such things as daily are used and had in councils of lords and prelates ghostly and worldly, and also among merchants and other common people. And this book is made for the need and profit of all good folk, as far as they in reading or hearing of it shall understand and feel the aforesaid subtle deceits that daily are used in the world: not to the intent that men should use them, but that every man should eschew and keep himself from the subtle false shrews, that they be not deceived. Then whoever wishes to have a true understanding of this material, must often and many times read in this book, and earnestly and diligently mark well that which he reads—for it is set subtly, like as you shall see in the reading of it—and not only once to read it. For in a single reading a man shall not find the right understanding, nor comprise it well, but reading it often shall cause it to be well understood. And for those who understand it shall be right joyous, pleasant, and profitable.

Prologue to *The Enead* (1490)

After having made, translated, and attained diverse works, having no works in hand, with I sitting in my study, where lay many diverse pamphlets and books, it happened that to my hand came a little book in French, which lately had been translated from Latin by some noble clerk of France, which is named Eneydos, written in Latin by that noble poet and great clerk Virgil. Of which book I looked over and read therein how, after the general destruction of the Great Troy, Aeneas departed, bearing his old father Anchises upon his shoulder, his little son Iolus in his hands, his wife, along with many other people, following, and how he shipped and departed with all the story of his adventures that he had before he came to the attainment of his conquest of Italy, as all along shall be showed in this present book. In which book I had great pleasure, because of the fair and honest terms and words in French, which I never saw to-fore like, nor none so pleasant nor so well ordered, which book as me seemed should be much requisite to noble men to see as well for the eloquence as the histories.

How well that many hundred years passed was the said book of Aenead with other works made and learned daily in schools, especially in Italy and other places, which history the said Virgil made in meter. And when I had advised myself in this said book, I deliberated and concluded to translate it into English. And forthwith I took a pen and ink and wrote a leaf or two, which I oversaw again to correct it. And when I saw the fair and strange terms therein, I doubted that it should not please some gentlemen which of late blamed me, saying in my translations I had overly curious terms, which could not be understood by common people, and desired me to use old and homely terms in my translations. And fain would I satisfy every man and so to do took an old book and read therein, and certainly the English was so rude and broad that I could not well understand it.

And also my lord abbot of Westminster did show to me lately certain evidence written in old English for to reduce it into our English now used. And certainly it was written in such wise that it was more like to Dutch than English. I could not reduce nor bring it to be understood. And certainly our language now used varies far from that, which was used and spoken when I was born.

For we Englishmen are born under the domination of the moon, which is never steadfast, but ever wavering, waxing one season and waneth and decreaseth another season, and that common English that is spoken in one shire varies in another. Insomuch that in my days it happened that certain merchants were in a ship in the Thames for to have sailed over the sea into Ireland, and for lack of wind they tarried at the forland, and went to land for to refresh themselves. And one of them named Sheffelde, a mercer, came in to a house and asked for meat, and especially he asked for eggs. And the good wife answered that she could speak no French. And the merchant was angry, for he also could speak no French, but he wanted to have eggs. And she understood him not. And then at least another said that he would have "eyren." And then the good wife said that she understood him well. Lo, what should a man in these days now write, eggs or "eyren"? Certainly it is hard to please every man because of the diversity and change of language. For in these days, every man who is of any reputation in his country will utter his communications and matters in such manners and terms that few men shall understand them. And some honest and great clerks have been with me and desired to write the most curious terms that I could find. And thus between plain rude and curious, I stand abashed. But in my judgment, the common terms that are daily used are lighter to be understood than the old and ancient English. And for as much as this present book is not for a rude uplander to labor therein nor read it, but only for a clerk and a noble gentleman that feels and understands death in feats of arms in love and in noble chivalry. Therefore, in a mean between both, I have reduced and translated this said book into our English and not overly rude nor curious, but in such terms as shall be understood by God's grace according to my copy. And if any man will enter suitably in reading of it and finds such terms that he cannot understand, let him go read and learn Virgil or the Epistles of Ovid, and there he shall see and understand all easily, if he has a good reader and informer. For this book is not for every rude and unlearned man to see, but the clerks and very gentlemen that understand gentleness and science.

Then I pray all them that shall read in this little treatise to hold me for excused for the translation of it. For I acknowledge myself ignorant of the knowledge to undertake on myself such a high and noble work. But I pray Master John Skelton, lately created Poet Laureate in the University of Oxford, to oversee and correct this said book. And to address and expound where shall be found faults, to those that require it. For him I know for sufficient, to expound and Englishify every difficulty that is therein, for he has lately translated the Epistle of Tulle and the Book of Dyodorus Syculus, and diverse other works out of Latin into English, not in rude and old language, but in polished and ornate terms, craftily, as he that has read Virgil, Ovid, Tully, and all the other noble poets and Orators unknown to me; and he has also read the nine muses and understands their musical sciences, and to which of them each science is appropriate. I suppose he has drunk of Helicon's well.

And then I pray him and such others to correct, add, or diminish where he or they shall find faults, for I have but followed my copy in French as closely as possible. And if any word be said well therein, I am glad. And if otherwise, I submit my said book to their correction. Which book I present unto the high born, my forthcoming natural and sovereign lord Arthur, by the grace of God, Prince, of Wales, Duke of Cornwall, and Earl of Chester, first begotten son and heir unto our most dread natural and sovereign lord and most Christian king, Henry the VII, by the grace of God King of England and of France and lord of Ireland, beseeching his noble grace to receive it and thanks from me, his most humble subject and servant. And I shall pray unto almighty God for his prosperous increasing in virtue, wisdom, and humanity, that he may be equal with the most renowned of all his noble progenitors and so to live in this present life that, after this transitory life, he and we all may come to everlasting life in Heaven.

EPILOGUE TO CHAUCER'S *House of Fame* (1483)

I find no more said of this work as far as I can understand. This noble man Geoffrey Chaucer finished at the said conclusion of the meeting of lies and truth, whereas they are checked and may not depart of which work, as it seems to me, as craftily made, and worthy to be read and known. For in it he touches right great wisdom and understanding. And thus in all his works he excels, in my opinion, all other writers in our English. For he writes no empty words, but all his matter is full of high and quick meaning. To him ought to be given lauds and praise for his noble craft and writing. For from him have all others borrowed and taken, in all their good sayings and writings. And I humbly beseech and pray you to remember his soul in your prayers, upon which and upon all other Christian souls I beseech almighty God to have mercy. Amen.

"Prohemye" to *The Canterbury Tales,* Second Edition (1484)

Right thanks, praise and honor ought to be given unto the clerks, poets, and historiographers who have written many noble books of wisdom on the lives, passions, and miracles of holy saints, of histories, of noble and famous Acts and deeds, and of the chronicles since the beginning of the creation of the world unto this present time, by which we are daily informed and have knowledge of many things which we should not have known if they had not left to us their created monuments. Among whom and especially before all others, we ought to give a singular praise unto that noble and great philosopher Geoffrey Chaucer, the which, for his ornate writing in our tongue, may well have the name of a laureate poet. For he through his labor embellished, ornamented, and made fair our English. In this realm was had rude and incongruous speech, as yet it appeared in old books, which at this day ought not to have place among nor be compared to his beauteous volumes and ornate writings, in which he made many books and treatises of many a noble history, both in meter and in rhyme and prose. And those so craftily made that he comprehended his materials in quick and high sentence, eschewing prolixity, casting away the chaff of superfluity, and showing the picked-out grain of sentence utterly by crafty and sugared eloquence. Of which among all other of his books I suppose temperate by the grace of God the Book of the Tales of Canterbury, in which I find many a noble history of every estate and degree, first rehearsing the conditions and array of each of them as properly as possible is to be said, and afterward their tales which are of nobles, wisdom, and gentleness, mirth and also of true holiness and virtue. Wherein he finished this said book, which book I have diligently overseen and duly examined to the end that it be made according to his own making.

For I find many of the said books which writers have abridged and left out many things, and in some places have set certain verses that he never made nor set down in his book. Of which books, so incorrect was one brought to me six years since which I supposed had been very true and correct. And according to the same I did imprint a certain number of them, which anon were sold to many diverse gentlemen, of whom one gentleman came to me and said that this book was not in accordance in many places to the book that Geoffrey Chaucer had made. To which I answered that I had made it according to my copy, and by me was nothing added nor diminished. Then he said he knew a book which his father had and much loved, that was very true, and according unto his own first book by him made, and said, moreover, if I would imprint it again, he would get me the same book for a copy; though howbeit he knew well that his father would not gladly depart from it.

To which I said in the case that he could get me such a book, true and correct, I would at once endeavor myself to imprint it again, for to satisfy the author where before I had erred in hurting and defaming his book in diverse places by setting in some things that he never said nor made, and leaving out many things that he made which are requisite to be set in it. And thus we fell in accord. And he full gently got from his father the said book and delivered it to me, through which I have corrected my book, as here, after all, along with the aid of almighty God, shall follow, to whom I humbly beseech to give me grace and aid to achieve and accomplish to his praise, honor and glory. And all ye that shall in this book read or hear, will, of your charity, remember among your deeds of mercy the soul of the said Geoffrey Chaucer, first author and maker of this book, and also that all we who shall see and read therein may so take and understand the good and virtuous tales, that they may profit the health of our souls, that after this short and transitory life we may come to everlasting life in Heaven. Amen.

NOTES

1   Hanawalt, *Growing Up in Medieval London: The Experience of Childhood in History* (Oxford: Oxford UP, 1993) 82

2   M.T. Clanchy, *From Memory to Written Record, England 1066-1307*, 2nd ed. (Oxford: Blackwell, 1993) 234.

3   Hanawalt, *Growing Up in Medieval London* 83.

4   Frederick J. Furnivall, ed. *The Babees Book, Aristotle's ABC, Urbanitatis, Stans Puer ad Mensam, The Lytille Childrennes Lytil Boke, The Bokes of Nurture of Hugh Rhodes and John Russell, Wynkyn de Worde's Boke of Kernynge, The Booke of Demeanor, The Boke of Curtasye, Seager's Schoole of Vertue, &c. with Some French & Latin Poems on Like Subjects.* EETS o.s. 32 (London: N. Trübner and Co., 1868) 181–87.

5   *The Babees' Book: Medieval Manners for the Young: Done Into Modern English From Dr. Furnivall's Texts,* ed. Edith Rickert (London: Chatto and Windus, 1923) 4.

6   Cited in Hanawalt, *Growing Up in Medieval London* 241, n. 12.

7   John Rastell, *Three Rastell Plays,* ed. Richard Axton (Cambridge: D.S. Brewer, 1979); cited in Nicholas Orme, *Medieval Schools: From Roman Britain to Renaissance England* (New Haven, CT: Yale UP, 2006) 58.

8   William Nelson, ed., *A Fifteenth Century School Book* (Oxford: Clarendon P, 1956) 20.

9   Beatrice White, ed., *The Vulgaria of John Stanbridge and the Vulgaria of Robert Whittinton,* EETS, o.s. 187 (London: Kegan Paul, Trench, and Trübner, 1932); quoted in Orme 116.

10 White, *The Vulgaria of John Stanbridge;* cited in Nelson, *A Fifteenth Century School Book* xiv.

11 Orme 118.

12 Derek Pearsall, *The Life of Geoffrey Chaucer* (Cambridge: Basil Blackwell, 1992) 33.

13 William Courtenay, *Schools and Scholars in Fourteenth Century England* (Princeton, NJ: Princeton UP, 1987) 29, 33.

14 The amount of time it took to acquire the doctorate was gradually reduced from approximately 15 years in the beginning of the fourteenth century to ten years by 1350. See Courtenay 42.

15 *Translations and Reprints from the Original Sources of European History, published for the Dept. of History of the University of Pennsylvania,* Vol. II:3 (Philadelphia, U of Pennsylvania P, 1897–1907) 19–20.

16 Charles Homer Haskins, *The Rise of Universities* (1923; Ithaca, NY: Cornell UP, 1990) 60–62.

17 Pierre Bersuire, *Metamorphosis Ovidiana Moraliter. Explanata: Paris, 1509,* ed. Stephen Orgel (New York: Garland, 1979) Book XV, prologue; our translation.

18 Russell A. Peck, "Chaucer and the Nominalist Questions," *Speculum* 53.4 (1978): 749.

19 Dante Alighieri, *La Vita Nuova,* ed. Tommaso Casini (Firenze: Sansoni, 1962), III, 20–22. Translations are Mark Musa's; SEE Dante Alighieri, *Vita Nuova,* trans. Mark Musa (Oxford: Oxford UP, 1992) 7.

20 Petrarch, "Letter X.4," *Letters on Familiar Matters (Rerum familiarium libri IX-X),* trans. Aldo S. Bernardo (Baltimore, MD: The Johns Hopkins UP, 1982) 69.

21 Richard de Bury, *The Love of Books: The Philobiblon of Richard de Bury,* trans. E.C. Thomas (New York: Cooper Square Publishers, 1966) 8. The remaining portions of this chapter have been considerably revised from an earlier article; SEE Laurel Amtower, "The Challenge of Philology and Comparative Study of the Late Middle Ages," *Yearbook of Comparative and General Literature* 51 (2003–04): 7–16.

22   C. Paul Christianson, *A Directory of London Stationers and Book Artisans 1300-1500* (New York: Bibliographic Society of America, 1990) 22.

23   Richard de Bury, *The Philobiblon* (Berkeley, CA: U of California P, 1948) 8.

24   William Blades, *The Biography and Typography of William Caxton, England's First Printer* (London: Kegan Paul, Trench, Trübner and Co, 1897) 63.

25   Seth Lerer, *Chaucer and His Readers* (Princeton, NJ: Princeton UP, 1995) 147.

26   Curt F. Bühler, *William Caxton and his Critics: A Critical Reappraisal of Caxton's Contributions to the Enrichment of the English Language* (Syracuse, NY: Syracuse UP, 1960) 27.

27   Bühler 29.

CHAPTER VII

"Magyk Natureel"
Science, Medicine, Psychology, and Alchemy

INTRODUCTION

O ur subtitle, by implying that there are neat distinctions to be made between medieval psychology, science, medicine, and alchemy, is more revealing of modern than of medieval ways of thinking. As citizens of post-enlightenment Western societies, we separate psychologists from physicians, podiatrists from pediatricians. A high degree of specialization is evident in our intellectual habits and in our professional circumstances. The two are, of course, related: when we gather knowledge about the world and its operations, we do so by consulting experts, who restrict themselves to particular subjects. No self-respecting modern scholar would attempt a book like the medieval cleric Bartholomew Anglicus's monumental *On the Properties of Things*, which, as its title indicates, collects information on everything from manners to medicines. Modern experts tend to devote books to a single literary author or to an obscure disease. Our assumption is that those who restrict themselves to one topic are more reliable than those who tackle many. In short, we think about professional authority as a function of specialization.

This was not the case in the Middle Ages. When it came to medicine, in fact, the opposite was true: "the more elite the physician, the more general the practice. Specialization in particular kinds of care—eye conditions, hernia, midwifery (the last practiced only by women)—was a mark of low status."[1] Like physicians, medieval scholars tended to be learned about a wide variety of subjects, and when they explained particular phenomena, they relied on the full extent of their learning. Comprehensive works like *On the Properties of Things* or the *Secreta Secretorum*, which offers advice on matters as diverse as physiognomy, politics, matrimony, and alchemy, exemplify medieval approaches to the gathering of knowledge. The popularity of these books was partly due to economic factors: before the printing press, books were scarce and expensive, and those that collected knowledge on an array of subjects were therefore desirable. But this popularity also reveals something about medieval habits of thought. Although medieval thinkers made distinctions, organized knowledge in systems, and accumulated expertise in certain fields, the lines they drew among disciplines were not hard and fast. The ability to make connections was often prized above the ability to observe disciplinary boundaries. Specialization of the sort that we take for granted is, for reasons too complicated to discuss here, one of the many legacies of the printing revolution. It had no place in medieval universities, where students who might incline towards one field were nevertheless expected to be familiar with state of the art knowledge in all fields. The pedagogical ideal of the medieval university was, as the prominent science historian David Lindberg puts it, the creation of the "universal scholar." Because of this goal, "work in one realm inevitably influenced achievements in the others. The interpenetration of disciplines could be very deep."[2] The one prohibition was against members of other faculties addressing matters of religious doctrine; only theologians were free to range across all the disciplines.[3]

MEDIEVAL SCIENCE: THEORY AND PRACTICE

Not all of those who tended to the sick in the Middle Ages were educated. Medical practitioners ranged from unlettered "empirics," who based their authority on their own experience; to surgeon-barbers and surgeons, who practiced what was thought of as a craft and who therefore served an apprenticeship to a master; to university-trained physicians, who based their authority on their extensive learning rather than on clinical experience.[4] Surgeons could and did attain a level of affluence and recognition, often through the cure of well-regarded patients. The English surgeon John of Arderne (1307-77), for example, listed several noblemen and clergymen among successfully cured patients in his treatise on anal fistulas.[5] Arderne is sometimes regarded as a model for Chaucer's Physician, but it seems more likely that the "Doctour of Phisik" was a university-educated physician. The title of doctor was, after all, reserved for university graduates.[6] These enjoyed the most elevated status among medical practitioners because they were highly educated—the doctorate in medicine in the Middle Ages required a significant commitment of time and energy, as it does nowadays.[7] The English physician John Landreyn, whose patients included Edward the Black Prince, apparently devoted 26 years of his life to obtaining his various degrees.[8] Like such university-educated physicians, Chaucer's "Doctour of Phisik" is "grounded in astronomye," and conversant with classical and Arabic authorities (GP 414, 430-34). A modern reader might be surprised by the diversity of the doctor's intellectual background. But it is in fact orthodox: medical curricula emphasized anatomy and physiology, to be sure, but also logic, rhetoric, and astronomy.

Although medical schools did achieve an exceptional independence in medieval universities, the arts were thus considered crucial to the physician's "magyk natureel." The classical author Galen (AD 129-?), the foremost medical authority throughout the Middle Ages, insisted that a good physician needed to be a philosopher. An emphasis on broad, eclectic learning also marks Anglicus's description of the medical diagnostician's work. He must forget:

> nothing that belongs to the evil, also that he [must] be diligent and busy in the things that belong to the craft of medicine, and he must be aware and advised in all things. Also, to heal and save effectually he needs to know that complexions of men, compositions, mixtures and blends both of members and of humours, and the dispositions of times, conditions of male and female, and age. For one medicine is needed in winter and another in summer; and one in the beginning of the evil, and another at the peak, and another at the passing of the disease; one in childhood and in youth, another in middle age, and another in old age; one in males and one in females.[9]

Where today's doctors might look to identify a microscopic bacterium as the cause of a disease, a medieval physician considered everything—age, sex, behavior, time, season, environment, planetary alignment. He focused on "the individual and his constitution and his circumstances," which included the so-called "non-naturals" affecting health, like rest, diet, exercise, and emotional disturbances.[10] The human body was thought to be so intimately connected to the cosmos that even the arrangement of the planets influenced its condition and its effective treatment. The plague proved a real challenge to early medical views because these included no viable models for highly infectious diseases; one theory was that the "conjunction of Saturn and Jupiter had poisoned the upper atmosphere, and the envenomed vapors had entered through the pores into the bodies of men."[11] Chaucer's "Knight's Tale" glances at this theory in Saturn's reference to himself as "the fader of pestilence" (2469). Like most of his contemporaries, Chaucer believed in the influence of astrological bodies on human bodies. In his *Treatise on the Astrolabe*, he asserts that "everich of these 12 signes [of the zodiac] hath respect to a certeyn parcel of the body of man, and hath it in governaunce."[12] The importance of astrological influence accounts for the professional pride that Chaucer's Doctor takes in his ability to "fortunen the ascendent / Of his ymages for his pacient" (GP 417-18). By the standards of his day—standards that emphasized a grounding in a range of disciplines—the "Doctour of Phisik" is a knowledgeable man indeed, capable of considering intelligently the multiple influences that might impact his patients' health.

Chaucer's designation of the Physician's expertise as "magyk natureel" forms an apt introduction to the topic of medieval science. By blurring the categories of natural and supernatural, this expression conveys the interdisciplinary nature of medieval intellectual inquiry. It also emphasizes that the pursuit of knowledge had not yet separated itself from other human pursuits, including those associated with magic, religion, and spirituality. In fact, the Middle English word for a scholar—"clerk" or "cleric"—implies membership in the spiritual orders. Medieval universities existed primarily for the benefit of the clergy; most medieval scholars and physicians were clergymen; and the most influential of them were often major theologians, like St. Thomas Aquinas (*c*. 1225-74), a key figure in medieval scholasticism. Scholastic philosophers emphasized the applicability of reason to matters of faith. According to Aquinas, dialectic—a method of reasoning that reconciles contradictory arguments through debate—and logic could lead to the discovery and understanding of spiritual truths. Their position on reason led scholastic philosophers to embrace the secular works of the classical authors, and to interpret them in a way that made them consistent with Christian belief. Albertus Magnus (*c*. 1206-80), one of the most famous medieval scholars, and Aquinas were major contributors to the Christianization of Aristotle, whose complete body of works only became available in Latin translations over the course of the thirteenth century. Both taught at the University of Paris, a city described by another clergyman on its faculty, Anglicus, as the medieval counterpart to classical Athens, a "mother of wisdom."

Because it was not just a philosophical approach but also a pedagogical system, the scholastic synthesis of reason and faith influenced intellectual life throughout the late Middle Ages. In accordance with the theoretical emphasis of scholasticism, the universities taught the interpretation of the standard authorities, but they did not provide much by way of empirical learning. Chaucer establishes the credentials of his physician by emphasizing his familiarity with Hippocrates, Galen, and the Arabian scholar Avicenna. These were, in fact, the authorities taught in the medical faculties. Lindberg points out that "the disciplines that we now consider part of the scientific enterprise were largely 'bookish' in the Middle Ages." Even when medical dissections were carried out, they served to illustrate an authoritative text, and "a theory that was satisfactory for philosophical, astrological, or numerological reasons was unlikely to be displaced, however difficult it might be to demonstrate" empirically. [13] As we mentioned in Chapter 6, the stubbornly deductive nature of much medieval scholarship—its tendency to make the particulars conform to authoritative generalizations—has caused it to be ridiculed in later, more "enlightened" periods. Indeed, the so-called birth of modern science is closely associated with a turn to inductive reasoning; Vesalius, Copernicus, William Harvey, and Galileo, historians of science assert, were revolutionaries because instead of accepting authoritative opinions, they derived their hypotheses from the evidence. But modern scientists nevertheless owe a debt to medieval scholastics for their passionate advocacy of learning, for endowing universities like the ones in Paris and Oxford with prestige, and for vigorously asserting the role of reason in an age of faith. From the perspective of a hyper-specialized age, there is also something admirable about the breadth, the ingenuity, and the disciplinary fluidity of the best medieval scholarship.

One area where the synthetic and deductive habits of scholastic thought are evident is medieval cosmology. Discussions about the nature of the universe considered not just physics and metaphysics but also theology. In the geocentric view of the universe that the Middle Ages inherited from Aristotle and his contemporaries, the earth was at the center of a series of nesting spheres, whose complicated movements accounted for the diurnal and cyclical motions of the planets. The exact number of spheres was a matter of debate. Some scholars limited the spheres to eight—the seven associated with the planets and one for the fixed stars. Others, like Aquinas, surmised the existence of additional spheres like the empyrean heaven and the crystalline or aqueous heaven. Where the theory of the first eight spheres was to some extent developed in response to empirical observation, the suggestion of additional spheres derived from readings of and commentaries on *Genesis*. The empyrean heaven was the heaven that God created on the first day—home to the angels. The heaven that God created on the second day is, according to this theologically informed cosmology, the visible heaven containing the seven planetary spheres and the fixed stars. Scholars deduced the existence of additional heavens from their interpretation of the most authoritative text of them all—the Bible.

Although the blending of natural philosophy and theology in the medieval period is remarkable, scholarly and doctrinal points of view could not always be reconciled, and occasionally theoretical speculations did run afoul of church doctrine. Ecclesiastical authorities responded from time to time by attempting to curb the spread of rationalism. Between 1270 and 1277, the Bishop of Paris, Étienne Tempier, condemned over 200 propositions, most of which concerned matters of natural philosophy, some of which illustrious figures like Thomas Aquinas adhered to, and many of which derived from Aristotle's teachings. Aristotle argued, for example, that the world is eternal, a position incompatible with the Christian view of Creation.[14] The church did not just raise objections to such theoretical points. Any cleric who transformed his knowledge into a source of income was in potential violation of his vows of poverty. Those who practiced applied forms of science also aroused the suspicion of church authorities, especially when these practitioners were involved in technological innovation or experimentation. The attempt to improve on nature through human art or technology was considered a form of blasphemy, an attempt to out-perform God. Artists, not just scientists, were subject to recriminations and anxieties on this account, and concerns about the potentially blasphemous nature of his art run throughout Chaucer's works. The habitual citation of ancient texts by medieval experts and writers was, among other things, a rhetorical way of deflecting the troubling charge of innovation. New inventions, like the printing press, were often regarded with such distrust that they were labeled instruments of the devil.

Not surprisingly, the emergent tension between scientific expertise and religious belief finds its way into medieval literature. The Chester "Nativity," for example, includes an apocryphal incident, in which Joseph hires a midwife, Salome. Salome's services prove unnecessary when the birth of Christ brings with it no messy labor: Mary feels no pain and, as Joseph underlines, remains a "clean maid" (513). The midwife, disturbed by this unprofessional turn of events, asserts that "was never woman clean may / and child without man" (514-15). The medical empiric's opinion, based on her professional experience, thus openly conflicts with Christian doctrine. When she seeks support for her skeptical hypothesis by touching Mary "in her private parts," Salome's hand shrivels up. She only recovers use of it when she accepts the Virgin birth. The pageant's expositor explains that "her hand rotted" as a clear sign "that unbelief is a foul sin" (699-701). By dramatizing Salome's astonishing trespass, the pageant issues a warning against rationalism and the doubts it promotes.[15]

In other cultural documents, scientific practitioners also stand accused of serious transgressions against religion. Although Chaucer makes clear that his physician is no charlatan, for example, he does cast doubt on the doctor's character. The doctor is more familiar with secular authorities than with Christian ones: "his study was but litel on the Bible" (GP 438). When the narrator calls attention to the physician's love of gold, he invites us to pass more specific judgment still. As medicine developed into a secular profession, its practitioners, many of whom were in orders, became vulnerable to the accusation that they were trying to turn a profit from acts that should be performed for the sake of charity. Disgruntled patients who brought suit against their doctors in medieval courts emphasized the financial aspect of medical transactions. For instance, Thomas Birchester complained that while his doctor had "undertaken at Southwark for a suitable fee to cure the said Thomas well and proper of a certain illness which incapacitated him," he was instead "very much the worse, to the said Thomas's loss of forty marks" (SEE COURT CASES, BELOW). Not only had Thomas not been cured, but he had been conned—or so concluded the jury, who awarded the plaintiff monetary damages. For physicians and frauds alike, the recurrent epidemics of the plague were especially profitable. "The General Prologue" implies that the Doctor benefited greatly from the times of "pestilence" (442).

The more medicine became commercialized, the more it became vulnerable to negative representation. In *Piers Plowman*, the allegorical figure Phisik has an unbecoming taste for gold (B.IV. 270). Through its deployment of the old tropes of sin as disease and of Christ as healer, *Piers* also contrasts the efficacy of spiritual "medicine," as administered by priests, to that of the medicine practiced by (for example) Sire Penetrans Domos, whose ministrations paralyze his patient.[16] The mountebank doctor—a fixture of English comedy after Ben Jonson—also makes his first recorded appearance in the drama of this period.[17] *The Croxton Play of the Sacrament*'s Master Brundiche is a confidence man: given the proper financial motivations, "though a man were right healthy, he [Brundiche] could soon make him sick."[18] Although Brundiche has affiliations with the quack in the folk play, his perfidy assumes new meaning in a Christian context, which contrasts the fraudulent promises of the doctor to the miraculous powers of Christ. Jonathas, a rich Jewish merchant who loses his hand while conducting experiments on the Host—he cannot accept the idea that a "cake" can be God's "flesh and blood" (200-03)—refuses Brundiche's professional services and orders his servants to beat this self-professed "man all of science" off stage. The repentant merchant then accepts the doctrine of transubstantiation and miraculously recovers his hand. He thus becomes, like Salome, a figure of rationalist skepticism reformed. By including the episode with Master Brundiche, the anonymous dramatist brings the problem of rationalism home, as a conflict between "two locally available methods of healing"—medicine and religion, the healer and the Healer.[19] As in *Piers*, the conflict is resolved in favor of the latter.

Although medical practitioners were sometimes accused of fraudulence, this charge was leveled more frequently against adherents of another discipline—alchemy. Alchemists sought to isolate a substance called "elixir" (from the Arabian *al-iksir*) or "philosopher's stone." While in some tracts elixir is valued exclusively as a catalyst in the transmutation of base metals into gold, other works suggested that it could also prolong human life or bestow immortality. In late medieval Europe, even as alchemy came under increasing suspicion, its medicinal applications may have contributed to the search for, and experimentation with, pharmaceutical cures.[20] Unlike university scholars, alchemists had a practical purpose in mind, which explains their pioneering efforts in experimentation and technological innovation. Alchemists thought that the material conditions of human existence could be transformed through applied science. Although treatises claimed for this practice a spiritual role—the transmutation of material objects required the assistance of God and implied a spiritual transformation of the self—alchemy was heavily censured by the medieval church. The alchemists' belief in the progressive force of technology contrasted sharply with the official position of the church and therefore challenged its monopoly on learning. In an attempt to ward off criticism, alchemical writers cloaked their craft in mystery: its "great secrets" were carefully guarded, passed from master to student, and wrapped in language comprehensible only to the initiated. Presented thus, the idea of the transmutation of metals proved seductive enough to withstand criticism and failure. Several late medieval kings, including Henry IV, forbade the practice of alchemy; others, like Edward III, actively patronized alchemists, in the hopes that these would replenish the royal coffers.[21] Yet despite the criticism of the church and the prevailing fraud that largely characterized the profession, the "subtle science of holy Alchemy" may be considered the shabby forebear of modern chemistry and pharmacology.[22]

Like most medieval alchemists, the Canon of *The Canterbury Tales* appears to concern himself mainly with the task of transforming base metals into precious ones.[23] Chaucer conveys the ambiguous status of alchemy in early English culture when his Yeoman describes it variously as an art, a science, and an "elvysshe craft" (CYT 751). Despite acknowledging a range of perspectives, however, the Yeoman's tale takes a condemnatory view of the matter. It describes its protagonist not just as a fraud but as a "feend" (CYT 984), who "wolde infecte al a toun / Thogh it as greet were as Nynevee" (CYT 973-74). According to the Yeoman, alchemy corrodes the "sely innocents" who sell their "body and good" (CYT 1289) to realize its lurid fantasy of transmuting base metals into gold. The only transformations that actually occur, however, are in the physical appearance and spiritual condition of alchemical practitioners, who wager their "savacioun" for the promise of "multiplicacioun" (CYT 848-49). Smelling of brimstone and looking like goats, the initiated pursue forbidden knowledge to find only their own total destruction. Some readers have found in "The Canon's Yeoman's Tale" a prophetic denunciation of modernity, particularly of the "blind materialism" that "leads to a complacent faith in science that despises God."[24] Others, noting that Chaucer uses the adjective "elvysshe" elsewhere to describe himself, see in the negative representation of alchemy the reflection of Chaucer's anxieties about being an artist, that is, a maker of multiple new and potentially subversive truths.[25] In either case, the tale expresses misgivings, of a theological nature, about the possible abuses of those with an "over-great wit."

To be sure, not all of Chaucer's contemporaries saw in alchemy satanic potential. Thomas Norton offers a sharp contrast to Chaucer's take on the issue by arguing that the "subtle science of holy Alchemy" presents a path to spiritual enlightenment and that only souls in grace can apprehend its secrets (SEE BELOW). Despite their disagreement, both authors share the premise that the concerns of alchemy cannot be separated from those of theology. The same might be said about any mode of inquiry in the Middle Ages. The practice of alchemy intersected not just with religion but also with other forms of intellectual endeavor, like medicine. The list of medical authorities that Chaucer cites and the list of alchemical authorities in Norton's *Ordinal of Alchemy* coincide: both refer to Avicenna and al-Rhazi or Razis, two Arabian scholars who wrote influential compendiums and commentaries.

As the case of alchemy suggests, licit forms of intellectual inquiry overlapped not just with one another but also with less licit forms. When the editors of *The Riverside Chaucer* gloss the Physician's "magyk natureel" as his "science" (30, n. 416), they obscure one such relationship: between early medical and magical practices. Science and magic are not always easily distinguished in early English discourses. A seventeenth-century English translation of Giambattista della Porta's treatise on magic, for example, echoes Chaucer on his Doctor:

> There are two sorts of Magick: the one is infamous, and unhappy, because it has to do with foul spirits, and consists of Enchantments and wicked Curiosity; and this is called Sorcery; an art which all learned and good men detest; neither is it able to yield any truth of Reason or Nature, but stands merely upon fancies and imaginations, such as vanish presently away, and leave nothing behind them .... The other Magick is natural; which all excellent wise men do admit and embrace, and worship with great applause; neither is there any thing more highly esteemed, or better thought of, by men of learning. The most noble Philosophers that ever were ... this was the Science which they professed ... (SEE DOCUMENTS SECTION)

"Science" seems here to be synonymous with "white magic." The distinction between white magic and black magic—between the siblings Merlin and Morgan le Faye in the Arthurian myths—is a long-standing one; however, as the case of alchemy illustrates, the difference between "wicked" and appropriate forms of expertise was unstable in early English society. One person's scientist was another person's necromancer. Like many alchemical and medical treatises (SEE our selections from the Italian Trotula and from the Middle English Gilbertus Anglicus, which was aimed at laymen), books on magic included collections of recipes. Even learned doctors believed in magical and folkloric remedies, such as the use of precious stones to protect against poison. Medicines were often endowed with magical attributes. For example, theriac—a concoction of viper's flesh—was supposed to be a universal antidote to poison and to cure a range of diseases, especially those caused by an excess of phlegm or melancholy. Anglicus recounts a common anecdote about this revered drug that emphasizes its magical qualities:

> To heal or to hide leprosy, as Plato says, best is a red adder with a white belly .... this medicine helps with many evils; as he [Plato] tells the story of the blind man, to whom his wife gave an adder with garlic instead of an eel, that it might slay him, and he ate it, and after that by much sweat, he recovered his sight good and clear. (423–27)

The viper's flesh heals because it induces sweat: its heating properties counteract the melancholic coolness thought to cause leprosy and blindness. The difference between magical and medical remedies is hard to tell in part because they derive from the same theories about the human body and, indeed, about the constitution of all matter.

The Elements

Although medieval intellectual culture was characterized by lively debate, everyone—alchemists and astrologers, physicists and physicians, poets and prelates—agreed that matter was composed of four elements: earth, water, air, and fire. These elements did not exist in pure form; instead, material objects, including animals and human beings, were composites in different proportions. Each of the elements was distinguished by its qualities; fire, for example, was hot and dry, where earth was cold and dry. The four qualities associated with the four elements—moisture, dryness, hotness, and coldness—are the ones that Galen defines in our selection as "primary and elementary"; all other qualities, he writes, derive "from the combination of these, they will be found to be in each animal of a number corresponding to its *sensible elements* [emphasis in the original]." The qualities of any given object resulted, in other words, from the proportion of elements that constituted the object. In a world where all things were arranged along hierarchies, the elements were not created equal. Fire and air were superior to the baser elements of water and earth; in the form of vital heat and breath, these two higher elements made life possible. The classical philosopher Empedocles (492-432 BC) had first advanced the view of the elemental nature of all matter; Plato, Aristotle, and Galen had subscribed to it; and, by the late Middle Ages, it had hardened into accepted fact. In the fourteenth and fifteenth centuries, moreover, the translation of scientific writing into the vernacular made elemental theory—as well as its derivatives, humour theory and physiognomy—available to literate audiences all over England.[26] Late medieval writers assume their readers' familiarity with these theories, which constituted a common frame of reference. Even Chaucer's barnyard animals have a smattering of knowledge about the elements.

Elemental theory proved attractive and enduring because it was a total theory; it could, with some effort, be made to account for all phenomena, from the behavior of the planets to the health of the individual human being. Proportion and mixture (also called temperament) were key features of all such explanations; the variations among living organisms, for example, were a function in part of their relative heat. According to Aristotle, all living things had a "soul" or life-principle. In plants, the life-principle was limited to the "vegetative" soul, which was responsible for things like growth and nutrition; animals added to the vegetative soul a "sensitive soul," which governed things like passions, appetites, and perceptions. Having attained a higher stage of perfection, human beings had a higher proportion of air and fire in their constitution, which enabled their development of a rational intellect. In this world view, differences between organisms are a matter of degree rather than kind; in fact, organisms were themselves composed of the same stuff as everything else in the world. No wonder physicians had to consider environmental causes and planetary alignment in the treatment of disease: mind, body, and universe were joined in a complex and mutually constitutive relationship.[27]

In accordance with elemental views, similarity and continuity underlie medieval accounts of the human being's relationship to the world and the other animals in it. The fabulous transformations of medieval romances reflect this sense of a fundamental connection among all things. In "The Wife of Bath's Tale," an old hag transforms herself into a young maiden by means of a kiss. Those versed in elemental theory might countenance such a transformation more readily than we do, because sexual ardor produced a heating effect which might counteract the cooling associated with aging. There is a kind of logic—similar to the logic that informs alchemical descriptions of the transmutation of metals—at work in the shape-shifting of medieval romances. Given that differences among creatures (or metals) are not absolute and stable but relative and unstable, under extreme circumstances, like the ones depicted in the romances, one thing can be transformed into another. Even the distinction between human and animal—a foundation of all systems of human categorization—is not absolute; for example, in Marie de France's "Bisclavret," the central character transforms himself into a wolf. Werewolves were not considered only the purview of fiction; late medieval subjects were prone to believe in werewolves.[28] The cultural prominence of the werewolf helps explain the phenomenon of lycanthropia—a kind of madness, allegedly brought about by an excess of cold and dry qualities (or melancholia), in which the patient imagined himself a wolf (SEE OUR EXCERPT).

Although werewolf lore most dramatically expresses the perceived connection between human and animal, it is evident everywhere in medieval culture—in the fondness of writers for animal imagery and analogies, for example, or in the popularity of animal fables and bestiaries. Bestiaries—a genre devoted to the description of animals—epitomize the medieval tendency to think of humans and animals as sharing the same traits. They describe the fox as "a fraudulent and ingenious animal," with a demonic nature (White excerpt), while the peacock finds himself accused of lechery (Bartholomew Anglicus excerpt). As our selections suggest, the bestiaries' descriptions work as illustrations of moral truths or religious concepts; for example, the entry on the cock includes a meditation on the significance of the cock's crow which preceded Peter's confession in the Bible. Bestiaries also allegorized and naturalized social realities.[29] The conventional iconography of the lion was closely tied to the monarchy, while descriptions of birds of prey as aristocrats convey the naturalness of social hierarchies.[30] What bestiaries did not provide was reliable and objective information about animals; there was, in fact, "no scientific study of animals" as such in the Middle Ages.[31]

Medieval literary works follow bestiaries in ascribing certain anthropomorphic traits to certain animals. The popular tales of Reynard the Fox immortalized this creature as a type of ingenuity and duplicity; in "The Nun's Priest's Tale," Chaucer describes the fox as a "fals flatour," full of "trecherye" (3325, 3329). Chaucer's animals generally behave more like human beings than like animals. His model for Pertelote, for example, must have been a medieval housewife, not a medieval chicken. A similar point could be made about Chaunticleer, or the lovesick falcon in "The Squire's Tale" or the highly articulate bird menagerie of *The Parliament of Fowls*. While his animals act like humans, Chaucer's figurative language often breaches the gap between the species in the other direction— making humans like animals. The comment about the Miller's beard being "as any sowe or fox . . . reed" (GP 552), for example, reveals something about the Miller's character. This "stout carl" (GP 545) with his "thombe of gold" (GP 563) shares in the fox's elemental nature, including its tendency towards aggression and fraudulence. Similarly, when Gawain lies to his host in *Sir Gawain and the Green Knight*, he receives only the gift of "this foul fox pelt" (1944) as a just indictment of his actions. Commonly held assumptions about animals helped medieval writers develop thematic points with remarkable economy.

If elemental theory could cast light on the relationship between humans and animals, it also explained differences among humans, like those associated with gender. Men were inherently superior to women because they had a higher proportion of fire and air in their constitution. The baser elements literally dominated in women. According to Galen's influential "one-sex model," women and men shared the same sexual organs; what made women different is that they lacked the necessary heat to eject theirs. Famously, Galen urged his readers to accept the homology between male and female organs by envisaging the expulsion of the latter: "Think too, please, of... the uterus turned outward and projecting. Would not the testes [ovaries] then necessarily be inside it? Would it not contain them like a scrotum? Would not the neck, hitherto concealed inside the perineum but now pendant, be made into the male member?"[32] Instead of being different in kind from men, women were different in degree—they were colder, inverted versions of men. On the hierarchy of living organisms, women represented a step between the more perfect men and the less perfect animals. The elemental coldness ascribed to women in the Galenic model helped explain not just cultural stereotypes and psychological characteristics but also physiological distinctions, accounting for everything from "feminine timidity" to "menstruation."[33]

Both Galen and Aristotle proposed theories of human generation that reflected the gendered assumptions of elemental theory. During the heat of sexual congress, Galen argued, male and female would produce the sperm or seed that gave form to the matter of the womb (which, as our selection makes clear, he identified with the base element of earth). Because male seed is hotter, and therefore more potent and more perfect, it has a greater influence on the offspring produced. Aristotle's so-called "one-seed" model is more radical still in assigning power to the male: the woman provides only the baser matter while the male seed fashions that matter and endows it with spirit. The scholar Thomas Laqueur describes this model for conception as "the male having an idea in the female body."[34] Because of their paramount importance to the medical curriculum, Galen and Aristotle's theories of human generation determined late medieval views on the matter. Men were considered the active principle and women the passive receptacle (this assumption is reflected in the commonplace literary metaphor of women as vessels). These views helped foster a whole series of stereotypes, including the association of women with the body and men with reason. Medieval theories of human sexuality reflected and reinforced the patriarchal arrangement of early societies: men *were* more perfect than women; sons *were* images of their father; women *were* passive vessels for the transmission of male identity.

THE HUMOURS AND HUMAN TEMPERAMENT

Elemental theory informed not just late medieval ideas regarding gender and sexuality but also notions of sickness and of health. Human health was considered a function of the complexion or temperament, the qualities resulting from the mixture of the elements. A person's complexion was controlled by the four bodily humours (or fluids)—blood, choler (red or yellow bile), melancholy (black bile), and phlegm—concocted out of the elements through the digestive processes of the body. Each humour manifested a combination of the qualities associated with the elements: phlegm, for example, is cold and moist, whereas choler is hot and dry. Just as the elements were arrayed along a hierarchy, so were the humours. Blood, claims Bartholomew Anglicus, "is perfectly heated" and "purified," whereas melancholy is "more earthy and the dregs of the other." The hotter, more active humours—blood and choler, which Anglicus describes as "overheated"—were associated with masculinity, and the colder, more passive ones—phlegm and melancholy—with femininity. Perfect health resulted from a well-balanced complexion, sickness from an excess of one or more humours. As Anglicus explains it, "these four humours if they are in even proportion in quantity and quality, they feed all the bodies that have blood and make them perfect and keep them in the being and state of health; contrariwise, if they are uneven in proportion and infected, then they breed evils" (SEE BELOW). A good physician needed therefore to know, as Chaucer's Doctor does, "the cause of everich maladye, / Were it of hoot, or coold, or moyste, or drye, / And where they engendred, and of what humour" (GP 419-21). The provenance of the disease helped the physician prescribe the appropriate cure.

Because humoural theory conceived of the body as a container of fluids, one of the body's distinguishing characteristics was its permeability to external forces. Seasonal changes had an impact on human complexions: spring caused an increase in blood, summer in bile, autumn in melancholy, and winter in phlegm. The opening lines of *The Canterbury Tales*, in which "swich licour" (GP 3) suffuses veins, engendering growth in plants and desire in human beings, celebrate the penetrating and revitalizing effect of spring on all living creatures. Alterations in planetary dominance, responsible for seasonal changes, also affected the human body; the ascendancy of Saturn triggered the advent of winter and a correspondent rise in phlegm. In this schema, the planetary alignment at a person's birth helped determine that person's disposition. The Wife of Bath attributes the particularities of her temperament to the conjunction of the planets Venus and Mars at her birth—a sensible explanation for her combativeness, given that Mars induced an increase in choler (WP 610-12).[35] Astrological influences did not just exert power over a human being at birth, they also affected his or her health for the duration of life. In the theory of the plague discussed above, the poisonous vapors generated by the conjunction of Jupiter and Saturn were thought to have entered victims through their pores, thereby upsetting their bodies' humoural balance and producing the tell-tale buboes.

The body was not just vulnerable to environmental forces but also to human intervention. Most medical cures, with the exception of surgery, involved a manipulation of the body's permeability; suggested treatments for the plague, for example, included abstention from hot baths and spicy foods, both of which opened the pores to the disease.[36] Although in the case of the plague these measures failed, selective administration of food and drink was generally thought an effective way of rectifying humoural imbalance. Physicians advised patients about their diets, urging them to refrain from foods that might exacerbate their condition and encouraging the consumption of foods that might soothe it. According to Galen, those suffering from melancholia should avoid the flesh of "goats, oxen, bulls, asses, camels, foxes, dogs, hares, wolves and boars," as well as cabbage and heavy red wine.[37] Given the known elemental qualities of certain foods, details about a literary character's diet—Chaucer's Monk's taste for roast game or his Summoner's addiction to "garleek, onyons, and eek lekes" (GP 634)—gave medieval readers information about the character's temperament. Like sought out like in a humoural world, and a sanguine man, like the Monk, would be naturally drawn to the sanguine meats that helped maintain his complexion. The Summoner, with his fiery temper, his inflamed complexion, and his love of hot foods, is probably suffering from an excess of choler.[38] One way for a medieval physician to have treated a patient like the Summoner would be to restrict his access to these foods.

Confronted with an imbalanced temperament, a physician could also administer a drug or "electuary" that counteracted the patient's disease. The basic approach of medieval pharmacology was to neutralize imbalance through the principle of opposition. Thus, Anglicus advocates treating leprosy, caused by an excess of cold melancholy, with red viper flesh, a substance so hot that it caused patients to sweat. All plants, animals, and minerals were endowed with the elemental qualities that made them potential remedies, and medieval works often make references to these pharmaceutical qualities. Descriptions of animals specify medicinal uses for their organs; the gall of the boar, for example, is an aphrodisiac because of its heating properties (SEE Bartholomew Anglicus EXCERPT). As we have seen, sexual consummation required the expenditure of heat, while aging had a cooling effect. Long before Viagra, old men like Chaucer's January therefore relied on an array of "electuaries"—"ypocras, clarree, and vernage" and "spices hoote"—to combat impotence and "encreessen" their "corage" in bed (MerT 1806-08).

Experts could determine a particular substance's qualities by external signs, like temperature and color; hence the medieval doctor's preoccupation with examining his patient's urine (a diagnostic procedure known as uroscopy). A patient whose urine felt hot and was tinged with red probably suffered from an excess of blood. The color of all objects—not just urine—provided a reliable index of their elemental condition. In his discussion of leprosy, Anglicus insists on the *red* viper, because the heating presence of blood added to the viper's medicinal effectiveness against the melancholic nature of the disease. All of the humours were associated with particular colors; yellow, or yellowish-red pointed to the presence of choler, white to phlegm, and black to melancholy. In "The Nun's Priest's Tale," when Pertelote, attributes Chaunticleer's dream about a beast "bitwixe yellow and reed" (4092) to a "greete superfluytee / Of youre rede colera" (2928), she makes an uncontroversial diagnosis.[39] But when she counsels Chaunticleer to purge himself "bynethe and eek above" from his "humours hoote" by taking laurel and hellebore, she demonstrates her own ignorance (NPT 2954). The herbs that she prescribes were considered hot and dry—far from curing Chaunticleer, they would have exacerbated his condition.

The hen's enthusiastic endorsement of "laxatyf[s]" (NPT 2943) points to another method by which medical practitioners manipulated the humoural body of their patients: if you could not achieve your goal by controlling the patient's diet, or administering herbs and drugs, you could always try purgation. Methods of purgation included laxatives, emetics, and bleedings; all three aimed at restoring corporeal balance by removing excessive fluids or humours. Purgative methods are significant in a consideration of medieval habits of thinking, because they readily lend themselves to symbolic meaning. The therapeutic practice of bleeding, for example, provides one context for the many literary and dramatic descriptions of wounds and wounding. In *Sir Gawain and the Green Knight*, the Green Knight's tonic effect on the decadent court of King Arthur is expressed in part through such blood imagery. When the Green Knight extracts "a little blood" from Gawain's neck (2315), he provokes Gawain's confession and his spiritual purgation. Because of the centrality of blood sacrifice to Christianity, purgation often evokes religious meanings, as it does here in *Gawain*. But purgative practices had social and political connotations as well. According to the anthropologist Mary Douglas, "the human body is always treated as an image of society."[40] The way that people imagine illness and cure in the human body influences how they conceive of illness and cure in the body politic; in the case of the Middle Ages, where the metaphor of the body politic was endemic, the emphasis on balance and purgation helps explain phenomena like the expulsion of the Jews (SEE CHAPTER 1) or the massacre of the Flemish (SEE CHAPTER 8).

The humoural concepts of balance and purgation are still very much part of our own vocabulary. We refer to people as "unbalanced," for example, and when someone loses their temper, we accuse of them of being "overheated." Many other words associated with elemental thinking survive in modern English—"temperament," "complexion," "sanguine," "choleric," "phlegmatic," and "melancholy," to name a few. But they survive in altered form, and when we read medieval works, we have to be careful that our familiarity with these words does not obscure their historically specific meanings. When we describe someone as being "overheated" nowadays, we speak metaphorically. But in medieval thought, choler, the bodily fluid associated with rage and anger, is literally "hot": it alters the quality of the body in which it manifests itself. The same thing might be said for the heat of sexual congress. While we think about erotic heat as a metaphor, medieval subjects thought about it as real, affecting the physical states of the lovers. Emotions during this period are imagined as occurring in the body and as forming part of it. They are physical—not just mental—events. Humour theory makes little allowance for some of the central distinctions of post-Enlightenment Western thinking—between the body and the soul, "between psychology and physiology," "between the mental and the physical."[41] Medieval medicine, in its emphasis on the connection between physiological and psychological phenomena (even love was seen as a kind of physical illness, called erotic melancholy), was a lot more like modern-day holistic medicine—which often shares an emphasis on the spirit and on purgation—than like mainstream Western medicine, with its almost exclusive focus on the body.

The cases of the Chester Salome and the *Play of the Sacrament*'s Jonathas, discussed above, illustrate the medieval tendency to fuse body and soul: in these characters, the spiritual failure to believe results in physical disintegration. When Salome and Jonathas accept spiritual truth, they also recover their bodily integrity. The Chester Herod is not so lucky. His attempted murder of the Christ child culminates in his own spectacular decomposition: Herod's "arms" and "legs rotten" (421) on stage, in full view of the audience. Herod assumes that the rotting—a form of leprosy?—is a sign that he is "damned" (420). Here, as elsewhere in medieval culture, the body is a dependable indicator of the condition of the soul. The tendency to see the soul and the body as one entity encouraged cultural practices like the ostracism of lepers and increased the burden on the very sick, whose diseases could be—and often were—assigned moral origins.

Just as a person's physical state derived from his or her mixture of humours, so did his or her mental state. You could therefore reliably "judge of the virtues and manners of man by their complexion" (SEE THE EXCERPT FROM *The Secreta Secretorum* IN THE DOCUMENTS SECTION). The science of physiognomy, as this practice was known, taught that most humans fit one of four "complexions": they were sanguine, phlegmatic, choleric, or melancholy. As the treatise reproduced below notes, "these four complexions derive from the four humours of the body"; they are also arranged along a hierarchy, with sanguine temperaments considered nobler and more masculine than the other ones. The treatise describes the traits associated with each of the complexions; the sanguine man, for example, "shall be hardy enough, of good will and without malice, he shall be fleshy, his complexion shall be quick to hurt and to impair because of his tenderness, he shall have a good stomach, a good digestion, and a good deliverance [evacuation of bowels and bladder]: and if he be wounded he shall soon be whole, he shall be free and liberal, of fair appearance and active enough of body." The domination of a humour in a particular temperament expressed itself in the person's personality ("hardy and without malice") and the person's physique ("of fair appearance"). A whole range of physical traits—from the thickness of the hair to the timbre of the voice to the color of the face—could provide reliable information about someone's temperamental disposition.

Medieval physiognomy is of obvious interest to students of literature, since poets and dramatists relied on it for their characterizations. Chaucer makes explicit reference to physiognomy as an explanation for his characters' personalities: in the General Prologue, he informs us that the Franklin's "complexioun ... was sangwyn" (333) while the Reeve is a "sclendre colerik man" (587). Both comments raise appropriate expectations in regards to how these characters behave and the kinds of stories they tell. The writer of our treatise on physiognomy would recognize in the Reeve's response to the Miller's tale, for example, the choleric man's tendency "quick to feel wrath" and his love of "hasty vengeance." Even when he does not explicitly categorize his pilgrims according to their humours, Chaucer gives us detailed clues to their complexions. The Miller's hairiness, the Pardoner's goatish voice, and the Wife's gap-toothed smile all assume significance in a physiognomical scheme.[42] Chaucer constructs faces—and bodies—in order to help us see minds.

Since a powerful emotion was a physical event, humoural theory could account not just for a person's basic disposition but also for the transformation of that person under stress. It thus made available what John Block Friedman calls a "literary vocabulary of emotion": changes in the color of the face or the motion of the eyes were among the most frequently utilized means of indicating changes of the heart.[43] In Chaucer's *The Book of the Duchess*, for example, a knight "clothed al in blak" (457) advertises his emotional distress through his complexion, which is "piteous pale and nothing red" because the "blood was fled for pure drede / Doun to hys herte, to make hym warm" (470, 490-91). By focusing on how the lack of blood leaves the knight's "hewe … grene / and pale" (495), Chaucer contrasts the knight's formerly sanguine complexion with his current grief-induced melancholia. The knight has even lost his facial hair, a sign of masculine heat, to his excess of cold melancholy: "upon hys berd," he has "but little her" (456). The Black Knight suffers from a disease that afflicts many a medieval literary hero, including Chaucer's Arcite: the "loveris maladye / Of Hereos," which, "lyk manye," is "engendred of humour malencolik" (KT 1373-76).[44] As we saw in Chapter 5, love sickness most often struck those in unconsummated or unrequited relationships, such as the ones celebrated in the courtly love tradition. Consummation, with its attendant heat, was one possible cure for this condition.

Melancholy is of special interest, from a literary point of view, not just because of its association with love. Since the classical period, melancholics had been credited with a special disposition towards poetic inspiration and visionary dreams.[45] Many medieval works reproduce a nexus of associations between love, poetry, dreams, and melancholy. *Pearl*, *Piers Plowman*, *The Legend of Good Women*, *The House of Fame*, *The Parliament of Fowls*, and *The Book of the Duchess* all make use of dream visions. In these works and in medieval intellectual circles more generally, the status of dreams— where do they come from? could they have prophetic content? or is their content merely psychological?—is a matter of debate. An early commentator, Macrobius (c.395-c.423; SEE EXCERPT BELOW), argued that some dreams had a divine origin and therefore conveyed prophetic truth. This view carried great weight in the late Middle Ages when dream books, such as the *Somnium Danielis*, styled as a corollary to Daniel's interpretations of dreams in the Bible, were compiled. These delineated types of dreams and their attendant interpretations. The Wife of Bath's dream of a bloody bed, which she interprets as an omen of future wealth, derives from such a compilation. Macrobius also allowed, along with other scholars, that some dreams could be physiologically induced. Indeed, Aristotle argued that dreams were symptomatic of a humoural disorder; although their content might reveal something about a person's complexion, they could not reveal much about the future. Chaucer reproduces the terms of this debate in "The Nun's Priest's Tale," where Chaunticleer cites Macrobius, Cicero, and Daniel in defense of his argument that dreams are prophetic, while Pertelote insists that dreams are signs of humoural indisposition.[46]

Whatever his own stance on the matter, Chaucer was clearly interested in the physiological origin and psychological content of dreams. Oftentimes his dream visions are attributed to a melancholy narrator. In *The Book of the Duchess*, his narrator tells us that he has been sick for eight years, and scholars agree that the narrator's symptoms are consistent with a diagnosis of melancholia. Geffrey has a hard time sleeping, he suffers from despondency, and he has been indulging himself in melancholy reading (including an Ovidian tale about a melancholy lady who dreams about her dead husband). Only after establishing his own condition does the narrator recount the "swete ... sweven" conjured up by his mind (276-77), the bulk of which concerns his encounter with the mournful Black Knight. Pertelote observes that "the humour malencolie / Causeth ful many a man in sleep to crie / For feere of blake beres" and, presumably, the same is true for black knights (NPT 2934-35). Significantly, the narrator suggests that Macrobius would be unable to interpret his dream, indicating that this dream reveals the narrator's psychology rather than prophetic truth. Thus, although Chaucer's treatment of dreams adheres to medieval medical lore on the matter, he also seems prescient of modern psychological theories, in which dreams are the expression of the dreamer's subconscious. The black Knight reflects the narrator's melancholia in subtle and sophisticated ways, thereby helping the narrator to gain a critical distance and pass judgment on his own condition.[47] This act of judgment might in turn lead to a cure; according to Thomas Aquinas, the rational intellect that distinguished humans from animals could exert control over the humoural nature that humans shared with animals. Chaucer arguably identifies in the analysis of dreams a therapeutic benefit of the sort claimed by psychoanalysts. His dream visions thus blur the firmest boundary of them all: the one between medieval and modern approaches to science.

DOCUMENTS

ON THE NATURAL FACULTIES. GALEN (170 AD)

The Greek physician Galen (129- 210 AD) was the foremost authority on
medicine throughout the Middle Ages (and beyond). A prolific and brilliant
writer, Galen catalogued and commented on the achievements of medical experts before him, including most notably Hippocrates (*c.* 460 BC),
while also describing his own theoretical and practical advances. Galen's
influence on the history of Western medicine cannot be overestimated.
The works of Hippocrates and of Galen formed the basis of the medical
curriculum at medieval universities. Our excerpt is from *On the Natural
Faculties*; it describes the role played by the elemental qualities in human
generation and in human constitutions.

> I.VI: Let us speak then, in the first place, of Genesis, which,
> as we have said, results from *alteration* together with *shaping*.
>   The seed having been cast into the womb or into the earth (for
> there is no difference), then, after a certain definite period, a great
> number of parts become constituted in the substance which is
> being generated; these differ as regards moisture, dryness, coldness
> and warmth, and in all the other qualities which naturally derive
> therefrom. These derivative qualities, you are acquainted with, if
> you have given any sort of scientific consideration to the question
> of genesis and destruction. For, first and foremost after the qualities
> mentioned come the other so-called *tangible* distinctions, and after
> them those which appeal to taste, smell, and sight. Now, tangible
> distinctions are hardness and softness, viscosity, friability, lightness,
> heaviness, density, rarity, smoothness, roughness, thickness and
> thinness; all of these have been duly mentioned by Aristotle. And
> of course you know those which appeal to taste, smell, and sight.
> Therefore, if you wish to know which alternative faculties are primary
> and elementary, they are moisture, dryness, coldness, and warmth, and
> if you wish to know which ones arise from the combination of these,
> they will be found to be in each animal of a number corresponding
> to its *sensible elements*. The name *sensible elements* is given to all the
> *homogeneous* parts of the body, and these are to be detected not by
> any system, but by personal observation of dissections.

II.VIII: Now in reference to the *genesis of the humours,*
I do not know that any one could add anything wiser than what has
been said by Hippocrates, Aristotle, Praxagoras, Philotimus and many
others among the Ancients. These men demonstrated that when the
nutriment becomes altered in the veins by the innate heat, blood is
produced when it is in moderation, and the other humours when it
is not in proper proportion. And all the observed facts agree with this
argument. Thus, those articles of food, which are by nature warmer
are more productive of bile, while those which are colder produce
more phlegm. Similarly of the periods of life, those which are
naturally warmer tend to more bile, and the colder to more phlegm.
Of occupations also, localities and seasons, and, above all, of natures
themselves, the colder are more phlegmatic, and the warmer more
bilious. Also cold diseases result from phlegm, and warmer ones from
yellow bile. There is not a single thing to be found which does not
bear witness to the truth of this account. How could it be otherwise?
For, seeing that every part functions in its own special way because
of the manner in which the four qualities are compounded, it is
absolutely necessary that the function [activity] should be either
completely destroyed, or, at least hampered, by any damage to the
qualities, and that thus the animal should fall ill, either as a whole, or
in certain of its parts.

Also the diseases which are primary and most generic are four
in number, and differ from each other in warmth, cold, dryness
and moisture. Now, Erasistratus himself confesses this, albeit
unintentionally; for when he says that the digestion of food becomes
worse in fever, not because the innate heat has ceased to be in due
proportion, as people previously supposed, but because the stomach,
with its activity impaired, cannot contract and triturate as before ...

Of the Four Complexions (14ᵀᴴc)

These excerpts, our translation of a Middle English poem included in
Henry Person's *Cambridge Middle English Lyrics*, pithily illustrate the tendencies associated with an excess of each of the four humours.

Choleric Disposition
The choleric [is] forward and full of deception
Ireful in heart, prodigal in expense,

Hardy also and his behavior is sly.
Slender and small, full light in existence,
Right dry of nature for the great surging
of heat, and the Choleric hath this sign:
He is commonly of color citrine.

Sanguine Disposition

Of gifts large in love has [the sanguine person] great delight
Jocose and glad, always gleaming with cheer
Of ruddy color mixed somewhat with white,
Disposed to be kind, to be a singer,
Hardy, I know, manly and bold of cheer
Of the Sanguine also it is a sign
To be demure, rich, courteous, and benign.

Phlegmatic Disposition

The phlegmatic is somnolent and slow,
With humors gross, replete, and abundant,
Spitting noxious substances. The phlegmatic is known
By his dull mind and his inability,
To craft or carry out any subtle art.
Fat of kind is the phlegmatic. Men may trace
And know them best by the fatness of their face.

Melancholic Disposition

The melancholy thus men espy:
He is thoughtful and set in covetousness,
Replenished, full of fretting envy.
His heart allows him to spend in no wise;
Treason, envious fraud can he well devise
Coward of kind when he should be a man
You will know him by his visage pale and wan.

Of the Science of Physiognomy from the Secreta Secretorum (1422)

In the Middle Ages, people believed that the outward aspect of a person gave reliable indications of his or her temperament and character. The techniques for interpreting these indications formed part of the widely respected science of physiognomy. One of the best sources for physiognomical lore is a collection of works known as the *Secreta Secretorum*, or *Secret of Secrets*. A translation of the Arabic *Kitāb sirr al-asrār*, the *Secret of Secrets* exists in numerous European versions, dating back to the twelfth century. Most medieval readers believed the *Secreta Secretorum's* claim that it was written by Aristotle for the instruction and edification of Alexander the Great. Although at first the treatise probably focused on matters of government, over the years materials covering medical, scientific, alchemical, and occult knowledge were added, giving the work its present encyclopedic nature. Our translation is based on Robert Steele's edition of a 1422 English version, entitled *The Gouernaunce of Prynces; or, Pryvete of Pryveteis*.

OF PHYSIOGNOMY

Physiognomy is a science which judges of the conditions or virtues and manners of people, by the tokens or signs that appear in the fashion or making of the body, and especially of the face and of the voice and of the color. One general aspect of physiognomy is to judge of the virtues and manners of man by their complexion. There are four complexions, because a man is either sanguine, or phlegmatic, or choleric, or melancholy. And these four complexions derive from the four humours of the body, which answer to the four Elements, and to the four times of the year. The blood is hot and moist to the likeness of the air; phlegm is cold and moist after the kind of water; choler hot and dry after kind of fire; melancholy cold and dry after kind of earth. The sanguine by kind should love joy, laughing, and the company of women, and much sleep and singing; he shall be hardy enough, of good will and without malice; he shall be fleshy; his complexion shall be quick to hurt and to impair because of his tenderness; he shall have a good stomach, a good digestion, and a good deliverance [evacuation of bowels and bladder]; and if he be wounded he shall be soon be whole, he shall be free and liberal, of fair appearance and active enough of body. The phlegmatic by kind he should be slow, sad, very still, and slow of answer; feeble of body, easily fall into a palsy [or fit]; he shall be big and fat, he shall have a feeble stomach, a feeble digestion, and good deliverance. And as his manners, he shall be piteous, chaste, and little desire the company of women. The choleric kind he should be lean of body, his body is hot and dry, and he shall be somewhat rough; and quick to feel wrath and quick to appease; of sharp wit, wise, and of good memory, a great meddler, very large and foolhardy, active of body, hasty of word and of answer; he loves hasty vengeance; desirous of the company of women more than he needs. He should have a good enough stomach, especially when it is cold. The melancholy man should be lean of body and dry, he should have good appetite of meat, and commonly he is a glutton and good deliverance [evacuation] he has of his belly. And as to his manners, he should be pensive and slow, and of still will, still and timid, and not much of a meddler. He is slower to anger than a choleric man, but he holds his wrath longer; he is subtle of imagination and of handiwork. And the melancholy men are wont to be subtle workmen. The sanguine men should be ruddy of color. The phlegmatic white and pale; the choleric should have yellow color somewhat mixed with red; the melancholy should be somewhat black and pale.

Of the Physiognomy of the Hair

Soft hair is a sign of fear, and hard hair is sign of hardiness and strength, and that appears in diverse beasts. For the hare and the sheep are very timid, and have very soft hair. And the lion and the boar are very strong, and have strong hair. Also in fowls, the kind that have hard feathers are strong and courageous, like the cock, and those that have soft feathers are full of fear, like the turtle doves and curlews. So are diverse peoples, in relation to the region in which they dwell. For those who dwell toward the north are strong and courageous, and have hard hair. And those who dwell toward the south are timid and have soft hair, like the people of Ethiopia. Plenty of hair on the belly is a sign of a talker, full of words, and they are like to birds which have plenty of feathers in the belly.

Of the Complexion of the Voice
As It Follows Here Next

A strong voice and well-heard, like a trumpet, is a token of a bold and hardy man. A small voice and feeble, like a woman's voice, is a sign of a faint man. And therefore the strong and hardy beasts have strong and high voices, as lions, bulls, and hounds; and cocks, stronger and more courageous than other birds, sing higher and stronger. Of the hare we see the contrary is true.

Of the Color of the Face It Is Here to Wit

When a man has a face like and of the color of the flames of a fire, he is wrathful, and by kind he should be quick to anger. The foresaid tokens of figures and movements and likeness of face are the most certain among all other tokens. And it is to wit to judge a man after one token it is great folly, but you should reward all the signs, and if many or all accord, than you can more surely judge; and what part the most of signs and tokens he holds, hold yourself to that part.

Of the Tokens of the Courageous, the Coward, the Bitter Man, the Piteous Man, and the Lecher

Eleven tokens signal strength and courage. The first is hard hair; the second is even stature of body; the third is great stature of bones and ribs, and of hands and of feet; the fourth is a large belly, drawn back to him; the fifth great and massy muscles; the sixth a big, sinewy neck, not very fat; the seventh is a big breast and broad, elevated and somewhat fat; the eighth large haunches of good proportion; the ninth grey or brown eyes, like camel hair, that are not overly open or close; the tenth brown color in all the body; the eleventh a sharp, straight forehead, not greatly lean nor all full, neither all wrinkled.

A little face and lean, and wrinkled, little dead-looking eyes, little of stature and low, and of feeble movement: these are the tokens of cowardice.

The tokens of the bitter man: he hath the head bowed and stooping as a man pensive and full of thought, he is black of color, a lean visage and wrinkled, not rough, and black hair smooth.

The piteous and merciful man is signaled by white color, and clean, the eyes ready to weep, gladly they love new, piteous stories … and when they hear piteous stories easily they weep, and especially after [they drink] wine. They are … without malice, they love women, and often they beget daughters. In proverbs it is said that the piteous man has three virtues, that is, to wit: wisdom, dread, and honesty; and the tyrant or the cruel man, the contrary.

The lecher often times is white of color, the hair rough, big, and black; rough temples, large eyes, rolling swiftly in sight like a crazy man; of such an appearance are beasts in rut.

Of the Conditions of Women

The most open variance in beasts is that one is male and that other female, and after their differences we understand that the manners

and virtues of every other changes. For among all beasts that are
nourished or tamed by the wit of man, the females are most meek
and easiest to teach and least worthy. And because of that they are
feeblest of body and less able to defend themselves, and the same
is it with wild beasts. But women are more moveable and varied,
especially from evil [causes], than men are. For just as they are feebler
of body and of complexion, so in the same manner they are endowed
with less reason. And therefore they get angry easily and hastily ask
for vengeance. And they withstand temptation very poorly, especially
the temptation of fleshly delight.

OF THE NOSE

They that have great noses are easily given to covetousness, and are
disposed to concupiscence, and are much like oxen. And they that
have the butt of the nose big and round are rude of wit and likened
to swine. And they that have the butt of the nose sharp are strongly
angry and likened to dogs. And they that have round noses and not
sharp are hardy and bold and are likened to lions. A stooping nose,
broad between the brows, is a token of a courageous man like to
the eagle. Those that have the nose crooked and the forehead round,
perchance upward, are lecherous and angry and like to apes. Open
nostril betokens anger; for when a man is angry, his nostrils open.

OF THE FACE

Those that have big, fleshy faces are disposed to concupiscence of
fleshly lusts. A lean face is a sign of study and business; a fat face
[of] fearfulness; and a little face, a little heart. A great and broad face
betokens sloth in manner, as oxen and asses. A straight little face of
poor appearance betokens a hard and hungry heart. An open face and
fair seeming betokens a liberal heart; a little small forehead betokens
little wit, hard to teach, and of ill condition. The forehead all round,
a hard wit; a long oversized forehead, a slow wit; a square forehead
of mean greatness betokens fierceness and courage; a plain straight
forehead betokens a flatterer; the forehead somewhat troubled in
aspect signals fierceness and hardiness.

OF THE EYES

Those that have red eyelids usually love well wine and are great
drinkers; heavy eyelids betoken a good sleeper; little eyes betoken
a little heart and a slow [one]; big eyes betoken a rude wit; mean

eyes, neither great nor small, betoken a good complexion without vice. Deep eyes, malice; over-open eyes, as if they were thrust out, commonly betoken a fool; somewhat deep eyes betoken hardiness; but eyes neither too deep nor too far out but in between are best.

Of Color

Those men that are overly black are dreadful and like the Egyptians and Ethiopians; and those that are overly white are dreadful, like to women. Those men that are between black and white, the color is a token that they are strong and hardy. Those that are yellow of color are courageous and like lions. Those that are red men are perceptive and treacherous, and full of cunning, like foxes. Those that are pale and troubled in color are fearful, for they bear the color of fear in their foreheads. Those that are of red color are hasty and eager, for when a man is chafed by running and other movement, he waxes red. Those that have a burning color like the flames of a fire, are easily angered; and those that have such color about the breasts are always angry; and that is evident because when a man is really angry, he feels that his breast is burning. And those men that have about the neck and the temples great ruddy veins are wrathful and hugely angry; and that is apparent because a man that is angry has the same passion. Those that have the face somewhat ruddy are shamefast and tokens of honesty show in their face; those that have the cheeks all red as they are drinking is a token that they love right well good wine.

An Arab Opinion of the Crusaders' Medicine (12THc)

As is true of medicine more broadly considered, late medieval surgery owed much to Arabian expertise. The encyclopedic works of scholars like Rhazes and Avicenna made available a substantial amount of information about surgical technique, much of it derived from Greek sources like Hippocrates and Galen. Clearly, this Arabian report, by Usámah, a doctor who claims to have witnessed the barbarian practices that he describes, is cognizant of the Arabian advantage when it came to matters of medical knowledge. The report may reflect Arabian opinions about Western cultures more accurately than it does Western surgical practices. According to Nancy Siraisi, an authority on early medicine, the "confident butchery" here described "cannot have been characteristic," since the amputation of limbs on living persons was rare before the sixteenth century. [48]

A case illustrating their curious medicine is the following:

The lord of al-Munaytirah wrote to my uncle asking him to
dispatch a physician to treat certain sick persons among his people.
My uncle sent him a Christian physician named Thabit. Thabit was
absent but ten days when he returned. So we said to him, "How
quickly hast thou healed thy patients!" He said:

"They brought before me a knight in whose leg an abscess had
grown; and a woman afflicted with imbecility. To the knight I applied
a small poultice until the abscess opened and became well; and the
woman I put on diet and made her humour wet."

Then a Frankish physician came to them and said, "This man
knows nothing about treating them." He then said to the knight,
"Which wouldst thou prefer, living with one leg or dying with two?"
The latter replied, "Living with one leg." The physician said, "Bring
me a strong knight and a sharpe axe." A knight came with the axe.
And I was standing by. Then the physician laid the leg of the patient
on a block of wood and bade the knight strike his leg with the axe
and chop it off at one blow. Accordingly he struck it—while I was
looking on—one blow, but the leg was not severed. He dealt another
blow, upon which the marrow of the leg flowed out and the patient
died on the spot. He then examined the woman and said, "This is
a woman in whose head there is a devil which has possessed her.
Shave off her hair." Accordingly they shaved it off, and the woman
began once more to eat their ordinary diet—garlic and mustard.
Her imbecility took a turn for the worse. The physician then said,
"The devil has penetrated through her head." He therefore took a
razor, made a deep cruciform incision on it, peeled off the skin at the
middle of the incision until the bone of the skull was exposed and
rubbed it with salt. The woman also expired instantly. Thereupon I
asked them whether my services were needed any longer, and when
they replied in the negative I returned home, having learned of their
medicine what I knew not before.

I have, however, witnessed a case of their medicine which was
quite different from that.

The king of the Franks had for treasurer a knight named
Bernard... who (may Allah's curse be upon him!) was one of the
most accursed and wicked among the Franks. A horse kicked him
in the leg, which was subsequently infected and which opened in
fourteen different places. Every time one of these cuts would close
in one place, another would open in another place. All this happened

while I was praying for his perdition. Then came to him a Frankish physician and removed from the leg all the ointments which were on it and began to wash it with very strong vinegar. By this treatment all the cuts were healed and the man became well again. He was up again like a devil ...

A Lollard View on Bodily and Spiritual Blindness (14ᵀᴴc-15ᵀᴴc)

As the following excerpt from a medieval sermon illustrates, physical blindness was often associated with spiritual blindness. In Chaucer's "The Merchant's Tale," January becomes blind soon after marrying his inappropriately young wife. His blindness is both sign and consequence of his inability to perceive his own motivations and of his arrogant belief that he can control May. Blindness was especially associated with a lack of judgment in the period; as January finds out, "he who mysconceyveth, mysdemeth"(MerT 2410)—he who misconceives misjudges. Gloria Cigman includes the original in her *Lollard Sermons*.

> But for as much as blindness may be in the soul, it happens often that one may not know the way, nor see to go therein to heavenly Jerusalem. Therefore the gospel tells specifically that our Lord Jesus healed a man of his bodily blindness, who cried busily after his sight, and made him for to see, in order to teach us to desire fully in our hearts, and to cry busily to God with our mouths after a ghostly sight, which is the greatest help that may be to know this way, and readily without, erring to go therein.
>
> ...And just as there are many manners of bodily blindness, right so, there are many manners of ghostly blindness: there is blindness in belief; there is blindness in deeds, and blindness in deeming [judgment].
>
> ...And this both in secular judges and in churches, when they, for any presents or meed, will not see what is right, but judge according to wrong and fear not their God, as it is said in the old proverb: "The poor be hanged by the neck; a rich man by his purse ...." In this also [blindness of judgment] are all other hypocrites who can see a mote in another man's eye, but they cannot see a beam in their own; that is, they can see a fault in their brother's deeds, but set naught by the greater in their own.

From *De Coitu* (On Intercourse).
Constantinus Africanus (11thc)

In "The Merchant's Tale," January reads up on all the best aphrodisiacs in order to enjoy his wedding night with his new bride, May. The book Chaucer refers to is the notorious *De Coitu*, a medical treatise that was considered scandalous for the frank way with which it dealt with sex. Its author, Constantinus Africanus, a Muslim who had converted to Christianity during the eleventh century, was responsible for changing the way the Western world viewed medicine and health through his introduction and translation of Arabic medical treatises into Latin. *De Coitu*, despite its titillating topic, covers many new and important topics for the medieval world, including information on how the male reproductive system works and the various disorders that may occur therein. It is possible that January's sudden onset of blindness after his marriage is directly related to his overindulgence in marital sex.

> ... Intercourse is ... good for people with plenty of non-viscous
> phlegm provided they are robust, because the humour is evacuated
> by coitus—it becomes scanty because the heat generated by the rapid
> movements of intercourse condenses and dries. However, if this kind
> of phlegmatic person is debilitated, frequent intercourse will be very
> harmful, because it will make his body extremely cold and weak. If
> you ask why we distinguish between the virtue of the strong and the
> weak, we say that intercourse is good for a man of strong virtue but
> does harm to the weak man by changing the complexion of his body
> to the greatest possible cold and weakness. Galen, indeed, said that
> frequent intercourse dries out the body and makes it slack; and some
> think that intercourse does not warm the body, but always chills it.
> Nonetheless, when there is virtue and strong natural heat, the body
> is warmed by intercourse; though if the virtue is weak, intercourse
> warms during the act itself, but afterwards chills very powerfully. We
> therefore distinguish between strong and weak virtue and say that to
> those of strong virtue intercourse does good, because it warms them,
> and that it harms those of weak virtue by chilling them, as Galen says.
>   Intercourse is useful in another way: to a man with excessive
> fumes in his body which destroy its temperance. If such a humour
> is confined in the body and not dissolved, it does serious damage.
> But if the man has intercourse, the superfluities are dissolved and
> the body is rested, cooled, and relieved—provided the intercourse

is not frequent but only performed when necessary. We said that
intercourse is beneficial in two ways. Rufus's opinion is that
intercourse relieves harmful bodily conditions and calms madness.
It is good for melancholics, recalls madmen to their senses, and frees
lovers of their passion (provided they can lie with some other whom
they desire). Thus Galen says that every wild animal is fierce before it
has intercourse, but is tamer afterward.

Hippocrates says that intercourse does harm to anyone whose
illness is becoming worse. At this point we should show why animals
become weak, and why it happens that some men suffer paralysis
and melancholy at the time of intercourse; others have tremor, a bad
smell, a swelling of the stomach during the act, a kind of buzzing,
or a headache afterwards. We say then, that when semen is emitted,
the humour lost by the body is a substantial one, drawing its essence
from the vital organs; it is not like the humour lost by excretion,
because this latter is incidental and, being superfluous, is cast off by
the organs. Hippocrates says the same thing in his book on the foetus:
when we emit semen willfully, weakness often follows ....

Galen says the same thing in his book on semen, when he speaks
of those who have intercourse too often: not only does a humour
come from the organs, but the vital spirit also leaves with the semen
through the arteries. So it is hardly surprising that someone who
has intercourse too often will be weakened. For when the body
is drained of these two substances, and lustful man thinks only of
pleasure, the vital spirit is dissipated; many have died in this way, and
no wonder ....

From *On the Properties of Things*. Bartholomew Anglicus (13ᵗʰc)

As we saw in the documents at the end of CHAPTER 2, Bartholomew
Anglicus's *On the Properties of Things* was among the most widely read
books of the late Middle Ages. The fourth book of *On the Properties of
Things* concerns the human body; from it, we drew our first two selections—the description of the elements that constitute all matters and
the description of the concoction of the humours. The other selections
are from the seventh book, which is devoted to the subject of medicine
and covers a variety of ailments from diarrhea to leprosy. Our translated
excerpts are based on John Trevisa's Middle English translation of the
Latin original.

On the Elements

Man's body is made of four elements: of earth, water, fire, and air; and each has its own qualities. Four qualities are called the first and principal ones, to wit: heat, cold, dryness, and wetness; and they are called the first qualities because they slide first from the elements into the things that are made of elements. They are also called the principal qualities because from them come all secondary effects. Two of these qualities are called *active* "able to work": heat and coldness. The other two, dryness and wetness, are called *passive* "able to suffer." And so as these qualities have mastery, the elements are said active or passive, "able to do or suffer."

On the Concoction of Humours

A humour is a fleeting substance indeed, and it is bred and comes of a gathering of the element qualities.... For humour is the principal material of bodies that have feeling and chief help in their working, and that because it nourishes and feeds [the body]. Constantinus says that the humours are called the children of the elements, for every one of the humours comes from a quality of the elements. And there are four humours: blood, phlegm, choler, and melancholy. And they are called simple in comparison to the members and the limbs [of the body], though they be compounded in comparison to the elements, whose children they are.

These four humours, if they are in even proportion in quantity and quality, they feed all the bodies that have blood and make them perfect and keep them in the being and state of health; contrariwise, if they are uneven in proportion and infected, then they breed evils. These humours are needful to the making of the body and to the ruling and keeping thereof; and also to restore what is lost in the body....

These four humours are bred in this manner: when meat is seized in the place of seeping, that is the stomach, first, its more subtle and fleeting part that the physicians call *phtisinaria* is drawn through certain veins to the liver, and there by the working of a kind of heat it is changed into the four humours. The breeding of them begins in the liver, but it does not end there. First, by working, heat turns what is cold and moist into the type called phlegm, and then what is hot and moist into the type of blood, and then what is hot and dry into the type of choler, and then what is cold and dry into the type of melancholy. Then the process is as follows: phlegm is bred as a humour half heated; second, blood that is perfectly heated; the third, choler that is overheated; and the last, melancholy, that is more earthy and the dregs of the other. And such is the order, as Avicenna says: the breeding of the elements is straight and again the same, for air is bred of fire, and fire of air, and every element of the other.... So in the humours is one part that is light and comes upwards, and that is choler; another as it were drags and goes downwards, and that is melancholy; the third is as it were raw, that is phlegm; and the fourth is blood, purified and cleansed of other humours. And therefore by the mixture of other humours, blood changes kind and color; for by blending with choler it seems red, and by melancholy, it seems black, and by phlegm, it seems watery and foamy.

On Leprosy

Leprosy is a universal corruption of members and of humours ... Constantinus says that every *elephantia* or leprosy begins principally from the corruption of melancholy. Therefore Constantinus says that leprosy is cool and evil and dry, and comes of strongly rotting black choler, and is seen in every extremity of the body. And it comes of four rotting humours that were strong, and that were corrupted, and changed into black choler.... The four types of leprosy have some common signs and tokens, and some special signs by which their particular type is especially known. Universally this evil [leprosy] hath such tokens and signs: in them the flesh is notably corrupt, the shape is changed, the eyes become round, the eyelids are shriveled, the sight gleams, the nostrils are striated and shriveled and shrunk; and especially in *lyonyna* [a type of leprosy] the nostrils are straight and shriveled and shrunk; the voice is hoarse in *elephancia* [another type of leprosy], swellings grow in the body, and many small botches and whelks, hard and round, in the legs; and in the other extremities feeling is somewhat taken away. The nails are unpolished and bunchy, as if they were scabs, and the fingers shrunk and crooked, and the hands dry. The breath is corrupt, and often healthy men are infected with its stench. The flesh and skin is oily, insomuch that they may throw water thereon, and it does not get wet, but the water slides off, as if it were off a wet hide. There is also itching, sometimes with scabs and sometimes not. Also on the body there are diverse specks, now red, now black, now wan, now pale. On the legs, there are many specks and whelks, which are sometimes seen and then vanish; sometimes they break out and then they shrink again. And among the whelks of the legs if you find one that is bigger and fouler than the others, it is a token that the leprosy is fastened and confirmed. The tokens of leprosy are most seen in the extremities, as in the feet, legs, and face; and namely in wasting and diminishing of the muscles of the body . . . .

Leprosy comes of diverse causes, other than the foresaid humours, like dwelling and living and keeping company and often talking with leprous men; for the evil is contagious and infects other men. Also it comes of fleshly lying with a woman soon after a leprous man has lain with her . . . .

In these manners and in many others, the evil of leprosy breeds in man's body. But howsoever it be engendered, it is only curable by God's hand if it be confirmed. But it may be somewhat hidden and helped, so that it destroys [the patient] not so quickly. The patient shall beware of meats and especially of such that breed melancholy, and also of meats that overheat the blood . . . . And if blood is the cause, as in *allopucia*, then he shall first have his blood let, and then be purged with proper medicines . . . . To heal or to hide leprosy, as Plato says, best is a red adder with a white belly, if the venom is taken away, and the tail and the head smitten off, and the body stewed in leeks, taken often and eaten; in the same way, give the patient often to drink of wine in which it [the adder] rots. And this medicine helps with many evils; as he [Plato] tells the story of the blind man, to whom his wife gave an adder with garlic instead of an eel, that it might slay him, and he ate it, and after that by much sweat, he recovered his sight good and clear.

ON PRACTICING MEDICINE

To give decent and true medicine against diverse illnesses and perils, a good physician needs to look well about him and be fully aware and well advised, for nothing hurts sick men more than the lack of knowledge and negligence of the physicians. On the physician's side, it is necessary that he forgets nothing that belongs to the evil, also that he be diligent and busy in the things that belong to the craft of medicine, and he must be aware and advised in all things. Also, to heal and save effectually he needs to know that complexions of men, compositions, mixtures and blends both of members and of humours, and the dispositions of times, conditions of male and female, and age. For one medicine is needed in winter and another in summer; and one in the beginning of the evil, and another at the peak, and another at the passing of the disease; one in childhood and in youth, another in middle age, and another in old age; one in males and one in females. And he needs to know the causes and occasions of evils, for medicines may never be sure to take if the cause of the evil is unknown. Also he needs to know the complexions, virtues, and workings of medicinal things, for only if he knows what medicine is simple, what compounded, what cold and what hot, what worsens and what amends the body, what maintains health, what heals sickness, what hardens and constrains, what loosens and works as a laxative, he may never surely pass forth and work in medicine. Also therefore he needs to know the qualities of herbs and other medicinal things and diversity of degrees, what is hot and dry, what is cold and moist, in what degree, if he will not err in his office .... Also when he sees that the evil comes of repletion, he helps it by voiding of the matter and by scarce diet. And if it comes of abstinence, he helps it with repletion.

Also the office of a good physician stands in inquisition and searching of the causes and circumstances of the evil, for he searches and seeks the cause by sight, by handling and groping, by uroscopy ....

Then consider that a physician visits often the houses and countries of sick men, and seeks and searches the causes and circumstances of the sicknesses, and arrays and brings with him divers and contrary medicines; and he does not refuse to grope and handle, and to wipe and cleanse privy members and the wounds of sick men. And he gives to all men hope and trust of recovering and of health; and he says that he will softly and easily burn that which shall be burnt, and cut that which shall be cut. And lest the whole part should corrupt, he spares not to burn or to cut off the part that is rotted, and if a part in the right side aches, he suffers it not to smite the left side. A good leech [doctor] leaves not cutting or burning for the weeping of the patient; and he hides and covers the medicine, though it be bitter; that it be not against the sick man's heart, and he refrains the sick man from meat and drink; and lets him of whose health there is neither hope nor trust of recovering have his own will; and does away rotted and dead flesh that is disposed to corruption with bitter and fretting medicines; and cleanses running scabs with drying medicines.

A good physician takes heed to the matter of the evil and of the place of the matter and also of the might and the strength of the patient, and thereby he varies his medicine.

VARIOUS REMEDIES. GILBERTUS ANGLICUS (13ᵀᴴC)

The following excerpts are based on a fifteenth-century Middle English translation of Gilbertus Anglicus's treatise, mentioned in the "General Prologue" of *The Canterbury Tales*. The treatise collects medicinal recipes and organizes them by reference to specific conditions. The details it offers—including descriptions of how to diagnose conditions—suggest that it is designed in part for lay consumption; according to its modern editor, the translation may be "a very early example of the 'self-help' manual."[49] As such, the Middle-English Gilbertus Anglicus participates in the fourteenth- and fifteenth-century trend in the translation and popularization of scientific writings. The Middle English original exists in a modern edition by Faye Marie Getz.

ON TOOTHACHES

In a man's teeth been diverse grievances: ache, worms, stinking, rottenness. Ache comes in diverse manners: sometimes, it comes of the head and of the humour of the head that falls down into the teeth, and than commonly the over-teeth ache. Sometimes, it comes of the stomach, and then the nether teeth ache. Sometimes, it comes of the hot meats that a man eats, or of the cold, or of a sudden changing from hot meats to cold, or of right sour meats or right keen, or of corrupt meats that stick between the teeth .... Sometimes, the ache comes of corrupt humours that are at the root of the teeth. And if it comes of heat of the head, the cheeks are to swell, and red, and hot. In ache that comes of cold, there is paleness of the cheek and cold of the teeth. And if it comes of moistness, there is swelling and softness of the cheek, and if it comes of dryness, there is hardness and little swelling with the ache. And so if the cheek be dark red, the ache is very keen. And if it is of phlegm, they are very white and the ache comes with heaviness. Of blood comes redness and swelling of the cheeks. Of melancholy comes dark ... cheeks, with little swelling, and great heaviness in the ache. And if it comes of the head, it may be known by grievance of the head. If it comes of a keen humour among the teeth, it makes worms in the teeth, or it makes the teeth hollow. And if it comes of the head and there be no rheum, let him bleed on the head vein of the arm. And if the body be full of blood, let him bleed at the vein that is under the tongue. And that is good for this grievance, and for the breast, and to make a man to have a clear voice. But if it comes of cold, let him not bleed at no vein, but let him be cupped in the pit of the neck. And if it comes of rheum, make that the humours flow not to the teeth, and if it comes of heat, with fumigations of roses soaked in water, or other cold herbs…And if the rheum is of cold, make a fumigation of incense. And in both causes, a fumigation of henbane and of leek seed is good. And if it comes of the stomach, let him chew purslane or solanum or belladonna with vinegar and purge the stomach of corruption. A plaster to lay upon the temples to staunch the flowing of the humour that comes from the head shall be made of mastic [resin made from the mastic tree], of bole [a type of red earth], of sandragon [red juice or resin from the dragon tree], and the white of an egg. And it is good to lay cold plasters to the chin with a quantity of mint mixed therewith. But if the ache be full great, lay a plaster outside of henbane or of opium. And mix gum resin, myrrh, and opium together, and lay to the tooth or the teeth, or myrrh with vinegar, or henbane by itself. But if it be of rheum, lay thereto no vinegar, and namely if the ache be on the side, but make a plaster of roses, and of water lilies, and henbane with pellitory [a medicinal, herbaceous plant] or cumin. And if all this helps not, it seems that the ache comes of some worm, or that the teeth is pierced by some corrupt humour, or rotted. And if it be with swelling of the cheek, it is a token of a disease of the gums. And if the ache be grievous without swelling, it is token of a worm. For the toothache: take gum resin, and of gum ivy, and powder of oak gall, and powder of ginger, and grind them together. And then make of them balls of the quantity of a filbert, and sew it all in a cloth. And then wet it in vinegar and lay to the tooth. Or take nine leaves of sage, and nine sprigs of red nettle, and nine peppercorns in the same manner.

On Feebleness of Sight

Feebleness of sight comes in many manners, as by sickness of the eyes, as I have told before; or of sickness of the head, and than it is helped by healing of that sickness; or of grievance of the stomach, which may be amended by healing of the stomach. Other times the feebleness of the eye comes of feebleness of her spirits. And here, thou must understand that such spirits are small bodies that are in a man's eye. And they are the instruments that the sight sees with; for such spirits receive the light of those things that a man sees. And therefore when they are feeble, needs the sight must be feeble.

For this sickness a magpie is good in this manner: pluck her, and take out her guts, and burn the remnant in a new earthen pot well stopped above. And make thereof powder and use it in thy meats, and drinks, and collyriums [medicine applied to the eyes]. This powder is also good for the cardiacle [a disease characterized by pain in the heart, palpitation, feebleness, and sweating], and for melancholy, and other cold sicknesses . . . . Also take the [mag]pie, and pluck her, and take out her guts, and soak the other matters in white wine until the wine is consumed and the flesh departed from the bones. Then stamp it all together, and put it in a vessel, and let the thin flow from the thick three days. Then take a small linen cloth and wet in that liquor, and put thereof in the eye both within and without, for it does away the darkness and the smarting of the eye, and the redness, and the ache, and comforts the spirits. Also, nettle seed is good for darkness of eyes, and the water that the seed is soaked in; also the water of euphrasy [medicinal herb], of celidone [a fabulous stone allegedly found in the stomach of a swallow], of rue, of agrimony [medicinal herb], of fennel, of roses, is good for the sight. Also, soak tormentil [medicinal herb] in wine and drink the wine. Then lay of that soaked herb on the eye, and within nine days it shall see. Also, take the juice of fennel and of ground ivy and set it in the sun three days in a brazen vessel. And after do thereof in the eye. Or mix the juice of ground ivy and honey together; or make a plaster of powdered cumin and white wine and lay it on his eye, but lay a cloth between. Or take the juice of wormwood and of rue, the same amount of both, and put in the eye; or take the juice of rue and honey and mix them together and put into the eye. And it shall make the flowing of water to cease. Or take ginger, and the juice of fennel, and white wine, and mix them together. And dry them in the sun and do thereof in the eye. Or take the juice of celidone, and of rue, and of morning dew, and honey, of each the same amount. And dry it in the sun and after do thereof in the eye. Also the water of these herbs: of euphrasy, celidon, rue, agrimony, fennel, and of roses, are good for feeble sight . . . .

ON LYCANTHROPIA (6ᵀᴴC)

The sixth-century treatise *De Melancholia*, by Aetius, included an influential account of the disease of lycanthropia, in which the patient imagined himself a wolf. Medieval and early modern medical treatises frequently recycled its lurid depiction of this disease. Our version is based on an English translation of Tomaso Garzoni's treatise on madness (1586), entitled *The Hospitall of incurable fooles* (London, 1600).

> Among these humours of melancholy, the physicians place a kind
> of madness by the Greeks called Lycanthropia, termed by the
> Latins *Insania Lupina*, or wolves' fury, which brings a man to this
> point … that in February he will go out of the house in the night
> like a wolf, hunting about the graves of the dead with great howling,
> and pluck the dead men's bones out of the sepulchers, carrying
> them about the streets, to the great fear and astonishment of all them
> that meet him. And the foresaid author affirms, that melancholic
> persons of this kind, have pale faces, soaked and hollow eyes, with
> a weak sight, never shedding one tear to the view of the world,
> a dry tongue, extreme thirst, and they want spittle and moisture
> exceedingly; where he also alleged that he saw two mightily troubled
> and oppressed with such an humour. But in this point Foruaretto of
> Lugo may serve for a notable example, who suffering this madness in
> his imagination and cogitative parts (for all men agree not touching
> the memory) he went one night into the Jew's churchyard, where
> there had been lately buried an old Jew, more than four score years
> of age, he having been sick more than six years of a dropsy, and
> taking up this body upon his shoulders, he went to a spacious place
> before the castle playing with this dead carcass, as if he had been at
> balloon [a ball game, in which a player struck a large inflated ball
> with his arm, which was defended by a bracer of wood], and crying
> out sometimes serve, sometimes send it home to me, now strike, then
> play. He by little and little raised up all that quarter, and the rumor
> went from hand to hand, through all the Hebrew families, that this
> man had disinterred master Simon, (for so was the dead Jew called)
> whereupon there presently grew a Synagogue of immeasurable
> laughter in their presence, when they saw this fool, how he took one
> of his legs by the small [short end] instead of a bracer [the wooden
> bracer used on the player's arm, SEE ABOVE], and the body full of
> garbage for a balloon, at every blow his hydropical tonnage [filled
> with too much fluid, as with dropsy] issuing forth, which was a
> fortnight's work for that people, to allay the stench thereof only ….

Two Medical Cases (late 14thc)

The following two cases are early examples of what we would nowadays call malpractice suits. Despite our modern skepticism regarding medieval medical practices, these suits reveal that medieval patients did expect to get better under their physicians' care. When treatment failed, as it had in these cases, blame attached itself to the practitioner, who was thought inadequate, but not to the practices themselves, so that the existence of these accusations "is in itself evidence that practitioners were normally thought of as competent."[50] In the second case here included, in fact, the defendant is found guilty because of the expert testimony that his peers provided.

Lewis the Leech, 1390

Lewis the leech, a Lombard, was attached to answer Thomas Birchester on a plea of why, whereas the said Lewis had undertaken at Southwark for a suitable fee to cure the said Thomas well and proper of a certain illness which incapacitated him, the aforesaid Lewis there applied his cure upon the aforesaid Thomas so negligently and recklessly that the said Thomas was very much the worse, to the said Thomas's loss of forty marks, so it is said.... Lewis, on Monday before the Feast of the Purification of the Blessed Mary in the seventh year of the reign of king Richard the Second at Southwark [February 1, 1384], undertook there for a suitable fee to cure the said Thomas of a certain illness which incapacitated him, that is to say, a certain injury in the kidneys near his privy parts and under the skin of his body, the aforesaid Lewis there applied his cure upon ... Thomas so negligently and recklessly that the said Thomas was very much the worse, whereby he says that he is wronged and has suffered loss to the value of a hundred marks.... And the aforesaid Lewis comes in his own person and denies all tort ... And he says that the aforesaid Thomas came to the said Lewis ... and asked Lewis to help him for payment with an illness in his stomach which incapacitated him. And the said Lewis applied his cure upon the said illness of the stomach and healed him thereof, without the said Lewis ever undertaking that he would cure the said Thomas of any injury under his skin near his privy parts. And he is ready to prove this by the country, etc. And the jury likewise came. And chosen, tried, and sworn for this purpose with the assent of the parties, they say on their oath that the aforesaid Lewis undertook the cure of the aforesaid Thomas in healing him of the aforesaid injury under his skin near his privy parts...And they assess the aforesaid Thomas's damages on the aforesaid account at ten pounds.

RICHARD CHEYNDUT, 13 FEBRUARY 1377

Richard Cheyndut was committed to prison for having undertaken to cure Walter, son of John del Hull, pinner, of a malady in his left leg, whereby, owing to his lack of care and knowledge, the patient was in danger of losing his leg, as was testified by John Donhed, John Garlikhuth, and Nicholas the Surgeon, three surgeons who had viewed the leg by order of the Mayor. The latter reported that it would require great experience, care, and expense if the leg were to be cured without permanent injury. A jury in this action found for the plaintiff with 50s. damages.

ON NATURAL MAGIC (16ᵀᴴc)

Where we tend to think of magic and of science as opposites, people in the middle ages and the Renaissance regarded these activities as compatible. The similarities between magic and science were, in fact, much easier to discern than the differences; both made wide use of herbal remedies, for example, and both involved the collection and application of knowledge to effect change. Our passage is taken from an English translation of a work by John Baptista Porta first published in Italy in 1558. The title, *Naturall Magick* (London, 1658), should ring a bell for those familiar with the description of Chaucer's Physician in "The General Prologue."

> There are two sorts of magic. The one is infamous, and unhappy, because it has to do with foul spirits, and consists of enchantments and wicked curiosity, and this is called sorcery—an art which all learned and good men detest; neither is it able to yield any truth of Reason or Nature, but stands merely upon fancies and imaginations, such as vanish presently away, and leave nothing behind them.... The other magic is natural, which all excellent wise men do admit and embrace, and worship with great applause—neither is there any thing more highly esteemed, or better thought of, by men of learning. The most noble philosophers that ever were, Pythagoras, Empedocles, Democrites, and Plato, forsook their own countries, and lived abroad as exiles and banished men, rather than as strangers; and all to search

out and to attain this knowledge, and when they came home again, this was the science which they professed, and this they esteemed a profound mystery. They that have been most skillful in dark and hidden points of learning, do call this knowledge the very highest point, and the perfection of natural Sciences, insomuch that if they could find out or devise amongst all natural sciences, any one thing more excellent or more wonderful than another, that they would still call by the name of magick. Others have named it the practical part of natural philosophy, which produces her effects by the mutual and fit application of one natural thing unto another.

ON ANIMALS (12ᵀᴴC AND 13ᵀᴴC)

The following descriptions of animals are typical of the medieval tradition in that they emphasize symbolic and allegorical associations over scientific detail. The eagle, for example, is endowed with all the traits of human monarchs. Our excerpts include our translated entries from Book 12 and 18 of Bartholomew Anglicus's *On the Properties of Things*, which concern birds and animals. The other descriptions come from T.H. White's classic translation of a twelfth-century medieval bestiary. We have reproduced both works' description of the fox, to show the common fund of associations between them, associations shared by medieval writers, who made frequent symbolic use of the fox.

ANGLICUS ON THE EAGLE
Now it is to speak of birds and fowls in particular and first is the eagle that has principality among the fowls (as queen of fowls). Among all manner, kinds of divers fowls, the eagle is the most liberal and free of heart, as Pliny says, for the prey that she takes, but it be for great hunger, she eats it not alone but puts it forth in common to fowls that follow her, but first she takes one portion and part. And therefore often other fowls follow the eagle for hope and trust to have some part of her prey. But when the prey that is taken is not sufficient to herself, then as a king that takes heed of the community, she takes the bird next to her and gives it among the others and serves them with this ....

And the eagle is called *aquila* and has that name because of sharpness of eye, as Isidore says; for she has so strong and so sharp and so clear sight, as it is said, that when she is borne and flees up into the air and hovers above the sea so high so that … from so great highness she sees a small fish swimming in the sea and she falls down anon as if she were a stone and takes suddenly the fish …

ANGLICUS ON THE PEACOCK

And the peacock is a bird that loves not his children, for the male seeks out the female and searches out her eggs to break them, so that he may occupy himself more in lechery. And the female dreads this and busily hides her eggs lest the peacock finds them. As Aristotle says, the peacock has an unsteadfast and evil-shaped head, as it were the head of a serpent, and with a crest, and he has … a blue breast, and a tail full of distinguished and high eyes of wondrous fairness, and he has foul and wrinkled feet. And he wonders at the fairness of his feathers, and rears them up as it were a circle about his head, and then he looks to his feet, and sees the foulness of his feet, and like as he were ashamed he lets his feathers fall suddenly, and all the tail downward, as though he took no heed of the fairness of his feathers. And he has a horrible voice, and as one says, he has the voice of a fiend, the head of a serpent, the pace of a thief. And …. Pliny says that the peacock is envious of men's profit and swallows his own dirt because it is very medicinal.

ANGLICUS ON THE BOAR

The boar is so fierce a beast, and also so cruel, that for his fierceness and his cruelness, he despises and sets nothing by death, and he charges full spitefully against the point of a spear of the hunter. And although he be smitten or stuck with a spear through the body, yet because of the greater ire and cruelty that he has in his heart, he charges his enemy, and takes comfort and heart and strength in avenging himself on his adversary with his tusks. And he puts himself in peril of death with a wondrous fierceness against the weapon of his enemy. And he has in his mouth two crooked tusks right strong and sharp, and with them breaks and rends cruelly those that withstand him. And he uses the tusks instead of a sword, and he has a hard shield, broad and thick in the right side, and puts that always against the weapon that pursues him, and he uses that brawny muscle instead of a shield to defend himself. And when he spies a peril that should befall, he whets his tusks and rubs them against trees, and tries by that rubbing against trees, to see if the points of his tusks be all blunt. And if he feels that they be blunt, he seeks an herb which is called oregano, and gnaws it and chews it, and cleanses and comforts the roots of his teeth therewith by its virtues, as Avicenna says....

Pliny says that the urine of the boar is medicine for diseases of the ears if it is mixed with the oil of roses...Also he says that the gall of the boar excites to engendering [in other words, it functions as an aphrodisiac].

Anglicus on the Fox

A fox is called Vulpes, and has that name which means as it were "wallowing feet aside," and he goes never forthright, but always aslant and with fraud. And he is a false beast and deceiving, for when he lacks meat, he feigns himself dead, and then fowls come to him, as it were to a carrion. Then he takes them and slays them and devours them, as Isidore says.... The fox limps always, for the right legs are shorter than the left legs. His skin is very hairy, rough, and hot; his tail is great and rough; and when a hound tries to take him by the tail, the dog gets his mouth (and teeth) full of hair, which stops it. The fox fights with the badger for dens, and he defiles the badger's den with urine and with dirt, and has so the mastery over him through fraud and deceit, and not through strength. The fox lives in places and dens under the earth and steals and devours more tame beasts than wild ones.... Between the fox and the badger is a kind of wrath and often the fox overcomes the badger more by guile than by might and strength.

He is a gluttonous beast and devours much and therefore engenders blind children as do the lion and the wolf, as Aristotle says.... For as Solinus says, in all beasts that engender incomplete brood, the cause is gluttony, for if nature suffered them to abide until they were complete, they would slay their mothers with sucking....

The fox is a stinking beast and corrupts often the places that he lives in continually by making them barren. His belly is white and so is his neck under the throat and his tail is red and so is his back. His breath stinks and his biting is sometimes venomous, as Pliny says. And when hounds pursue him, he draws his tail between his legs; and when he sees that he may not escape, he gathers urine in the tail that is full hairy and rough and throws that urine on the hounds that pursue him; and the stench of that urine is horrible to the hounds and therefore the hounds sometimes spare him. The fox feigns himself tame in time of need, but by night he waits his time and doeth shrewd deeds.

And though he be right guileful in himself and malicious, yet he is good and profitable in use of medicine, as Pliny says.... For his grease and marrow helps much against the shrinking of sinews, as it is said.

A BESTIARY ON THE FOX

VULPIS the fox gets his name from the person who winds wool (*volupis*)—for he is a creature with circuitous pug marks who never runs straight but goes on his way with tortuous windings.

He is a fraudulent and ingenious animal. When he is hungry and nothing turns up for him to devour, he rolls himself in red mud so that he looks as if he were stained with blood. Then he throws himself on the ground and holds his breath, so that he positively does not seem to breathe. The birds, seeing that he is not breathing, and that he looks as if he were covered with blood with his tongue hanging out, think he is dead and come down to sit on him. Well, thus he grabs them and gobbles them up.

The Devil has the nature of this same.

With all those who are living according to the flesh he feigns himself to be dead until he gets them in his gullet and punishes them. But for spiritual men of faith he is truly dead and reduced to nothing.

Furthermore, those who wish to follow the devil's works perish, as the Apostle says: "Know this, since if you live after the flesh you shall die, but if you mortify the doings of the foxy body according to the spirit you shall live." And the Lord God says: "They will go into the lower parts of the earth, they will be given over to the power of the sword, they will become a portion for foxes."

A BESTIARY ON THE COCK

The COCK (*gallus*) is called the cock because it gets castrated. It is the only member of the bird family whose testicles are removed. Indeed, the ancients used to call the Galli (the priests of Cybele) the "cut-offs."

Just as a lioness takes her name from a lion or a dragoness from a dragon, so does a hen take hers (*gallina*) from the cock (*gallinus*).

Their limbs, they say, are eaten mixed with liquid gold.

Cockcrow is a pleasant thing of a night, and not only pleasant but useful. It is nice to have it about the place. It wakes the sleeping, it forewarns the anxious, it consoles the traveler by bearing witness to the passage of time with tuneful notes. At the cock's crowing the robber leaves his wiles, the morning star himself wakes up and shines upon the sky. At his singing the frightened sailor lays aside his cares and the tempest often moderates, waking up from last night's storm. At his crowing the devoted mind rises to prayer and the priest begins again to read his office. By testifying devotedly after the cockcrow Peter washed away the sin of the Church, which he had incurred by denying Christ before it crowed. It is by this song that hope returns to the sick, trouble is turned to advantage, the pain of wounds is relieved, the burning of fever is lessened, faith is restored to the fallen, Christ turns his face to the wavering or reforms the erring, wandering of mind departs and negation is driven out. Confession follows. Scripture teaches that this did not happen by chance, but by the will of our Lord.

A Bestiary on the Lion

LEO the Lion, mightiest of beasts, will stand up to anybody.

The word "beasts" should properly be used about lions, leopards, tigers, wolves, foxes, dogs, monkeys, and others which rage about with tooth and claw—with the exception of snakes. They are called Beasts because of the violence with which they rage, and are known as "wild" (*ferus*) because they are accustomed to freedom by nature and are governed (*ferantur*) by their own wishes. They wander hither and thither, fancy free, and they go wherever they want to go.

The name "Lion" (*leo*) has been turned into Latin from a Greek root, for it is called "*leon*" in Greek—but this is a muddled name, partly corrupted, since "*leon*" has also been translated as "king" from Greek into Latin, owing to the fact that he is the Prince of All Animals.

They say that the litters of these creatures come in threes. The short ones with curly manes are peaceful: the tall ones with plain hair are fierce.

The nature of their brows and tail-tufts is an index to their disposition. Their courage is seated in their hearts, while their constancy is in their heads. They fear the creaking of wheels, but are frightened by fires even more so.

A lion, proud in the strength of his own nature, knows not how to mingle his ferocity with all and sundry, but, like the king he is, disdains to have a lot of different wives.

Scientists say that Leo has three principal characteristics.

His first feature is that he loves to saunter on the tops of mountains. Then, if he should happen to be pursued by hunting men, the smell of the hunters reaches up to him, and he disguises his spoor behind him with his tail. Thus the sportsmen cannot track him.

It was in this way that our Savior (i.e., the Spiritual Lion of the Tribe of Judah, the Rod of Jesse, the Lord of Lords, the Son of God) once hid the spoor of his love in the high places, until, being sent by the Father, he came down into the womb of the Virgin Mary and saved the human race which had perished. Ignorant of the fact that his spoor could be concealed, the Devil (i.e., the hunter of humankind) dared to pursue him with temptations like a mere man. Even the angels themselves who were on high, not recognizing his spoor, said to those who were going up with him when he ascended to his reward: "Who is this King of Glory?"

The Lion's second feature is that when he sleeps, he seems to keep his eyes open.

In this very way, Our Lord also, while sleeping in the body, was buried after being crucified—yet his Godhead was awake. As it is said in the *Song of Songs*, "I am asleep and my heart is awake," or, in the Psalm, "Behold, he that keepeth Israel shall neither slumber nor sleep."

The third feature is this, that when a lioness gives birth to her cubs, she brings them forth dead and lays them up lifeless for three days—until their father, coming on the third day, breathes in their faces and makes them alive.

Just so did the Father Omnipotent raise Our Lord Jesus Christ from the dead on the third day. Quoth Jacob: "He shall sleep like a lion, and the lion's whelp shall be raised."

So far as their relations with men are concerned, the nature of lions is that they do not get angry unless they are wounded.

Any decent human ought to pay attention to this. For men do get angry when they are not wounded, and they oppress the innocent although the law of Christ bids them to let even the guilty go free.

The compassion of lions, on the contrary, is clear from innumerable examples—for they spare the prostrate; they allow such captives as they come across to go back to their own country; they prey on men rather than on women, and they do not kill children except when they are very hungry.

Furthermore, lions abstain from over-eating: in the first place, because they only take food and drink on alternate days—and frequently, if digestion has not followed, they are even in the habit of putting off the day for dinner. In the second place, they pop their paws carefully into their mouths and pull out the meat of their own accord, when they have eaten too much. Indeed, when they have to run away from somebody, they perform the same action if they are full up.

Lack of teeth is a sign of old age in lions.

They copulate the backward way. Nor are they the only ones, but also Lynxes, Camels, Elephants, Rhinoceroses, Tigers, and Hyenas.

When they first have babies, they produce five whelps. Then, one by one, they reduce the number in succeeding years. Finally, when they have come down to one, the maternal fertility disappears and they become sterile forever afterward . . . .

FROM *The Ordinal of Alchemy*. THOMAS NORTON (1477)

Thomas Norton (*c.* 1433-1513) was reputed England's leading alchemist during the reign of Edward IV. His *Ordinal of Alchemy* (1477) shares the concerns of all medieval works on the subject: how to make the philosopher's stone described in Arabian texts and how to transform base metals into precious ones. The philosopher's stone, or elixir—familiar to fans of the Harry Potter series—was credited with a range of powers, from the transmutation of metals to the granting of eternal life. Several medieval authorities, including Avicenna (980-1037), the great Arabian scholar whom Norton cites, denied the possibility of a real transmutation of metals, but the idea proved seductive enough to withstand criticism and failure. As Norton's emphasis on religious matters indicates, alchemy had a spiritual side as well as a mundane one: it offered a path to purification and enlightenment, and its secrets could be fully apprehended only by souls in grace. Although Norton promises to explain everything in a "plain and homely style," his description of how to make philosopher's stone, not surprisingly, rivals that of his colleagues in its use of obscure jargon. The "Proem" of his book, here reproduced, should be of particular interest to students of Chaucer's *Canterbury Tales*. Norton shares many of the Canon Yeoman's observations regarding alchemical language. As a speaker who demystifies the very rhetorical strategies that he then employs, Norton also resembles Chaucer's Pardoner. Our translation is based on the 1975 edition by John Reidy for the Early English Text Society. The word "clerk" has been translated variously as cleric or scholar; readers should remember that most scholars were also men of the cloth.

> To the honor of God, one in persons three,
> This book is made so that laymen can see,
> And scholars also after my decease,
> Whereby all laymen who take pains
> To seek by alchemy great riches to win,
> May find good counsel before they such work begin,
> And great deceptions they can hereby eschew,
> And by this doctrine know false men from true.
> Nevertheless scholars great secrets here may learn,
> But all laymen shall find here cause to fear,
> And to beware of false illusions
> Which multipliers [alchemists] work with their arguments.
> Because I do not desire worldly fame,
> Except your good prayers, unknown shall be my name,
> That no man hereafter should search or look,
> But wisely consider the flowers of this book.
> If you search every state which is within mankind,
> Many people may you find
> Who become interested in alchemy
> Only out of appetite for wealth and luxury,
> Like popes and cardinals of dignity,
> Archbishops and bishops of high degree,
> Like abbots and priors of religion,
> Like friars, hermits, and priest, many a one,
> And kings, with princes, lords great of blood,
> For every estate desires this good,
> And merchants also, who dwell in the fire
> Of burning covetousness, crave this thing;
> And common workmen will not be left out,
> For they love this craft as much as the lords.
> Like goldsmiths, whom we should the least reprove,
> Since the sights of their craft moves them to belief,
> But it's a wonder that weavers deal with such works,
> Freemasons and tanners and poor parish clerks,
> Stainers (of windows) and glaziers will not cease to try,
> And even silly tinkers will take pains,

With great presumptuousness, but yet some color was
For all such men who give tincture to glass.
But many artificers have been overly swift,
With credulous haste to smoke away their goods,
And all be it that loss makes them smart,
Yet ever in hope continued their heart,
Trusting sometime to speed right well,
Of many such truly I can tell,
Who in this hope continued all their life,
Whereby they became poor and failed to thrive.
It had been good for them to have left off
Betimes, because they found nothing but taunts,
For truly he that is not a great scholar,
Is foolish and lewd to meddle with that work.
You may well trust it is no small thing,
To know all the secrets pertaining to mine,
For it is a most profound philosophy,
The subtle science of holy Alchemy,
About which science I here intend to write,
Although I should not write in too complicated a fashion,
Because he that wishes the common people to teach,
He must for them use plain and common speech.
Even though I write in plain and homely fashion,
No good man should such writing despise.
All the masters who write of this solemn work,
They make their books to many men full dark,
Through poetry, and parables, and metaphors also,
Which to scholars cause much pain and woe,
Because when it comes time to test their practice,
They lose their investments, as men see every day.
Hermes, al-Razi, Geber, and Avicenna,
Merlin, Ortolane, Democritus, and Morienus,
Bacon and Ramon, with many other authors,
Write ambiguously, and Aristotle also;
For when they write about this with their pen,
With their cloudy explanations they stupefy men.
From laymen, from scholars and from every man,
They hide this art so no man can gain access to it
Through their books, although they give such good reasons,
That many people are brought into despair.

Yet Anaxagoras wrote plainest of them all,
In his book about natural conversions,
Of all the old fathers that ever I found,
He best disclosed this science's ground,
Thereby causing Aristotle's great envy,
Who rebukes him unrightfully,
In many places, which I can report,
Trying to ensure I would not to him [Anaxagoras] resort.
For he had great learning and love,
God have his soul in bliss with him above.
And such as sowed the envious seed,
God forgive them their misdeed.
....
    My pity constrains me
To show the truth in words plain and few,
So that you may from false doctrine flee,
If you give credence to this book and to me,
Avoid the books full of recipes,
For all such recipes are full of deceit;
Trust not such recipes, and learn well this cause,
Nothing is wrought but by its proper cause;
Wherefore any practice falls far behind,
Where knowledge of the cause is not in mind,
Therefore remember evermore wisely,
To work only when you know how & why.
Also he that would in this art proceed,
Must learn to avoid falsehood indeed,
For truth is the good which this art must guide,
Wherefore you may never to falsehood slide,
But steadfastly your mind must be set,
False colored metal never to counterfeit,
Like those who use blanchers [whitening] or citrinations [yellowing]
That will not withstand examinations,
To make false plate as they can,
Or to beguile money from some good true man.
But God has made that of this blessed art,
All those who are false shall have of it no part.
He must have grace that would for this art sue,
Therefore of right this person must be true,
Also he may not be troubled in his mind,

With outward charges which this art would find;
And he that would have his intent,
He must have riches sufficient.
In many ways he may not look,
But only pursue the order of this book,
Named the Ordinal of Alchemy,
The great creed, the perpetual standard;
For just as the Ordinal sets for priests out
The service of the days as they go about,
So the effects of all the unordered books in Alchemy,
Are in this book here laid out orderly.
Therefore this book to an Alchemist wise,
Is a book of incomparable price,
Whose truth shall never be defiled,
Although it appears in a homely way compiled.
And as I had this art by grace from heaven,
I give you the same here in chapters seven,
As largely as I by my fidelity may,
By license of the dreadful Judge of doomsday.
The first chapter shall all men teach,
What manner of people may this science reach,
And why the true science of Alchemy
Is by old fathers called blessed and holy.
In the second chapter may be seen
How to enjoy this practice without great pain.
The third chapter, for the love of one,
Shall truly disclose the matter of our stone,
Which the Arabians call the Elixir,
What it is made of you shall there understand.
The fourth chapter teaches the gross work,
A foul labor not meant for a clerk,
In which is found much great travail,
With many perils, at which many fail,
The fifth chapter is about the subtle work,
Which God ordained only for a clerk,
But only a few scholars can it comprehend,
Therefore to few men is this science sent.
The sixth chapter is about the concord and love
Between low nature and the heavenly sphere above,
True knowledge whereof greatly advances clerics,

And greatly furthers our wondrous works.
The seventh chapter shall teach you truly,
The fearful control of all fires.
Now the Sovereign Lord God speed me and guide me,
For to my matters will I now proceed.
Praying all men who find this book,
To keep my soul in mind in their prayers,
And that no man for better nor worse,
Change my writing, for dread of God's curse,
For a sentence shall not seem immediately intelligible,
There may wise men find some marvelous secret knowledge;
And the changing of even one syllable,
May make this book unprofitable.
Therefore trust not to one reading or two,
But 20 times would not be overstating,
Because it contains many a ponderous sentence,
Even if it falls short of eloquence,
But the best thing that you to have done,
Is to read many books, including this one.

"On Dreams." Macrobius (c. 395-423)

The fifth-century grammarian and philosopher Macrobius was considered one of the leading authorities on the nature and interpretation of dreams throughout the Middle Ages. His *Commentary on the Dream of Scipio* takes as its subject Cicero's *Dream of Scipio*, in which the elder Scipio appears to his grandson and describes the afterlife and the nature of the universe. Our excerpt covers one of the most influential parts of Macrobius's commentary: his elaborate system for categorizing and interpreting dreams. Chaucer cites Macrobius as an authority on this topic several times, including in "The Nun's Priest's Tale" and in *The Book of the Duchess*.

(1) After these prefatory remarks, there remains another matter to be considered before taking up the text of *Scipio's Dream*. We must first describe the many varieties of dreams recorded by the ancients, who have classified and defined the various types that have appeared to men in their sleep, wherever they might be. Then we shall be able to decide to which type the dream we are discussing belongs.

(2) All dreams may be classified under five main types: there is the enigmatic dream, in Greek *oneiros*, in Latin *somnium*; second, there is the prophetic vision, in Greek *horama*, in Latin *visio*; third, there is the oracular dream, in Greek *chrematismos*, in Latin *oraculum*; fourth, there is the nightmare, in Greek *enypnion*, in Latin *insomnium*; and last, the apparition, in Greek *phantasma*, which Cicero, when he has occasion to use the word, calls *visum*.

(3) The last two, the nightmare and the apparition, are not worth interpreting since they have no prophetic significance.

(4) Nightmares may be caused by mental or physical distress, or anxiety about the future: the patient experiences in dreams vexations similar to those that disturb him during the day. As examples of the mental variety, we might mention the lover who dreams of possessing his sweetheart or of losing her, or the man who fears the plots or might of an enemy and is confronted with him in his dream or seems to be fleeing him. The physical variety might be illustrated by one who has overindulged in eating or drinking and dreams that he is either choking with food or overburdening himself, or by one who has been suffering from hunger or thirst and dreams that he is craving and searching for food or drink or has found it. Anxiety about the future would cause a man to dream that he is gaining a prominent position or office as he hoped or that he is being deprived of it as he feared.

(5) Since these dreams and others like them arise from some condition or circumstance that irritates a man during the day and consequently disturbs him when he falls asleep, they flee when he awakes and vanish into thin air. Thus the name *insomnium* was given, not because such dreams occur "in sleep"—in this respect nightmares are like other types—but because they are noteworthy only during their course and afterwards have no importance or meaning.

(6) Virgil, too, considers nightmares deceitful: "False are the dreams (*insomnia*) sent by departed spirits to their sky." He used the word "sky" with reference to our mortal realm because the earth bears the same relation to the regions of the dead as the heavens bear to the earth. Again, in describing the passion of love, whose concerns are always accompanied by nightmares, he says: "Oft to her heart

rushes back the chief's valour, oft his glorious stock; his looks and words cling fast within her bosom, and the pang withholds calm rest from her limbs." And a moment later: "Anna, my sister, what dreams (*insomnia*) thrill me with fears?"

(7) The apparition (*phantasma* or *visum*) comes upon one in the moment between wakefulness and slumber, in the so-called "first cloud of sleep." In this drowsy condition he thinks he is still fully awake and imagines he sees specters rushing at him or wandering vaguely about, differing from natural creatures in size and shape, and hosts of diverse things, either delightful or disturbing. To this class belongs the incubus, which, according to popular belief, rushes upon people in sleep and presses them with a weight which they can feel.

(8) The two types just described are of no assistance in foretelling the future; but by means of the other three we are gifted with the powers of divination.

We call a dream oracular in which a parent, or a pious or revered man, or a priest, or even a god clearly reveals what will or will not transpire, and what action to take or to avoid.

(9) We call a dream a prophetic vision if it actually comes true. For example, a man dreams of the return of a friend who has been staying in a foreign land, thoughts of whom never enter his mind. He goes out and presently meets his friend and embraces him. Or in his dream he agrees to accept a deposit, and early the next day a man runs anxiously to him, charging him with the safekeeping of his money and committing secrets to his trust.

(10) By an enigmatic dream we mean one that conceals with strange shapes and veils with ambiguity the true meaning of the information being offered, and requires an interpretation for its understanding. We need not explain further the nature of this dream since everyone knows from experience what it is. There are five varieties of it: personal, alien, social, public, and universal.

(11) It is called personal when one dreams that he himself is doing or experiencing something; alien, when he dreams this about someone else; social, when his dream involves others and himself; public, when he dreams that some misfortune or benefit has befallen the

city, forum, theater, public walls, or other public enterprise; universal, when he dreams that some change has taken place in the sun, moon, planets, sky, or regions of the earth.

(12) The dream which Scipio reports that he saw embraces the three reliable types mentioned above, and also has to do with all five varieties of the enigmatic dream. It is oracular since the two men who appeared before him and revealed his future, Aemilius Paulus and Scipio the Elder, were both his father, both were pious and revered men, and both were affiliated with the priesthood. It is a prophetic vision since Scipio saw the regions of his abode after death and his future condition. It is an enigmatic dream because the truths revealed to him were couched in words that hid their profound meaning and could not be comprehended without skillful interpretation.

It also embraces the five varieties of the last type. (13) It is personal since Scipio himself was conducted to the regions above and learned of his future. It is alien since he observed the estates to which the souls of others were destined. It is social since he learned that for men with merits similar to his the same places were being prepared as for himself. It is public since he foresaw the victory of Rome and the destruction of Carthage, his triumph on the Capitoline, and the coming civil strife. And it is universal since by gazing up and down he was initiated into the wonders of the heavens, the great celestial circles, and the harmony of the revolving spheres, things strange and unknown to mortals before this; in addition he witnessed the movements of the stars and planets and was able to survey the whole earth.

(14) It is incorrect to maintain that Scipio was not the proper person to have a dream that was both public and universal inasmuch as he had not yet attained the highest office but, as he himself admitted, was still ranked "not much higher than a private soldier." The critics say that dreams concerning the welfare of the state are not to be considered significant unless military or civil officers dream them, or unless many plebeians have the same dream.

(15) They cite the incident in Homer when, before the assembled Greeks, Agamemnon disclosed a dream that he had had about a forthcoming battle. Nestor, who helped the army quite as much with

his prudence as all the youth with their might, by way of instilling confidence in the dream said that in matters of general welfare they had to confide in the dream of a king, whereas they would repudiate the dream of anyone else.

(16) However, the point in Scipio's favor was that although he had not yet held the consulship or a military command, he—who himself was destined to lead that campaign—was dreaming about the coming destruction of Carthage, was witnessing the public triumph in his honor, and was even learning of the secrets of nature; for he excelled as much in philosophy as in deeds of courage.

(17) Because, in citing Virgil above as an authority for the unreliability of nightmares, we excerpted a verse from his description of the twin portals of dreams, someone may take the occasion to inquire why false dreams are allotted to the gate of ivory and trustworthy ones to the gate of horn. He should avail himself of the help of Porphyry, who, in his *Commentaries*, makes the following remarks on a passage in Homer presenting the same distinction between gates: "All truth is concealed. (18) Nevertheless, the soul, when it is partially disengaged from bodily functions during sleep, at times gazes and at times peers intently at the truth, but does not apprehend it; and when it gazes it does not see with clear and direct vision, but rather with a dark obstructing veil interposed."

(19) Virgil attests that this is natural in the following lines: "Behold— for all the cloud, which now, drawn over thy sight, dulls thy mortal vision and with dank pall enshrouds thee, I will tear away."

(20) If, during sleep, this veil permits the vision of the attentive soul to perceive the truth, it is thought to be made of horn, the nature of which is such that, when thinned, it becomes transparent. When the veil dulls the vision and prevents its reaching the truth, it is thought to be made of ivory, the composition of which is so dense that no matter how thin a layer of it may be, it remains opaque.

NOTES

1   Nancy Siraisi, *Medieval and Early Renaissance Medicine: An Introduction to Knowledge and Practice* (Chicago, IL: U of Chicago P, 1990) 38.

2   David C. Lindberg, ed., "Introduction," *Science in the Middle Ages* (Chicago, IL: U of Chicago P, 1978) xiii–xiv.

3   Pearl Kibri and Nancy G. Siraisi, "The Institutional Setting: The Universities," in *Science in the Middle Ages*, ed. David C. Lindberg (Chicago, IL: U of Chicago P, 1978) 132.

4   For learning and rationality as the two qualities defining university-trained physicians, SEE R.K. French, *Medicine Before Science* (Cambridge: Cambridge UP, 2003).

5   Siraisi 172.

6   Huling E. Ussery, *Chaucer's Physician: Medicine and Literature in Fourteenth-Century England* (New Orleans, LA: Tulane University, 1971) 65–68; Siraisi 21.

7   French 2.

8   Ussery 9.

9   Bartholomew Anglicus, *On the Properties of Things: Trevisa's Translation of Bartholomaeus Anglicus'* De Proprietatibus Rerum, ed. M.C. Seymour (Oxford: Clarendon P, 1975); our translation.

10   French 158.

11   Charles H. Talbot, "Medicine," in *Science in the Middle Ages*, ed. David C. Lindberg (Chicago, IL: U of Chicago P, 1978) 414.

12   Geoffrey Chaucer, "A Treatise on the Astrolabe," *The Riverside Chaucer*, ed. Larry D. Benson (New York: Houghton Mifflin, 1987) 668–69.

13   Lindberg xii; Siraisi 91.

14   William A. Wallace, "The Philosophical Setting of Medieval Science," in *Science in the Middle Ages*, ed. David C. Lindberg (Chicago, IL: U of Chicago P, 1978) 105.

15   All references to the Chester Cycle are to *The Chester Mystery Cycle: A New Edition with Modernised Spelling*, ed. David Mills (East Lansing, MI: Colleagues P, 1992).

16   Rosanne Gasse, "The Practice of Medicine in Piers Plowman," *The Chaucer Review* 39.2 (2004): 177–97.

17   This figure also shows up in the oral tradition of mummer's plays; SEE David Lawton, "Sacrilege and Theatricality: The Croxton *Play of the Sacrament*," *Journal of Medieval and Early Modern Studies* 33.2 (2003): 287.

18   *The Play of the Sacrament*, in *Medieval Drama*, ed. David Bevington (Boston, MA: Houghton Mifflin, 1987) 776. All references are to this edition.

19   Victor Sherb, "The Earthly and Divine Physicians: *Christus Medicus* in the Croxton *Play of the Sacrament*," in *The Body and The Text: Comparative Essays in Literature and Medicine*, ed. Bruce Clarke and Wendell Aycock (Lubbock, TX: Texas Tech UP, 1990) 162.

20   Robert P. Multhaug, "The Science of Matter," in *Science in the Middle Ages*, ed. David C. Lindberg (Chicago, IL: U of Chicago P, 1978) 379.

21 H.L. Ogrinc Will, "Western Society and Alchemy, 1200-1500," *Journal of Medieval History* 6 (1980): 103-32.

22 Lee Patterson, "Perpetual Motion: Alchemy and the Technology of the Self," *SAC* 15 (1993): 50-54; See also John Read, *Prelude to Chemistry: An Outline of Alchemy, Its Literature and Relationships* (Cambridge, MA: MIT Press, 1966).

23 Patterson, "Perpetual Motion" 50; on the need for divine aid, SEE Sheila Fisher, *Chaucer's Poetic Alchemy: A Study of Value and Its Transformation in The Canterbury Tales* (New York: Garland, 1988) 200.

24 See Charles Muscatine, *Chaucer and the French Tradition* (Berkeley, CA: U of California P, 1957) 213-21.

25 Mark J. Bruhn, "Art, Anxiety, and Alchemy in *The Canon Yeoman's Tale*," *The Chaucer Review* 33.3 (1999): 294; and Patterson, "Perpetual Motion" 55. For Chaucer's knowledge of alchemy, SEE Pauline Aiken, "Vincent of Beauvais and Chaucer's Knowledge of Alchemy," *Studies in Philology* 41.3 (1944): 371-89.

26 Irma Taavitsainen and Paivi Pahta, eds., *Medical and Scientific Writing in Late Medieval English* (Cambridge: Cambridge UP, 2004).

27 Gail Kern Paster, *Humoring the Body: Emotions and the Shakespearean Stage* (Chicago, IL: U of Chicago P, 2004) 136, 4, 10.

28 Jerry Stannard, "Natural History," in *Science in the Middle Ages*, ed. David C. Lindberg (Chicago, IL: U of Chicago P, 1978) 435.

29 Debra Hassig, "Introduction," in *The Mark of the Beast: The Medieval Bestiary in Art, Life, and Literature*, ed. Debra Hassig (New York: Garland, 1999) xi-xix.

30 Margaret Haist, "The Lion, Bloodline, and Kingship," in *The Mark of the Beast: The Medieval Bestiary in Art, Life, and Literature*, ed. Debra Hassig (New York: Garland, 1999) 3-16.

31 Stannard 429-60, 430.

32 Galen, *On the Usefulness of the Parts of the Body*, trans. Margaret Tallmadge May (Ithaca, NY: Cornell UP, 1968) 2: 628-29.

33 Siraisi 103.

34 Thomas Laqueur, *Making Sex: Body and Gender from the Greeks to Freud* (Cambridge, MA: Harvard UP, 1990) 35.

35 Walter Clyde Curry, "More About Chaucer's Wife of Bath," *PMLA* 37.1 (1922): 48.

36 Talbot 414.

37 Quoted in Carol Falvo Heffernan, *The Melancholy Muse: Chaucer, Shakespeare, and Early Medicine* (Pittsburgh, PA: Duquesne UP, 1995) 13.

38 For the Summoner as choleric, SEE Laurel Braswell-Means, "A New Look at an Old Patient: Chaucer's Summoner and Medieval Physiognomia," *The Chaucer Review* 25.3 (1991): 266-75.

39 Pauline Aiken, "Vincent of Beauvais and Dame Pertelote's Knowledge of Medicine," *Speculum* 10.3 (1935): 281-87.

40 Mary Douglas, *Natural Symbols: Explorations in Cosmology*, 2nd ed. (London: Barrie and Jenkins, 1973) 98-99.

41 Paster 5.

42 Walter Clyde Curry, *Chaucer and the Medieaval Sciences*, 2nd ed. (London: Barnes and Noble, 1960); on the Reeve, SEE Walter Clyde Curry, "Chaucer's Reeve and Miller," *PMLA* 35.2 (1920): 189-209.

43 John Block Friedman, "Another Look at Chaucer and the Physiognomists," *Studies in Philology* 78 (1981): 139, 146.

44 John Livingston Lowes, "The Loveres Maladye of Heroes," *Modern Philology* 11.4 (1914): 491-546.

45 Heffernan 7, 22.

46 Michael St. John, *Chaucer's Dream Visions: Courtliness and Individual Identity* (Aldershot and Burlington, VT: Ashgate, 2000) 10.

47 St. John 20-62.

48 Siraisi 157.

49 Gilbertus Anglicus, *Healing and Society in Medieval England: A Middle English Translation of the Pharmaceutical Writings of Gilbertus Anglicus*, ed. and trans. Faye Marie Getz (Madison, WI: U of Wisconsin P, 1991) xvi.

50 Siraisi 42.

CHAPTER VIII

"To Flaundres Wol I Go"

International Influences and Exchanges

INTRODUCTION

LATE MEDIEVAL CONCEPTIONS OF THE WORLD

*A*mong the stage properties required for a performance of the Chester Cycle is a medieval *mappa mundi* ("map of the world"). R.M. Lumiansky and David Mills propose that this map served as part of the set, a visualization of the universe that God creates at the beginning of the pageant.[1] Since the Banns [an announcement of the plays read in the streets] refer to the set for this pageant as "Paradise," we can assume that the Drapers' wagon was decorated—lavishly, perhaps—to evoke the Garden of Eden, complete with its tree of knowledge. According to medieval maps and travelogues, Eden had a geographical location: it was "the highest land on earth," as Mandeville writes in his *Travels*, "so high it touches the sphere of the moon" (SEE DOCUMENTS BELOW). The Chester map probably followed convention in assigning Paradise a place above Asia at the top of the world. Medieval maps usually organized the three known continents in a so-called T-O formation, where the "T" represents rivers dividing the world into three continents, with Europe and Africa taking up the lower section of the circle and Asia the upper. Jerusalem—the premier destination for medieval pilgrims—was located at the center to reflect its religious significance, while England was squashed into the lower left corner. As this description suggests, *mappae mundi* differ from modern maps in that they pay more heed to religious ideology than to accuracy and proportion or to political boundaries. Their primary purpose was to testify to God's shaping hand in human affairs.

Medieval maps, plays, and travelogues can tell us a lot about how medieval subjects perceived their world. Despite their apparent differences, these works attest to common assumptions about the relations between geography, history, and individual identity. If geography was to a large extent cosmographic—reflecting spiritual truth rather than actual experience—so was history, which revealed divine providence just as surely as the shape of the world did. In fact, the two—geography and history, place and event—often appear indistinguishable in medieval artifacts. The famous Hereford map, for example, gives reliable information about pilgrimage and trading routes in Western Europe but provides no such information for Asia and Africa. Instead, it represents in tableau form several of the biblical incidents staged by the cycle plays, including Noah's Flood (the biblical event that also helps Chaucer's "hende" Nicholas to convince the carpenter to hole up in his attic) and the expulsion of Adam and Eve from Eden. These same biblical narratives determine Mandeville's account of the Eastern landscape: Paradise is the one place on earth, he tells us, left unaffected by Noah's flood.

If we imagine the draper who played the Chester God wearing his gilded mask, standing near the edge of his wagon, and unrolling his cloth map towards the audience, we can see that this prop imported into the pageant rich possibilities of meaning. It provided a visual tableau of God's omnipresence in the world. It also supplied an instantaneous verification of God's assertion that "Now heaven and earth is made" (5). Depending on its quality and size, the Chester map might have given the audiences of the plays a detailed illustration of God's creation, from the "fowls in the firmament flying" to the "great whales in the sea swimming" (58-59). The Hereford map, probably similar to the one used in the Chester Cycle, depicts the beasts specified by the Chester God as well as other, less common ones, like hump-backed camels, flying salamanders, and beaked, horned satyrs. It includes in its exhaustive catalogue of bizarre figures the *cynocephali*—the dog-headed people that Bartholomew Anglicus describes in our excerpt—and the "tigolope," a web-footed humanoid. Many of the map's creatures derive from the same classical sources as the creatures described in contemporary travelogues and geography primers. Like these other works, the Hereford map evinces a quasi-anthropological interest in alternative modes of organizing experience; it represents, for example, the funeral practices of the "essedones," who preferred to eat their dead parents rather than subject them to the humiliation of becoming food for worms. *Mappae mundi* are encyclopedic in their representation of familiar and fantastical life forms.

Although we might expect the theologically driven perspective to be challenged by empirical evidence, pilgrims to the Holy Land tended to share in a cosmographic view of the world. *The Book of Margery Kempe*, for example, focuses on Margery's suffering and on her affective response to the sacred places in the East; it records little by way of ethnographic or geographic detail. European travelers to Asia and Africa were also interested in finding evidence of Christianity there, in the form of actual Christians like the Nubians (Ethiopians) or mythical ones like Prester John. The real and imagined presence of Christians in Asia and Africa helped address European anxieties regarding a central contradiction of the medieval world: the East was the place of origin and salvation for Christians, but it was mainly inhabited by nonbelievers. The desire to resolve that contradiction informed the actions of crusaders, missionaries, and conquistadors; according to his diary, Christopher Columbus set sail for India hoping to effect the conversion of its people.[2] *Mandeville's Travels*, which imagines a world inhabited by Christians and would-be Christians, might have owed its popularity to its characterization of the world as a stage for Christianity.[3]

On the whole, European travelers to the East saw what they expected to see—authoritative descriptions of the world determined individual travelers' actual experiences of it, especially insofar as these were moved by religious goals. For pilgrims to the Holy Land, the Bible provided the surest travel guide, one that domesticated the alien landscapes by reference to familiar stories.[4] Pilgrims also frequently recorded their experiences for others' use; some 526 accounts of pilgrimages to the Holy Land survive for the period of 1100-1500.[5] Margery Kempe, for example, modeled her pilgrimage—and her description of it—on Birgitta of Sweden's (*c.* 1303-73).[6] Readers and travelers alike granted full authority to books like *Mandeville's Travels* and viewed their fantastical representations as factual accounts. In fact, Mandeville's status as a fictional narrator was not fully recognized until the nineteenth century, and Columbus used the *Travels* as a source when planning his circumnavigation of the world. Surviving letters suggest that until his dying day the great explorer remained convinced that he had landed on the islands near Cathay (China) that Mandeville describes.[7]

Not surprisingly, the characters in the cycle plays, drawn from biblical history, often evoke a cosmographic sense of the world. In the Wakefield "Herod the Great," for example, the messenger claims that Herod's sovereignty extends

From Paradise to Padua to Mount Flascon,
From Egypt to Mantua unto Kemptown,
From Sarceny to Susa, to Greece it abounds,
Both Normandy and Norway laud his crown
His renown
Can no tongue tell,
From heaven unto hell.[8] (42-51)

Herod's messenger follows late medieval maps and travelogues in locating paradise, hell, and heaven in the geographical world. The effect of this speech is ironic. The audience understood the pervading cosmographic structure to which Herod's own anachronistic curses to "God's dear nails" (116) unwittingly referred—Christ's "renown" *really* united the world. The messenger's speech thus derives its particular force from the audience's knowledge to which he is not privy. Beginning with the "Creation of Paradise" and ending with "Judgment Day," the cycle plays stage temporally what medieval maps represent spatially—a world united in Christ (Christ hovers over the world in the Hereford map). In the Wakefield pageant, the threat that the pagan tyrant poses to the Christian community is thus contained by the overall structure of the plays. At once alien and ridiculous, Herod's antics must have provoked fear but also laughter.

The world view of much medieval art and literature asserts the fundamental coherence of the Christian world by inviting medieval subjects to think of Europe as homogeneous. Indeed, medieval maps, paintings, and plays provide some of the visual images that were so important to medieval Christianity. The appearance of Christ in the plays and paintings, dressed in a manner similar to the viewer, illustrates a characteristic tendency of the medieval imagination. The "juxtaposition of the cosmic-universal and the mundane particular [ensured that] however vast Christendom might be, and was sensed to be, it manifested itself variously" to particular communities as "replications of themselves."[9] In plays, as in many medieval paintings, the town becomes a microcosm of the larger Christian community, its history a replica of the larger Christian history, its Christ tangibly present as He was elsewhere in the Christian world.[10]

This widespread sense of Christian cohesiveness was accompanied by the exclusion of "others"—the enemy "turks" of medieval crusades, the pagan figures of the drama, the monsters haunting the margins of the maps, and the "satyrs and other men wondrously shaped" who crowd accounts of the Far East (SEE Bartholomew Anglicus, BELOW). Because, during the medieval period, little actual information was available regarding Africa and Asia,[11] Western representations relied on a handful of sources and a great deal of imagination.[12] The pagans, monsters, and cannibals that populate Asia in the medieval European imagination share affinities with Cain, the first biblical murderer, excluded by divine decree from the godly community. According to medieval legends, Cain bore a divine sign—most commonly, a horn—which turned him into one of the monstrous figures that the *mappae mundi* depict and Mandeville and Anglicus describe. Mandeville is often praised for his celebration of Asian diversity and his sympathetic treatment of Muslims; however, he follows an orthodox line of thinking when he claims that Asians descend from Noah's son Ham, in whose "time many devils came in the likeness of men and lay with the women of his race and begat on them giants and other monsters of horrible shape—some without heads, some with dog's heads, and many other misshapen and disfigured men."

These biblical readings of race establish European superiority by literally demonizing the non-European other. As such, they form part of a pervasive discourse of differentiation, of which the most violent expression is the crusades, which in the earlier Middle Ages had united Christian knights in the repeated attempt to wrest control of the Holy Land from Eastern hands. Although they failed to secure Jerusalem, the crusades made a lasting impact on Western culture. The adventures of the crusaders became a favorite topic of late medieval literature, as we saw in Chapter 5. The thirteenth-century Middle-English romance *Richard Coeur de Lion* celebrates, for example, the crusading king's ruthless treatment of the Saracens; when ambassadors from Saladin come to negotiate a truce, Richard serves them roasted Saracen heads, which he himself proceeds to eat with great gusto. The primal conflict between Muslim and Christian is a staple of medieval romance, even if this conflict is resolved in a variety of ways. In many works, like *The Chanson de Roland* (1100), the conversion of the pagan knight signals the superiority of the Christian religion just as surely as, if a little less brutally than, Richard's cannibalism.[13] This strain of medieval literature proved a rich one in England, leading variously to Chaucer's "The Man of Law's Tale," Spenser's *Faerie Queene* (1596), and Shakespeare's *Othello* (1604).

The topic of medieval world views is one likely to make modern subjects, used to more scientific approaches to geography, feel smug and superior. But in fact the dualistic thinking that marked the West's relationship to the Middle East in medieval accounts has left a lasting legacy, one perhaps more easily detected these days than it was 20 years ago. As an example of this phenomenon, we have included Mandeville's anecdote about the Muslim warlord Catolonabes, who, well aware of the power of religious ideology to determine actual experience, turns young men into assassins by promising them "dalliance" with maidens in his "Paradise" (SEE BELOW).

ENGLAND AND THE CONTINENT

Although late medieval society was not nationalistic in a modern sense, fourteenth-century and fifteenth-century representations of Flanders and the Flemish—or Lombardy and the Lombards, or France and the French—suggest that English people were beginning to fashion an identity in opposition to their European neighbors. The discourses of differentiation that shaped this emergent identity aimed at a range of continental neighbors. Some countries, however, were more frequent targets than others, because of their importance to the English way of life. Xenophobic views of Flanders, for example, can ironically be explained by its proximity to England and its significance as a trading partner. Designating Flanders as a separate space—where prodigious quantities of beer were drunk and huge piles of money made—was a crucial step in the development of a specifically English identity. France, in a similar geographic relation to England, did not lend itself as easily to this purpose as Flanders. For one thing, the English monarchy was Anglo-Norman and therefore retained close ties to the French language and French culture (as we saw in Chapter 1, the so-called Hundred Year's War was fought over the titles of "English" monarchs to French dominions). In addition, England's relationship with France was marked by a sense of cultural and linguistic inadequacy. In the course of his work, for example, Chaucer apologizes six times for the poverty of his language; as Ardis Butterfield puts it, "linguistic superiority" was "a privilege [that] belonged to those who wrote and spoke in Latin and French."[14] When Chaucer's Prioress insists on speaking French "after the scole of Stratford ate Bowe" (GP 125), she tries—and fails—to lay claim to that privilege. If the English felt inadequate in regards to French culture, however, they could and did learn to feel superior towards Flanders.

The comparisons that began to characterize English thinking about Europe during this period lead to the development of commonly held stereotypes. Our excerpt from the *Libelle of English Policy* (1436), which argues that controlling the seas would bring "profit" and "worship and salvation to England and all English men," provides a good illustration of this phenomenon:

> You have heard that two Flemings together
> Will undertake, before they go anywhere
> Before they rise once, to drink a barrel full
> Of good beer; so hard do they drink and pull,
> Under the board they piss as they sit.

Like modern ethnic jokes, these lines provoke laughter at the expense of a stereotyped "other" and thus enforce a sense of distinction based on national origin. The joke relies on shared assumptions: everyone has "heard" what "Flemings" are really like. And indeed, late medieval English literature routinely imagines the Flemish as drunkards. It is no coincidence that in *Piers Plowman* the prostitute Pernele of Flanders appears in a tavern. This stereotype informs Chaucer's decision to set his amoral Pardoner's tale—about three lubricious sots—in Flanders as well, a place he describes as festering with "riot, hazard, stywes, and taverns" (ParT 465). Insofar as none of the analogues and sources for the tale shares this setting, we may conclude that it reflects a conscious choice on Chaucer's part. David Wallace notes that while "it would be difficult to isolate a discourse of England in Chaucer... there is a discourse of Flanders. As a discourse, this bears some relation to a territory called Flanders, has consequences for those tagged as Flemish, but speaks most eloquently of the anxieties and desires of its English authors." Wallace further suggests that the references to Flanders and northern France in *The Canterbury Tales* aim "to raise a snicker from Chaucer's first audience."[15] Unanimous laughter at a clearly demarcated "other" is an effective way of building a sense of community, as Chaucer well knew.

Many late medieval works invite us to construe Flanders as a tavern writ large—a place of drunken, hedonistic excess—and to pass moral judgment accordingly. These works also urge their audiences to think of themselves as superior *in kind* to the vilified "Flemings." The political theorist Benedict Anderson associates this form of comparative thinking with the emergence of nationalism: nationalists view their nation as "'the best' in a competitive, *comparative field*."[16] Anglicus's mid-thirteenth-century description of the Flemish offers a contrast to these later representations, which might be called proto-nationalistic. According to Anglicus, the Flemish are "fair of speech, sad of bearing, honest of clothing, peaceable to their own neighbors, true and trusty to strangers." Although Anglicus makes generalizations based on nationality, by and large they are not disparaging (his description of Ireland is an exception), nor do they reflect a clear hierarchical understanding of the countries' relationships to one another. His book bears no mark of the "discourse of Flanders" that shapes *The Canterbury Tales*, *Piers Plowman*, and *The Libelle*.

Several factors contributed to the changes in English habits in their relationship to continental Europe during the late medieval period. Chaucer's description of the Squire's activities draws attention to one of them—England's prolonged war with France, discussed in Chapter I. During this century-long conflict, an unprecedented number of Englishmen were sent over to the regions mentioned in "The General Prologue" for diplomatic or military reasons. The reference to the squire's "chyvauchie" may indeed evoke a specific expedition, the so-called "crusade" that Richard II sent to Flanders in 1383, which resulted ingloriously in the sacking of the unfortified town of Ypres.[17] Once on the continent, men like the squire—soldiers and diplomats and servants—were able to note firsthand their similarities to and differences from their European neighbors. Chaucer himself is an example of this phenomenon. He traveled to Europe throughout the late 1360s, the 1370s, and the 1380s on royal business (SEE the "Mandate for Payment" IN THE DOCUMENTS BELOW). Scholars conjecture that one of Chaucer's first trips, to Navarre in southern France in 1366, involved a secret mission to Pedro of Castile (or Pedro the Cruel, as he was known for good reasons), an ally of the English in their wars against France. Chaucer also participated in his patron John of Gaunt's failed 1369 expedition to northern France; this expedition was one of many opportunities he had to travel "in Flaundres, in Artoys, and in Pycardie" (GP 85–86).[18] These regions are the birthplace of the *fabliaux*, a literary genre to which a number of *The Canterbury Tales* belong, including "The Miller's Tale" and "The Shipman's Tale." Chaucer seems to acknowledge a debt to these foreign places when his turn comes in *The Canterbury Tales*, since his tale of Sir Thopas, learned "longe agoon" (1999), is set in Flanders.

Not all of Chaucer's royal missions were militaristic in purpose; in 1372, for example, he went to the Italian city of Genoa to discuss the possibility of extending certain royal privileges to its merchants. The trip included a stop in Florence where he was first exposed to the ideas of the Italian Renaissance. Italy was far ahead of England in its cultural and economic development; in wealthy city-states like Florence, a thriving, secular, and mercantile society encouraged the making of money and of beautiful things. The latter were, of course, meant to display the former. The early humanist emphasis on worldly achievements encouraged an unparalleled flowering of letters, and many scholars identify 1341, the year that the poet Francesco Petrarca had himself named poet laureate before the Roman senate, as the beginning of the Renaissance. Petrarch (1304-74) and Boccaccio (1313-75) were still alive when Chaucer first visited Italy. Although it is unlikely that the young Englishman met these venerable old men, their works—and those of Dante (1265-1321), their illustrious predecessor—made a lasting impact on him, as he adopted and adapted Italian literary techniques throughout his career. Arguably the most significant debt Chaucer—and through him, English literature—owes to the Italian tradition was a new respect for the powers of the vernacular—the common or native language as opposed to the Latin favored by the clerical and political elite.[19] Dante had insisted that Italian could become as eloquent as Latin in *De Vulgari Eloquenti* (1303-05?) and, through his other works, had established it as a viable medium for great literature. Chaucer is often credited with doing for the English language what Dante did for the Italian; ironically, a specifically English literature originates in an Englishman's encounter with Italian letters. This shift away from Latin and towards the vernaculars played a crucial role in the emergence of nationalistic sensibilities in Europe. By choosing to write in English, Chaucer contributed to this shift—as did Wyclif, when he made available a vernacular Bible in 1382, and the English government, when it started using English for governmental purposes after 1362.

As Chaucer's mission to Italy suggests, the burgeoning mercantile economy of late medieval Europe encouraged exchanges of all kinds. Indeed, scholars of the medieval drama think it no accident that English drama flourished in the eastern towns, where trade with the Low Countries (roughly the area covered by modern Belgium and the Netherlands) was most active. The civic drama of the English towns shares many themes, preoccupations, and formal qualities with the plays put on in Flemish towns. Here, too, Alexandra Johnston argues, "the influences, in all probability, flowed from the continent to England." In her analysis of the activities of the Mercers in York, Johnston demonstrates that the men who traded with the Low Countries were often the same men who made decisions about staging the York Cycle. These "Merchant Adventurers," an organized group of English merchants involved in the wool trade on the continent, had experienced the flourishing dramatic traditions of the Low Countries and were attempting to replicate it at home. The whole morality tradition in England may be a Flemish export. The majority of extant morality plays—including *The Castle of Perseverance* (1405-25?), *Mankind* (1465-70?), and *Wisdom* (1465-70?)—hail from East Anglia, the region of England most closely involved in trade with Flanders.[20] *Everyman* (c. 1495), long considered the best of the English morality plays, is a translation of *Elckerlijc*, a Flemish play which won first prize at a *rederijkers* (or rhetoricians) contest in Antwerp in 1485 (these contests, sponsored by the Flemish Chambers of Rhetoric, have left hundreds of plays as opposed to the handful of surviving English manuscripts). The language of *Elckerlijc* suggests that the playwright targeted a mercantile audience. At least one member of this audience—the one who commissioned or produced the translation—thought the message relevant to Flemish and English merchants alike. In his influential *From Mankind to Marlowe*, David Bevington argues for the centrality of what he calls the "popular and indigenous" morality tradition to the development of English tragedy in the sixteenth century.[21] If indeed Flemish—rather than just indigenous—"popular" modes of theater helped set the stage for Marlowe and Shakespeare, then English letters may owe as important a debt to the Low Countries as to France or Italy.

Everyman is the first "English" play for which we have a printed text. This fact points us to another set of crucial exchanges, that is, those involving the printing trade. Early English printers relied almost entirely on continental expertise. With the exception of William Caxton (1422-91), the first English printer, most of London's early printers were in fact immigrants themselves. The English-born Caxton, as we saw in Chapter 6, learned his trade in Cologne and practiced it in Bruges before setting up shop in Westminster in 1476.[22] He had a successful career in Flanders; in 1463, he became acting governor for the Merchant Adventurers there and then moved into the service of Margaret, Duchess of Burgundy (and sister to the King of England). Of the 70 books that Caxton printed in English, 20 were his own translations from French, Latin, and Dutch or Flemish. One of his most successful imports was *The Historie of Reynart the Foxe* (1481), fables satirizing the pretensions of the clergy and the aristocracy, which Caxton translated from the Flemish.[23]

The peculiar combination of mercantile and military interests that tied England to the Low Countries helps explain the place that Flanders earned in the late medieval English imagination. The town of Calais, where Chaucer first landed on his 1369 expedition, best emblematizes this combination, even though it is technically in northern France. First captured by Edward III in 1347, Calais became the English gateway to the continent. Edward rid Calais of its original inhabitants and settled it with English people; it remained under English control until 1558. In 1363, Calais became a staple port, a center for the exportation of various commodities, including the English wool crucial to the Flemish cloth-weaving industry. The customs charged on this wool were a major source of revenue for the English monarchy through the period under consideration in this book. The additional charges meant that English wool cost Flemish cloth-makers more than twice what it cost their English rivals.[24] After Calais became a staple port, Flemings had to "travel to English territory to buy English wool with English-minted coin to finance the war that was their ruin."[25] Chaucer held the post of Controller of Wool Custom from 1374 to 1386 and was therefore in a good position to understand the interde-pendence of the English wool and the Flemish cloth-making industries.

Because Calais became the preferred point of entry for English soldiers and merchants alike, many Englishmen traveling abroad were, for all intents and purposes, delivered first to Flanders. When Chaucer situates Sir Thopas's birthplace in that "fer countree, / In Flaundres, al biyonde the see" (TST 718-19), he relies on English familiarity—and the con-tempt it breeds—for humoristic effect. Some of the most powerful men in Chaucer's England, including Lionel of Antwerp and his brother John of Gaunt, shared the dubious distinction of being "Yborn ... in Flaundres." Their birthplaces provide one index of England's investment in this region: Gaunt was named after Ghent, where at the time of his birth his father Edward III had been negotiating an important political and economic alliance.[26] The aristocratic Duke of Lancaster, arguably the most powerful man in England, was associated throughout his life with a city of wealthy Flemish merchants. Chaucer's uneasy juxtaposition of chivalric and mer-cantile motifs in "Sir Thopas"—the title character is a "knight fair and gent" whose various parts, in a parody of the courtly *blazon*, are likened to mercantile commodities, such as "scarlet in grayn" (a kind of cloth) and "saffroun" (an expensive spice)—comments on the predatory ambitions that defined the English response to Flanders.

At the same time, however, Chaucer may be deriding mercan-tile pretensions to aristocratic privilege. By the time he composed *The Canterbury Tales*, Flanders was one of the richest and most densely popu-lated areas of Europe, despite a turbulent history of foreign invasion and civil conflict. Two of its cities, Bruges and Antwerp, were major European centers for monetary exchange. The thriving economy encouraged an unprecedented urbanization so that, by the fourteenth century, over 30 per cent of Flemings were living in cities. This urbanization in turn caused cer-tain social changes to occur earlier in Flanders than in the rest of Europe: wealthy merchants constituted a powerful bourgeoisie which slowly, but surely, usurped the French aristocracy ostensibly ruling Flanders. Not sur-prisingly, given its economic and political centrality, Flanders became a bone of contention between the French and the English (much later, the

French emperor Napoleon would characterize Belgium as a gun pointed at England's heart). Its own allegiances were necessarily divided, as the Flemish economy depended on English wool and French grain alike. To generalize somewhat incautiously, during the Hundred Years' War, the Counts of Flanders were French sympathizers while the Flemish people were sympathetic to the English. When Edward III signed the 1340 treaty in Ghent, he signed it with the Flemish townsmen, led by Jacob van Arteveldt, and not with Louis of Nevers, the Count of Flanders. Louis of Nevers had, in fact, placed stringent strictures on commerce with England; these had led the weavers and cloth-makers of Ghent, Ypres, and Bruges to rebel, and, under the leadership of van Arteveldt, these Flemish cities were self-governing for a period of eight years (1338-45). The English king appears to have treated the commoner van Arteveldt for all intents and purposes like a prince of Flanders.[27] Although the Counts of Flanders eventually reclaimed power, and relations with the English were complicated accordingly, the Flemish *burgers* (citizens) had established themselves as forces of change.

It is therefore not surprising that in many late medieval English works Flanders stands for the innovations that threaten traditional society—commercialization, urbanization, mercantilism, and social mobility. Chaucer, in particular, plants the root of such phenomena firmly in Flemish soil. In "The Shipman's Tale," for example, the husband heads to Bruges while his wife sells herself at home. The plot of the tale—in which his financial dealings clear the way for her erotic transgressions—urges us to consider how economic forces erode traditional values and power structures. Helen Fulton argues convincingly that relationships which in other tales "are shown to be governed by social protocols are here controlled by market forces." The tale emphasizes the parallel activities of wife and husband, thus equating what we would call banking with a form of prostitution. Both activities are sterile, producing nothing of concrete value to the community.[28] Flanders, with its burgeoning population and lack of arable land, had made an art out of making something out of nothing. As the *Libelle* puts it:

> ... what is Flanders also?
> And who says, naught; there wealth is all gone.
> For the little land of Flanders is
> But a staple to other lands, in truth,
> And all that grows in Flanders, grain and seed,
> May not a month feed those in Breda.

This ability to turn a profit out of "naught" (nothing and naughtiness) is one that Chaucer associates with his most morally dubious characters—the Pardoner, obviously, but also the Wife of Bath, whose cloth-making capacities rival those of weavers from Ghent and Ypres. The Wife of Bath knows all about Flemish "clooth-making" (GP 447) and, like the wife in "The Shipman's Tale," she knows how to "selle" herself as well (WP 478). The association is not a spurious one. For a variety of reasons, including the lax application of sexual misconduct laws and the local system of inheritance, which did not privilege first-born sons, Flemish women enjoyed a much greater degree of independence than their English counterparts. According to one historian, "sex was so open in Ghent that there is little evidence of prostitution" while "Bruges had numerous brothels." Flemish women resident in England often resorted to prostitution to make a living.[29] Stereotypes about the sexual profligacy of Flemish women developed accordingly and made their way into the English literary tradition. From Langland's Pernele of Flanders (*Piers Plowman* C.VI) to Marston's *Dutch Courtesan* (1605) to Daniel Defoe's *Moll Flanders* (1722), women advertise their easy virtue by an association with the Low Countries.

The impact of late medieval constructions of difference was enduring in less quantifiable ways as well. The stereotype of the drunken foreigner is one that the English eventually applied to the Irish, with famously disastrous consequences for that nation. As David Wallace suggests, *The Libelle*, which urges the English to adopt an expansionist agenda and concludes by advocating English occupation of the "wild" but "fertile" space of Ireland, provides a connection between English ways of talking about continental "others" and English ways of talking about the Irish.[30] The habits of imagining Flanders as a land of sinful pleasures, including the sexual variety, may also help explain why early modern English explorers, like Sir Walter Raleigh, likened the process of colonization to sexual possession. Judging by the number of surviving manuscripts, *The Libelle* enjoyed a lasting and broad-based appeal. Lord Burghley, Elizabeth I's chief minister, owned a copy. Given that his government initiated English imperial policy towards Ireland and the Americas, *The Libelle*'s attitudes towards the Flemish may well have helped structure the world as we know it.

The Stranger in Their Midst

Despite the favor it found in the highest political circles, the *Libelle* was probably written by and for members of the London mercantile class.[31]

Although some of these merchants evolved their attitudes towards their continental counterparts while traveling abroad, this was by no means the only way that English people encountered what we would call foreigners. Late medieval London had a substantial population of alien merchants, who came mainly from Germany and Italy, and of cloth-workers, who came from Flanders. The consequences of late medieval discourses of differentiation were felt most directly by these residents of London. Some stayed only temporarily, while others immigrated on a more permanent basis. Although official English policy emphasized the benefits to be derived from the presence of alien merchants (largely because the duties they paid enriched the king's coffers), the difficulties that they encountered suggest that individual attitudes often failed to reflect the official stance on the matter. As might be expected given these circumstances, in the literature of the time the figure of the alien resident merchant is a suspect one.

To be a merchant at all, in medieval times, was to fall outside the traditional model for society, which emphasized a tri-partite division of labor (SEE CHAPTER 2). Because he did not fight, pray, or work, "the medieval merchant was a marginal, even deviant figure, whose disposition towards change and adaptation might lead to innovation."[32] Merchants were fundamentally different from most other medieval subjects in that they secured contracts with strangers for money.[33] The judgment that a conformist, rooted society brought to bear on such innovators was compounded in the case of aliens, those risk-takers and adventurers who had left their homelands to make careers elsewhere. As is the case in our society, the fact that alien residents provided services that natives were unwilling or unable to perform inspired further resentment and suspicion. The arts of making "something out of nothing"—that is, prostitution and banking—were often described as immigrant problems. If the Flemish were associated with prostitution, the Italians were despised for their involvement in banking. *Piers Plowman*, for example, singles out the Lombards—who had taken over banking activities in England from the Jews after their expulsion in 1290—for condemnation: while proffering economic advice, Reason warns the king against the "Lumbardus of Lukes, that leven by lone as the Jewes" (C.IV. 194). The 1376 Commons petitioned the king to banish Lombard merchants for practicing usury, for introducing the vice of sodomy to England, and for being no better than "Jews, & Saracens & Privy Spies."[34] In both instances, the Lombards are characterized in terms of their resemblance to pagan others—the old discourses of differentiation, that is, are being applied in new ways.

Many late medieval works similarly conflate the pagan "other" with the alien resident merchant. In the *Croxton Play of The Sacrament*, for example, the merchant Aristorius introduces himself as a "merchaunte mighty, of a royall araye," whose business takes him to "all maner of londys." Aristorius confidently asserts that his wealth allows him to live as a "lordys pere" and to impose his will on the "world so wide" (89-124).[35] His lengthy boast, which specifically identifies mercantile behavior as a manifestation of the will to power, recalls in its details the speeches of the cycle drama's pagan tyrants. Notice, however, that this is a speech assigned to a *Christian* merchant, who is characterized in terms of his willingness to travel for money, and whose power is a function of his wealth, not of his usurpation of Christ's throne. Aristorius is so committed to making a profit that he sells the Host to some Jewish merchants intent on desecrating it. When he eventually repents his evil ways, he agrees "nevermore for to bye nor sell" (915) and returns to "his own contré" (972). The life of alien merchant was not one easily assimilated to prevailing notions of virtue; only by foregoing his profession and by returning home, can Aristorius assure his salvation.

In "The Man of Law's Tale," which includes a mercantile motif missing in analogues by Boccaccio and Gower, Chaucer raises more subtle concerns about the activities of alien merchants. The Man of Law claims to have heard his story from a merchant who is "goon many a yeere" (MLT, 132)—precisely the sort of adventurer who exchanged the safety of home for the possibility of wealth abroad. The tale itself features "a compaignye of chapmen riche" (MLT 135-36), of unspecified origins and religion, who conduct business in Rome and return with loaded ships to Syria. The narrator calls attention to the goods that these men bring to trade:

> Clothes of gold, and satyns riche of hewe.
> Hir chaffare was so thrift and so newe
> That every wight hath deyntee to chaffare
> With hem, and eek to sellen hem hire ware. (MLT 136-40)

But the price that the Romans pay for tolerating these merchants and desiring their wares turns out to be quite high. The merchants export tales about the beautiful and virtuous Constance to Syria. This strange cultural "chaffare," like a form of medieval advertising, incites the desire of the Sultan of Syria, who promptly converts to Christianity and proposes marriage to the lady. Chaucer dwells at some length over the painful fate of this young woman married into a "strange" and "barbre nacioun" (MLT

268, 281). He also emphasizes what might be called the secondary function of medieval merchants—their sometimes unofficial role as diplomats
and spies, purveyors of stories, "tidynges," and information (MLT 181) to
foreign princes.[36] In its attention to how one form of exchange between
men (mercantile) spirals into another (marriage), the tale evokes a whole
host of anxieties about the ability of alien merchants to penetrate a culture
and make off with its prized possessions.

These anxieties were pervasive, and English citizens attempted
throughout this period to control the activities of alien merchants. Most
obviously, their practices were the source of litigation and legislation. In
response to a 1377 petition from his subjects, for example, Edward III
agreed that his citizens were disadvantaged by some of the activities of
aliens and decreed "that no stranger shall in the future sell any merchan-
dize in the same city, or in the suburb thereof, any Statutes and Ordinances
made to the contrary notwithstanding; saving always unto the merchants
of the Hanse of Almaine their liberties unto them by us and our progenitors granted and confirmed." The majority of alien merchants, in other
words, were limited to the import/export business; they could not trade
within England or among themselves. By 1378, however, some of these
restrictions were already being lifted by Parliament.[37] For those in power,
the profit principle trumped other considerations. The Hanse of Almain,
granted an exemption from the 1377 restrictions, was the most powerful company of alien merchants in late medieval London and one of
the most powerful in all of Europe. A league of allied cities (including
Lübeck, Cologne, and Hamburg) located on important trading routes,
the Hansards managed to obtain important royal "liberties" because of
the money they brought into royal coffers. The confiscation of a Hansard
ship in 1389 by enterprising and envious Englishmen, however, suggests
that even at the height of its power, the Hanse confronted significant
problems. International commerce was no career for the faint of heart in
late medieval England.

Although the Hanse merchants did receive compensation for their
illegally confiscated goods, justice was not readily accessible to England's
alien residents. The murders of two Italian merchants—Nicholas
Sardouche in 1368 and Janus Imperial in 1379—suggest that the authori-
ties tended to be lenient towards Englishmen who murdered foreigners.
Both men were killed in apparent street brawls. In the case of Janus
Imperial, however, compelling evidence has brought the scholar Paul
Strohm to argue that the murder was an ordered hit. Imperial was a
Genovese merchant who operated under Richard II's special protection

and who dabbled in diplomacy on the side. At the time of his death, he was in the process of negotiating a treaty for Genoa which would have allowed all his countrymen to bypass the Calais staple port in favor of Southampton and thus to pay duties directly to Richard II—privileges that, as Richard's letter patent shows, Imperial himself already enjoyed. Although this treaty would profit the king, it stood to disadvantage London merchants involved in the wool trade. This treaty had been a long time in the making; on his 1372-73 trip to Italy, Chaucer was charged with broaching the subject of opening certain English ports to Genovese ships. One of the rumors flying around in London at the time of Imperial's murder is that the proposed treaty would "destroy and ruin all the wool merchants in London" (SEE John Algor's confession, BELOW). On 26 August 1379, John Kirkby and John Algor, employees of London merchants, sought out Imperial and picked a fight with him. Imperial had been enjoying the late summer evening—he was sitting outside on a log—when Kirkby and Algor approached him. Over the course of the fight, Algor distracted Imperial's servants, while Kirkby dealt him three different wounds, including "two mortal wounds, each of them seven inches long and deep into the brain" (SEE BELOW). Although the murder was premeditated, neither Algor nor Kirkby attempted to flee; apparently, they felt that they would never be prosecuted. Indeed, jury after jury proved reluctant to convict. Only by resorting to unusual tactics—like categorizing the murder as an act of treason, because it violated the king's letters of safe conduct—were the royal authorities able to convict and execute Kirkby. Algor received a royal pardon. And the wool merchants who at the very least approved and more probably ordered the murder were never directly implicated at all.

Taken together, the documents in the Imperial case offer a fascinating glimpse into commonly held attitudes towards strangers and contemporary methods of investigation and jurisprudence. Xenophobia, when combined with commercial interests, seems to have enabled the English juries to overlook crime. Clearly, Imperial's behavior—he was allegedly "annoyed and clearly began to lose his temper"—received as much scrutiny as his murderers'. Jurors cited Imperial's anger in support of their conclusions that the murderers had acted in self-defense; when all was said and done, and despite strong evidence to the contrary, "no fewer than thirty-seven different citizens of London, proven and sworn for jury duty, stood firmly behind the claim that Kirkby and Algor acted on their own, without malice aforethought, and in self-defense." The case of Janus Imperial can finally be explained only by reference to "an irrational fear of otherness, a xenophobia implicated in, but exceeding, any computation of profit and loss."[38]

The layout of medieval London may well have exacerbated such xenophobia. It certainly facilitated the demonstration of it in violence. Those seeking aliens, like Kirkby and Algor, knew where to find them. For example, near London Bridge on upper Thames Street, the Hanse of Almain had a trading post that included a church, warehouses, and sleeping quarters. All Hanse merchants resided at the "Steelyard," as it was known. The nearby neighborhood of St. Martin's Vintry housed many of the city's aliens, including the Flemish. Chaucer grew up here; St. Martin's was located in the Vintry ward, just one block down Thames Street from the house of his father John. During Chaucer's lifetime, there were nearly 1,000 Flemish immigrants in London, by far the largest alien group in the city. Most Flemish residents were not merchants but cloth-workers who had left their homeland in the wake of civil conflict and economic upheaval. They were resented in part because the locals suspected them of taking English jobs.[39] Court records suggest that Flemish immigrants endured systematic harassment throughout the period. They were accused of theft, prostitution, organizing "covens" or conspiracies, and being "notorious malefactors."

The xenophobic hatred of the Flemish found its most violent expression in the so-called "Massacre of the Flemish," which took place during the Peasant's Revolt in 1381 (discussed in Chapter 1). According to the *Anonimalle Chronicle*, one of the first acts of the rebels, once they reached London, was the razing of a Flemish brothel near London Bridge. Taking advantage of the chaos occasioned by the revolt, a mob gathered the next day at St. Martin's Vintry, dragged out the Flemish immigrants who had sought refuge in the church, and beheaded them in the street. The mob then proceeded to rob the other aliens who lived nearby. Despite the relative lack of reference to the Peasant's Revolt in Chaucer's work, it hit close to home since the Vintry was his boyhood neighborhood. This should, perhaps, make us pause over the following lines in "The Nun's Priest's Tale":

> Certes, he Jakke Straw and his meynee
> Ne made nevere shoutes half so shrille
> Whan they wolden any Flemyng kille,
> As thilke day was made upon the fox. (3394-97)

Chaucer transforms the beheading of 30 to 40 foreigners into a humorous simile, used to describe the behavior of animals; with one blow, he dehumanizes both the peasant rebels and their innocent foreign victims. It is, as Derek Pearsall notes, a "brutally trivializing reference" to a horrific event.[40] These chilling lines suggest a form of complicity—hard to define, but undeniable—between the Chaucerian "snicker" that deprives the Flemish of their humanity and the sword strokes that deprived them of their lives.

Documents

Information for Pilgrims (c. 1500)

These excerpts, translated from a pamphlet entitled *Information for Pilgrims unto the Holy Land* (c. 1500), exemplify the sort of advice that pilgrimage reports dispensed. The pamphlet also includes information about foreign currencies, lists of words, itineraries, and so on. Unlike modern travel writing, which devotes itself to description of landscapes and cultural habits as well as to practical matters, the focus here is almost exclusively on practical matters like safety.

> If man shall journey in a ship ... then choose you a chamber as near the middle of the ship as you can for there is less rolling or tumbling to keep your brain and stomach in temper. And in the same chamber keep your things in safeguard. And buy yourself in Venice a padlock to hang on the door when you shall go on land.
>
> Also see that the said patron gives you every day hot meat twice at two meals ... at dinner and the afternoon at supper. And that the wine that you shall drink be good and the water fresh and not stinking....
>
> Also take good heed of your knives and other small things that you bear about you because the Saracens will go talking by you and make good cheer but they will steal from you if they can.
>
> Also when you shall take your ass at the port of Joppa, stay not long behind your fellows; if you come early you can choose the best mule or ass that you can because you will pay no more for the best

than the worst. And you must give your ass man there a groat [coin] of Venice for courtesy. And do not go too far in front of or behind your fellows because of the shrews.

Also when you shall ride to Jordan take with you out of Jerusalem bread, wine, water, and hard-boiled eggs and choose such victuals as you can keep for two days because on that whole journey there are none to buy.

Also keep one of your bottles of wine … if you go up to the place where our lord Jesus Christ fasted 40 days. It is appallingly hot and very high.

FROM *Mandeville's Travels* (1356-57?)

Purportedly written by a knight from St. Albans, England, *The Voyage and Travel of Sir John Mandeville* (1356-57?) is a patchwork of carefully woven together sources. The author was probably more widely read than traveled and relied almost entirely on second-hand accounts; he or she endowed the book with coherence through the creation of a fictional narrator, the eponymous wandering knight, who shares his observations about the Holy Land and the mysterious regions beyond it. This medieval travelogue enjoyed an immediate and lasting popularity, of which the three extant medieval translations into English from the French original offer one index. Our excerpt includes the descriptions of Paradise and of the mythical Prester John, the emperor of an idealized Christian state located in India. Mandeville's book, here, owes much to the immensely popular letter supposedly written by this figure, which began circulating in Europe as early as 1165. We also include an account of the villainous Catolonabes (a figure based on the historical Hasan ben Sabbah, leader of an extreme Muslim sect known as the Assassins). *The Voyage and Travel of Sir John Mandeville* repeatedly insists that the world can be circumnavigated; it inspired, among other things, Columbus's epoch-changing journeys. Mandeville's descriptions of the world's strange wonders—"marvelous" is a favorite adjective—exerted a powerful influence on the English literary imagination. As a first-person observer of human behavior, Mandeville also offers an important precedent for Chaucer's experiments with point of view and narration.

Noah had three sons, Sem [Shem], Cham [Ham], and Japhet. Ham was the one who saw his father's privy parts naked as he lay asleep, and went to his brothers and showed that sight in scorn; and so afterwards his father, when he knew of it, cursed him. But Japhet went backwards to his father and covered his private parts. These three sons of Noah divided the earth between them after the Flood. Shem, because he was the eldest chose the best and largest part, which is towards the East, and it is called Asia. Ham took Africa, and Japhet took Europe. Ham was the richest and mightiest of the brothers; and from him came many more descendants than from his other brothers. From one of his sons called Chus [Cush] came Nimrod the giant, who was the first king there ever was; and he began to build the Tower of Babel. In his time many devils came in the likeness of men and lay with the women of his race and begat on them giants and other monsters of horrible shape—some without heads, some with dog's heads, and many other misshapen and disfigured men. Of the kindred of Ham came the pagans and different kinds of men in the isles of India.... And of Shem, so they say, came the Saracens; and of Japhet the people of Israel and we who live in Europe.

From this land men go into the land of Bactria, where there are many wicked and cruel men. In this land there are trees that bear wool, like that of sheep, of which they make cloth. In this land too there are many hippopotami, which live sometimes on dry land and sometimes in the water; they are half man and half horse. And they eat men, whenever they can get them, no meat more readily. And in that land are many griffons, more than in any other country. Some men say they have the foreparts of an eagle and the hind-parts of a lion; that is indeed true. Nevertheless the griffon is bigger and stronger than eight lions of these countries and ... bigger and stronger than a hundred eagles. For certainly he will carry to his nest in flight a great horse with a man on his back, or two oxen yoked together, as they work together at the plough. He has talons on his feet as great and as long as the horns of oxen, and they are very sharp. Of these talons men make cups to drink out of and the ribs of his feathers they make into strong bows to shoot with.

From this land of Bactria men go many days' journeys to the land of Prester John, who is Emperor of India; and his land is called the isle of Pentoxere.

This Emperor Prester John has many different countries under his rule, in which are many noble cities and fair towns, and many isles

great and broad. For this land of India is divided in isles on account
of the great rivers which flow out of Paradise and run through
and divide up his land. He also has many great isles in the sea. The
principal city of the isle of Pentoxere is called Nise; the Emperor's
seat is there, and so it is a noble and rich city. Prester John has under
him many kings and many different peoples; and his land is good and
wealthy, but not so rich as the land of the Great Khan of Cathay. For
merchants do not travel so much to that land as to the land of Cathay,
for it is too long a journey. And also merchants can get all they need
in the isle of Cathay—spices, golden cloth, and other rich things; and
they are reluctant to go to Pentoxere because of the long way and
the dangers of the sea....

This same royal King Prester John and the Great Khan of Tartary
are always allied through marriage; for each of them marries the
other's daughter or sister. In the land of Prester John there is a great
plenty of precious stones of different sorts, some so big that they
make from them dishes, bowls, cups and many other things too
numerous to mention.

Now I shall speak of some of the principal isles of Prester John's
land, and of the royalty of his state, and of what religion and creed he
and his people follow. This Emperor Prester John is Christian, and so
is the greater part of his land, even if they do not have all the articles
of the faith as we clearly do. Nevertheless they believe in God as
Father, Son, and Holy Ghost; they are a very devout people, faithful
to each other, and there is neither fraud nor guile among them.... In
the land of Prester John there are many marvels. Among others there
is a vast sea of gravel and sand, and no drop of water in it. It ebbs and
flows as the ocean itself does in other countries, and there are great
waves in it; it never stays still and unmoving. No man can cross that
sea by ship or any other way; and so it is unknown what kind of land
or country is on the far side. And though there is no water in that
sea, yet is there great plenty of good fish caught on its shores; they are
very tasty to eat, but they are of different shape to the fish in other
waters. I, John Mandeville, ate of them and so believe it, for it is true.

And three journeys from the sea are great mountains, from which
flows a large river that comes from Paradise. It is full of precious
stones, without a drop of water. It runs with it great waves through
the wilderness into the gravelly sea, and then it disappears. Each week
for three days this river runs so fast that no man dares enter it, but on
other days people go into it when they like and gather the precious

stones. Beyond that river towards the wilderness is a great plain, set among the hills, all sandy and gravelly, in which there are, as it seems, trees which at the rising of the sun begin to grow, and a fruit grows on them; they grow until midday, and then they begin to dwindle and return back into earth, so by sunset nothing is seen of them. No man dare eat of this fruit, or go near it, for it looks like a deceptive phantom. That is accounted a marvelous thing, as well it may be.

In this wilderness are many wild men with horns on their heads; they dwell in woods and speak not, only grunting like pigs. And in some woods in that land are wild dogs, that will never come near to a man, any more than foxes do in this country. There are birds, too, that of their own nature speak and call out to men who are crossing the desert, speaking as clearly as if they were men. These birds have large tongues and five claws on each foot. There are others that have only three claws on each foot, and they do not speak so well or clearly. These birds are called parrots, as I said before.

This same King and Emperor Prester John, when he goes to battle against his enemies, has no banner borne before him; instead there are carried before him three crosses, of fine gold, which are very large and tall and encrusted with precious stones. Ten thousand men at arms and more than a hundred thousand foot soldiers are detailed to look after each cross, in the same way as men guard a banner or standard in battle or wherever. And this number of men is always assigned to the guarding of these crosses whenever the Emperor goes to battle; this is not counting the main army, or certain lords and their men who are ordered to be in the Emperor's own division, and also not counting certain wings whose job it is to forage. And when he rides with his private company in time of peace, there is carried before him a wooden cross, without gold or painting or precious stones, in remembrance of the Passion of Christ who died on a wooden cross. He also has carried in front of him a golden plate full of earth, as a token that notwithstanding his great nobleness and power he came from the earth and to the earth he shall return. And there is carried before him another vessel full of gold and jewels and precious stones, like rubies, diamonds, sapphires, emeralds, topazes, chrysolites, and many others, as a token of his nobility, power, and might.

I shall now tell you of the arrangement of Prester John's palace, which is usually at the city of Susa. That palace is so wealthy, so noble, so full of delights that it is a marvel to tell of. For on top of the main tower are two balls of gold, in each of which are two great fair carbuncles, which shine very brightly in the night. The chief gates of the palace are precious stones, which men call sardonyx, and the bars are ivory. The windows of the hall and the chambers are of crystal. All of the tables they eat off are of emeralds, amethysts, and, some, of gold, set with precious stones; the pedestals that support the tables are, in the same way, of precious stone .... The frame of his bed is of sapphire, well set in gold, to make him sleep well and to destroy lustful thoughts—for he only lies with his wives on four set occasions in the year, and even then for the sole purpose of engendering children ....

Next to the isle of Pentoxere, which is Prester John's, is another long and broad isle called Mulstorak [Malazgirt]; it is under Prester John's lordship. In this isle there is great plenty of goods and riches. Once there was there a rich man called Catolonabes, and he was powerful and marvelously cunning. He had a fair strong castle, standing on a hill, and he had strong high walls built around it. Inside the walls he made a beautiful garden and planted in it all kinds of trees bearing different kinds of fruit. He had all kinds of sweet-smelling and flowering herbs planted too. There were many fair fountains in that garden, and beside them lovely halls and chambers, painted marvelously delicately in gold and azure with different stories; there were different kinds of birds, worked by mechanical means, which seemed quite alive as they sang and fluttered. In that garden he put all the kinds of birds and beasts he could get to please and delight a man. He also put there beautiful maidens, not older than fifteen, the loveliest he could find, and boys of the same age; they were all clad in clothes of gold. These he said were angels. He also had three lovely wells made of precious stones enclosed in jasper and crystal, and other precious stones set in gold. He built conduits under the earth so that, when he wished, one of these wells would run with honey, another with wine, and another with milk, from these conduits. This place he called Paradise. And when any young noble of the country came to him, he led him into this Paradise and showed him all these things I have mentioned. He secretly had minstrels in a high tower where they could not be seen, playing on different instruments of music. He said they were God's angels, and that that place was the Paradise God grants to those He loves, saying, *Dabo uobis terrram fluentem lac et mel*, which means "I shall give you a land flowing with milk and honey."

Then this rich man gave these youths a kind of drink which quickly made them drunk; then they were more blinded than before, and they thought they had indeed been in bliss. He then told them that if they would put themselves in danger of death for his sake, when they were dead they would come to his Paradise and would evermore be of the age of the maidens, that they would evermore live with them and have pleasure and dalliance with them and they should still remain always a virgin; and that after a certain time he would put them in a yet fairer Paradise, where they would see God in His majesty and bliss and joy. Thereupon they all agreed to do what he wanted. Then he would tell them to go to such and such a place and slay some lord or man of the area who was his enemy; that they were to have no fear, for if they were killed he would put them in Paradise. Thus he had many lords of the country assassinated; and many of these young men were killed in the hope of having the Paradise that he promised them....

A little way from that place towards the river Phison (the Ganges) is a great marvel. There is a valley between two hills, about four miles long; some men call it the Vale of Enchantment, some the Vale of Devils, and some the Vale Perilous. In this valley there are often heard tempests, and ugly, hideous noises, both by day and by night.... This valley is all full of devils and always has been, and men of those parts say it is an entrance to Hell. There is much gold and silver in this valley, and to get it many men—Christian and heathen—come and go into that valley. But very few come out again—least of all the unbelievers—for all who go therein out of covetousness are strangled by devils and lost. In the middle of the valley under a rock one can clearly see the head and face of a devil, very hideous and dreadful to see; nothing else is seen of it except from the shoulders up. There is no man in the world, Christian or anyone else, who would not be very terrified to see it, it is so horrible and foul. He looks at each man so keenly and cruelly, and his eyes are rolling so fast and sparkling like fire, and he changes expression so often, and out of his nose and mouth comes so much fire of different colors with such an awful stench, that no man can bear it. But good Christian men, however, who are firm in the faith, can enter that valley without great harm if they are cleanly confessed and absolved and bless themselves with the sign of the Cross; then the devils will not harm them.... My companions and I, when we came near that valley and heard all about it, wondered in our hearts whether to trust ourselves totally to the mercy of God and pass through it; some turned aside and said they would not put themselves in that danger. There were in our company two Friars Minor of Lombardy, who said they would go through that valley if we would go with them; so what with their encouragement and the comfort of their words, we confessed cleanly and heard Mass and went into the valley, fourteen of us together. But when we came out we were only nine. We never knew what became of the remainder, whether they were lost or turned back, but we never saw them again.... And my companions and I went through the valley, and saw many marvelous things, and gold and silver and precious stones and many other jewels on each side of us—so it seemed to us. But whether it really was as it seemed, or was merely illusion, I do not know. But because of the fear that we were in, and also so as not to hinder our devotion, we would touch nothing we saw: for we were more devout then than we ever were before or after, because of the fear we had on account of devils appearing to us in different guises and of the multitude of dead men's bodies that lay in our path....

Now I shall tell you why this Emperor is called Prester John. There was once an Emperor in that land who was a noble and brave prince; he had many knights with him who were Christian, like he has who is now Emperor. And one day this Emperor thought that he would like to see the manner of the service in Christian churches. At that time, Christian men occupied many countries towards those parts.... And so it fell that this Emperor and a Christian knight who was with him entered a church in Egypt on the Saturday in Whit week, when the Bishop was holding an ordination service. The Emperor watched the service, and the way priests were made, and how solemnly and devoutly they were ordained. He then asked the knight what sort of people these were who were being ordained, and what they were called; the knight said they were priests. Then the Emperor said that no longer would he be called King or Emperor, but priest instead, and that he would take the name of the first priest who came out of the church. It happened that the first priest to come out of the church was called John; and so that Emperor and all the other Emperors since have been called Prester John, that is, Priest John....

Of Paradise I cannot speak properly, for I have not been there; and that I regret. But I shall tell you as much as I have heard from wise men and trustworthy authorities in those countries. The Earthly Paradise, so men say, is the highest land on earth; it is so high it touches the sphere of the moon. For it is so high that Noah's flood could not reach it, though it covered the rest of the earth. Paradise is encircled by a wall; but no man can say what the wall is made of. It is all grown over with moss and with bushes so that no stone can be seen, nor anything else a wall might be made of. The wall of Paradise stretches from the south to the north; there is no way into it open because of ever burning fire, which is the flaming sword that God set up before the entrance so that no man should enter. In the middle of Paradise is a spring from which come four rivers, which run through different lands. These rivers sink down into the earth inside Paradise and then run many a mile underground; afterwards, they rise up out of the earth again in distant lands.... And men say that all the fresh rivers of the world have their beginning in the spring that wells up in Paradise.

And you should realize that no living man can go to paradise. By land no man can go thither because of the wild beasts in the wilderness, and because of the hills and rocks, which no one can cross; and also because of the many dark places that are there. No one can go there by water either, for those rivers flow with so strong a current, with such a rush and such waves that no boat can sail them. There is also such a great noise of waters that one man cannot hear another, shout he ever so loudly. Many great lords have tried at different times to travel by those rivers to Paradise, but they could not prosper in their journeys; some of them died through exhaustion from rowing and excessive labor, some went blind and deaf through the noise of waters, and some were drowned through the violence of the waves. And so no man, as I said, can get there except through the special grace of God.

On Various Countries. BARTHOLOMEW ANGLICUS (13ᵗʰc)

As we saw earlier, in Chapters 2 and 7, Bartholomew Anglicus's *On the Properties of Things* was among the most widely read books of the late Middle Ages. Our translated excerpts are based on Trevisa's Middle English translation of the Latin original.

ON ENGLAND

England is the most island of Ocean, and is surrounded all about by the sea, and departed from the roundness of the world, and called sometimes Albion: and had that name of white rocks, which were seen on the sea cliffs. And by continuance of time, lords and noble men of Troy, after that Troy was destroyed went from thence, and were accompanied with a great navy, and fortuned to the cliffs of the foresaid island, and that by revelation of their feigned goddess Pallas, as it is said, and the Trojans fought with giants, both with craft and with strength, and conquered the island, and called the land Britain, by the name of Brute that was prince of that host: and so the island called Britain, as it were an island conquered of Brute that time, with arms and might. Of this Brute's offspring came most mighty kings. And who that hath liking to know their deeds, let him read the story of Brute.

And long time after, the Saxons won the island with many and divers hard battles and strong, and their offspring had possession after them of the island, and the Britons were slain or exiled, and the Saxons parted the island among them, and gave every province a name, by the property of its own name and nation, and therefore they called the island Anglia, by the name of Engelia the queen, the worthiest duke of Saxony's daughter, that had the island in possession after many battles. Isidore said, that this land is called Anglia, and hath that name of Angulus, a corner, as it were land set in the end, or a corner of the world. But Saint Gregory, seeing English children to sell at Rome, when they were not christened, and hearing that they were called English: according with the name of the country he answered and said: Truly they be English, for they shine in face right as angels: it is need to send them message, with word of salvation. For as Bead said, the noble kind of the land shone in their faces. Isidore said, Britain, that now called Anglia, is an island set afore France and Spain, and contains about 48 times 75 miles. Also therein be many rivers and great and hot wells. There is great plenty of metals, there be enough of the stones agates, and of pearls, the ground is special good, most apt to bear corn and other good fruit. There be, namely, many sheep with good wool, there be many harts and other wild beasts; there be few wolves or none, therefore there be many sheep, and may securely be left without ward, in pasture and in fields, as Beda saith.

England is a strong land and a sturdy, and the most plenteous corner of the world, so rich a land that it never needs the help of any land, and every other land needs help of England. England is full of mirth and of game, and men oft times able to mirth and game, free men of heart and with tongue, but the hand is more better and more free than the tongue.

On Flanders

Though Flanders be little in space, yet it is wealthy of many special things and good. For this land is plenteous and full of pasture, of cattle, and of beasts, royal and rich of the best towns, havens of the sea, and of famous rivers, and well nigh all about is moistened with the Scaldelia [the river Schelde]. The men thereof be seemly and fair of body and strong, and they get many children. And they be rich of all manner of merchandises and goods, and generally fair and seemly of face, mild of will, and fair of speech, sad of bearing, honest of clothing, peaceable to their own neighbors, true and trusty to strangers, passing witty in wool craft, by their crafty working a great part of the world is succored and helped in woolen clothes. For of the principal wool which they have out of England, with their subtle craft be made many noble cloths, and be sent by sea also by land into many diverse countries.

On India

And as among all countries and lands India is the greatest and most rich: so among all lands India is most wonderful. For as Pliny said, India abounds in wonders. In India be many huge beasts bred, and more greater hounds than in other lands. Also there be so high trees that men may not shoot to the top with an arrow, as it is said. And that makes the plenty and fatness of the earth and temperateness of weather, of air, and of water. Fig trees spread there so broad, that many great companies of knights may sit at meat under the shadow of one tree. Also there be so great reeds and so long that every piece between two knots bear sometime three men over the water. Also

there be men of great stature, passing five cubits in height, and they
never spit, nor have never headache nor toothache, nor sore eyes,
nor they be not grieved with passing heat of the sun, but rather
made more hard and sad therewith. Also their philosophers that they
call Gymnosophists stand in most hot gravel from the morning till
evening, and behold the sun without blemishing their eyes. Also
there, in some mountains be men with soles of the feet turned
backwards, and the foot also with eight toes on one foot. Also there
be some with hounds' heads, and be clothed in the skins of wild
beasts, and they bark as hounds, and speak none other wise; and they
live by hunting and fowling; and they be armed with their nails and
teeth, and be full many, about six score thousand he said. Also among
some nations of India be women that bear never child but once,
and the children wax white-haired as soon as they be born. There
be satyrs and other men wondrously shaped. Also in the end of East
India, about the rising of Ganges, be men without mouths, and they
be clothed in moss and in rough hairy things, which they gather off
trees, and live commonly by odor and smell at the nostrils. And they
neither eat nor drink, but only smell odor of flowers and of wood
apples, and live so, and they die anon in evil odor and smell. And
other there be that live full long, and age never, but die as it were
in middle age. Also some be hoary in youth, and black in age. Pliny
rehearses these wonders, and many more.

On Ireland

Ireland is called Hibernia, and is an island of the Ocean in Europe,
and is near to the land of Britain, and is more narrow and straight
than Britain, but it is a more plenteous place .... In this land is much
plenty of corn fields, of wells and of rivers, of fair meads and woods,
of metal and precious stones. For there is gendered a six-cornered
stone, that is to wit, Iris, that makes a rainbow in the air, if it be set
in the sun. And there is jet found, and white pearls. And concerning
the wholesome air, Ireland is a good temperate country. There is little
or none passing heat or cold, there be wonderful lakes, ponds, and
wells. For there is a lake, in which if a stag or a pole of tree ... tarries
a long time therein, the part that is in the earth turns into iron, and
the part that is in the water turns into stone, and the part that is
above the water, abides still in its kind of tree. There is another lake
in which if you throw rods of hazel, it turns those rods into ash: and
in the same way if you cast ashen rods therein, they turn into hazel.

Therein be places in which dead carrions never rot but abide there uncorrupt. Also in Ireland is a little island, in which men die not, but when they be overcome with age, they be borne out of that island to die without. In Ireland is no serpent, no frogs, nor venomous adder; but all the land is so contrary to venomous beasts that if the earth of that land be brought into another land, and sprinkled on the ground, it slays serpents and toads. Also venomous beasts flee Irish wool, skins and furs of animals. And if serpents or toads be brought into Ireland by shipping, they die anon.

Solinus speaks of Ireland, and says the inhabitants thereof be fierce, and lead an inhuman life. The people there use to harbor no guests, they be warriors, and drink men's blood that they slay, and wash first their faces therewith, right and unright they take for one .... Men of Ireland be singularly clothed and unseemly arrayed and scarcely fed, they be cruel of heart, fierce of cheer, angry of speech, and sharp. Nonetheless they be free hearted, and fair of speech and goodly to their own nation, and namely those men that dwell in woods, marshes, and mountains. These men be pleased with flesh, apples, and fruit for meat, and with milk for drink and given themselves more to plays and to hunting, than to work and travail.

From *The Libelle of English Policy* (15ᵀᴴc)

The Libelle of English Policy makes an early and radical argument for securing the seas as a means of expanding English commercial and military power. This treatise was probably written shortly after the Duke of Gloucester raided Flanders in 1436; a reference to these events, reproduced below, describes the animalistic Flemish in flight from the English Duke. *The Libelle* is a repository of unflattering stereotypes about Flemish people: they are louts, drunkards, cowards, and parasites. Although *The Libelle* reserves its most vituperative descriptions for the Flemish, it does not spare other trading partners, including the Italians. Our translation is based on Sir George Warner's edition of the poem.

> OF THE COMMODITIES OF SPAIN AND FLANDERS
> And when these said merchants discharged be
> Of merchandise in Flanders, near the sea,
> Then they are charged again with merchandise,
> That to Flanders belongs full richly,

Fine cloth of Ypres, that is called better than ours,
Cloth of Kortrijk, fine cloth of all colors,
A lot of fustian [a kind of cloth] and also linen cloth.
But you Flemings, if you be not contentious,
You know you make the great substance
Of your cloth out of our English wool.
Than does it not sink in man's brain
But that it must, this merchandise of Spain,
Pass both in and out at our cost?
He that says nay in wit is like an ass.
Thus if this sea were kept, I dare well say,
We should have peace with those grounds twain;
For Spain and Flanders are as each other's brother,
And neither may well live without the other.
They may not live to maintain there degrees
Without our English commodities,
Wool and tin, for the wool of England,
Sustains the common Flemings, I understand.
Then, if England would its wool restrain
From Flanders, this follows, it's certain:
Flanders of needs must with us have peace
Or else it is destroyed . . . .

Thus, if the sea be kept, take heed of this,
If these two lands come not together,
So that the fleet of Flanders cannot pass,
So that it cannot in the narrow sea be brought
Into the Rochelle to fetch the famous wine,
Nor into Brittany's bay for its salt so fine,
What is then Spain, what is Flanders also?
And who says, naught; there wealth is all gone.
For the little land of Flanders is
But a staple to other lands, in truth,
And all that grows in Flanders, grain and seed,
May not a month feed those in Breda.
What has then Flanders, be Flemings loved or loathed,
But a little matter and Flemish cloth?
By working our wool Flemish commons
Live substantially, this is their government,

Without which they may not live at ease;
Thus must they starve or with us have peace.

ON THE FLEMISH
You have heard that two Flemings together
Will undertake, before they go anywhere
Before they rise once, to drink a barrel full
Of good beer; so hard do they drink and pull,
Under the board they piss as they sit.
This comes of covenant of a worthy wit.
Outside of Calais in their breeches they shat,
When they fled home and when they leisure lacked
To hold their siege; they went soft like a doe,
Lucky was that Fleming that might pack off and go.
For fear, they turned back and hurried fast,
Milord of Gloucester made them so aghast
With his coming and sought them in their land
And burnt and slew what he took in hand,
So that our enemies dared not abide nor stay;
They fled to mew [a coop for fowl], they durst no more appear.

OF THE COMMODITIES OF IRELAND AND ...
CONQUERING OF WILD IRISH
Why speak I thus so much of Ireland?
For also much as I can understand,
It is fertile for thing that there do grow
And multiply, look who so lust to know,
So large, so good and so commodious,
That to declare is strange and marvelous.
For of silver and gold there is the ore
Among the wild Irish, though they be poor,
For they are rude and have no skill;
So that, if we had there peace and good will,
To mine and fine and metal for to pure,
In wild Irish might we find the cure.

COURT CASES (14THC)

The following court cases offer us valuable glimpses into the life of the London immigrant. Although aliens enjoyed some privileges, they also operated under legal restrictions. The penalties exacted for violating these prohibitions ranged from the confiscation of illegally retailed goods to imprisonment. Flemish immigrants show up regularly in the court records of the period; they belonged to the largest alien group in London, brought there because of economic and political problems in their own country and because of the burgeoning textile industry in England. The English were wary of these immigrant "evildoers," who were accused of stealing English jobs, associated with prostitution (as in the Martyn case), and suspected of illegal conspiracies (the "covens" referred to in the Gyles/atte Hyde case).

> Zenobius Martyn, who had been indicted in Langbourne Ward as a common bawd and associate of prostitutes, admitted his offence and put himself on the mercy of the court. He also admitted that, though he was not a freeman of the City, he kept a lodging-house for aliens and had acted as a broker against the ordinances of the City, and that he had admitted to his house men of ill-fame, evildoers, thieves, and prostitutes. He was committed to prison ...

> Baldewyn Gyles and Gerard atte Hyde, bailiffs of the Flemish weavers, were committed to prison because they had allowed certain workmen to go about preventing others, including the masters of their craft, from working, and because they refused to certify the names of these offenders to the Mayor .... Baldewyn Gyles and Gerard atte Hyde ... were attached and committed to prison for refusing to inform the Mayor and Aldermen of divers evildoers among the Flemish weavers, who made covens and assemblies in the City and suburbs, also for having levied unlawful tolls from Lambekyn Ruyt and others, and further for having told the above weavers that they need not work, thus allowing them to wander about the City to the grave damage of the common people. On the Monday following the said bailiffs were released on the mainprise of John Yonkere, John Otemele, and John Persoun for their appearance on Thursday after the Feast of All Saints, on condition that they repaid the said Lambekyn the money unjustly taken. When the day came it was found that they had not repaid the money. Thereupon John Yonkere,

John can Everden, John Otemele, John Persoun, Henry Nauger, John Van Loo, and Lenin van Dyke became sureties for payment and for the appearance of the bailiffs before the Mayor and Aldermen when required. At the same time the above mainpernors, together with Peter Sterteway, Henry Cloffhamer, William van Aughten, Gerard van Brugge, John Maaz, Peter van Thelbroke, Lodewic Fynk, Giles van de Baaz, Michael Mummard, John Brunols, John van Legh, John Omekyn, Peter de Gotham, John Gaunsterman and John van Wettre became sureties for the good behavior of all Flemish weavers, who were forbidden to hold any covens, leagues, or assemblies in the future, or to levy any subsidies from the men of their mystery except on behalf of the infirm, blind, and lame. The mainpernors also undertook to inform the Mayor and Aldermen if they could not by themselves cope with any evildoers in their mystery.

The Murder of Janus Imperial (1379)

On 26 August 1379 the Genovese merchant Janus Imperial was murdered in front of his residence. The attempts of the authorities to bring the suspects, John Kirkby and John Algor, to justice were repeatedly thwarted by the reluctance of the various juries involved. As Paul Strohm notes, Kirkby and Algor were in the employ of Richard Preston and John More, "leading merchant-capitalists of London." In his confession Algor cites gossip that involved John Philpot and Nicholas Brembre, both of whom served as Mayor of London at various times. As we noted above, the victim was an alien merchant, who enjoyed Richard II's protection. A trial before Chief Justice Cavendish, attended by some of the most powerful people in the country, including John of Gaunt, failed to produce a conviction, since the jury insisted that the suspects had acted alone and in self-defense. The skeptical justices returned Algor and Kirkby to custody; they were moved first to Nottingham then to Northampton; and Algor turned king's evidence and confessed. We reproduce several of the legal documents connected with the case, including Algor's confession.

From the Letter Patent of Richard II (6 March 1378)

Know that, whereas on the advice of our council we have granted to Janus Imperial of Genoa, master of a certain tarit [ship] called "The Holy Mary of Genoa," that he can bring a tarit, whatever

kind of tarit it is, laden with merchandise to any port he pleases in
our realm of England and can take it thence, laden with wool and
other merchandise bought in England by himself or his agents, to his
own country and not elsewhere, paying to us and to others before
they pass outside our said realm the customs and subsidies and other
moneys due ... we, wishing to provide of grace for the safety and
security of the said master and the aforesaid tarit, whatever kind it
be, have taken the said master and the aforesaid tarit and merchandise
and the sailors of said tarit, with the goods with which it happens
to be laden, into our safe and secure conduct and under our special
protection and defense in coming to whatsoever port he pleases in
our realm of England .... And so we order you not to inflict and,
insofar as you are able, not to allow to be inflicted by others any
wrong, loss, mischief, arrest, violence hindrance, or injury upon the
said master or the said sailors or the aforesaid tarit in coming with
merchandise to our aforesaid realm .... And should any wrong or
injury be done them, you are to have it redressed without delay and
properly amended, always provided that the said master [pays his
customs and subsidies and moneys].

FROM THE INDICTMENT SENT TO THE KING'S CHANCERY

It happened that on Saturday after the Feast of St. Bartholomew the
Apostle in the third year of the reign of King Richard, second after
the Conquest of England [27 August 1379], a certain Janus Imperial
of Genoa lay slain in the house where he resided in the lane and
parish of St. Nicholas Acon in Langbourne Ward, London, wherefore
Nicholas Dymcock, coroner of London, Thomas Cornwallis and
John Bosham, sheriffs of the said city, on hearing about it, went there
on the same Saturday and, having summoned before them upright
and law-worthy men of the aforesaid Langbourne Ward and of three
other adjacent wards ... they diligently inquired of said men upon
a view of the aforesaid Janus Imperial's body how and in what way
he came to his death .... They say on their oath that ... the aforesaid
Janus Imperial of Genoa was wickedly and feloniously slain at night
shortly before curfew by certain malefactors and disturbers of the
present king's peace, and the jurors are at the moment completely
ignorant of their names and cognomens and how and in what
way it happened because the said felony was committed at night,
as aforesaid. [the jurors were granted two days to "make more

satisfactory inquiry" but claimed still to be unable to shed light on the event; they were reconvened a month later on September 27].

At that Tuesday the aforesaid jurors appeared again. And they say on their oath that on the aforesaid Friday after the Feast of St. Bartholomew the Apostle ... as Janus Imperial of Genoa was sitting in the high street at night shortly before curfew on a certain log, which lay outside the door of the house where he resided, and four of the said Janus Imperial's servants ... were standing chatting together in front of him in the same place, a certain John Kirkby, mercer, and John Algor, grocer, came there during that time, crossing the street between Imperial and his servants. And, as they were thus crossing there and coming between them, it so happened that John Kirkby suddenly and by no wish of his own then trod unwittingly on Janus Imperial's feet, whereupon the said Janus Imperial was annoyed and clearly began to lose his temper. Thereupon, the aforesaid servants of Janus Imperial, realizing this, severely reprimanded the aforesaid John Kirkby and John Algor, asking them why they had done such a thing to their master. And John Algor, being incensed thereon against the said servants ... immediately drew a knife of his called a baslard. And the said John Algor then and there made an attack upon Janus Imperial's servants with that baslard and struck them wickedly and wounded some of them in various parts of their bodies and ill-treated them against the king's peace. Thereupon Janus Imperial got up and came between them, shouting for peace and angrily asking John Algor and John Kirkby the reason why they thus struck and beat his servants. When this was said, the aforesaid John Kirkby at once drew a sword which he wore on him, and of his own wrongdoing the said John Kirkby with the said sword wrongfully cut away the right side of Janus Imperial's chin, dealing Janus Imperial a wound that was not fatal. And afterwards the said John Kirkby feloniously struck Janus Imperial another time with the aforesaid sword right across his head and at the back of his head on the crown and seriously wounded him, felling the said Janus Imperial to the ground in the aforesaid street and dealing him on his head two mortal wounds, each of them seven inches long and deep into the brain. And as soon as this was done, Janus Imperial was carried as it were half-living by his friends into the aforesaid house where he resided ... and there he died soon afterwards from the aforesaid fatal wounds. And the dead body of the said Janus Imperial was there

viewed by the abovesaid coroner and jurors, and two fatal wounds
were seen on his head, as aforesaid, along with the wound on his
chin that was not fatal. And so the jurors also say that John Kirkby
feloniously slew the said Janus Imperial for the aforesaid reason
and not out of any malice aforethought or previous quarrelling
between them.... And the aforesaid coroner and sheriffs persistently
questioned the jurors whether any person or persons procured,
assented to, or in any way assisted the aforesaid felony. And they were
also asked if any person or persons had wittingly harboured John
Kirkby and John Algor after the said felony was committed. They say
on their oath that there was no one....

FROM JOHN ALGOR'S CONFESSION, DECEMBER 1380

He and Kirkby "met each other in a certain street called Cheap in
London after the sunset and proceeded thence to Lombard Street
and thence to a lane near Lombard Street, called St. Nicholas Acon
Lane, where a certain Janus Imperial of Genoa, merchant, lodged,
in order to search out the said Janus Imperial. And when they had
arrived there and saw him sitting on a log outside his door, with
his servants standing around him, the said John Algor said to the
aforesaid John Kirkby that he wished that Janus Imperial could be
slain on this account, namely, because the said Janus Imperial was
suing before the king's council to obtain the release of a certain ship
which the servants of Richard of Preston, his master, and the servants
of John Philpot of London had captured in war upon the sea and
from which the said Richard of Preston and John Philpot would
have a hundred pounds in profit, that is to say, fifty pounds each,
and the suit was for the purpose of preventing the aforesaid Richard
and John Philpot from having the profit which would have accrued
to them in this matter; and also because he frequently heard from
rumor and gossip in the households of Nicholas of Bramber, William
Walworth, and the aforesaid Richard of Preston and John Philpot in
London among their servants that the aforesaid Janus Imperial would
destroy and ruin all the wool merchants in London and elsewhere
within the realm of England in the event that he could bring to a
conclusion what he had in mind. And John Algor immediately went
past the aforesaid Janus Imperial and came back three times, on each
occasion stumbling over Janus Imperial's feet for the sake of picking
a quarrel between them. And one of Janus's servants, noticing this,
went up to the aforesaid John Algor with a drawn baslard in his hand,

[asking] why he had done this to his master ... [the rest conforms to the previous accounts of the murder]

THE RIGHTS OF ALIENS AND THE PETITION OF THE HANSARDS (1389)

The rights and practices of alien merchants were the source of much litigation and legislation, as the selections below show. The Hanse of Almain [Germany], mentioned in both, was the most powerful company of alien merchants in late medieval London and its trading post, near London Bridge, was a thriving commercial institution throughout the late middle ages and early Renaissance. It closed down after Elizabeth I expelled the League from London in 1598.

> ### THAT NO STRANGER SHALL SELL BY RETAIL, ETC.
> Edward, by the grace of God, King of England and France, and
> Lord of Ireland, to the Sheriffs of London, greeting. Whereas at the
> supplication of our well-beloved and trusty, the Mayor, Aldermen
> and citizens of our city of London, unto us by their Petition in our
> last Parliament exhibited, and there, with the assent of the prelates,
> peers, and nobles of our realm of England, us in the same Parliament
> assisting, endorsed, we have, by our letters patent granted, for
> ourselves and our heirs, unto the before-named Mayor, Aldermen,
> and citizens of the city aforesaid, and their successors, that no stranger
> shall in future sell any merchandize in the same city, or in the
> suburb thereof, any Statutes and Ordinances made to the contrary
> notwithstanding; saving always unto the merchants of the Hanse of
> Almaine their liberties unto them by us and our progenitors granted
> and confirmed, as in the same letters is more fully contained—We
> do command you, that you cause our letters aforesaid, and all matters
> therein contained, within your bailiwick, in such places as you shall
> deem most expedient, on our behalf publicly to be proclaimed,
> and from henceforth by all persons there strictly to be observed,
> according to the tenor of the letters aforesaid. Witness myself, at
> Westminster, this fourth day of December, in the fiftieth year of our
> reign in England, and of our reign in France thirty-seven.

THE PETITION OF THE HANSARDS

To the very noble and very gracious lord, the chancellor of England [William of Wykeham, Chancellor of England from 1389 to 1391], Conrad Fynk, Gerard Clambeck and Warner Heynson, merchants of Almain and of the Hansa, make humble supplication that whereas on the 28TH day of January last the said suppliants with a ship called *The Saint Mary Knight*, one-half of Kampen and the other half of Lübeck, laden with 40 lasts of barrels of herrings, that is 9 lasts belonging to the said Conrad, 5 lasts to the said Gerard, 8 lasts to Withman Claiston, 6 lasts to the said Warner Heynson, 6 lasts to Hubert Bowman, and to Peter Scale of Dortrecht in Holland and Alard Henrison burgess of Kampen, 3 lasts each, the said Warner being merchant for Peter and Alard, were sailing upon the sea towards Southampton there to sell the said herring, and they sailed as far as the Isle of Wight. Here there came upon them two ships of Plymouth, the one of Cok Wille and the other of Richard Rawe of Plymouth, and these Englishmen wrongfully took their said ship and herring bringing them to the port of Weymouth, to the great damage and loss of the said suppliants, because the last was sold there for £5 what was well worth £6 at Southampton, of which there were in the hands of John Gold of Weymouth the money for 21 lasts; this money the said John Gold delivered and it is in the hands of Sir John Ravenser, clerk, by virtue of two writs purchased of you, very noble lord, whereby the said merchants have received 7 lasts except 1 barrel, while the master has received for his freight 4 lasts. And so the said merchants of Almain and of the Hansa ought to have 23 lasts 1 barrel, and Peter Scale 3 lasts, and Alard Henrison of Kampen 3 lasts; and also they have expended upon the suit from then until now 23 marks, and since the men of Cok Wille and Richard Rawe have the money for 8 lasts 1½ barrels, wherefore in their presence the council of our lord the king granted to the said suppliants that if they could bring and show letters of their lord the Duke of Gueldres and of other towns they should be delivered and have full restitution and deliverance of their goods. Hereupon they have brought three letters of the Duke of Gueldres, three letters of the town of Lübeck, two letters of the town of Delbrück, two letters of the town of Dortrecht, and two letters of the town of Kampen certifying and demonstrating how said goods belong to the said merchants; nevertheless they have no deliverance. So may it please your very noble and very gracious lordship to consider this matter and ordain for it remedy, so that they may have restitution of their money in arrear, for love of God and in the way of charity.... And the said suppliants will always give good proof by the evidences aforesaid that the aforesaid merchandise belongs to the said merchants.

Be it remembered that in the Octaves of Holy Trinity during the present year, because of the aforesaid Conrad as attorney and proctor of the aforesaid Gerard Clambeck and Withman Claiston offered and exhibited divers letters testimonial before the council of the lord the king testifying that the goods and chattels aforesaid should of right belong to the aforesaid merchants, wherefore it was adjudged and decreed by the said council that the £105 remaining in the hands of the aforesaid John Ravenser should be entirely delivered to the said merchants. Whereupon the said John at the mandate of the venerable father William of Wykeham, bishop of Winchester, chancellor of England, delivered the £105 to the aforesaid Conrad.

The Massacre of the Flemish (1381)

The Massacre of the Flemish took place during the so-called Peasant's Revolt, on Friday, 14 June 1381. The three excerpts below describe this event. The neighborhood of St. Martin's Vintry, the church from which the rebels dragged their Flemish victims, was a known haunt of alien merchants and was located just one block down Thames Street from the house of Chaucer's father John. In 1364, John Chaucer had stood surety for his fellow vintner and neighbor Richard Lyons, the powerful merchant killed by the rebels in the aftermath of the slaughter of the Flemish. Lyons served as collector of customs; when Chaucer was appointed controller in 1374, Lyons became, for all intents and purposes, his direct superior.

From the *Anonimalle Chronicle*

At the same time the commons had it proclaimed that whoever could catch any Fleming or other aliens of any nation, might cut off their heads; and so they did accordingly. Then they took the heads of the archbishop and of the others and put them on wooden poles, and carried them before them in procession through all the city as far as the shrine of Westminster Abbey, to the contempt of themselves, of God and of Holy Church: for which reason vengeance descended on them shortly afterwards. Then they returned to London Bridge and set the head of the archbishop above the gate, with the heads of eight others they had executed, so that all who passed over the bridge could see them. This done, they went to the church of St Martin's in the Vintry, and found therein thirty-five Flemings, whom they dragged outside and beheaded in the street. On that day were beheaded 140 or 160 persons. Then they took their way to the places of Lombards and other aliens, and broke into their houses, and robbed them of all their goods that they could discover. So it went on for all that day and the night following, with hideous cries and horrible tumult.

From Froissart's *Chronicles*

Then the captains, as John Ball, Jack Straw, and Wat Tyler, went throughout London and a twenty [thirty] thousand with them, and so came to the Savoy in the way to Westminster, which was a goodly house [by the Thames] and it pertained to the duke of Lancaster. And when they entered, they slew the keepers thereof and robbed and pilled [pillaged] the house, and when they had so done, then they set fire on it and clean destroyed and burnt it. And when they had done that outrage, they left not therewith, but went straight to the fair hospital of the Rhodes called Saint John's, and there they burnt the house, hospital, minster, and all. Then they went from street to street and slew all the Flemings that they could find in church or in any other place, there was none respited from death. And they brake up divers houses of the Lombards and robbed them and took their goods at their pleasure, for there was none that durst say them nay. And they slew in the city a rich merchant called Richard Lyon, to whom before that time Wat Tyler had done service in France; and on a time this Richard Lyon had beaten him, while he was his varlet, the which Wat Tyler then remembered, and so came to his house and strake off his head and caused it to be borne on a spear-point before him all about the city.

From the *City of London Letter-Book H*

Upon the same day there was also no little slaughter within the City, as well of natives as of aliens. Richard Lyons, citizen and vintner of the said City, and many others, were beheaded in Cheapside. In the Vintry also, there was a very great massacre of Flemings, and in one heap there were lying about forty headless bodies of persons who had been dragged forth from the churches and their houses; and hardly was there a street in the City in which there were not bodies lying of those who had been slain. Some of the houses also in the said city were pulled down, and others in the suburbs destroyed, and some too, burnt.

Mandate of Payment to Geoffrey Chaucer (11 November 1373)

The following is our translation of a mandate for payment, issued by Edward I, to cover the expenses that Chaucer incurred while conducting the king's "secret business" in Genoa and Florence. It is one of several documents included in the *Chaucer Life Records* showing that the king employed Chaucer abroad. Although Chaucer visited the Italian cities as a paid employee of Edward I, he clearly found time to soak up their vibrant literary traditions.

> Edward, by the grace of God etc., to the treasurers and barons and chamberlains of our exchequer, greetings. We ask you that you take account ... of our beloved esquire Geoffrey Chaucer of the journey that he lately undertook in our service to parts of Genoa and Florence for some of our secret business; allowing to the said Geoffrey Chaucer for the entirety of the said journey, from the day he left our city of London for that cause until his return the same wages per day as are allowed other esquires of his estate going similarly abroad on our business ... as well as reasonable costs for his passage and return over the sea and also for the diverse messengers that he needed to accomplish our above mentioned requests. And what you will find reasonably due to the said Geoffrey by that same account you aforesaid treasurer and chamberlains will make payment to him from our treasury. Given under privy seal at Westminster the 11 day of November in the forty-seventh year of our reign of England and the thirty-fourth of France.

Notes

1. R.M. Lumianksy and David Mills, "Development of the Cycle," in *The Chester Mystery Cycle: Essays and Documents*, ed. R.M. Lumiansky and David Mills (Chapel Hill, NC: U of North Carolina P, 1983) 179. All references to the Chester Cycle are to *The Chester Mystery Cycle: A New Edition with Modernised Spelling*, ed. David Mills (East Lansing, MI: Colleagues Press, 1992).

2   Iain Macleod Higgins, *Writing East: The "Travels" of Sir John Mandeville* (Philadelphia, PA: U of Pennsylvania P, 1997) 5.

3   Linda Lomperis, "Medieval Travel Writing and the Question of Race," *Journal of Medieval and Early Modern Studies* 31:1 (Winter 2001): 147-64.

4   Mary Campbell, "'The Object of One's Gaze': Landscape, Writing, and Early Medieval Pilgrimage," in *Discovering New Worlds: Essays on Medieval Exploration and Imagination*, ed. Scott Westrem (New York: Garland Publishing, 1991) 6.

5   Donald Howard, *Writers and Pilgrims: Medieval Pilgrimage Narratives and Their Posterity* (Berkeley, CA: U of California P, 1980) 17.

6   Rosalynn Voaden, "Travels with Margery: Pilgrimage in Context," in *Eastward Bound: Travel and Travellers, 1050-1550*, ed. Rosamund Allen (Manchester: Manchester UP, 2004) 184.

7   "Introduction," *The Travels of Sir John Mandeville*, trans. C.W.R.D. Moseley (Penguin: Penguin Books, 1983) 32.

8   All references to *Magnus Herodes* are to *The Wakefield Pageants in the Towneley Cycle*, ed. A.C. Cawley (Manchester: Manchester UP, 1958) 64-77. On this passage, SEE also Martin Stevens, "From *Mappa Mundi* to *Theatrum Mundi*," in *From Page to Performance: Essays in Early English Drama*, ed. John Alford (East Lansing, MI: Michigan State UP, 1995) 38. Stevens takes this passage to be evidence that the "world from every perspective is shaped for the spectator as the ubiquitous stage"(38); he does not note the extent to which this passage represents an inversion of cosmography rather than the thing itself.

9   Benedict Anderson, *Imagined Communities: Reflections on the Origin and Spread of Nationalism* (London: Verso, 1983) 29.

10 On Christ's presence in medieval towns, SEE also Peter Womack, "Imagining Communities," in *Culture and History, 1350-1600: Essays on English Communities, Identities, and Writing*, ed. David Aers (Detroit, MI: Wayne State UP, 1992); James 1-28.

11 Bernard Hamilton, "The Impact of the Crusades on Western Geographical Knowledge," in *Eastward Bound: Travel and Travelers, 1050-1550*, ed. Rosamund Allen (Manchester: Manchester UP, 2004) 15-33.

12 Scott Westrem, "Introduction," *Discovering New Worlds: Essays on Medieval Exploration and Imagination*, ed. Scott Westrem (New York: Garland, 1991) xix.

13 Carol F. Heffernan, *The Orient in Chaucer and Medieval Romance* (Cambridge: D.S. Brewer, 2003) 11.

14 Ardis Butterfield, "Chaucer's French Inheritance," in *The Cambridge Companion to Chaucer*, ed. Piero Boitani and Jill Mann (1986; Cambridge: Cambridge UP, 2003) 20.

15 David Wallace, "In Flaundres," *Studies in the Age of Chaucer* 19 (1997): 63-91, p. 72.

16 Anderson 17. On the concept of uniqueness in nationalist thinking, SEE also Liah Greenfeld, *Nationalism: Five Roads to Modernity* (Cambridge, MA: Harvard UP, 1992) 12. For the well-established connections between print technology and emergent nationalism, SEE Anderson 42-46; and Adrian Hastings, *The Construction of Nationhood: Ethnicity, Religion, and Nationalism* (Cambridge: Cambridge UP, 1997) 20-24.

17 Wallace 71.

18 On Chaucer's journeys, SEE Pearsall, *The Life of Geoffrey Chaucer* 51-55, 102-09.

19 On this, SEE also David Wallace, "Chaucer's Italian Inheritance," in *The Cambridge Companion to Chaucer*, 2nd ed., ed. Piero Boitani and Jill Mann (Cambridge: Cambridge UP, 2003) 37, 40, 42.

20 Alexandra Johnston, "Traders and Playmakers: English Guildsmen and the Low Countries," *England and the Low Countries in the Late Middle Ages*, ed. Caroline M. Barron and Nigel Saul (New York: St. Martin's P, 1995).

21 David Bevington, *From Mankind to Marlowe* (Cambridge, MA: Harvard UP, 1962) 2.

22 A.S.G. Edwards, "Continental Influences on London Printing and Reading in the Fifteenth and Early Sixteenth Centuries," in *London and Europe in the Later Middle Ages*, ed. Julia Boffey and Pamela M. King (London: Centre for Medieval and Renaissance Studies, 1995) 229-56.

23 Edwards 244.

24 David Nicholas, *Medieval Flanders* (New York: Longman, 1992) 274.

25 Wallace 67.

26 Nicholas 236, 220.

27 Nicholas 220.

28 Helen Fulton, "Mercantile Ideology in Chaucer's Shipman's Tale," *The Chaucer Review* 96 (2002): 311-28; Patterson, *Chaucer and the Subject of History*.

29 Nicholas 315-16. On Flemish women as prostitutes in medieval England, SEE also Lacey 24-82, 49.

30 Wallace 88-89.

31 Carol M. Meale, "*The Libelle of Englyshe Polycye* and Mercantile Literary Culture in Late-Medieval London," in *London and Europe in the Later Middle Ages*, ed. Julia Boffey and Pamela M. King (London: Centre for Medieval and Renaissance Studies, 1995) 225.

32 Kathryn Reyerson, "The Merchants of the Mediterranean: Merchants as Strangers," *The Stranger in Medieval Society*, ed. F.R.P. Akehurst and Stephanie Cain Van D'Elden (Minneapolis, MN: U of Minnesota P, 1997) 2.

33 Jenny Kermode, *Medieval Merchants: York, Beverley, and Hull in the Later Middle Ages* (Cambridge: Cambridge UP, 1998) 159.

34 Quoted in Derek Pearsall, "Strangers in Late-Fourteenth-Century London," in *the Stranger in Medieval Society*, ed. F.R.P. Akehurst and Stephanie Cain Van D'Elden (Minneapolis, MN: U of Minnesota P, 1997) 53.

35 The Croxton *Play of the Sacrament*, in *Early English Drama*, ed. John Coldewey (New York: Garland, 1993) 274-305.

36 On this, SEE also Heffernan, *The Orient in Chaucer* 30-33.

37 Pearsall, "Strangers" 46-62.

38 Strohm, "Trade, Treason, and the Murder of Janus Imperial," *Journal of British Studies* 35 (1996): 19.

39 Pearsall, "Strangers" 57.

40 Pearsall, "Strangers" 59.

BIBLIOGRAPHY

Aers, David. *Chaucer*. Brighton, Sussex: Harvester P, 1986.

——, ed. *Culture and History, 1350-1600: Essays on English Communities, Identities, and Writing.* Detroit, MI: Wayne State UP, 1992.

Aiken, Pauline. "Vincent of Beauvais and Chaucer's Knowledge of Alchemy." *Studies in Philology* XLI.3 (1944): 371-89.

——. "Vincent of Beauvais and Dame Pertelote's Knowledge of Medicine." *Speculum* 10.3 (1935): 281-87.

Akehurst, F.R.P. and Stephanie Cain Van D'Elden, eds. *The Stranger in Medieval Society*. Medieval Cultures Vol 12. Minneapolis, MN: U of Minnesota P, 1997.

Alford, John, ed. *From Page to Performance: Essays in Early English Drama.* East Lansing, MI: Michigan State UP, 1995. 25-49.

Alighieri, Dante. *The Literary Criticism of Dante Alighieri.* Trans. Robert S. Haller. Lincoln, NE: U of Nebraska P, 1973.

——. *La Vita Nuova.* Ed. Tommaso Casini. Firenze: Sansoni, 1962.

——. *Vita Nuova.* Trans. Mark Musa. Oxford: Oxford UP, 1992.

Allen, Rosamund, ed. *Eastward Bound: Travel and Travellers, 1050-1550.* Manchester: Manchester UP, 2004.

Amtower, Laurel. "The Challenge of Philology and Comparative Study of the Late Middle Ages." *Yearbook of Comparative and General Literature* 51 (2003-04): 7-16.

Amtower, Laurel, and Dorothea Kehler, eds. *The Single Woman in Medieval and Early Modern England: Her Life and Representation.* Tempe, AZ: Medieval and Renaissance Text Society, 2003.

Anderson, Benedict. *Imagined Communities: Reflections on the Origin and Spread of Nationalism.* London: Verso, 1983.

Anglicus, Bartholomew. *On the Properties of Things: John Trevisa's Translation of Bartholomaeus Anglicus' De Proprietatibus Rerum.* Ed. M.C. Seymour. Oxford: Clarendon P, 1975.

——. *Bertholomeus De proprietatibus rerumi.* London, 1535.

——. *Bartholomew Anglicus*. Ed. Robert Steele. New York: Cooper Square, 1966.

Anglicus, Gilbertus. *Healing and Society in Medieval England: A Middle English Translation of the Pharmaceutical Writings of Gilbertus Anglicus*. Ed. Faye Marie Getz. Wisconsin Publications in the History of Science and Medicine 8. Madison, WI: U of Wisconsin P, 1991.

Armstrong, Dorsey. "Gender, Marriage, and Knighthood: Single Ladies in Malory." In *The Single Woman in Medieval and Early Modern England: Her Life and Representation*, eds. Laurel Amtower and Dorothea Kehler. Tempe, AZ: Medieval and Renaissance Text Society, 2003.

The Babees' Book: Medieval Manners for the Young: Done Into Modern English From Dr. Furnivall's Texts. Ed. Edith Rickert. London: Chatto and Windus, 1923

Baker, Denise Nowakowski, ed. *Inscribing the Hundred Years' War in French and English Cultures*. SUNY Series in Medieval Studies. Albany, NY: State U of New York P, 2000.

Baldwin, Frances Elizabeth. *Sumptuary Legislation and Personal Regulation in England*. Johns Hopkins University Studies in Historical and Political Science, Series XLIV: 1. Baltimore, MD: The Johns Hopkins P, 1926.

Barber, Richard. *Edward, Prince of Wales and Acquitaine*. New York: Charles Scribner's Sons, 1978.

——. *The Knight and Chivalry*. New York: Charles Scribner's Sons, 1970.

Barron, Caroline M., and Nigel Saul, eds. *England and the Low Countries in the Late Middle Ages*. New York: St. Martin's P, 1995.

Bennett, H.S. *The Pastons and Their England: Studies in an Age of Transition*. 2nd ed. Cambridge: Cambridge UP, 1951.

Bennett, Michael J. "*Sir Gawain and the Green Knight* and the Literary Achievement of the North-West Midlands: The Historical Background." *Journal of Medieval History* 5 (1979): 63-88.

Bernard of Clairvaux. *The Letters of St. Bernard of Clairvaux*. Trans. Bruno James. London: Burns Oates, 1953.

——. *The Works of Bernard of Clairvaux*, Vol. 7. Trans. Conrad Greenia. Kalamazoo, MI: Cistercian Publications, 1977.

Bersuire, Pierre. *Metamorphosis Ovidiana Moraliter. Explanata: Paris, 1509*. Ed. Stephen Orgel. New York: Garland, 1979.

The Bestiary: A Book of Beasts: Being a Translation From a Latin Bestiary of the Twelfth Century. Ed. T.H. White. New York: Putnam, 1960.

Bevington, David. *From Mankind to Marlowe: Growth of Structure in the Popular Drama of Tudor England*. Cambridge, MA: Harvard UP, 1962.

——, ed. *Medieval Drama*. Boston, MA: Houghton Mifflin, 1987.

Binski, Paul. *Medieval Death: Ritual and Representation*. Ithaca, NY: Cornell UP, 1996.

Blades, William. *The Biography and Typography of William Caxton, England's First Printer*. London: Kegan Paul, Trench, and Trübner, 1897.

——, ed. *The Life and Typography of William Caxton*. 1861; New York: Burt Franklin, 1966.

Blamires, Alcuin, Karen Pratt, and C.W. Marx, eds. *Woman Defamed and Woman Defended: An Anthology of Medieval Texts*. New York: Oxford UP and Clarendon P, 1992.

Bloch, Marc. *Feudal Society*, Vol. 2. Trans. L.A. Manyon. Chicago, IL: U of Chicago P, 1961.

Boccaccio, Giovanni. *The Decameron*. Trans. G.H. McWilliam. Harmondsworth: Penguin, 1972.

——. *Boccaccio On Poetry: Being the Preface and the Fourteenth and Fifteenth Books of Boccaccio's Genealogia Deorum Gentilium*. Trans. Charles G. Osgood. New York: Bobbs-Merrill Company, 1956.

Boffey, Julia, and Pamela M. King, eds. *London and Europe in the Later Middle Ages*. London: Centre for Medieval and Renaissance Studies, 1995.

Boitani, Piero, and Jill Mann, eds. *The Cambridge Companion to Chaucer*. 2nd ed. Cambridge Companions to Literature. Cambridge and New York: Cambridge UP, 2003.

Bonet, Honoré. *The Tree of Battles of Bonet: An English Version with Introduction*. Ed. and trans. G.W. Coopland. Cambridge, MA: Harvard UP, 1949.

Bowers, John M. "Chaucer After Retters: The Wartime Origins of English Literature." In *Inscribing the Hundred Years' War in French and English Cultures*, ed. Denise N. Baker. Albany, NY: State U of New York P, 2000. 91–125.

Braswell-Means, Laurel. "A New Look at an Old Patient: Chaucer's Summoner and Medieval Physiognomia." *The Chaucer Review* 25.3 (1991): 266–75.

Brie, Friedrich W.D., ed. *The Brut, or The Chronicles of England*. London: Kegan Paul, Trench, Trübner and Co. 1908.

Brown, Peter. *Chaucer At Work: The Making of the Canterbury Tales*. New York: Longman, 1994.

Bruhn, Mark J. "Art, Anxiety, and Alchemy in *The Canon Yeoman's Tale.*" *The Chaucer Review* 33.3 (1999): 288-313.

Bühler, Curt F. *William Caxton and His Critics: A Critical Reappraisal of Caxton's Contributions to the Enrichment of the English Language.* Brewster House Typographical Series 3. Syracuse, NY: Syracuse UP, 1960.

Bull, Marcus. "Origins." In *The Oxford Illustrated History of the Crusades*, ed. Jonathan Riley-Smith. Oxford: Oxford UP, 1995. 13-33.

Butterfield, Ardis. "Chaucer's French Inheritance." *The Cambridge Companion to Chaucer*, ed. Piero Boitani and Jill Mann. Cambridge: Cambridge UP, 2003.

Campbell, Bruce. "The Land." In *A Social History of England, 1200-1500*, ed. Rosemary Horrox and W.M. Ormrod. Cambridge and New York: Cambridge UP, 2006. 179-237.

Campbell, Mary. "'The Object of One's Gaze': Landscape, Writing, and Early Medieval Pilgrimage." In *Discovering New Worlds: Essays on Medieval Exploration and Imagination*, ed. Scott Westrem. New York: Garland Publishing, 1991. 3-15

Cannon, Christopher. "Chaucer and Rape: Uncertainty's Certainties." *Studies in the Age of Chaucer* 22 (2000): 67-92.

——. "*Raptus* in the Chaumpaigne Release and a Newly Discovered Document Concerning the Life of Geoffrey Chaucer." *Speculum* 68 (1993): 74-94.

Capellanus, Andreas. *The Art of Courtly Love.* Trans. John Jay Parry. New York: Columbia UP, 1990.

Cave, Roy C., and Herbert H. Coulson. *A Source Book for Medieval Economic History.* 1936; Cheshire, CT: Biblo and Tannen, 1965.

Cawley, A.C., ed. *The Wakefield Pageants in the Towneley Cycle.* Old and Middle English Texts 1. Manchester: Manchester UP, 1958.

Charles, Lindsey, and Lorna Duffin. *Women and Work in Pre-Industrial England.* The Oxford Women's Series. London and Dover, NH: Croom Helm, 1985.

Chaucer, Geoffrey. *The Riverside Chaucer.* 3rd ed. Ed. Larry Benson. Boston, MA: Houghton Mifflin, 1987.

The Chester Mystery Cycle: A New Edition With Modernised Spelling. Ed. David Mills. Medieval Texts and Studies Vol 9. East Lansing, MI: Colleagues P, 1992.

Childs, Wendy R. "Moving Around." In *A Social History of England, 1200-1500*, ed. Rosemary Horrox and W.M. Ormrod. Cambridge and New York: Cambridge UP, 2006. 260-75.

Christianson, C. Paul. *A Directory of London Stationers and Book Artisans, 1300-1500*. New York: Bibliographical Society of America, 1990.

Cigman, Gloria, ed. *Lollard Sermons*. EETS o.s. 294. Oxford: Oxford UP, 1989.

Clanchy, M.T. *From Memory to Written Record, England 1066-1307*. 2nd ed. Oxford and Cambridge, MA: Blackwell, 1993.

Clanvowe, John. *The Works of Sir John Clanvowe*. Ed. V.J. Scattergood. Cambridge: D.S. Brewer, 1975.

Clarke, Bruce, and Wendell Aycock, eds. *The Body and The Text: Comparative Essays in Literature and Medicine*. Lubbock, TX: Texas Tech UP, 1990. 161-71.

Coldewey, John C. *Early English Drama: An Anthology*. New York: Garland, 1993.

Compton Reeves, Albert. *Pleasures and Pastimes Medieval*. Stroud, Gloucestershire: Sutton Publishing, 1998.

Cooper, W.R., ed. *The Wycliffe New Testament (1388): An Edition in Modern Spelling with an Introduction, the Original Prologues and the Epistle to the Laodiceans*. London: British Library, 2002.

Coss, Peter. "An Age of Deference." In *A Social History of England, 1200-1500*, ed. Rosemary Horrox and W. Mark Ormrod. Cambridge: Cambridge UP, 2006. 31-73.

——. *The Lady in Medieval England, 1000-1500*. Mechanicsburg, PA: Stackpole Books, 1998.

Courtenay, William J. *Schools and Scholars in Fourteenth-Century England*. Princeton, NJ: Princeton UP, 1987.

Crotch, W.J.B. *The Prologues and Epilogues of William Caxton*. EETS o.s. 176. 1928; London: Oxford UP, 1956.

Crowe, Martin M., and Clair C. Olson, eds. *Chaucer Life Records*. Oxford: Clarendon P, 1966.

Curry, Walter Clyde. *Chaucer and the Mediaeval Sciences*. 2nd ed. New York: Barnes and Noble, 1960.

——. "Chaucer's Reeve and Miller." *PMLA* 35.2 (1920): 189-209.

——. "More About Chaucer's Wife of Bath." *PMLA* 37.1 (1922): 30-51.

Dahmus, Joseph Henry. *William Courtenay, Archbishop of Canterbury, 1381-1396*. University Park, PA: Pennsylvania State UP, 1966.

de Bury, Richard. *The Love of Books: The Philobiblon of Richard de Bury*. Trans. E.C. Thomas. New York: Cooper Square Publishers, 1966.

——. *The Philobiblon*. Berkeley, CA: U of California P, 1948.

de Charny, Geoffroi. *The Book of Chivalry of Geoffroi de Charny*. Ed. Richard W. Kaeuper and Elspeth Kennedy. Philadelphia, PA: U of Pennsylvania P, 1996.

Delany, Paul. "Constantinus Africanus' *De Coitu*: A Translation." *Chaucer Review* 4 (1970): 55-65.

Dinshaw, Carolyn. *Chaucer's Sexual Poetics*. Madison, WI: U of Wisconsin P, 1989.

Dobson, R.B. *The Peasants' Revolt of 1381*. New York: St. Martin's P, 1970.

Douglas, Mary. *Natural Symbols: Explorations in Cosmology*. 2nd ed. London: Barrie and Jenkins, 1973.

Dryden, John. "The Preface to Fables Ancient and Modern." In *John Dryden*. New York: Oxford UP, 1987. 552-70.

Durandus, William. *The Symbolism of Churches and Church Ornaments: A Translation of the First Book of the Rationale Divinorum Officiorum*. Trans. and ed. John Mason Neale and Benjamin Webb. London: Gibbings and Company, 1906.

Dyer, Christopher. *An Age of Transition?: Economy and Society in England in the Later Middle Ages*. The Ford Lectures. Oxford and New York: Oxford UP, 2005.

——. *Standards of Living in the Later Middle Ages: Social Change in England c. 1200-1500*. New York: Cambridge UP, 1989.

Edwards, A.S.G. "Continental Influences on London Printing and Reading in the Fifteenth and Early Sixteenth Centuries." In *London and Europe in the Later Middle Ages*, ed. Julia Boffey and Pamela M. King. London: Centre for Medieval and Renaissance Studies, 1995. 229-56.

Elias, Norbert, Eric Dunning, *et al*. *The Civilizing Process: Sociogenetic and Psychogenetic Investigations*. Rev. ed. Oxford and Malden, MA: Blackwell, 2000.

Fisher, Sheila. *Chaucer's Poetic Alchemy: A Study of Value and Its Transformation in The Canterbury Tales*. Garland Publications in American and English Literature. New York: Garland, 1988.

French, R.K. *Medicine Before Science: The Rational and Learned Doctor From the Middle Ages to the Enlightenment*. Cambridge and New York: Cambridge UP, 2003.

Friedman, John Block. "Another Look at Chaucer and the Physiognomists." *Studies in Philology* 78 (1981): 138-52.

——. "Henryson's *Testament of Cresseid and the Judicio Solis*." *Modern Philology* 83.1 (1985): 12-21.

Froissart, Jean. *Chronicles of England, France, Spain, and the Adjoining Countries*. Trans. Thomas Johnes London, 1855.

——. *Chronicles*. 3rd ed. Trans and ed. Geoffrey Brereton. Penguin Classics. Baltimore, MD: Penguin Books, 1978.

——. *Chroniques*. Trans. Lord Berners. Ed. G.C. Macauley. London, 1895.

Fulton, Helen. "Mercantile Ideology in Chaucer's Shipman's Tale." *The Chaucer Review* 96 (2002): 311-28.

Furnivall, Frederick J., ed. *The Babees Book, Aristotle's ABC, Urbanitatis, Stans Puer ad Mensam, The Lytille Childrennes Lytil Boke, The Bokes of Nurture of Hugh Rhodes and John Russell, Wynkyn de Worde's Boke of Kernynge, The Booke of Demeanor, The Boke of Curtasye, Seager's Schoole of Vertue, &c. with Some French & Latin Poems on Like Subjects*. EETS o.s. 32. London: N. Trübner and Co., 1868.

Galen. *Galen on the Natural Faculties*. Trans. Arthur John Brock. Cambridge, MA: Harvard UP, 1963.

——. *On the Usefulness of the Parts of the Body. De Usu Partium*. Trans. Margaret Tallmadge May. Cornell Publications in the History of Science. Ithaca, NY: Cornell UP, 1968.

Garzoni, Tomaso. *The Hospitall of incurable fooles*. London, 1600.

Gasse, Rosanne. "The Practice of Medicine in Piers Plowman." *The Chaucer Review* 39.2 (2004): 177-97.

Gee, Henry, and William John Hardy. *Documents Illustrative of English Church History*. London: Macmillan, 1896.

Ginsberg, Warren, ed. *Wynnere and Wastoure and the Parlement of the Thre Ages*. TEAMS Middle English Texts. Kalamazoo, MI:, Medieval Institute Publications, 1992.

Glanville, Ranulf de. *The Treatise on the Laws and Customs of the Realm of England Commonly Called Glanvill*. Ed. G.D.G. Hall. Oxford: Clarendon P, 1993.

The Goodman of Paris: A Treatise on Moral and Domestic Economy by a Citizen of Paris. Ed. and trans. Eileen Power. New York: Harcourt Brace, 1928.

Gower, John. *The Major Latin Works of John Gower: The Voice of One Crying, and the Tripartite Chronicle.* Trans. Eric W. Stockton. Seattle, WA: U of Washington P, 1962.

Greenfeld, Liah. *Nationalism: Five Roads to Modernity.* Cambridge, MA: Harvard UP, 1992.

Grigsby, Bryon Lee. *Pestilence in Medieval and Early Modern English Literature.* Medieval History and Culture Vol 23. New York: Routledge, 2004.

Gross, Charles, ed. *Select Cases from the Coroners' Rolls A.D. 1265-1413 with a Brief Account of the History of the Office of Coroner.* Publications of the Selden Society Vol. 9. London: Bernard Quaritch, 1896.

Haist, Margaret. "The Lion, Bloodline, and Kingship." In *The Mark of the Beast: The Medieval Bestiary in Art, Life, and Literature,* ed. Debra Hassig. New York: Garland, 1999. 3-21.

Hall, Edward. *Hall's Chronicle; Containing the History of England, During the Reign of Henry the Fourth, and the Succeeding Monarchs, to the End of the Reign of Henry the Eighth, in Which Are Particularly Described the Manners and Customs of Those Periods.* 1809; New York: AMS P, 1965.

Hallam, Elizabeth, ed.. *Chronicles of the Crusades: Eye-Witness Accounts of the Wars Between Christianity and Islam.* London: Weidenfeld and Nicolson, 1989.

Hamilton, Bernard. "The Impact of the Crusades on Western Geographical Knowledge." In *Eastward Bound: Travel and Travellers 1050-1550,* ed. Rosamund Allen. Manchester: Manchester UP, 2004. 15-34.

Hammond, Peter W. *Food and Feast in Medieval England.* Rev. ed. Stroud, Gloucestershire: Sutton Publishing, 2005.

Hanawalt, Barbara. *Growing Up in Medieval London: The Experience of Childhood in History.* New York: Oxford UP, 1993.

——. *The Ties That Bound: Peasant Families in Medieval England.* New York: Oxford UP, 1986.

Haskins, Charles Homer. *The Rise of Universities.* Ithaca, NY: Cornell UP, 1979.

Hassig, Debra, ed. *The Mark of the Beast: The Medieval Bestiary in Art, Life, and Literature.* New York: Garland, 1999.

Hastings, Adrian. *The Construction of Nationhood: Ethnicity, Religion, and Nationalism*. Cambridge: Cambridge UP, 1997.

Heffernan, Carol Falvo. *The Melancholy Muse: Chaucer, Shakespeare, and Early Medicine*. Duquesne Studies, Language and Literature Series Vol 19. Pittsburgh, PA: Duquesne UP, 1995.

——. *The Orient in Chaucer and Medieval Romance*. Studies in Medieval Romance. Cambridge: D.S. Brewer, 2003.

Hieatt, Constance B., and Sharon Butler, eds. *Curye on Inglysch: English Culinary Manuscripts of the Fourteenth Century*. New York: Oxford UP, 1985.

Higgins, Iain Macleod. *Writing East: The "Travels" of Sir John Mandeville*. The Middle Ages Series. Philadelphia, PA: U of Pennsylvania P, 1997.

Horrox, Rosemary, and W.M. Ormrod, eds. *A Social History of England, 1200-1500*. Cambridge and New York: Cambridge UP, 2006.

Howard, Donald Roy. *Writers and Pilgrims: Medieval Pilgrimage Narratives and Their Posterity*. Berkeley, CA: U of California P, 1980.

Hudson, Anne. *The Premature Reformation: Wycliffite Texts and Lollard History*. New York: Oxford UP, 1988.

——, ed. *Selections From English Wycliffite Writings*. Cambridge and New York: Cambridge UP, 1978.

Hufton, Olwen H. *The Prospect Before Her: A History of Women in Western Europe*. New York: Alfred Knopf, 1996.

Hugh of Saint Victor. *Hugh of Saint Victor: On the Sacraments of the Christian Faith*. Trans. Roy J. DeFerrari. Cambridge: Medieval Academy, 1951.

Information for Pilgrims unto the Holy Land. London, *c.* 1500.

Jaeger, C. Stephen. *Ennobling Love: In Search of a Lost Sensibility*. Philadelphia, PA: U of Pennsylvania P, 1999.

——. *The Origins of Courtliness: Civilizing Trends and the Formation of Courtly Ideals 939-1210*. Philadelphia, PA: U of Pennsylvania P, 1985.

James, Mervyn. "Ritual, Drama, and Social Body in the Late Medieval English Town." *Past and Present* 98 (1983): 1-28.

Jerome. *The Principal Works of St. Jerome.* Trans. W.H. Fremantle. Oxford: James Parker and New York: Christian Literature Company, 1893.

John of Garland. *Morale Scolarium.* Trans. Louis John Paetow. Berkeley, CA: U of California P, 1927.

John of Salisbury. *The Policraticus.* Trans. Cary J. Nederman. Cambridge: Cambridge UP, 1990.

Johnston, Alexandra. *England and the Low Countries in the Late Middle Ages.* New York: St. Martin's P, 1995.

Jones, Terry. *Who Murdered Chaucer.* New York: St. Martin's P, 2003.

Keen, Maurice. *Chivalry.* New Haven, CT: Yale UP, 1984.

——. *English Society in the Later Middle Ages, 1348-1500.* Penguin Social History of Britain. London and New York: Penguin Books, 1990.

Kelly, John. *The Great Mortality: An Intimate History of the Black Death, the Most Devastating Plague of All Time.* New York: HarperCollins, 2005.

Kempe, Margery. *The Book of Margery Kempe.* Trans. B.A. Windeatt. London: Penguin, 1985.

——. *The Book of Margery Kempe.* Ed. Lynn Staley. TEAMS Middle English Texts. Kalamazoo, MI: Medieval Institute Publications, 1996.

Kermode, Jennifer. *Medieval Merchants: York, Beverley, and Hull in the Later Middle Ages.* Cambridge Studies in Medieval Life and Thought Series 4: 38. Cambridge and New York: Cambridge UP, 1998.

Kibri, Pearl, and Nancy G. Siraisi. "The Institutional Setting: The Universities." In *Science in the Middle Ages,* ed. David C. Lindberg. Chicago, IL: U of Chicago P, 1978. 120-44.

Knighton, Henry. *Knighton's Chronicle 1337-1396.* Trans. G.H. Martin. Oxford Medieval Texts. Oxford and New York: Clarendon P and Oxford UP, 1995.

Lacey, Kay E. "Women and Work in Fourteenth and Fifteenth Century London." In *Women and Work in Pre-Industrial England,* ed. Lindsey Charles and Lorna Duffin. London: Croom Helm, 1985. 24-83.

Langland, William. *Piers Plowman: A New Translation of the B-Text.* Ed. A.V.C. Schmidt. The World's Classics. Oxford and New York: Oxford UP, 1992.

Laqueur, Thomas Walter. *Making Sex: Body and Gender From the Greeks to Freud.* Cambridge, MA: Harvard UP, 1990.

Lawton, David. "Sacrilege and Theatricality: The Croxton *Play of the Sacrament.*" *Journal of Medieval and Early Modern Studies* 33.2 (2003): 281-309.

Leadam, I.S., and J.F. Baldwin, eds. *Select Cases before the King's Council 1243-1482.* 1918; Abingdon, UK: Professional Books, 1978.

Lerer, Seth. *Chaucer and His Readers.* Princeton, NJ: Princeton UP, 1995.

Lewis, C.S. *The Allegory of Love.* Oxford: Oxford UP, 1936.

Leyser, Henrietta. "Piety, Religion, and the Church." In *The Oxford Illustrated History of Medieval England,* ed. Nigel Saul. Oxford: Oxford UP, 1997. 174-206.

The Libelle of Englyshe Polycye: A Poem on the Use of Sea-Power, 1436. Ed. Sir George Warner. Oxford: Clarendon P, 1926.

The Liber Albus: The White Book of The City of London, compiled A.D. 1419, by John Carpenter (common clerk) and Richard Whittington (mayor). Trans. Thomas Riley. London: Richard Griffin, 1861.

Lindberg, David C., ed. *Science in the Middle Ages.* Chicago, IL: U of Chicago P, 1978.

Llull, Ramon. *The Book of the Order of Chivalry.* In *Chaucer: Sources and Backgrounds,* ed. Robert P. Miller. New York: Oxford UP, 1977.

——. *The Book of the Ordre of Chyvalry or Knyghthode.* Amsterdam: Walter J. Johnson, 1976.

Lomperis, Linda. "Medieval Travel Writing and the Question of Race." *Journal of Medieval and Early Modern Studies* 31:1 (Winter 2001): 147-64.

Lowes, John Livingston. "The Loveres Maladye of Heroes." *Modern Philology* 11.4 (1914): 491-546.

Lumiansky, R.M., and David Mills, eds. *The Chester Mystery Cycle: Essays and Documents.* Chapel Hill, NC: U of North Carolina P, 1983.

Lydgate, John. *The Minor Poems of John Lydgate.* Ed. Henry Noble MacCracken. EETS, o.s. 192. London: Oxford UP, 1934.

Machaut, Guillaume de. *The Capture of Alexandria.* Trans. Janet Shirley. Cornwall: Ashgate, 2001.

Macrobius, Ambrosius Aurelius Theodosius. *Commentary on the Dream of Scipio.* Trans. William Harris Stahl. Records of Civilization, Sources and Studies 48. 1952; New York: Columbia UP, 1990.

Malory, Sir Thomas. *Le Morte Darthur.* Ed. Helen Cooper. Oxford: Oxford UP, 1998.

Mandeville, John. *The Travels of Sir John Mandeville*. Ed. and trans. C.W.R.D. Moseley. Penguin Classics. Harmondsworth and New York: Penguin Books, 1983.

Mankind. In *Early English Drama: An Anthology*. Ed. John C. Coldewey. New York: Garland, 1993. 105–35.

Marcus, Jacob Rader, and Marc Saperstein, eds. *The Jew in the Medieval World: A Source Book, 315-1791*. Rev. ed. Cincinnati, OH: Hebrew Union College P, 1999.

Mate, Mavis E. "Work and Leisure." In *A Social History of England*, ed. Rosemary Horrox and W. Mark Ormrod. Cambridge: Cambridge UP, 2006. 276-92.

Matthew of Paris, *Matthew of Paris's English History*. Trans. Rev. J.A. Giles. New York: AMS P, 1854.

Meale, Carol M. "*The Libelle of Englyshe Polycye* and Mercantile Literary Culture in Late-Medieval London." In *London and Europe in the Later Middle Ages*, ed. Julia Boffey and Pamela M. King. London: Centre for Medieval and Renaissance Studies, 1995.

Multhaug, Robert P. "The Science of Matter." In *Science in the Middle Ages*, ed. David C. Lindberg. Chicago, IL: U of Chicago P, 1978.

Muscatine, Charles. *Chaucer and the French Tradition: A Study in Style and Meaning*. Berkeley, CA: U of California P, 1957.

Myers, A.R., and David C. Douglas, eds. *English Historical Documents, 1327-1485*. English Historical Documents Vol. 4. New York: Routledge, 1969.

A Myrour to Lewde Men and Wymmen: A Prose Version of the Speculum Vitae, Ed. From B.L. Ms Harley 45. Ed. Venetia Nelson. Middle English Texts Vol. 14. Heidelberg: Winter, 1981.

Nelson, William, ed. *A Fifteenth Century School Book*. Oxford: Clarendon P, 1956.

Nicholas, David. *Medieval Flanders*. New York: Longman, 1992.

Norton, Thomas. *Thomas Norton's Ordinal of Alchemy*. Ed. John Reidy. EETS n.s 272. New York: Oxford UP, 1975.

Orme, Nicholas. *Medieval Schools: From Roman Britain to Renaissance England*. New Haven, CT: Yale UP, 2006.

Paster, Gail Kern. *Humoring the Body: Emotions and the Shakespearean Stage*. Chicago, IL: U of Chicago P, 2004.

Patterson, Lee. *Chaucer and the Subject of History*. Madison, WI: U of Wisconsin P, 1991.

——. "The Living Witnesses of Our Redemption: Martyrdom and Imitation in Chaucer's Prioress's Tale." *Journal of Medieval and Early Modern Studies* 31.3 (2001): 507-60.

——. "Perpetual Motion: Alchemy and the Technology of the Self." *SAC* 15 (1993): 25-57.

Pearsall, Derek Albert. *The Life of Geoffrey Chaucer: A Critical Biography*. Blackwell Critical Biographies. Oxford and Cambridge, MA: Blackwell, 1992.

——. "Strangers in Late Fourteenth-Century London." In *The Stranger in Medieval Society*, eds. F.R.P. Akehurst and Stephanie Cain Van D'Elden. Minneapolis, MN: U of Minnesota P, 1997. 46-62.

Peck, Russell A. "Chaucer and the Nominalist Questions." *Speculum* 53.4 (1978): 745-60.

Pendrill, Charles. *London Life in the 14th Century*. New York: Adelphi, 1925.

Person, Henry A., ed. *Cambridge Middle English Lyrics*. Rev. ed. Seattle, WA: U of Washington P, 1962.

Petrarch. *Letters on Familiar Matters (Rerum familiarium libri IX-X)*. Trans. Aldo S. Bernardo. Baltimore, MD: The Johns Hopkins UP, 1982.

Piponnier, Françoise, and Perrine Mane. *Dress in the Middle Ages*. Trans. Caroline Beamish. New Haven, CT: Yale UP, 1997.

Pizan, Christine de. *The Book of the City of Ladies*. Trans. Earl Jeffrey Richards. New York: Persea, 1982.

——. *The Book of the Duke of True Lovers*. Trans. Thelma S. Fenster. New York: Persea, 1991.

——. *Christine de Pizan's Letter of Othea to Hector*. Trans. Jane Chance. Newburyport, MA: Focus Publishing, 1990.

——. *The Writings of Christine de Pizan*. Ed. and trans. Charity Cannon Willard. New York: Persea, 1993.

Platt, Colin. *King Death: The Black Death and Its Aftermath in Late-Medieval England*. Toronto: U of Toronto P, 1996.

The Play of the Sacrament. In *Medieval Drama*, ed. David Bevington. Boston, MA: Houghton Mifflin, 1987. 754-88.

Pollard, A.J. *Late Medieval England, 1399-1509*. Longman History of Medieval England. New York: Longman, 2000.

Porta, John Baptista. *Naturall Magick*. London, 1658.

Rastell, John. *Three Rastell Plays: Four Elements, Calisto and Melebea, Gentleness and Nobility*. Tudor Interludes Vol 1. Ed. Richard Axton. Cambridge: D.S. Brewer, 1979.

Read, John. *Prelude to Chemistry: An Outline of Alchemy, Its Literature and Relationships*. Cambridge, MA: MIT P, 1966.

Reyerson, Kathryn. "The Merchants of the Mediterranean: Merchants as Strangers." In *The Stranger in Medieval Society*, ed. F.R.P. Akehurst and Stephanie Cain Van D'Elden. Minneapolis, MN: U of Minnesota P, 1997.

Richards, Earl Jeffrey. "The Uncertainty in Defining France as a Nation in the Works of Eustache Deschamps." In *Inscribing the Hundred Years' War in French and English Cultures*, ed. Denise N. Baker. Albany, NY: State U of New York P, 2000. 159-75.

Riley, Henry Thomas, ed. and trans. *The City of London Letter-Book H, in Memorials of London and London Life in the 13th, 14th, and 15th Centuries, being a series of extracts, local, social, and political*. London: Longmans, Green, and Co., 1868.

Riley-Smith, Jonathan, ed. *The Oxford Illustrated History of the Crusades*. Oxford: Oxford UP, 1995.

Robbins, Rossell Hope. *Early English Christmas Carols*. New York: Columbia UP, 1961.

Robert of Clari. *The Conquest of Constantinople*. Trans. Edgar Holmes McNeal. 1936; New York: Columbia UP, 2005.

Robertson, D.W. *A Preface to Chaucer: Studies in Medieval Perspectives*. Princeton, NJ: Princeton UP, 1962.

Robin Hood and the Friar. Ed. Mary Blackstone. *PLS Performance Text #3*. Toronto: Poculi Ludique Societas, 1981.

Rose, Mary Beth, ed. *Women in the Middle Ages and the Renaissance: Literary and Historical Perspectives*. Syracuse, NY: Syracuse UP, 1986.

Ross, James Bruce, and Mary Martin McLaughlin, eds. *The Portable Medieval Reader*. London: Penguin, 1977.

Saint Augustine. *On Christian Doctrine*. Trans. D.W. Robertson, Jr. Indianapolis, IN: Bobbs-Merrill Educational Publishing, 1958.

Saul, Nigel, ed. *The Age of Chivalry: Art and Society in Late Medieval England.* Leicester: Brockhampton P, 1995.

——. *Richard II.* Yale English Monarchs. New Haven, CT: Yale UP, 1997.

Savage, Anne, and Nicholas Watson, eds. and trans. *Anchoritic Spirituality: Ancrene Wisse and Associated Works.* Mahwah, NJ: Paulist P, 1991.

Sayles, G.O., ed. *Select Cases in the Court of King's Bench.* London: B. Quaritch, 1971.

Schulenburg, Jane Tibbets. "The Heroics of Virginity: Brides of Christ and Sacrificial Mutilation." In *Women in the Middle Ages and the Renaissance,* ed. Mary Beth Rose. Syracuse, NY: Syracuse UP, 1986. 30-72.

Setton, Kenneth M. *The Papacy and the Levant, 1204-1571,* Vol. 1. Philadelphia, PA: The American Philosophical Society, 1976.

Sherb, Victor. "The Earthly and Divine Physicians: *Christus Medicus* in the Croxton *Play of the Sacrament.*" In *The Body and The Text: Comparative Essays in Literature and Medicine,* ed. Bruce Clarke and Wendell Aycock. Lubbock, TX: Texas Tech UP, 1990. 161-71.

Siraisi, Nancy G. *Medieval and Early Renaissance Medicine: An Introduction to Knowledge and Practice.* Chicago, IL: U of Chicago P, 1990.

Sir Gawain and the Green Knight. Trans. Marie Boroff. New York: Norton, 1967.

St. John, Michael. *Chaucer's Dream Visions: Courtliness and Individual Identity.* Studies in European Cultural Transition Vol 7. Aldershot and Burlington, VT: Ashgate, 2000.

Stannard, Jerry. "Natural History." In *Science in the Middle Ages,* ed. David C. Lindberg. Chicago, IL: U of Chicago P, 1978. 429-60.

Statutes of the Realm, 12 vols. Record Commission: London, 1810-28.

Steele, Robert, ed. *Three Prose Versions of the "Secreta Secretorum."* EETS e.s. 74. London: Kegan Paul, Trench, and Trübner, 1898.

Stevens, Martin. "From *Mappa Mundi* to *Theatrum Mundi.*" In *From Page to Performance: Essays in Early English Drama,* ed. John Alford. East Lansing, MI: Michigan State UP, 1995. 25-49.

Strohm, Paul. *Hochon's Arrow: The Social Imagination of Fourteenth-Century Texts.* Princeton, NJ: Princeton UP, 1992.

——. *Social Chaucer.* Cambridge, MA: Harvard UP, 1989.

——. "Trade, Treason, and the Murder of Janus Imperial." *Journal of British Studies* 35 (1996): 1-23.

Taavitsainen, Irma, and Päivi Pahta. *Medical and Scientific Writing in Late Medieval English.* Studies in English Language. Cambridge and New York: Cambridge UP, 2004.

Talbot, Charles H. "Medicine." In *Science in the Middle Ages,* ed. David C. Lindberg. Chicago, IL: U of Chicago P, 1978. 391-428.

Thatcher, Oliver J. *The Library of Original Sources.* New York: University Research Extension, 1907.

Thomas, A.H., ed. *The Calendar of Select Pleas and Memoranda of the City of London Preserved among the Archives of the Corporation of the City of London at the Guildhall (1381-1412).* Cambridge: Cambridge UP, 1929.

Thorndike, Lynn, ed. *University Records of Life in the Middle Ages.* New York: Columbia UP, 1944.

Thrupp, Sylvia L. *The Merchant Class of Medieval London, 1300-1500.* Chicago, IL: U of Chicago P, 1948.

Tout, T.F. *Chapters in the Administrative History of Mediaeval England: The Wardrobe, the Chamber, and the Small Seals.* New York: Manchester UP, 1967.

Translations and Reprints From the Original Sources of European History, published for the Dept. of History of the University of Pennsylvania. Philadelphia, PA: U of Pennsylvania P, 1897-1907.

Tyerman, Christopher. *England and the Crusades 1095-1588.* Chicago, IL: U of Chicago P, 1988.

Usámah. *An Arab-Syrian Gentleman and Warrior in The Period of the Crusades: Memoirs of Usámah Ibn-Munqidh.* Trans. Philip K. Hitti. Princeton, NJ: Princeton UP, 1987.

——. *The Autobiography of Ousama.* Trans. George Richard Potter. London: Routledge, 1929.

Usk, Thomas. *The Testament of Love.* Ed. R. Allen Shoaf. Kalamazoo, MI: Medieval Institute Publications, 1998.

Ussery, Huling E. *Chaucer's Physician: Medicine and Literature in Fourteenth-Century England.* Tulane Studies in English Vol 19. New Orleans, LA: Tulane University, 1971.

Vale, Juliet, and Malcolm Vale. "Knightly Codes and Piety." In *The Age of Chivalry: Art and Society in Late Medieval England,* ed. Nigel Saul. Leicester: Brockhampton P, 1995. 24-35.

Voaden, Rosalynn. "Travels with Margery: Pilgrimage in Context." In *Eastward Bound, Travel and Travellers, 1050-1550,* ed. Rosamund Allen. Manchester: Manchester UP, 2004. 177-95.

Wallace, David. "Chaucer's Italian Inheritance." In *The Cambridge Companion to Chaucer*, ed. Piero Boitani and Jill Mann. Cambridge: Cambridge UP, 2003. 36-57.

——. "In Flaundres." *Studies in the Age of Chaucer* 19 (1997): 63-91.

Wallace, William A. "The Philosophical Setting of Medieval Science." In *Science in the Middle Ages*, ed. David C. Lindberg. Chicago, IL: U of Chicago P, 1978. 91-111.

Walsingham, Thomas. *The Chronica Maiora of Thomas Walsingham*. Trans. David Preest. Woodbridge: The Boydell P, 2005.

——. *Chronicon Angliae II*. Ed. Edward Maunde Thompson. Rolls Series 64. 1874; Wiesbaden: Kraus Reprint, 1965.

——. *The St. Albans Chronicle: The Chronica Maiora of Thomas Walsingham*. Ed. and trans. John Taylor, Wendy R. Childs, and Leslie Watkiss. Oxford: Clarendon P, 2003.

Warrington, John, ed. *The Paston Letters*. Rev. ed. London: J.M. Dent and Sons, 1956.

Waugh, Scott L. *England in the Reign of Edward III*. Cambridge: Cambridge UP, 1991.

Westrem, Scott D. *Discovering New Worlds: Essays on Medieval Exploration and Imagination*. New York: Garland, 1991.

White, Beatrice, ed. *The Vulgaria of John Stanbridge. And the Vulgaria of Robert Whittinton*. EETS 187. London: Kegan Paul, Trench, and Trübner, 1932.

Wickham, Glynne William Gladstone. *English Moral Interludes*. London: J.M. Dent and Sons, 1976.

Will, H.L. Ogrinc. "Western Society and Alchemy, 1200-1500." *Journal of Medieval History* 6 (1980): 103-32.

Womack, Peter. "Imagining Communities." In *Culture and History, 1350-1600: Essays on English Communities, Identities, and Writing*, ed. David Aers. Detroit, MI: Wayne State UP, 1992. 91-145.

Wright, Thomas, and James Orchard Halliwell, eds. *Reliquiae Antiquae: Scraps from Ancient Manuscripts, Illustrating Chiefly Early English Literature and the English Language*. 1843; New York: AMS, 1966.

Wyclif, John. *Wyclif: Select English Writings*. Ed. Herbert E. Winn. London: Oxford UP, 1929.

SOURCES

Berners, Lord (translator) and **G.C. Macauley** (editor)
"The Massacre of the Flemish," from Jean Froissart's *Chroniques*, trans. Lord Berners, ed. G.C. Macauley
(London, 1895) 155.

Blamires, Alcuin (translator)
"Sermon 66," from *Women Defamed and Women Defended*. Trans. by Alcuin Blamires (Oxford: Oxford
University Press, 1992). Reprinted by permission of Oxford University Press.

Brereton, Geoffrey (translator and editor)
"Coronation of Bolingbroke," "Death of Richard II," "Free Companies," "Henry IV's Words to
Richard II, Upon Richard's Abdication" and "Order of the Garter," from Jean Froisssart's
Chronicles, 3rd ed., trans. and ed. by Geoffrey Brereton (1968; New York: Penguin, 1979)
p. 148-49, 460-66, 468-69. Copyright © Geoffrey Brereton 1968. Reprinted by permission
of Penguin Books Ltd.

Brock, A. J. (translator)
"On the Natural Faculties," from *Galen, Loeb Classical Library Volume 71*, translated by A. J. Brock,
Cambridge, Mass: Harvard University Press, 1916. The Loeb Classical Library ® is a registered
trademark of the President and Fellows of Harvard College. Reprinted by permission of
Harvard University Press.

Bury, Richard de
"The Philobiblon," from Richard de Bury's *The Philobiblon* (Berkeley, CA: University of California
Press, 1948) 13-16.

Cannon, Christopher
"Chaucer and the Raptus of Cecily Chaumpaigne," from Christopher Cannon's "Raptus in the
Chaumpaigne Release and a Newly Discovered Document Concerning the Life of Geoffrey
Chaucer," *Speculum* 68 (January 1993): 89-90.

Cave, Roy C. and Herbert H. Coulson
"Apprenticeship Contracts," from Roy C. Cave and Herbert H. Coulson's "17. Apprenticeship in the
Weaving Industry," in *A Source Book for Medieval Economic History* (1936; New York: Biblo
and Tannen, 1965) 256-57.

Cooper, W.R. (editor)
"First Epistle to the Corinthians," from *The Wycliffe New Testament (1388): An Edition in Modern
Spelling with an Introduction, the Original Prologues and the Epistle to the Laodiceans*, ed.
W.R. Cooper (London: British Library, 2002) 278-80.

Coopland, G.W. (translator and editor)

"The Tree of Battles," from *The Tree of Battles of Honore Bonet: An English Version with Introduction*, ed. and trans. G.W. Coopland (Cambridge, MA: Harvard University Press, 1949) 125.

Dahmus, Joseph

"A Punishment for Lollardy" and "The Register of William Courtenay," from Joseph Dahmus' *William Courtenay: Archbishop of Canterbury 1381-1396* (University Park, PA: The Pennsylvania State University Press, 1966) 145-46. Reprinted by permission of Penn State University Press.

DeFerrari, Roy J. (translator)

"The Two Powers," from *Hugh of Saint Victor: On the Sacraments of the Christian Faith*, trans. Roy J. DeFerrari (Cambridge: Medieval Academy, 1951) 256, 259-60. Reprinted by permission of the Medieval Academy.

Delany, Paul

"De Coitu," from Paul Delany's "Constantinus Africanus' 'De Coitu': A Translation." *Chaucer Review* 4 (1970): 60-61. Reprinted by permission of Penn State University Press.

Dobson R.B. (translator and editor)

"The Massacre of the Flemish," translation from the *Anonimalle Chronicle*, in *The Peasant's Revolt of 1381* (New York, St. Martin's Press, 1970) 162. Reprinted by permission of Bedford/St. Martin's Press. All rights reserved

Gewirth, Alan and Cary Nederman (translators)

"The Defender of Peace," from Marsilius of Padua's *defensor pacis*, trans. Alan Gewirth and Cary Nederman (New York: Columbia University Press, 2001) 357-58. Copyright © 2001 Columbia University Press. Reprinted by permission of Columbia University Press.

Giles, Rev. J. A. (translator)

"Hugh of Lincoln," from *Matthew of Paris's English History, Vol. III.*, trans. Rev. J.A. Giles (London, Henry G. Bohn, 1854). Reprint AMS Press, New York. 114-141.

Hall, G.D.G. (editor)

"The Ways in Which a Person Can Be Made Free," from *The Treatise on the Laws and Customs of the Realm of England Commonly Called Glanvill*, ed. G.D.G. Hall (Oxford: Clarendon Press, 1993) 57-60, 108. Reprinted by permission of Oxford University Press.

Haller, Robert S. (editor)

"Letter to Can Grande," from *The Literary Criticism of Dante Alighieri* edited by Robert S. Haller. Copyright © 1973 by the University of Nebraska Press. Copyright © renewed 2001 by the University of Nebraska Press. Reprinted by permission of the University of Nebraska Press.

Hieatt, Constance B. and Sharon Butler (editors)

"A Feast fit for a King" and "Fourteenth-Century Menus from MS Cosin V. III. 11 (C): A. Historical
Documents," from *Curye on Inglysch: English Culinary Manuscripts of the Fourteenth Century*,
ed. Constance B. Hieatt and Sharon Butler (New York: Oxford University Press, 1985).
Reprinted by permission of Oxford University Press.

Hitti, Philip K. (translator)

"An Arab Opinion of the Crusaders' Medicine," from *An Arab-Syrian Gentleman and Warrior in
the Period of the Crusades: Memoirs of Usámah Ibn-Munqidh*, translated by Philip K. Hitti
(Princeton: Princeton University Press, 1987). Reprinted by permission.

Kaeuper, Richard W. and Elspeth Kennedy (editors)

"The Book of Chivalry," from *The Book of Chivalry of Geoffroi de Charny*, ed. Richard W. Kaeuper
and Elspeth Kennedy (Philadelphia: University of Pennsylvania Press, 1996) 87, 91. Reprinted
by permission of Penn State University Press.

Marcus, Jacob Rader and Marc Saperstein (editors)

"The Papal Bull Defending the Jews," from *The Jew in the Medieval World: A Source Book: 1315-1791*,
Rev. ed., ed. Jacob Rader Marcus and Marc Saperstein (Cincinnati, OH: Hebrew Union
College Press, 2000) 170-72. Printed by permission of the Hebrew Union College Press.

Martin, G.H. (translator and editor)

"The Battle of Poitiers," "The Plague" and "The Plague and Its Aftermath," from *Knighton's Chronicle
1337-1396*, ed. and trans. G.H. Martin (Oxford: Clarendon Press, 1995) 95-99, 103-05, 143-45.
Reprinted by permission of Oxford University Press.

Meyers, A.R. and David C. Douglas (editors)

"Close Roll," "Deposition of Richard II," "Statutes of the Realm," "Statute on Livery and
Maintenance," "St. Joan's Appearance to Deliver France," "Studies Necessary Before Admission
as a Master of Arts," "The Commons Protest Against the Misbehavior of the Scholars and
Clerks of Oxford," "The Merciless Parliament," "The Poll Tax" and "The Statutes of New
College, Oxford," from *English Historical Documents 1327-1485*, ed. A.R. Meyers and
David C. Douglas (New York: Routledge, 1969) 62-63, 70, 126-27, 154-56, 242-43, 407-14,
887-89, 890-91, 1116. Reprinted by permission of Routledge, a division of the Taylor and
Francis Group LLC.

Moseley, Charles W.R.D. (translator)

"Mandeville's Travels" and "On Amazons," from *The Travels of Sir John Mandeville* by Sir John
Mandeville, translated with an introduction by Charles W.R.D. Moseley (Penguin Classics,
1983). This translation, introduction and notes copyright © C. W.R.D. Moseley 1983.
Reprinted by permission of Penguin Books Ltd.

Nelson, William (editor)

"A Fifteenth Century School Book," from *A Fifteenth Century School Book*, ed. William Nelson (Oxford: Clarendon Press, 1956) 20, 28, 29, 33, 35, 43, 54, 64. Reprinted by permission of Oxford University Press.

Osgood, Charles G. (translator)

"Genealogy of the Gentile Gods," from *Boccaccio On Poetry: Being the Preface and the Fourteenth and Fifteenth Books of Boccaccio's Genealogia Deorum Gentilium*, trans. Charles G. Osgood (New York: Bobbs-Merrill Company, Inc., 1956). Reprinted by permission of Bobbs-Merrill, Inc.

Parry, John Jay (translator)

"The Art of Courtly Love," from *The Art of Courtly Love* by Andreas Capellanus, translated by John Jay Parry. Copyright © 1990 Columbia University Press. Reprinted by permission of Columbia University Press.

Potter, George Richard (translator)

"Relations with the Franks," from Ousama Ibn Mounkidh's *The Autobiography of Ousama*, trans. George Richard Potter (London: Routledge, 1929) 176-77.

Power, Eileen

"The Goodman's Instructions on Hosting, Cooking, and Serving," Eileen Power, from *The Goodman of Paris: A Treatise on Moral and Domestic Economy by a Citizen of Paris* (New York: Harcourt Brace, 1928).

Pratt, Karen (translator)

"The Lamentations of Matheolus," from *Women Defamed and Women Defended*, translated by Karen Pratt (Oxford: Oxford University Press, 1992). Reprinted by permission of Oxford University Press.

Richards, Earl Jeffrey (translator)

"On Amazons," from *The Book of the City of Ladies* by Christine de Pizan, translated by Earl Jeffrey Richards. Copyright © 1982, 1998 by Persea Books. Reprinted by permission of Persea Books, Inc. (New York).

Riley, Henry Thomas (translator and editor)

"The Massacre of the Flemish," from *The City of London Letter-Book H*, in *Memorials of London and London Life in the 13th, 14th, and 15th Centuries, being a series of extracts, local, social, and political* (London: Longmans, Green, and Co., 1868) 450.

Robertson Jr., D.W. (translator)

"On Christian Doctrine," from Saint Augustine's *On Christian Doctrine*, trans. D.W. Robertson, Jr. (Indianapolis, IN: Bobbs-Merrill Educational Publishing, 1958). Reprinted by permission of Bobbs-Merrill, Inc.

Savage, Anne and Nicholas Watson (translators)

"The Ancrene Wisse." Excerpts from *Anchoritic Spirituality: Ancrene Wisse and Associated Works*, translated and introduced by Anne Savage and Nicholas Watson, Copyright 1991 by Anne Savage and Nicholas Watson. Paulist Press, Inc., New York/Mahwah, NJ. Reprinted by permission of Paulist Press, Inc. www.paulistpress.com.

Sayles, George Osborne (editor)

"The Murder of Janus Imperial" and "Two Medical Cases," from *Select Cases in the Court of King's Bench under Richard II, Henry IV and Henry V*, ed. George Osborne Sayles. Selden Society, Vol. 88, 1971. Reprinted by permission of the Selden Society.

Shirley, Janet (translator)

"The Capture of Alexandria," from Guillaume de Machaut's *The Capture of Alexandria*, trans. Janet Shirley (Cornwall: Ashgate, 2001) 149-150, 151, 154. Reprinted by permission of Ashgate publishing.

Stahl, William Harris (translator)

"On Dreams," from Macrobius, Ambrosius Aurelius Theodosius's "Book One: Chapter III," *Commentary on the Dream of Scipio*, trans. William Harris Stahl (1952; New York: Columbia University Press, 1990) 87-92. Copyright ©1952, 1990 Columbia University Press. Reprinted by permission of Columbia University Press.

Stockton, Eric (translator)

"Vox Clamantis," from John Gower's *The Major Latin Works of John Gower*, trans. Eric Stockton (Seattle, WA: University of Washington Press, 1962) 161-62, 165-66, 166-68, 171-72, 182-84, 260, 270, 280, 290. Reprinted by permission of the University of Washington Press.

Taylor, John, Wendy R. Childs and Leslie Watkiss (translators and editors)

"John Ball" and "Letter From Richard Revoking Their Liberties," from *The St Albans Chronicle: The Chronica Maiora of Thomas Walsingham I, 1376-1394*, ed. and trans. John Taylor, Wendy R. Childs and Leslie Watkiss (Oxford: Clarendon Press, 2003) 523, 545. Reprinted by permission of Oxford University Press.

Thomas, A.H. (editor)

"Court Cases," from *Calendar of Plea and Memoranda Rolls: Preserved among the Archives of the Corporation of the City of London at the Guildhall: A.D. 1364-1381*, ed. A.H. Thomas (Cambridge: Cambridge University Press, 1929) 41, 65-66, 139, 151, 206; "Court Cases," from *The Calendar of Select Pleas and Memoranda of the City of London Preserved among the Archives of the Corporation of the City of London at the Guildhall (1381-1412)*, ed. A.H. Thomas (Cambridge: Cambridge University Press, 1929) 18-19, 22-23. Reprinted by permission of Cambridge University Press.